The Letters of William Lloyd Garrison

EDITED BY

WALTER M. MERRILL AND LOUIS RUCHAMES

PUBLISHER'S NOTE

A word of explanation about the cooperation of the editors of this edition. Some time before 1960, each of the editors, unknown to the other, had embarked on the task of editing Garrison's letters. Each had secured a publisher: Professor Merrill, Harvard University Press; Professor Ruchames, University of Massachusetts Press. On learning accidentally of one another's efforts, the editors decided to cooperate in issuing one edition. The University of Massachusetts Press and Harvard University Press, after discussions, concluded that the latter should assume responsibility for publishing the work.

In arriving at their decision to cooperate, the editors agreed to combine the letters which each had gathered separately as well as to unite in a systematic search for letters that had thus far been overlooked. Repositories of manuscript letters, including libraries, state and local historical societies, and manuscript dealers, in the United States and abroad, were checked. In a number of instances, collections of uncatalogued letters were also searched and several hundred new letters have been discovered and incorporated in the collections.

Two significant changes have been made in the editorial plans since the publication of volume IV. Upon the death of Professor Ruchames in 1976, Professor Merrill undertook to complete the project. The estate of Professor Ruchames turned over to Professor Merrill such letters as had been collected for the 1870s, and the final volume of this edition will carry both scholars' names. Owing to the bulk of extant material from Garrison's last two decades, volume V as well as volume VI will contain a selection of Garrison's letters. Those not included in these last volumes will be microfilmed by University Microfilms International.

In the allocation of responsibilities, the editors have divided the material by periods as follows:

1822–1835—Walter M. Merrill	1850–1860—Louis Ruchames
1836–1840—Louis Ruchames	1861–1867—Walter M. Merrill
1841–1849—Walter M. Merrill	1868–1879—Walter M. Merrill and Louis Ruchames

William Lloyd Garrison in 1867,
from an oil portrait by Edwin T. Billings

The Letters of
William Lloyd Garrison

Volume V

LET THE
OPPRESSED
GO FREE
1861-1867

EDITED BY WALTER M. MERRILL

The Belknap Press of Harvard University Press
Cambridge, Massachusetts
London, England
1979

Library of Congress Cataloging in Publication Data (Revised)

Garrison, William Lloyd, 1805–1879.
The letters of William Lloyd Garrison.

Includes bibliographical references.
CONTENTS.—v. 1. I will be heard, 1822–1835.—
v. 2. A house dividing against itself, 1836–1840,
edited by L. Ruchames.—v. 3. No union with
slaveholders, 1841–1849.—v. 4. From disunionism to the
brink of war, 1850–1860, edited by L. Ruchames.—v. 5.
Let the oppressed go free, 1861–1867.
1. Slavery in the United States—Anti-slavery
movements—Sources. 2. United States—Social
conditions—To 1865—Sources. 3. Garrison,
William Lloyd, 1805–1879. 4. Abolitionists—United
States—Correspondence. 5. Social reformers—United
States—Correspondence. I. Title.
E449.G245   326'.0924   75-133210
ISBN 0-674-52660-0 (v. 1)
ISBN 0-674-52665-1 (v. 5)

The preparation of this volume of *The Letters of William
Lloyd Garrison* was made possible in part through a grant from
the Program for Editions of the National Endowment for the
Humanities, an independent federal agency.

For Cinda

ACKNOWLEDGMENTS

I note with appreciation the many contributions made by individuals and institutions to this volume of Garrison's letters. The financial support that made the project possible was generously provided by two sources. Since March of 1970 the National Endowment for the Humanities has granted the major funds. Drexel University has paid some overhead costs, has provided office space, and has during most of the period for the production of this volume released me from half of my teaching responsibilities.

Four institutions, major depositories of Garrison's letters, and their staffs have provided substantial assistance in the preparation of this volume and of the entire edition: Boston Public Library, James Lawton, curator of manuscripts; Houghton Library, Harvard College, William H. Bond, librarian, Rodney G. Dennis, curator of manuscripts; Massachusetts Historical Society, Stephen T. Riley, until recently director; Sophia Smith Collection, Smith College, Mary-Elizabeth Murdock, director.

Although the excellent research assistance of individuals, historical societies, and libraries is acknowledged within the Notes, several contributors deserve special mention for their personal efforts and for their continuing interest in the project: American Antiquarian Society, William L. Joyce, curator of manuscripts; American Baptist Historical Society; Astor, Lenox and Tilden Foundations of the New York Public Library; Cayuga County Historical and Genealogical Referral Center (New York); Chicago Historical Society; Columbia County (New York) Historical Society; Columbia University Libraries, Kenneth A. Lohf, librarian for rare books and manuscripts; Concord (Massachusetts) Free Public Library; Connecticut Historical Society, Thompson R. Harlow, director, Melancthon W. Jacobus, curator of prints; Cornell University Library; Detroit Public Library, Burton Historical Collection; Essex Institute (Salem, Massachusetts), Dorothy M. Potter, former librarian; Fitchburg Historical Society (Massachusetts), Eleanora F. West, li-

Acknowledgments

brarian; Friends Historical Library of Swarthmore College, Nancy P. Speers, assistant; David Lloyd Garrison; Willard Heiss; Historical Library of the Religious Society of Friends (Dublin), Olive C. Goodbody, curator; Historical Society of Old Newbury (Massachusetts), Wilhelmina V. Lunt, curator; Clara M. Houck; Sarah P. Huntington; Illinois State Historical Library; Martin Kaufman; Knox Memorial Mansion (Maine); Dorothy Koval, former assistant to Professor Louis Ruchames; Library of Congress, John C. Broderick, chief of manuscript division; Library of the College of Physicians of Philadelphia, Lisabeth M. Holloway, associate curator, historical materials; Ethel G. Mann; National Archives and Records Service, Military Archives Division; New Hampshire Historical Society; New-York Historical Society, James J. Heslin, director; Oberlin College Library and Archives; Old Dartmouth Historical Society Whaling Museum (Massachusetts), Richard C. Kugler, director; Onondaga Historical Association (New York), Richard N. Wright, president; Rhode Island Historical Society, Nathaniel N. Shipton, manuscript curator; Schlesinger Library, Radcliffe College; Natalie Kiliani Shastid; Grace P. Smith; Edward W. Stanley; Syracuse University Library, Carolyn A. Davis, manuscript librarian; Vermont Historical Society; Western Reserve Historical Society (Ohio); Wichita State University Library, Michael D. Heaston, formerly curator of special collections, Dale R. Schrag, social sciences reference librarian; William L. Clements Library, University of Michigan, John C. Dann, curator of manuscripts. Finally, I am especially grateful to Anthony W. Shipps, librarian for English, Main Library, Indiana University, for his expert assistance in identifying quotations for volume III as well as volume V.

I also wish to acknowledge the able assistance in both research and editing of a seasoned staff, which has included (not necessarily at the same time) Marion E. Jarrett, Alice J. Nearing, Susan C. Overath, William B. Remington, Frank Saul, Judith A. Scheffler, Patricia P. B. Wells, Scott M. Wilds, and Nancy Zurich.

Ancillary to the Philadelphia staff has been a group of researchers responsible for out-of-town research: Ruth Bell, Gary Bell, and Hilda Armour in Boston; Esther Katz and Ilana Stern in New York; and Nancy Sahli in Washington.

I deeply regret that the untimely death of Dr. Louis Ruchames on June 3, 1976, interrupted an editorial collaboration of a decade.

W.M.M

Philadelphia

x

CONTENTS

List of Illustrations   xiii

Editorial Statement   xv

Abbreviations of Works Cited   xviii

Calendar of Garrison's Extant Correspondence

    1861–1867   xix

   I. Secession and Civil War: 1861   1

  II. Preliminary Proclamation: 1862   59

 III. War for Freedom: 1863   131

 IV. Lincoln Reappraised: 1864   178

  V. Jubilee and Dissension: 1865   245

 VI. Retirement and Financial Security: 1866   364

VII. Honors and Awards: 1867   439

    Index of Recipients   569

    Index of Names   571

LIST OF ILLUSTRATIONS

Frontispiece

William Lloyd Garrison in 1867. From an oil portrait by Edwin T. Billings. Garrison mentions the portrait in his letter to Francis Jackson Garrison of April 16, 1867.

Courtesy of Mechanics Hall, Worcester County Mechanics Association.

Following page 128

"Watch Meeting, Waiting for the Hour, Dec. 31st. 1862." From an oil painting by William Tolman Carlton. Garrison wrote to President Lincoln about this painting in his letter of January 21, 1865.

Courtesy of The White House.

Three wood engravings after Thomas Nast, the famous cartoonist who was to invent the Republican elephant and the Democratic donkey in 1874:
"Emancipation," published in Philadelphia by Samuel Bott, 1865.
"(?) Slavery is Dead(?)," *Harper's Weekly,* January 12, 1867.
"Verdict, 'Hang the D—— Yankee and Nigger,'" *Harper's Weekly,* March 23, 1867.

All, courtesy of the Library of Congress.

Following page 212

"Eminent Opponents of the Slave Power." An engraving by John Chester Buttre, New York City, 1864.

Courtesy of the Library of Congress.

Wendell Phillips in 1861

Courtesy of the Library of Congress.

"'Marching On!'—the Fifty-fifth Massachusetts Colored Regiment Singing John Brown's March in the Streets of Charleston, February 21, 1865." Wood engraving, *Harper's Weekly,* March 18, 1865. The officer on horseback may be Lieutenant Colonel Charles B. Fox, then in command of the regiment; among other officers was Lieutenant George Thompson Garrison.

Courtesy of the South Carolina Historical Society.

xiii

List of Illustrations

Photograph of the flag-raising ceremony at Fort Sumter on the anniversary of the fort's surrender, April 14, 1865.
Courtesy of the Library of Congress.

Following page 318

Lieutenant George Thompson Garrison, between 1863 and 1865. Photograph by Chandler Seaver, Jr., Boston.
Courtesy of the Sophia Smith Collection, Smith College Library.

William Lloyd Garrison, Jr., about 1863. Photograph by Chandler Seaver, Jr., Boston.
Courtesy of the Sophia Smith Collection, Smith College Library.

Wendell Phillips Garrison, June 1861. Photograph by Chandler Seaver, Jr., Boston.
Courtesy of the Sophia Smith Collection, Smith College Library.

Photograph of Garrison and Fanny Garrison Villard, about 1866.
Courtesy of the Sophia Smith Collection, Smith College Library.

Francis Jackson Garrison, April 1, 1863. Photograph by Chandler Seaver, Jr., Boston.
Courtesy of the Sophia Smith Collection, Smith College Library.

Helen E. Garrison, about 1865.
Courtesy of the late Marian K. Chubb.

"Rockledge," the house at 125 Highland Street, Roxbury, where Garrison and his family lived from 1864 to 1879. Photograph by Augustine H. Folsom, Boston. Purchased in 1904 by the Episcopal Sisters of Saint Margaret, the house was for many years used as a nursing home for black women and children. Since 1963, when the building was enlarged, the original house has been used primarily as a residence for the sisters on the staff.
Courtesy of the Sophia Smith Collection, Smith College Library.

EDITORIAL STATEMENT

VOLUME V, unlike earlier volumes of Garrison's letters, is an anthology, a selection of approximately forty percent of the letters for the period 1861–1867. Although I have attempted to choose the most important and interesting letters for this printed volume, I disclaim the prescience to single out precisely the letters most useful to present and future historians and scholars. I have included most of the letters concerned with national and international events as well as representative family letters. Fortunately, the responsibility for making the selection has been mitigated by the fact that all those letters not included in this volume will be available on microfilm through University Microfilms International, and will follow the same basic format as the printed edition. This microfilm is important not only because it supplements the printed volume, but also because it includes letters gathered from many obscure sources.

As in earlier volumes, the text of the letters has been established from the most reliable source, whether manuscript, typed, or printed, with exact sources specified in the descriptive notes. The letters have been arranged insofar as possible in chronological order, though in the case of several letters written on the same day the arrangement is alphabetical according to the names of the recipients. The letters have been grouped by year, with each year introduced by a brief essay describing the letters and supplying biographical and historical comment.

Format of the Text

1. Each letter is numbered and placed in its chronological position.

2. Since all the letters are from Garrison, a uniform heading, with recipient's name in its usual spelling, has been adopted.

3. A uniform date line is also used, with Garrison's wording sup-

plied verbatim, and additional information, when necessary, given in square brackets. In those letters dated by Garrison at the bottom of the text, the date has been supplied twice: in square brackets at the beginning and as intended by Garrison at the end.

Text of the Letters

1. The salutation is uniformly placed but follows Garrison's original wording.

2. The text of each letter is supplied as presented in its source, including errors in spelling, in punctuation, and in diction, though cancellations have been omitted and obvious slips, such as the repetition of a word, have been silently corrected.

3. The complimentary close and signature are uniformly placed, worded, and punctuated as in the source, although the form in letters that are not autographs may be at variance with Garrison's usual practice.

4. Simple postscripts are uniformly placed following Garrison's signature. Marginal notations clearly intended as postscripts are transcribed as such, with notes explaining their position in the manuscript. Marginal notations intended to be read as comments within the text are so placed.

5. The following editorial symbols are used:

[. . .] A lacuna in the source. When the lacuna consists of more than a word or two, a description is supplied in the notes.

[   ] Editorial insertion.

⟦   ⟧ Garrison's brackets.

☞   ☜ Garrison's method of emphasis.

Descriptive Notes

1. An unnumbered source note immediately follows the text of the letter, with no abbreviations except ALS for "autograph letter signed" or AL for "autograph letter" without signature. Sources other than autographs are described.

2. Previous publications of the letter known to the editor are indicated.

3. Whenever the condition of the source interferes with transcription, it is described.

4. Efforts have been made to identify all recipients.

Editorial Statement

Notes

1. Consecutively numbered notes are placed following the descriptive notes.

2. Cross-references are frequently made between printed and microfilmed letters, so that they can be preserved in the context of Garrison's correspondence for the period.

3. Every effort has been made to identify persons, references, allusions, and quotations appearing in the text of the letters. Persons and references identified in the printed volume are not annotated a second time in the supplement.

4. Biblical quotations or allusions have been verified or identified in the King James version. Shakespearean quotations and allusions have been traced through the standard concordance: John Bartlett, *A Complete Concordance . . . of Shakespeare* (New York, 1967), which follows the Globe edition of 1891.

5. The following commonly used secondary sources are not cited: *Appleton's Cyclopaedia of American Biography, Dictionary of American Biography, Dictionary of National Biography, Encyclopaedia Britannica, Oxford Companion to American Literature, Oxford Companion to English Literature,* and *National Cyclopaedia of American Biography.*

ABBREVIATIONS OF WORKS CITED

AWT. Walter M. Merrill, *Against Wind and Tide: A Biography of Wm. Lloyd Garrison* (Cambridge, Mass., 1963).

FJG. Francis Jackson Garrison, unpublished diaries, Merrill Collection of Garrison Papers, Wichita State University Library, Wichita, Kansas.

HWS. Elizabeth Cady Stanton, Susan B. Anthony, and Matilda Joslyn Gage, *History of Woman Suffrage*, 3 vols. (Rochester, N.Y., 1881–1887).

Letters. The Letters of William Lloyd Garrison, ed. Walter M. Merrill and Louis Ruchames, Vols. I–IV (Cambridge, Mass., and London, 1971–1975).

Life. Wendell Phillips Garrison and Francis Jackson Garrison, *William Lloyd Garrison, 1805–1879: The Story of His Life, Told by His Children*, 4 vols. (New York, 1885–1889).

micro. Microfilm supplement to *The Letters of William Lloyd Garrison 1861–1867* (University Microfilms International, Ann Arbor, Mich.).

Mott. Frank Luther Mott, *American Journalism: A History, 1690–1960*, 3d ed. (New York, 1962).

NAW. Edward T. James, ed., *Notable American Women 1607–1950: A Biographical Dictionary*, 3 vols. (Cambridge, Mass., 1971).

OHAP. Samuel Eliot Morison, *Oxford History of the American People* (New York, 1965).

PMHS. Proceedings of the Massachusetts Historical Society.

Sheffeld. Charles A. Sheffeld, ed., *History of Florence, Mass., including a Complete Account of the Northampton Association of Education and Industry* (Florence, Mass., 1895).

ULN. Winifred Gregory, ed., *American Newspapers, 1821–1936: A Union List of Files Available in the United States and Canada* (New York, 1937).

ULS. Edna Brown Titus, ed., *Union List of Serials in Libraries of the United States and Canada* (New York, 1965).

Weld-Grimké Letters. Gilbert H. Barnes and Dwight L. Dumond, eds., *Letters of Theodore Dwight Weld, Angelina Grimké Weld and Sarah Grimké, 1822–1844* (Gloucester, Mass., 1965).

CALENDAR OF GARRISON'S
EXTANT CORRESPONDENCE 1861–1867

Numbered letters are printed in this volume. All others appear in the University Microfilms supplement.

    To Jacob Merrill Manning; Boston, January 8, 1861

    To Lydia Mott; n.p., [after January 14, 1861]

1.   To Oliver Johnson; Boston, January 19, 1861

    To Edmund Quincy; Boston, January 24, 1861

    To Robert F. Wallcut; Boston, February 15, [1861]

2.   To Helen E. Garrison; Boston, February 23, 1861

3.   To Charles Sumner; Boston, February 26, 1861

    To Henry Wilson; Boston, February 26, 1861

    To John A. Andrew; Boston, February 28, 1861

    To John A. Andrew; Boston, March 8, 1861

4.   To John S. Rarey; Boston, March 20, 1861

    To Charles Sumner; Boston, March 22, 1861

    To Samuel Gridley Howe; Boston, April 1, 1861

    To John S. Rarey; Boston, April 5, 1861

    To Charles Sumner; Boston, April 6, 1861

    To Aaron M. Powell; n.p., [before April 15, 1861]

5.   To Oliver Johnson; Boston, April 19, 1861

    To Oliver Johnson; Boston, April 23, 1861

    To Thomas B. Drew; Boston, April 25, 1861

6.   To James S. Gibbons; Boston, April 28, 1861

    To Francis Jackson; Boston, May 5, 1861

7.   To Oliver Johnson; Boston, May 9, 1861

8.   To George T. Downing, John V. DeGrasse, and Robert Morris; Boston, May 13, 1861

9.   To Aaron M. Powell; Boston, May 14, 1861

    To William Lloyd Garrison, Jr.; Boston, May 29, 1861

    To Walker and Wise; Boston, June 18, 1861

    To Oliver Johnson; Boston, June 28, 1861

10. To Oliver Johnson; Boston, July 3, 1861

    To Unknown Recipient; Boston, July 20, 1861

    To Charles Sumner; Boston, July 25, 1861

    To Wendell Phillips Garrison; Boston, July 27, 1861

11. To Wendell Phillips Garrison; Valley Falls, R.I., August 9, 1861

    To Francis Jackson Garrison; Valley Falls, R.I., August 11, 1861

    To Wendell Phillips Garrison; Providence, R.I., August 13, 1861

    To Unknown Recipient; Boston, September 1, 1861

12. To Gerrit Smith; Boston, September 5, 1861

13. To Henry T. Cheever; Boston, September 9, 1861

    To William and Mary Howitt; Boston, September 14, 1861

    To Frank A. Kilton; Boston, October 1, 1861

14. To Oliver Johnson; Boston, October 7, 1861
15. To James Miller McKim; Leicester, Mass., October 13, 1861
     To Helen E. Garrison; New York, October 21, 1861
16. To Helen E. Garrison; Philadelphia, October 29, 1861
     To Charles Sumner; Boston, November 5, 1861
     To Maria Weston Chapman; Boston, November 15, 1861
     To William Lloyd Garrison, Jr.; Boston, November 15, 1861
     To James Miller McKim; Boston, November 22, 1861
     To William Rounseville Alger; Boston, November 25, 1861
17. To Oliver Johnson; Boston, December 6, 1861
18. To Samuel J. May; Boston, December 6, 1861
19. To Helen E. Garrison and Children; n.p., [December 10, 1861]
20. To Charles Sumner; Boston, December 20, 1861
21. To Oliver Johnson; Boston, December 22, 1861
     To Theodore Tilton; Boston, December 22, 1861
22. To Oliver Johnson; Boston, December 26, 1861
     To Oliver Johnson; Boston, December 29, 1861
     To Charles H. Brainard; Boston, January 1, 1862
     To Oliver Johnson; Boston, January 7, 1862
     To Edward Percy; Boston, January 10, 1862
     To Oliver Johnson; Boston, January 10, 1862
     To John M. Hawks; Boston, January 11, 1862
     To Oliver Johnson; Boston, January 11, 1862
     To Edwin Marble; Boston, January 20, 1862
     To George W. Julian; Boston, January 31, 1862
23. To Charles Sumner; n.p., [c. January 31, 1862]
24. To Annie Brown; Boston, February 2, 1862
     To Aaron M. Powell; Boston, February 16, 1862
     To Robert F. Wallcut; Boston, February 20, [1862]
25. To George Thompson; n.p., [February 21, 1862]
     To Eliza Frances Eddy; Boston, February 28, [1862]
26. To George Thompson; n.p., [February 28, 1862]
27. To James McKay; Boston, March 4, 1862
28. To George Thompson; n.p., [March 7, 1862]
     To Oliver Johnson; Boston, March 13, 1862
29. To Henry I. Bowditch; Boston, March 18, [1862]
     To Oliver Johnson; Boston, March 18, 1862
30. To Anna E. Dickinson; Boston, March 22, 1862
31. To Anna E. Dickinson; Boston, March 27, 1862
32. To Anna E. Dickinson; Boston, March 30, 1862
     To Oliver Johnson; Boston, March 30, 1862
33. To Anna E. Dickinson; Boston, April 3, 1862
34. To George W. Julian; Boston, April 13, 1862
     To Oliver Johnson; Boston, April 17, 1862
     To Oliver Johnson; Boston, April 24, 1862
     To George W. Julian; Boston, April 28, 1862
     To Thomas R. Lounsbury; Boston, April 28, 1862

To Walker and Wise; Boston, April 28, 1862
To William Lloyd Garrison, Jr.; Boston, May 1, 1862
To John A. Andrew; Boston, May 20, 1862
35. To Charles B. Sedgwick; Boston, May 20, 1862
To Wendell Phillips; Boston, May 24, [1862]
To Oliver Johnson; Boston, June 2, 1862
To Helen E. Garrison; Philadelphia, June 9, 1862
36. To Helen E. Garrison; New York, June 10, 1862
37. To Aaron M. Powell; New York, June 10, 1862
To Francis Jackson Garrison; Boston, July 13, 1862
38. To Julia M. Friend; Boston, July 31, 1862
To C. H. Hazard; Boston, July 31, 1862
39. To Oliver Johnson; Boston, July 31, 1862
40. To Wendell Phillips Garrison; Boston, August 1, 1862
To Francis Jackson Garrison; Boston, August 2, 1862
41. To Elizabeth Buffum Chace; Boston, August 7, 1862
To Oliver Johnson; Boston, August 7, 1862
42. To Wendell Phillips Garrison; Boston, August 10, 1862
To Charles Sumner; Boston, September 5, 1862
43. To Oliver Johnson; Boston, September 9, 1862
To Fanny Garrison; Boston, September 14, 1862
To Fanny Garrison; Boston, September 18, 1862
To Oliver Johnson; Boston, September 18, 1862
To Oliver Johnson; Boston, September 21, 1862
To Elizabeth Buffum Chace; Boston, September 22, [1862]
To Fanny Garrison; Boston, September 22, 1862
44. To Fanny Garrison; Boston, September 25, 1862
To Oliver Johnson; Boston, September 25, 1862
To Theodore D. Weld; Boston, September 29, 1862
To Helen E. Garrison; Peacham, Vt., October 4, 1862
To Helen E. Garrison; Peacham, Vt., October 7, 1862
45. To Helen E. Garrison; Peacham, Vt., October 8, 1862
46. To Helen E. Garrison; White River Junction, Vt., October 9, 1862
47. To Helen E. Garrison; Braintree, Vt., October 10, 1862
48. To Helen E. Garrison; Burlington, Vt., October 14, 1862
To Theodore Tilton; Boston, October 23, 1862
To Milo A. Townsend; Boston, October 27, 1862
To Sydney Howard Gay; Boston, October 31, 1862
49. To Oliver Johnson; Boston, December 14, 1862
50. To John Greenleaf Whittier; Boston, January 10, 1863
51. To Ralph Waldo Emerson; Boston, January 13, 1863
To Charles Sumner and Henry Wilson; Boston, January 17, 1863
To Louisa Gilman Loring; Boston, January 27, 1863
52. To Oliver Johnson; Boston, March 10, 1863
53. To Theodore Tilton; Boston, March 10, 1863
To William and Mary Howitt; Boston, March 16, 1863
To Theodore Tilton; Boston, March 16, 1863

54. To John A. Andrew; Boston, April 6, 1863
55. To Samuel J. May; Boston, April 6, 1863
    To Theodore D. Weld; Boston, April 6, 1863
    To Mary A. Estlin; Boston, April 10, 1863
56. To Elizabeth Pease Nichol; Boston, April 10, 1863
    To Andrew Paton; Boston, April 10, 1863
    To George Thompson; Boston, April 10, 1863
57. To Milo A. Townsend; Boston, April 16, 1863
58. To Oliver Johnson; Boston, May 5, 1863
59. To Daniel Ricketson; Boston, May 10, 1863
60. To Helen E. Garrison; New York, May 14, 1863
    To Samuel J. May; Boston, June 5, 1863
61. To Theodore Tilton; Boston, June 5, 1863
    To Samuel J. May; Boston, June 6, 1863
    To Milo A. Townsend; Boston, June 9, 1863
62. To George Thompson Garrison; Boston, June 11, 1863
63. To Horace Greeley; Boston, June 30, 1863
64. To Samuel J. May; Boston, July 5, 1863
65. To Oliver Johnson; Boston, July 14, 1863
    To Oliver Johnson; Boston, July 25, 1863
    To Mary M. Brooks; Boston, July 30, 1863
66. To George Thompson Garrison; Boston, August 6, 1863
    To Francis Jackson Garrison; Plymouth, Mass., August 22, 1863
    To William Lloyd Garrison, Jr.; Plymouth, Mass., August 24, 1863
    To Loring Lothrop; Boston, September 7, 1863
    To Robert C. Waterston and Charles F. Barnard; n.p., September
       8, 1863
    To Charles W. Slack; Boston, October 12, 1863
    To William F. Channing; Boston, October 15, 1863
    To S. R. Warfel; Boston, October 15, 1863
    To Franklin B. Sanborn; Boston, October 16, 1863
    To Daniel C. Colesworthy; Boston, October 17, 1863
    To Anna Loring; Boston, October 29, 1863
67. To Aaron M. Powell; Boston, October 31, 1863
68. To Gerrit Smith; Boston, October 31, 1863
    To Oliver Johnson; Boston, November 5, 1863
    To Alfred H. Love; Boston, November 9, 1863
69. To George W. Julian; Boston, November 12, 1863
    To Charles Sumner; Boston, November 12, 1863
70. To Arthur Tappan; Boston, November 12, 1863
71. To James Miller McKim; Boston, November 14, 1863
    To Oliver Johnson; Boston, November 22, 1863
    To Oliver Johnson; Boston, November 26, 1863
    To Charles G. Ames; Boston, November 28, 1863
    To Oliver Johnson; Boston, December 15, 1863
    To Oliver Johnson; Boston, December 20, 1863

To Samuel May, Jr.; Boston, December 20, 1863
To Wendell Phillips Garrison; Boston, December 27, 1863
72. To Francis Gardner; Boston, January 13, 1864
To Henry Wilson; Boston, January 13, 1864
73. To Horace Greeley; Boston, February 5, 1864
To John A. Andrew; Boston, February 12, 1864
74. To Oliver Johnson; Boston, February 16, 1864
To Wendell Phillips Garrison; Boston, February 18, 1864
75. To Ellen Wright; Boston, February 19, 1864
76. To Henry Wilson; Boston, February 20, 1864
To Oliver Johnson; Boston, March 14, 1864
To James Miller McKim; Boston, March 14, 1864
77. To John M. Forbes; Boston, March 22, 1864
78. To Gerrit Smith; Boston, March 29, 1964
79. To Wendell Phillips Garrison; n.p., April 14, 1864
To Gideon Welles (with Wendell Phillips); Boston, April 14, 1864
80. To Gideon Welles; Boston, April 14, 1864
81. To Charles Sumner; Boston, April 19, 1864
82. To Oliver Johnson; Boston, April 28, 1864
To John A. Andrew; Boston, April 30, 1864
To Elizabeth Buffum Chace; Boston, April 30, 1864
To Oliver Johnson; Boston, May 6, 1864
To Helen E. Garrison; New York, May 10, 1864
83. To Helen E. Garrison; New York, May 13, 1864
To Harriet Winslow Sewall; Boston, May 21, 1864
To John and Hannah Cox; Boston, May 29, 1864
To Helen E. Garrison; Longwood, Pa., June 4, 1864
84. To Helen E. Garrison; Hamorton, Pa., June 6, 1864
85. To Helen E. Garrison; Baltimore, June 8, 1864
86. To Helen E. Garrison; Washington, June 9, 1864
87. To Helen E. Garrison; Washington, June 10, 1864
88. To Helen E. Garrison; Philadelphia, June 11, 1864
To Helen E. Garrison; Philadelphia, June 13, 1864
89. To Oliver Johnson; Boston, June 17, 1864
To Samuel May, Jr.; Boston, June 17, 1864
90. To Oliver Johnson; Boston, June 20, 1864
91. To Charles Sumner; Boston, June 26, 1864
To James Manning Winchell Yerrinton; Boston, June 29, 1864
92. To Wendell Phillips Garrison; Boston, June 30, 1864
93. To Lucy McKim; Boston, July 11, 1864
94. To Francis W. Newman; n.p., [July 15, 1864]
95. To Francis W. Newman; n.p., [July 22, 1864]
To Francis Jackson Garrison; Boston, August 11, 1864
To Helen E. Garrison; Peterboro, N.Y., September 6, 1864
96. To Samuel J. May; Peterboro, N.Y., September 6, 1864
97. To Helen E. Garrison; Syracuse, N.Y., September 10, 1864

	To Samuel J. May; Auburn, N.Y., September 12, 1864
	To Helen E. Garrison; Auburn, N.Y., September 14, 1864
	To Unknown Recipient; n.p., [October 20, 1864]
	To J. R. W. Leonard; Boston, November 25, 1864
98.	To Oliver Johnson; Boston, November 26, 1864
99.	To Benjamin F. Butler; Boston, December 13, 1864
100.	To Charles Eliot Norton; Boston, January 13, 1865
101.	To John A. Andrew; Boston, January 17, 1865
102.	To Nathaniel P. Banks; Boston, January 21, 1865
103.	To John M. Forbes; Boston, January 21, 1865
104.	To Abraham Lincoln; Boston, January 21, 1865
105.	To Abraham Lincoln; Boston, February 13, 1865
	To Oliver Johnson; Boston, February 15, 1865
	To Henry C. Wright; Boston, February 18, 1865
106.	To Howard M. Jenkins; Boston, February 28, 1865
107.	To Charles King Whipple; Boston, March 13, 1865
	To Henry C. Wright; Boston, March 14, 1865
108.	To Jacob Horton; Boston, March 17, 1865
109.	To Helen E. Garrison; New York, April 7, 1865
110.	To Helen E. Garrison; n.p., April 9, 1865
111.	To Helen E. Garrison; Charleston, S.C., April 15, 1865
112.	To Helen E. Garrison; New York, May 10, 1865
113.	To Oliver Johnson; Boston, May 21, 1865
114.	To Wendell Phillips Garrison; Boston, May 25, 1865
115.	To George Trask; Boston, May 27, 1865
116.	To Oliver Johnson; Boston, May 28, 1865
	To Samuel May, Jr.; Boston, June 5, 1865
	To Helen E. Garrison; New York, June 7, 1865
	To Helen E. Garrison; Longwood, Pa., June 8, 1965
	To Helen E. Garrison; Longwood, Pa., June 11, 1865
	To Helen E. Garrison; Roxbury, June 20, 1865
	To Helen E. Garrison; Boston, June 22, 1865
	To Helen E. Garrison; Roxbury, June 25, 1865
	To Fanny Garrison; Boston, June 30, 1865
	To Helen E. Garrison; Boston, June 30, 1865
117.	To Lydia Maria Child; Boston, July 10, 1865
	To Helen E. Garrison; Boston, July 10, 1865
	To Helen E. Garrison; Roxbury, July [17], 1865
	To Helen E. Garrison; Boston, July 20, 1865
118.	To Helen E. Garrison; Roxbury, July 23, 1865
119.	To Henry Villard; Roxbury, August 10, 1865
	To Samuel May, Jr.; Boston, August 14, 1865
	To Francis Jackson Garrison; Roxbury, August 17, 1865
120.	To James Miller McKim; Boston, September 11, 1865
	To Ellen Wright Garrison; Boston, September 12, 1865
	To James and Lucretia Mott; Boston, September 12, 1865
121.	To Henry Villard; Boston, September 12, 1865

122.　To James Miller McKim; Boston, September 14, 1865
　　　To George W. Grandey; Boston, September 15, 1865
123.　To Edwin M. Stanton; Boston, September 15, 1865
　　　To Henry Miles; Boston, September 28, 1865
124.　To James Miller McKim; Boston, October 1, 1865
125.　To Henry C. Wright; Boston, October 2, 1865
　　　To George W. Grandey; Boston, October 8, 1965
126.　To Henry Miles; Boston, October 8, 1965
127.　To Elizabeth Pease Nichol; Boston, October 9, 1865
　　　To John Nichol; Boston, October 9, 1865
128.　To Helen E. Garrison; n.p., October 12, 1865
129.　To James Miller McKim; Roxbury, October 15, 1865
　　　To James Miller McKim; Boston, October 19, 1865
　　　To Samuel J. May; Boston, October 19, 1865
　　　To Benjamin Franklin Peixotto; Boston, October 20, 1865
　　　To Andrew H. Caughey; Boston, October 22, 1865
　　　To Alfred T. Goodman; Boston, October 29, 1865
　　　To William H. Herndon; Boston, October 29, 1865
　　　To James Miller McKim; Roxbury, [October 29, 1865]
130.　To Maria Weston Chapman; Syracuse, N.Y., October 31, 1865
131.　To Helen E. Garrison; Syracuse, N.Y., October 31, 1865
132.　To Helen E. Garrison; Syracuse, N.Y., November 1, 1865
133.　To Helen E. Garrison; Lockport, N.Y., November 2, 1865
134.　To Helen E. Garrison; Meadville, Pa., November 5, 1865
　　　To Helen E. Garrison; en route from Meadville, Pa., to Warren,
　　　　Ohio, November 6, [1865]
135.　To Helen E. Garrison; Cleveland, Ohio, November 9, 1865
　　　To William Lloyd Garrison, Jr.; Cleveland, Ohio, November 9,
　　　　1865
136.　To Helen E. Garrison; Toledo, Ohio, November 10, 1865
137.　To Helen E. Garrison; Adrian, Mich., November 13, 1865
　　　To William H. Herndon; La Porte, Ind., November 15, 1865
138.　To Helen E. Garrison; La Porte, Ind., November 16, 1865
139.　To Helen E. Garrison; Chicago, November 17, 1865
　　　To William H. Herndon; Chicago, November 17, 1865
140.　To James Miller McKim; Chicago, November 17, 1865
　　　To William F. Phillips; Chicago, November 17, 1865
　　　To Helen E. Garrison; Chicago, November 20, 1865
141.　To Helen E. Garrison; Princeton, Ill., November 21, 1865
　　　To Milo A. Townsend; Galesburg, Ill., November 21, 1865
142.　To Helen E. Garrison; Springfield, Ill., November 24, 1865
143.　To Wendell Phillips Garrison; Springfield, Ill., November 25,
　　　　1865
144.　To Helen E. Garrison; Lafayette, Ind., November 27, 1865
145.　To William H. Herndon; Lafayette, Ind., November 27, 1865
　　　To Helen E. Garrison; Indianapolis, November 29, 1865
146.　To Helen E. Garrison; Cincinnati, December 1, 1865

147. To Helen E. Garrison; Pittsburgh, December 3, 1865
      To Marius R. Robinson; Pittsburgh, December 4, 1865
      To Samuel May; Roxbury, December 10, 1865
148. To Samuel J. May; Roxbury, December 10, 1865
149. To Henry Villard; Roxbury, December 10, 1865
150. To Wendell Phillips Garrison; Roxbury, December 14, 1865
151. To Charles Sumner; Boston, December 14, 1865
152. To Oliver Johnson; Boston, December 23, 1865
      To Henry C. Wright; Boston, December 25, 1865
      To Amasa Walker; Boston, December 29, 1865
153. To Wendell Phillips; Roxbury, January 1, 1866
154. To James B. Yerrinton; Boston, January 1, 1866
      To James Manning Winchell Yerrinton; Boston, January 1, 1866
155. To Fanny Garrison Villard; Roxbury, January 7, 1866
      To James Miller McKim; Boston, January 11, 1866
      To Wendell Phillips Garrison; n.p., January 18, 1866
      To Rebecca and Anna Lowell; Roxbury, January 18, 1866
156. To Sarah Salisbury Tappan; Boston, January 25, 1866
157. To Fanny Garrison Villard; Boston, January 27, 1866
158. To Harriet Beecher Stowe; n.p., [January 1866]
159. To Theodore Tilton; Boston, February 3, 1866
      To Henry C. Wright; Roxbury, February 9, 1866
160. To Oliver Johnson; Roxbury, February 11, 1866
161. To George W. Julian; Boston, February 11, 1866
      To James Miller McKim; Roxbury, February 11, 1866
162. To Charles Sumner; Boston, February 11, 1866
163. To Fanny Garrison Villard; Boston [Roxbury], February 11, 1866
164. To Edwin L. Godkin; n.p., [February 15, 1866]
165. To Helen E. Garrison; Philadelphia, February 16, 1866
      To Helen E. Garrison; Washington, February 19, 1866
166. To Wendell Phillips Garrison; Washington, February 22, 1866
      To Samuel J. May; Roxbury, March 1, 1866
      To James Miller McKim; Roxbury, March 3, 1866
167. To Fanny Garrison Villard; Roxbury, March 3, 1866
      To Helen E. Garrison; Auburn, N.Y., March 7, 1866
168. To Theodore Tilton; n.p., [March 8, 1866]
      To Fanny Garrison Villard; Roxbury, March 11, 1866
      To Sidney H. Morse; Roxbury, March 19, 1866
169. To Ira Steward; Boston, March 20, 1866
170. To Ellen Wright Garrison; Roxbury, March 23, 1866
171. To Wendell Phillips Garrison; Roxbury, March 25, 1866
      To Oliver Johnson; n.p., March 30, [1866]
172. To James Miller McKim; Roxbury, March 31, 1866
      To Helen E. Garrison; Providence, R.I., April 2, 1866
      To Fanny Garrison Villard; Providence, R.I., April 2, 1866
      To Helen E. Garrison; Providence, R.I., April 3, 1866
      To Helen E. Garrison; Providence, R.I., April 4, 1866

To Elizabeth Cady Stanton; Providence, R.I., April 5, 1866
To Edwin A. Studwell; Providence, R.I., April 5, 1866
To Helen E. Garrison; Providence, R.I., April 6, 1866
To Helen E. Garrison; Providence, R.I., April 7, 1866
To Helen E. Garrison; Providence, R.I., April 8, 1866
To Helen E. Garrison; Providence, R.I., April 10, 1866

173. To Wendell Phillips Garrison; Providence, R.I., April 10, 1866
To Helen E. Garrison; Providence, R.I., [April] 11, 1866
To Francis Jackson Garrison; Providence, R.I., April 12, 1866
To Helen E. Garrison; n.p., [April 13, 1866]

174. To Edwin A. Studwell; Providence, R.I., April 13, 1866
To John G. Palfrey; Boston, April 20, 1866
To James Miller McKim; Roxbury, April 24, 1866
To Lyman Abbott; Boston, May 7, 1866
To James Miller McKim; Roxbury, May 7, 1866

175. To Samuel May, Jr.; Roxbury, May 7, 1866
To Henry Villard; Roxbury, May 19, 1866

176. To Fanny Garrison Villard; Roxbury, May 25, 1866
To Fanny Garrison Villard; Roxbury, June 1, 1866
To Wendell Phillips Garrison; Roxbury, June 3, 1866
To Samuel J. May; Roxbury, June 6, 1866

177. To Wendell Phillips Garrison; Roxbury, June 14, 1866
To Charles Sumner; Roxbury, June 29, 1866
To Ticknor and Fields; Roxbury, July 5, 1866

178. To Fanny Garrison Villard; Roxbury, July 6, 1866
To George Putnam; Roxbury, July 7, 1866
To Bayard Taylor; Boston, July 15, 1866
To Francis Jackson Garrison; Roxbury, July 17, 1866
To Wendell Phillips Garrison; Roxbury, July 17, 1866

179. To Fanny Garrison Villard; Roxbury, July 19, 1866

180. To Helen E. Garrison; Orange, N.J., July 23, 1866
To Francis Jackson Garrison; New York, July 24, 1866

181. To Helen E. Garrison; Orange, N.J., July 28, 1866
To Helen E. Garrison; Orange, N.J., July 30, 1866
To Francis Jackson Garrison; n.p., [August 4, 1866]
To Francis Jackson Garrison; Roxbury, August 7, 1866
To Fanny Garrison Villard; Roxbury, August 11, 1866
To Wendell Phillips Garrison; Roxbury, August 13, 1866
To Fanny Garrison Villard; Roxbury, August 17, 1866
To Fanny Garrison Villard; n.p., [August 23, 1866]
To Franklin B. Sanborn; Roxbury, September 8, 1966
To Samuel J. May; Roxbury, September 18, 1866
To Fanny Garrison Villard; Roxbury, September 21, 1866
To Fanny Garrison Villard; n.p., September 28, 1866
To Fanny Garrison Villard; Roxbury, October 12, 1866
To Francis Jackson Garrison; Roxbury, October 19, 1866
To Francis Jackson Garrison; Roxbury, October 26, 1866

To Samuel May, Jr.; Roxbury, October 29, 1866
To Samuel J. May; Roxbury, October 30, 1866
To Caroline Weston; Boston, November 1, 1866
182. To Fanny Garrison Villard; Roxbury, November 2, 1866
To Caroline Weston; Roxbury, November 7, 1866
To Francis Jackson Garrison; Roxbury, November 23, 1866
To Fanny Garrison Villard; Roxbury, November 23, 1866
183. To Fanny Garrison Villard; Roxbury, November 30, 1866
184. To Francis Jackson Garrison; Roxbury, December 7, 1866
To Charles Sumner; Boston, December 13, 1866
To Samuel J. May; Roxbury, December 18, 1866
To Francis Jackson Garrison; Roxbury, December 21, 1866
To Francis Jackson Garrison; n.p., December 28, 1866
To Samuel May, Jr.; Roxbury, December 30, 1866
To James Miller McKim; Roxbury, December 31, 1866
185. To James Russell Lowell; Roxbury, January 1, 1867
To Francis Jackson Garrison; Roxbury, January 4, 1867
To Wendell Phillips Garrison; Roxbury, January 14, 1867
186. To Francis Jackson Garrison; Roxbury, January 18, 1867
187. To Samuel May, Jr.; Roxbury, January 24, 1867
188. To Oliver Johnson; Roxbury, January 25, 1867
189. To Fanny Garrison Villard; Roxbury, February 1, 1867
To Oliver Johnson; Roxbury, February 5, 1867
To Fanny Garrison Villard; n.p., [February 9, 1867]
To Elizabeth Buffum Chace; Roxbury, February 18, 1867
To John S. Clark; Roxbury, February 19, 1867
190. To Fanny Garrison Villard; Roxbury, February 19, 1867
To Nathaniel Barney; Roxbury, February 20, 1867
To Fanny Garrison Villard; Roxbury, February 24, 1867
To James Miller McKim; New York, February 27, 1867
191. To Helen E. Garrison; New York, February 28, 1867
To Francis Jackson Garrison; Roxbury, March 5, 1867
To Samuel May, Jr.; Roxbury, March 10, 1867
To Francis Jackson Garrison; Roxbury, March 19, 1867
To Benjamin Snow, Jr.; Roxbury, March 26, 1867
To Francis Jackson Garrison; Roxbury, March 27, 1867
To Wendell Phillips Garrison; Roxbury, March 27, 1867
To Fanny Garrison Villard; Roxbury, April 2, 1867
192. To Samuel May, Jr.; Roxbury, April 5, 1867
193. To Lucretia Mott; Roxbury, April 8, 1867
To Fanny Garrison Villard; n.p., [April 9, 1867]
194. To Francis Jackson Garrison; Roxbury, April 16, 1867
To James Miller McKim; Boston, April 17, 1867
To Samuel May, Jr.; Boston, April 17, 1867
To James Miller McKim; Roxbury, April 19, 1867
To William C. Nell; Roxbury, April 20, 1867

To Francis Jackson Garrison; Roxbury, April 23, 1867
To James Miller McKim; Roxbury, April 23, 1867
195.   To William C. Nell; Roxbury, April 23, 1867
To Fanny Garrison Villard; n.p., April 30, 1867
196.   To John A. Kennedy; Roxbury, May 1, 1867
To Alfred H. Love; Roxbury, May 1, 1867
To Henry C. Wright; Roxbury, May 3, 1867
To Unknown Recipient; Roxbury, May 5, 1867
197.   To Samuel May, Jr.; Roxbury, May 7, 1867
To Lyman Abbott; Roxbury, May 8, 1867
To James Miller McKim; Roxbury, May 8, 1867
198.   To Helen E. Garrison; at sea, [May 9, 1867]
199.   To Helen E. Garrison; at sea, May 15, [1867]
200.   To Helen E. Garrison; Liverpool, May 18, 1867
201.   To Helen E. Garrison; Paris, May 24, 1867
202.   To Helen E. Garrison; Paris, May 31, 1867
203.   To Helen E. Garrison; Paris, June 7, 1867
204.   To Richard D. Webb; Paris, June 9, 1867
To Helen E. Garrison; Paris, [June] 11, 1867
205.   To Samuel May, Jr.; Paris, June 11, 1867
To Elizabeth Pease Nichol; Paris, June 12, 1867
206.   To William Lloyd Garrison, Jr.; Paris, June 14, 1867
To William Robson; Paris, June 14, 1867
207.   To Richard D. Webb; Paris, June 14, 1867
To Elizabeth Pease Nichol; London, June 18, 1867
To Richard Monckton Milnes, Lord Houghton; London, June 26, 1867
To Mary A. Estlin; London, June 27, 1867
To John Mawson; London, June 27, 1867
To Elizabeth Pease Nichol; London, July 1, 1867
To Elizabeth Pease Nichol; Gateshead, July 9, 1867
208.   To S. Alfred Steinthal; Edinburgh, July 15, 1867
To Helen E. Garrison; Edinburgh, July 16, 1867
209.   To Elizabeth Pease Nichol; Glasgow, July 23, 1867
To Mary A. Estlin; Glasgow, July 24, 1867
To Helen E. Garrison; London, July 26, 1867
To Elizabeth Pease Nichol; London, July 28, 1867
210.   To Oliver Johnson; London, July 30, 1867
211.   To William Lloyd Garrison, Jr.; London, July 31, 1867
To Elizabeth Pease Nichol; London, August 1, 1867
212.   To Helen E. Garrison; Paris, August 12, 1867
To William Lloyd Garrison, Jr.; Paris, August 14, 1867
213.   To Samuel May, Jr.; Paris, August 20, 1867
To Robert Rae; Geneva, August 30, 1867
214.   To Helen E. Garrison; Chillon, September 4, 1867
215.   To William Lloyd Garrison, Jr.; Interlaken, September 11, 1867

216.   To Ellen Wright Garrison; Interlaken, September 12, 1867
To Thomas Phillips; Lucerne, September 25, 1867
To Helen E. Garrison; Lucerne, September 26, 1867
217.   To Helen E. Garrison; Frankfurt, October 3, 1867
To Thomas Phillips; Frankfurt, October 3, 1867
To Fanny Garrison Villard; Frankfurt, October 4, 1867
218.   To Fanny Garrison Villard; London, October 11, 1867
To William Lloyd Garrison, Jr.; London, October 12, 1867
To Elizabeth Pease Nichol; London, October 12, 1867
To Henry C. Wright; London, October 12, 1867
To Arthur Albright; London, October 14, 1867
To Fanny Garrison Villard; London, October 15, 1867
To Helen E. Garrison; n.p., [October 19, 1867]
To Rachel A. Albright; Manchester, October 23, 1867
To Rachel A. Albright; Liverpool, October 26, 1867
To Elizabeth Pease Nichol; Liverpool, October 26, 1867
To Wendell Phillips Garrison; Roxbury, November 10, 1867
To Oliver Johnson; Roxbury, November 11, 1867
To Edmund Quincy; Roxbury, November 11, 1867
To Josiah Quincy; Roxbury, November 11, 1867
219.   To Fanny Garrison Villard; Roxbury, November 12, 1867
220.   To Henry Villard; Roxbury, November 12, 1867
To George W. Stacy; Roxbury, November 15, 1867
To Henry C. Wright; Roxbury, November 25, 1867
To Fanny Garrison Villard; n.p., December 3, 1867
To Helen E. Garrison; Providence, R.I., December 5, 1867
To Helen E. Garrison; Providence, R.I., December 6, 1867
To Wendell Phillips Garrison; Roxbury, December 8, 1867
To Samuel J. May; Roxbury, December 9, 1867
221.   To Henry C. Wright; Roxbury, December 9, 1867
To Wendell Phillips Garrison; Roxbury, December 10, 1867
222.   To Oliver Johnson; Roxbury, December 11, 1867
To Charles Eliot Norton; Roxbury, December 11, 1867
223.   To Fanny Garrison Villard; Roxbury, December 12, 1867
To Wendell Phillips Garrison; Roxbury, December 13, 1867
224.   To Lyman Abbott; Roxbury, December 14, 1867
225.   To Jacob Horton; Roxbury, December 14, 1867
226.   To Wendell Phillips Garrison; Roxbury, December 18, 1867
To Oliver Johnson; Roxbury, December 18, 1867
To Alfred H. Love; Roxbury, December 18, 1867
To Elizabeth M. Powell; Roxbury, December 18, 1867

I SECESSION AND CIVIL WAR: 1861

WITHIN HIS OWN LIFETIME Garrison's reputation underwent a striking metamorphosis. In 1831 he was generally considered an impulsive, vituperative, self-righteous fanatic; by 1861 he was firmly established as one of the most responsible and most influential of abolitionists. In fact, as editor of *The Liberator* and president of the American Anti-Slavery Society, he was the acknowledged spokesman for radical antislavery opinion. In the twentieth century an analogous transformation of Garrison's reputation has occurred, from the deprecation by revisionist historians in the 1930s to the praise by historians writing since the civil rights movement of the 1960s. Recent historians have considered Garrison and other abolitionists moral heirs of revolution and personal leaders of powerful impact on social and political forces. They have credited the abolitionist agitation not with the outbreak of hostilities between the North and the South but with social reform generated as a result of that conflict.[1]

For nonresistant Garrison the outbreak of the war was a profoundly disturbing event. Ever since the 1830s he had proclaimed on innumerable occasions his dedication to pacifist principles. The following statement, which appeared in *The Liberator*, September 28, 1838, represented his position: "We cordially adopt the non-resistance principle; being confident that it provides for all possible consequences, will ensure all things needful to us, is armed with

---

1. See, for example, Howard Zinn, "Abolitionists, Freedom-Riders, and the Tactics of Agitation," *The Antislavery Vanguard*, ed. Martin B. Duberman (Princeton, 1965), pp. 417–451; Bertram Wyatt-Brown, "William Lloyd Garrison and Antislavery Unity," *Civil War History*, 13:5–24 (March 1967); Martin B. Duberman, "The Abolitionists and Psychology," *Ante-Bellum Reform*, ed. David Brion Davis (New York, 1967), pp. 38–45.

omnipotent power, and must ultimately triumph over every assailing force."

Even before making this statement, however, he had learned not to condemn the use of force by others when it led in the direction of emancipation. As early as the second issue of *The Liberator* (January 8, 1831), he discussed *Walker's Appeal*, a pamphlet that urged insurrection of the slaves, written by David Walker, a free Negro residing in Boston. Little as he liked the methods recommended by Walker, he blamed not him but "our guilty countrymen, who put arguments into the mouths, and swords into the hands of the slaves." The following summer a slave named Nat Turner literally put swords into the hands of slaves and killed fifty-four whites—men, women, and children. For this insurrection, Garrison blamed the whole country and its guilty oppression of the black man.

Two years before the outbreak of the Civil War, Garrison's nonresistance was put to a more crucial test. John Brown marched on Harpers Ferry on October 16; twelve days later Garrison wrote his first editorial on the "well-intended but sadly misguided" action. He prophesied that the execution of Brown and his associates—to occur December 2—"will be sowing seed broadcast for a harvest of retribution. Their blood will cry trumpet-tongued from the ground, and that cry will be responded to by tens of thousands in a manner that shall cause the knees of the Southern slave-mongers to smite together as did those of Belshazzar of old!"[2]

Garrison's position as nonresistant reacting to the war in 1861 is consistent with his earlier response to *Walker's Appeal* and to the raid at Harpers Ferry. He was convinced, as he said in an editorial in *The Liberator* on June 14, that adherence to nonresistance principles in the past would have been preferable to war, would in fact have obviated both the war itself and the institution of slavery. But, the argument continues, given "the present deadly conflict," such an application of peace principles is "impracticable." The nonresistant abolitionist must bring himself to support the North, for "it is impossible not to wish success to the innocent, and defeat to the guilty party."

Lincoln's election to the Presidency in 1860 caused considerable agitation among "the Southern slave-mongers," and on December 20, South Carolina protested by seceding from the Union. In *The Liberator*, January 4, Garrison was ecstatic that the guilty union had been broken: "'The covenant with death' is annulled . . . at least, by the action of South Carolina. . . . Hail the approaching ju-

2. *The Liberator*, October 28, 1859.

bilee, ye millions who are wearing the galling chains of slavery; for, assuredly, the day of your redemption draws nigh, bringing liberty to you, and salvation to the whole land!" His ecstasy was soon mitigated by the claim of critics that there was no essential difference between Garrison's disunion and southern secession.

On April 19 (the day the North declared a blockade on southern ports), Garrison denied in another editorial that the two positions were analogous. He argued that there were only two valid grounds for secession—one constitutional, the other revolutionary. Although South Carolina and other seceding states claimed the constitutional right to secede, asserting that the federal government did not protect their full property rights, they were in error. For the Constitution did, in fact, protect property rights, even the right to own slaves. Nor, Garrison said, could the Confederate states plead revolutionary grounds for secession under the Declaration of Independence, since there was no "long train of abuses and usurpations." In effect, "the South has rent the Union asunder without being able to show a bruise or a scratch, or an outrage of any kind." By contrast, northern abolitionists had every right to urge disunion in order to disassociate themselves from the South, which was "the most lawless, desperate, barbarous, mobocratic, tyrannical and profligate body of wrongdoers, to be found in the world." Garrison's new emphasis was reflected in the superscription on page 1 of *The Liberator* at the top of the right column. On December 13, 1861, he changed it from "The United States Constitution is a 'covenant with death, and an agreement with hell'" to "Proclaim Liberty throughout all the land, to all the inhabitants thereof."

It was also on April 19 that Garrison penned in a letter to Oliver Johnson his immediate reaction to the Civil War, urging that abolitionists be patient and uncritical of Lincoln, of the Republican party, and of the war, and await "the salvation of God." As he put it in a letter to Johnson on April 23 (micro.), 'Let us *all* stand aside, when the North is rushing like a tornado in the right direction." And so, in April 1861, Garrison, the nonresistant who had for two decades preached "No Union with Slaveholders," was in effect conniving at a bloody war designed to preserve that very union. From Garrison's point of view, it was now all right to preserve the Union, provided slavery was abrogated in the process. As the months of 1861 passed, Garrison planned *sub rosa* a campaign to influence public opinion concerning abolition. He wrote to the Reverend Henry T. Cheever on September 9 that "consultations are going on in this city with reference to . . . a wide use of the newspaper press in the publication of able and telling articles, simultaneously, printed on slips, and sent privately for insertion—all bearing upon the extinction of slavery by the exercise of the war power."

In the meantime, Garrison's attitude toward Lincoln was changing, as can be seen in his editorials in *The Liberator*. On February 15 he said: "It is much to the credit of Mr. Lincoln, that he has maintained his dignity and self-respect intact, and gives no countenance to any of the compromises that have yet been proposed." Following the inaugural address, he commended him (March 8) for his "moderation towards the factious secessionists," and his "disposition at once to uphold the laws, and, as far as possible, to avoid the shedding of blood in civil strife. . . . It must be conceded, even by his bitterest opponents, that the new President has met the trying emergency with rare self possession and equanimity."

Subsequently, however, after Lincoln had, in effect, annulled General Frémont's premature emancipation proclamation, Garrison, his patience as agitator worn thin, accused Lincoln (September 20) of "serious dereliction of duty in not making it applicable to all the other slave states in revolt," suggesting that "either the government must abolish slavery, or the independence of the Southern Confederacy must be recognized." After Lincoln's message to Congress toward the end of the year, Garrison said (December 6) that he could commend Lincoln only for his brevity. In a letter of the same date to Oliver Johnson he wrote, "What a wishy-washy message from the President! It is more and more evident that he is a man of very small calibre. . . . He has evidently not a drop of anti-slavery blood in his veins; and he seems incapable of uttering a humane or generous sentiment respecting the enslaved millions in our land."

A relatively small proportion (even smaller than the selection in this volume indicates) of the letters Garrison wrote during 1861 were concerned with historical events of national and international significance. Many of them discussed interesting but less crucial events, such as his wife's and his own birthday, their mutual ill health, the death of Francis Jackson, the preaching of Henry Ward Beecher, the rights of animals (especially horses), and the use of balloons in warfare.

The letters of 1861 show Garrison as a family man and curious observer as well as a reformer who saw, above the smoke of battle, the vision of a free and peaceful land.

1

TO OLIVER JOHNSON

Boston, Jan. 19, 1861.

Dear Johnson:

It will be a fortnight, to-morrow, since I have been out of doors. I have had a very severe cold, or succession of colds, (for I am growing more and more susceptible to such attacks,) and a slow fever hanging about me; and though the latter seems to be broken up, I am still weak, so as to make any effort burdensome.

It is on this account I have not replied to your letter, giving me an extract from Mary Ann's, relative to her vision of a plot in embryo for a murderous assault upon our dear and noble friend, Wendell Phillips.[1] I thought it best, on the whole, to say nothing to him about it; but that his precious life is in very great danger, in consequence of the malignity felt and expressed against him in this city since the John Brown meeting, there is no doubt among us.[2] Hence, we are quite sure of a mobocratic outbreak at our annual meeting on Thursday and Friday next; and though some of us may be exposed to personal violence, Phillips will doubtless be the object of special vengeance. The new mayor, Wightman, is bitterly opposed to us, refuses to give us any protection, and says if there is any disturbance, he will arrest our speakers, together with the Trustees of Tremont Temple![3] What a villain! I should not wonder if blood should be shed on the occasion; for there will be a resolute body of men present, determined to maintain liberty of speech. Whether an attempt will be made to break up the A. S. Festival at the Music Hall, on Wednesday evening, remains to be seen.[4] But all will work well in the end.

Phillips is to speak at the Music Hall to-morrow forenoon, before Mr. Parker's congregation, and another violent demonstration is anticipated.[5] Mayor Wightman refuses to order the police to be present to preserve order. This makes the personal peril of Phillips greater than it was before.

I am anxious to hear from you or Mary Ann a little more specifically about her startling prevision. Was the scene located in her mind as to time or place—relating to our approaching anniversary or some other occasion—or wholly indefinite as to such particulars? You know I believe in such revelations—i. e., that it is *sometimes* given to individuals to foresee future events; and, therefore, knowing how receptive Mary Ann is in this direction, I feel quite desirous of getting further particulars.[6]

Dark as the times are, beyond them all is light. I would have nothing changed, for this is God's judgment day with our guilty nation, which really deserves to be visited with civil and servile war, and to be turned inside out and upside down, for its unparalleled iniquity. I fervently trust this pro-slavery Union is broken beyond the possibility of restoration by Northern compromises; yet, when I see our meetings every where mobbed down, and the cities swarming with ruffians in full sympathy with the Southern traitors, and the Northern pulpits more satanic than ever, as far as they speak out against Abolitionism, and the Republican party constantly "shivering in the wind," I am not sure but *the whole country* is to come under the bloody sway of the Slave Power—for a time—as it has not yet done.

Faithfully yours,

W. L. Garrison.

Oliver Johnson.

☞ Did not Mary Ann have a fearful vision, two or three years ago, when at the Davises in Providence,[7] respecting the breaking up of this Union–blood flowing at Washington–&c., &c.? I wish she could recall the particulars.

ALS: Garrison Papers, Boston Public Library; partly printed in *Life*, IV, 3–4. For more information regarding mob violence at this time see the letter to Lydia Mott, [after January 14, 1861] (micro.).

Oliver Johnson (1809–1889), newspaper editor and journalist, had been closely associated with Garrison and the antislavery movement since 1831. From 1844 to 1848 he was Horace Greeley's assistant on the New York *Tribune;* in 1853 he became, along with Sydney Howard Gay, coeditor of the *National Anti-Slavery Standard,* serving as editor between 1858 and 1865. After the Civil War he held various editorial posts in New York City. Most pertinent of them, since Garrison became a frequent contributor to the paper, was that of associate editor of the *Independent* (1865–1870).

Johnson married twice. His first wife was Mary Anne White (1808–1872), an assistant matron at the female branch of Sing Sing prison and an effective agitator for prison reform; later in life she made some reputation lecturing on anatomy and physiology to female audiences. She supposedly had clairvoyant powers. His second wife was Jane Abbott, the daughter of John S. C. Abbott; she bore Johnson a daughter, his only child.

1. Wendell Phillips (1811–1884), Boston born and Harvard educated, both at the college and at the law school, had been Garrison's associate since 1837. Phillips supported Garrison's position as abolitionist and even contributed to the support and education of his namesake among Garrison's sons. In the middle sixties, however, differences were to develop between the two men, first over the disposition of the Francis Jackson bequest and then over the continuance of the Massachusetts and the American Anti-Slavery societies.

2. Despite the bloody acts he perpetrated in Kansas and Virginia, John Brown (1800–1859) had become the martyred hero even to nonresistants like Garrison. In this letter Garrison refers to a meeting sponsored by the Massachusetts Anti-Slavery

Society at Tremont Temple in Boston on December 3, 1860, to commemorate the first anniversary of Brown's execution. When the meeting was violently disrupted by a mob intent on preserving the Union, it was dismissed, to be reconvened at the Joy Street Church that evening so that it could condemn the mob action. Unfortunately, some of the black members of the audience were attacked on their way home after the meeting. Garrison also makes oblique reference to Phillips' having been mobbed while speaking at the Music Hall on December 16. Possibly he was in addition, thinking of two thwarted meetings in New York state on January 14, one at Rochester and one at Utica. (*The Liberator*, December 7, 14, 21, and 28, 1860; January 18 and 25, 1861.)

3. Joseph Milner Wightman (1812–1885) had a long career of public service in Boston, including a term in the Massachusetts legislature and three years (1856–1858) on the Board of Aldermen, in the last year becoming its president. In 1860 he was elected mayor of Boston on the Democratic and Union ticket but was defeated for reelection in 1862. In his last years (1880–1885) he served on the Board of Registrars of Voters. (Obituary, New York *Tribune*, January 26, 1885.)

At the annual meeting of the Massachusetts Anti-Slavery Society, January 24–25, there was a considerable amount of disruptive heckling, for which Garrison blamed Mayor Wightman, whom he thought guilty of "flagrant violation of his oath of office." (*The Liberator*, February 1, 1861.)

As Garrison indicates, this meeting was held in Tremont Temple, a Baptist church building, whose large auditorium was often used for reform meetings. (*Sketches and Business Directory of Boston and Vicinity, 1860–1861*, Boston, 1861, pp. 109–110.)

4. Garrison refers to the twenty-seventh National Anti-Slavery Subscription Anniversary, a social event that initiated the yearly meeting of the Massachusetts Anti-Slavery Society. It was held at the Music Hall, located at Winter Street and Bumstead Place, a regular meeting place for Boston abolitionists. Admission was by invitation only, although "all who hate slavery, and wish to become subscribers to the funds" were invited to pick up invitations at the Anti-Slavery Office, 221 Washington Street, or "from the Ladies at their homes." There is no evidence of disturbance at the festival. (*The Liberator*, January 18, 1861.)

5. Wendell Phillips delivered his speech, "The Lesson of the Hour," on schedule and without interruption, perhaps owing to the police protection provided by the city. *The Liberator* reported that upon leaving the hall Phillips and his party "found Winter Street lined by crowds of genteel ruffians." (*The Liberator*, January 25, 1861.)

Theodore Parker (1810–1860), a graduate of the Harvard Divinity School, became in 1837 minister of the Unitarian church in West Roxbury, Mass., and in 1852 minister of the Twenty-Eighth Congregational Society of Boston, which held services at the Music Hall. One of the most learned and controversial of Unitarians, he was also an active abolitionist who used his pulpit in the cause of reform. Convinced that abolition could be effected only by violent means, he became a supporter of John Brown in 1858.

6. For other references to Garrison's interest in clairvoyance, spiritualism, and the like, see his entry in the Index.

7. Thomas Davis (1806–1895) emigrated from Ireland to Providence, R.I., where he became a jewelry manufacturer. He later served as a state senator (1845–1853), a United States congressman (1853–1855), and a state representative (1887–1890). He married (1) Eliza Chace (c. 1809–1840), the friend of Helen Garrison; and (2) Paulina Kellogg Wright (1813–1876); both women were active abolitionists.

Paulina Wright Davis, with her first husband, Francis Wright, had worked for the antislavery cause, temperance, and woman's rights. Since 1850 she had devoted herself to woman's rights and had organized the first National Woman's Rights Convention at Worcester. Between 1853 and 1855 she published at her own expense the *Una*, a monthly periodical, and in 1868 she helped to found the New England Woman Suffrage Association. (*NAW; HWS*, I, 283–289.)

2

TO HELEN E. GARRISON

Boston, Feb. 23, 1861.

My Beloved Wife:

Your feet stand upon the summit-level of half a century. To-day completes your fiftieth year! Our dear children and I most lovingly congratulate you on the auspicious event, not on account of increasing age, but because of the prolongation of your life to this hour, in good health.[1] We desire to present to you such a token of that love as will prove alike useful and ornamental, though utterly inadequate, and therefore wish you to accept the accompanying gold watch, which will mark the hours as they fly till time with you shall be no longer, and you shall enter that heavenly sphere where there shall be neither death nor decay, but "all are as the angels of God."[2] With its every tick will beat in unison our hearts' affectionate pulsations towards you, subject, however, to "no variableness, nor shadow of turning."[3]

As a wife, for a period of more than twenty-six years, you have left nothing undone to smooth the rugged pathway of my public career —to render home the all-powerful magnet of attraction, and the focal point of domestic enjoyment—to make my welfare and happiness at all times a matter of tender solicitude—and to demonstrate the depth and fixedness of that love which you so long ago plighted to me. If I have not been profuse with lip acknowledgments of your constancy and worth, be assured it is not because I have not clearly perceived and fully appreciated them, but because words ever seem expressionless in such a case. The highest praise is conveyed where no fault is ever found with the manner in which you discharge the daily household responsibilities resting upon you, but, on the contrary, every thing is satisfactorily recognized as complete and perfect. Whatever of human infirmity we may have seen in each other, I believe few have enjoyed more unalloyed bliss in wedded life than ourselves.

As a mother, you have ever been watchful, devoted, unwearied. Our children will always have cause to be grateful for the manner in which you have consulted their comfort, safety and happiness,— sparing no labor in their behalf, and folding them in the arms of your motherly affection.

As for the future—

"Serene will be our days and bright.
And happy will our nature be,
When love is an unerring light,
And joy its own security."[4]

Dear wife and mother! we unitedly join in giving you our fervent benediction, and wishing you many a happy birth-day.

In behalf of all the children,

Your loving husband,

Wm. Lloyd Garrison.

Helen Eliza Garrison.

ALS: William Lloyd Garrison Papers, Massachusetts Historical Society; Garrison's transcription of this letter (marked "copy" in an unknown hand) is preserved in the Garrison Papers, Boston Public Library. The letter is also printed, with a few minor changes, in *Helen Eliza Garrison, A Memorial* (Cambridge, Mass., 1876), pp. 30–31.

Helen Eliza Garrison (1811–1876), Garrison's wife since 1834, was the daughter of George and Sarah Thurber Benson of Providence, R.I., and subsequently of Brooklyn, Conn. Although in personality diffident and retiring, Helen brought to the marriage qualities in which Garrison was deficient. She was punctual, orderly, and efficient and had the temerity to remind her husband of engagements and editorial deadlines. Frugal and foresighted and more aware of financial problems than he, it was Helen who struggled to keep the family solvent. Never herself directly involved in antislavery agitation, she shared Garrison's convictions and supported him in many ways, by running the family efficiently and by entertaining his friends and associates. At the date of this letter Helen was in good health, but she was to suffer a stroke in December 1863, which left her an invalid the remaining thirteen years of her life.

1. Five Garrison children were living at this time, three young men, a sixteen-year-old girl, and a twelve-year-old boy.

George Thompson Garrison (1836–1904) passed from job to job, coming nearest to distinguishing himself as a second lieutenant in the 55th Massachusetts, a Negro regiment. George married his cousin Anne Keene Anthony in 1873.

William Lloyd Garrison, Jr. (1838–1909), who married Ellen Wright in 1864, pursued a reasonably successful career in business, working first as a bank cashier and, by 1865, as a wool broker. Garrison depended on his second son to look after his financial affairs.

Wendell Phillips Garrison (1840–1907) was the most capable of the Garrison sons. In 1865 he was to become literary editor of *The Nation,* a position he held until 1906. With his younger brother, he was to write the four-volume life of his father, published between 1885 and 1889. Wendell married Lucy McKim in 1865; she died in 1877. In 1891 Wendell married Anne McKim Dennis.

Helen Frances (Fanny) Garrison (1844–1928) was the beloved daughter who was to marry Henry Villard in 1866. In the last years of the century the Villards lived in one of the most elaborate mansions on Madison Avenue in New York City, where Fanny became one of the city's outstanding hostesses. In her later years Mrs. Villard gave much of her time to philanthropic and social work; she served, for example, as a member of the advisory board of the National Association for the Advancement of Colored People. As World War I approached, she worked increasingly for the cause of peace and nonresistance.

Francis (Frank) Jackson Garrison (1848–1916), the youngest of the children, became an editor and publisher, and was co-author of the official biography of

Garrison. In 1879 he married Mary Pratt, who died in 1882; in 1891 he married
Theresa Holmes.
2. An adaptation of Matthew 22:30.
3. James 1:17, with the substitution of "nor" for "neither."
4. William Wordsworth, "Ode to Duty," stanza 3.

3

TO CHARLES SUMNER

Boston, Feb. 26, 1861.

Dear Mr. Sumner:

It gives me great pleasure to introduce to your friendly consideration the bearer of this, Capt. James H. Holmes, of New Mexico, but,
formerly, one of the bravest defenders of Kansas against Border-
Ruffian invasion—a modest, unassuming man, but full of enthusiasm and indomitable perseverance in the cause of impartial freedom—disinterested in his efforts, and willing to sacrifice and to be
sacrificed for the good of others.[1] He has resided for the last two
years in New Mexico, exploring the territory, taking notes of its
condition and capability, &c., with a view to shaping its institutions
in accordance with the principles of justice and humanity.[2] It is for
this purpose he visits Washington, to communicate, as a reliable
witness, what information he possesses for the guidance of President Lincoln in his appointments for that territory, upon which so
much will depend in regard to its future destiny. His mission is a
vastly important one, and I earnestly trust he may have a fair opportunity to unfold it. New Mexico must be speedily saved to freedom,
or it will pass into the hands of the slave oligarchy, to be moulded
as they like.

It is truly astonishing that Mr. C. F. Adams should consider this a
matter of trivial concern, on the ground that less than a score of
slaves are now in that territory.[3] I doubt the accuracy of that statement; but a single slave held legally, *ad libitum*, will suffice to control legislation, and determine the action of any State or territory.

While the wavering manifested by several prominent Republicans is much to be deplored, your own straight-forward course, and
that of several others in the Senate and House, in accordance with
the solemn pledges made before the election, are worthy of the
highest commendation.[4] All compromises with the South will be
equally wicked and futile. The only alternative is, the abolition of
slavery, or the "crushing out" of liberty in every part of our country.

For one, I desire to thank you for declaring in the Senate, that the

petition from Boston, asking for any compromise to propitiate the
South, did not represent the sentiment even of the city, but was
signed by multitudes ignorantly and recklessly, the left hand not
knowing what the right did.[5] I wish it were in your power to have
that list of names critically examined. I am quite sure that hundreds
of names would be proved to be mere "men of straw." I have been
told that the names of Wendell Phillips, Henry Ward Beecher,
Theodore Parker, (!) and my own, were appended to it.[6] This is possible, but hardly credible. Still, excepting the Border-Ruffian returns in Kansas,[7] I do not believe there was ever a petition more
impudently and fraudulently presented to a legislative assembly
than the one from this city.

I congratulate you upon being the special object of the *Courier's*
malignant abuse.[8] Do not fear of being fully sustained by Massachusetts in your boldest utterances. And how posterity will decide
is easily seen.

Would to God that the people of the North, without distinction of
party, could see that the time has come for a separation from the
South, in the spirit of peace, and in obedience to the "Higher
Law"! Is it not self-evident that we are, and must be, with slave institutions in one section and free institutions in the other, two nations?

Think of the necessity for Mr. Lincoln to get through Baltimore in
the darkness of night, as if he were a felon of the deepest dye![9]

What will inauguration day bring forth?[10] Heaven only knows.
There is no crime too dreadful to be committed by the dealers in
human flesh. I have no belief in the possibility of maintaining the
Seat of Government at Washington.

Thanking you for the many documents you have so kindly sent to
me, from time to time, and hoping you will be divinely strengthened for whatever cross you may yet be called to bear, I remain,

Yours, for universal emancipation,

Wm. Lloyd Garrison.

Hon. Charles Sumner.

ALS: Charles Sumner Papers, Harvard College Library.

Garrison wrote on behalf of Holmes to Henry Wilson on the same day (micro.).

Charles Sumner (1811–1874), a graduate of Harvard College and Law School,
served as United States senator from 1851 until his death. A Radical Republican and
by 1861 chairman of the Senate Committee on Foreign Relations, Sumner consistently supported the abolition of slavery and the establishment of civil rights; he was
one of the politicians most admired by Garrison.

1. James H. Holmes, the editor of the Santa Fé *Republican*, served as secretary of
state in New Mexico in 1861. In this post he opposed so-called patriotic but actually

repressive measures. No other information about him is available. (Chris Emmett, *Fort Union and the Winning of the Southwest*, Norman, Okla., 1965, p. 254.)

The Border Ruffians were proslavery Missourians who came into Kansas to disrupt elections and harass opponents of slavery.

2. By "New Mexico" Garrison means Arizona and parts of Nevada and Colorado, as well as the present state.

3. Charles Francis Adams (1807–1886), the Harvard-educated son of John Quincy Adams, was a lawyer by training and a politician by preference. By 1861 he had served in the Massachusetts legislature (1840–1845), edited ten volumes of the works of his grandfather, John Adams, and been elected to Congress (in 1858). In December 1860 he had heard testimony from Judge John S. Watts, nine years a resident of New Mexico, to the effect that it was unlikely that slavery would ever develop in New Mexico, despite its intention to enter the Union as a slave state. In fact, Judge Watts explained, there were only eleven slaves in the territory. (Martin Duberman, *Charles Francis Adams, 1807–1886*, Palo Alto, Calif., 1968, pp. 235–243.)

4. Among the Republicans who approved the admission of New Mexico without any restriction in regard to slavery were Mason W. Tappan of New Hampshire and William A. Howard of Michigan. (Duberman, *Charles Francis Adams*, pp. 228, 241.) When the measure came to the House, it was tabled by a vote of 115 to 71, twenty-six Republicans voting not to table. In fact, New Mexico was not admitted as a state until 1912. (David Potter, *The South and the Sectional Conflict*, Baton Rouge, La., 1968, p. 248.)

5. Garrison refers to the petition in support of the Crittenden compromise read in the Senate on February 12, 1861, which was signed by 22,313 Massachusetts citizens. Senator John J. Crittenden of Kentucky had presented five constitutional amendments proposing extension of the line of the Missouri Compromise west to the Pacific, thus protecting slavery in the territory to the southwest. Sumner replied to the petition, alleging that the signers of it were ignorant of the real nature of Crittenden's compromise, and using in his speech the biblical expression Garrison quotes, an adaptation of Matthew 6:3. On February 18, Sumner presented a memorial from the town of Hopkinton, Mass., which stated antislavery views much more consistent with "the principles of the Commonwealth." (Benjamin P. Thomas, *Abraham Lincoln*, New York, 1952, pp. 229, 985.)

6. Henry Ward Beecher (1813–1887), son of Lyman Beecher and brother of Harriet Beecher Stowe, was probably the most powerful, most popular, and, ultimately, the most controversial minister of his day. At first an independent Presbyterian and then a Congregational minister, he had been pastor of churches in Cincinnati and Indianapolis before accepting calls to the Park Street and Old South churches in Boston and then to the newly formed Plymouth Church in Brooklyn Heights, N.Y. As minister in Brooklyn he became a national and then an international figure; attending his sermons was a signal event not only for his parishioners but also for visitors to New York. From the pulpit he displayed extraordinary emotional and physical vigor in discussing not only religion but politics and reform. He wrote for newspapers and periodicals and published books on a variety of subjects. Ultimately his life was marred by one of the most spectacular of nineteenth-century domestic scandals, when Theodore Tilton sued him for adultery with his wife. (Paxton Hibben, *Henry Ward Beecher: An American Portrait*, New York, 1927.)

7. A reference to the elections of 1854 and 1855, in which the Border Ruffians stuffed ballot boxes in order to defeat antislavery candidates.

8. The Boston *Courier*, founded in 1803, had, after the retirement of long-time editor Joseph T. Buckingham, become proslavery. In recent months the *Courier* had disparaged Sumner as a bachelor inhabiting an ivory tower. The paper was especially angered by Sumner's opposition to Crittenden's compromise proposals, calling him a "maniac, fiend, fool," and concluding that it is "a gross and a foul libel upon us to say that we are not in favor of compromise." (See especially Boston *Daily Courier*, February 13, 1861.)

9. After his election Lincoln came by special train from Springfield to Washing-

ton, making many stops and speeches en route; but the Pinkerton detective agency warned of an assassination plot and persuaded him to travel secretly from Philadelphia to Washington by way of Harrisburg and Baltimore. (Thomas, *Abraham Lincoln*, pp. 242–244.)

10. The inauguration was on March 4. Security precautions were taken, but no hostile incidents occurred.

4

TO JOHN S. RAREY

BOSTON, March 20, 1861.
JOHN S. RAREY, ESQ.:

DEAR SIR—

Though wholly a stranger to you, permit me to express the high gratification I have felt in listening to your sensible and excellent instruction, and in witnessing your simple but humane and effectual method, respecting the training of horses, however vicious they may be.

Twenty years ago, on my first visit to Dublin, Ireland,[1] I made the acquaintance of a most amiable and worthy gentleman,—WILLIAM H. DRUMMOND, D. D., Honorary Member of the Belfast Natural History Society; and on taking leave of him, he kindly put into my hands a thin volume written by himself, entitled "THE RIGHTS OF ANIMALS, AND MAN'S OBLIGATION TO TREAT THEM WITH HUMANITY."[2] I read it with inexpressible delight, every page of it indicating a truly benevolent spirit, and inculcating, by apt illustrations and the most cogent reasoning, lessons of kindness to the whole animal creation. My heart actually leaped within me as I read the expressive title, "THE RIGHTS OF ANIMALS"! I was myself then, as now, engaged in vindicating "THE RIGHTS OF MAN"; but here was a claim even for animals, affirming the possession, on their part, of certain absolute and inherent rights, which could not be disregarded without great wrong, as well as positive suffering; and, yet, which had been systematically violated through ignorance, caprice, thoughtlessness, or brutality, to the infliction of an amount of suffering and crime beyond all power of computation:—

> "O man! tyrannic lord, how long, how long
> Shall prostrate nature groan beneath your rage,
> Awaiting renovation?"[3]

Truly, "the whole creation groaneth and travaileth in pain together until now."[4] The causes of this state of things are manifold,

13

but not such as to forbid the hope of a general redemption, in the progress of light and knowledge. Hence, I regard yours as a messianic mission in behalf of the brute race, who, though incapable of articulate speech, possess feeling, memory, instinct, forecast, a certain power of reasoning, with large capacity for enjoyment and suffering; and whose claims to rational and humane consideration, at the hands of man, ought ever to be sacredly regarded. It is true, the sphere of your benevolent labors is confined mainly to the treatment of the horse, that noblest and most valuable of domesticated animals, and perhaps the most shamefully outraged of them all; but the sound philosophy upon which you base your theory, and the lessons of patience, kindness and self-government which you teach, embrace "every beast of the earth"[5] as well. Thus you are destined to exert a wide influence, favorable to the cause of suffering humanity, in all its complicated phases. You are instructing men, not less than subduing horses. Few can listen to your words, or witness your dealings with the most intractable animals, without feeling ashamed that they have given so little attention to the nature and capacity of the horse, and also painfully conscious of gross neglect, or irrational conduct, or positive barbarity, in their past treatment of him. It is desirable therefore, that your exhibitions should be as widely extended as possible, and witnessed by people of every tongue and clime. To this end, may your life long be spared!

Your method of controlling, almost to instantaneous obedience, every horse submitted to your hands, is as simple as its results are almost miraculous. There is no mystery, no legerdemain about it. Not a wound is made, not a blow given, not a wrathful word uttered: all is quietly done, with serenity and confidence, in a friendly spirit, the termination of the struggle being as sure as the law of gravitation. The transformation wrought in the spirit of the animal must be as singular to him as it is surprising to the spectator. "Old things are passed away; and behold, all things are become new!"[6] Where, only a few minutes before, all was obstinacy, nervous excitability, furious temper, ungovernable control, and imminent personal peril—now are witnessed ready obedience, unshrinking firmness, a docile spirit, and absolute safety even with the heels of the horse in close contact with your naked head. For years a nuisance or a terror, and subjected to the worst usage in order to break his will, he now stands erect, "clothed and in his right mind,"[7] requiring but a look or word to insure prompt obedience! A conquest like this is as sublime as it is beneficent.

The field of your labors expands to a boundless extent. You are needed every where in the two-fold capacity of teacher and savior. If it be true that

"Man's inhumanity to man makes countless thousands mourn,"[8]

it is equally true that his barbarity to fish, and fowl, and cattle, mightily augments the sum of mortal agony. The lesson of humanity is the slowest, if not the hardest, to be learnt by mankind. It constitutes no part of our educational processes, from the primary school to the university; whereas, it should be the earliest taught, and the soonest reduced to practice. But how many, who assume to fill the high and responsible office of instructor, are capable of instilling it into the plastic minds committed to their charge? How many are able to present an exemplification of its power and beauty in their own persons? True, there is much less of brutality in our schools than in by-gone days; but the reign of violence is only mitigated, not fully ended. If the wildest horse that ever bounded over plain or prairie can be easily controlled by kind and judicious treatment, surely this renders inexcusable a tyrannous severity in the government of children and youth. Your method is a fresh and striking demonstration of the proverb, that "like begets like."[9] Love responds to love; friendship to friendship; gentleness to gentleness; and likewise force to force, and hatred to hatred. "Overcome evil with good"[10] is the process of redemption marked out by Jesus: it is equally yours, as applied to the brute creation. Exalt your mission of philanthropy by a clear perception of its scope and importance. Go on, taming both man and beast, and showing them their exact relations to each other. We, Anglo-Saxons, being somewhat ferocious and exceedingly stubborn in our nature, need "line upon line, and precept upon precept," to make us noble and good toward each other, and to those whose place in the scale of mankind is lower than our own.[11]

The ancient proverb says, "A merciful man is merciful to his beast."[12] If this be the test of character, how many can be safely measured by it? Human conduct, however, is often strangely paradoxical.

What you have already achieved, Mr. Rarey, as an educator in the treatment of animals, seems almost to warrant a literal interpretation of the prophecy of the arrival of a period when "the wolf shall dwell with the lamb, and the leopard shall lie down with the kid; and the calf and the young lion and the fatling together; and a little child shall lead them. And the cow and the bear shall feed; their young ones shall lie down together; and the lion shall eat straw like the ox. And the sucking child shall play on the hole of the asp, and the weaned shall put his hand on the cockatrice's den."[13]

Yours, for the recognition of "the rights of man" and "the rights of animals,"

WM. LLOYD GARRISON.

Printed: *The Liberator*, March 22, 1861; a rough draft is preserved in the Merrill Collection of Garrison Papers, Wichita State University Library.

John Solomon Rarey (1827–1866) was a well-known horse trainer who began his career in 1852 and by 1857 was instructing Queen Victoria and the royal family. Between 1858 and 1862 he made extensive tours through Europe, the Middle East, and the United States, demonstrating and teaching his various skills. In 1856 he published *The Modern Art of Taming Wild Horses. (Who Was Who in America, 1607– 1896*, revised ed., 1967.)

1. Garrison had arrived in Dublin on July 28, 1840, and spent three days visiting Richard D. Webb. (*AWT*, p. 173.)

2. William Hamilton Drummond (1778–1865) was the minister of the Strand Street Church in Dublin from 1815 until his death. In addition, he had a considerable reputation as poet, translator, and author of numerous pamphlets. He was also active in the Belfast Natural History and Philosophical Society, which was at that time the only museum facility in the city. In addition to the essay cited by Garrison (London, 1838), which urges kindness to animals and condemns hunting, cockfights, and vivisection, he was known for *The Battle of Trafalgar* (1806), *The Giant's Causeway* (1811), and a translation of *The First Book of T. Lucretius Carus on the Nature of Things* (1808). (Letters to the editor from J. R. H. Greeves, hon. secretary and treasurer, Belfast Natural History and Philosophical Society, Northern Ireland, June 27 and July 17, 1972.)

3. James Thomson, *The Seasons*, "Autumn," lines 1189–1191.

4. Romans 8:22.

5. Genesis 1:30, 9:2, or 9:10.

6. II Corinthians 5:17, with the addition of the conjunction.

7. Luke 8:35 or Mark 5:15.

8. Robert Burns, "Man Was Made to Mourn," stanza 7.

9. A proverb of Roman origin.

10. Romans 12:21.

11. Garrison's quotation is adapted from Isaiah 28:10. In *The Liberator*, March 29, 1861, Garrison corrects this sentence as follows: "for 'each other,' read 'all mankind,' and for 'mankind,' read 'creation.'"

12. The proverb is probably of biblical origin; see Proverbs 12:10.

13. Isaiah 11:6–8, slightly adapted.

5

TO OLIVER JOHNSON

Boston, April 19, 1861.

Dear Johnson—

I thank you for your letters, keeping me posted in regard to our prospects of a disturbance at our approaching anniversary.[1] It is an interesting statement that you make respecting the early anti-slavery antecedents of Mr. Kennedy, the Superintendent of your City Police, and it is gratifying to be assured that he and his force are disposed to give us all the protection which exigencies may require.[2] [Wendell] Phillips, Quincy, and myself, however, have just had a consultation, upon the state of things, and we are unitedly of the opinion that, at this critical juncture, it will be the wisest and best not to attempt to hold more than *one* public meeting, anniversary week,—namely, in the morning of Tuesday, the 7th of May, in Rev. Dr. Cheever's Church,—omitting the meeting at the Cooper Institute in the evening; and by their desire I write to request you to apprise the agent of the Institute that we shall hold no meeting therein, leaving him free to engage it to any other party or society wanting it for that evening; and if he cannot let it, then to pay him for the hall as though we had used it.[3]

Now that civil war has begun, and a whirlwind of violence and excitement is to sweep through the country, every day increasing in intensity until its bloodiest culmination, it is for the abolitionists to "stand still, and see the salvation of God,"[4] rather than to attempt to add any thing to the general commotion. It is no time for minute criticism of Lincoln, Republicanism, or even the other parties, now that they are fusing for a death-grapple with the Southern slave oligarchy; for they are instruments in the hands of God to carry forward and help achieve the great object of emancipation, for which we have so long been striving. The war is fearfully to scourge the nation, but mercy will be mingled with judgment, and grand results are to follow, should no dividing root of bitterness rise up at the North. All our sympathies and wishes must be with the government, as against the Southern desperadoes and buccaneers; yet, of course, without any compromise of principle on our part. We need great circumspection and consummate wisdom in regard to what we say and do, under these unparalleled circumstances. We are rather, for the time being, to note the events transpiring, than seek to control them. There must be no needless turning of popular violence upon ourselves, by any false step of our own. Therefore, whether we should be likely to excite it or not, by holding an evening meeting at the Institute, we deem it soundly prudent not to attempt to hold it. We ought not *wholly* to forego our anniversary if we can help it; but events may so shape themselves before the morning of the 7th, that even that public meeting had better not be held. None can tell what a day may bring forth.[5]

We were all taken aback by P's speech at New Bedford—it was so unlike him, in various particulars.[6] No wonder the pro-slavery press had seized upon it approvingly in part. It was simply not well-digested or guardedly expressed. His discourse on Sunday next, at Music Hall, will make all right, no doubt.

Simply omit from the call in the Standard, the notice of the evening meeting at the Institute, without making any reference whatever to it in the Standard.[7]

Yours, hopefully and strongly,

Wm. Lloyd Garrison.

ALS: Garrison Papers, Boston Public Library; partly printed in *Life*, IV, 21–22.

1. The annual meeting of the American Anti-Slavery Society, of which Garrison was president, was normally held in New York City in May. Garrison and other abolitionists did decide to postpone indefinitely that meeting and others. (*The Liberator*, April 26 and May 3, 1861.)

2. John Alexander Kennedy (1803–1873), who was the superintendent of police in New York in 1861, had guaranteed the society protection in the event of violence. Formerly secretary of an antislavery society in Baltimore, Kennedy, prior to 1827, had been Benjamin Lundy's partner in publishing the *Genius of Universal Emancipation*. (*Life*.)

3. Edmund Quincy (1808–1877), son of Josiah Quincy, a Harvard graduate and a minor man of letters, had been an active abolitionist since 1837. On a number of occasions during Garrison's absence (notably in 1843, 1846, and 1847) he had been substitute editor of *The Liberator*. In 1844 he became one of the editors of the *National Anti-Slavery Standard*. Although Quincy occasionally differed with Garrison (for instance, concerning the Free-Soil party and the Sabbath question in 1848), he wholeheartedly supported Garrison most of the time. (*AWT*.)

George Barrell Cheever (1807–1890), educated at Bowdoin College and Andover Theological Seminary, had since 1846 been the minister of the Congregational Church at Union Square in New York. Cheever, a vigorous abolitionist and even a supporter of John Brown, was to become bitterly critical of Lincoln and, after the war, an advocate of Radical Reconstruction. (Robert M. York, *George B. Cheever, Religious and Social Reformer, 1807–1890*, Orono, Me., 1955, pp. v–xi.)

Cooper Institute (or Cooper Union) was founded in 1857 by Peter Cooper (1791–1883) to provide working people with free education in the evenings. Located in a brownstone building on the corner of Third Street and Fourth Avenue, the institute contained in addition to a library a large auditorium. (Frederick Taber Cooper, *Rider's New York City: A Guide Book for Travelers*, New York, 1924, p. 211.)

4. Exodus 14:13, with the substitution of "God" for "the Lord."

5. An adaptation of Proverbs 27:1.

6. Wendell Phillips delivered two lectures before the New Bedford Lyceum in the spring of 1861: "The Crisis" on March 19 and "The Times" on April 9 (reported in the press as "The Present Crisis"). Summaries of the lectures appeared in the New Bedford *Evening Standard*, March 20 and April 10. Garrison may well have been "taken aback" by remarks like the following on April 9: "we have no right to deny the South a separate form of government"; the North will never endorse such a war," for "it violates expediency as well as principle. You cannot conquer ideas with bullets." In the speech in Boston to which Garrison refers Phillips voiced sentiments that seemed quite the opposite of those he expressed in New Bedford.

7. The *National Anti-Slavery Standard* was founded in 1840 to serve as the official organ of the American Anti-Slavery Society. Sustained largely through funds raised at annual antislavery fairs, its editorial staff included over the years, besides Johnson, Lydia Maria Child, David Lee Child, Sydney Howard Gay, Wendell Phillips, and Parker Pillsbury. Despite frequent financial difficulties, the *Standard* continued publication until 1870.

6

TO JAMES S. GIBBONS

Boston, April 28, 1861.

J. S. Gibbons, Esq.

My Dear Friend—I am much obliged to you for your advisory and interesting letter, received yesterday. You will see, by an official notice in the Standard and Liberator, that the Executive Committee of the American Anti-Slavery Society have deemed it expedient to postpone the anniversary in May until a more suitable period.[1] Heaven grant there may be no occasion for holding another, unless to celebrate the jubilee! For the present, at least, the abolitionists are justified in suspending their usual operations. The civil war now raging in the land is, on the part of the Administration, technically and ostensibly to defend the "stars and stripes," and maintain the government against conspirators and traitors; but it is really a struggle between the free and the slave States—i. e., between freedom and slavery—between free institutions and slave institutions—between the ideas of the nineteenth and those of the twelfth century. All the slave States make common cause with each other, the border ones being the most dangerous and detestable of them all. The Cabinet ought never, for one moment, to have recognized neutrality on the part of Virginia and Maryland, except as arrant disloyalty.[2] It is manifest that the sentiment of the North is far ahead of the action of the Cabinet, and demands more vigorous measures—not acting merely on the defensive in trying to save the Capital, but carrying the conflict southward with irresistible energy.

You may well be astonished at the almost miraculous change which, in the course of a single fortnight, has taken place in the feelings and purposes of all classes in your city, (as it has throughout the North,) in relation to the South. That change you describe, in a very amusing and graphic manner, in your sketch of the "Billy Wilson's men," whose ferocious desperation Divine Justice seems to be concentrating into a flaming thunderbolt, to hurl at the heads and homes of Southern oppressors, by whom they have hitherto been controlled and directed against the cause of liberty.[3]

So tremendous and wholly unexpected to the slave oligarchy are the military gatherings of the North for the preservation of the Union, that I am inclined, now, to think the South will no longer make any offensive assaults, in which case the present Northern furore may as suddenly go down as it has been aroused—leaving the spirit of "compromise" and "conciliation" to come in, and re-duce the North to a worse submission than she has ever yet evinced. The war, in itself, presents some paradoxical aspects.

Give my warmest love to your dear wife and children, and to John and Rosa, whom not to see anniversary week will be a great bereavement.[4]

Yours, truly,

Wm. Lloyd Garrison.

ALS: Autograph Collection, Essex Institute, Salem, Mass.; extract printed in Sarah Hopper Emerson, ed., *Life of Abby Hopper Gibbons* (New York, 1897), I, 290–292.

James Sloan Gibbons (1810–1892) was a New York merchant and banker who made frequent financial contributions to the abolitionist cause. By 1842 he was so closely associated with the abolitionists and especially with the *National Anti-Slavery Standard* that the New York Meeting of Friends officially disowned him. During the New York draft riots of 1863, Gibbons' home was ransacked.

1. The executive committee at this time consisted of the following: Garrison, Francis Jackson, Edmund Quincy, Maria W. Chapman, Wendell Phillips, Anne W. Weston, Sydney Howard Gay, Samuel May, Jr., William I. Bowditch, Charles K. Whipple, Henry C. Wright, and Charles Follen, Jr. (*National Anti-Slavery Standard*, May 19, 1860.)

2. Lincoln's cabinet at the time consisted of the following: Edward Bates, attorney general; Mason Blair, postmaster general; Simon Cameron, secretary of war; Salmon P. Chase, secretary of the treasury; William H. Seward, secretary of state; Caleb B. Smith, secretary of the interior; and Gideon Welles, secretary of the navy.

Garrison refers to the fact that Lincoln and his cabinet had been more lenient with Virginia and Maryland than with some of the other southern states, owing to their strategic locations in relation to Washington. In fact, the state convention of Virginia, meeting in Richmond on February 13, 1861, had voted to waive secession with the hope that a compromise could be worked out with the new administration. Garrison considered any compromise with Virginia equivalent to guaranteeing "slave-holders some forty or fifty years more of power." In the case of Maryland, Lincoln and the cabinet had done what they could to placate the state legislature and avoid provoking incidents. (*The Liberator*, March 29, 1861; *OHAP*, p. 612.)

3. Although the Gibbons sketch has not been otherwise identified, "Billy Wilson's men" refers to a particularly rowdy part, perhaps a battalion, of the New York regiment led by Colonel Elmer Ellsworth. Billy Wilson (died 1874) had raised this regiment in 1861. (Allan Nevins and Milton Halsey Thomas, eds., *The Diary of George Templeton Strong*, New York, 1952, III, 137, 149; IV, 543.)

4. Abigail Hopper Gibbons (1801–1893), a friend of James and Lucretia Mott, as well as of Ralph Waldo Emerson, was the third child of humanitarian and abolitionist Isaac Tatem Hopper (1771–1852) and Sarah Tatum Hopper. She was active in abolition, woman's rights, and prison reform and during the Civil War served as a nurse in the camps and hospitals. The Gibbons' children at the time of this letter were Sarah H. (1835–1918), Julia (born 1837), and Lucy (1839–1936). Julia never married. Sarah married William Emerson in 1863 and in 1897 published in two volumes the *Life of Abby Hopper Gibbons*. Lucy married author, educator, and poet James Herbert Morse in 1870. The sisters were active in philanthropy and in the woman suffrage movement.

John and Rosa DeWolf Hopper, who were married in 1845, were Abigail Hopper Gibbons' brother and sister-in-law. John (1815–1864) was a lawyer by training but worked as agent for the New England Mutual Life Insurance Company. He was physically disqualified from service in the army but, nevertheless, contributed financial support to the northern cause. (Margaret Hope Bacon, *Lamb's Warrior: The Life of Isaac T. Hopper*, New York, 1970; Benjamin Kendall Emerson, *The Ipswich Emersons, A.D. 1636–1900* . . . , Boston, 1900; Sarah Hopper Emerson, ed., *Life of Abby Hopper Gibbons*, New York, 1897; Sarah T. Thayer, "Mrs. Abby Hopper Gibbons," *Charities Review*, 2, No.7: 379–389, May 1893; obituaries, New York *Times*, July 21, 1864, New York *Daily Tribune*, July 20, 1864.)

7

TO OLIVER JOHNSON

Boston, May 9, 1861.

Dear Johnson:

I have delayed answering your letters,[1] knowing that we were to have a meeting of the Executive Committee to-day; and now that it has been held, I lose no time in communicating the result.

No proposition was made to discontinue the Standard; but the question naturally arose, how, with the limited means of the [American Anti-Slavery] Society, and the prospect of an empty treasury at no distant day, in consequence of the pecuniary drainage that will every where be made by the war, it could be carried through another year. Of course, the strongest desire to avoid its discontinuance, if possible, was expressed; my own feeling being, at all times, that every other operation or agency of the Society should give way, if necessary, in order to keep the Standard alive; and that when this cannot be done, it will be tantamount to the extinction of the Society itself. We voted unanimously to do our best to raise the necessary means, and shall take the requisite steps without delay.

As it is possible that the thought may have passed into your mind, that the Standard is deemed of little interest or importance, it may be gratifying to you to know that no such feeling was expressed by any member of the Committee. The only question raised, the only one discussed, was,—With the prospect before us, can the necessary funds be raised? In every respect, the Standard is highly creditable to our Society. It is handsomely printed; it is edited with marked ability; its correspondence is highly talented and interesting; and its selections uniformly discriminating and excellent. It ought to have a subscription list larger than that of the Independent;[2] but its fidelity to principle, its uncompromising opposition to slavery, renders this impracticable. Nevertheless, it is a little singular that its circulation continues so extremely limited, and its income so very small. It does not meddle with "extraneous" matters, like the Liberator, and is very faithful to its position as an official organ. Probably both papers will always be meagrely supported, no matter what may be the change in public sentiment on the subject of slavery; for with that change will come a readiness on the part of papers to which no odium is attached to meet the demands of the hour, on a popular scale.

In regard to the Bugle, the Committee unanimously voted to comply with the proposition, contained in M. R. Robinson's letter, to supply its paid subscribers with the Standard, to the extent that may be required; the Hovey Committee being willing to make our Society whole in the matter.[3] To such subscribers of the Bugle as now take the Standard, whatever they may have pre-paid on it can be carried to their credit on their Standard account in the future.

The Bugle has been conducted in a most uncompromising spirit, and I am sorry it must be discontinued. It has sometimes erred, I think, in harshness of criticism, and in the lack of a comprehensive view of the growth of public sentiment through political action; and its tone respecting the war partook, I also think, of a somewhat morbid character. Nevertheless, it never showed any sign of faltering, and was always up "to high-water mark."

You speak of wishing to retire from the Standard. I do not wonder at this, for you have had a heavy burden to carry, and have a right to an honorable discharge; but I trust you will hold on "while a shot remains in the locker,"[4] or a competent person can be found to fill your place.

Understanding that some sensitiveness is felt and expressed by some in our ranks at the appearance of the American flag in the Standard, notwithstanding the motto over and under it, the Committee deem it advisable to have it quietly withdrawn.[5]

Wm. I. Bowditch is our new Treasurer. Mr. Jackson will probably not survive the summer.[6]

Faithfully yours,

W. L. G.

☞ We need great circumspection in what we write and publish concerning the present anomalous war, which, after all, *may* end less hopefully for freedom than we desire.

☞ As we expected, some dissatisfaction is expressed in certain quarters at the discontinuance of our anniversaries in New York and Boston; but all the Committee, and abolitionists generally, unite in the wisdom and policy of the measure.

☞ When you write again, please let me know how many letters George Thompson has contributed to the Standard since last October.[7]

ALS: Garrison Papers, Boston Public Library.

1. In a letter dated May 7, 1861, Johnson urged Garrison to help continue the publication of the much-needed *National Anti-Slavery Standard.* (Anti-Slavery Letters to Garrison and Others, Boston Public Library.)

2. The *Independent,* a Congregational newspaper, had been one of the more limited New York publications until Theodore Tilton became its managing editor in 1856. He converted it into an influential, liberal organ with numerous distinguished contributors, including Henry Ward Beecher, Elizabeth Barrett Browning, Louis Kossuth, James Russell Lowell, William H. Seward, and John Greenleaf Whittier. After the discontinuance of *The Liberator* in December 1865, Garrison himself became a frequent contributor of both letters and articles.

3. The *Anti-Slavery Bugle,* founded in August 1845 in Salem, Ohio, as the official organ of the Ohio Anti-Slavery Society, had ceased publication shortly before the date of Garrison's letter. Oliver Johnson had served as editor from 1849 to 1851.

Marius R. Robinson (1806–1878) was minister, orator, editor, and devoted abolitionist. A graduate of the University of Nashville, he had studied at the seminary there before moving to Cincinnati to teach free blacks. In 1836–1837 he had assisted James G. Birney in editing the *Philanthropist* and from 1851 to 1859 had edited the *Anti-Slavery Bugle.* (Russel B. Nye, "Marius Robinson, a Forgotten Abolitionist Leader," *Ohio State Archaeological and Historical Quarterly,* 55:138–154, 1946; *Life,* IV, 409. Robinson's death date is incorrectly given in the Nye article.)

Charles Fox Hovey (1807–1859) was a prosperous Boston merchant and abolitionist who had frequently contributed financial support to the cause, ultimately in the form of a bequest of approximately one-quarter of his estate ($40,000). The "Hovey Committee" were the trustees empowered with full discretion to administer this fund; they consisted of Stephen S. and Abby Kelley Foster, Garrison, Francis Jackson, Wendell Phillips, Parker Pillsbury, Charles K. Whipple, and Henry C. Wright. The money was dispensed for a variety of antislavery works at the rate of $8,000 per year over a five-year period.

4. A naval colloquialism.

5. The masthead, which illustrated the *Standard* column "Chronicles of War," was printed in the issues for April 27 and May 4, 1861. The American flag, which appeared with a liberty cap atop the staff, was sandwiched between two slogans: "Proclaim LIBERTY throughout the land, unto all the Inhabitants thereof" and "To-day the Slave asks God for a sight of this Banner.—WENDELL PHILLIPS."

6. William Ingersoll Bowditch (1819–1909), son of Nathaniel and Mary Ingersoll Bowditch, received both his bachelor's and his law degrees from Harvard. By profession a conveyancer and trustee, he was marginally active in the antislavery movement, having been elected in 1860 to serve one term on the executive committee of the American Anti-Slavery Society. (Letter to the editor from Nathaniel R. Bowditch, Philadelphia, August 15, 1972; *Standard,* May 19, 1860.)

Francis Jackson (1789–1861) was a wealthy Boston merchant and active Garrisonian abolitionist. He frequently gave financial support both to Garrison and to the cause. He served for many years as president of the Massachusetts Anti-Slavery Society and as vice-president of the American Anti-Slavery Society. In 1848 Garrison named his youngest child for Jackson. Jackson died in November 1861, leaving an antislavery bequest, the disposition of which led to a controversy that proved divisive among abolitionists.

7. George Thompson (1804–1878) was the English politician and reformer who had been a radical and active abolitionist since the early 1830s. By 1831, as agent of the London Anti-Slavery Society, he was agitating for abolition in the British West Indies. It was he who successfully guided the emancipation bill through Parliament in 1833. That same year Garrison on his first trip to England met Thompson and persuaded him to visit the United States in 1834. Between September 1834 and December 1835 he lectured on abolition in this country, expressing radical views so much like Garrison's that the Boston mob of October 1835 sought him as much as his American counterpart. On subsequent trips to America in 1850 and in 1864–1867 he

was honored rather than reviled. American abolitionists were grateful to him for his help in presenting to British audiences the northern point of view during the Civil War. By the late 1860s, as can be seen by reading Garrison's letters, he had lost much of his fire as a public speaker and was hard pressed to support himself and his family.

No letters from Thompson appeared in the *Standard* during the period mentioned.

8

TO GEORGE T. DOWNING, JOHN V. DeGRASSE, and ROBERT MORRIS

Boston, May 13, 1861.

Messrs. George T. Downing, John V. De Grasse, and Robert Morris:

Gentlemen—

You apprise me of a meeting to be held this evening in the Joy Street Church, in this city, by our colored fellow-citizens, with reference to the Haytian emigration scheme, and desire me to express my views respecting it. This I must do very briefly, for want of time to go into the consideration of the subject with that thoroughness which its importance demands.

It is well known to you, that I have always strenuously opposed the scheme of the American Colonization Society,—not because it proposed to aid such colored persons as might wish to go to Africa, in order to better their condition, for this might be a generous act under appropriate circumstances,—but solely on account of the iniquitous doctrines and hateful designs of that Society, all tending to perpetuate slavery, and to make the condition of the free colored population as hopeless as possible in this their native land.[1] Let me congratulate you all, that the power of the Colonization Society for evil, to any extent, has passed away, by the general enlightenment of the public mind through the Anti-Slavery agitation.

Within a few months past, overtures have been made, by the President of Hayti, to colored Americans to make themselves citizens of that republic.[2] How ought these to be regarded?

1. As to their nature. They are certainly generous, and unquestionably to be relied upon as made in good faith.

2. As to the motive prompting them, on the part of the Haytian government: I see no reason to doubt its benevolence and purity. It can have no design, from such a source, either to entrap emigrants or to injure the cause of the colored people, whether bond or free, in this country. So broad and liberal an invitation is at least very

strong, if not conclusive evidence that Hayti is advancing in civilization, wealth and enterprise, and aspires to be a populous and powerful nation.

3. As to the expediency of emigrating. This resolves itself simply into the question of individual feeling; for as no compulsion is connected with it, whoever goes will do so voluntarily; and this right of locomotion and adventure naturally belongs to every human being.

> "The world is all before us where to choose,
> And Providence our guide."[3]

4. As to the probable results of it. No doubt, in many cases there will be good success; in others, disappointment and loss. Every thing will depend upon the character and spirit of the emigrants. In all lands, some never fail to thrive; others are ever poor and shiftless. In such cases, generally, the cause is organic, and no change of circumstances can essentially alter it. Thus far, the emigrants appear to be satisfied with the change they have made, with a few exceptions.

If you desire to know whether, as a general rule, I would advise colored persons to emigrate to Hayti, even on the generous terms proposed by its government, my reply is, decidedly, no. Hence it is that I have given no encouragement to that scheme, or to any other similar scheme, in the columns of the Liberator. One unavoidable evil attending it is to unsettle the minds of the colored people themselves, in regard to their future destiny; to inspire the mischievous belief in the minds of the white people, that they can yet be effectually "got rid of"; and to keep law and custom unfriendly to them; so as to induce their departure to a foreign land. In proportion to the magnitude and success of the scheme will be this evil. A few thousands may be colonized without any perceptible effect of this kind; but plans for a general exodus, I believe, would have a very injurious effect upon the cause of the enslaved, and those already free.

This is their native land. Here they are to remain, as a people, as long as men are left to tread upon the soil; here they are gradually, but surely, to rise in the scale of civilization and improvement; here their fetters are to be broken, and their rights restored. All the signs of the times indicate that a death-blow has been given to the accursed slave system; and when that shall be abolished, the way will be opened for a glorious redemption. Complexional prejudice shall swiftly disappear, injurious distinctions cease, and peace and good will every where reign. Though I have no word of censure to bestow upon any one emigrating to Hayti, but, on the contrary, wish him all possible success, yet I specially honor the colored man who cherishes this faith in the future, and is willing to stand firmly in his lot here, even though it be a hard one, manfully laboring for "the good time coming," at whatever present cost to himself, and bearing his cross which in due time a just God shall change into a crown of glory.

Your faithful and untiring advocate,

Wm. Lloyd Garrison.

ALS: Collection of Howard DeGrasse Asbury, Hollis, N.Y.

George T. Downing (1819–1903) was a free Negro who lobbied for abolition and civil rights. As early as 1837 he was involved in petitioning the New York legislature for abrogation of the property requirement for Negro voting. In 1855 he established a station on the Underground Railroad in Newport, R.I., and in the same year he was a delegate to the Colored National Convention in Philadelphia. In August 1859 he was chairman of the convention of New England Negroes in Boston. (Benjamin Quarles, *Black Abolitionists*, New York, 1969, passim; obituary, Boston *Globe*, July 23, 1903; letter to the editor from Howard DeGrasse Asbury, September 28, 1971.)

John V. DeGrasse (1825–1868) was a Negro physician practicing in New York City, who had received his medical degree from Bowdoin College in 1849 and been admitted to the Boston Medical Society in 1854. Although his education had been financed by the American Colonization Society with the understanding that he would practice in Liberia, in fact he remained in the United States. During the Civil War he was an assistant surgeon with black troops. (Letters to the editor from Howard DeGrasse Asbury, September 28, 1971, and from Ruth Bell, researcher, March 6, 1972.)

Robert Morris (died 1882) was a prominent Boston Negro lawyer devoted to aiding members of his race, both fugitive and free. In 1852 he petitioned the military committee of the Massachusetts legislature to establish a Negro company. In 1855 he was active in the movement to integrate the public school system in the state. (Quarles, *Black Abolitionists*, passim.)

1. Opposition to the American Colonization Society (founded in 1817), culminating in his *Thoughts on African Colonization* in 1832, had been Garrison's first crusade as an abolitionist. (Aileen S. Kraditor, *Means and Ends in American Abolitionism: Garrison and his Critics on Strategy and Tactics, 1834–1850*, New York, 1967; see also *Letters*, I.)

2. Nicholas Fabre Geffrard (1806–1879), a mulatto, took office as president of Haiti in 1859, following a coup overthrowing his predecessor, Soulouque, Faustin I. Geffrard appointed James Redpath (see *Letters*, IV, 704) as commissioner of emigration, and Haitian emigration bureaus were set up in Boston and New York. Some sixteen hundred Negroes were sent out to Haiti but few remained, owing to the corruption and inefficiency of the Haitian government. Although Geffrard's rule was relatively enlightened, he in turn was overthrown in 1867. (L. L. Montague, *Haiti and the United States, 1714–1938*, Durham, N.C., 1940.)

3. John Milton, *Paradise Lost*, XII, lines 646–647.

9

TO AARON M. POWELL

Boston, May 14, 1861.

My dear Aaron:

Thanks for your interesting letter. It is very pleasant to hear from you, with incidental reference to your dear Anna, to father, mother, Lizzie, and George. I shall always regret that I was not present at your marriage. Had I not expected to be in New York, as usual, anniversary week, I should doubtless have been at Ghent at the time referred to.

A word in regard to the postponement of our annual meeting. No doubt it is regretted by some, but, as far as I can learn, it is generally deemed a wise measure. The life of our glorious Anti-Slavery cause is in no wise dependant upon an unbending adherence to the observance of times and seasons. There is a time to speak, and a time to keep silent;[1] a time to hold meetings, and a time to omit them. Here, all the members of our Executive Committee, and others of the "household of faith,"[2] came spontaneously to the same conclusion, in regard to the expediency of postponing our anniversaries, in view of the unparalleled war excitement, which probably will be still greater as blood flows, victims are slain, and the conflict waxes to the gate. Technically, the war is to restore the old state of things —fugitive slave law, and all; practically, it is a geographical fight between North and South, and between free and slave institutions.[3] Of the great body of soldiers who have enlisted at the North, comparatively few have any intention or wish to break down the slave system; but God, "who is above all, and greater than all,"[4] and who

"—moves in a mysterious way,
His wonders to perform,"[5]

is making use of them to do "a strange and terrible work,"[6] in righteousness. I neither deprecate his justice, nor desire to see peace through compromise. I believe this state of things is hopeful, compared with what it was six months ago.

I am glad to know that you are pleased with my views of the war, as expressed through the Liberator.[7] Matters are so complex in some cases, so paradoxical in others, that it is difficult to write so as not to be misunderstood or misrepresented.

So, you are coming to Worcester with Anna on Saturday, and propose extending your visit to Boston. We are all desirous of giving you both our warmest welcome, and shall be ready to greet you at any time. If you can make it convenient to come to Boston on Thursday or Friday of next week, it will enable me to give you more of my time than during the first part of that or any subsequent week. Thursday, I am like Bunyan's pilgrim in sight of the cross, released from my pack for several days. I believe he had a longer respite. But come whenever most convenient to you.

I write in haste, and have time to add nothing more, except that we all desire to be most lovingly remembered to all under the family roof.

Truly yours,

Wm. Lloyd Garrison.

Aaron M. Powell.

ALS: Friends Historical Library, Swarthmore College; extract printed in Aaron M. Powell, *Personal Reminiscences* (New York, 1899), p. 46.

Aaron Macy Powell (1832–1899), a Friend active in abolition and other reform movements, was a farmer turned teacher. He was the son of Townsend (1807–c. 1888) and Catherine Macy Powell, who had two other children at this time, Elizabeth and George T. Aaron Powell was married to Anna Rice; the couple had one daughter, who died in early childhood. He edited the *National Anti-Slavery Standard* from 1865 to 1870. Later Powell was editor of the *National Temperance Advocate* and of the *Philanthropist*, official organ of the American Purity Alliance, of which he was a founder and at the time of his death the president. In 1880 he and Anna moved to Plainfield, N.J. (Letter to the editor from Mary L. Thomas, Columbia County Historical Society, Kinderhook, N.Y., August 7, 1972; testimonial written on the death of Aaron M. Powell by the Plainfield, N.J., Monthly Meeting of Friends, October 15, 1899.)

1. A reference to Ecclesiastes 3:7.
2. Galatians 6:10.
3. The Fugitive Slave Law was enacted by Congress in 1850 as a part of the compromise proposals of Henry Clay. This law, which provided for the return of escaped slaves to their masters, was so unpopular in the North that the Underground Railroad was devised to help escaping slaves reach Canada.
4. Possibly an allusion to John 10:29.
5. William Cowper, "Light Shining Out of Darkness," *Olney Hymns*, stanza 1, lines 1–2.
6. A possible allusion to Psalms 65:5.
7. In four successive weeks, beginning April 19, Garrison had printed editorials about secession and the war. On April 19, he distinguished on moral grounds between northern disunion and southern secession. "The former is based on the eternal fitness of things, and animated by a noble, disinterested, and philanthropic spirit. The latter is the concentration of all diabolism." On April 26 he described public response to the war with an enthusiasm hardly consistent with his own nonresistant principles: "In support of it, there is such an uprising in every city, town and hamlet at the North—without distinction of sect or party—as to seem like a general resurrection from the dead! . . . Neutrality will not be tolerated. The change in Northern feeling since the capture of Fort Sumter is total, wonderful, indescribable—uniting the most discordant, and reconciling the most estranged." On May 3 he insisted that the real issues of the war concerned not Union but slavery. "If this war shall put an end to that execrable system, it will be more glorious in history than that of the Revolution." In the final editorial on May 10 he expressed his confidence that emancipa-

tion was nearer than the abolitionists had thought. "The present struggle cannot fail to hasten it mightily, in a providential sense."

10

TO OLIVER JOHNSON

Boston, July 3, 1861.

Dear Johnson:

I am sorry that you cannot be at the Framingham Grove to-morrow, and yet glad that you are to be with the friends at Providence, with whom, I doubt not, you will have a very pleasant time.

I shall be at home the remainder of the week, and glad to see you, if you can make it convenient to come to the city.

The state of the times makes the pecuniary prospects of the American A. S. Society quite inauspicious; expecially as Mrs. Chapman has abandoned the idea of holding another Anti-Slavery Festival, which (as the Fair before it) has been our main dependance for means to sustain the [National Anti-Slavery] Standard in special.[1] She is satisfied that little or nothing is to be hoped from our friends across the ocean, who seem to be singularly muddled about the war here, and who have hitherto contributed nearly one half of all the moneys obtained at the Fair and Festival. So she has no hope of any success in making another attempt; and thus our pecuniary sheet anchor is suddenly swept away. This makes the continuance of the Standard so problematical. Still, we shall make a vigorous effort to keep the flag flying. "Don't give up the ship," said the dying Lawrence; and this should be the spirit animating the abolitionists in regard to the Standard.[2] We shall send out our appeals shortly, hoping for the best.

Give my warm regards to Thomas and Paulina [Davis], and to Mary Ann [Johnson].

Ever faithfully yours,

Wm. Lloyd Garrison.

Oliver Johnson.

ALS: Garrison Papers, Boston Public Library.

1. Maria Weston Chapman (1806–1885), the widow of Boston merchant Henry G. Chapman, was one of the leading spirits of both the Massachusetts and the Boston Female Anti-Slavery societies. A frequent contributor to *The Liberator*, she also published a number of antislavery pamphlets.

2. The quotation is usually attributed to Captain James Lawrence (1781–1813), a naval officer who distinguished himself during the War of 1812. However, the only

fully authenticated use of the exhortation is that by Oliver Hazard Perry on the flag-ship *Lawrence* during the battle of Lake Erie, September 10, 1813.

11

TO WENDELL PHILLIPS GARRISON

Valley Falls, Aug. 9, 1861.

My Dear Son:

We received your letter from North Becket just as we were leaving for this place yesterday afternoon, and were much relieved and gratified to hear that every thing had gone so pleasantly with you and our dear Franky. Our Florence friends deserve special thanks for their kind hospitality.[1] I am sorry, for George's sake, that he did not leave in season to meet you there.

We expect to be gone till Saturday evening, next week. In the meantime, you and Catharine must provide for yourselves according to your taste.[2] Our grocer will let you have any thing on my account until my return, as I spoke to him about it; and so will Mr. W., our meat provider at Boylston market.[3]

I have seen no advertisement in regard to the vacancy in the Latin School, but understand there are three applicants for it, beside yourself. Mr. McGill says it will doubtless be given to the one Mr. Gardner prefers; so that, if he seconds your motion, your chance may be considered good.[4] Mr. McGill thinks it would be well to place the letters you have received from Felton[5] and others in Mr. Gardner's hands, to be laid before the Committee. At any rate, would it not be well to call upon Mr. Gardner, and see how the case stands?

If you can read the proof of the outside of the Liberator, and assist in reading the inside, it would be an accommodation. Mr. Whipple, however, has promised to attend to it, and you need not put yourself to any trouble about it.[6]

I wish, however, you would (if you can) go to the Anti-Slavery Office[7] every day, see what letters are sent to my address, open and examine them—if any are important for me to see before my return, send them to me at Providence, care of Henry Anthony; if not important, file them till I get home.[8] All communications for the Liberator may be handed over to Mr. Whipple.

I wish Winchell to send me, on Monday, to Providence, by express, (if convenient,) his report of my afternoon remarks at Abington [Massachusetts] on the 1st of August, and I will return it on Tuesday, so as to cause no delay.[9] I prefer to revise what I speak so utterly without premeditation. Be particular to send to care of Henry Anthony, 9 Benevolent Street, Providence.

Your loving father,

W. L. G.

ALS: Garrison Papers, Boston Public Library.

1. According to Frank Garrison's diary, he and his brother Wendell stayed in Florence, Mass., "at Mr. S. Hill's," no doubt the home of Samuel L. Hill (1806–1882), a leading organizer of the Northampton Association of Education and Industry, who had remained in Florence and continued in the silk manufacturing business. (FJG, August 1, 1861; Sheffeld.)

2. Catharine Knapp Stetson Benson (born 1808), whose name Garrison sometimes spells "Catherine," was the sister of Garrison's friend James A. Stetson and the wife of George W. Benson, Helen's brother. George Benson had recently moved to Lawrence, Kan., and Catharine and the family stayed behind for a time. (John S. Barry, *A Genealogical and Biographical Sketch on the Name and Family of Stetson, 1634–1847*, Boston, 1847; see also the letter to Edward Percy, January 10, 1862 [micro.].)

3. Boylston Market, designed by Charles Bulfinch, was built in 1810 at the corner of Boylston and Washington streets. (Walter Muir Whitehall, *Boston, A Topographical History*, Boston, 1959, p. 69.)

4. Wendell Phillips Garrison, who had graduated from Harvard on July 17, hoped for but did not obtain a teaching position at the Boston Latin School. (FJG, July 17, 1861; letter to Wendell Phillips Garrison, August 13, 1861 [micro.].)

Edward H. Magill was the submaster of the Boston Latin School in 1861. (*Catalogue of the Latin Grammar School in Boston*, Boston, 1861.)

Francis Gardner (1812–1876), a graduate of the Boston Latin School and of Harvard, had become submaster of the school in 1836 and master in 1851. (Obituary, Boston *Daily Advertiser*, January 12, 1876.)

5. Cornelius Conway Felton (1807–1896) had become Eliot Professor of Greek Literature at Harvard in 1834 and president of the university in 1860. He was the author of several books, the most popular of which, *Greece, Ancient and Modern*, was to appear in 1867. (*Who Was Who in America*.)

6. Charles King Whipple (1809–1900), who sometimes assisted with the editing of *The Liberator*, was assistant editor of the *Non-Resistant* and treasurer of the New England Non-Resistance Society. In 1859 he had been appointed a member of the Hovey Fund Committee. (*Life*.)

7. The office of the Massachusetts Anti-Slavery Society, which was moved several times during the existence of the society, was located in 1861 in the Washington Building at 221 Washington Street, Boston. The same office housed *The Liberator* until its final issue, served as a meeting place for functions of the Society, and was a clearing-house for antislavery publications that were advertised frequently in *The Liberator*. (*The Liberator*, passim.)

8. Henry Anthony (1802–1879) of Providence, R.I., was the husband of Mrs. Garrison's sister Charlotte and the brother of naturalist John Gould Anthony, whose daughter married George Thompson Garrison in 1873. The Anthony family was relatively conservative on the slavery question. (Charles L. Anthony, *Genealogy of the Anthony Family from 1495 to 1904*, Sterling, Ill., 1904; Lillie Buffum Chace Wyman and Arthur Crawford Wyman, *Elizabeth Buffum Chace, 1806–1899, Her Life and Its Environment*, Boston, 1914, I, 137.)

9. James Manning Winchell Yerrinton (1825–1893) and his father, James Brown Yerrinton (1800–1866), were for many years the printers of *The Liberator*. Highly skilled as a phonographic (shorthand) reporter, the son was the official reporter for

the Massachusetts Anti-Slavery Society, often recording speeches by Garrison, Phillips, and others. (*Life.*)

Garrison had spoken in Abington, Mass., in commemoration of the West Indian emancipation, showing how good emancipation had been for business in the islands and bewailing the ineptness of the northern war effort, especially that of General Winfield Scott. The speech was printed in *The Liberator*, August 9, and in the *National Anti-Slavery Standard*, August 10, 1861.

12

TO GERRIT SMITH

Boston, Sept. 5, 1861.

Dear Mr. Smith:

My old and esteemed friend, Mr. William P. Powell, having informed me of his peculiar situation, and the application he has made to you for a loan to enable him to start in what promises to be a good business in the city of New York, in connection with his son, a promising young man, who has recently completed a medical and surgical education in England, I volunteer to say in his behalf, that I have long known him as an upright and worthy man, full of intelligence and of high aims, remarkable for business capacity and executive talent, hitherto (until expending his means nobly in the education of his children) abundantly able to "paddle his own canoe," a loving husband and father, a fast friend, and a true and clear-sighted abolitionist.[1]

I sincerely hope it may be in your power to extend to him the loan he needs, as it may be the turning point in his destiny, and probably that of his son, on whose education he has expended so much; but I will add nothing more than this, because you know precisely what you are able to do, and, never so happy as when aiding and blessing others, needing no urging in any case. The appeals to you for assistance, I am sure, must be "legion," and oftenly provokingly absurd and unreasonable. In this case, it is meant to be a *bona fide* business transaction. Mr. Powell is "the soul of honor,"[2] and possesses a commendably sensitive and independent spirit; and, if life and health be spared, he will assuredly leave nothing undone to repay all that you may be able to do for him; for his word is better than most men's bond.[3] An excellent opportunity presents itself for him and his son to open a druggist store in the city of New York, the latter engaging in professional practice. There is no other regularly educated colored physician in New York, except Dr. James McCune Smith;[4] and as the colored population is probably not less than twenty-five or thirty thousand in that city, (to say nothing of the white,) the chance for success is highly favorable.

I feel a deep interest in this case, because of the worthiness of Mr. Powell, because of his noble efforts to educate his children, and because the help he needs may, if obtained, lift him at once to a sphere of industrial and successful activity; and without it he may be embarrassed and crippled for life.

I know you will write to him in the frankest manner as the tried friend, generous and eloquent advocate, and disinterested and intrepid supporter of the cause of the colored race universally.

Your recent letters to Mr. Lovejoy, Mr. Breckinridge, and the Democratic Committee, have been perused by me, as well as by many thousands, with the greatest pleasure and interest.[5] They indicate how thorough is your restoration to health, and that you are "complete in all things, lacking nothing."[6] But, pray, while losing no suitable opportunity to bear your effective testimonies in behalf of freedom and justice, take care not to tax your brain and strength beyond what prudence dictates.

Give my warm and high regards to dear Mrs. Smith, of whom all who know her speak to me in the most laudatory terms.

Are you not greatly cheered by Fremont's Proclamation?[7] Is it not "the beginning of the end," and is not the end near?

Yours, to break every yoke,[8]

Wm. Lloyd Garrison.

Hon. Gerrit Smith.

ALS: Gerrit Smith Collection, Syracuse University Library.

Gerrit Smith (1797–1874) was a wealthy New York state landowner and philanthropist. Basically more conservative than Garrison, Smith had been an abolitionist since the 1830s but came to believe in political action and ultimately violence as essential instruments for emancipation. In February 1858, when John Brown came to see him in Peterboro, N.Y., he promised support for the militant abolitionist's plans. After the raid at Harpers Ferry, Smith was so deeply affected by public criticism of him as an accessory that he became mentally unbalanced for several months. During the Civil War he consistently supported the Union side, campaigning for Lincoln in 1864 and for Grant in 1868. He favored a moderate Reconstruction policy and in 1867 was one of several who signed a bail bond to release Jefferson Davis. He published several books, including *Religion of Reason* (1864) and *Speeches and Letters of Gerrit Smith on the Rebellion* (2 vols., 1864–1865).

After a brief marriage to Wealtha Ann Backus (January–August 1819) Smith married in 1822 Ann Carroll Fitzhugh (1805–1875), the daughter of Colonel William Fitzhugh of Maryland and later of Hampton, N.Y. The Smiths had four children, of whom a son and a daughter lived to maturity. (Thomas J. C. Williams, *A History of Washington County, Maryland* . . . , Baltimore, 1968, I, 136–140.)

1. William Peter Powell, the Negro keeper of a boardinghouse in lower Manhattan, was active in the Underground Railroad movement and the founder and later superintendent of a Negro sailors' home. The father of seven children, he spent ten

years in England educating his four oldest sons, including William Peter Powell, Jr., the physician for whom he was currently trying to borrow $700 to set up a pharmaceutical business. His efforts were apparently unsuccessful. (William P. Powell to Gerrit Smith, September 4, 1861, Gerrit Smith Collection, Syracuse University Library.)

2. Garrison perhaps quotes from Oliver Goldsmith, *The Vicar of Wakefield*, chapter 31.

3. Garrison refers to the classic proverb that had been used by a number of English and continental writers since the Renaissance.

4. James McCune Smith (1813–1865) was undoubtedly the most scholarly and perhaps the most distinguished American Negro of his day. Born in New York City and educated abroad (receiving bachelor's and medical degrees from the University of Glasgow), he practiced in his native city, where he was probably the first American Negro to operate a drugstore. Dr. Smith was an active abolitionist, an editor, and the author of many articles and pamphlets on slavery, abolition, and the comparative anatomy of the races. He was well known to Gerrit Smith, who in 1846 chose him and two other Negroes to distribute 120,000 acres of land to deserving black families in New York City.

5. Owen Lovejoy (1811–1864) was a brother of the martyred abolitionist Elijah P. Lovejoy, with whom he had been closely associated in Alton, Ill. Following his brother's death in 1837, he became a Congregational minister; for seventeen years as the pastor of a church in Princeton, Ill., he persistently bore testimony against the evils of slavery. Although he remained a sincere abolitionist, following his election to the Illinois legislature in 1854 his major interest shifted to politics. He was one of the founders of the Republican party in his state and became an unswerving admirer and supporter of Lincoln. In 1856 Lovejoy was elected to Congress; two years later he threw all his energies into Lincoln's unsuccessful campaign for election to the United States Senate. Although on the issue of slavery he had been one of the most radical and outspoken of congressmen, in 1861 he did introduce a resolution calling for the implementation of the Fugitive Slave Law. The following year it was he who replied to Garrison's attacks on the President. On the other hand, it was also he who proposed the bill to abolish slavery in all the territories. Lincoln called Lovejoy "my most generous friend." (For Gerrit Smith's letter to Lovejoy, July 12, 1861, attacking him for his support of the Fugitive Slave Law, see *The Liberator*, August 2, 1861.)

Robert J. Breckinridge (1800–1871) of Kentucky, after being trained as a lawyer and briefly practicing his profession, studied theology and was by 1832 installed as the controversial minister of the Second Presbyterian Church of Baltimore. In 1845 he began his third career, as an educator, by becoming president of Jefferson College (Pennsylvania). Two years later he was appointed superintendent of the public school system in Kentucky, a post he held until 1853, when he became a professor at Danville Theological Seminary. On July 23, 1861, Gerrit Smith wrote Breckinridge, defending Lincoln's war policy against the charge that he had acted unconstitutionally. (For Smith's letter see *The Liberator*, August 9, 1861.)

Smith's letter to the New York state Democratic committee (dated August 13, 1861) urged them to put patriotism above party by supporting the Republicans against the rebels. (See *The Liberator*, August 23, 1861.)

6. Not identified.

7. John Charles Frémont (1813–1890) had a spectacular although ultimately anticlimactic career. Born in Georgia, he had been to South America and had explored sections of the Middle and Far West before being elected in 1850 as one of the first two senators from the new state of California. In 1856 he was a Republican candidate for President, and upon the outbreak of the Civil War Lincoln appointed him major general in charge of the Western Department. On August 30, 1861, Frémont proclaimed martial law throughout Missouri and proclaimed as free all slaves whose masters actively supported the enemy. This emancipation, though supported by abolitionists, proved premature, and Lincoln relieved Frémont of his command, appointing him in March 1862 to a relatively insignificant post in western Virginia.

From this command he was also removed when Stonewall Jackson defeated him in the Shenandoah Valley campaign. Following the war Frémont engaged in various unsuccessful business ventures, losing the money he had earlier accumulated. He served between 1878 and 1883 as the territorial governor of Arizona. (For further information about Frémont's proclamation, see *The Liberator*, September 13 and 20, 1861.)

8. Isaiah 58:6.

13

TO HENRY T. CHEEVER

Boston, Sept. 9, 1861.

Dear Mr. Cheever:

I have delayed answering your letter till now, because I wished to lay your proposition for a national Anti-Slavery Convention, in relation to the war, before the Executive Committee of the American A. S. Society. They held a meeting, a day or two since, and considered the matter in the most friendly and deliberate manner. The conclusion to which they unanimously came was, that such a Convention, called by the parties and persons suggested by you, "pronounced abolitionists," would be more likely to excite popular prejudice at this crisis, and thus to damage a movement for the abolition of slavery under the war power, than to do good. So long as the government is in direct and deadly conflict with the Slave Power, it seems to us the part of wisdom to avoid conspicuity as radical abolitionists in convention assembled, and to merge ourselves, as far as we can without a compromise of principle, in the onward sweeping current of Northern sentiment.

In order, however, to further the grand object you have in view, —namely, persuading the government to put an end to slavery as the only feasible method of terminating the war, and rendering a true peace possible,—consultations are going on in this city with reference to the best method of influencing "the powers that be,"[1] on this particular subject. We are to have another conference tomorrow afternoon at Dr. Howe's office,[2] at which your brother, Dr. [George B.] Cheever, will probably be present; so that, through him, doubtless, you will be apprised of the precise scope of the new movement, which contemplates a wide use of the newspaper press in the publication of able and telling articles, simultaneously, printed on slips, and sent privately for insertion—all bearing upon the extinction of slavery by the exercise of the war power; and also contemplates the circulation of a memorial for signatures, with the same object in view, to be presented at the opening of the next Congress.

The real difficulty lies in the case of the so-called loyal slaveholders. How are they to be propitiated, and satisfactorily disposed of? Cannot Congress be asked to give them a pecuniary equivalent for their slaves, *as a conciliatory measure,* without recognizing or implying the right of property in man? That is a question for grave consideration. If we can devise a petition, which all but the inveterately pro-slavery can sign, no doubt an immense number of signatures can be obtained, and this will greatly aid and strengthen the government in the right direction. Events, however, may render even this spur unnecessary.

Yours, with warm regards,

Wm. Lloyd Garrison.

Rev. Henry T. Cheever.

ALS: Cheever Papers, American Antiquarian Society; printed in the American Antiquarian Society *Proceedings,* 46: 94–95 (1936).

Henry Theodore Cheever (1814–1897), like his older brother George B. Cheever a graduate of Bowdoin College and a Congregational minister, was an active abolitionist. The purpose of the meeting of "pronounced abolitionists" proposed by Cheever was to devise ways to force the President to emancipate the slaves. (Robert M. York, *George B. Cheever, Religious and Social Reformer, 1807–1890,* Orono, Me., 1955.)

1. Romans 13:1.
2. Samuel Gridley Howe (1801–1876), after receiving a medical degree from Harvard in 1824, spent six years serving as a surgeon in the war for Greek independence, before returning to Massachusetts to run a school for the blind. He agitated for many educational and prison reforms, as well as for abolition, and for a time in 1843 co-edited the antislavery *Commonwealth.* He later became so deeply involved with the John Brown raid at Harpers Ferry that he was temporarily exiled to Canada. An active supporter of the North during the Civil War, he served on many governmental committees, including the Sanitary Commission and the President's Inquiry Commission. He married reformer Julia Ward (1819–1910) in 1843.

14

TO OLIVER JOHNSON

Boston, Oct. 7, 1861.

My dear Johnson:

I am greatly obliged to you for your letter; and will certainly try to accept your kind overture to spend a day or two (including a Sunday) with you and Mary Ann in New York, either on my way to the Pennsylvania meeting, or on my return from it.[1] I will decide, and let you know which it shall be, as soon as the time for the meeting is definitely fixed. It will give me great pleasure to see any persons whom you may wish to invite together socially on my account.

Mr. May arrived in the city, to-day, from his New York trip, and expressed gratification at having seen you at the office, though he thinks you are looking as if you had had a large burden to carry for some months past.[2]

You feelingly allude to the remarkable unity of views which has always existed between us, without consultation, in every critical period through which the Anti-Slavery cause has passed. This has been as gratifying to me as to you; for I have always regarded you as possessing an unusually clear perception of things, and a great deal of that common sense, than which nothing is more uncommon. Your absolute disinterestedness has shown that your eye was single from the beginning, and therefore your whole body has been full of light. "All things are made manifest in the light."[3] I have never had a suspicion that we should very widely differ in our judgment of things; and yet I have known that, in forming and expressing your own opinions, you have always adhered to your convictions of right, independently and conscientiously, without stopping to ask whether they were embraced or rejected by any others.

After all the progress that has been made, how much of the old pro-slavery venom remains at the North! And how the serpents hiss and shake their rattles whenever a direct blow is given to the dragon of slavery—as in the case of Fremont and Sumner! It is more and more evident, that the support given to the government by such papers as the New York Journal of Commerce and Bennett's Herald, and the Boston Courier and Post, is nothing but the basest dissimulation to effect a treasonable end. They would incomparably prefer the reign of Jeff. Davis and eternal slavery, than to see the Union preserved and slavery abolished by a Republican administration.[4] Yet Mr. Lincoln is so infatuated as to shape his course of policy in accordance with their wishes, and is thus unwittingly helping to prolong the war, and to render the result more and more doubtful! If he *is* 6 feet 4 inches high, he is only a dwarf in mind.

We have had our friend, E. H. Heywood, sick with a brain fever at our house for nearly three weeks.[5] He is now slowly recuperating, and spending a few days with our beloved friend Francis Jackson, who, happily, is now in such a comfortable state of health as to be in the streets every day. What a wonderful raising up from the brink of the grave in his case!

Please convey to Theodore Tilton the assurances of my warm personal regards, and my appreciation of his talents and reformatory labors.[6] He has placed me under special obligations by his friendly attentions, from time to time. Tell him I shall so far try to comply with his hospitable overture as at least to break bread with him at his own table. In the severe bereavement which he and his estimable wife have been called to suffer, in the death of their darling child,[7] I very strongly participate. All our household desire to be kindly remembered to them, and to Mary-Ann and yourself.

Unswervingly yours,

Wm. Lloyd Garrison.

Oliver Johnson.

ALS: Garrison Papers, Boston Public Library.

1. The annual meeting of the Pennsylvania Anti-Slavery Society was to begin October 24 and was to confirm the resolve specified in the call: that the society should remain loyal to antislavery principles as well as to the government now fighting the South. (*National Anti-Slavery Standard*, October 19 and November 2, 1861.)

2. Samuel May, Jr. (1810–1899), the cousin of Samuel J. May, was one of Garrison's closest friends and most loyal supporters. In the middle 1860s he agreed with Garrison regarding the dissolution of the antislavery societies. He served with Garrison as one of the trustees in charge of the Francis Jackson bequest. In 1866 he became a member of the committee charged with raising funds for a national testimonial to Garrison and was subsequently the committee's paid secretary. He was also among those to eulogize Garrison at his funeral. (*Life.*)

3. Matthew 6:22 and Ephesians 5:13, adapted.

4. Garrison groups together what he considered the "satanic press." Although founded in 1827 by abolitionist Arthur Tappan, the New York *Journal of Commerce* had become in Garrison's words, "a villanous paper," formerly proslavery and in 1861 pro-compromise. The New York *Herald* was founded in 1835 by the "satanic Scotchman" James Gordon Bennett (1795–1872), who as editor had supported Douglas for President and continued to be recalcitrant concerning abolition. The Boston *Courier* has been identified in the letter to Charles Sumner, February 26, 1861, n. 8. At this time it was considered a leading Copperhead journal. The Boston *Morning Post*, founded in 1831, was before the war the leading organ for Massachusetts Democrats. Recently, it had turned ambivalent about slavery, becoming almost as much a Copperhead journal as the *Courier*. (*Life;* Mott.)

Jefferson Davis (1808–1889), originally from Kentucky and a graduate of West Point, had seen service in the Mexican War and been a senator from Mississippi (1847–1851) before becoming President of the Confederacy. Following the Civil War he was imprisoned for two years; he spent the rest of his life pursuing unsuccessful business ventures.

5. Despite the brain fever, Ezra H. Heywood (1829–1893) survived for many years. He was a graduate of Brown University and one of the few abolitionists who opposed the war. At the time of Garrison's letter he was general agent, pro tem, for the Massachusetts Anti-Slavery Society. Although Garrison disagreed with Heywood's vigorous opposition to the war, he did give him and his fellow pacifists space in *The Liberator* for expression of their views. Between 1872 and 1893 Heywood published a reform journal called *The Word.* In 1873 he organized the Union Reform League and the New England Free Love League. On several occasions he was arrested for publishing obscene material. (*Who Was Who in America;* see also the letter to Samuel May, Jr., August 11, 1858, *Letters,* IV, 545, n. 3; Peter Brock, *Pacifism in the United States,* Princeton, N.J., 1968.)

6. Theodore Tilton (1835–1907), after acquiring experience on the New York *Tribune* and studying at the Free Academy (later the College of the City of New

York), became in 1853 a member of the staff of the New York *Observer*, a Presbyterian weekly. In 1855 he married Elizabeth Richards, who taught Sunday school in Henry Ward Beecher's Plymouth Church in Brooklyn. The following year Tilton left the *Observer* to become managing editor of the New York *Independent*, and in 1863 he became editor-in-chief, a post he was to hold until the end of 1870. His allegation of an adulterous relationship between his wife and Beecher forced him to resign his position. The resulting inconclusive trial and the publicity ruined not only his marriage but also his reputation and his finances. He lived out his last years in Paris writing and publishing poetry and fiction.

7. Not certainly identified.

15

TO JAMES MILLER MCKIM

Leicester, Oct. 13, 1861.

My dear McKim:

I am here, spending a day or two with my beloved friend, Mr. May, and his pleasant family.[1]

Not seeing in the last Standard any official notice of the annual meeting of the Pennsylvania Anti-Slavery Society, and having received no letter from you respecting it since your return home from Boston, I think it not improbable that your Committee[2] are still deliberating whether, on the whole, it is best to hold your anniversary as usual, or to set it aside as we did the annual meeting of the American A. S. Society and the New England Convention, in view of the war and the troublous state of the times. I do not know (if it is still an open question) that I have any advice to offer you in regard to your meeting. You are the best judges of your own affairs. There seems to be a fresh development of pro-slavery malignity created by Fremont's proclamation of freedom to the slaves of the rebellious slaveholders in Missouri, which is rather heightened than mitigated by the President's interposing letter;[3] and this has been still more aggravated, in our section of the country, by the recent emancipation speech of Charles Sumner;[4] all indicating a readiness to resort to mobocratic violence against the abolitionists, as in days gone by, under the pretence of saving the Union, whenever an opportunity is presented. Now, as abolitionists, we are not to be deterred from holding any meeting by any probable or certain outbreak of popular indignation against us, as thirty years of unyielding, straight-forward persistency, on our part, have plainly demonstrated; but as the time for our convening together is not necessarily a matter of principle, but always discretionary, and as we are to be somewhat guided by the state of events, in what manner to use our machinery, we have not only the right, but it is our duty, to deliberate well how we may best subserve the cause which is so dear to our hearts. While the present war continues, and the armies of the South are fiercely confronting those of the North, I am very reluctant, for one, needlessly to provoke the spirit of mobocracy by any ill-timed movement, and thus to encourage the Southern rebels in their dark and desperate conspiracy. No doubt all our Pennsylvania friends participate in this feeling. In their decision, therefore, respecting the anniversary of the Pennsylvania A. S. Society, whether to hold or to postpone it, I shall most cordially unite.[5] Let me hear from you about it, as soon as convenient.

I suppose that you have been daily expecting to see the Address of the Executive Committee of the American A. S. Society, on the relations of our cause to the war, (which you suggested should be written when you were with us,) but, as yet, it remains to be prepared. The Committee desired me to write it; and I made the attempt, which was partially completed, as you will see by my "Restatement of the Principles, Measures and Objects of the American Anti-Slavery Society," published in a recent number of the Liberator; but, while the Committee liked it very much, in itself considered, they generally seemed to consider (Wendell Phillips in special) that something more brief, and in a more popular form, would be preferable. On my motion, therefore, Mr. Phillips was unanimously requested by our Committee to prepare the address, which he reluctantly half promised to do, but we have waited in vain for it to this hour, and in all probability shall continue to be disappointed.[6] If, therefore, you have been delaying the calling of your anniversary in the hope of receiving the address, and distributing it more or less extensively in advance in Pennsylvania, this will apprise you that any longer waiting on your part will be useless. I regret the disappointment, for I think the present position of the American A. S. Society, in regard to the Government, the Constitution, and the war, should be officially defined. In view of the ground covered, I endeavored to condense my "Restatement" (already alluded to) as much as possible; and I thought it desirable that our principles, measures and object, from the beginning, should again be rehearsed, because many new readers would undoubtedly be made by the state of the times. But if Mr. Phillips would only take the time to shape an address, in accordance with his ideas of the fitness of things, I am sure it would admirably meet all our wishes.

My wife is here with me, and unites in proffering the most affectionate regards to Mrs. McKim and your children,[7] as well as yourself, and all the members of the anti-slavery household of faith[8] in your attractive region. Mr. and Mrs. May send their assurances of high respect and esteem.

Your strongly attached friend,

Wm. Lloyd Garrison.

J. Miller McKim.

ALS: Dreer Collection, Historical Society of Pennsylvania.

James Miller McKim (1810–1874) was educated at Dickinson College and Andover Theological Seminary. In 1835 he became minister of the Presbyterian church at Womelsdorf, Pa., but soon resigned his ministry to devote himself entirely to abolition. He was active in the Pennsylvania as well as the American Anti-Slavery Society and for a time was editor of the *Pennsylvania Freeman*. He was a staunch supporter of John Brown and one of the leaders in the Underground Railroad.

McKim's ties with the Garrisons were close not only because of mutual interest in reform but also through two marriages. McKim's daughter, Lucy, married Wendell Phillips Garrison in 1865, and after her death (1877), Wendell married McKim's niece and adopted daughter, Anne McKim Dennis. In 1865 McKim helped finance *The Nation*, with which his son-in-law was for many years associated. (Obituary, Wendell Phillips Garrison, New York *Times*, March 1, 1907.)

1. Mrs. Samuel May, Jr., was the former Sarah Russell (born 1813), third daughter of Nathaniel P. and Sarah Tidd Russell. The Mays' children were Adeline (born 1836), Edward (born 1838, married Mary M. Blodgett), Joseph Russell (born 1844), and Elizabeth Goddard (born 1850). (Samuel May, John Wilder May, and John Joseph May, *A Genealogy of the Descendants of John May*, Boston, 1878, pp. 31–32.)

2. The executive committee of the Pennsylvania Anti-Slavery Society consisted of the following: James Mott, president; Robert Purvis, vice president; Thomas Whitson, vice president; James Miller McKim, corresponding secretary; Isaac Flint, recording secretary; Sarah Pugh, treasurer; Mary Grew, E. F. Pennypacker, Thomas Garrett, John Cox, George Atkinson, Lucretia Mott, B. Fussell, and Wilmer Atkinson. (*National Anti-Slavery Standard*, November 2, 1861.)

3. Frémont's premature proclamation was dated August 30, 1861. When General Frémont refused to rescind his proclamation, Lincoln modified it with his own.

4. Charles Sumner's speech before the Republican Convention at Worcester, Mass., which was reported in *The Liberator*, October 4, 1861, accused Lincoln of dereliction of duty in delaying to proclaim emancipation.

5. The Pennsylvania Anti-Slavery Society scheduled the meeting for October 24. (*Standard*, October 19, 1861.)

6. Although Garrison's statement was printed in *The Liberator* of October 4, Phillips' revision never appeared. Garrison's statement asserted that the old order must not be restored after the war and that the government must choose either to acknowledge the independence of the South or to "abolish slavery throughout the land."

7. Sarah Allibone Speakman (1813–1891) had married J. Miller McKim in 1840. Like her husband she was an ardent abolitionist.

The McKims had two children, Lucy (1842–1877) and Charles Follen. Lucy, who attended the Eagleswood School at Raritan, N.J. (run by Theodore and Angelina Grimké Weld), was a piano teacher. In 1862 she accompanied her father to the Sea Islands on a trip sponsored by the Port Royal Relief Committee. She became interested in the slave songs she heard and transcribed them in musical notation. She published two of the songs, "Poor Rosy, Poor Gal" and "Roll, Jordan, Roll," and planned to publish more, but was disappointed in the extent of their sale. After their marriage, Wendell Phillips Garrison encouraged her to do editorial work and review books for *The Nation*. In 1867 she published (with William Francis Allen and Charles Pickard Ware) *Slave Songs of the United States*, which is still the best extant source for slave music. Lucy and Wendell had three children, Lloyd McKim, Philip McKim, and Katherine McKim Garrison. Lucy's long illness after the birth of her children resulted in paralysis, heart disease, and eventual death. (*NAW*; for Garrison's opinion of his daughter-in-law, see his letter to Wendell Phillips Garrison, June 30, 1864.)

Charles Follen McKim (1847–1909), who was a good friend of Francis Jackson Garrison, graduated from Harvard and studied art and architecture in Paris. He became a distinguished New York architect and leading member of the famous firm of McKim, Mead, and White, which designed in classical and Renaissance style many of the most important buildings of the period, including the extraordinarily elaborate group of houses on New York's Madison Avenue, between Fiftieth and Fifty-first streets, commissioned by Henry Villard in 1882, and the Boston Public Library.

8. Galatians 6:10.

16

TO HELEN E. GARRISON

Philadelphia, Oct. 29, 1861.

Dear Wife:

Having had to do pretty much all the talking since we left Boston, I have left Wendell to do nearly all the writing.[1] He has kept you posted as to our movements up to Saturday last, when we were with Joseph A. Dugdale at Isaac and Dinah Mendenhall's at Hamorton.[2] On the afternoon of that day, we were carried over to the residence of our dear friends, John and Hannah Cox, at Longwood, where we received such a welcome as you and I experienced when we were there a few years ago.[3] Oliver and Mary Anne Johnson were in our company. A few friends were with us in the evening—among them, Chandler and Hannah Darlington, Sarah Pugh, and Abby Kimber.[4] It threatened to be a wet and dreary Sunday; but, fortunately, it proved to be a very fine day, and our gathering in the Progressive Friends' cosy meeting-house was a very full one—persons coming in every direction from a distance of fifteen miles. It was a very choice collection indeed. After reading portions of Scripture, I spoke for upwards of an hour, and was listened to with gratifying interest. I was followed by Thomas Curtis,[5] (not a Friend, but a materialist,) who undertook to argue that we could not expect any thing better than slavery to exist while the people were taught to believe in the Calvinistic doctrine of the atonement! I replied to him, showing the utter absurdity of such an idea. I was followed by Anna Dickinson, of Philadelphia, a young woman of nineteen, of Quaker origin, who spoke with remarkable oratorical fluency at our West Chester meetings, and not less so on this occasion.[6] Joseph A. Dugdale made a short prayer, and closed the meeting. A number of us then returned to the Mendenhalls to dine, where others joined us, and we spent a couple of hours very pleasantly. I should have stated that, Sunday morning before meeting, William Cox drove Oliver, Mary Anne, and Wendell to Bayard Taylor's charming residence, where they received a warm welcome from Bayard and the whole family.[7] I went there in the afternoon, and was also very cordially greeted by them all. Bayard's German wife has a very pleasant face, and is said to be an excellent woman and wife. They have but one child, a girl four or five years old. The house is spacious, unique, and of large dimensions. Bayard owns more than a hundred acres of very choice land, all in one lot, and beautifully diversified and situated. Bayard remembered seeing Fanny in Boston when he last lectured there, and of his own accord inquired after her, in a complimentary manner. Didn't that show a retentive memory?

We returned, after a brief interview, going by the new residence which Benjamin and J. Elizabeth Jones are building for themselves at Kennett, where they intend henceforth to abide.[8] We took tea and spent the evening at Chandler Darlington's, with a large company, and then went to John Cox's to spend the night. Yesterday (Monday) morning, we took the cars for Philadelphia, accompanied by Oliver, Mary Anne, Sarah Pugh, Abby Kimber, and Anna Dickinson, arriving at 10 o'clock. According to previous agreement, we met Mary Grew[9] at the Anti-Slavery Office, and then proceeded to Sarah Pugh's residence, where we took a lunch; and then Sarah and Mary went with us, and also Oliver and Mary Anne, to the Girard College, where we were shown through the various apartments, and then went on the vast marble roof, to gaze upon one of the most expansive and beautiful prospects to be found in the country.[10] The Superintendent of the schools is a Mr. Stephens, the son of my old anti-slavery friend in Plymouth by that name.[11] He was very glad to see us. Returning, we took the steam-cars, and came out to the cottage now occupied by our dear friends, Miller McKim and wife, where we now are. We have had here a right royal time. Last evening, a large circle was convened to welcome us—among them, James and Lucretia Mott, and Dr. Furness and his son.[12] The company did not break up till 11 o'clock. The inquiries after you were and have been, all along, very affectionate and sincere; and your absence is so uniformly regretted, and the remembrance of your visit is so pleasantly cherished, that I am very sorry I did not insist on your coming with me.

We are now just leaving to go to James Mott's, where we are to spend the day and night, and to meet another large circle. Edward M. Davis is expected home to-day, fresh from Fremont, and I hope to learn many particulars from him respecting the Missouri campaign.[13] To-morrow we shall pass in the city, making various calls; in the evening, we shall attend the Female Sewing Circle.[14] Thursday morning, we are off for New York, and expect to go to Ghent on Saturday morning. We shall not be home before Tuesday morning —perhaps later. Our health is perfect. You are all in our thoughts, wherever we move. This is darling Franky's birthday. May his photographic be perfect, and his years long in the land! I am forced to close abruptly. Love to George, Fanny, Frank, and Kate—to dear Mr. [Francis] Jackson, Mr. [Charles K.] Whipple, Mr. Wallcut, &c.[15]

With boundless affection, ever yours,

Wm. Lloyd Garrison.

ALS: Garrison Papers, Boston Public Library.

1. The letters written by Wendell Phillips Garrison to his mother at this period apparently have not been preserved.

2. Joseph A. Dugdale (1810–1896), born of Quaker parents in Bristol, Pa., was alternately farmer, teacher, and minister. He was active in the temperance and anti-slavery movements, and as a result of his forthrightness and his aid to runaway slaves, he was disowned by the Green Plain, Ohio, monthly meeting, where he and his wife, Ruth, had been members since 1835. By 1857 Dugdale was living in Hamorton, Pa., southwest of Philadelphia, for he is listed in the minutes of the Progressive Friends there at that date. In 1862 Dugdale moved to Mount Pleasant, Ia. (Obituary, *Friends' Intelligencer*, March 21, 1896; Otelia Cromwell, *Lucretia Mott*, Cambridge, Mass., 1958, pp. 114–115.)

Isaac Mendenhall (1806–1882) married Dinah Hannum (1807–1889) in 1831. They were affiliated with the Progressive Friends of Longwood (see note 3) and lived at Hamorton. (Henry Hart Beeson, *The Mendenhalls: A Genealogy*, n.p., 1969; William Mendenhall, *History, Correspondence, and Pedigrees of the Mendenhalls of England and the United States Relative to their Common Origin and Ancestry*, Cincinnati, 1865.)

3. John (1786–1880) and Hannah Peirce Cox (1797–1876), Friends active in abolition and other reforms, were living at Longwood, the Peirce family home in Chester County, Pa. John and Hannah were married in 1823; he was a farmer, she had been briefly a teacher. Together they established a station of the Underground Railroad in their home. In 1853 they were founders of the Progressive Friends of Longwood, a liberal organization that attracted reformers and sponsored meetings concerning current social issues.

4. Chandler (1800–1879) and Hannah Monaghan Darlington (1808–1883), who had been married since 1832, were members of the Progressive Friends and lived on a farm near the town of Kennett Square. (Gilbert Cope, *Genealogy of the Darlington Family: A Record of the Descendants of Abraham Darlington of Birmingham, Chester County, Pennsylvania*, West Chester, Pa., 1900.)

Sarah Pugh (1800–1884) was one of the more prominent members of the Philadelphia Female Anti-Slavery Society; in 1840 she was one of that society's repudiated woman delegates to the World's Anti-Slavery Convention in London. (*Memorial of Sarah Pugh: A Tribute of Respect, From her Cousins*, Philadelphia, 1888.)

Abby Kimber (1804–1871), another Philadelphia abolitionist, was the daughter of Emmor Kimber, the Quaker schoolmaster who had established the Kimberton Boarding School for Girls in his Chester County home in 1818. Abby and her sister taught in the family school. (Sidney Arthur Kimber, *The Descendants of Richard*

Kimber: A Genealogical History of the Descendants of Richard Kimber of Grove, Berkshire, England, Boston, 1894; Cromwell, *Lucretia Mott,* passim.)

5. Not identified.

6. Anna Elizabeth Dickinson (1842–1932) was the daughter of Philadelphia Quaker merchant and abolitionist John Dickinson. Having begun her career as a public speaker on woman's rights as early as January 1860, in 1861 she was discharged from a job in the United States mint for calling General George B. McClellan's dilatory policy treasonable. In subsequent years she lectured around the country on abolition and other reforms and also tried unsuccessfully to be an actress. Ultimately she was to publish several books, including a novel. (*NAW.*)

7. John William Cox (1835–1901), the youngest child of John and Hannah Cox, was as a boy actively involved with his parents in the Underground Railroad, assisting his father to drive wagonloads of escaping slaves on to further stations. He moved to California in 1886 and spent the rest of his life there. (Obituary, *Friends' Intelligencer,* July 20, 1901; R. C. Smedley, *History of the Underground Railroad,* Lancaster, Pa., 1883, pp. 276, 302.)

Bayard Taylor (1825–1878) was a professional traveler, an editor, a minor but prolific man of letters, and a translator. He published many popular travel books and volumes of poor verse and poorer fiction. He also edited and worked for various papers and journals, including the *Saturday Evening Post,* the New York *Tribune,* and the *Literary World.* He translated Goethe's *Faust* (2 vols., 1870–1871). After 1860 Taylor and his second wife, Marie Hansen, the daughter of Danish astronomer Peter Andreas Hansen, lived at Cedarcroft, the "charming residence" to which Garrison refers. Their daughter was Lilian Bayard Taylor (1858–1940), who attended Vassar and subsequently married German physician Otto Kiliani. (Albert H. Smyth, *Bayard Taylor,* Boston and New York, 1905; John W. Jordan, *Encyclopedia of Pennsylvania Biography,* New York, 1916; Marie Hansen Taylor, with Lilian Bayard Taylor Kiliani, *On Two Continents: Memories of Half a Century,* New York, 1905.)

8. Benjamin Smith Jones (1812–1862) and Jane Elizabeth Jones (1813–1896) of Salem, Ohio, were editors of the *Anti-Slavery Bugle* (1847–1849), official organ of the Ohio American Anti-Slavery Society between 1845 and 1861. (*The Liberator,* July 11, 1845, and May 10, 1861; *Life.*)

9. Mary Grew (1813–1896) was the daughter of the Reverend Henry Grew and his third wife, Kate Merrow. A resident of Philadelphia since 1834, she was for many years an active abolitionist, serving as corresponding secretary of the Philadelphia Female Anti-Slavery Society until its dissolution in 1870. She served for several terms as a member of the executive committee of the Pennsylvania Anti-Slavery Society, and for a time was coeditor of that society's organ, the *Pennsylvania Freeman.* After 1840 she gave increasingly of her energies to the woman's rights movement. In 1869 she became the first president of the Pennsylvania Woman Suffrage Association, a position she held until 1892. (*NAW.*)

10. Girard College, a school in Philadelphia for orphan boys, was founded in 1833 and opened in 1848, thanks to a bequest from the financier and merchant Stephen Girard. (Cheesman A. Herrick, *History of Girard College,* Philadelphia, 1927.)

11. Lemuel Stephens, Jr. (1814–1892), was a Harvard graduate who had done graduate work at Göttingen and Berlin. During the 1860s he was professor of science, history, rhetoric, and other subjects at Girard College in Philadelphia. His father (born 1786), of Plymouth, Mass., had been an active abolitionist as early as 1835. (Herrick, *History of Girard College;* William T. Davis, *Plymouth Memories of an Octogenarian,* Plymouth, 1906; *Letters,* III, 571, 572.)

12. James Mott (1788–1868), son of Long Island Quakers Adam and Anne Mott, was educated at Nine Partners boarding school near Poughkeepsie, N.Y., where he subsequently became a teacher. In 1811 he married Lucretia Coffin. After eight prosperous years in the cotton commission business, he transferred to the woolen business for reasons of conscience. At about the same time, he aligned himself with the liberal Hicksite Quakers, adhering to that faction when they split off from the orthodox Friends in 1827. A founder of the American Anti-Slavery Society in Phila-

delphia in 1833, he and Lucretia represented the Pennsylvania Anti-Slavery Society at the World's Anti-Slavery Convention in London in 1840. The Motts were also active in the cause of woman's rights. James Mott's last years were spent in helping to found Swarthmore College. (Anna Davis Hallowell, *James and Lucretia Mott, Life and Letters,* Boston, 1884.)

Lucretia Coffin Mott (1793–1880) was one of the most prominent and outspoken critics of the slave system and of the injustices toward women in nineteenth-century America. The daughter of Nantucket Quakers Thomas and Anna Folger Coffin, she, like her husband, was educated and later taught at Nine Partners School. Following her marriage she taught in a Philadelphia Quaker girls' school and cared for the needs of her growing family. In 1818 she began to speak out in meeting and by 1821 was officially accepted as a Quaker minister. Like her husband a founder of the American Anti-Slavery Society in 1833, she afterward established the Philadelphia Female Anti-Slavery Society and served for many years as its president. She and Elizabeth Cady Stanton issued the call for the famous Seneca Falls woman's rights convention in 1848. (Hallowell, *James and Lucretia Mott;* Cromwell, *Lucretia Mott.*)

William Henry Furness (1802–1896) was the first pastor of the Unitarian church in Philadelphia (1825–1875). He was the author not only of many hymns but also of a number of significant works concerned with the historical Jesus as distinguished from the theological Christ. He was one of the first American scholars to study and translate German literature.

The son referred to here may have been Horace Howard Furness (1833–1912), the Shakespearean scholar, who, like his father, was an active abolitionist.

13. Edward Morris Davis (1811–1887) was a Quaker, a nonresistant, and an abolitionist. Despite his religion and philosophy he became a Union officer in the Civil War, serving as a captain on Frémont's staff. His wife was Maria Mott (born 1818), the second daughter of Lucretia and James Mott. (*Life;* Hallowell, *James and Lucretia Mott; The War of the Rebellion: A Compilation of the Official Records of the Union and Confederate Armies,* 1st series, Washington, 1881, III, 542.)

For information about Frémont in Missouri, see the letter to Gerrit Smith, September 5, 1861, n. 7.

14. Garrison probably refers to the Philadelphia Female Anti-Slavery Society. (Cromwell, *Lucretia Mott,* p. 49.)

15. Robert Folger Wallcut (1797–1884) was graduated from Harvard in 1817 and soon afterward was ordained a Unitarian minister. A close friend of Garrison, he took an interest in abolition early in life and for many years (1846–1865) was bookkeeper for *The Liberator.* Thereafter he worked for the Freedmen's Commission, in 1876 becoming a clerk in the Boston Custom House. He was one of the pallbearers at Garrison's funeral. (*Life,* II, 422, 477; letter from Garrison to Charles Sumner, August 7, 1869 [micro.].)

17

TO OLIVER JOHNSON

Boston, Dec. 6, 1861.

Dear Johnson:

I do not know when we shall have a meeting of our Executive Committee; but as Mr. [Samuel] May [Jr.] has sent to me your letter to him, in regard to sending copies of the Standard to members of Congress, I will venture to assume the responsibility of advising you to send one hundred to such persons in the Senate and House as you think best, during the session. I have no doubt that they will be eagerly and profitably read by those receiving them, and that the Committee will readily sanction such a distribution. Now is the time to put forth every available instrumentality to give the death-blow to slavery. The Standard will do our cause special service at Washington.

What a wishy-washy message from the President![1] It is more and more evident that he is a man of very small calibre, and had better be at his old business of splitting rails than at the head of a government like ours, especially in such a crisis. He has evidently not a drop of anti-slavery blood in his veins; and he seems incapable of uttering a humane or generous sentiment respecting the enslaved millions in our land. No wonder that such villanous papers as *the Journal of Commerce, the Express*,[2] Bennett's *Herald,* and the Boston *Courier* and *Post*, are his special admirers and champions! If there be not soon an "irrepressible conflict" in the Republican ranks, in regard to his course of policy, I shall almost despair of the country.

In fact, I shudder at the possibility of the war terminating without the utter extinction of slavery, by a new and more atrocious compromise on the part of the North than any that has yet been made. We must continue to brand as accessories of the Southern traitors all those who, now that the government can rightfully do it under the war power, denounce and oppose the emancipation of those in bondage. A curse on that Southern "loyalty" which is retained only by allowing it to control the policy of the administration!

What a matter of congratulation it is that your lawless and profligate Mayor Wood has been ejected from his office![3] I hope we, in Boston, shall imitate so good an example, on Monday next, by ousting from the mayoralty one of the same kidney, J. M. Wightman; but his re-election is not improbable.

How much I was indebted to you while I was in New York! Especially for that memorable interview with the party at Mrs. Savin's.[4] Her kindness is most gratefully remembered. Please give my regards to her, to Mary Anne, and the household.

Yours, heart and soul,

Wm. Lloyd Garrison.

N.B. All last week, I was confined to the house by a violent inflammation of the right eye, but it is now better. My wife was at the same time confined to her bed, and under daily medical attendance, in consequence of a severe and painful congestion of the stomach, or something equivalent to it. She is now convalescent, though still weak.

What has got into Ward Beecher, that he denounces emancipation by the government?[5] I see all the pro-slavery journals are copying his ill-timed, ill-digested, absurd, and practically pro-slavery sentiments, with "thanksgiving." I was too unwell to attend his lecture in this city on "The Camp and Country," but, though its funny parts elicited some applause, I am told, yet, as a whole, it "made the judicious grieve,"[6] and damaged rather than added to the reputation of the lecturer.[7] "The way of peace he knows not."[8]

ALS: Garrison Papers, Boston Public Library; partly printed in *Life*, IV, 33–34.

1. On December 3, 1861, President Lincoln delivered a message to Congress. Although the speech covered various issues, abolitionists were concerned primarily with its omission of the emancipation question. (*National Anti-Slavery Standard*, December 7, 1861.)

2. The New York *Express*, founded by James and Erastus Brooks in 1836 as a Whig paper, had by the date of Garrison's letter become staunchly Democratic. (Mott, pp. 261–262.)

3. Fernando Wood (1812–1881) had been prominent in New York City politics since 1834. In the 1840s he served a term in Congress, was a dispatch agent for the State Department, and made a fortune in the California gold rush. In the 1850s he became a power in Tammany Hall and was twice elected mayor of New York. He served for many years in the federal House of Representatives (1863–1865 and 1867–1881).

4. Sarah S. Savin and her husband, Augustus Savin (1817–1895), a seaman of French parentage, operated a New York boardinghouse at 90 East Twelfth Street, where Oliver Johnson and his family were living at the time. The Savins, who were married in 1848, had three children: Frank W., Harrison, and Carrie. (New York city directories; obituary, New York *Tribune*, October 26, 1895. Carrie Savin is further identified in the letter to Oliver Johnson, December 29, 1861 [micro.].)

5. On Thanksgiving Day (November 26) Beecher had spoken in Plymouth Church on the topic "Modes and Duties of Emancipation," opposing slavery only cautiously, for he expressed fear that the federal government would overstep its constitutional prerogatives if it freed the slaves. "The conflict must be carried on *through* our institutions, not over them. Revolution is not the remedy for rebellion," he said. (Henry Ward Beecher, *Patriotic Addresses in America and England, from 1850 to 1885, on Slavery, the Civil War, and the Development of Civil Liberty in the United States* . . . , Boston and Chicago, 1887, pp. 322–341.)

6. Shakespeare, *Hamlet*, III, ii, 29.

7. Beecher spoke satirically at Tremont Temple in Boston on November 26, 1861, giving what the *Standard* called "an elaborate eulogy on war, as a promoter of civilization and improvement . . . ," thereby "treating the gravest subjects with unscrupulous levity." (*Standard*, December 7, 1861.)

8. Isaiah 59:8.

1 8

TO SAMUEL J. MAY

Boston, Dec. 6, 1861.

Dearly beloved Friend:

You know, from long experience, how incorrigible I am on the score of dilatoriness as a correspondent, and have recently had fresh evidence of the fact; and so I have only, like a self-convicted criminal, to plead guilty, and submit without murmuring to the proper sentence. Allow me to say, however, in mitigation, that all last week I was confined to my house by a severe inflammation of the right eye; and, as if to sympathize fully with me, wife came down with illness the same day, and was confined to her bed and under regular medical treatment for several succeeding days. We are now both convalescent.

I feel complimented by your wishing me to lecture in Syracuse on slavery and the war, but I cannot think of going so far from home for that purpose. You very kindly offer to prepare the way for my lecturing in Utica and other places; and this would be a strong anti-slavery inducement to make you a visit, (whose face and home I long to see again,) were it not that I so easily subject myself to violent catarrhal attacks by exposure at this inclement season of the year, that I deem it prudent to remain at home, and labor only in this vicinity.

Mr. [Wendell] Phillips tells me that, so many are his engagements already, he sees no chance of getting an evening to lecture in Syracuse, highly as he appreciates your overture, and glad as he would be to accept it if he could.

All honor to the mayor of Syracuse, and to the police, and to the city itself, for having so nobly vindicated the freedom of speech in the person of Frederick Douglass![1] That handbill was villanously well calculated to stir up the base mobocratic element, which, undoubtedly, would have been rampant on the occasion, had not such efficient measures been taken to meet and suppress it.

Wendell [Phillips Garrison], and all the rest of us, gratefully appreciate your interest in his welfare. He has one or two scholars[2] whom he is temporarily instructing, to accommodate absent teachers; but as there is soon to be a vacancy in the Latin School, he will again try to get the appointment; though I fear the hunkerish[3] committee will be prejudiced against him on account of being the son of his father! We are all delighted to hear that Joseph has been so fortunate in New York city: he deserves it.[4]

Mr. Jackson's death took us all by surprise, it was so sudden.[5] We feel that a strong and reliable pillar has fallen. In addition to his gifts to personal friends, he left ten thousand dollars for anti-slavery purposes, and five thousand for the woman's rights movement, and two thousand for the benefit of fugitive slaves. His bequest, to cover all the expenses of Franky's education, and in aid of my family, was extremely generous—being $4,000—not $5,000 as generally published. It will help me to bear the large expense to which my conspicuity and relation to the anti-slavery cause unavoidably subjects me, on the score of hospitality, &c.; the receipts of the Liberator not covering my expenses by considerable. Last spring, Mr. Jackson apprised me that he should leave enough for Franky's education at Harvard;[6] but, beyond that generous act, I expected nothing, of course.

Aunt Charlotte [Coffin][7] is with us a good deal, much to our gratification, and also our aid and comfort; for she is ever busy in useful matters, and knows well how to co-operate with wife.

And now, accept all our most loving remembrances, and let them be given to your wife, and daughter, and son, who are with you in Syracuse; and may Heaven's choicest blessings rest upon you all![8] So prays

Your admiring and loving friend,

Wm. Lloyd Garrison.

S. J. May.

☞ For weeks I have been trying to find room in the Liberator for your excellent Fast Sermon, or a part of it, and will do so yet.[9]

ALS: Garrison Papers, Boston Public Library.

Samuel J. May (1797–1871) was the Unitarian minister who had married Garrison and Helen Benson in 1834. He was Garrison's friend and close associate from 1830 until his death. During his career he served churches in Brooklyn, Conn. (1822–1836), South Scituate, Mass. (1836–1842), and Syracuse, N.Y. (1845–1867). For many years a reformer as well as a minister, he had been a founder of both the Massachusetts and the American Anti-Slavery societies. In Syracuse he was active in the Underground Railroad, helping many slaves to escape. His wife was Lucretia Flagge Coffin May (see n. 8). He was the author of *Some Recollections of our Antislavery Conflict* (1869).

1. Frederick Douglass (1817–1895) was born in Tuckahoe, Md.; he was the son of Harriet Bailey and an unknown white father. Escaping from slavery in 1838, he moved to New York City, where he assumed the name of Douglass. Three years later, after a successful speech before the convention of the Massachusetts Anti-Slavery Society, his career as an abolitionist began. He became an agent of the Massachusetts society and was soon one of the most popular and successful of antislavery lecturers. In 1845 he published *Narrative of the Life of Frederick Douglass*, and during the next two years he traveled in England and Ireland. On his return in 1847, he established, against Garrison's advice, a Negro abolitionist paper, the *North Star*, which was published continuously for seventeen years. During the Civil War Doug-

lass recruited for the Massachusetts 54th and 55th Negro regiments; following the war he was appointed minister to Haiti. In 1884 he married, as his second wife, a white woman, Helen Pitts.

Douglass' lecture, "The Rebellion, its Cause and its Remedy," to be delivered in Syracuse November 14, 1861, was anticipated in the city with trepidation, especially after the circulation of a hostile handbill headed "Nigger Fred Coming." But the recently elected mayor, Charles Andrews (1827–1918), kept order with an augmented police force, and the lecture proceeded on schedule. Andrews, who had formerly been district attorney for Onondaga County, subsequently became associate judge and then chief justice of the New York Court of Appeals. (Frederic May Holland, *Frederick Douglass: The Colored Orator,* New York, 1891, p. 285.)

2. Not identified.

3. That is, extremely conservative.

4. Joseph May (1836–1918) was the fourth child of Samuel J. May. He graduated from Harvard in 1857 and from Cambridge Divinity School in 1865. The same year he married Harriet Charles Johnson, sister of Eastman Johnson. In 1876 he became the minister of the First Unitarian Church in Philadelphia. It is not clear what constituted Joseph May's good fortune in New York City. (Samuel May, John Wilder May, and John Joseph May, *A Genealogy of the Descendants of John May,* Boston. 1878.)

5. Francis Jackson had died on November 14.

6. Francis Jackson Garrison never went to Harvard.

7. The sister (1809–1889) of Mrs. Samuel J. May (see below).

8. Lucretia Flagge Coffin May (c. 1802–1865) was the daughter of Peter Coffin, a Portsmouth, N.H., merchant who later moved to Boston. She married Samuel J. May in 1825 and bore him four sons and a daughter: Joseph (1827–1828); John Edward (1829–c. 1902), who married Kate Pomroy Horton in 1866; Charlotte Coffin (1833–1909), who married Alfred Wilkinson in 1854; Joseph (identified in n. 4); and George Emerson (1844–1906), who married Caroline M. Mathews in 1865 and Alice Haven in 1867. Thus the son "with you in Syracuse" could have been either John Edward or George Emerson.

9. Although Fast Days in New England were traditionally held not in the fall but in the spring, May preached a Fast Day sermon in Syracuse on September 26, concerned with the war and the way in which the sin of slavery had generated collective national guilt. (*The Liberator* printed an abbreviated version of the sermon, entitled "Repentance Alone Can Save Us," on December 13.)

19

TO HELEN E. GARRISON AND CHILDREN

[December 10, 1861.]

Wm. Lloyd Garrison to his Wife and Children greeting:—

To-day, December 10th, 1861, he completes his 56th year; and, thanks to their affectionate remembrance, never has he had a birthday in which he was so well *suited* before. There are many, he is aware, out of his family,—and especially in the land of Secession, —who would like to give him, on any day, "a good *dressing*," but not in the same sense, nor according to the same pattern. For example—they would be pleased to see him wearing a *"coat* of tar and feathers"; but this fine broadcloth one, he thinks, is much to be preferred, as a matter of fitness and comfort. Come what may, however, he does not mean to play the "turn-coat," even though somebody has discovered that "one good turn deserves another." He cannot find words to express his love for his wife and children, and the amount of blessedness they have afforded him, because none such are to be found in any vocabulary; but he invokes upon them all whatever blessings Heaven may be able to bestow, and trusts that every succeeding birthday may find them steadily advancing in knowledge, goodness and truth, until clothed upon with the robes of immortal life.[1]

The beautiful photographic volume presented by his dear Fanny and Franky is a precious token of their loving regards. Its contents —"the counterfeit presentments"[2] of those whom he loves, admires and honors—are of exceeding value, and will be cherished by him "till time shall be no longer."[3]

AL: Garrison Papers, Boston Public Library.

1. An allusion to II Corinthians 5:4.
2. Shakespeare, *Hamlet*, III, iv, 54.
3. An adaptation of Revelation 10:6.

20

TO CHARLES SUMNER

Boston, Dec. 20, 1861.

Dear Mr. Sumner:

A short time since, I was waited upon by a very worthy and intelligent German, named Winter, from Poughkeepsie, N.Y., (who brought with him a letter of recommendation from Rev. Mr. Cutting, of that place,) for the purpose of asking my judgment respecting a voluminous work that he had written on the reconstruction of society.[1] On examining it, I could give him no encouragement as to his getting it published at the present time. The numerous designs of public buildings, private residences, squares, gardens, &c., &c., accompanying it, all designed and executed by himself, were exceedingly beautiful and attractive, indicating rare artistic genius and skill on his part.

I found him thoroughly intelligent and radical on the question of slavery, particularly with reference to its bearings on the present rebellion, and the duty of seizing the present favorable opportunity to abolish that hateful system.

Enclosed, I send you some designs he has made in regard to the employment of balloons, on a new principle, by Gen. McClellan, or by any other of the army officers.[2] He solicits your friendly offices in having them submitted to Prof. Lowe, or to any other scientific person acquainted with ballooning, believing as he does that they will prove of great service as against the common enemy.[3] Should they challenge attention, on close examination, and his presence be needed at Washington for consultation and arrangement, a line to this effect, addressed to him at Poughkeepsie, would be promptly attended to.

Thanks for your eloquent eulogy upon the late Senator Baker, (which I have published in the Liberator this week,) and its forcible application to slavery as the primary cause of his untimely death, as it is of all our national woes.[4] Be in no wise daunted, but rather strengthened and stimulated, by the abusive clamors and assaults following all your efforts, on the part of the "satanic press," and unprincipled demagogues generally. These are surer evidences of the wisdom, goodness and nobility of your course, than all the praises of your numerous friends and admirers. You may confidently make "the safe appeal of truth to time,"[5] and rely upon a universal verdict of approval at no distant day. To be in the right is as surely to be allied to victory as that God reigns. When there is howling in the pit, there is special rejoicing in heaven.

There is much that I would like to write about, but want of time forbids.

I hope some one will keep an accurate account of the petitions presented, from time to time, in both houses, asking for the abolition of slavery under the war power—where from, the number of signatures, &c., &c. It will be useful for publication.

I trust no countenance will be given to the absurd and preposterous scheme, suggested by the President, for acquiring foreign territory with a view to the colonization of the colored population of this country. They are all needed where they are.[6]

I am rejoiced to see a proposition before Congress for the abolition of slavery in the District of Columbia.[7] That is the first step in order.

Faithfully yours,

Wm. Lloyd Garrison.

Hon. Charles Sumner.

ALS: Charles Sumner Papers, Harvard College Library; extract printed in *The Works of Charles Sumner* (Boston, 1872), VI, 139.

1. Although the identity is uncertain, Garrison may refer to Julius Winter, listed in the 1862 Poughkeepsie city directory as an architect. In an earlier letter to Sumner, Garrison mentions that Winter was an ingenious designer and mathemati-

cian, as well as the author of an elaborate but unpublished work on "Communism and Social Reform." (See the letter to Charles Sumner, November 5, 1861 [micro.].)

H. P. Cutting was the minister of a church on Cannon Street; he is frequently mentioned between 1861 and 1863 in the Poughkeepsie *Daily Eagle*.

2. For a discussion of the use of balloons during the Civil War see F. Stansbury Haydon, *Aeronautics in the Union and Confederate Armies* (Baltimore, 1941). Winter is not mentioned in this book, but there had been considerable interest in ballooning during 1861 owing to the exploits of Thaddeus S. C. Lowe. (See n. 3.)

George Brinton McClellan (1826–1885), a graduate of West Point in 1846, had become a major general upon the outbreak of the Civil War. Having prevented Confederate military occupation of West Virginia, he was appointed commander of the Division of the Potomac, but his reluctance to engage the enemy tried President Lincoln's patience. In 1864 McClellan was nominated as the Democratic candidate for President and ran on a platform calling for immediate cessation of hostilities. After the war he worked on construction of a steam warship, and he served in his last years as governor of New Jersey (1878–1881).

3. Thaddeus S. C. Lowe (1832–1913) was a scientist and inventor who pioneered in the use of balloons for air travel. In 1861 he had in fact suggested to Simon Cameron, the secretary of war, that balloons might have a military potential.

4. Edward Dickinson Baker (1811–1861) was one of the most versatile and ubiquitous figures of his day. Born in England, he had settled with his family in Philadelphia, moved to Indiana and then to Illinois, and become a distinguished lawyer and orator. He was twice elected to Congress from Illinois, and he commanded a brigade in the Mexican War. From the Middle West he moved to California and then to Oregon, and was elected to the Senate in the fall of 1860. Given charge of a brigade in 1861, to avoid resigning as senator he refused the ranks of brigadier and major general. He was killed in action at Ball's Bluff, October 22, 1861.

Sumner's eulogy of Baker was printed in *The Liberator,* December 20, 1861.

5. John Greenleaf Whittier, "For Righteousness' Sake," line 35.

6. In his message to Congress of December 3, 1861, Lincoln did indeed recommend colonization in a "congenial climate" as a means of dealing with liberated slaves. The New York *Times,* in commenting on the speech as a whole, objected to this scheme, saying that it was too expensive and that the freed slaves would be needed in the United States to work the land.

7. In fact, the act abolishing slavery in the District of Columbia was not passed by Congress until April 1862.

21

TO OLIVER JOHNSON

Boston, Dec. 22, 1861.

Dear Johnson:

Your letter, in regard to the success attending the delivery of Phillips's lecture at the Cooper Institute, is cheering indeed; for I had some anxiety about it, especially in view of the Herald's malignant efforts to create a disturbance. Fortunate is it for your city that it has such a Chief of Police, with such determined men under him.[1]

This morning, at the Music Hall, Phillips's discourse on Ideas in their relation to Events, was listened to by an immense audience,— showing his hold upon the popular interest.[2] It was, of course, able and instructive, and well received, but not so brilliant and effective as some of his efforts.

I wish I could be present to hear Mr. Tilton's speech.[3]

You and he very kindly urge me to lecture in your city on the 2d or 7th of January, as the committee may judge best, and think there would be a large attendance. Considering the size of the Institute hall, I am afraid the number present would look rather meagre, and really *be* so, in case of a storm, (which I am pretty sure to raise in such cases)—still, be the assembly few or many, I am willing to "bear witness to the truth"[4] before them, in the best manner I am able, if, on further consideration, you and dear Theodore deem it best to announce me. But, I pray you, think carefully of it. Remember that Sumner drew because of his Senatorial position and career —Phillips because of his oratorical fame, besides being helped by the Herald—Tilton is justly a growing favorite, and no doubt will have a flattering reception. Had you not better let the series of lectures terminate with his, rather than to run the risk of a decided falling off in interest and attendance? I say this with reference to popular effect, and not because I am not as ready to speak where only "two or three" are drawn together, as where thousands congregate.[5] As for the remuneration, beyond my travelling expenses, give yourself no anxiety about it. Should I come, I am quite willing to "run for luck" on that score, according to the success of the meeting. To the hands of you both, I commit myself, and will cheerfully abide by your concurrent judgments. If that decision be, "Come," you can advertise me for the evening of Jan. 2d or 7th, (as named in your letter,) as may be most convenient for you; but, other things being equal, I should prefer the evening of the 2d, as Phillips is to give his "Fraternity" lecture here on the 7th.[6]

Again—consider the matter well before deciding.

I was "taken all aback" by the announcement, that Drs. Bacon and Thompson are to be succeeded by Henry Ward Beecher as editor of the Independent; but I think it will be a popular change, and I am sure there will be none of the sectarian meanness and bitterness, so frequently evinced in the lucubrations of Bacon and Thompson, in the editorials of Mr. Beecher.[7] How he will be able to find any time to attend to his editorial duties is what puzzles me. But, in T. T., he will have an excellent auxiliary.

I hope Mary Anne is in better health, and Victoria quite restored.[8]

At home we are all in good health, and the whole family desire to be cordially remembered to you & wife.

Ever yours,

Wm. Lloyd Garrison.

Oliver Johnson.

ALS: Garrison Papers, Boston Public Library; extract printed in the *National Anti-Slavery Standard*, December 28, 1861.

1. Wendell Phillips' speech, with its enthusiastic support of the war, was delivered in New York City on December 19 and printed in the New York *Daily Tribune*, December 20; in *The Liberator*, December 27; and in the *National Anti-Slavery Standard*, January 4, 1862. In the issue for December 28 the *Standard* described the *Herald's* attempt "to create a disturbance" as follows: "*The Herald* had endeavored, by mendacious appeals to popular ignorance and passion, to excite a mob, but its efforts in this direction were fruitless. The Superintendent of Police [John A. Kennedy] was present with a numerous force, ready for any emergency, and with a fixed determination to maintain the freedom of speech."

2. The foregoing passage from Garrison's letter describing Phillips' speech at the Music Hall on December 22 was quoted by Johnson in the *Standard* for December 28 as "Extract from a private letter, dated Boston, Dec. 22"; Garrison in effect became the reporter for Phillips' lecture.

3. Theodore Tilton spoke at the Cooper Institute on December 26 on the subject "The Latest Questions of the War," his basic conclusion being that the only way to put down the rebellion was to eliminate slavery, its cause. "The lesson of the hour is the freedom of the slave," he said. "Better fitted than I to teach it, was the man who stood here a week ago; I mean Wendell Phillips. Better fitted than I to teach it, will be the man who is to stand here a few weeks hence. I mean William Lloyd Garrison. As to myself, I have somehow drifted in between them, like a cock-boat between the Pillars of Hercules." (*Standard*, January 4, 1862.)

4. John 18:37, with "to" substituted for "unto."

5. An allusion to Matthew 18:20.

6. In fact, Garrison spoke the week following Phillips' speech on the topic "The Abolitionists, and their Relations to the War." The *Standard* reported on January 18 that although the attendance was not so large as for Phillips, "the speech evidently made a very deep impression, sweeping away old prejudices and misconceptions, and setting the anti-slavery cause in a light so clear as to carry conviction to every candid mind." (The text of Garrison's lecture was printed in the *Standard*, February 1, 1862.)

In his speech, "The Times," at Tremont Temple in Boston on January 7, Phillips expressed grave concern over the prospect for northern military success, although he praised the efforts of Northerners, if not of Lincoln's cabinet. (*The Liberator*, January 17, 1862.)

7. Leonard Bacon (1802–1881) and Joseph P. Thompson (1819–1879) had more in common than the fact that they had been editors of the New York *Independent*. Both went to Yale and to Andover Theological Seminary, both became Congregational ministers and authors, and both were moderate abolitionists.

8. Victoria Knight Smith (1837–1865) was the daughter of Jane Charlotte and Holland Lorenzo Knight and the niece of Mary Anne Johnson (Oliver's wife). In 1859 she married Dr. Henry M. Smith. See also the letters to Oliver Johnson, September 9, 1862, and to Helen E. Garrison, June 8, 1865 (micro.). (Almira Z. White, *Genealogy of the Descendants of John White*, Haverhill, Mass., 1905, p. 145.)

2 2

TO OLIVER JOHNSON

Boston, Dec. 26, 1861.

Dear Johnson:

Yours is just received. I will consider myself pledged to be with you at the time specified in your letter; and you may announce my subject as suggested by you—"The Abolitionists, and their Relations to the War." I shall probably deem it safest to be in New York the night before the delivery of my lecture.

I am wishing a flattering attendance at the Cooper Institute, this evening, for our friend [Theodore] Tilton; but I do not see how you can gather such audiences as you have had, with tickets at 25 cents.

E. H. Heywood acquitted himself most creditably, on Tuesday evening, in his lecture on "Common Sense" before the Fraternity.[1] As it was Christmas eve, only about two-thirds of the usual number were present.

You will see in the Liberator, this week, the speech of Mr. Phillips, delivered at New York, as revised and corrected by himself. And such revision, correction, alteration, and addition you never saw, in the way of emendation![2] More than two columns of the Tribune's[3] report were in type before P. came into our office; and the manipulation these required was a caution to all reporters and typesetters! I proposed to P. to send his altered "slips" to Barnum as a remarkable curiosity, and Winchell suggested having them photographed![4] But P. desired to make his speech as complete and full as he could, and I am glad you are to receive it without being put to any trouble about it. Doubtless, you will be requested to make some new alterations; for he is constantly criticising what he has spoken, and pays no regard to literal accuracy. This speech will be eagerly read, as it touches ably upon many interesting points.

Gerrit Smith at Peterboro', and Charles Sumner at Washington, both write to me in discouraging tones as to the prospects before us. The Administration has neither pluck nor definite purpose. What tremendous events will hinge upon an actual war with England![5]

Please give my kindest remembrances to Mary-Anne, Mrs. [Augustus] Savin, and others of the pleasant household.

Yours, in all weathers,

Wm. Lloyd Garrison.

Oliver Johnson.

ALS: Garrison Papers, Boston Public Library; partly printed in *Life*, IV, 39.

1. The Parker Fraternity was a liberal lecture series founded by Theodore Parker (see *Letters*, IV, 29, n. 2) in 1858. It was open to both men and women, who were asked to speak on all the crucial issues of the day, some of which were not tolerated on other platforms. Heywood had spoken to the fraternity at Tremont Temple on December 24, urging that "the Union be re-established on the ruins of slavery! Pluck up this rebellion by the roots and brandish it in triumph over the enemy!" (*The Liberator*, January 3, 1862.)

2. Wendell Phillips' speech, "The War," delivered at the Cooper Institute on December 19, was printed in the New York *Daily Tribune*, *The Liberator*, and *National Anti-Slavery Standard* (see the previous letter, n. 1). The *Tribune* version was presumably a reporter's literal transcription of the speech as delivered. The revisions Garrison refers to were many stylistic changes, largely insignificant, as well as expansions of the original text. *The Liberator* and the *Standard* reprinted the same revised version.

Phillips made six sizable interpolations: only one is a noteworthy addition to the content of his address. Two-thirds of the way through he compares slaveholders with the French nobility before the Revolution, which depended on inherited privilege for continuance. He says further, "I would claim of Congress . . . a solemn act abolishing slavery throughout the Union, securing compensation to loyal slaveholders. As the Constitution forbids the States to make and allow nobles, I would now, by equal authority, forbid them to make slaves or allow slaveholders." In this scheme, compensation in the form of money would be paid to former slaveholders as a spur to southern industry and agriculture. Such a move, Phillips continues, would save the Union and bind "the negro to us by the indissoluble tie of gratitude—the loyal slaveholder by strong self-interest." Although the idea of compensation to slaveholders was not original with Phillips, this addition to his text is significant because he takes up and articulates once again a practical solution for reachieving union by means of a tactic that would theoretically assure the economic homogeneity of northern and southern institutions.

3. The New York *Tribune* was founded by Horace Greeley in 1841. Under his tasteful and energetic editing, the paper became known as the best daily newspaper in the country. One of the *Tribune's* hallmarks was its devotion to progressive political causes, including abolitionism.

4. Phineas Taylor Barnum (1810–1891), the outstanding American showman, had by the time of Garrison's letter diverted and hoaxed the public for some twenty years.

James Manning Winchell Yerrinton is identified in the letter to Wendell Phillips Garrison, August 9, 1861, n. 9.

5. The danger of war with Great Britain centered around an incident known as the *Trent* affair. On November 8, 1861, Captain Charles Wilkes of the U.S.S. *San Jacinto* boarded the *Trent*, a British mail steamer in Boston harbor, and seized Confederate diplomatic agents James M. Mason and John Slidell, holding them for a time at Fort Warren. The British considered the incident an affront to their national honor. Although northerners cheered Wilkes's action as brave and patriotic, Lincoln was persuaded by Charles Sumner to release the prisoners, averting threats of British hostilities.

II PRELIMINARY PROCLAMATION: 1862

PART FROM THE correspondence with his English friend and associate George Thompson, Garrison's letters for 1862 show relatively little concern for the catastrophic political and military events of the period; comment on national issues was reserved for his editorials and speeches. In *The Liberator*, January 10, for instance, he argued for the abolition of slavery under the war power, stating that it was "the solemn duty and exalted privilege of the Government, UNDER THE WAR POWER, in this terrible emergency, as a matter of self-preservation, to seek the utter suppression of the rebellion through the abolition of slavery, its murderous cause." It was this argument that he repeated frequently until the preliminary Emancipation Proclamation in September. When the New York *Journal of Commerce* upbraided him for the shift in his constitutional position, alluding to Benedick in *Much Ado About Nothing* and his statement, "When I said I would die a bachelor, I did not think I should live till I were married," he gave this humorous answer in his speech at Cooper Union in New York: "When I said I would not sustain the Constitution, because it was 'a covenant with death, and an agreement with hell,' *I had no idea that I would live to see death and hell secede. . . .* Hence it is that I am now with the Government, to enable it to constitutionally stop the further ravages of death, and to extinguish the flames of hell forever."[1]

During 1862, despite his resolution to stand "loyally by the government as such, on the battle-field or in any other capacity,"[2] Garrison continued to be hostile toward the President. He expressed fear that "the present glorious opportunity to put an end to slavery

1. *The Liberator*, January 24, 1862.
2. *The Liberator*, September 26, 1862.

may be allowed to pass unimproved by the Government."³ He became increasingly critical of Lincoln for tolerating the dilatory tactics of General McClellan. He was annoyed with Lincoln's veto of General Hunter's emancipation order for the area of Georgia, South Carolina, and Florida: "The President is still disposed to treat the dragon of slavery as though it was only a wayward colt."⁴ He remained critical when, following the inconclusive federal victory at Antietam, Lincoln issued the preliminary Emancipation Proclamation, and condemned the provision that fugitive slaves of masters loyal to the government be returned to servitude. Nor was his hostility mitigated when in December Lincoln proposed a constitutional amendment to reimburse slaveholders for loss of slave property. "This," Garrison said, ". . . closely borders upon hopeless lunacy. It will assuredly excite the astonishment of all Europe, the derision of the Southern traitors, and the pity of every true friend of freedom. It would, in our judgment, warrant the impeachment of the President by Congress as mentally incapable of holding the sacred trusts committed to his hands."⁵ Realizing that the Proclamation was to take effect on January 1, Garrison closed the year with more hope: "The eventful day indicated in this Proclamation is at hand, and, as it draws near, the hearts of all true friends of Freedom are palpitating with hope and fear as to its enforcement or possible modification."⁶

Although Garrison had himself been critical of Lincoln as President, he was concerned that England support the northern cause during the war. His concern was intensified by the many letters that he and other abolitionists had received during 1861, from English friends and associates, in which there had been much criticism of Lincoln and the northern role in the war.

In *The Liberator* for February 21, 1862, Garrison published anonymously selections from those letters, in which the war was called "the American Revolution of 1861," and it was argued that the southern states had a right "to choose their own form of government." It was also said that the North had little chance of defeating the South. One correspondent suggested that if Lincoln had had as the major goal of the war not the preservation of the Union, but the emancipation of the slaves, the English reaction would have been quite different. Garrison's response to these letters was in the form of three long and important letters to George Thompson that he

3. *The Liberator*, March 21, 1862.
4. *The Liberator*, May 23, 1862.
5. *The Liberator*, December 5, 1862.
6. *The Liberator*, December 26, 1862.

printed in three successive issues of the paper (February 21, 28, and March 7). In these letters, he reviewed for British consumption the facts regarding the outbreak of the war, asserted once more the central constitutional argument, and defended the American abolitionists in their support of the government of the North. His most vituperative response was expressed in the first letter, which was concerned largely with the most outspoken and hostile of the English letters he reprinted.

Less important and far-reaching than the letters to Thompson was Garrison's correspondence with Anna E. Dickinson, from which four of his letters are printed in this volume. The correspondence began in the spring of 1862, when Garrison received from the nineteen-year-old Philadelphian an appeal for help in scheduling lectures in New England. (She had already had some success lecturing on woman's rights and on the national crisis.) The resulting lectures in Boston charmed the audiences, and Garrison was profusely thanked for discovering her. Miss Dickinson's letters of this period, which have been preserved at the Library of Congress, give fascinating glimpses of Garrison and his family.[7]

Many of Garrison's letters of 1862 concern family matters; ill health and good health; lectures—George Thompson's, Wendell Phillips', and his own; his travels to "immense, dirty, bustling, turbulent" New York City and elsewhere; his continuing interest in spiritualism and homeopathic medicine; and his feelings, as the father of four sons, about serving in the army.

7. *AWT*, pp. 282, 371.

---

2 3

TO CHARLES SUMNER

[c. January 31, 1862]

Dear Mr. S.

The bearer of this, Dr. David Thayer, a much respected physician of large practice in this city, visits Wash[ingto]n as the authorized agent of the Mass[achusetts]. H[omœopathic]. S[ociety]. to exert what influence he can towards securing the passage, through Congress, of a bill, conceding to Hom[eopathic]. practitioners the same right to be employed in the army as is granted to practitioners of the Allopathic school.[1] I do not know what your preferences may be as between the two modes of practice; but as it is not a question of individual choice, but one of strict and impartial justice, I have no doubt you will be inclined to give the matter your candid consideration, and to vote against any proscription.

I need not add, that it is too late in the day to attempt to stamp the Hom. treatment as quackery, or to subject it to ridicule and contempt. It has won for itself the highest position in Europe, and is extending itself in every direction in this country. For intelligence, moral wealth, and medical acumen, its practitioners, as a body, will compare most favorably with any other class of physicians in the world; and in their career they have exhibited a conscientiousness of conviction, and a firmness of purpose, (in many cases under sore persecution,) worthy of all admiration. The results of their practice are the best evidences of its superiority. At any rate, they have a right to ask to be placed on the same footing with others, leaving the sick and wounded of the army to decide for themselves whether they will be doctored in one way or another.

AL: Merrill Collection of Garrison Papers, Wichita State University Library. The manuscript appears to be a rough draft. Since this letter opens with the same sentence as does a letter to George Washington Julian dated January 31, 1862 (micro.), it seems probable that it was written on the same day.

1. David Thayer (born 1813), educated at Phillips Academy, Andover, and Union College, with a medical degree from Berkshire Medical Institute, was one of the leading American homeopathic physicians; he was president of the Massachusetts Homœopathic Society (founded in 1846) and in 1870 of the American Institute of Homœopathy. An active abolitionist, Thayer was a friend of Garrison, who himself had greater confidence in homeopathic than in the more orthodox allopathic medical treatment. The homeopathic method, which had originated in Germany in the late eighteenth century, dispensed for treatment of disease small quantities of those drugs that would produce in unaffected patients the same symptoms as the disease. (Egbert Cleave, *Cleave's Biographical Cyclopedia of Homœopathic Physicians and Surgeons*, Philadelphia, 1873, pp. 481–482.)

Although it is known that Massachusetts Senator Henry Wilson presented to the Senate a petition requesting what Dr. Thayer sought, there is no evidence that a bill was passed or even discussed. (*Journal of the Senate of the United States of America, Being the Second Session of the Thirty-Seventh Congress*, Washington, 1862, pp. 155–160.)

24

TO ANNIE BROWN

Boston, Feb. 2, 1862.

Dear Miss Brown:

In answer to your letter just received, I will state that Mr. R. J. Hinton is in Col. Jennison's Brigade in Missouri, and a regular correspondent of the Boston Traveller.[1] I presume, however, that a letter directed to Leavenworth, Kansas, would be more likely to reach him than if sent any where else.

Please give my high regards to your excellent mother, and to all the members of the family at home.[2]

Yours, to break every yoke,[3]

Wm. Lloyd Garrison.

Miss Annie Brown.

ALS: Eldridge Collection, Henry E. Huntington Library.

Annie Brown (1843–1926), born in Richfield, Ohio, was the eighth child of John Brown and Mary Anne Day Brown. As a young woman of fifteen she managed her father's eccentric household on the Maryland border prior to the invasion of Harpers Ferry. Her experiences during this period provided the basis for the impressions and the information she later conveyed to John Brown's biographers, including Franklin Sanborn, Richard Hinton, and Oswald Garrison Villard. (Letter to the editor from Stephen B. Oates, Department of History, University of Massachusetts, Amherst, August 1, 1973.)

1. Richard J. Hinton (1830–1901), born in London and a resident of New York City since 1851, had a diversity of occupations and interests. He worked as a printer, but also studied medicine and topographical engineering. Having demonstrated his dedication to abolition by assisting in the formation of the Republican party, he moved in 1856 to Kansas, where he served as correspondent for the Boston *Evening Traveller* and three New York papers (the *Times*, the *Tribune*, and the *Herald*) and helped to found several new papers in Kansas. Closely associated with Brown, though not a participant in the raid at Harpers Ferry, Hinton was among those who considered a plan for rescuing him from jail. During the Civil War Hinton served as first lieutenant adjutant and recruited and commanded black troops. In 1865 he became acting inspector general of the Freedmen's Bureau. In his later years he lived in Washington, traveled abroad, and continued to contribute widely to American newspapers. (William E. Connelley, "Col. Richard J. Hinton," *Kansas Historical Collections*, 7: 486–493, 1901–1902; Oswald Garrison Villard, *John Brown, 1800–1859: A Biography Fifty Years After*, New York, 1943, p. 570.)

Charles Ransford Jennison (born 1834) was a physician who moved in 1854 from New York state to Kansas, where he became a leader in the Kansas free-state movement and a supporter of John Brown. He and his band of some forty men virtually defeated the proslavery forces in the state. In 1861 he was appointed colonel in the First Kansas Cavalry, and he served for a time as commander of Fort Leavenworth. In 1865 and again in 1867 he was elected to the state legislature; in 1871 he became a state senator. (*United States Biographical Dictionary*, Kansas volume, Chicago, 1879.)

Appearing first as the *American Traveller* in 1825, the paper had been published since 1845 as the Boston *Evening Traveller;* after 1912 it was combined with the Boston *Herald.* At the time of Garrison's letter the managing editor was Garrison's former fellow apprentice on the Newburyport *Herald,* Joseph B. Morse. (Edwin A. Perry, *The Boston Herald and its History,* Boston, 1878; Mott, p. 560; *Life.*)

2. Mary Anne Day Brown (1816–1884) had married John Brown in 1833 after the death of his first wife. She bore him thirteen children, of whom six lived till adulthood: Annie, Ellen, Oliver, Watson, Salmon, and Sarah. After her husband's execution she moved west: to Iowa in 1862 and to Red Bluff, Calif., in 1864, where she was awarded financial aid by the town. (Fresno [Calif.] *Bee*, December 14, 1941; Villard, *John Brown.*)

3. Isaiah 58:6, adapted.

2 5

TO GEORGE THOMPSON

[February 21, 1862.]

MY DEAR FRIEND AND COADJUTOR:

In common with the great body of Abolitionists in this country, I have been greatly surprised,—not at the ignorance pervading England in regard to American affairs, for this I found to be universal, in many cases to a ludicrous extent, on my several visits, and time seems to have done little or nothing to enlighten it since I was last with you in 1846,—but at the general obfuscation of mind among *our English anti-slavery co-laborers,* respecting the nature of the civil war now going on in America, the bearing it has upon the cause of liberty in its broadest significance, and the position occupied by those with whom they have so long, so disinterestedly, and so generously coöperated for the peaceful extinction of negro slavery, by moral and religious instrumentalities, on this side of the Atlantic. To us, they appear to have lost all power of discrimination as to the great issues presented, and therefore all power of correct reasoning; while, to their vision, we, the hitherto uncompromising enemies of slavery, appear to have abdicated our high position of unswerving principle for the low ground of political expediency, in order, for once, to be on the popular side—deceiving ourselves with the idea, that we shall win the victory over the great dragon of slavery all the more readily by pursuing such a course! Certainly, there is a total misapprehension on one side or the other. I think it is with them; and though, in view of all that has been written and published on the subject, I almost despair of removing that misapprehension in the slightest degree, yet, by the love I bear them, I feel impelled to address this letter to you—hoping it may not be wholly in vain.

As for yourself, you need nothing from me, either by way of information or guidance, at this particular juncture. Before I read any of the admirable speeches which you have made on the American question, or knew any thing of your sentiments pertaining to it, I felt sure that your judgment would be sound, and your verdict just, as between our Government and the Southern traitors who have so perfidiously risen in rebellion against it. Your mastery of American affairs is absolute: the key to unlock them is SLAVERY, and of that key you took possession when you first came to this country in 1834, and have ever since used it with all possible skill, diligence and success. You have had the advantage of a residence here; and though it subjected you to bitter opprobrium and great peril at that time, nevertheless, it enabled you to traverse a wide extent of country, to gather a large amount of valuable information, and to understand the precise relations subsisting between the Federal and State Governments, with their special, diverse, but not conflicting sovereignties.[1] There are few Americans who are so well posted in the history of this country as yourself, while there is scarcely any one in England who seems to have any intelligent knowledge of it. Almost all your writers and public speakers are ever blundering in regard to the constitutional powers of the American Government, as such, and those pertaining to the States, in their separate capacity. Mr. Bright, in his masterly speech at Rochdale, evinced a power of analysis and correct generalization worthy of the highest praise; and has secured for himself the thanks and admiration of every true friend of free institutions.[2] His case is as exceptional, however, as it is creditable.

I am sure that you, my dear friend, will not deem it presumption when I say, that, of all persons, the Abolitionists are most capable of understanding the rise, progress and tendency of the present struggle in this country, and the least liable to be jaundiced in vision or biased in judgment. For more than thirty years they have been tried and tempted in every conceivable manner; yet they have stood firm and unyielding. Lifted infinitely above all sectional considerations and selfish aims—dead to all partisan appeals—in conflict with Church and State, because of their complicity with slavery—waiving in many instances the exercise of the elective franchise, for conscience' sake—and world-wide in the doctrines they inculcate and the spirit they breathe—their position is one of the highest moral elevation, enabling them to retain uncommon clearness of vision, and to exhibit rare integrity of character. As they have never cherished towards the South any other feelings than those of good will, not withstanding her brutal and murderous spirit towards them, they cannot be justly suspected of being swayed by popular feeling at the present time. In the midst of unparalleled excitement, they are calm and steadfast; still pursuing their glorious object, without turning to the right hand or to the left; still bearing such testimonies as the times demand; still speaking the truth "without concealment and without compromise"; still "rightly dividing the word,"[3] and making the freedom of the slave the paramount object of their regard. Yet—strange to say—their consistency, in some instances almost their integrity, has been called in question by their English anti-slavery friends, who assume to understand matters three thousand miles off, and to see the most intricate operations that long distance, a great deal better than those of us who are on the ground, and whose knowledge of men and things, and of the growth of public sentiment and the causes of this rebellion, is equally comprehensive and absolute.

If you will turn to the fourth page of the present number of the *Liberator,* you will see specimens of numerous letters that have been received by various persons from these excellent, beloved, well-meaning, but thoroughly confused English friends.[4] The first writer takes the preposterous ground that "the North [meaning the American Government] has no more right to control the South than Austria has to control Hungary, or Russia Poland"! He insists that "the North is simply fighting for empire," but that it would have made no difference, in his estimation, "even if the policy of the North had been to extinguish slavery"! To cap the climax of his infatuation, he declares, "Every lover of liberty, (!) whose personal feelings do not warp his judgment, will wish success to the South at this present crisis"! Was there ever greater incoherency of speech than this? Nay, he sweepingly declares, "All charges of treason and conspiracy and robbery mean nothing but the expression of revengeful feelings or disappointed ambition"! But, even assuming the truth of them all, he affirms that they are all "perfectly justified as against the North, by the present attitude and behavior of the North itself"! He even proceeds to justify the atrocious robberies perpetrated by the South by pleading, "If the South had not availed itself of the opportunities (!) of arming itself, &c. &c., where would it have been now, in the face of the overwhelming power of the North?" As if that "overwhelming power" would have been called into action, had not the South, while professing allegiance to the Government, treacherously seized the national arsenals, armories, navy-yards, fortifications, &c., to carry on its treasonable work, and to enable it to seize the very Capital itself as the seat of its dominion!

I have seen no positions more absurd, no sentiments more revolting, in any of the Southern journals, than these. On this subject, our worthy friend is clearly demented. Yet, with singular complacency, he "wants the Abolitionists of America to take a broader and wider and deeper view of this subject than they have done"—so broad and wide and deep that they will see in Jeff. Davis the incarnation of the spirit of outraged liberty, and in Southern treason an exhibition of the purest patriotism! He thought they were "universal men," but to his great grief he finds "they have nearly all sunk from this sublime height to the level of Americans"—"they have fallen from that lofty and majestic eminence on which they stood, into a position in which they stand little higher, at the best, *and in some respects lower*, than the community around them"! Our reproving friend says he is, "frank and outspoken," but his assertions and impeachments are none the less astounding. I deny their truthfulness, while I am sure he has spoken his sincere convictions, and I honor him for keeping nothing concealed. He is simply laboring under a strange hallucination of mind, which it is to be hoped will soon disappear; for it is causing him "to call good evil, and evil good, and to put light for darkness, and darkness for light."[5]

Whether the Southern rebellion be viewed from a Governmental or an Abolition stand-point, it presents no feature which is not abhorrent to reason, justice and humanity; and the sternest condemnation of an indignant universe should be meted out to those who concocted it.

First—as to the Government. It is based upon the doctrine, that the people have a right to choose their own rulers, and to be governed by their own laws, in accordance with the Constitution of their adoption. At the last Presidential election, the slave oligarchy failed for the first time to carry their point, and the free States triumphed in the election of Abraham Lincoln. Without waiting for his inauguration, five of the slave States rose in rebellion, organized a hostile confederacy, and endeavored to seize the national capital. Six more slave States were added to the number in the course of a few months, and, combined, they aimed at the subjugation of the whole country to their bloody sway.[6] Perjury, lynch law, robbery on a gigantic scale, piracy on the high seas, treason of the blackest dye, marked their entire career. They fired upon the national flag, captured Fort Sumter, drove out every vestige of governmental authority from their dominions, proclaimed themselves independent, declared adhesion to the old Union punishable with outlawry, imprisonment or death, and committed atrocities of the most revolting character upon those who refused to betray their country. It was not an oppressed people rising up in defence of their rights, or to overthrow a tyrannical dynasty, but a desperate man-stealing oligarchy bent upon the extinction of free institutions universally. Any attempt to make their case analogous to that of our revolutionary fathers, or to find justification in the doctrines laid down in the Declaration of Independence, is not only futile, but an insult to the memories of the signers of that great charter of human rights. There is nothing to warrant it. The rebels had suffered no oppression, and were threatened with no injustice; on the contrary, they had always shaped the policy of the country, and had their own way. Mr. Lincoln was elected to the Presidency as constitutionally as was Washington, Adams, or Jefferson; the Constitution he was sworn to uphold in its integrity was unchanged in letter or spirit; a Kentuckian by birth, and no Abolitionist, his natural tendency was to desire to propitiate the South, even to a humiliating degree. Neither he, nor the party by whom he was chosen, had any more thought or intention of interfering with the "peculiar institution" of the South, than of annexing the United States to Great Britain or Austria. Besides, even if the new Administration had been inclined to transcend its rightful authority, adverse to Southern interests, it was powerless to do so; for the Supreme Court was thoroughly pro-slavery as then (and even now) constituted, and the Democratic party held the mastery in both houses of Congress, at the very time the rebellion took place; so that no action, detrimental to the South, could have obtained any legislative or judicial sanction whatever. Mr. Lincoln, had it not been for the treasonable withdrawal of the slave States, would have been wholly at the mercy of his political opponents in the formation of his Cabinet, in all his official appointments, and in determining the character of his measures: he could have been check-mated in every direction. On no recognized theory of government—much less that of democratic equality—could they be justified in throwing off their allegiance, and making war upon that Union in which they had always had the lion's share of honor, emolument, office, power and protection; or in trampling upon that Constitution which was originally made as dictated by themselves, and to the maintenance of which their faith stood plighted before the world. But, without the shadow of an excuse, they perfidiously banded together, in a treasonable manner, for the most iniquitous purposes; resorting to every villanous expedient to consummate their diabolical object; and they have ever since been menacing with their forces the very seat of Government itself. Their avowed object was and is the boundless extension and absolute perpetuity of their accursed slave system, which they have made the cornerstone of their confederacy. They openly deny and deride the glorious self-evident truths embodied in the Declaration of Independence; they avow their detestation of the doctrine of popular sovereignty, as fraught with all conceivable mischief; and they pronounce "free society" at the North, and throughout the world, an utter failure.

Under these circumstances, my dear friend, is it not astounding that any on your side of the Atlantic, claiming to be governed by the principles of honor, the dictates of morality, and the feelings of humanity,—especially in the Anti-Slavery ranks,—should be so bewildered in judgment, or so jaundiced in vision, as to regard the

South in the attitude of Hungary to Austria, or Poland to Russia!—
should vindicate her right to withdraw as she has done, and arraign
the Government as tyrannical in endeavoring to crush her foul conspiracy against God and man?—or, at least, should avow that, as between the contending parties, there is little or nothing to choose,
"being six on one side, and half a dozen on the other"—and where
they utter one rebuke of the doings of the slaveholding banditti,
give vent to a score of bitter denunciations of the American Government, because it is not willing to fall down, and let "bloody treason
flourish over it"? Such conduct is quite inexplicable, and extorts
the exclamation—

> "O judgment, thou art fled to brutish beasts,
> And men have lost their reason!"[7]

The charge is cruelly false, that the Government "is simply fighting for empire." It is acting, not aggressively but in self-defence,
without malice or passion, having first allowed itself to be driven to
the wall, by a mistaken and dangerous forbearance, as no other
strong Government ever yet did. It is contending, not for "empire"
in itself considered, but for its right to exist over the territory embraced by the republic, with those limitations and prerogatives
which are so carefully defined by the Constitution for the promotion of the general welfare, and for the common defence. It is a renewal of the old revolutionary struggle to vindicate the right of THE
PEOPLE to form and administer their own government, but against a
despotism incomparably more to be feared and abhorred than was
that of the mother country in "the times that tried men's souls."[8]
Mr. Lincoln, as the legitimate President of the United States, had
no alternative but to proceed, with all the forces at his command, to
put down the rebellion; and had he not done so, he would have
been guilty of perjury, and a traitor to the Government he was
elected by the people to uphold.

You perceive, therefore, as between the rebels and the Government, that the American Abolitionists could not but give their sympathy and support to the latter, as wholly innocent of any wrong to
the South, either inflicted or premeditated; and that, in so doing,
they have not compromised their principles, nor turned aside a
hair's breadth from their well-defined course. Whatever may be the
issue they now take with the Government, it is not as to its entire
rectitude in its treatment of the Southern slaveholding rebellion,
viewed from the stand-point of constitutional authority and obligation. Upon that issue, whether as American citizens, or as impartial
umpires between contending parties where the most momentous

interests are at stake, they have no difficulty in rendering a decisive verdict in favor of the Government.

I will address you again on this subject.

Your fellow-laborer in the cause of universal freedom,

WM. LLOYD GARRISON.

Printed: *The Liberator*, February 21, 1862; partly printed in *Life*, IV, 47. Although a fragmentary manuscript in Garrison's hand (consisting of six closely written and edited pages) is preserved in the Merrill Collection of Garrison Papers, Wichita State University Library, this transcription is from *The Liberator*, which contains the entire letter and is factually more accurate.

1. Garrison refers to Thompson's hectic and often dangerous sojourn in the United States between October 1834 and November 1835.

2. John Bright (1811–1889), member of the House of Commons successively from Durham, Manchester, and Birmingham, was one of the most conscientious and influential of English reformers. After 1868 he was to hold several posts in Gladstone's government. On December 4, 1861, Bright called for peaceful arbitration of the *Trent* affair, urging his countrymen to support the cause of the North; it was the first such stand by a politically prominent Englishman. (George M. Trevelyan, *The Life of John Bright*, Boston, 1925.)

3. II Timothy 2:15.

4. Garrison refers to three letters (two from England, one from Scotland) printed anonymously in *The Liberator*, February 21, 1862, and his quotations from them represent accurately their line of argument.

5. Garrison adapts Isaiah 5:20.

6. Garrison refers to the following states: South Carolina, Alabama, Florida, Mississippi, Georgia, Louisiana, Texas, Virginia, Arkansas, North Carolina, and Tennessee. (*OHAP.*)

7. Garrison alludes to Shakespeare, *Julius Caesar*, III, ii, 197, and quotes III, ii, 110–111.

8. Garrison changes the verb from the present to the past tense in the famous passage from Thomas Paine, *The Crisis*, No. 1, December 23, 1776.

---

2 6

TO GEORGE THOMPSON

[February 28, 1862.]

MY DEAR FRIEND AND COADJUTOR:

I have expressed my profound astonishment, that, among the professed friends of freedom and progress in England, there should be any division of sentiment as to the cause, nature and object of the Southern rebellion, and the right and duty of the Government, under the Constitution, to exert all its power to suppress it. This division, I am confident, could not exist, if they would make an analogous case on their own soil. Suppose that England, Scotland, Ireland and Wales were originally colonial dependencies of France; but, in consequence of the oppressive treatment of the mother country, they had been compelled to declare their independence, and, after a long and bloody struggle, they had obtained its recognition. To secure their liberties, they found it necessary to enter into "solemn league and covenant" with each other, and to form their national and State governments upon a common basis—making the Federal Constitution "the supreme law of the land," and the voice of the majority decisive in the election of their officers. Suppose that Ireland, in consequence of her "peculiar institutions," had insisted upon having extraordinary privileges conceded to her, by which she had been enabled to control the government and shape its policy to promote her special interests, for more than half a century. Suppose that, during all that period, while she was enjoying every recognized right and privilege throughout the republic, she was perfidious to all her constitutional obligations and duties—denying the guaranteed right of freedom of speech and of the press on her soil, applying lynch law in numberless instances to the citizens of England, Wales and Scotland found within her limits, and continually bullying and insulting the whole country. Suppose that, partly to prevent an open rupture, partly for lack of true courage, and partly from selfish considerations, the other portions of the country had allowed her to have her own way, "like a spoiled child," till, at last, in order to have a vestige of liberty and equal political rights left in the land, it became necessary for them to break from her thraldom, and to take the reins of government legally into their own hands, in order to subserve the interests of freedom. Suppose that a Presidential election was made the trial of strength between the parties, at the ballot-box, as by law provided; that Ireland had entered into it professedly in good faith, nominating her own candidate, and agreeing to abide the verdict of the people; and that, being defeated, she had raised the standard of rebellion, and proclaimed her independence—treacherously seizing upon all the national property and defences within her domains, and endeavoring to get possession of London itself, from which to issue her imperial decrees. And suppose, finally, that her avowed object for taking this traitorous course was to make that system of human bondage, which is "the sum of all villainies,"[1] the cornerstone of her new government, and to overturn all the institutions of freedom. Under such circumstances, what would the people of England, Scotland and Wales say, if, while their own government was exerting its constitutional authority to put down the rebellion, and to preserve the unity of the country,—not for purposes of "conquest" or oppression, but to promote the general welfare,—those claiming to be the friends of freedom in other lands should declare that they could see no essential difference between the contending parties; that it was a mere political struggle, in the decision of which the civilized world had no interest; that Ireland had a right to secede, and steal what she could, and the British Government had no right to "coerce" her; and that, in fact, she was "more sinned against than sinning,"[2] and therefore should be permitted to take her course? I need not attempt to depict the astonishment and indignation they would express in such a contingency.

It is no defence to quote the words of the American Declaration of Independence—"All governments derive their just powers from the consent of the governed"; for, surely, that political axiom was never meant to justify or extenuate perfidy, robbery, lynch law, and a long catalogue of bloody crimes! Besides, the South had helped to make the American Constitution, and it was shaped expressly so as to secure her approval; she voted to make it supreme over the whole country; she registered her oath to support it; under it she had found peace, security, and the largest indulgence; in the disposal of its offices and emoluments she had obtained vastly more than her fair proportion; no change had been effected, none even proposed, in its letter or spirit, adverse to her interests; yet she shamelessly violated her plighted faith, causelessly lifted the heel of rebellion, impudently insisted that she had been grievously insulted and outraged by the north, wreaked her diabolical vengeance upon all within her reach who dared to advocate the old Union, and instituted a bloody reign of terror for the reign of constitutional liberty!

Granted that there are cases in which "rebellion" is laudable, and "treason" a sublime duty—rebellion against the iniquitous decrees of a fiercely despotic power, and treason against the powers of darkness. Granted that "resistance to tyrants is obedience to God."[3] But the South has rebelled against no such decrees, and she is playing the traitor in order to establish the dominion of the devil, and to enlarge the boundaries of hell. Her spirit, contumacy, aim, effort, are all infernal. Justice is trodden under her feet; humanity bleeds under her murderous lash; liberty she dreads, abhors, and banishes from her soil; mercy she derides, and philanthropy she laughs to scorn. Honest, free, compensated labor is not to her taste; she delights in plundering the needy, in imbruting the helpless, in stealing and buying and selling fathers and mothers, husbands and wives, parents and children; and her fury "burns to the lowest hell"[4] when she is rebuked for her infamous conduct, and admonished to put away her iniquities. In her domains are the habitations

of cruelty; in her skirts is the "blood of the souls of the poor inno-
cents."[5] By a divine decree, her system of chattel slavery is sinking
her lower and lower in the scale of civilization, impoverishing her
resources, turning her fertile soil to barrenness, nourishing every
form of sensual indulgence, filling her brain with madness and her
heart with murder, promoting violence and lawlessness among all
classes, and making pandemonium the fitting symbol of her actual
condition. It has so thoroughly demonized her that appeals to reason, to justice, to the law of eternal rectitude, are not only inopera-
tive, but they seem to inflame her passions, and to stimulate her to
the perpetration of still bloodier crimes. She is an outlaw in the universe of God.

This is not to deal in vituperation: it is truthfully, though in-
adequately, to describe her character and situation. Promise what
she may, there is no reliance to be placed upon her word: she delights in lying and perjury. All her accusations against the North are
the basest of calumnies, coined and circulated for the worst of purposes. She is so cursed by slavery that she is insensible to shame,
recreant to every sentiment of honor, and dead to every appeal of
conscience. Her rebellion is the culmination of her slaveholding
wickedness: it has been characterized throughout by that satanic
spirit which deems it incomparably "better to reign in hell than
serve in heaven."[6]

These things being so, my dear friend, do you marvel at my astonishment that there should be found in England a disposition,—in
some cases even in the Anti-Slavery ranks,—to defend the right of
the South in dismembering the republic, and setting up a confederacy based expressly upon CHATTEL SLAVERY; and, consequently, to
represent the American government as seeking her subjugation by
despotic power, in violation of the doctrines embodied in the Declaration of Independence, and for no higher purpose than the conquest of empire? This indicates a strange obliquity of vision, or a
surprising want of accurate intelligence. As well take the part of the
wolf against the lamb—of the highwayman against his victim—of
the murderer against the man who is endeavoring to defend his life.
The government is innocent of wrong in this case, except that of
dealing with the rebellion too forbearingly, and hesitating to strike
the only effective blow that can be struck for its suppression. The
South is wholly, inexcusably, horribly in the wrong, in all her declarations and measures, her methods and objects, from first to last.
Of course, I do not believe that the great body of the intelligent and
moral people of England are disposed to countenance anything like

the lawlessness on the part of the South: but, at the same time, it is certain that they have not given that earnest sympathy and cordial approval to the American government in its attempt to restore the peace and unity of the republic, which the friends of freedom here had a right to expect.

I have not, thus far, made any reference to the connection subsisting between the government and Southern slavery, under the Constitution, because that is a distinct matter, to be determined by another standard. The first question to be settled is,—Has the South any justification for her revolt on the ground of oppressive and unconstitional treatment on the part of the government? Certainly, none at all. Whatever the words "factious," "seditious," "rebellious," "treasonable" mean in their worst sense, is applicable to her case; and therefore, *wholly aside from the question of slavery*, every lover of order and public tranquillity is bound to pass sentence of condemnation upon her, and to desire her humiliation and defeat in every encounter with the government.

It is objected abroad, that the government forfeits its claim to respect and sympathy, because it allows the fugitive slaves of loyal masters to be given up, and refuses to make this a war for the abolition of slavery. But is it any worse, in these particulars, than it was before the rebellion, when it obtained the hearty recognition and good will of the British people? Surely, my position, as an abolitionist, in relation to the government, for a quarter of a century, will shield me from the suspicion of desiring to extenuate or overlook its constitutional complicity with slavery; but this is certain—bad as the Constitution is, it has at last become so intolerable to the Southern slave-traffickers that they will no longer live under it, and they make it a capital offence for any Southern man to profess allegiance to it. An avowed Unionist among them stands in as great peril of his life as though he were an "ultra abolitionist." Let him dare to unfurl "the stars and stripes" as the flag to which he owes loyalty, and they will either smother him in its folds, or hang him to the first lamp-post. When they are ferociously eager to shoot President Lincoln and every member of his Cabinet,[7] and declare eternal hostility to the Union, common sense dictates that the government is none the less, but all the more, to be favorably regarded by the friends of freedom on that account, whether at home or abroad.

Having thus disposed of the GOVERMENTAL aspect of this question, in order to show that the abolitionists are fully justified in the course they are pursuing, and also that the friends of freedom in Europe ought to be united in sustaining the American government

in its efforts to crush this slaveholding rebellion, I shall next proceed to consider its ANTI-SLAVERY bearings.

Your attached and faithful friend,

WM. LLOYD GARRISON.

GEORGE THOMPSON, Esq.

Printed: *The Liberator*, February 28, 1862; the first page of Garrison's rough draft,
marked "Letter II," is preserved in the Merrill Collection of Garrison Papers, Wichita State University Library.

1. John Wesley, *Journal*, February 12, 1772.
2. Shakespeare, *King Lear*, III, ii, 60.
3. A reference to the motto on Thomas Jefferson's seal, "Rebellion to tyrants is
obedience to God."
4. Deuteronomy 32:22.
5. Jeremiah 2:34.
6. John Milton, *Paradise Lost*, I, 263.
7. Lincoln's cabinet in 1862 consisted of the following: William H. Seward
(State), Salmon P. Chase (Treasury), Montgomery Blair (Post Office), Gideon Welles
(Navy), Caleb B. Smith (Interior), Edwin M. Stanton (War).

27

TO JAMES McKAY

BOSTON, March 4, 1862.

COL. JAMES McKAYE:

Dear Sir,—

I feel honored by the invitation which has been extended to me,
in behalf of the Committee of Arrangements, to be present at a public meeting to be held at the Cooper Institute, in New York, on
Thursday evening next. Other engagements will prevent my attendance, except in spirit. Most heartily do I subscribe to the statement in your call, that the "hostile and traitorous power, calling itself 'The Confederate States,' instead of achieving the destruction
of the nation, has thereby only destroyed slavery; and that it is now
the sacred duty of the National Government, as the only means of
securing permanent peace, national unity and well-being, to provide against its restoration."[1] Whoever else may have the folly or
hardihood to do so, the Southern traitors themselves will not deny
the validity of this statement. In raising the standard of rebellion
they voluntarily and defiantly assumed all the responsibilities of
their perfidious act, and declared themselves ready and eager to
meet all its consequences, whether extending to the confiscation of

their property, the emancipation of their slaves, the outlawry of their persons, or the forfeiture of their lives. Whatever claims they once had upon the Constitution, as loyal citizens of the United States, ceased the first moment they declared themselves out of the Union, set up their hostile confederacy, and made war upon the Government. The punishment of treason is death. Death is the extinction of all constitutional rights. In such a case, the power of the Government, in the exercise of its legitimate functions, is absolute; and, surely, it is not for those who have halters around their necks to call it in question. It is now the glorious prerogative of the Government to "create a soul under the ribs of death,"[2] by proclaiming liberty to every bondman at the South, and by establishing upon her soil "democratic institutions founded on the principles of the Declaration of Independence."

In view of their recent staggering defeats, the Southern traitors will not deny that they have failed to destroy the Republic; or that, solely to guard and perpetuate slavery and slave institutions, they have plunged the country into all the horrors of civil war; and, therefore, that the abolition of slavery is "the only means of securing permanent peace and national unity."[3] They instinctively perceive and frankly avow, that there is an "irrepressible conflict"[4] between liberty and slavery, free institutions and slave institutions; and they are consistently carrying out their anti-republican doctrines. Fearful as is the guilt they have incurred, I hold that they are to be far less abhorred than those at the North, who, under the mask of loyalty, are for treasonable ends denying to the Government the right to remove the source of the rebellion, and to uproot the cause of all our national troubles. I prefer the Charleston *Mercury* to the New York *Journal of Commerce*, the Richmond *Enquirer* to the New York *Herald*, the Norfolk *Day-Book* to the Boston *Courier*. Give us the devil, "going about like a roaring lion seeking whom he may devour," rather than the devil in the garb of "an angel of light," trying to deceive even the very elect![5]

Over the so-called "Confederate States," ever since his inauguration, President Lincoln has been as unable to exercise governmental jurisdiction as over China or Japan. They have rendered it impossible for any officer of the Government to exist, or any law of the land to be enforced, within their limits. They have trampled upon the national flag, made the slightest manifestation of loyalty to the Union perilous to life, exhibited entire unanimity of sentiment in their treasonable designs, and as thoroughly ignored all constitutional relations and obligations as though no such instrument as the Constitution of the United States had ever been heard of. Nor, to this hour, is their position changed one hair's breadth. Hitherto they have acted under a temporary provisional arrangement; now they are acting under a recognized Constitution, designed to be permanent, and have duly inaugurated a President, with all the machinery of independent government.[6] Their treason is now organized and consolidated rebellion, compelling obedience to its bloody decrees in the name of law and order, and by virtue of constitutional authority. Their avowal is still one of undying hostility to that Union which they once professed to adore, and to that Constitution which they formerly lauded as the perfection of human reason, the bulwark of national security, the ark of civil and religious liberty. Their voice is still for war—fierce, revengeful, sanguinary, fratricidal war—"war to the knife, and the knife to the hilt."[7] They have left nothing undone to destroy the Government, to paralyze every branch of industry, to jeopard the safety of peaceful and prosperous commerce, to throw upon the shoulders of the loyal North a crushing weight of debt and taxation, to fill the land with lamentation and woe, and to redden the soil with blood. Thus they have forfeited all rights and immunities; they have brought upon themselves all the tremendous penalties of treason; they have challenged the Government to mortal combat, and staked every thing upon the issue. Not one of their Northern abettors is so audacious as to deny the right of the Government, under these circumstances, to confiscate their property to the fullest extent—property in houses and lands, in ships and goods, in cattle and swine—property recognized as legitimate throughout the world, and in all ages; but when it is proposed to include slave property also, which is based upon robbery and oppression, and therefore has no rightful existence in this or in any other land, then a hue-and-cry is instantly raised, in the name of the Constitution, against the exercise of this right, as though it were a sacrilegious act! Is not this palpable complicity with the Southern traitors, and ought it not to excite universal indignation and abhorrence? It is a vicious rejection of the law of nations for the basest purposes, and a practical betrayal of the Government itself. But it needs no other answer than is contained in the following truthful declaration of John Quincy Adams:[8]—"From the instant that the slaveholding States become the theatre of war, civil, servile or foreign, from that instant the war powers of Congress extend to interference with the institution of slavery, *in every way in which it can be interfered with* . . . Not only the President of the United States, but the Commander of the Army, *has power to order the universal emancipation of the slaves.*"[9]

The Government, then, being clothed with this power, and refusing to wield it, is to be held as responsible for the continuance of slavery as though it had just created the system, and reduced four millions of the people to the condition of chattels. It occupies to the slave population the position which Pharaoh did to the children of Israel in Egypt. It can "let the people go,"[10] and blow the trump of jubilee throughout the land; and not to do so is to evince infatuation and to court destruction. Every hour that it delays is pregnant with future judgments,—symbolized by the plagues of frogs and lice, of fire and hail, of locusts and darkness, the murrain of beasts, and the slain of the first-born in the old Egyptian kingdom.[11] Every hour that it delays, it is to be held responsible for a fearfully criminal waste of life and treasure, and for the needless prolongation of a rebellion more desperate in spirit and design than any to be found in the annals of the world. It has now an opportunity to strike a blow for justice, humanity, freedom, the rights of mankind, and to terminate the most dreadful system of oppression that ever cursed the earth, that has never been equalled in beneficence and glory. To allow this opportunity to pass unimproved, no matter on what pretence, will be such comprehensive iniquity as only He can measure and punish whose command is, "Execute judgment in the morning, and deliver him that is spoiled out of the hand of the oppressor, lest my fury go out like fire, and burn that none can quench it, because of the evil of your doings."[12]

Let the will of God be done, and let all the people say, Amen![13]

Yours, to break every yoke,[14]

WM. LLOYD GARRISON.

Printed: *The Liberator,* March 7, 1862.

James Morrison McKay (1805–1888), whose name Garrison misspells, was the father of actor and dramatist Steele MacKaye. He was a lawyer, first in Buffalo and then in New York City. During the Civil War, as a member of the Union League Club and the Loyal Publication Society, he worked so hard for the Union cause that in 1862 Lincoln secretly appointed him one of three commissioners charged with investigating the conditions of the slaves in the South. (Percy MacKaye, *Epoch: The Life of Steele MacKaye,* New York, 1927).

1. Garrison quotes from the call from the meeting in New York on March 6. The names of those on the committee of arrangements, which included prominent men from many fields, and the full text of the call for the meeting were printed in *The Liberator,* March 7, 1862.

2. John Milton, *Comus,* line 562.

3. The North had enjoyed a series of victories in the early part of 1862, the most notable of which were Grant's defeat of General John B. Floyd at Fort Donelson, which practically reinstated Tennessee in the Union, and the assault on Shiloh, Tenn., which cost some 13,000 federal troops. (*OHAP.*)

4. William H. Seward, speech of October 25, 1858.

5. The Charleston *Mercury,* founded in 1822, expressed extreme proslavery views. During the Civil War it was owned and edited by Robert Barnwell Rhett, Jr.,

who, though a loyal Confederate, inveighed against the "imbecility" of Jefferson Davis and his government and the inefficiency of southern generals. The paper ceased publication in 1868. (Mott.)

The Richmond *Enquirer* was first issued in 1804, succeeding Meriwether Jones's *Examiner*. Ably edited by Thomas Ritchie, it was encouraged by President Jefferson and soon became one of the most influential voices of the Democratic party. After the Nat Turner insurrection, the *Enquirer* spoke out against slavery, but public opinion soon suppressed these views. The paper continued to be published until 1877. (Mott; *ULN*.)

The Norfolk (Va.) *Day-Book* (1857–1880) was several times suppressed by federal authorities during the Civil War. (*ULN*.)

The quotation is adapted from I Peter 5:8.

6. The Confederate Constitution, adopted March 11, 1861, was modeled on the Constitution of the United States, with important differences. State sovereignty was to be maintained, members of the cabinet were to have seats in Congress, protective tariffs were to be discouraged, and slavery was to be recognized and protected in all Confederate territory.

7. Possibly Garrison alludes to Byron, *Childe Harold's Pilgrimage*, Canto I, stanza 86, line 9.

8. John Quincy Adams (1767–1848), sixth President of the United States.

9. Garrison quotes from two speeches Adams delivered in the House of Representatives, the first (down to the three dots, signifying a break) on May 25, 1836, during a debate concerning the furnishing of food to fugitives from the Indian hostilities in Georgia and Alabama; the second in April 1842, during the debate on the Haverhill Petition. Garrison quotes exactly, except for the substitution in the first sentence of "the" for "your" before "slaveholding" ("slave-holding" in Adams). The capital letters in the words "Commander" and "Army" and the italics are also his. (Charles F. Adams, "John Quincy Adams and Martial Law," *PMHS*, 2d ser., 15:436–479, January 1902.)

The commander of the army from November 1861 to July 1862 was George B. McClellan.

10. Exodus 7:16.

11. Garrison refers to Exodus 8:12.

12. Jeremiah 21:12.

13. A possible reference to Matthew 6:10 and Deuteronomy 27:15.

14. Isaiah 58:6.

---

2 8

TO GEORGE THOMPSON

[March 7, 1862]

MY DEAR FRIEND AND COADJUTOR:

There are some of our Anti-Slavery friends in England, who are not disposed to give any countenance to the rebels, or to wish them any success; nevertheless, they have no cheering word for the North, and evince no sympathy with the Government. They are neither on one side nor on the other; they cannot perceive that the struggle has any particular connection with the cause of negro emancipation in special, or of human liberty in general. Hence, they marvel at the deep interest taken in it by the American Abolitionists, and have sorrowfully come to the conclusion that, in sustaining the Government, we have abandoned our high vantage ground, lowered our moral standard, and allowed ourselves to be carried headlong by a strong tide of popular feeling. Their sincerity is not to be questioned; and, for one, I thank them for their friendly solicitude and admonitory counsel, while none the less wondering at what seems to me their lack of sound discrimination as pertaining to American affairs at the present crisis.

How is it, after so many years of faithful and generous coöperation, that they fail to see the intimate relation of this Southern rebellion to the Anti-Slavery movement; or to find in it the most cheering evidence of the growing power and victorious march of that movement? Have they forgotten the state of the country before the banner of immediate emancipation was flung to the breeze— how the slave oligarchy held unquestioned sway over the religion and politics, the government and legislation, the press and the pulpit, the literature and business of the whole country? Then "order reigned in Warsaw"[1]—despotism supreme on the one hand, and subjugation absolute on the other. Then quietude prevailed throughout the land—the quietude of the grave, where there is "no work nor device," and where "the dead do all forgotten lie."[2] Then there was no agitation, but all was peace—the peace engendered by universal moral degeneracy and the rankest political corruption. At length, in the order of divine appointment, the Anti-Slavery struggle commenced, that henceforth there should be neither peace nor quietude, but rather tumult and strife, until the overthrow of the republic through incorrigible impenitence, or its salvation through the liberation of every bondman, and obedience to the Higher Law. Have they forgotten, by some inexplicable loss of memory, the long eventful history of that struggle—how, from the time that the first number of the *Liberator* made its ominous appearance, the Southern dealers in human flesh instinctively clutched at every weapon their brutality could wield, and resorted to every device their villainy could frame, in order to suppress all discussion of the question of slavery? These haughty oppressors had every thing on their side, excepting God and justice. The North was swarming with religious and political accomplices, who left nothing undone to prevent the spread of the new heresy. Abolitionism was every where fiercely denounced, and its advocates,—"like angels' visits, few and far between,"[3]—were universally ridiculed, insulted, ostracised. Mob violence became epidemic. No Anti-Slavery meeting could be held in any village or hamlet, however remote or obscure, without hostile demonstrations. You, my dear

Thompson, knew by early experience and a memorable residence here, what trials and perils thronged in the pathway of the faithful advocate of the slave at that tumultuous period. But the struggle went on—every inch of ground being as desperately contested by the minions of the slavocracy as was ever field of battle. Year after year, Abolitionism was hissed down, howled down, mobbed down, voted down, trodden down, but would not stay down. Over it the powers of hell could exercise no control, and maintain no mastery. In every encounter, it grew stronger, and more assured of ultimate victory. In vain did the church excommunicate it, the pulpit anathemize it, the press calumniate and caricature it; the mob assail it; in vain were scoff, and sneer, and falsehood, and deception, and menace, and violence resorted to; in vain did wealth, and respectability, and piety, and political demagoguism combine their ample means and mighty forces to crush it out of existence; it was never defeated in argument, nor intimidated by numbers, nor compelled to relinquish the ground on which it stood, because based upon reason, supported by justice, inspired by humanity, and guarded by an omnipotent arm. Steadily but surely, it has won its way from heart to heart, from fireside to fireside, from city to city, from one extremity of the country to the other, till it can no longer be safely trifled with or despised. All the while, naturally and inevitably, by the law of repulsion, the slave oligarchy have been growing more and more seditious, and rendered more and more uncomfortable in their relations to the North. At length, the vast moral change effected in public sentiment, through the Anti-Slavery movement, culminated at the ballot-box in a political triumph of the Free States on the territorial issue, by the election of Abraham Lincoln, the candidate of the Republican party. This triumph indicated no wish or design to interfere with slavery as already existing in the Slave States, or to repudiate any of the pro-slavery guarantees contained in the Constitution; but it showed a determination to allow no further territorial expansion of slavery, and for the first time entrusted the policy of the government to the hands of the North. The political campaign was hotly contested; and I am confident that there was not an English Abolitionist who did not regard its result as a triumph to the cause of freedom, and as indicating a hopeful and progressive state of things in the United States. Certainly, the Southern lords of the lash looked upon it as a most disastrous defeat; it filled them with rage and despair; it proclaimed that the day of their tyrannical dominion was ended; it drove them to open rebellion.

By their own recorded declarations, they would have seceded just as promptly if John C. Fremont had been elected four years previous; for their motto has always been to "rule or ruin."[4] They would have broken up the Union at any period, from George Washington down to Abraham Lincoln, if there had then been the same relative growth of Anti-Slavery sentiment as now. In short, they came into the Union only to play the part of masters and overseers, not only to their slaves, but to the whole country. They cared nothing for a republican form of government, provided they could be the governing party. Their usurpation being overthrown, and despairing of ever reëstablishing it, they have gone out like the unclean spirits of old, but not without rending the body.

Is not this a hopeful state of things? Is it to be regarded as a very slight or a very dubious matter by any friend of the slave on either side of the Atlantic? Granted that the North is still far from being up to the true Anti-Slavery standard; that the Government still hesitates to strike the one decisive blow, which it may lawfully give, to crush the rebellion and terminate the war, without returning evil for evil; that a fugitive slave is occasionally sent back from the camp by an upstart officer; that there is danger of future compromises, as the federal forces march on to victory. Nevertheless, the fact stands "open and palpable as a mountain,"[5] that it is owing to the increasing strength and general prevalence of Anti-Slavery sentiment at the North, that these slaveholding conspirators have seceded in hot haste, declaring that with them endurance has passed its bounds, and they will never again consent to be in the same Union with the people of the Free States. Are we, as Abolitionists, never to recognize that we have made any progress, because we have not yet effected all that we have been so long struggling to accomplish? For one, I am disposed to shout and sing, "Glory! Halleluia!" And when it is reproachfully said by the enemies of freedom, that, had it not been for the Abolition agitation, there would have been no secession, I accept the statement as a splendid tribute to the power of truth, the majesty of justice, and the advancement of the age. Of course, if there had been no slaveholders in the land, there would have been no Abolitionists—no pro-slavery mobs—no civil war— no dissolution of the Union—but freedom, peace, prosperity and happiness would have been the inheritance of the people from the Atlantic to the Pacific. Let the responsibility rest and the retribution fall on the heads of the oppressors!

Yours, for the jubilee,

WM. LLOYD GARRISON.

GEORGE THOMPSON, ESQ.

Printed: *The Liberator*, March 7, 1862.

1. The words of General François Sebastiani in the Chamber of Deputies, September 16, 1831. (Alexandre Dumas, *Memoirs of a Physician*, Philadelphia, 1850, IV, chapter 3.)
2. Garrison quotes from Ecclesiastes 9:10 and apparently alludes to 9:5.
3. Thomas Campbell, *The Pleasures of Hope*, Part II, line 378.
4. Garrison inverts the verbs in John Dryden, *Absalom and Achitophel*, Part I, line 174.
5. An adaptation of Shakespeare, *1 Henry IV*, II, iv, 249.

2 9

TO HENRY I. BOWDITCH

14 Dix Place, March 18 [1862].

Dr. H. I. Bowditch:

My Dear Friend—

I am much obliged to you for your note, and for sending me Mr. Emerson's explanatory letter to you.[1] That letter is entirely satisfactory, and will be a relief to the mind of Mr. Place as it is to my own; though, until this explanation, I think we were warranted in regarding the remark of Mr. Emerson, "Oh, Mr. Garrison is a one-sided man," as having special reference to my abolitionism, and not to a lack of credentials on the part of Mr. Place.[2]

Allow me to keep Mr. E's letter a day or two, that I may show it to Mr. Place.

The bearer of this, Mr. L. H. Mitchell, a member of the Freshman Class in Harvard College, has called upon me for advice in regard to his situation.[3] I have no other knowledge of him than what his very excellent and flattering recommendations afford; but these (especially the one from Rev. Dr. Peabody) amply suffice to inspire the highest confidence and the warmest interest in his case.[4] Mr. Mitchell will explain to you how he is situated, and what he proposes, to insure against loss any benevolent and kind-hearted friend of education, who may be willing to loan him the small sum he needs to enable him to complete his collegiate course. Dr. Peabody says—"Second to no member of his class, perhaps to no member of college, as a mathematician, he holds a high rank in every other department and on the general scale, and will *in all probability* be chosen to one of the scholarships at the close of the present term." Under these circumstances, it would be very sad to have Mr. Mitchell compelled to leave college, and be cut off irretrievably from accomplishing the laudable object he has in view, for the want of the pecuniary assistance he is lacking, and desirous of obtaining at the present time. I send him to you,—not to deepen *your* burdens, which, in the service of humanity and science and literature, are always heavy, because of your ever kind and generous nature,—. but to obtain your advice, and to ascertain whether, in the range of your acquaintance with persons of pecuniary means, you can think of any one, (gentleman or lady,) who would be likely to take an interest in Mr. M's case, if not to make him a *protégé*, at least to loan him the amount he needs, to make it possible for him to obtain the scholarship so near his grasp, and of which he is evidently so deserving; and thus to make his future one full of promise to himself, and of usefulness to his race. Should any such person occur to you, I am sure of your sympathy and good will in the case.

Yours, with the warmest regards,

Wm. Lloyd Garrison.

ALS: Merrill Collection of Garrison Papers, Wichita State University Library.

Henry Ingersoll Bowditch (1808–1892), the eminent Boston physician, was a brother of William Ingersoll Bowditch. At the date of this letter he was Jackson Professor of Clinical Medicine at the Harvard Medical School. He had been an ardent supporter of Garrison since 1834 and was one of those who established the National Testimonial for Garrison in 1866.

1. Unfortunately, since the letter of transcendental essayist and poet Ralph Waldo Emerson (1803–1882) has apparently not been preserved, we cannot clarify the situation to which Garrison refers.

2. Garrison probably refers to William Henry Place (born 1836), originally from Providence, who had served briefly in the Union navy before being discharged as the result of an injury. He was currently a successful builder and contractor in his native city; later he was to move to Brooklyn, Conn. (*Representative Men and Old Families of Rhode Island*, Chicago, 1908, II, 1102.)

3. Lebbeus Horatio Mitchell (1833–1916) first graduated with honors in mathematics from Union College and was then, according to the quinquennial folder, admitted to Harvard on probation in August 1861. The reports of the class of 1865 indicate that he left Harvard after his freshman year to join the army and to fight in many of the major battles of the Civil War. He was honorably discharged in 1864 and subsequently was admitted to the Harvard senior class, graduating in civil engineering —perhaps as the first Negro to do so—in July 1865. After studying mining engineering for two years in Germany, he worked for the khedive of Egypt and elsewhere, and ultimately became a professor at Cornell University and editor of the *American Journal of Mining*. He spent his last years, impoverished and ill, at the United States Soldiers' Home near Los Angeles. (Secretary's Letterbook, Class of 1865, and other records, Harvard Archives.)

4. Andrew Preston Peabody (1811–1893) graduated from Harvard College at the age of fifteen, entered Harvard Divinity School in 1829, and became a Unitarian minister three years later. In 1860 Harvard appointed him Plummer Professor of Christian Morals. At the time of Garrison's letter Peabody was serving as acting president of the college.

3 0

TO ANNA E. DICKINSON

Boston, 14 Dix Place,
March 22, 1862.

Dear Miss Dickinson:

In answer to your letter of inquiry about giving your lecture in Boston, I will state that we have had so many lectures delivered upon the war and its issues, during the present lecturing season, that there is no probability that you would be able to meet the expenses of a hall, &c., in case you should make the attempt. Besides, you would labor under the great disadvantage of not being publicly known.

I have succeeded, however, in doing better for you than in running any such risk. The committee of the late Theodore Parker's congregation, on the strength of my representation of your speaking ability, have very kindly consented to have you fill the desk on Sunday forenoon, April 6th, (the earliest arrangement they can make,) and deliver your lecture on "The National Crisis."[1] This will ensure you the immense Music Hall without any cost, a good audience, and I presume the usual fee of twenty dollars.

On conferring with the Anti-Slavery Committee,[2] I am happy to say that they would like to have you deliver the same lecture in various towns in Massachusetts, averaging three evenings a week, (if your strength will allow,) for four consecutive weeks, or until the time for holding the annual meeting of the American Anti-Slavery Society at New York. In case you are willing, they will make all the arrangements for the meetings, send you to reliable families where you will be made welcome, and see that you receive satisfactory remuneration. This will furnish you a good opportunity to make yourself known to the public as a lecturer, and I trust will be but the beginning of extended labors in the field of freedom, humanity and progress.

Though you can come through to Boston in one day from Philadelphia, arriving here about 6 P. M., still you had better leave on Friday morning, the 4th, instead of Saturday, the 5th, in order to be "on the safe side," as against any unforeseen detention.

Whether you can stay the desired four weeks in this State, or not, please let me know, by return mail, whether you will lecture before the Music Hall congregation at the time named. If so, I will be at the depot Friday evening previous, to conduct you to my house.

I was very much gratified to hear, by a letter from Dr. Longshore, that your lecture was well attended in Philadelphia, and very approvingly received.[3] I have no doubt it will be well received here.

Yours, for the jubilee,

Wm. Lloyd Garrison.

P.S. It may be that, here and there, you may have an opportunity to speak on woman's rights.

ALS: Papers of Anna Elizabeth Dickinson, Library of Congress.

1. The lecture at the Music Hall was postponed. (See Garrison's letter to Anna E. Dickinson, March 30, 1862.)
2. That is, the executive committee of the Massachusetts Anti-Slavery Society.
3. Dr. Longshore has not been identified.

3 1

TO ANNA E. DICKINSON

Boston, March 27, 1862.

Dear Miss Dickinson:

I am glad to get your letter in answer to mine, announcing your acceptance of the arrangements proposed for your lecturing in Boston and other places in Massachusetts.

I find I was in error in calculating that you could *seasonably* come through the same day from Philadelphia to Boston. Should you leave P., in the morning train for New York, you would doubtless be able to connect there with the afternoon train for Boston, via Springfield; but, even in that case, you would not arrive here until after midnight—i.e., about one o'clock in the morning—a most unsuitable hour. So that, if you desire to come through by the land route, it will be necessary for you to leave P. in the afternoon train of Thursday, April 3, and spend the night in New York, and then take the morning train for Boston, which is due here about half past five, P.M.

Or, if you have no objection to coming by way of the Sound, and prefer not to be detained over night in New York, then you can leave P. on Friday morning and take the afternoon boat for either Fall River, Stonington or Norwich, and so arrive in Boston early Saturday morning, which would be amply in season. If you decide to take this course, then I would advise you to take the Fall River boat, as you will get more sleep, and arrive here just as soon. But you may prefer to come by the way of Stonington or Norwich, and the boats are all admirable.

Please let me know which route you will take, and at what time, and I will endeavor to be at the depot at the time of your arrival. Should any thing happen to prevent my doing so, all you need do will be to hand a hackman the check for your baggage, and then order him to drive to my house, (which is near three depots,) 14 Dix Place.[1]

You will need all the voice you can well command to be distinctly heard in Music Hall, on account of its immense size. It is some eighty feet from the floor to the wall, and much better adapted to singing than speaking. Most of the female lecturers fail for lack of voice, and this has led those who are opposed to female speaking sneeringly to say, that if God had intended it, he would have given the necessary vocal powers. I am pretty confident that you will be able to make yourself heard generally, and the more you practice, the easier it will be for you. Do not feel hurried, but speak with deliberation, and do not allow yourself to be confined to the reading of your manuscript more than you can help, as that restrains action, and more or less affects the quantity of the voice.

Yours, with my best wishes,

Wm. Lloyd Garrison.

(Over.)

Anna E. Dickinson.

P.S. You will see, by this week's Liberator which I send you, that I have noticed your coming, and also your lecture in Philadelphia.[2]

ALS: Papers of Anna Elizabeth Dickinson, Library of Congress.

1. Fourteen Dix Place was the Garrison family residence from April 1853 through August 1864. The address is sometimes given as 579 Washington Street to indicate the single public access to Dix Place from Washington Street. (*Boston Atlas*, 1874, plate R; Wendell Phillips Garrison and Francis Jackson Garrison, compilers, *Words of Garrison*, Cambridge, Mass., 1905, pp. 134–135.)

The three depots near Garrison's house were the Boston and Worcester at the intersection of Lincoln and Beach streets, the Boston and Providence at the intersection of Providence and Pleasant streets, and the Old Colony at Kneeland and Cove streets. (Nineteenth-century maps of Boston, Boston Public Library.)

2. In *The Liberator*, March 28, 1862, Garrison reported that young Anna had received great acclaim for her speech "The Present War," delivered in West Chester at the annual meeting of the Pennsylvania Anti-Slavery Society in October. He also reported favorably on a repetition of the speech in Philadelphia in March, and said that the Committee of the Twenty-Eighth Congregational Society of Boston had invited her to deliver a speech in the Music Hall on April 6.

3 2

TO ANNA E. DICKINSON

Boston, March 30, 1862.

Dear Miss Dickinson:

I wrote to you, a day or two since, stating that I had made an arrangement for you to lecture before the late Theodore Parker's congregation on Sunday next, April 6th; but, to-day, I am informed by the Committee, that this arrangement will have to be deferred until the fourth Sunday in April, (27th,) in consequence of a blunder having been made by one of their number,—as Rev. M. D. Conway, of Cincinnati, is engaged to speak next Sunday, Ralph W. Emerson the Sunday after, and Wendell Phillips on the 20th.[1] This need not, I think, materially change the time of commencing your labors in this State, in other places; but as Mr. May, our General Agent, has returned to Leicester, I must first consult him on this subject, and will write to you about it with the least possible delay.[2] So, do not leave home until you hear from me again. I am sorry any mistake has been made about the time of your speaking at Music Hall; but I am none the less gratified that the Committee have so kindly consented to have you occupy the desk at the time now fixed, (27th April,) on the strength of my recommendation of you; and I trust and believe that they will have no occasion to regret the arrangement.[3]

In replying to this, you had better determine how many times you think you can lecture each week, without detriment to your health, or too great a strain upon your vocal powers.

Possibly, so considerable a delay may, by the course of events, make it necessary for you to modify your lecture, to some extent; but of this you will easily be able to judge.

Very truly yours,

Wm. Lloyd Garrison.

Miss Anna E. Dickinson.

ALS: Papers of Anna Elizabeth Dickinson, Library of Congress.

1. Moncure D. Conway (1832–1907), originally from Virginia and a graduate of Dickinson College and Harvard Divinity School, was a recent convert to the cause of abolition. In 1856 he was dismissed as minister of the Unitarian church in Washington, D.C., because of his antislavery views. Subsequently, he became minister of the First Congregational Church in Cincinnati. In April 1863 Conway went on a lecture tour to England, where he became involved in a controversy with James M. Mason, Confederate diplomatic commissioner, which may have helped dissuade the British from official recognition of the Confederacy. (For a more detailed description of this controversy, see Introduction III, "War for Freedom: 1863.") Conway stayed on in

London for twenty years as minister of the radical South Place Chapel, Finsbury, a post he held again between 1892 and 1897. A frequent contributor to such magazines as *The Atlantic Monthly* and the *Dial*, he also wrote a life of Thomas Paine and edited his works.

2. Samuel May, Jr., was, at the time this letter was written, general agent of the Massachusetts Anti-Slavery Society. (*The Liberator*, March 28, 1862.)

3. Miss Dickinson spoke in Boston, not on the twenty-seventh (on which date she spoke at the Unitarian church in New Bedford, Mass.) but on the twentieth. She spoke with great power and eloquence, attributing the Civil War to slavery and urging emancipation. (For a brief but enthusiastic report of her Boston lecture see *The Liberator*, April 25; reports of other presentations of the same lecture, including the one at New Bedford, were printed in the issues for April 18 and May 2.)

3 3

TO ANNA E. DICKINSON

Boston, April 3, 1862.

Dear Miss Dickinson:

I wrote to you, a few days since, stating that a mistake had been made in regard to the time of your lecturing in Music Hall, by one of the committee of arrangements; and that no vacancy occurs until the fourth Sunday in this month, which I have definitely engaged you to fill at that time. I have as yet received no reply to my letter, though I trust it has been received.

I now write to say, that this postponement need not delay your coming to this State. Mr. [Samuel] May [Jr.] has already made arrangements for you to lecture in Fall River on Wednesday evening next; and it is necessary, in order to prevent disappointment there, that we should receive a definite answer from you, as, until we do so, we can proceed no further in making appointments for you.[1] Please, therefore, write to me by return of mail, unless you have already done so.

In case you have not written, and cannot come, and have not time to inform me by mail seasonably, then be sure to send me a telegraphic despatch at once to this effect:—

"Cannot go to Fall River. Particulars by letter."

Taking it for granted, however, that you will be able to come, I suggested to you, in my last letter,[2] that you could leave home on Tuesday morning, and take the Fall River boat in the afternoon (at 5 o'clock, I suppose) at New York, which would land you at F. R. early on Wednesday morning. You will then remain on board of the boat until my friend, Dr. J. M. Aldrich, shall call for you to take you to his house.[3]

Mr. May suggests that, possibly, you may have an objection to coming on in the boat, on account of sea-sickness; though I think you will experience nothing of the kind. But should you prefer, you can take the 8 o'clock night train for Boston on Tuesday evening, which would bring you here by daylight, and on arriving you could take a hack for my house, 14 Dix Place, and in the course of the day go to Fall River, which is about 54 miles from Boston.

Yours, truly,

Wm. Lloyd Garrison.

Miss A. R. Dickinson.

☞ I am sure that my good friend, Oliver Johnson, will be happy to show you any attention in New York—such as going either to the steamboat or the railroad depot, as you may choose. The Anti-Slavery Office is 5 Beekman Street, up one flight of stairs.

ALS: Papers of Anna Elizabeth Dickinson, Library of Congress.

1. The lecture in Fall River, Mass., was enthusiastically reported in *The Liberator*, April 18, 1862.
2. Garrison mistakenly refers to his letter of March 27 as though it were his last letter, whereas he had also written Miss Dickinson on March 30.
3. Little is known of Dr. J. M. Aldrich except that he practiced "miscellaneous" medicine in Fall River. The term "miscellaneous" apparently suggests that he was neither a regular nor a homeopathic physician. (Samuel W. Butler, compiler, *Medical Register and Directory of the United States*, Philadelphia, 1877.)

34

TO GEORGE W. JULIAN

Boston, April 13, 1862.

Dear Sir:

I was much gratified to receive a letter from you, a short time since, in which you kindly expressed the hope that I would visit Washington, and deliver the concluding lecture of the course which has been attended with such cheering success in the cause of universal emancipation.[1] No official invitation having been extended to me by the committee of arrangements, I, of course, have had none to accept or to decline; but, if one had been sent to me, I should have been compelled to decline it, in consequence of the impaired state of my health. My speaking apparatus is getting to be more and more out of tune, in consequence of a growing bronchial difficulty; and I am still laboring under a severe and long protracted cold. My presence at Washington, however, were I in "the right trim,"[2] would be of no consequence, after such a succession of able and eloquent speakers, whose advent in such a place, under such encouraging auspices, is truly an epoch in our national history.

Of course, I felt greatly delighted at the generous reception accorded to Mr. Phillips. It has evidently been as gall and wormwood[3] to the half traitorous pro-slavery spirits at the North; and their malignant spite was speedily manifested on his appearance at Cincinnati.[4] But the recoil of their cowardly and brutal attack has been overwhelming, and he has since received the most flattering attentions, and drawn crowded and enthusiastic audiences, wherever he has lectured. He has not yet returned home, having been compelled to change his original programme, and to lecture many more times than he contemplated, in consequence of the interest excited in him, arising from the Cincinnati mob.

The abolition of slavery in the District of Columbia, by the present Congress, is an event of far-reaching importance, and will make the session especially honorable in the history of the country.[5] All honor to the Republican party for having accomplished the good work, through its Senators and Representatives; and let infamy rest upon the Democratic party for having opposed the measure! I take it for granted that President Lincoln will sign the bill.

So far as the war is concerned, I have no faith in any effort to restore unity and peace to the republic, that does not include the total abolition of slavery by the Government, under the war power; and I fervently pray that the Government may have the courage and the justice to proclaim this the year of jubilee.[6]

My principal object, however, in writing to you, is to invite you to attend the annual meeting of the American Anti-Slavery Society, which is to be held in the city of New York May 6th; and to be among the speakers either at the morning session at Rev. Dr. [George B.] Cheever's church, or at the evening session at Cooper Institute, as you may prefer.[7] This I do by the unanimous wish of the Executive Committee. Of course, all your expenses will be gladly covered. Trusting it will be in your power to come, I remain,

    Yours, with high regards,

                             Wm. Lloyd Garrison.

Hon. G. W. Julian.

☞ I congratulate you on the delivery of your admirable speech, and will yet try to find room for it in the Liberator, if possible.[8]

ALS: Giddings-Julian Papers, Library of Congress.

    George Washington Julian (1817–1899) was born in Wayne County, Ind. After teaching school, studying law, and being admitted to the bar in 1840, he became a member of the state legislature in 1845. Three years later he was elected to Congress as a Free-Soil candidate. In 1856 he helped found the Republican party at the convention in Pittsburgh. In 1860 he was again sent to Congress, and subsequently was reelected four times. Always an outspoken abolitionist, Julian became a Radical Republican and a leader in the impeachment proceedings against President Johnson. In 1868 he proposed a constitutional amendment for woman's suffrage, one of the reforms that most concerned him. In his later years he contributed many articles to periodicals and published a number of volumes of recollections and speeches. Between 1885 and 1889 he served as surveyor general of New Mexico.

1. Garrison refers to a lecture course at the Smithsonian Institution sponsored by the Washington Lecture Association and scheduled between December 13, 1861, and March 21, 1862. Among the speakers were Orestes Brownson, Ralph Waldo Emerson, Horace Greeley, Wendell Phillips, and Gerrit Smith, but not Garrison. (Washington *Evening Star,* December 1861 to March 1862, passim.)

2. A nautical term meaning that the sails are properly adjusted for the desired course.

3. An allusion to Lamentations 3:19.

4. Wendell Phillips was on a western lecture tour, which included stops in Harrisburg, Cincinnati, and Chicago. His reception was worst in Cincinnati, where heckling and threatened violence from the audience at the opera house forced him to discontinue his speech. He was also thought to have been pursued by a mob, but escaped uninjured. (*National Anti-Slavery Standard,* April 5, 1862.)

5. The bill in question, which called for "the release of certain persons held to service or labor in the District of Columbia," was introduced on December 6, 1861, referred to the Committee on the District of Columbia on December 19, and approved and signed by President Lincoln on April 16, 1862. Among other provisions, the law demanded immediate emancipation and appropriated $100,000 to aid freed Negroes and to establish colonies in Haiti, Liberia, and elsewhere. (*The Statutes at Large, Treaties, and Proclamations of the United States of America from December 5, 1859, to March 3, 1863,* Boston, 1863, XII.)

6. In Leviticus 25 and 27 there are several references to "the year of jubile."

7. Julian was not among the speakers reported in *The Liberator,* May 16, 1862.

8. The speech for which Garrison is trying to find room may well be Julian's address of January 14, 1862, before the House of Representatives, extracts from which were printed in *The Liberator,* May 2, 1862. Julian says that since slavery and freedom cannot live together without leading to devastating war, slavery must be abolished and the country reconstructed in freedom.

---

3 5

TO CHARLES B. SEDGWICK

Boston, May 20, 1862.

Dear Mr. Sedgwick:

I am sorry that I am unable to furnish you with any information beyond what, in all probability, you have already obtained, concerning the emancipation of slaves under the war power. As far as I know, the instances have been comparatively rare. The example of Bolivar, in South America, you are familiar with; but I know not where reliable statistics are to be found in regard to it.[1] The slaves in Hayti were proclaimed free for the support of the republic then threatened.[2] Mr. Phillips tells me there was a History of Slavery published in Cincinnati, not long ago, and quite comprehensive; but no copy of it is to be found in Boston.[3] Some valuable information is contained in "Gurowski's History of Slavery," treating chiefly of classical and middle-age slavery; but no copy of it is to be had here.[4] Fortunately, Gurowski is at present in Washington, employed in Seward's department, I believe.[5] Perhaps you have already conferred with him.

Yesterday, the great body of the people of this State were rejoicing over the glorious proclamation of Gen. Hunter.[6] To-day, a wet blanket is thrown upon the flame of popular enthusiasm by President Lincoln's veto. What giving and taking, what blowing hot and blowing cold, we have upon this slavery question! The government is neither for God nor the Adversary. With what undignified haste the President comes forward to veto an act which he is not yet sure has taken place; for he relies solely upon a newspaper report, and does not wait to hear officially from Gen. Hunter! True, there is no doubt that the reported proclamation has been put forth; but the President, before taking action upon it, was bound in courtesy and good faith to hear direct from Gen. Hunter, and to learn his reasons for taking such a course. Depend upon it, this veto will serve to increase the disgust and uneasiness felt in Europe at our shilly-shallying course, to abate the enthusiasm of the army and the friends of freedom universally, and to inspire the rebels with fresh courage and determination. It seems to me that infatuation pervades the President and his Cabinet, and the future is pregnant with sorrow and disaster. But God reigns over all, and the folly as well as the wrath of men he will cause to praise him.

Yours, for no compromise,

Wm. Lloyd Garrison.

Hon. Charles B. Sedgwick.

ALS: Charles B. Sedgwick Collection, Syracuse University Library. This letter is printed by courtesy of Sarah K. Auchincloss, Syracuse, N.Y.

Charles Baldwin Sedgwick (1815–1883), a lawyer of Syracuse, N.Y., was in 1859 elected to Congress, where he served for two terms before returning to his law practice. He was married first to Ellen Chase Smith (1812–1846), with whom he had two surviving children, Ellen Amelia (1841–1924) and Charles Hamilton (1846–1924); his second wife was Deborah W. Gannett (1825–1901), a teacher and reformer; she had four daughters who survived infancy. (*Biographical Directory of the American Congress;* Charles M. Sedgwick, *A Sedgwick Genealogy,* New Haven, 1961, pp. 111–133.)

1. Simón Bolívar (1783–1830), the son of a noble Venezuelan family, became the republican hero and liberator from Spanish rule of Venezuela, Colombia, Peru, and Bolivia, which was named for him.

2. The slaves in Haiti had been freed by decree in May 1791, but a rebellion subsequently resulted in repeal of the decree. By 1796, however, the Negro revolu-

tionary Toussaint L'Ouverture had become ruler of the island, and under his government the slaves were considered freed.

3. Although several antislavery works are known to have been published in Cincinnati at this period, none corresponds to the book described by Garrison. (*National Union Catalogue, Pre–1956 Imprints.*)

4. Count Adam Gurowski (1805–1866) was a Polish revolutionary who immigrated to the United States in 1849. He became a journalist and wrote articles on European life for the weekly Boston *Museum;* he also worked on the *New American Cyclopedia.* He was the friend of many prominent literary figures and the persistent critic of Lincoln, who is said to have called him the only potential assassin he took seriously. In 1860 Gurowski published *Slavery in History,* the book to which Garrison refers. Although he became a clerk in Washington in 1861 and never rose to a post of any importance, he was not loath to write frankly and critically to men in high places. He published a three-volume diary between 1862 and 1866, a historical source of some importance. (Le Roy H. Fischer, *Lincoln's Gadfly, Adam Gurowski,* Norman, Okla., 1964.)

5. William Henry Seward (1801–1872) was a lawyer who became a New York state legislator in 1830 and governor in 1838. In 1848 he was elected to the United States Senate. After refusing to accept Clay's compromise in 1850 he developed antislavery views unusually liberal for a politician. In a famous speech in 1858 he described the struggle for abolition as "an irrepressible conflict." In 1861 he became secretary of state, a post in which he functioned with exceptional skill and good judgment throughout the Lincoln and Johnson administrations.

By the date of the letter in question, however, Garrison was convinced that Seward was compromising his antislavery principles. Indeed, Seward had said in a speech on January 13, 1861, "we cannot always do what seems to be absolutely the best." In a letter to Lydia Mott written after January 14, 1861 (micro.), Garrison pronounced judgment: "Shame on the truckling, compromising spirit of Seward and Weed!" In *The Liberator* for January 18 he reprimanded Seward for "a compromise of principles to propitiate and preserve wrongdoers of the South." In February 1867, when Seward had become a central figure in the Johnson administration, Garrison castigated him as worse than the President himself (see Introduction VII, "Honors and Awards: 1867").

6. David Hunter (1802–1886) was graduated from West Point in 1822, but in 1836 he resigned from the army to go into business in Chicago. Upon the outbreak of the Civil War he was commissioned brigadier general of volunteers. In March 1862 he assumed command of the Department of the South, and at Fort Pulaski, Ga., he issued his famous order liberating all slaves held in federal hands in his territory. By proclamation President Lincoln annulled the order on the grounds that General Hunter had exceeded his authority. Although he served several stints of court-martial duty, he also commanded in the field, with indifferent success. He accompanied the body of Lincoln on its journey to Springfield, Ill., and was president of the commission that tried the conspirators. Following his retirement from service in 1866, he became president of the Special Claims Commission and of the Cavalry Promotion Board.

---

3 6

TO HELEN E. GARRISON

New York, June 10, 1862.

My Dear Wife:

I wrote a few hasty lines to you yesterday, while in the Anti-Slavery Office at Philadelphia, which I suppose you will receive in the course of to-day. After I sent it, I went to see dear Mary Grew's father, who has been so very ill, hoping to see her also.[1] I found the venerable invalid sitting up in his chair, poring over the Bible, and looking very feeble indeed, though he is slowly recuperating as the warm weather advances. He evidently was very glad to see me, and we spent half an hour together in interesting conversation. Susan was also present, and inquired very particularly after you and the children; and she confused me not a little by asking how the remedy for the catarrh she sent me so long ago had operated![2] Of course, I had to admit that I had made but a partial trial of it, and to thank her for her kindness. They were expecting Mary momently when I had to leave.

On my return to the office, who should I see but dear Lucretia Mott, just from her trip to New Jersey and New York, and looking exceedingly well? Was there ever her match in completeness of character on earth? She gave me a *carte de visite*[3] of her husband, better by far than the one she sent to Franky, which I enclose as a present for the dear boy, to be substituted for the other one in our collection.

After taking a lunch with Robert Purvis of ice cream, strawberries, &c., we went to his beautiful home at Byberry.[4] Hattie, his young handsome daughter, met us at the steamboat landing with his carriage, and drove us to their residence, about two miles' distant.[5] I found Mrs. Purvis still very deeply afflicted at the recent loss of their beautiful and noble son, and tried to give her some words of consolation.[6] In the evening, we had a large party of friends, including the Pierces from Bristol, and enjoyed ourselves very agreeably.[7] They came to see me eight miles.

This morning, Robert drove me to Bristol to see the Pierces in return, where I had a warm welcome, and then took the cars for New York. I shall remain here till Thursday morning, then go to Ghent. At tea-time on Saturday, have a plate for me at the table.

I shall see Catharine [Benson], Dr. Percy, &c., to-morrow.[8]

Boundless love to the dear ones.

Yours, most affectionately,

Wm. Lloyd Garrison.

Helen E. Garrison.

ALS: Garrison Papers, Boston Public Library.

1. Henry Grew (1781–1862) was born in Birmingham, England, but as a youth went to Boston and then to Providence, R.I., where he rebelled against his Congregationalist upbringing and became a Baptist. In 1807 he took over the pastorate of the First Baptist Church of Hartford, but left after four years because of disagreement with the prevailing views of the church members. He lived for a time in Boston again, but by 1834 had become a resident of Philadelphia. Although he was always

an earnest abolitionist, his fundamentalist views precluded his advocating equal rights for women. As a representative from Pennsylvania to the 1840 World's Anti-Slavery Convention in London, he did not believe that women, including his own daughter Mary, should be seated as equal participants in the convention. (Obituary, *The Liberator*, August 15, 1862; *Centennial Memorial of the First Baptist Church of Hartford, Connecticut*, Hartford, 1890, pp. 192–194.)

2. Susan Grew (c. 1804–1881) was Henry Grew's daughter by his first wife, Susannah Pitman (died 1809), and granddaughter of the elder Isaac Pitman of Providence. (J. N. Arnold, *Vital Records of Rhode Island, 1636–1850*, Providence, 1891, XVII, 335.)

3. Small card photograph.

4. Robert Purvis (1810–1898) was the son of a Charleston cotton broker who was also an abolitionist and of a woman from Morocco who had been sold into slavery but freed upon the death of her mistress. Purvis moved to Philadelphia where he came under the influence of Garrisonians. In 1833 he was one of the founders of the American Anti-Slavery Society; in 1838 he was a founder and became president of the Pennsylvania Underground Railroad Society. Although he remained a loyal supporter of Garrison during the schism of 1840, he became alienated from him during the mid 1860s. By June 1868 he was to call Garrison the Benedict Arnold and Judas Iscariot of the antislavery cause. Late in their lives the two men were reconciled. (For information about the estrangement and reconciliation, see Garrison's letters to Helen E. Garrison, February 16, 1866, and June 8, 1868, and one to Purvis, of November 21, 1878.)

5. Hattie Purvis (born 1839) was the daughter of Robert and Harriet Forten Purvis (see n. 6). She was a friend of the Mott grandchildren as well as of Ellen Wright Garrison, William Lloyd, Jr.'s wife. It is thought that she attended Eagleswood, the school in New Jersey run by Theodore and Angelina Grimké Weld and Sarah Grimké. (Letter to the editor from Dorothy Sterling, author of *Speak Out in Thundertones* [1973], February 24, 1975.)

6. Harriet Forten Purvis (died c. 1875) was the daughter of James Forten, a leader in the black community in Philadelphia during the early 1800s. She was one of the four Negro signers of the founding charter of the Philadelphia Female Anti-Slavery Society. (Benjamin Quarles, *Black Abolitionists*, New York, 1969, p. 27.)

Robert Purvis, Jr., had died on March 19, 1862, after a long illness, at the age of twenty-eight. He was a well-liked and respected young man. Lucretia Mott and J. Miller McKim were among the speakers at his funeral, and he was buried at the Friends meetinghouse in Byberry. (Obituary, *The Liberator*, April 4, 1862.)

7. The Pierce family of Bristol, Pa., included Joseph S. (c. 1818–1911) and his brothers Charles W. and Joshua, all ardent abolitionists. Charles was active in the Underground Railroad. (Doron Green, *A History of the Old Homes on Radcliffe Street, Bristol, Pennsylvania*, Bristol, 1938; *A History of Bristol Borough*, Camden, N.J., 1911.)

8. Edward R. Percy (died 1875), a graduate of the New York College of Physicians and Surgeons in 1850, was a practicing physician in New York. In 1852 he married Anna Elizabeth Benson, the daughter of George W. Benson, Garrison's brother-in-law, and Catharine Knapp Stetson Benson. (*Medical Register, New York, New Jersey, and Connecticut*, New York, 1875–1876.)

37

TO AARON M. POWELL

New York, June 10, 1862.

Dear Aaron:

I have just arrived in this immense, dirty, bustling, turbulent city, on my return from the Progressive Friends' meeting at Longwood [Pennsylvania].[1] I intend remaining here until Thursday morning, when I purpose taking the regular morning boat for Hudson, (should the weather be propitious—if not, the railroad train,) and hope to be with you and the beloved ones at Ghent at early tea-time.

I went to Longwood in company with Oliver Johnson and Theodore Tilton. We had the warmest greetings and received the kindest hospitality from our Longwood friends, and enjoyed ourselves in "a right royal manner." Seven consecutive meetings were held; and as the burden of public speaking rested chiefly on Tilton and myself, you may imagine we both feel a good deal jaded; especially as we had an immense amount of private talking to do with old and young. The more I see of Theodore, the more I appreciate his many fine qualities, and feel that, should his life be spared, he is destined to be "a burning and a shining light"[2] in the cause of humanity and progress.

It fell to my lot to draw up the "Testimonies" this year on Slavery, the Rebellion, and Peace, and they were accepted unanimously, without amendment.[3] Some of the old school Quakers will think they read queerly, as a matter of style at least, emanating from a "Society of Friends"; but they must be reminded that it is a *"Progressive* Society," and therefore the repudiation of the old stereotyped phraseology.

I expected to find, in consequence of the convulsions of the times, a good deal of contrariety of opinion and feeling concerning the war and the duty of the government; but I was agreeably disappointed. There was entire unity of the spirit and concurrence of judgment. A memorial was adopted, addressed to President Lincoln, urging him to abolish slavery without delay; and Thomas Garrett, Oliver Johnson and Alice Eliza Hambleton were appointed delegates to go to Washington, and in person present it to the President. They will go.[4]

Nature now presents her handsomest features and her richest attire. Every thing in your region must be looking very attractive: of that I hope to judge in a day or two. But, conceding the fact as settled, I must nevertheless ask, Aaron, "Did you ever see the Boston Common?"[5] And, if so, "then I guess you never did see any thing like that!"—of course, I mean precisely like it.

But, "wind and weather permitting," we will have a peep together from Bunker Hill at Ghent,[6] and see how the scenery compares with the view from Bunker Hill at Charlestown.[7]

Present my loving regards to your dear wife, father, mother, Lizzie, and George, and believe me

Ever faithfully yours,

Wm. Lloyd Garrison.

Aaron M. Powell.

ALS: Collection of William W. Layton, Washington, D.C.; extract printed in Aaron M. Powell, *Personal Reminiscences* (New York, 1899), p. 44.

1. Held June 5–7.
2. John 5:35.
3. The "Testimonies" condemned the South and supported the North, concluding that only the freedom of all American slaves could insure a satisfactory peace.
4. The "Memorial to the President" exhorted Lincoln to free every slave. On June 20 Lincoln received the delegation, which included, in addition to those mentioned by Garrison, William Barnard and Dinah Mendenhall; Senator Wilmot introduced them. Although Lincoln agreed that slavery was wrong, he disagreed with the delegation regarding the ways and means of its removal; he was convinced that the South would ignore a proclamation of emancipation. (*National Anti-Slavery Standard*, June 14, 1862; *The Liberator*, June 27, 1862.)

Thomas Garrett (1789–1871) was a hardware merchant and toolmaker who had been an active abolitionist for many years, having joined the Pennsylvania Abolition Society in 1818. His home in Wilmington, Del., was a refuge for fugitive slaves, and his efforts on their behalf were such that the state of Maryland offered a $10,000 reward for his arrest.

Alice Eliza Hambleton was a founder of the Progressive Friends in May 1853. In the letter to Helen E. Garrison, June 9, 1862 (micro.), Garrison refers to her as "Alice B. Hambleton," apparently mistaking her middle initial; unless, indeed, she was married to either Thomas or Eli Hambleton, who were also members of the Progressive Friends meeting; in which case "B" could have been the initial of her maiden name. (Letter to the editor from Nancy Speers, Friends Historical Library, Swarthmore College, November 20, 1972.)

5. Boston Common is a park of some forty-five acres located in the center of the city. The Common had been a public reservation since 1634; in 1859 it was supplemented by the adjoining twenty-four-acre Public Garden. (Walter Muir Whitehill, *Boston, A Topographical History*, 2d ed., Boston, 1968, pp. 35, 241.)

6. Garrison refers to a hill owned by a Mr. Bunker and commanding a breathtaking view of the Hudson River Valley and Catskill Mountains. (Aaron M. Powell, *Personal Reminiscences*, New York, 1899, p. 44.)

7. In 1843 a monument was completed on Breed's Hill in commemoration of the Battle of Bunker Hill. Although Breed's Hill is often mistaken for Bunker Hill, it is likely Garrison refers to the real Bunker Hill nearby, which, at 110 feet, is some thirty-five feet higher than Breed's Hill.

3 8

TO JULIA M. FRIEND

Boston, July 31, 1862.

Dear Mrs. Friend:

I duly received your letter, and read it with deep interest. My reply has been unintentionally delayed.

You write in relation to the contemplated visit of my esteemed friend, Henry C. Wright, to England, and express heartfelt concern of mind lest it may result in great bodily suffering, and final dissolution, on account of the extraordinary effect of a sea voyage upon his constitution.[1] You state, as a medium, that you have had a clairvoyant vision of the whole distressing scene, and urge me strongly to exert my influence to have him abandon the undertaking. You say, finally, that you would not have ventured to press this matter upon my attention, if you had not understood that I was a believer in spiritual phenomena.

It is true that, during the last ten years, I have seen a variety of "manifestations," of such a striking character, and under such circumstances, as to compel me, by sheer force of evidence, to believe in their spirit origin; yet I should be slow to abandon any well-considered plan, merely because it was discountenanced in some message from that mysterious sphere. Still, (as is the fact in the present case,) as various other mediums, unknown to each other, in different parts of the country, have had substantially the same impressions and apprehensions as your own, in regard to the result of Mr. Wright's visit abroad, I think such testimonies or admonitions deserve to be seriously considered, and to have their proportionate weight in making up a final conclusion.

Whether H. C. W. would ever be permitted to return to his native land in the flesh, or not, the terrible experience he met in crossing and re-crossing the Atlantic, some years ago, in respect to sea-sickness, makes it quite certain that he will suffer as much, to say the least, in the same way, should he make the voyage. At his period of life, he would probably suffer more. Now, as no special duty calls him abroad to require any such risk—as it is to be simply a visit of friendship, for the sake of "auld lang syne"—as there is imminent danger of a conflict with England, growing out of a probable recognition of the Southern Confederacy, in which case the situation of H. C. W. in England would be a very delicate and embarrassing one—and as his labors were never more needed here in the Anti-Slavery cause, and in the broad field of reform, than now—I am happy to inform you that, on mature consideration of the whole subject with me, Mr. Wright has abandoned the idea of going to England, and I shall announce the fact in the Liberator of next week.[2]

Respectfully yours,

Wm. Lloyd Garrison.

Mrs. J. M. Friend.

ALS: Garrison Papers, Boston Public Library.

Little is known about Julia M. Friend except that she was the author of *The Chester Family: Or the Curse of the Drunkard's Appetite* (Boston, 1869), a book taking the form of letters to Henry C. Wright. She is listed in Boston city directories only for 1870 and 1871, in which she is described as a clairvoyant living in boardinghouses on Harrison Avenue.

1. Henry Clarke Wright (1797–1870) of Sharon, Conn., originally a hatmaker, became a minister in 1823. From 1835, when he joined the New England Anti-Slavery Society, Wright was closely associated with Garrison in all his reforms, especially abolition and nonresistance. He spent many years lecturing in Great Britain and was a frequent correspondent to *The Liberator*. He wrote many antislavery tracts, including a number of works for children. (*AWT.*)

Presumably Wright's traumatic experience with seasickness occurred on his voyage to England in 1842 or his return to the United States in 1847. (*Life; Letters*, III, see Index.)

2. In the issue for August 15, Garrison announced that Wright had decided to postpone his trip to England indefinitely, owing to the "delicate relations" with England during the war and to the "pressing demands" of the antislavery cause in the United States.

39

TO OLIVER JOHNSON

Boston, July 31, 1862.

Dear Johnson:

I was in no hurry to obtain the photographic negative, and, of course, am greatly obliged to you for the trouble you took in procuring it for me. I have not opened the package since it was received, in consequence of the absence of Mr. Seaver, who will strike off copies from the plate when he returns to the city.[1] Of course, you shall have one of the first impressions.

You forgot to send me the photographer's bill. Please enclose it in your next letter, that I may settle it.

My "college oration" is almost completed, and will be entirely so to-day.[2] I have written it out in full, as you and [James Miller] McKim advised, and so I feel great relief in knowing certainly what I am going to say. But, oh! the bondage and drawback of reading it, as though I had never seen it before!—for I cannot remember two sentences consecutively. Such confinement in delivery will be extremely irksome to me, and, I fear, tedious to the audience; but I am "in for it," and must do the best I can.

My theme will be, "Our National Visitation"—solidly anti-slavery, with nothing particularly interesting to abolitionists, with not a bit of imagination or a single "rhetorical flourish," but a straight-forward arraignment of our national guilt and an exposition of the cause of the war, and the duty of the government at this crisis. How it will suit, I cannot tell; but, you know how the old injunction runs, in a similar exigency, "Thou shalt speak all my words unto them, whether they will hear, or whether they will forbear."[3]

By the way, I have not seen in any paper, except the Standard, any announcement that I am to speak at Williamstown.[4] The *Traveller*, of this city, contained a notice, (editorial,) státing when the exercises would come off, and that two orations would be delivered —one by Professor Fowler,[5] and "the other by *another person*"! Laughable, isn't?

Should to-morrow prove fair, we shall undoubtedly have a large gathering at our First of August celebration at Abington. Phillips says he shall not speak more than ten minutes, but will probably speak longer than he now contemplates.[6] You shall have the proceedings as fast as we can put them in type, leaving you to publish as much or as little of them as you choose. It is not necessary for you to devote much space to them; so, consult your convenience.

I have read the discussion you have had in the *Herald of Progress*, respecting the Progressive Friends' last anniversary at Longwood. I am surprised our friend A. J. D. should have drawn such unwarrantable inferences from so simple a matter as that of changing the time of holding the anniversary.[7] Your replies were to the point, and very satisfactory. I am glad you were allowed fair play.

The published copies of the proceedings, which you kindly forwarded to me, I am distributing judiciously.[8] I hope you will take special care to send copies to President Lincoln and his Cabinet. Also to each of the Governors of the loyal States.

Give my most affectionate regards to Theodore Tilton, and my thanks for his last letter, calling my attention to Brownson's able article on the right and duty of the government, under the war power, to abolish slavery at this crisis.[9] I have not yet been able to do any thing with it, for lack of room.

All the children are away in the country, except George.

With kindest remembrances to Mary Anne, and to Mrs. [Augustus] Savin and household, I remain,

Ever truly yours,

Wm. Lloyd Garrison.

ALS: Garrison Papers, Boston Public Library; partly printed in *Life,* IV, 57.

1. Francis Seaver of the firm Seaver and Lothrop, 27 Tremont Row, Boston, has not been further identified. The photograph of Garrison in question is used as an illustration for this volume. (See also the letter to Oliver Johnson, August 7, 1862 [micro.].)

2. Garrison's speech, which was delivered before the Adelphic Union Society of Williams College as part of the commencement exercises on August 4, was printed in the *National Anti-Slavery Standard,* September 13, 1862.

3. Ezekiel 2:7.

4. In the *Standard* of July 26 Garrison's speech is announced, but no mention is made of Fowler.

5. Philemon Halsted Fowler (1814–1879) was graduated from Princeton Theological Seminary in 1836; he became a Presbyterian minister in Washington, D.C., then in Elmira, and finally in Utica, N.Y., retiring in 1874. In 1866 he was a member of a committee to unite all the Presbyterian factions in the North. The unification did not take place until 1870, at which time Fowler was named moderator of the New School Presbyterian General Assembly. He wrote *Historical Sketch of Presbyterianism within the Bounds of the Synod of Central New York* (1877) and several other smaller volumes. He was given an honorary doctor of divinity degree at the Williams College commencement.

6. Wendell Phillips was the principal speaker at the celebration of the anniversary of the emancipation in the British West Indies. He expressed confidence in Lincoln's intention to free the slaves, but criticized him for failure to act forcefully and to fire General McClellan. By contrast, Moncure D. Conway, one of the other speakers, condemned Lincoln and his entire administration as unworthy of support. (*Standard,* August 9 and 16, 1862.)

7. Andrew Jackson Davis (1826–1910) was a clairvoyant and hypnotist who acquired a considerable reputation in the 1840s for his supernatural and extrasensory powers. A popular lecturer and voluminous writer, he was interested successively in mysticism, occult phenomena, mesmerism, and spiritualism. He and his second wife, Mary Robinson Love Davis, having settled in Orange, N.J., in 1859, published the spiritualist *Herald of Progress* between 1860 and 1864. In that paper for June 28, 1862, Davis refers to a statement in the *Standard* that the Progressive Friends closed the session of its yearly meeting on Saturday "when notice was given that Mr. Garrison, Mr. Tilton, and others would attend the 'usual religious meeting' on Sunday." Davis commented: "Are our Progressive Friends afraid that something a little irreligious will creep into the 'yearly' meetings of their 'religious society' on Sunday . . .?" In the issue for July 12, Oliver Johnson's letter to the editor is printed, in which he insists that all the meetings are religious.

8. Garrison apparently refers to the proceedings of the tenth yearly meeting of the Progressive Friends, held June 5–7.

9. Possibly Garrison refers to Brownson's article "Slavery and the War," printed in *Brownson's Quarterly Review,* October 1861.

Orestes A. Brownson (1803–1876) was a New England clergyman who began as a Presbyterian and then became a Universalist, next a Unitarian, and finally a Roman Catholic. A liberal thinker and reformer, he agreed with the socialist ideas of Robert Dale Owen and Fanny Wright and was one of the founders of the Workingmen's party. He was an influential journalist, in 1838 establishing the *Boston Quarterly Review,* in which he attacked inheritance and penal laws as well as organized religion. Later he was associated with the *Democratic Review* of New York and in 1844 he returned to publication of his own Boston paper, renaming it *Brownson's Quarterly Review*. After his conversion to Catholicism in 1844, the review lost many subscribers. Brownson was a friend of Henry David Thoreau, George Ripley of Brook Farm, and other social theorists, as well as John C. Calhoun; he also wrote books on religion, spiritualism, and government.

4 0

TO WENDELL PHILLIPS GARRISON

Boston, August 1, 1862.

My dear Son:

I have just returned from the 1st of August celebration at Abington; and though feeling somewhat jaded, (having had to do the "presiding" all day,) I must improve the only hour I shall have before leaving for Williamstown, by sending you a few lines, in answer to yours of the 27th, dated at Lancaster [New Hampshire].

For the last three days, prior to this, it "rained like the deluge," accompanied with thunder and lightning of the most "striking" character. This morning, it was extremely foggy, and still threatened rain; nevertheless, we had a large company, and probably ten or fifteen hundred at the Grove.[1] Our morning session was held in the Town Hall, as a matter of prudence; at which J. Sella Martin, Moncure D. Conway, and Wendell Phillips, made capital speeches, such as the times demand.[2] At noon, the sun emerged brilliantly, and we all went into the Grove for a pic-nic, where we held our afternoon session. The speakers were Daniel Foster, Dr. Rock, Wm. Wells Brown, George W. Stacy, Henry C. Wright, Rev. Samuel Green, (who was sentenced to ten years' imprisonment for having in his house a copy of Uncle Tom's Cabin, in the loyal (?) State of Maryland, Rev. Mr. Gloucester, of Brooklyn, N. Y., and Rev. Mr. Ames, of Illinois.[3] Their speeches were necessarily brief, but all exceedingly pertinent and impressive. On the whole, I think we have never had a celebration surpassing it in interest.

Of the family, only George was with me; and he, at the close, went down to Plymouth with his friend Drew, to be gone till Monday.[4] I have no doubt he will have a very pleasant time.

While I am gone to Williamstown, your mother will probably make a visit to the Southwicks at Grantville.[5] I shall try to reach home by Tuesday evening.

My address is not quite completed, but nearly so. It is simply a serious, straight-forward anti-slavery arraignment of the guilt of the nation, and showing why the present national visitation has come upon us. I have written it without a metaphor, or a single flight of the imagination, or any thing to relieve its sombre aspect. To old abolitionists it would be trite, but to the mass of my audience it will, perhaps, be "as good as new." It will, of course, be distasteful to some; but, "whether they will hear, or whether they will forbear,"[6] they shall have it all. One gets weary, however, in the constant affirmation of those moral truisms which would seem to be as plain to every mind as the midday sun is to the vision.

Your letters have all been read by us with a great deal of pleasure and interest. That dated at Lancaster brings up a host of reminiscences of our visits to that beautiful village when we sojourned at Northumberland.[7] It was pleasant to hear about the Bellows family, John Wilson, the Marshalls, &c.[8] I really wish I could have been with you.

It is gratifying to know that you are getting along so well with the boys, and that you have met with no mishap on the way.[9] Give my regards to them, and tell them I trust, for their sake and their father's, they will "persevere in well-doing to the end."[10] It will be a memorable excursion for you all. Continue to be cautious not to overtax the physical powers of the lads, nor to run any unnecessary risks.

Your mother has gone to Dorchester, to be at an exhibition with William where Mrs. Jamison's Anne is to take a part.[11] She was greatly alarmed, the other night, when the lager beer saloon near us took fire. It was a very narrow escape from an extensive conflagration.

Franky writes that he thinks of returning home a week from to-morrow. He has had a first rate time of it.

Your loving father,

W. L. G.

☞ I send you a few stamps, thinking they may be convenient. Are you greatly troubled for change?

☞ We have had our dining-room carpet varnished to-day.[12]

☞ I send you the Liberator, Traveller, &c.

☞ Jaded, from day to day, by your pedestrianising, it must be a task for you to write any letters in addition to those which you send to Mr. Stephenson.[13] But a letter to Willie answers for us all.

☞ It now looks as if Washington might be taken before Richmond.

☞ Fanny finds the sweetest "Concord" where she is visiting.

ALS: Garrison Papers, Boston Public Library; partly printed in *Life*, IV, 57.

1. Island Grove Park (on Wilson Place, off Washington Street) in Abington, Mass., was a favorite meeting place for antislavery and temperance groups. The August First anniversary of emancipation in the British West Indies was regularly celebrated there. (*Massachusetts, a Guide to Its Places and People*, Cambridge, Mass., 1937.)

2. J. Sella Martin (c. 1825–1876), a Negro from North Carolina, had been the minister of the Twelfth Baptist Church on Joy Street in Boston since 1859. His career carried him to various parts of the United States and Europe. He solicited funds for the Ohio Freedmen's Aid Society in England, where he spent most of the war years. Following the war he was politically active in the south, first in Alabama and Mississippi and in 1868 as a postmaster in Louisiana. He succeeded Frederick Douglass as editor of the *New National Era*. (Letter to the editor from Ruth Bell, researcher, May 8, 1972.)

3. Daniel Foster (1816–1864) was a native of Hanover, N.H., who had gone to Kansas in 1857 on an abolitionist mission and who had hoped to establish "a liberal reformatory free church." Because of local opposition he was eventually imprisoned; on April 11, 1862, *The Liberator* printed a letter from the Namaha County jail in which Foster appealed for funds to found a high school. In August 1862 he became a chaplain with the Massachusetts 33rd Regiment; in November 1863 he was mustered into a black regiment, the North Carolina Volunteers, as captain and chaplain. He was killed in action on September 30, 1864. (*The Liberator*, June 21, 1861, and November 25 and December 9, 1864.)

John Swett Rock (1825–1866) was a black man of many distinctions. After studying medicine (graduating from the American Medical College in 1852), dentistry, and law, he practiced all three professions in Boston. He was also an active antislavery lecturer and a proficient translator from the French for *The Liberator*. He was the first black man to be received on the floor of the House of Representatives. (Letter to the editor from Ruth Bell, researcher, September 17, 1972.)

William Wells Brown (c. 1816–1884), the son of a slave mother and reputedly of a white father, escaped to Ohio in 1834, intending to go to Canada. Assuming the name of the Quaker, Wells Brown, who had helped him escape, he became an effective lecturer for the Western New York Anti-Slavery Society and the Massachusetts Anti-Slavery Society. He was also active in temperance, woman's suffrage, and prison reform. In 1849 he went to England and Paris, where he represented the American Peace Society at an international peace congress. During his five years abroad he promoted various reforms and even studied medicine. He was the author of many books about slavery and the Negro.

George Whittemore Stacy (1809–1892) was a minister, printer, and abolitionist of Milford, Mass. (*Life;* see also *Letters*, IV, 682, descriptive note.)

Samuel Green was a black Methodist minister from Dorchester County, Md. Although he was a free black, in 1857 he was tried and sentenced to ten years in the Baltimore jail for helping slaves to escape. Part of the evidence used against him was a copy of Harriet Beecher Stowe's *Uncle Tom's Cabin* found in his house. After five years Governor Augustus W. Bradford released him. (*The Liberator*, July 4 and August 15, 1862.)

James Gloucester was the son of John Gloucester, a former slave who founded the First African Presbyterian church in Philadelphia in 1807. Like his father, Gloucester was a minister; he organized the Siloam Presbyterian Church in Brooklyn, serving as its pastor from 1847 to 1851. He was also editor of the *Zion Standard and Weekly*. (Carter G. Woodson, *The History of the Negro Church*, Washington, D.C., 1921; Andrew E. Murray, *Presbyterians and the Negro—A History*, Philadelphia, 1966; Jesse Belmont Barker, *A History of the Work of the Presbyterian Church among the Negroes in the U.S.A.*, New York, 1936.)

Charles Gordon Ames (1828–1912) was ordained a minister in 1849. After serving in Tamworth Iron Works, N.H., he moved to St. Anthony Falls, Minn., where in 1855 he began editing the first Republican paper in the state, the Minnesota *Republican*. In 1859 he moved to Bloomington, Ill. During the war he lectured extensively on behalf of the Union and abolition. His last years were spent as minister of the Church of the Disciples in Boston.

4. Probably Thomas Bradford Drew, identified in the letter to Helen E. Garrison, June 7, 1867.

5. Joseph Southwick (1791–1866) was an abolitionist of long standing, having been a founder of the American Anti-Slavery Society in 1833. His wife was Thankful Hussey Southwick (1792–1867), daughter of Quaker abolitionist Samuel Hussey. She was a member of the Boston Female Anti-Slavery Society and, in 1838, a member of the executive committee of the New England Non-Resistance Society. Garrison delivered the eulogy at her funeral. (Sarah Hussey Southwick, *Reminiscences of Early Anti-Slavery Days*, Cambridge, Mass., 1893.)

By "Grantville" Garrison apparently means Granville, Mass., which is located west of Springfield near the Connecticut border.

6. Ezekiel 2:7.

7. Garrison refers to Northumberland in Coos County, N.H., at the mouth of the Upper Ammonoosuc River. He and his family vacationed there in July and August 1860. See *Letters*, IV, 677–689.

8. The Marshalls and John Wilson possibly belong to the same families referred to in *Letters*, IV, 689, 691. There was a Lancaster merchant named Charles Bellows, but whether Garrison refers to his family in uncertain. (Letter to the editor from William Copeley, assistant librarian, New Hampshire Historical Society, February 6, 1975.)

9. "The boys" whose walking tour Wendell was supervising were the sons of John H. Stephenson (see n. 13); they have not been further identified.

10. Possibly an allusion to II Thessalonians 3:13.

11. Anne Jameson was the daughter of Lucinda Lawrence Otis (1808–1886) and Thorndike C. Jameson of Providence. (Letter to the editor from Ruth Bell, researcher, October 16, 1971.)

12. Garrison probably refers to strips or pieces of painted canvas that were varnished and used as carpeting, no doubt precursors of linoleum and similar floor coverings.

13. John Hubbard Stephenson (1820–1888), a native of New Hampshire, was in early life a member of the firm of Stephenson and Plympton, millinery jobbers in Boston. His wife was Abigail Southwick, daughter of Joseph and Thankful. In 1868 he was to move to New York, where he founded an importing house. (Letter to the editor from Ruth Bell, researcher, November 1, 1971.)

41

TO ELIZABETH BUFFUM CHACE

Boston, Aug. 7, 1862.

I find your letter desiring to know what I intend doing, in case any of my sons are drafted for the war.

I have three sons of the requisite age—George, William and Wendell. Wendell is in principle opposed to all fighting with carnal weapons. So is William. In any case, they will not go to the tented field but will abide the consequences. George is inclined to think he shall go, if drafted, as he does not claim to be a non-resistant.

Your sons have not reached their majority, and consequently are still under recognized parental care.[1] Whether opposed in principle or not to all war, like my own sons, they are liable to be drafted and if they refuse to go when called, I presume neither pleas of conscience nor the claims of filial obedience will avail aught with "the powers that be." What the penalties of refusal will be, I do not know; but, no doubt, they can be made pretty severe in the matter of fine and imprisonment, unless substitutes are hired; and one conscientiously opposed to all war could not employ another to do what he could not do himself.

I do not know that I can give you any specific advice. The war is shaping itself, as a matter of necessity on the part of the government, into an Anti-Slavery war, more and more, and it seems to me cannot end in the suppression of the rebellion without at the same time exterminating slavery. Still, if I had no conscientious scruples as a peace advocate against enlisting so long as the government is struggling, avowedly and solely, to maintain "the Union as it was, and the Constitution as it is,"—"the old "covenant with death and the agreement with hell," I do not see how I, or any other radical abolitionist, could consistently fight to maintain it.[2] And it is my hope that George, though not a non-resistant, will take the penalties of disobedience as the friend and representative of the slave, until entire emancipation is the declared policy of the government.[3]

I do not object to my children suffering any hardships, or running any risks, in the cause of liberty and the support of great principles, if duty requires it; but I wish them to know themselves, to act from the highest and noblest motives, and to be true to their conscientious convictions.

I trust you and your husband will be spared the pain and anguish of seeing either of your sons drafted; and I am inclined to think the liability of a draft, unless a still larger requisition be made by the government, is growing less and less probable. You must give them the best advice in your power, but conjure them to act as duty may seem to require.

Have your sons returned from the White Mountains?

Wife unites with me in kindest regards to yourself and husband.[4]

Printed extract: Lillie Buffum Chace Wyman and Arthur Crawford Wyman, *Elizabeth Buffum Chace 1806–1899: Her Life and Its Environment* (Boston, 1914), I, 241–243.

Elizabeth Buffum Chace (1806–1899), daughter of early abolitionist Arnold Buffum and Rebecca Gould Buffum and wife of Samuel B. Chace (see n. 4), was an active abolitionist and an important leader in the woman's rights movement. In 1850 she was one of the sponsors of the National Woman's Rights Convention at Worcester, Mass.; following the Civil War she and Paulina W. Davis organized the Rhode

Island Woman's Suffrage Association, of which she was president from 1870 until her death. She was also an officer in the American Woman Suffrage Association and in 1872 went to London as a delegate to the International Congress on the Prevention and Repression of Crime. In addition to the sons mentioned below, the Chaces had two daughters, Elizabeth and Mary. (Wyman and Wyman, *Elizabeth Buffum Chace; NAW.*)

1. During the early months of the Civil War so many men volunteered to serve that conscription was not necessary. By the summer of 1862 the number of volunteers had diminished, and two draft acts followed: (1) the Federal Militia Act of 1862, which provided for the mustering in of the militia between the ages of eighteen and forty-five when called upon by the President, and which became effective August 4, when Lincoln issued a call for 300,000 men; (2) the Enrolment Act of 1863, which applied to men between ages twenty and forty-five, for whom calls were issued in the summer of 1863, the spring and fall of 1864, and the spring of 1865.

Of the Chace boys living at this time, Samuel Oliver (1843–1867), Arnold (born 1845), and Edward (1849–1871), only Samuel would have been subject to a draft call, and apparently in his case the issue did not arise. Although he was eager to enlist, he did not do so, in deference to his mother's strong opposition. Rhode Island's draft law made no provision for conscientious objection. (Eugene Murdock, *One Million Men: The Civil War Draft in the North*, Madison, Wis., 1971, pp. 6–9; Edward N. Wright, *Conscientious Objectors in the Civil War*, Philadelphia, 1931, pp. 49, 64; Wyman and Wyman, *Elizabeth Buffum Chace*, I, 216–220; *The Liberator*, September 26, 1862.)

2. In *The Liberator*, September 19 and 26, 1862, Garrison explained his views on the draft and its effect on nonresistants, pacifists, and abolitionists, concluding that each individual should be guided by his own conscience and prepared to take the consequences. (See *Life*, IV, 37, 58–59; for a discussion of conscientious objection during the Civil War, see P. Brock, *Pacifism in the United States*, Princeton, 1968, chapters 17–20.)

3. For more information about George Thompson Garrison and the Civil War, see the letters to him, June 11 and August 6, 1863.

4. Samuel Buffington Chace (1800–1870) was an orthodox Quaker born near Fall River, Mass., who entered into cotton manufacturing in that city. He married Elizabeth Buffum in June 1828, and in 1840 the Chaces moved to Valley Falls, near Providence, R.I., where Samuel operated a cotton mill with his brother Harvey. Their home became a station on the Underground Railroad. Compared with his wife, Chace was not prominent in the abolition movement, but he possessed the same philanthropic and antislavery sympathies as she did. (*Biographical Cyclopedia of Representative Men of Rhode Island*, Providence, 1881; Wyman and Wyman, *Elizabeth Buffum Chace.*)

4 2

TO WENDELL PHILLIPS GARRISON

Boston, August 10, 1862.

My Dear Son:

For the last ten days, the weather has been hot and sultry, without any intermission, accompanied with heavy showers and an unusual amount of thunder and lightning. If it has been the same with you, then you and the boys must have found pedestrianizing any thing but pleasurable; unless, indeed, you took only the morning and the dewy eve[1] to accomplish your walking tasks.

A week ago to-day, (Sunday,) I was at Pittsfield, and found it to be as beautiful and attractive as eye and heart could wish. I there met Professor [Philemon H.] Fowler, of Poughkeepsie, who, like myself, was on the way to Williamstown, to deliver one of the orations. Having nothing special to do, we went in the forenoon to Rev. Dr. Todd's church, but heard a stranger; and in the evening to the Episcopal church, and heard Dr. Huntington.[2] Dr. H's sermon was very well written, but, as I know him to be a trimmer and a formalist, it was to me "as empty as the whistling wind."[3] You know his style and manner. He is indulging in a little country recreation, and is looking sleek and in good condition. My aversion to a liturgy, with its responses, deepens every time I listen to it. The worship of God, as a set, mechanical, stereotyped observance, is to me nothing better than a solemn mockery; and it is sad to see so many otherwise sensible people who are duped by it.

I found Prof. Fowler to be a spiritualist, and also a medium. He says he sees and converses with spirits as readily as with any persons in the flesh; and that often, at night, they are so voluble around him, that he has to order them to "shut up," in order to get his needed repose! Webster, Choate, &c., are with him frequently.[4]

Monday morning, the young student, Mr. G. C. Brown, whose home is in Pittsfield, and who engaged me to give the address before the Adelphic Union Society,[5] drove us to Williamstown, a distance of twenty-two miles, in a sort of barouche, with a fine span of horses. The scenery throughout was a continual blending of the sublime and the beautiful, and some of the views of a very enchanting kind. We enjoyed our ride to the full.

The day was one of the most sultry of the season. I gave my address in the afternoon, at 4 o'clock, occupying an hour and a half. It was listened to with unbroken interest, and occasionally applauded, (it was too grave and serious for much applause,) and was evidently well received. At the close of it, Professor Bascom (who introduced me) expressed his gratification, and said he endorsed every word of it.[6] The audience was not very large, as twenty-five cents were asked for a ticket admitting the holder to both lectures. Hardly any of the Faculty were present, except Prof. Bascom. In the evening, Prof. Fowler gave his lecture, and spoke without manuscript or notes for nearly two hours and a half! His theme was "The Crisis," which he discussed with marked ability, and delivered with great energy and eloquence.

I have not seen, in any of the journals, any allusion made to our discourses. See what it is (not) to be popular!

Williamstown is charmingly located, nestling in the bosom of surrounding mountains, green and handsome to their summits.

I returned home Tuesday noon, and to my surprise found Franky, —his face in a battered condition, the result of being thrown from a wagon at Oakdale. It was a narrow escape for him. He could sympathize with Herb. and Benny, in the bruises they got from the accident at the well.[7] We were all startled to think how near it came being fatal in their case, and earnestly hope there will be no permanent scars left. It must have been an occasion of great anxiety to you.

Your mother sighs for the time when you and Fanny will be added once more to the family circle, which seems so lonely without you, that Willie prefers to stay at Dorchester, rather than to be in the city. I need not say, that I share in your mother's desire in this particular, though not in her anxiety.

There is nothing new to communicate. As usual, up to this time, "all is quiet along the Potomac."[8] Volunteering is going on rapidly in every part of the State, so that drafting will probably be required to a much less extent than was apprehended.

I send you a few papers, and enclose a few stamps.

Your mother, George and Franky send their warmest love. George goes to Hopedale on Monday, 18th inst. We look for Fanny Saturday.

Your affectionate father,

Wm. Lloyd Garrison.

ALS: Garrison Papers, Boston Public Library; partly printed in *Life*, IV, 57–58.

1. An adaptation of John Milton, *Paradise Lost*, I, 743–744.
2. John Todd (1800–1873), a graduate of Yale College and Andover Theological Seminary, after short pastorates in Northampton, Mass., and Philadelphia, settled in Pittsfield, Mass., as minister of the First Congregational Church, where he remained for the last thirty years of his life. His influence, owing partly to his many published books, was considerable. The stranger who occupied his pulpit has not been identified.
   Frederic Dan Huntington (1819–1904), an Amherst graduate, had reacted against his Calvinistic background and entered the Unitarian church, only to relinquish it for the Episcopal in 1859. Resigning a position at the Harvard College Chapel in 1860, he became rector of Emmanuel Church in Boston and subsequently priest of the Church of the Messiah. In 1869 he became the first bishop of the Diocese of Central New York.
3. Possibly an allusion to Shakespeare, *1 Henry IV*, V, i, 3–6.
4. Garrison refers to the famous statesmen of the first half of the nineteenth century, Daniel Webster (1782–1852) and Rufus Choate (1799–1859).
5. George Center Brown (1842–1892) attended Williams College and then studied law with Cott and Pingree in Pittsfield and at the Harvard Law School. Subse-

quently he moved to St. Louis, where he practiced law and worked as a newspaper correspondent. (Obituary Record of Williams College.)

The Adelphic Union Society was the oldest literary society at Williams; it sponsored debates and lectures by distinguished men, especially at commencement exercises. (Leverett Wilson Spring, *A History of Williams College,* Boston and New York, 1917).

6. John Bascom (1828–1911) of New York had been educated briefly as a lawyer and more extensively as a minister before settling on an academic career. He was first professor of rhetoric and oratory at Williams College (1855–1874), then president and professor of philosophy at the University of Wisconsin (1874–1887), and finally professor of political science at Williams (1891–1903). Bascom was the author of twenty books and many articles on a variety of religious, literary, and philosophical topics.

7. Herb and Benny have not been identified.

8. Garrison adapts Ethel Lynn Beers, "The Picket Guard," stanza 6, line 1. The phrase is supposed to have originated with General George B. McClellan and exasperated a country demanding action.

43

TO OLIVER JOHNSON

Boston, Sept. 9, 1862.

Dear Johnson:

I am such a laggard with the pen, in all epistolary matters, that I deserve to be cut off without a *pen*-sion, if not sent to the *pen*-itentiary; yet I am always *pen*-itential for my short-comings.

Certainly, I meant to have sent a reply to your first letter, in the *Liberator* bundle of Thursday; but I missed the opportunity; and just as I was about to sit down, and write a letter for the mail, yours of yesterday came to hand.[1]

I commend your anxiety in regard to the course to be pursued both by the *Standard* and the *Liberator,* respecting the present critical state of affairs; and fully agree with you, that there has never been a time when abolitionists should weigh their words (whether written or spoken) more carefully than now, in order to avoid needless persecution and baffle pro-slavery malignity. Our work, as abolitionists, is still to impeach, censure and condemn where we must, and approve when we can; but, in such an inflammable state of the country, the injunction, "Be ye wise as serpents, and harmless as doves,"[2] deserves to be carefully heeded. I have always believed that the Anti-Slavery cause has had aroused against it a great deal of uncalled for hostility, in consequence of extravagance of speech, and want of tact and good judgment, on the part of some most desirous to promote its advancement; but this is a drawback which has ever affected the success of reformatory movements, and grows out of the incompleteness of human development.

It is very desirable, as you intimate, that the *Standard* and the *Liberator* should harmonize, as far as practicable, in the mode of dealing with such correspondents as wish to make use of their columns to express their honest but often badly expressed sentiments on men and things. In common, on the ground of free discussion, we are both often called to publish what, on the score of good taste and fair criticism, we cannot endorse; but I grant a larger indulgence than it would be proper for you to do, seeing that no one else is responsible for the *Liberator* but myself; whereas, the *Standard* is the official organ of the American Anti-Slavery Society, and on that account should be conducted with more habitual circumspection. Still, I would have the *Standard* err on the side of liberality, rather than of exclusiveness, so as to always indicate its fearlessness of the most thorough investigation and the strongest dissent; while, at the same time, I would have you exercise your own good judgment, just as you have hitherto done, in determining what shall appear in the *Standard.* I do not feel that I can give you any advice, or that you need any. You did perfectly right, I think, in declining to publish Howland's attack on Mr. May; and it was certainly very unfair, on his part, to send it for simultaneous appearance in the *Standard* and *Liberator,* without intimating to either of us that he had done so.

As to the Ellenville Convention, I have not yet received any report of its proceedings, but presume it will come to hand this week.[3] In point of attendance, it was only a baker's dozen, until Sunday, when the threatened arrest of Powell caused a breeze, and brought out a fuller attendance.

Pillsbury tells me the meetings were dull, and quite dispiriting.[4] Should you receive the proceedings, in whole or in part, I would have you do with them just as you think best.

Your safeguard in publishing what is not to your taste, or what may be extravagant and undiscriminating in impeachment, is in making an editorial note of dissent, or in reminding the public that the editor does not hold himself responsible for the views or sentiments of correspondents, or for the action of any independent convention, whose proceedings may find a place, as a matter of intelligence, in the columns of the *Standard.*

I am growing more and more skeptical as to the "honesty" of Lincoln. He is nothing better than a wet rag; and it is manifest that, in the appointment of Halleck to be Secretary of War, and McClellan commander-in-chief of the army, he is as near lunacy as any one not a pronounced Bedlamite.[5] The satanic democracy of the North, and the traitorous "loyalty" of the Border States, have almost absolute control over him, and are industriously preparing the way for the overthrow of his administration, and the inauguration of, if not a reign of terror, at least one that will make terms with Rebeldom, no matter how humiliating they may be.

Only think of Washington, Harrisburg, Baltimore, and even Philadelphia, all threatened with immediate capture by the rebel forces, now encamped in full strength on the Maryland soil! I think they are very likely to succeed in their purposes. So in regard to Cincinnati and New Orleans. It seems to me we are virtually betrayed by our leaders.

Perhaps before this reaches you, Fanny may have called at your office. She has been on a brief visit to the [Aaron] Powells at Ghent, and will spend a few days with the Anthonys, at 86 State Street, Brooklyn.[6] It is her first visit, and I am anxious to have her make the most of it. She may conclude to stay a few days with Dr. [Edward] Percy and family. If Mary-Ann is at home, put Fanny in the way of seeing her and Mrs. [Augustus] Savin, as well as Mrs. [James S.] Gibbons, Dr. Smith and wife, &c., and consider me largely your debtor.[7]

The [John] Hoppers, I suppose, are rusticating in the country; but Fanny might call at John's office, and leave her card.

Give my kindest regards to Ward Beecher and Theodore Tilton. The *Independant* is speaking out bravely and eloquently, and I read it with lively interest.

How does the war affect your subscription list? The *Liberator*'s is minus at least two hundred.

Faithfully yours

W. L. G.

Handwritten transcription: Garrison Papers, Boston Public Library; partly printed in *Life*, IV, 62–63.

1. Johnson's first letter to Garrison, dated August 28, 1862, concerned a letter the *National Anti-Slavery Standard* received from Joseph A. Howland (died 1889), a well-known businessman and abolitionist of Worcester, Mass. Howland's letter criticized Samuel May, Jr., for encouraging enlistment in support of the Union, on the grounds that nonresistant abolitionists should not actively support the government in wartime. There followed in subsequent issues of *The Liberator* a minor controversy between Howland and May. (Anti-Slavery Letters to Garrison and Others, Boston Public Library; *The Liberator*, August 1, 8, 22, and 29, 1862.)

The contents of Johnson's second letter, which has not been found, can be inferred from Garrison's letter.

2. Matthew 10:16.

3. An antislavery convention was held at Ellenville, Ulster County, N.Y., August 28–30, 1862. Although it was not noted in *The Liberator*, the *Standard* reported on

September 13 that all the speakers (Parker Pillsbury, Susan B. Anthony, and Aaron M. Powell) asserted that the war was a by-product of slavery. The reference to Powell's arrest has not been explained.

4. Parker Pillsbury (1809–1898) left the ministry to become a lecture agent for the New Hampshire, the Massachusetts, and the American Anti-Slavery societies, successively. He also edited the *Herald of Freedom* (in Concord, N.H.) in 1840 and 1845 and the *National Anti-Slavery Standard* (in New York City) in 1866. His writings included *Acts of the Anti-Slavery Apostles* (1883).

5. Garrison errs in thinking that Henry W. Halleck (1815–1872), West Point graduate, lawyer, and engineer, was appointed secretary of war. Instead, on July 11, 1862, he was made military adviser to the President and given the title of general-in-chief. It is true that orders of the secretary of war were sometimes issued in his name. It was only after Grant was appointed lieutenant general and given command of all the armies that Halleck's status was clarified and he became chief of staff.

6. Edward Anthony (1807–1868) was the brother of Helen Garrison's brother-in-law Henry Anthony. In 1831 Edward had married Helen Maria Hastings Grieve. They had nine children, seven girls and two boys. He was president of the Lamaz Insurance Company in New York City. (Charles L. Anthony, *Genealogy of the Anthony Family from 1495 to 1904*, Sterling, Ill., 1904.)

7. Henry Mitchell Smith (1835–1901) was a graduate of the New York Medical College, a member of the American Institute of Homœopathy, and editor of the *Homœopathic Review*. (*Biographical Cyclopaedia of Homœopathic Physicians and Surgeons*, Chicago, 1893, p. 88; see also the letter to Oliver Johnson, April 16, 1859, *Letters*, IV, 620, n. 6.) Victoria Knight Smith has already been identified.

44

TO FANNY GARRISON

Boston, Sept. 25, 1862.

Dear Fanny:

Your mother has just received your letter of the 23d, and wishes me to acknowledge it for her with thanks and gladness, as she is too busy to answer it this morning.

The President's Proclamation is certainly matter for great rejoicing, as far as it goes for the liberation of those in bondage; but it leaves slavery, as a system or practice, still to exist in all the so-called loyal Slave States, under the old constitutional guaranties, even to slave-hunting in the Free States, in accordance with the wicked Fugitive Slave Law. It postpones emancipation in the Rebel States until the 1st of January next, except as the slaves of rebel masters may escape to the Federal lines. What was wanted, what is still needed, is a proclamation, distinctly announcing the total abolition of slavery.[1] Still, the proclamation commits the government, in due time, to the emancipation of more than three quarters of the whole slave population; and therein I, with you, and a great multitude of others, "do rejoice, and will rejoice."[2] The President can do nothing for *freedom* in a direct manner, but only by circumlocution and delay. How prompt was his action against Fremont and Hunter!

I have nothing special to write about. Mrs. Fish of Hopedale, is staying with us for a few days, prior to her joining her husband in Western New York.[3]

Birney Mann spent from Saturday to Wednesday with us.[4]

Mr. Bramhall and Mrs. Rand,[5] from Orange, spent an hour with us on Tuesday. They said they had left you at home, and were much pleased with your visit. I hope it was not so long protracted as really to put them to some inconvenience. It was very kind in Phebe to insist on your being with her two or three days.[6]

Should she accompany you home, you can come in the boat, if she prefers; but, otherwise, your mother and I think you had better come through by daylight, in the cars, via New Haven, even if you come alone. For we think you would not like to be alone in the ladies' cabin, during the night, on board of the boat; and you might be caught in a gale of wind, and be very sea-sick. You would be pretty sure, at any rate, to get very little sleep.

I am very glad you have seen Abby Patton, Lucy Stone, the two Misses Gibbons, &c., and I trust you will not fail to see dear Mattie Griffith.[7] I am sorry Rosa Hopper will not be able to give you a welcome, in consequence of her absence from the city.

Mother thinks you had better present Anna's little girl[8] either with a gown of some kind, or a nice pair of shoes, or some other token of love. I enclose some additional money, to be used at your discretion for this purpose.

As you may wish to have a card or two more of my photograph, I enclose a couple, to be given away or not as you may choose.

When you come back, I shall want you and your mother to try again at Seaver's.[9] I am not yet satisfied.

Be careful, and do not eat fruit in excess, as it is the season for temptation.

Mother, all the brothers, and Mary,[10] desire me to send loving remembrances.

We are glad to hear that Dr. [Edward] Percy has got a commission as surgeon, though we shall be sorry for Anna that he must be absent with the army.

Give her our warmest love. Our regret still lingers that she was unable to make us a visit.

Your loving father,

Wm. Lloyd Garrison.

ALS: Garrison Papers, Boston Public Library; extract printed in *Life*, IV, 62.

1. On September 22, 1862, President Lincoln announced that in one hundred days (on January 1, 1863) all slaves of any still rebellious states, or parts of any states specified by him, would be freed; those in already conquered states or loyal states were to be freed by other legislation. He also recommended a constitutional amendment that would provide compensation to all states abolishing slavery before 1900, guarantee the freedom of all slaves liberated by the Union army, with some form of remuneration to loyal masters, and implement a program of colonization for freed Negroes. Although the Emancipation Proclamation's significance has been widely debated, there is little doubt that it had a distinct impact on the international scene. By changing the Civil War into an antislavery crusade, Lincoln deterred from intervention those foreign governments determined to raise the economic blockade crippling their trade. England and France could hardly justify opposing the North once it was dedicated to the same philosophy that had effected abolition in their own countries.

2. Philippians 1:18.

3. William Henry Fish (1812–1880) was married to Anne Eliza Wright (born 1815). Although he was by profession a minister among the Independent Restorationists of the Massachusetts Association, he is chiefly remembered for his role in founding the Hopedale Community in Milford, Mass., where he lived between 1846 and 1855. With the help of Samuel J. May, he became the minister of the Unitarian church in South Scituate, Mass., in 1865. (For more complete information, see the letter to George Thompson Garrison, February 18, 1851, *Letters*, IV, 50, n. 4.)

4. Birney Mann (1847–1903) was the son of Daniel and Maria Dimock Mann of Sterling, Mass., and Boston. He was a friend and classmate of Francis Jackson Garrison at the Boston' Latin School and in adult life became an accomplished organist and piano teacher. His father was the dentist who treated Garrison in 1865–1866. (Letter to the editor from Frances P. Tapley, curator, Sterling Historical Society, Sterling, Mass., June 21, 1973; see also the letters to Helen E. Garrison, July 23, 1865; James Miller McKim, October 1, 1865; and Wendell Phillips Garrison, June 14, 1866.)

5. Cornelius Bramhall and his wife, Ann Rebecca Reed Bramhall, were active abolitionists, at first in Massachusetts and after 1855 in New York City and New Jersey. (See the letter to Ann R. Bramhall, August 8, 1856, *Letters*, IV, 400–402.) Mrs. Rand has not been identified.

6. Phebe has not been identified.

7. Abigail Jemima Hutchinson Patton (1829–1892), one of the famous Hutchinson antislavery singers, had toured extensively with her brothers John, Judson, and Asa from 1842 until her marriage in 1849 to Ludlow Patton. The Pattons lived in Orange, N.J. Even after her retirement Mrs. Patton sometimes joined the family group to sing on special occasions, such as the woman's rights conventions in Rochester in 1855 and in New York City in 1857, the Lincoln campaign in 1860, various meetings on behalf of the Union cause during the war, and the American Equal Rights Association convention in New York City in 1868. Her last public appearance was at the funeral of John Greenleaf Whittier in 1892. (*NAW.*)

Lucy Stone (1818–1893), whose father refused to send her to college, taught school, saved money, and paid her own way through Oberlin, graduating in 1847. The same year she began lecturing in public on woman's rights. In 1850 she was instrumental in calling the first national woman's rights convention in Worcester, Mass. After her marriage in 1855 to Henry Brown Blackwell, she retained her maiden name and worked even more intensively for woman's rights. She was among the founders of the leading woman's rights associations, including the American Equal Rights Association, the New Jersey Woman Suffrage Association, the National Woman Suffrage Association, and, with her daughter, Alice Stone Blackwell, the American Woman Suffrage Association. In 1870 she founded the *Woman's Journal*, of which she and her husband served as editors after the resignation of Mary A. Livermore. (Alice Stone Blackwell, *Lucy Stone, Pioneer of Woman's Rights*, Norwood, Mass., 1930.)

Garrison refers to Sarah, Julia, or Lucy Gibbons, already identified.

Martha Griffith (c. 1833–1906) had been left an orphan in Louisville, Ky.; she was raised by one of her father's female slaves. When she came of age, she freed all her slaves and went north. She published a volume of poems (1853) and the sensational, though fictional, *Autobiography of a Female Slave* (1856). In 1867 she married Albert G. Browne, Jr., a former correspondent for the New York *Tribune*, and settled in Boston. (Letter to the editor from Linda Anderson, assistant librarian, Kentucky Historical Society, June 20, 1974; *National Anti-Slavery Standard*, July 6, 1867.)

8. Charlotte Helen Percy (1860–1870). (Wendell Phillips Garrison, *The Benson Family of Newport, Rhode Island*, New York, 1872.)

9. Garrison refers to the photographer.

10. Not identified; probably a Garrison servant.

45

TO HELEN E. GARRISON

Peacham, Oct. 8, 1862.

Dear Wife:

We were again favored, yesterday, with good autumnal weather, and occupied ourselves chiefly in visiting the spot where Oliver was born, and where he spent his life till he was sixteen years old, when he went to Montpelier to learn "the art and mystery" of printing. The log cabin in which he first saw the light of heaven has long since been removed, and nothing remains to mark the spot but a portion of the cellar, filled with stones and weeds. His father occupied, at different periods, two or three other farms in that locality;[1] but the house in which Oliver lived all his conscious existence in this village, until going to Montpelier, is still in good repair, and occupied by a young farmer, with a good-looking wife and a pretty little boy. We went through the various rooms, and found them all neatly papered and presenting a very tidy appearance. Oliver showed us the room in which the family prayers were made, and scriptural selections read, with portions of Scott's Commentaries,[2] his father having been rigidly orthodox, and a deacon of the church. He also pointed out where he used to drive the oxen to their daily task, where he first learned to mow, where he flailed the wheat and shelled the corn, and did all that a poor farmer's boy is called to do, to secure the means of comfortable subsistence. We who live in the city have no conception of the amount of hard work performed in the interior, especially in a mountainous region like this, alike by the men, the women, and the children; for all are compelled, by the necessities of their position, to toil unremittingly, week in and week out. It would have made Franky stare to hear Oliver's recital of the amount and the various kinds of work he had to do as a small lad. Many funny reminiscences were called up by Oliver and his brother,[3] concerning the various persons that then lived in that vicinity, but who have either "shuffled off this mortal coil,"[4] or gone no one knows where. Every place has its odd characters, and Peacham appears to have had its full proportion.

Oliver was born on the slope of what is called Cow Hill, which is of high elevation, and one of the hardest eminences to surmount with team or carriage, the road being very rocky and much gullied. On the top the waters divide,—on one side running down, and ultimately finding their way into Lake Champlain, and on the other into the Connecticut river. The prospect, in every direction, is vast, majestic, and exceedingly beautiful.

While we were there, a handsome young heifer, of a mottled color, came toward me as if desirous of a better acquaintance, though a little coy at first. I patted her gently, and, moving from spot to spot to obtain different views, found that she followed me like an affectionate dog. Presently, some other persons joined us, and she left us to join some cows at a short distance. On getting into the road, and proceeding a short distance, on my return, I heard a looing sound, and on looking back saw my beautiful heifer close to the stone wall by the road, gazing intensely toward me, and still making a murmuring sound as much as to say, "Please don't leave me here, or else come and stay with me." The incident was quite touching to my feelings.

On getting to the village, I got hold of the Boston Journal of Monday, in which I saw that a sanguinary battle had taken place between the Federal and Rebel forces near Corinth, to the discomfiture of the latter; but nothing appears to be doing by McClellan and his army.[5] The Journal due to day will, no doubt, give some account of the Faneuil Hall meeting on Monday.[6] I was glad to see it announced that Richard Busteed would speak on the occasion, as well as Charles Sumner.[7]

A country life is exceedingly monotonous, presenting no other phase than that of habitual stillness and uniformity.

In the morning, we are off for White River junction and Braintree.
Your loving husband,

W. L. G.

ALS: Garrison Papers, Boston Public Library.

1. Oliver Johnson's father was Ziba Johnson (1770–1843), a carpenter by trade. Born in West Bridgewater, Mass., and residing after 1793 in Peacham, Vt., he was married three times. His first wife, the mother of Oliver and a deceased brother and sister, was Sally Lincoln (1770–1823). (Jennie Chamberlain Watts and Elsie A. Choate, *People of Peacham*, Montpelier, 1965, pp. 171–172.)

2. Thomas Scott (1747–1821), whose first American edition of the Bible, "with explanatory notes," was published in Philadelphia in 1810.

3. Oliver's brother was Ziba Leonard Johnson (1797–1890), who probably pursued the same vocation as his father, farming and carpentry, and who was married to Betsey Merrill (1800–1855). (Watts and Choate, *People of Peacham.*)

4. Shakespeare, *Hamlet,* III, i, 67.

5. Between October 3 and 5 there was fighting in Corinth, Miss., between Union forces under Rosecrans and Confederate under Price and Van Dorn. Although losses were heavy on both sides, the Confederates were defeated and withdrew. (E. B. Long, *The Civil War Day by Day,* Garden City, N.Y., 1971, pp. 274–275.)

6. The Boston *Journal,* to which Garrison refers, was founded as a Whig daily paper in 1833 by Captain John S. Sleeper and was then called the *Mercantile Journal.* In 1834 it became the *Evening Mercantile Journal,* in 1845 the *Daily Journal.* It attained its greatest prosperity during the Civil War under the editorship of Charles O. Rogers. After 1872 the paper was called the *Evening Journal;* it ceased publication in 1903. (*ULN;* Mott.)

The paper did report the ratification meeting which had been held at Faneuil Hall on October 6, 1862. At the meeting resolutions supported President Lincoln and rejoiced "that the cause of the country is now seen to be the cause of universal and impartial freedom."

7. Richard Busteed (1822–1898), an Irishman by birth, was a New York lawyer who served on the city's Corporation Council between 1856 and 1859. Although a supporter of Douglas in 1860, he became a strong Union man and in 1862 was appointed brigadier general of volunteers. In September 1863 he was named United States district judge for Alabama.

Sumner's speech was fully reported on the front page of the *Journal,* October 6, but Busteed is not mentioned.

---

4 6

TO HELEN E. GARRISON

White River Junction,
Oct. 9, 1862.

Dear Wife:

I know not what weather you are having in Boston; but yesterday it was as hot and sultry as in July; and we experienced the full power of the heat in an excursion to Devil's Mountain, about six miles from friend [Oliver] Johnson's residence.[1] We rode to within a mile of the base, and then picked our away along through the woods and over the rocks till we reached the summit. We were all wet through with perspiration, and felt a good deal fatigued; but we were amply repaid for our toil and sweat by the magnificent views we obtained, East, West, North and South. At the East and South, the gigantic White Mountain range were clearly visible to their tops, and we had a fine view of Camel's Rump and the Mansfield mountain,[2] the two most prominent elevations in Vermont. As the name imports, Devil's Mountain is a wild and rocky affair so as to present forbidding aspects; but, being bare on the summit, it enabled us to get the finest views in every direction. Directly below it, and far reaching, is an immense wilderness, covering an enormous bed of marle, and looking more glorious in its gorgeous apparel than an army with banners.[3] The jaunt repaid us many times over, sweltering though we were to the skin when we got home at tea-time. I sprained my left foot a little in coming down, and shall probably feel the effects of it for a few days so as to warn me against making any more ascensions at present. But I have had my fill of the sublime and beautiful, and shall be content with taking a more lowly position.

This morning, we (Oliver's brother accompanying us) came down to Barnet, in Leonard's wagon; and from thence took the train for this Junction—Oliver going East, with his brother, to see a half sister[4] at Andover, N.H.; and I waiting for the Boston train to take me to Randolph, where I shall meet Oliver to-morrow afternoon. I am occupying a portion of my time in writing this upon my knee, though, of course, I have nothing special to communicate.

On coming along in the cars from Barnet, one gentleman sitting back of us, in a clear, emphatic voice, spoke of the war as a just judgment of Heaven upon our land for its sin of oppression, and expressed the hope that the fire would continue to burn till the dross was removed, and the land thoroughly purified. This stirred up two others near him—gentlemen in pretence and appearance, one of them the President of the Railroad—who revealed the true democratic bile, and by their slang about the abolitionists showed they were as secesh in spirit as Jeff. Davis himself.[5] It was evident that they knew who I was; and they paid Massachusetts a compliment by expressing the wish that she might be set off from the rest of the Union. They were spiritedly replied to by the stranger who first spoke, and who proved to be a Dr. Smith, of Wisconsin, formerly of Ryegate, Vermont.[6] After many years' absence, he was here on a visit to bring up "the days o'auld lang syne" to his memory. We found him a very hearty abolitionist.

I see, by the Boston Journal, that the Faneuil Hall meeting was a great success, and that Sumner was the principal speaker.[7] His speech reads well, and no doubt was eloquently delivered. It seems that impudent and scatter-brained fellow, G. F. Train, undertook at the close to make a fool of himself, but was carried to the lock-up, with a shouting rabble after him as his sympathizers and backers.[8]

Though I am enjoying myself every hour of my absence, I shall be glad when the time is up that I have set for my return; for home grows dearer to me as I grow older, and the happiest place for me is 14 Dix Place, with you and the dear ones around me.

I think I shall improve the occasion, when at Burlington, (where I expect to lecture on Tuesday evening,) to go to Montreal, unless there should be an uncomfortable change in the weather, or the expense should prove greater than I can well meet at present.[9] War times demand economy, in every way; and therefore recreation is not to be freely indulged in, especially at remote distances. I do not know whether we shall have any hospitality proffered to us at Burlington; but I hope so, for hotel prices are high.

How you are all getting along, I hope to learn by a letter at Braintree or Burlington. I shall take it for granted that all is well.

Tell the children they are in my thoughts continually.

Lovingly yours,

W. L. G.

ALS: Garrison Papers, Boston Public Library.

1. Devil's Hill (altitude 2,058 feet) is located about four miles from the village of White River Junction. (*F. W. Beers' Atlas of Caledonia County, Vermont*, New York, 1869.)

2. That is, Camel's Hump and Mount Mansfield.

3. Song of Solomon 6:4 and 10.

4. Not identified.

5. Henry Keyes (1810–1870) of Newbury, Vt., was named president of the Connecticut and Passumpsic River Railroad in 1854. He also had an interest in several stage and steamboat lines as well as the Atchison, Topeka and Santa Fe Railroad, of which he became president in 1869. In addition to being a businessman, Keyes was a practical farmer, serving as president of the Vermont State Agricultural Society, and a politician; as chairman of the Vermont delegation to the Democratic convention of 1860 he nominated Stephen A. Douglas for President. (Frederic P. Wells, *History of Newbury, Vermont*, St. Johnsbury, Vt., 1902, p. 609.)

6. There were several Smith families in Ryegate, but this particular Dr. Smith remains unidentified.

7. *The Liberator* printed generous extracts from Sumner's speech of October 6 in the issue for October 10.

8. George Francis Train (1829–1904) had had a spectacular although eccentric career by the time of Garrison's letter. Early involved with a Boston shipping firm owned by a relative, he conducted business in cities ranging from Liverpool, England, to Melbourne, Australia, and made a considerable amount of money. After his return to the United States in 1856, he wrote extensively for the New York *Herald*, published many books, such as *Young America in Wall Street* (1857) and *Young America Abroad* (1857), and gave innumerable speeches. He also promoted street railroads in England and railroads in America. In 1862 he returned to Boston, where he was indeed jailed for his antics at the Faneuil Hall meeting. Train filled his remaining years with multitudinous and sensational activities, even being jailed for obscenity when he championed Victoria Woodhull and her "biblical" language. (See also Index entries for Train and the woman's rights movement.)

9. In fact, Garrison did not lecture at Burlington.

4 7

TO HELEN E. GARRISON

Braintree, Oct. 10, 1862.

Dear Wife:

Yesterday noon, I wrote upon my knee a hasty note at the White River junction depot, which was mailed at that place for you. After waiting there two hours and a half for the arrival of the Boston morning train for the North, at half past 2, P. M., I took the cars for Randolph—25 miles distant, one hour's ordinary ride; but our train proved "a slow coach," and we were almost three hours in accomplishing that short journey. We were detained a full hour on the way, in consequence of some breakage or disarrangement of the piston rod, &c.

I wrote to my friend, James Hutchinson, on Monday last, that I should be at the depot in that train; and, consequently, expected to see him on my arrival, to take me to his house.[1] But he was not there. As he lived three miles off, I had to hire a conveyance to Braintree, where I arrived at tea-time, taking Mr. and Mrs. Hutchinson entirely by surprise; as, it appears, they had not received my letter, in consequence of its having been directed to Braintree, instead of West Randolph, which is their post-office address—a piece of information James gave me in his letter sent to Peacham, which I happened to overlook. However, "all's well that ends well"—and as I was not looked for, the surprise was all the better.

James and his wife are a highly intelligent and admirably matched couple, extensively read, and unusually well cultured for the country. Their home receives all the anti-slavery lectures that come in this region, and on them devolves the labor of making arrangements for the meetings, &c. It was here that Miss Holley and Miss Putnam took special delight in visiting, as a matter of recreation.[2] Henry C. Wright has also spent considerable time here. The house stands in a retired spot, somewhat elevated, and yet is not solitary. Rev. Dr. Murdock, of Boston, and his family, (wife and four children,) boarded here during the summer.[3]

It has looked somewhat threatening as to rain, and a few drops fell early in the morning. I have just returned from a ride with Mr. and Mrs. Hutchinson over the hills, making a circuitous route to Randolph, and obtaining some of the finest views I have yet had in Vermont. To-morrow, should the weather prove favorable, we are to ascend a neighboring mountain, from which the prospect is said to be unusually grand and charming. But there is no need of going any where in particular, in Vermont, to see the sublime and beautiful: they are continually meeting your eye, which ever way you turn. ⟦Speaking of climbing, I am happy to say that my sprained foot and ankle are now quite well.⟧

The anti-slavery meetings advertised to be held by Mr. Foss in this village, on Sunday next, (which Oliver [Johnson] and I intended to address,) have been given up, we not being expected, and Mr. Foss having been summoned home by the sudden death of his son at Manchester, who, I believe, has recently returned from the army an invalid.[4] It is possible that we may speak on Sunday, either at Randolph or Braintree, as the Hutchinsons are very desirous we should; though I hardly feel in the mood to do so.[5] We shall decide the matter this afternoon, on the arrival of Oliver from the East.

I see that Gen. McClellan has acquiesced, passively, in the enforcement of the President's Emancipation Proclamation, and enjoins obedience upon the army; but he takes care to express no approval of it, and evidently means to do as little about it as possible, and yet preserve the semblance of loyalty.[6] Fremont seems to be effectually laid upon the shelf. The friends of freedom should be clamorous for his restoration to his post.

Tell Wendell I wish he would put into the Refuge of Oppression, in the Liberator of the 24th, some of the worst sayings of E. C. Bailey, Gen. James S. Whitney, and others, together with some of the resolutions adopted, at the Democratic Convention held at Worcester on the 8th inst.[7] The proceedings may be found in the Boston Journal of the 9th—though it is possible the Post of that date may have a more full account.[8]

I shall hope to get a line from you before I leave here. If not, then at Burlington.

I send the children a father's benediction.

Yours, lovingly,

W. L. G.

ALS: Garrison Papers, Boston Public Library.

1. About James Hutchinson, Jr. (1826–1911), a native of Randolph, Vt., few facts are known. He married Abby E. Flint (1828–1879) in 1847. He was a delegate to a state constitutional convention in 1856 and was to become an assistant judge of the county court in 1864. The farm at which Johnson and Garrison stayed is at Peth and is still owned by the Hutchinson family. (H. Royce Bass, *History of Braintree, Vermont*, n.p., 1883; letter to the editor from Muriel C. Thresher, curator, Braintree Historical Society, March 12, 1974.)

2. Sallie Holley (1818–1893) and Caroline F. Putnam (c. 1825–1917) had come to know each other in 1847 when they were students at Oberlin College. A decisive event at the college was a lecture by Abby Kelley Foster, who converted the young

women from the political abolitionism Miss Holley had acquired from her father to Garrisonianism. Following her graduation in 1851, Miss Holley became an agent of the American Anti-Slavery Society and lectured extensively for many years. Her interests included temperance, woman's rights, and the freedmen's cause. Following three years at Oberlin, Caroline Putnam became Sallie Holley's companion in reform; after her friend's death she continued to work for woman's suffrage and peace. (*NAW;* New York *Evening Post,* January 27, 1917.)

3. John Nelson Murdock (1820–1897), born in Oswego, N.Y., studied law and was admitted to the bar before becoming licensed to preach in the Methodist church. In 1842 he became a Baptist and served as minister in churches in Albion, N.Y., Hartford, Conn., and Boston. Between 1853 and 1856 he was coeditor of the *Christian Review;* he also served for many years as secretary of the Missionary Union. In 1854 Rochester University gave him an honorary doctor's degree. (*Baptist Encyclopedia, a Dictionary,* Philadelphia, 1883.)

Dr. Murdock's wife and children have not been identified.

4. Andrew Twombly Foss (1803–1875) was the first pastor of the Merrimac Street Baptist Church of Manchester, N.H., and lectured for abolitionism throughout New England and the Midwest. (Letter to the editor from Elizabeth Lessard, librarian, Manchester Historic Association, January 30, 1973; see also letter to Samuel J. May, September 11, 1854, *Letters,* IV, 317, n. 1.)

Eugene Kincaid Foss (c. 1836–1862), the only son of A. T. Foss, was a printer by trade. In the army he played in the cornet band of the 4th New Hampshire Regiment. Although taken sick while in the service, he had not seemed seriously ill, and so his death was sudden and unexpected. (Obituary, *The Liberator,* October 24, 1862; letter from A. T. Foss to Samuel May, Jr., October 7, 1862, printed in *The Liberator,* October 10.)

5. Garrison did speak at the Braintree meetinghouse on Quaker Hill on Sunday, October 12. It was reported that the audience was very large and that "Mr. Garrison's appeal for the slave was earnest and effective." (Bass, *History of Braintree,* pp. 46–47.)

6. McClellan's general order to the officers and soldiers of the Army of the Potomac (reprinted in *The Liberator,* October 10, 1862) calls attention to the Emancipation Proclamation, stating that the armed forces "are to be held in strict subordination to" civil authorities and that "the remedy for political errors . . . is to be found only in the action of the people at the polls." McClellan's view of emancipation as set forth in his autobiography is both sober and cautious. (George B. McClellan, *McClellan's Own Story,* New York, 1887.)

7. *The Liberator* of October 17 printed under the heading "Refuge of Oppression" resolutions adopted by the Democratic State Convention, including a protest against the Emancipation Proclamation and a censure of Lincoln for suspending *habeas corpus.* In the same column was reprinted an editorial from the Boston *Herald* (of which Edwin C. Bailey was editor), predicting a Democratic sweep in 1864 and urging that "the war be prosecuted to a speedy termination without regard to the whims of Wm. Lloyd Garrison, Abby Folsom, or Charles Sumner." There was also a column in the same issue of *The Liberator* signed C. K. W. (Charles K. Whipple, printer of the paper), reporting Bailey's speech at the convention and objecting to his censure of the suspension of *habeas corpus.*

Edwin C. Bailey (1816–1890) worked for many years for the Boston *Post* and subsequently acquired the Boston *Herald,* greatly increasing its circulation and adding, during the war, the Sunday *Herald.* He was postmaster of Boston between 1852 and 1857. In 1879 Bailey became editor-in-chief of the Boston *Globe* and in 1884 managing editor of the Boston *Star.* (Obituary, Boston *Evening Transcript,* August 21, 1890.)

James S. Whitney (1811–1878) was a successful Boston businessman who in 1835 had been commissioned brigadier general in the Massachusetts militia. Three years later he moved to Conway, N.H., and in 1851 and 1854 he was elected to the state legislature. Whitney was an earnest supporter of the Constitution who regarded

Charles Sumner as an abolitionist agitator and refused for many years to support him as a candidate for the United States Senate. At the time of his death he was president of the Boston Water Power Company and of the Metropolitan Steamship Company. (Frederick Clifton Pierce, *The Descendants of John Whitney . . .,* Chicago, 1895.)

8. The *Journal* for October 9 commented that the convention demonstrated welcome signs of weakness in the Democratic party. On October 10, the *Post* carried a lengthy but highly editorialized report of the convention, commending the Democratic party for putting aside partisan issues and supporting a slate virtually equivalent to the ticket of the People's party.

---

4 8

TO HELEN E. GARRISON

Burlington, Oct. 14, 1862.

Dear Wife:

Though the simple particulars of my jaunt can possess very little interest to you or the children, I will continue to narrate them, as helps to my memory on my return home.

Yesterday forenoon we occupied in ascending and descending a mountain in Braintree, about three miles from the residence of our friend [James] Hutchinson, he and his wife, and a young lady from Canada, going with us. It gave us some new views, on a magnificent scale, and we were well repaid for our labors. Near the base of the mountain, we passed through an extended grove of maple trees, the largest and finest I have yet seen in the State, from which a large quantity of maple sugar is annually made.

After dinner, we took a final leave of the Hutchinsons, who had for so many days kindly extended to us their hospitality, and rode to West Randolph, in a drenching rain, to take the cars for this place, where we arrived at 7 o'clock in the evening. The rain continued nearly the whole distance, and the weather was cold and cheerless. We went to the American House,[1] got our supper, and, being very weary, concluded we would retire early to get needed rest; but, just as we were proceeding to put our purpose in execution, Mr. Lawrence Goodhue Bigelow (whom I apprised by letter that I would be in Burlington that evening) came to our chamber, apologizing for not meeting us at the depot, as he was five minutes too late, and inviting us both to go to his residence—saying he should be happy to proffer his hospitality while we remained in the place, hoped we should be in no hurry to leave, and suggested at once various excursions on the Lake and in the neighborhood; nay, offering to go with us to North Elba to see John Brown's grave, driving us in his carriage—&c.[2] As we had booked ourselves for the night at the hotel, we told him that we would go to his house in the morning, after breakfast. He is a retired lumber merchant, and has a fine residence beautifully located in sight of the Lake. Accompanying him to our room at the hotel was a venerable looking man, named Sawyer, formerly a teacher in the College in this place, and a lawyer by profession; a great talker, full of wit and satire, and cherishing views of the war and its management under McClellan, Halleck, McDowell and Buell, and also of the satanic "Democracy," in entire accordance with my own.[3] Our interview did not break up until some time after 10. A good night's rest followed, though I was still suffering from my hoarseness. This morning, it gave promise of being a fine day, and, having eaten our breakfast, we proceeded to Mr. Bigelow's handsome residence, where we are now comfortably situated. In my letter to him, written at Peacham, I had authorized him, if he thought best, to get up a meeting for me this very Tuesday evening; and, having almost lost my voice, I was very nervous lest he had done so. But, fortunately, no arrangements for a lecture had been made, and I felt almost as happy as an emancipated slave.

At 10 o'clock, he, and his daughter and niece, went with us in the steamer America up Lake Champlain some forty miles to Port Henry, where are extensive iron furnaces to smelt the iron ore which is obtained in that vicinity in immense quantities.[4] We remained there about an hour, and then returned in the steamer Canada, arriving at Burlington at 5 o'clock, P. M. The excursion, up and down, was the most interesting one I ever made, throwing the Hudson river entirely into the shade, on the score of the grandeur, beauty and magnitude of the views, on both sides of the Lake. We could see, on one side, the vast range of Green Mountains which divide Vermont east and west,—including the Mansfield and Camel's Hump Mountains, the two highest in the State. On the opposite side, loomed up before us the Adirondack Mountains, in all their awful grandeur, where, at North Elba,

> "John Brown's body lies a-mouldering in the grave,
> But his soul is marching on."[5]

For the most part, the sky was somewhat overcast, though not to hide the view at any time; but on our return, when our boat was in a position directly opposite, in an air line, (though some twenty-five miles off,) where the noble dead was buried, the sun burst out effulgently, as he was near his setting, and covered the mountains with a [. . .][6] of glory, which I have never seen equalled, setting the clouds on fire, and enrapturing the eyes of all the passengers. It was a remarkable coincidence, and in superstitious times would have been deemed a miraculous display and interposition.

Lake Champlain is the widest directly opposite Burlington, about nine miles. The shore is very irregular, but fertile, and extremely beautiful as far as we went. You and the children would have enjoyed the trip beyond any thing you ever saw.

To-morrow, should the weather prove favorable, Mr. Bigelow is to drive us in his carriage to several interesting places in the vicinity. We may leave here Wednesday morning, or may remain till Thursday. Montreal we shall not visit; but we may conclude to visit Lake George, in case the steamers still run, in which case I shall not get home till next week. Otherwise, I shall try to be with you Saturday evening. I shall hope to hear from some one of you before I leave this place.

Should we not go to Lake George, we shall in all probability, on our way back, stop at the [Aaron] Powells at Ghent, at least for one night—as I expect to return by the way of Troy, Springfield and Worcester.

I am feeling very well, but my hoarseness is a great annoyance to me in the matter of conversation, and will probably continue till I get home, when I can better attend to it.

Burlington is all, in point of situation, that it was described to me. It lies on the Lake very much as Newburyport does on the Merrimack, and has no peer in New England, in the sublimity and beauty of its surroundings. Even 14, Dix Place, cannot compare with it, except on the score of its inhabitants! We are very fortunate in finding so kind and hospitable a friend in Mr. Bigelow. He has five children to match our own—three sons[7] and two daughters, two of the former being attached to the army of the Potomac, though the youngest is now here for more recruits.

Wherever we travel, we see soldiers hurrying to the seat of war, or to their several encampments. Poor fellows, how many of them are doomed never again to see their beloved State, or "home, sweet home!"

In all my journeyings, I carry you and the children in my heart of hearts, and regret that we cannot be all bodily together every step of the way. Glad as you and they may be to see me, my own joy on getting home will be equal in kind and degree.

Give my kindest regards to Charlotte Coffin, lady Otis, and all inquiring friends;[8] and accept, for yourself the heart's purest and warmest love of

Your husband,

Wm. Lloyd Garrison.

ALS: Garrison Papers, Boston Public Library.

1. A distinguished hotel at the corner of Main and St. Paul streets, which operated between 1808 and 1893. (Charles Edwin Allen, *About Burlington, Vermont,* Burlington, 1905; Hamilton Child, *Gazetteer and Business Directory of Chittenden County, Vermont, for 1882–1883,* Syracuse, N.Y., 1882.)

2. Lawrence Goodhue Bigelow (1810–1867) was a prosperous lumber dealer; he does not seem to have been a reformer. (Gilman Bigelow Howe, *Genealogy of the Bigelow Family of America . . .,* Worcester, Mass., 1890.)

John Brown's grave was at his farm in North Elba, to which his second wife, Mary, had removed the body following his execution. After 1870 the farm and grave were preserved by Kate Field and nineteen other interested persons; in 1896 the property was deeded to the state of New York, which has since maintained it as an historic site. (Letter to the editor from Edwin N. Cotter, Jr., superintendent, John Brown's Farm, Lake Placid, N.Y., August 22, 1974.)

3. Possibly Garrison refers to Gamaliel Bradford Sawyer (1801–1868), a lawyer admitted to the Chittenden County Bar in 1822. He was a literate and popular man, though he is not known to have been connected with the University of Vermont. (Letter to the editor from Mary C. Johnson, Vermont Historical Society, August 29, 1974.)

Irvin McDowell (1818–1885), after graduating from West Point in 1838 and serving in various capacities in the army, became a brigadier general in 1861 and commander of the army of the Potomac and the department of northeastern Virginia. After the disastrous first battle of Bull Run he was relieved of command, though he remained in charge of a division. After the second battle of Bull Run, during which he was in command of the third corps of the Army of Virginia, his conduct was censured and he was again removed. Although ultimately exonerated, he never afterward fought in the field. In his last days he moved to San Francisco, where he participated in many local activities.

Like McDowell a graduate of the Military Academy, Don Carlos Buell (1818–1898) was a professional soldier of varied experience. A brigadier general at the beginning of the Civil War, he helped organize the Army of the Potomac. By the time of Garrison's letter he had been promoted to major general, United States Volunteers. Though he had had early successes, expecially at Shiloh, he was much criticized for dilatory tactics in Tennessee and Kentucky. On October 8, 1862, he had engaged the forces of General Bragg at Perryville with uncertain effect; on the twenty-fourth he was to be relieved of his command. In 1864 he resigned from the army and took up mining in Kentucky.

4. Bigelow is known to have had two daughters: Susan A. (c. 1843–1872) and Elisabeth T. (c. 1846–1925); his niece has not been identified. (Letter to the editor from Mary C. Johnson, August 29, 1974.)

5. Although the words to the old tune have been attributed to many, Thomas Brigham Bishop has most often been given credit.

6. Illegible.

7. George H. (1838–1888), Lawrence L. or G. (1840–1879), and Lucius L. Bigelow (born c. 1842). (Letter to the editor from Mary C. Johnson, August 29, 1974.)

8. Garrison probably refers to Lucinda Smith Otis (1784–1865), widow of George A. Otis, who is identified in the letter to John A. Andrew, January 17, 1865.

"Watch Meeting, Waiting for the Hour, Dec. 31st. 1862,"
from an oil painting by William Tolman Carlton

"Emancipation," wood engraving after Thomas Nast,
published in Philadelphia by Samuel Bott, 1865

"(?) Slavery is Dead(?)," wood engraving after Thomas Nast,
Harper's Weekly, January 12, 1867

"Verdict, 'Hang the D—— Yankee and Nigger,'"
wood engraving after Thomas Nast,
Harper's Weekly, March 23, 1867

4 9

TO OLIVER JOHNSON

Boston, Dec. 14, 1862.

Dear Johnson:

In consequence of the fearful rise in the price of white paper, the Executive Committee of the American A. S. Society, at a meeting held to consider the subject, have unanimously decided to raise the subscription price of the Standard to $2.50 from the first of January, 1863; and they desire me to inform you of this change, that you may announce it in your next number, giving the reason for it in the enhanced price of printing material, and the state of the treasury of the Society.[1] Of course, the Committee have come to this conclusion most reluctantly; but they see no other way to meet the added expense. True, it may, and probably will, somewhat diminish the circulation of the Standard; but the risk must be taken, or we shall be compelled to suspend its publication even before the annual meeting,[2] for lack of means.

The Liberator must also change its subscription price from $2.50 to $3.00; and this may fatally cripple its circulation, and so end its existence. But the added expense of a thousand dollars on white paper can be met in no other way. To keep the price at $2.50 will certainly make it necessary to stop the paper, and to raise it to $3.00 may lead to a similar result. It is a desperate state of things; and all the more as the Liberator has been hitherto 50 cents dearer per annum than other weekly papers. Besides, the *Commonwealth* is likely to draw off subscribers, and to prevent the getting of new ones, as it is offered for $2.00; though it must sink a good deal of money, and may not be published more than one year.[3] If slavery were really abolished, I should care very little about the continuance of the Liberator or Standard, or the American Anti-Slavery Society, but, until emancipation come, I do hope these instrumentalities will remain in the field, as hitherto. At all events, we will (if need be) "go down with our colors nailed to the mast-head."[4]

I regret you were not able to get the official notice of the National Subscription Anniversary in the last Standard, on account of the shortness of the time.[5] Do not forget to add to the signers the names of Lydia Maria Child, Sarah Blake Shaw, and Abby Kelley Foster—placing that of Mrs. Child at the head of the list, as it stood last year.[6]

I write in such haste, for lack of time, that I can only add that I am, as always,

Faithfully yours,

Wm. Lloyd Garrison.

ALS: Garrison Papers, Boston Public Library; extract printed in *Life*, IV, 65, note 1.

1. The executive committee, consisting of William I. Bowditch, Maria W. Chapman, Charles Follen, Jr., Garrison, Sydney Howard Gay, Edmund Jackson, Samuel May, Jr., Wendell Phillips, Edmund Quincy, Anne Warren Weston, Charles King Whipple, and Henry C. Wright, met in a special emergency session. The *National Anti-Slavery Standard* printed the notice of the increase in subscription price December 20.

2. Usually held in the first full week of May.

3. The *Commonwealth*, established in 1861 as the weekly organ of the Emancipation League of Boston, was esteemed for its literary as well as its antislavery content; it was published from 1862 until 1869, with Moncure Conway as editor for the first two years and Franklin B. Sanborn from 1863 to 1869. (*Life*, IV, 48; *ULS*.)

4. Possibly Garrison adapts Walter Scott, *Marmion*, Introduction to Canto I, st. 10: "And nail'd her colors to the mast."

5. The twenty-ninth National Anti-Slavery Subscription Festival, which was announced in the *Standard* for December 20, took place January 28, 1863, and raised more than $3,600. A report of the festival was printed in *The Liberator*, February 20, 1863, and in the *Standard*, February 21, 1863.

6. Lydia Maria Francis Child (1802–1880) had acquired some distinction as an author of didactic novels before she married Boston lawyer David Lee Child, and the couple became prominent abolitionists. She wrote several effective works concerned with the cause: *An·Appeal in Favor of that Class of Americans Called Africans* (1833), *Correspondence between Lydia Maria Child and Governor Wise and Mrs. Mason* (1860), *The Right Way, the Safe Way* (1860), *The Freedmen's Book* (1865). She and her husband had also edited the *National Anti-Slavery Standard* from 1841 to 1849.

Sarah Blake Sturgis Shaw (1815–1902), daughter of Boston merchant Nathan Russell Sturgis, married her cousin Francis George Shaw. In 1863 Mrs. Shaw served on the board of managers of the National Anti-Slavery Subscription Anniversary. The Shaws entertained Garrison on a number of occasions. (*Life; The Liberator*, January 9, 1863; New York City Death Records, 1902.)

Abby Kelley Foster (1810–1887) was a Lynn schoolteacher who became a Garrisonian abolitionist through reading *The Liberator*. Already active as secretary of the Lynn Female Anti-Slavery Society, she became one of the founders of the New England Non-Resistant Society in 1838. The following year she began her career as agitator and lecturer for woman's rights. In 1845 she married Stephen S. Foster, and in 1856 she broke with Garrison and advocated the use of political action to effect abolition. In her later years she was increasingly occupied with the woman's rights movement. (*NAW.*)

III WAR FOR FREEDOM: 1863

GARRISON'S INITIAL REACTION to the preliminary Emancipation Proclamation in September 1862 was hardly enthusiastic, since he felt it should be more extreme. But the first week in January 1863, he delayed putting *The Liberator* to press in order to print (on January 2 as well as in many subsequent issues) the full text of the final Proclamation of January 1. In the Proclamation Lincoln enumerated the states then in rebellion and declared "all persons held as slaves, within said designated States and parts of States, are and hereafter shall be free." Garrison was excited and optimistic: "It is a great historic event, sublime in its magnitude, momentous and beneficient in its far-reaching consequences, and eminently just and right alike to the oppressor and the opressed, as well as imperatively called for by the fearfully imperilled state of the country. THE PEOPLE will sustain it—the army will receive fresh inspiration—and all Rebeldom be filled with consternation in view of their inevitable doom."

By spring, however, Garrison was beginning to rethink his position regarding both the Proclamation and the Constitution. On March 13 he wrote in *The Liberator* that since slavery was in open rebellion against both the Union and the Constitution, "we demand of the President, under the war power, a proclamation of IMMEDIATE AND UNIVERSAL EMANCIPATION! Every hour's delay is attended with danger, criminality, and a needless prolongation of the war." In a letter to Samuel J. May on April 6 he suggested that generals like Frémont, Butler, Sigel, and Phelps had been removed to propitiate Copperheads and that the Proclamation seemed to have had "little effect at the South." In an editorial on April 24 he recollected an earlier occasion when, on July 4, 1854, he publicly burned the Constitution. Should the war end, he said, with a compromise on the issue of slavery, "we shall again give that instrument to the consuming fire, and renew our protest against it as 'a covenant with death and an agreement with hell.' "

War became a personal reality for Garrison in the spring of 1863 when his oldest son, George Thompson, considered enlisting in the army. On June 11 Garrison wrote George an affectionate and touching letter in which he tried to be both a good father and a consistent nonresistant. He expressed his fears that as the son of a well-known abolitionist serving in a black regiment, the Massachusetts 55th, he would be subject to special danger. Despite his father's concern George did enlist in the 55th, and his service during the remainder of the war may well have been the most fulfilling period of his life.

During 1863 Garrison remained concerned about American relations with Great Britain and the possibility of British recognition of the Confederacy. He wrote Oliver Johnson on March 10, agreeing that Wendell Phillips, despite his "aversion to England," should undertake a British mission. At first Phillips was receptive, and Garrison endeavored to persuade him through associates in New York City. "It is a splendid opportunity for Phillips," he wrote, "to do pre-eminent service to the world-wide cause of liberty and international peace." Garrison also tried to induce Gerrit Smith to go to England, thinking that he and Phillips would be a winning combination, but Smith thought that Garrison himself would be the most appropriate person to visit England and offered to help raise funds for his expenses.

In the meantime, Moncure D. Conway, liberal minister and Virginian turned abolitionist, successfully raised money to finance his own mission to England. Garrison sponsored his trip, which began in April, to the extent of writing Conway several letters of introduction to British abolitionists. During this period the Confederacy has been represented in Europe by two diplomats—in England by James M. Mason (author of the Fugitive Slave Law) and in France by John Slidell. In November 1861 Mason and Slidell's mission had triggered the *Trent* affair, an international incident that could have led to war.[1] Predictably, Conway, recently arrived in London, had a difference of opinion with Mason during the summer of 1863, the altercation taking the form of letters printed in *The Times* of London on June 19. Mason expressed the view that the North was determined not so much to free the slaves, who would be freed anyway, as to subjugate the South. Conway promised that American abolitionists would oppose the war if the South began immediately

---

1. For more information concerning the *Trent* affair, see the letter to Oliver Johnson, December 26, 1861, n. 5.

to emancipate the slaves. In his reply Mason questioned Conway's authority to represent the abolitionists and insisted vehemently that the South would not negotiate with the North. Recognizing the importance of the controversy and feeling personally involved, owing to his prior support of Conway, Garrison stated his position in a letter to the New York *Tribune* (printed June 30, 1863). He denied that Conway represented American abolitionists any more than "every other eloquent and devoted friend of freedom who desires to see the rebellion speedily suppressed, and slavery as speedily abolished." He asserted also that the federal government was committed by the Proclamation to free the slaves and that it would be inappropriate "to solicit the traitors to do that . . . which has been wisely and constitutionally done by President Lincoln to save the Republic." Although many abolitionists reacted to the controversy in the way Garrison did, it may be that Conway's attack on Mason was an important factor in changing British public opinion and defeating in Parliament the Roebuck bill, which provided for British support of the Confederacy.

As usual, the letters of 1863 make reference to various abolitionists. In the spring Garrison writes about George Thompson's precarious financial position and the need for raising funds for him through an international testimonial in his honor. Wendell Phillips is mentioned frequently and respectfully. Garrison lists him first among the speakers he contemplated for the third-decade annual meeting of the American Anti-Slavery Society in Philadelphia in December. Although he was never a close associate, Theodore D. Weld does appear sporadically in the letters for this year; Garrison was especially pleased to receive his photograph.

At the end of the year an event occurred that was to alter the course of Garrison's family life. On the night of Tuesday, December 29, Helen Garrison suffered a severe stroke that left her left side paralyzed, her mind confused, and her speech impaired. Although of late her health had seemed good (early in the month she had especially enjoyed a trip to Philadelphia with her husband and two sons), she had had the warning of a slight paralytic attack in April of 1862. Symptoms from the new attack abated gradually, and for a time Garrison hoped for a complete recovery. Letters for subsequent years describe various treatments aimed at restoring her health, but she remained incapacitated until her death in 1876. Garrison carried in his mind for the rest of his life the indelible image of his invalid wife sitting by the window, awaiting his return.

50

TO JOHN GREENLEAF WHITTIER

Boston, Jan. 13, 1863.

Dear Whittier:

I am requested by the ladies, Managers of the National Anti-Slavery Subscription Anniversary[1] to be held in Music Hall on the evening of the 28th instant, to entreat you, (not for their sakes, but in behalf of the glorious cause of impartial liberty so long espoused by you and them,) to write an Emancipation poem,—if the spirit move, and may it do so powerfully!—to be read or sung on that occasion. Let it be your latest gift upon the altar of freedom and humanity. Be it long or short, it will be greatly prized and gratefully acknowledged.

Rejoicing that the great body of the slaves are declared free by the President's Proclamation, I remain, my dear W.,

Yours, to break *every* yoke,[2]

Wm. Lloyd Garrison.

J. G. Whittier.

ALS: The Whittier Home, Amesbury, Massachusetts.

John Greenleaf Whittier (1807–1892), the Quaker poet, abolitionist, and editor, had long been Garrison's friend and associate in the cause of abolition. In fact, Whittier's poetry had first been published in 1826, in Garrison's paper, the Newburyport *Free Press*. Although Whittier did write a poem ("The Proclamation") on the occasion of the Emancipation Proclamation, it is not known to have been connected in any way with the subscription anniversary.

1. The following is a list of managers of the National Anti-Slavery Subscription Anniversary as given in *The Liberator*, January 9, 1863: Lydia Maria Child, Mary Goddard May, Lydia M. Parker, Louisa Loring, Henrietta Sargent, Sarah Russell May, Helen E. Garrison, Anna Shaw Greene, Sarah Blake Shaw, Caroline C. Thayer, Mattie Griffith, Mary Jackson, Evelina A. Smith, Caroline M. Severance, Elizabeth N. Gay, Ann Rebecca Bramhall, Sarah H. Southwick, Sarah P. Remond, Mary Willey, Abby H. Stevenson, Sarah J. Nowell, Elizabeth von Arnum, Eliza Apthorp, Sarah Cowing, Abby Kelley Foster, Mary E. Stearns, Mary Elizabeth Sargent, Sarah C. Atkinson, Abby Francis, Mary Jane Parkman, Georgina Otis, Katherine Earle Farnum.
2. A reference to Isaiah 58:6.

5 1

TO RALPH WALDO EMERSON

Boston, Jan. 13, 1863.

Dear Mr. Emerson:

The annual National Anti-Slavery Subscription Anniversary is to be held at Music Hall, in this city, on Wednesday evening, 28th inst. The ladies who have the management thereof desire me to solicit your presence on that occasion, to say a cheering word as the spirit may prompt, in company with Wendell Phillips and M. D. Conway.[1] The design is not to exact a set speech. If it be among the possibilities, I trust you will gratify them, and the multitude of estimable friends of freedom and humanity who will be in attendance. Of course, whatever expense you may be put to will be gladly defrayed.

With high regard for your genius, virtue and philanthropy, I remain,

Yours, to break *every* yoke,

Wm. Lloyd Garrison.

R. W. Emerson, Esq.

ALS: Ralph Waldo Emerson Papers, Harvard College Library. This letter is printed by courtesy of the Ralph Waldo Emerson Memorial Association.

1. Neither Emerson nor Phillips attended the subscription anniversary. William Wells Brown, Moncure D. Conway, and Garrison spoke briefly, but their speeches were not reported or reprinted in the antislavery newspapers. (*The Liberator*, February 20, 1863; *National Anti-Slavery Standard*, February 7, 1863; Ralph I. Rusk, ed., *The Letters of Ralph Waldo Emerson*, 6 vols., New York, 1939.)

5 2

TO OLIVER JOHNSON

Boston, March 10, 1863.

Dear Johnson:

As soon as I got your letter of inquiry this forenoon, I went up to the Adjutant General's office[1] at the State House, and had a careful examination made of the Roster of the 16th Regiment, but no such name as James Lathrop could be found among either officers or privates. I then took the Boston Almanac, for 1862, which contained the names of all the men enlisted in all the Regiments; and my search was equally vain to find the name wanted. Unless Mary

Anne, therefore, can get some information much more explicit and definite from her mysterious visitant, it will be useless to look any further; and Jessie Long may still be permitted to indulge the pleasing hope that her "[lover]" may yet make his appearance in the flesh, to join his fate with hers.[2] The whole affair, however, is curious.

Your *carte de visite*, so kindly sent some days ago, is a decided improvement upon the former one, and received the unanimous preference of the household. We are, of course, very much obliged to you for it.

As soon as I got your letter which enclosed it, and which contained your earnestly expressed conviction that Phillips ought to go to England without delay, in view of the anti-slavery demonstrations bursting out in every part of the Kingdom, I sent it to him and his wife for their consideration; adding the expression of my own conviction of the immense value and importance of such a mission at such a grand historic period.[3] As he immediately left the city on a lecturing tour, I was not able to see him till some days afterward. But, knowing P's aversion to England, and remembering how severe had been his criticisms upon her since the war broke out, I did not dare indulge the slightest hope that he would give a moment's heed to the proposition.[4] I was gratified and encouraged, therefore, on talking the matter over with him, to hear him say that he would take the suggestion into serious consideration. And now that he is going to New York, and will take this along with him, I want you to renew the proposition, and to get Tilton, Smalley and Gay to bring their influence to bear upon his mind towards securing a favorable conclusion.[5] At the longest, he need not be absent, unless he chose, more than four months; during which time he could address crowded meetings in Liverpool, Manchester, Birmingham, London, Sheffield, Leeds, Newcastle, Edinburgh, Glasgow, &c., and do much towards confirming and securing the British public sentiment in opposition to any official recognition of the Southern Confederacy, and in hearty support of President Lincoln and the Government. It is a splendid opportunity for Phillips to do pre-eminent service to the world-wide cause of liberty and international peace. I do not think Mrs. Phillips will throw any obstacle in the way of his going. Before receiving your letter, I had earnestly entreated Gerrit Smith (on his late visit here) to go to England this spring, on precisely such a mission, believing he also would make a most favorable impression upon the public mind of that country, and in private do a great work for us. He modestly declined, for various reasons, but I got Mrs. Smith, and Mr. and Mrs. Miller, to second my motion, and I am not without hope that he will yet consent to take the trip.[6] In a note received from him at Albany, he says— "Your last words were, 'Remember England!' But to-night's news of the great Emancipation meetings in England makes me feel that she can get along very well without my help.[7] If any American Abolitionist visits England it must, I think, be you. To this end, the friends should make you up a purse of a thousand dollars; and I will contribute a hundred dollars of it." A handsome compliment, an ingenious evasion, and a generous overture! But I shall renew my importunity to have him go—and all the more, as he has never visited England, and on that account, as well as on that of his transatlantic fame as a philanthropist and champion of the slave, would be assure to attract great attention. If Phillips and he would go together! "What a team" they would be! There is scope for both of them.

Moncure D. Conway is endeavoring to raise the means to go to England in April, and, as a Virginian, in addition to the brilliancy of his talents, would be a potent witness as against [Jefferson] Davis, Mason, Slidell, &c.[8]

It will be thirty years in May since my first, and seventeen since my last visit to England. I confess, it would give me unspeakable joy to see my English, Scottish and Irish friends once more, nor should I hesitate to go if I could afford the expense. But I do not feel willing to go at the expense of others, as suggested by Mr. Smith, because I am already too deeply indebted to my friends on the score of pecuniary kindnesses; and having been three times across the Atlantic, I must consider the last my farewell visit.

Use all power of persuasion with Phillips to go, and I will do all I can to get Smith to change his mind.

I shall write to Theodore about a plan for the benefit of George Thompson, which I am sure will receive your approval and co-operation.[9]

Three of our family have been down with incipient diptheria— Wendell, Fanny, and Frank—but they are now convalescent. William to-day complains that his throat is badly affected.

With warm regards to Mary Anne, Mrs. Savin, &c., &c., I remain, Always yours,

Wm. Lloyd Garrison.

ALS: Garrison Papers, Boston Public Library.

1. William Schouler (1814–1872), who had earlier held a similar post in Ohio, was the adjutant general of Massachusetts between 1860 and 1867.

2. Although the curious affair involving the unidentified Jessie Long cannot be accurately described, James Lathrop could be James Roosevelt Lathrop (1844–1907) who did serve in the United States Cavalry in 1862 (the 6th rather than the 16th Reg-

iment) and who later became superintendent of Roosevelt Hospital in New York City. (Obituary, New York *Times*, March 13, 1907.)

The editor has accepted the reading of "lover" for the word Garrison inserted in quotation marks, although the correction in Garrison's hand makes the meaning difficult to decipher. It would seem that he first wrote "Jamy" and then wrote over it "lover."

3. George Thompson had been urging Phillips to go abroad to strengthen English support for the North, but his wife's illness prevented his going. (Oscar Sherwin, *Prophet of Liberty: The Life and Times of Wendell Phillips*, New York, 1958, p. 479.)

Ann Greene Phillips (1813–1886) was the daughter of wealthy Boston merchant Benjamin Greene. Orphaned at an early age, she had become interested in reform while living with her aunt and uncle, Maria W. and Henry G. Chapman. Despite her chronic ill health, she exerted a great influence on Wendell Phillips following their marriage in 1837. (Irving H. Bartlett, *Wendell Phillips, Brahmin Radical*, Boston, 1961.)

4. Phillips' speech at the Music Hall in Boston, December 4, 1861 (repeated in New York, December 29), clearly expressed his hostility to England. He said that notwithstanding the liberal middle class, English merchants and aristocrats were ready to commit the "selfish and treacherous" English government to the cause of the South. (*National Anti-Slavery Standard*, December 7, 1861; Wendell Phillips, *Speeches, Lectures, and Letters*, 1884; reprint, New York, 1968.)

5. George Washburn Smalley (1833–1916), a graduate of the Harvard Law School, had, with the help of Wendell Phillips, whose adopted daughter Phoebe Garnaut he had married in 1862, become a distinguished journalist. During the Civil War he served at the front as the New York *Tribune*'s war correspondent. Between 1866 and 1895 he was in charge of all the *Tribune*'s foreign correspondence.

Sydney Howard Gay (1814–1888), early trained as a lawyer, was a dedicated abolitionist and a professional journalist, editor, and author. He edited the *National Anti-Slavery Standard* between 1842 and 1856 and then joined the New York *Tribune* in 1857, becoming its managing editor after 1862. In 1867 he became managing editor of the Chicago *Tribune*, returning to New York after the fire of 1871 to be an editor of the *Evening Post*. He was the ghostwriter of a history of the United States for which his chief editor, William Cullen Bryant, received credit; he also published a biography of James Madison in 1884.

6. Gerrit Smith's daughter Elizabeth (1822–1911), who had married lawyer Charles Dudley Miller (1818–1896), was an early advocate of woman's suffrage; to her goes credit for designing the famous "Bloomer" costume. Mr and Mrs. Miller were among the signers of the call for the first National Woman's Rights Convention held in Worcester, Mass., in 1850. They had four children: Gerrit Smith (born 1845), Charles Dudley (1847), William Fitzhugh (1850), and Ann Fitzhugh (1856). Despite whatever influence the Millers and Garrison brought to bear, Gerrit Smith did not go to England. (*NAW;* Ralph V. Harlow, *Gerrit Smith, Philanthropist and Reformer*, New York, 1939, pp. 16–17.)

7. Shortly after Lincoln's Emancipation Proclamation there was a series of enthusiastic meetings in England supporting both the Proclamation and the Union cause. *The Liberator*, for instance, reported meetings in London and Bristol, some of which were organized by the Thompson-dominated London Emancipation Society. (*The Liberator*, February 20 and 27, 1863.)

8. Moncure D. Conway did go to England and became, in fact, the minister of the South Place Chapel in London, a post he held until 1884 and again from 1892 to 1897. (*Standard*, April 11, 1863.)

James Murray Mason (1798–1871), the grandson of Revolutionary statesman George Mason, was born in Georgetown, now a part of Washington, D.C. After graduating from the University of Pennsylvania and the law school at the College of William and Mary, he practiced his profession in Winchester, Va. He was elected to the state legislature in 1826, to Congress in 1837, and to the Senate in 1847, where he was serving at the beginning of the Civil War. The champion of southern rights, he had been the author of the Fugitive Slave Bill in 1850. In November 1861 he and John Slidell were sent as Confederate diplomatic commissioners to England and France respectively. Following the war he took refuge in Canada until a proclamation of amnesty enabled him to return to Virginia in 1868.

John Slidell (1793–1871), originally from New York City, was a Louisiana politician and Confederate diplomat. Having moved to New Orleans in 1819, he became in succession district attorney, member of Congress, and United States senator. He served the Confederacy in France during the war and remained in that country until his death.

9. Garrison initiated a testimonial for George Thompson in March 1863 and urged Theodore Tilton and Oliver Johnson to publicize the nonpartisan effort. Although little information is available concerning the testimonial, it is clear in later Garrison letters that the effort failed dismally. Suggestions for reviving the testimonial were to be made in 1867 while Garrison was in England, but Garrison himself thought such attempts would be inexpedient, since Thompson had alienated many of his friends. In 1869, however, a testimonial committee was to be organized with a goal of raising £2,000, and in 1870 at least part of that sum was presented to Thompson. (See the letters to Theodore Tilton, March 10, 1863, below, and March 16, 1863 [micro.].)

53

TO THEODORE TILTON

Boston, March 10, 1863.

My Dear Tilton:

You are so noble, generous and appreciative in your nature, that I not only have no hesitancy, but rather the greatest delight, in submitting for your consideration a proposition for a substantial pecuniary testimonial to George Thompson, Esq., for his splendid, untiring, and wonderfully successful efforts to call forth the old anti-slavery spirit of England in its grandest demonstrations, and to turn the current of English feeling into a Niagara against the Secession element in that country. To him, mainly, is our country indebted for this unexpected and immensely important change, both by the formation of the London Emancipation Society and by his lectures in every part of the Kingdom.[1] It seems to me, therefore, a most opportune period to show him a substantial appreciation for what he has done and is doing in this respect; and I cannot doubt that there are hundreds of gentlemen, in the various States, outside of the Abolition ranks, who, if personally appealed to, would readily, and in many cases generously, subscribe to raise a sum for the benefit of Mr. Thompson and his family, in view of such unsolicited, disinterested and valuable services. I would make the appeal not an Abolition one, but an American one, on the score of free institutions, and aid rendered our country and government at a most critical period. Thus no old or new prejudices would be excited, and the reasonableness of the appeal would commend it to every generous mind. I think such men as Gov. Andrew, [Charles] Sumner, Wilson, in our State, and others like them in other States, will be ready to favor the project, if not with publicity, at least privately; and, doubtless, there are liberal-minded merchants who would also respond.[2]

Please confer with [Sidney Howard] Gay, [George] Smalley, [Oliver] Johnson, [Henry Ward] Beecher, and any others you choose, about it, and let me know your conclusions as soon as convenient. Consult [Wendell] Phillips, as his counsel will be valuable and judicious. My impression is that a considerable sum can easily be raised; and if ever man deserved it, it is George Thompson, for what he has suffered at the hands of this guilty country, and nobly done to save her from destruction. Of course, the plan to be successful will require personal applications, near and remote, to be made in behalf of a responsible committee; but, in addition to this, I think an impetus might be given to it if the Tribune, Evening Post, (and I confidently count upon the good will of the Post,) and the Independent, should each refer to the meritorious services of Mr. Thompson for several months past, and suggest sending subscriptions to a Treasurer in New York,—either yourself or Mr. Gay, for instance,—as *a public testimonial*.[3]

When the whole amount shall have been raised, I would advise that an investment should be safely made of it for the relief of Mr. Thompson and family, to be used discreetly, with certain limitations. Of course, in the present ruinous rate of foreign exchange, I would not attempt to put it into gold; but let it remain on interest here, till exchange is nearly equal.

I enclose a printed slip, containing a letter from Mr. Thompson, referring to the lectures delivered by him; also, an abstract of one of his speeches; and an advertisement of a soiree in honor of his services. I have had a hundred copies printed, to be sent to gentlemen, with the appeal, who may need a little posting as to what Mr. Thompson has done. Can a committee of well known and respectable gentlemen be raised in your city to act in this matter, either for the city, the State, or on a wider scale?[4]

Ever truly yours,

Wm. Lloyd Garrison.

Theodore Tilton, Esq.

☞ Of course, Mr. Thompson knows nothing of this, and dreams of nothing of the kind.

ALS: William Lloyd Garrison Miscellaneous Manuscripts, New-York Historical Society.

1. Because of the inactivity of the British and Foreign Anti-Slavery Society, the London Emancipation Society was formed in 1862 to encourage the abolition of slavery and British support of the Union cause. George Thompson was chairman of the society, and John Stuart Mill, John Bright, and Newman Hall were active members. Branch societies were formed in Birmingham and in Manchester. (*Life; The Liberator,* February 6 and 27, 1863.)

2. John Albion Andrew (1818–1867), a native of Maine and a graduate of Bowdoin College, had moved to Boston in 1837, entering the bar in 1840. Andrew was a conscientious abolitionist and one of the organizers of the Free-Soil party. Active in local politics since the 1840s, he was elected governor of the state in 1860. In 1866–1867 he was chairman of the committee to raise funds as a testimonial to Garrison.

Henry Wilson (1812–1875), from a poor New Hampshire family, had risen from shoemaker to shoe manufacturer, to editor, to politician. Between 1848 and 1851 he edited the Boston *Republican*. Following 1840 he served in the Massachusetts legislature, being president of the state Senate in 1851–1852. In 1855 he was elected to the United States Senate, where for the next twenty years he was the champion of many controversial causes, including the abolition of slavery and prejudice and the establishment of rights and privileges for the working man.

3. Before the date of Garrison's letter, *The Liberator* had already taken the lead in publicizing Thompson's contribution to abolition and to the Union cause; in the issue for February 27 an abundance of material was printed. Although it is understandable that Garrison should expect the support of the New York *Evening Post*, which had for years been edited by William Cullen Bryant as a liberal and even pro-abolitionist organ, in fact neither that paper nor the *Tribune* printed material about Thompson at this time. Only the *Independent* responded. The issue for March 19, 1863, carried a laudatory biographical sketch of him, a note on a London soirée in his honor, and a suggestion that "the time has come . . . [for] some expression or testimonial" to him, though without a specific request for donations.

The further history of the *Post* is of interest, in that the paper was to be purchased in 1881 by Garrison's son-in-law, Henry Villard, and Wendell Phillips Garrison was to become its literary editor.

4. Since a committee such as Garrison suggests is not mentioned either in the abolitionist or the New York press, it would seem that it never materialized.

54

TO JOHN A. ANDREW

Boston, April 6, 1863.

Gov. Andrew:

Dear Sir—On the first day of January last, the President of the United States issued his Proclamation, emancipating forever three millions of slaves in Rebeldom, as a military necessity, and to bring the war to a speedy termination. A measure so in accordance with the claims of justice and humanity, and yet so needing the official sanction of every loyal State to give it efficacy, deserved to receive the cordial endorsement of the Legislature of Massachusetts at the earliest possible opportunity. That opportunity was fortunately presented almost as soon as the Proclamation made its appearance; but, though that body has been in session from the first week in January till now, it has taken no action upon the Proclamation, and therefore given it no sanction or even recognition. What should have been done early had better be done late, than not done at all.[1] Should the Legislature adjourn, without sustaining the President to the extent he has gone in this matter, an evil use will be made of the fact by the enemies of the Administration, and they will boldly claim that not even "radical, fanatical Massachusetts" was so radical or fanatical as to give her official endorsement to such an "unconstitutional" measure! As the Legislature will very shortly adjourn, there is no time to be lost. Pardon me for bringing this subject to your special attention. As all the fierce, "copperhead" opposition to the President is raised with special reference to the Proclamation,[2] and the vital issue is upon its being sustained, Massachusetts ought to put upon the historic page her most emphatic approval of his course.

Very truly yours,

Wm. Lloyd Garrison.

His Ex. Gov. Andrew.

ALS: John A. Andrew Papers, Massachusetts Historical Society.

1. Although the state legislature never passed a resolution specifically supporting the Emancipation Proclamation, on March 27, 1863, the governor proclaimed a day for fasting, humiliation, and prayer. Resolutions were passed on April 29, affirming the state's loyalty to the Union and the federal government and supporting "all the laws, acts, and proclamations by which the goverment aims to preserve the national integrity, and to enforce the national authority," as well as all efforts in the "cause of universal freedom and humanity." (Letter to the editor from Ruth Bell, researcher, January 20, 1972; *The Liberator,* May 1, 1863.)

2. The term "Copperhead" originated in the New York *Tribune,* July 20, 1861, in reference to Democrats critical of Lincoln's war policy. By extension, it came to mean any northerner sympathetic to the South.

55

TO SAMUEL J. MAY

Boston, April 6, 1863.

Dear friend May:

Your cousin [Samuel May, Jr.] writes to me from Leicester, that he learns that Theodore D. Weld lectured in Syracuse, a few days since; and as our Executive Committee are very desirous that he should be one of the speakers at the approaching anniversary of the American Anti-Slavery Society, in the Rev. Dr. [George B.] Cheever's church, I send a note for him, at a venture, informing him of their wishes—thinking it very probable that, if he is not in Syracuse, you will know where to send it, so that he get it with the least possible delay.[1] It is possible he may have gone to visit Gerrit Smith, at Peterboro', where he has a son who has long been a poor invalid.[2] Weld has never appeared on a public platform in the city of New York, and we trust he will now be disposed to come forward.

How pleasant it would be to me, and to many others, to see you at that anniversary! But as between that and the New England Anti-Slavery Convention,—if you cannot be present at both,—I would prefer to have you at the latter, as your visit would be much more enjoyable.[3]

How slow is the progress of the army and navy in subduing the rebellious South! I have no faith in [Henry W.] Halleck, Grant, or Banks, to say nothing of others.[4] The policy of the Administration is singularly paradoxical and self-defeating. Think of such men as Fremont, Butler, Sigel and Phelps laid upon the shelf, to propitiate the "copperhead" element of the North![5] No wonder the Proclamation of January 1st has produced so little effect at the South. But, perhaps, the more blindness and hardness of heart,—the more involved and desperate the struggle,—the more sure is the liberation of our enslaved countrymen. Freedom is to be won by judgment, not by repentance. No matter where a Pharaoh exists, or where a Moses and Aaron demand, in the name of the Lord, that he should let the oppressed go free. They will be driven from his presence, and he will require plague after plague before he will give up his prey.[6]

How vulgar and brutal, and yet how fearfully prevalent, is the spirit of colorphobia at the North! I am shocked to see how an all-wise God is constantly mocked and outraged in the person of the un-offending negro, even by those who claim to be refined, humane and Christian. Slavery has done a deadly and most atheistical work in engendering this spirit. It is to the soul as leprosy to the body.

The mildness of the past winter was any thing but favorable to the general health. As a family, we have had our share of illness. I have suffered a good deal from my implacable enemy, the catarrh. Wife, Wendell, Fanny and Franky have had the diptheria, but not of a malignant type. We are now all once more in usual health.

"Aunt" Charlotte Coffin calls to see us frequently, and is now at Dix Place, "as usual," she desires me to say—to which I will add, "as usual" assisting wife in the most indefatigable and disinterested manner, making her presence not only always most agreeable, but in every possible way truly serviceable. Wife often says that no such helpful visitor as herself ever comes within our doors. Charlotte sends her warmest love to you all, and reports all well at Roxbury.

How nobly George Thompson has labored to sustain our cause in England, and baffle the plots of the secessionists in that country! The friends of our Government ought to send him a handsome testimonial. I am about to make an effort in his behalf.

Give our household love to your dear wife and children.

Ever lovingly yours,

Wm. Lloyd Garrison.

Rev. S. J. May.

ALS: Garrison Papers, Boston Public Library.

1. Theodore Dwight Weld (1803–1895), although born in Connecticut, made his reputation as an abolitionist in New York state. First inspired by retired British army officer Charles Stuart, principal of Utica Academy, and later by Presbyterian revivalist Charles G. Finney, from 1830 on Weld was a dedicated abolition lecturer. He introduced many converts to the cause, including Arthur and Lewis Tappan, James G. Birney, Elizur Wright, Harriet and Henry Ward Beecher, and Angelina E. Grimké, whom he married in 1838. After directing an antislavery lobby for members of the House of Representatives, he continued to lecture throughout the United States. His most famous tract, *American Slavery As It Is* (1839), was an important source for Harriet Beecher Stowe's *Uncle Tom's Cabin.*

Garrison had written to Weld September 29, 1862 (micro.), asking him, on behalf of the Committee of the Theodore Parker Society, to speak at the Music Hall. He also wrote him on the same date (micro.) as this letter to May and persuaded him to speak at the Church of the Puritans during the annual meeting of the Amercican Anti-Slavery Society, held May 12–13. (*The Liberator,* May 22, 1863.)

2. Garrison refers to Theodore Grimké Weld (born 1841), who was in a sanatorium. (Benjamin P. Thomas, *Theodore Weld, Crusader for Freedom,* New Brunswick, N.J., 1950, pp. 192, 243.)

3. In a letter to Garrison printed in *The Liberator,* May 29, 1863, May expressed regret that "domestic duties" would prevent his attending the national meeting; he did, however, attend the anniversary of the New England Anti-Slavery Society, held in Boston May 28–30, and became president of the meeting.

4. Ulysses S. Grant (1822–1885) had graduated from West Point and served in the the Mexican War before entering active service in the Civil War as a brigadier general. Success in Tennessee advanced him to major general early in 1862. At the time of Garrison's letter, however, Grant's fortunes seemed to have reached their nadir. Twice, in November 1862 and in January 1863, his expeditions to Vicksburg had failed. Garrison had no way of foreseeing his brilliant capture of the city in July, his advancement to commander-in-chief, his defeat of Lee, and his election as President in 1868.

Nathaniel Prentiss Banks (1816–1894) was both soldier and politician. Having served in the Massachusetts Senate as early as 1849, he was elected to Congress in 1853, serving five terms in all, though not continuously. In 1858 he became governor of Massachusetts, serving until January 1861. He entered the army in 1861, with a commission as major general of volunteers, but late in 1862 he succeeded General Benjamin F. Butler as commander of the department at New Orleans, where he had to deal with a hostile civilian population, as well as take part in various military campaigns radiating from that city. Discharged in 1865, he returned to Congress, first as a Republican and in 1875 as a Democrat. Two years later he was returned to Congress as a Republican, and his final term he served as a Republican, having defeated Colonel Thomas W. Higginson in 1888.

5. Garrison exaggerates the situation by suggesting that the generals in question were removed "to propitiate the 'copperhead' element of the North," as the facts in the following paragraphs indicate.

John C. Frémont had been removed by Lincoln on November 2, 1861, only partly because of his premature proclamation two months earlier, which confiscated property and freed the slaves of rebellious Missourians. The mismanagement of his military department had hastened his replacement.

Benjamin Franklin Butler (1818–1893) was a distinguished criminal lawyer who before the Civil War was elected to both the Massachusetts House and Senate. A long-time interest in military matters led to his election as brigadier general of the Massachusetts militia, and soon after the beginning of the war he was made major general of volunteers. Despite his clever leadership in several actions, he was relieved after the disastrous battle of Big Bethel, being transferred to the command of the forts at Cape Hatteras and subsequently to the forces that occupied New Orleans, where his administration was certainly autocratic and probably corrupt. He was relieved of duties in New Orleans on December 16, 1862, and in 1863, probably after the date of Garrison's comment in this letter, he was assigned the command of eastern Virginia and North Carolina. Between 1866 and 1875 he served in Congress and was one of the leaders in the impeachment preceedings against President Johnson. In 1882, after several unsuccessful attempts, he was elected governor of Massachusetts.

Franz Sigel (1824–1902) was born and educated in Germany, where he led a revolutionary army in 1848. He immigrated to the United States in 1852. He was a teacher in New York City and a major in the state militia before moving to St. Louis in 1857, where he later became director of schools. During the Civil War Sigel rose from colonel to brigadier general to major general. In the spring of 1863, owing to ill health, he relinquished command of the 11th Corps of the Army of the Potomac; when he returned to duty that summer he was given a subordinate command with the department of the Susquehanna. Following the war he edited a German paper, the Baltimore *Wecker,* and in 1871 he became collector of internal revenue in New York City.

Garrison probably means John Wolcott Phelps (1813–1885) of Guilford, Vt. A professional soldier, he was a brigadier general in the volunteer service and participated in the taking of New Orleans. He wanted to organize the slaves as soldiers, but the government commander would not permit this and put the slaves to work in the city. As a result Phelps resigned in August 1862.

6. Isaiah 58:6 contains the phrase "let the oppressed go free"; but it seems more likely that Garrison is referring to Exodus 7:16, where God directs Moses to say to Pharaoh, "Let my people go." Garrison also alludes to Exodus 8, 9, and 10.

---

5 6

TO ELIZABETH PEASE NICHOL

Boston, April 10, 1863.

Ever Beloved Friend:

It will be thirty years, next month, since I first visited England; twenty-three since my second, and seventeen since my last. It has been strongly in my mind to commemorate the third decade by making another visit across the water this summer, but I am reluctantly compelled to forego that unspeakable enjoyment.

Let me introduce to you the bearer of this, Moncure D. Conway, a native Virginian, allied to the most respectable families in that State, and the author of two admirable works for the times, entitled "The Rejected Stone," and "The Golden Hour."[1] He is all heart and soul in the cause of the oppressed—abhors Southern secession and slavery, and understands them both thoroughly—and visits England for the purpose of testifying against them as a Southern man. He has a brilliant mind, and is a racy writer and speaker. His case is so remarkable, that it would be strange if he failed to create a sensation among your people. No such witness has ever before visited your country. He wittily says that, as the ostracised son of a slaveholder, he ought to be as good as a Southern contraband in drawing an audience. I trust his mission will be eminently useful to the cause of international peace and universal emancipation. As a pulpit preacher, (Unitarian,) he has been, like Abdiel, "faithful among the faithless found";[2] but his taste is not particularly clerical. Any attention you can show him will be very gratefully appreciated by us both.

While the course of the English government towards our own seems to be, if not flagrantly hostile, at least very unfriendly, in allowing so many piratical vessels to be built for the use of the Southern Confederacy, and to destroy our commerce, we are cheered and strengthened by the many popular demonstrations made in our behalf, these showing that the heart of the people is right, however perverse may be the tory and aristocratic element. Nevertheless, unless your government put a stop to the furnishing of iron clads for the piratical Confederates, it is to be feared that public exasperation here will culminate in demanding of the government a declaration of war against England, sooner or later.[3] Such an event is to be contemplated with horror; for both countries would be able to inflict the most frightful injuries upon each other, and cause immense suffering throughout the civilized world. God grant that none may be permitted to see a spectacle so revolting and unnatural! England can have no possible interest in the success of the Southern Confederacy. Slavery is as commercially unfruitful, as it is morally unjust and atrocious. Freedom is the life of the universe.

Are you never coming to America, as a matter of recreation?—if not in the midst of hot rebellious war, at least when peace shall have won the victory, and the jubilee for the oppressed been every where consummated—an event I hope not to be greatly prolonged before its realization.[4] You don't know how many here would re-joice to welcome you to their homes, in different parts of the coun-try; for you are remembered with the highest esteem and the sin-cerest affection.

Enclosed, you will find *cartes de visite* of myself and all the chil-dren—"the latest edition."[5] I regret that I have not a good one of my dear wife to send also but you shall have it when it can be ob-tained. Can you send me yours in return?

I have also forwarded a set to dear Eliza Wigham—the only dif-ference being in the attitude of my oldest son George.[6]

Your much attached friend,

Wm. Lloyd Garrison.

Elizabeth Pease Nichol.

ALS: Garrison Papers, Boston Public Library. On the date he composed this letter Garrison also wrote on behalf of Conway to George Thompson (micro.), to Mary Est-lin (micro.), and to Andrew Paton (micro.).

Elizabeth Pease Nichol (1807–1897), daughter of wealthy Quaker reformer Jo-seph Pease, was active in the movements to abolish slavery in the British West Indies, to curb British exploitation of India, and to promote free trade. In 1853 she married the distinguished astronomer John Pringle Nichol (1804–1859), of the Glas-gow Observatory. Mrs. Nichol was at the time of Garrison's letter one of the central figures among British reformers. She had been Garrison's close friend and supporter since their meeting in 1840. (Anna M. Stoddart, *Elizabeth Pease Nichol*, London and New York, 1899.)

1. Conway's two short books had been published in Boston in 1861 and 1862, the first by Walker, Wise, and Company, the second by Ticknor and Fields. They were both forceful pleas for the pursuit of the war on principles of liberty and justice that would forever abolish slavery. (*National Union Catalog, Pre–1956 Imprints*.)

2. An adaptation of John Milton, *Paradise Lost*, V, 897.

3. Garrison's appraisal of the serious situation arising out of Britain's furnishing piratical vessels for the Confederacy is not exaggerated. Considerable damage had already been done to northern commerce and to the blockade by ships like the *Nash-ville*, the *Florida*, and the *Alabama;* and now two ram-type ironclads, vessels far more advanced in destructive power than any in the northern navy, were under con-struction. Only the northern successes at Gettysburg and Vicksburg and especially the skillful diplomacy of American minister Charles Francis Adams were to prevent the delivery of the ships and a war between Great Britain and the United States.

4. In fact, Mrs. Nichol never did visit the United States.

5. Garrison sent recent card photographs.

6. Eliza Wigham (1820–1899), the daughter of John Wigham (died 1864) of Coan-wood, Northumberland, and his first wife, Jane Richardson of Whitehaven, was an ardent Quaker and reformer. She was made a minister in her meeting in 1867 and worked for many years in behalf of temperance, peace, woman's rights, and espe-cially abolition. She was active in the Ladies' Emancipation Society in Edinburgh, serving for a time as its secretary. The group supported Garrison's point of view and disassociated itself from the British and Foreign Anti-Slavery Society. (Letter to the editor from A. Baillie, senior assistant, National Library of Scotland, Edinburgh, Au-gust 22, 1973.)

5 7

TO MILO A. TOWNSEND

Boston, April 16, 1863.

Dear friend Townsend:

Agreeably to your request, I have called upon G. B. Johnson, in Brattle Street, and given him your introductory note.[1]

With regard to the Churn, he says we have had such a wintry spring, (the mean temperature of January having been several degrees warmer than that of March!) that there has been no advantageous opportunity presented satisfactorily to test it, so as to procure sales for the same; but he spoke very favorably of it, and seemed to think it would come into use in due season. He said he would report to me as soon as he had made any progress. I understood him to say that he had written to you on the subject. I am sorry that, at this time, he has no money to send you.

I was much pleased on examining the churn; and though I am not a connisseur in such matters, I do not see how it can be improved on the score of simplicity, and ease and efficiency of action.[2]

Of course, it will give me pleasure at any time to transmit, without charge, any funds that Mr. Johnson may put into my hands on your account.

With my best wishes for your welfare, and my regards to your dear wife, I remain,

Yours, for good churns and good deeds,

Wm. Lloyd Garrison.

Milo A. Townsend.

ALS: Collection of Charles W. Townsend, Darlington, Pennsylvania.

Milo A. Townsend (1816–1877) was a Quaker schoolmaster, abolitionist, reformer, and editor of the New Brighton (Pa.) *Times*. He was married to Elizabeth Updegraph Walker (1819–1906). (Letters to the editor from Charles W. Townsend, January 3 and March 8, 1971; see also the letter to Helen E. Garrison, August 16, 1847, *Letters*, III, 510.)

1. Of Giles B. Johnson it is known only that he operated an inventor's exchange at 41 Brattle Street, Cambridge, and that he lived in Roxbury. (Letter to the editor from Ruth Bell, researcher, January 31, 1972.)
2. Nothing more is known about the butter churn designed by Townsend.

5 8

TO OLIVER JOHNSON

Boston, May 5, 1863.

Dear Johnson:

I have nothing special to communicate in regard to the anniversary. I do not wish or intend to make any speech during the meetings.[1] Personally, I am tired of speech-making, and, therefore, am glad that we are apparently so near the end of our great conflict.

As for our morning meeting at Dr. [George B.] Cheever's, it will suffice for me to preside—read the scriptures, the resolutions, &c. These last I will try to have ready in printed slips for the reporters, but shall have to bring them with me, as I must be absent this coming Thursday and Friday in New Hampshire, to attend a Will case in Dover.[2] So, do not be uneasy, though you should fail to receive them by Saturday.

Weld writes me that he will try to be with us at the opening session. So the speakers can be advertised as Sloane, Weld, Purvis, and Phillips.[3]

As for the evening session, Tilton and Phillips are secured. I have written, by advice of the latter, to our friend Gerrit Smith, to see if he will consent to be "sandwiched" between them, in a speech of 30 or 40 minutes. I have done so, because he writes me that he would like to be in New York at that time, though he hardly expects to be able to do so. His letter generously enclosed a draft for one hundred dollars, in aid of our Society.

In case he should fail, perhaps Anna E. Dickinson would consent to speak on that occasion, if needed. *En passant*—is it not curious what a popular enthusiasm she has created wherever she has spoken? It is without a parallel.

If Dr. Cheever should feel like offering prayer, at our opening session in his church, it would be well to let him know it would, doubtless, be very acceptable to many. Of course, I shall not call upon any one, specifically, to do that service, but he can act freely upon the usual general invitation.

I shall calculate to leave for New York on Monday morning, via Springfield and New Haven, as usual.

The Committee who are to investigate the condition of the colored population of the country have intimated to Yerrinton that they would like to have him accompany them to New Orleans to report proceedings, &c.[4] Should he not go, he will report for us at New York. You shall duly be apprised of his decision.

It will be a great gratification to see you, and Mary Anne, and Tilton, and other cherished friends again, face to face.

To the call of the Progressive Friends' meeting, I see my name is appended; but I would prefer to have it omitted in the Standard, as the phraseology of the call, *"our* Religious Society," &c., places me in a more intimate and official connection than I have thought of assuming. True, I see Theodore's name is also appended, but I prefer to have mine quietly dropped.

Wendell Phillips will not go to England, though duly appreciating the invitation so generously extended in Mr. Chesson's letter.[5] It would be well for you to apprise Chesson of his decision, stating that at no time has Phillips intimated any purpose of visiting England, but that you and I, and other friends, were extremely desirous to have him go, if by any invitation or persuasion we could bring it about.

Ever affectionately yours,

Wm. Lloyd Garrison.

ALS: Garrison Papers, Boston Public Library.

1. Although Garrison made no formal speech at the anniversary meetings, which were held May 12 in the Church of the Puritans (Dr. Cheever's church), he did preside, and he spoke occasionally at the business meeting. (*The Liberator*, May 29, 1863.)

2. Details concerning the "Will case" have eluded conscientious research.

3. The advertisement was printed as specified by Garrison in *The Liberator*, May 8.

James Renwick Wilson Sloane (1823–1886) was a distinguished Presbyterian clergyman, scholar, and educator. At the time of this letter he was pastor of the Third Congregation of New York City, where he gained a wide reputation as an eloquent preacher and a dedicated abolitionist. In 1868 he was to resign his position to become a professor at the Theological Seminary of Allegheny, Pa., where he spent the rest of his life. (William M. Glasgow, *History of the Reformed Presbyterian Church in America*, Baltimore, 1888.)

Theodore Weld did attend the meeting and gave one of the speeches, though it was not reported in *The Liberator*. Sloane's speech was reported, and the full text was given for the speeches of Robert Purvis, Theodore Tilton, and Wendell Phillips. Neither Smith nor Dickinson, whom Garrison mentions as possible speakers, addressed the meetings. (*The Liberator*, May 22 and 29, 1863.)

4. Garrison refers to the Freedmen's Inquiry Commission, organized in January 1863 by Secretary of War Edwin M. Stanton, to investigate the condition of freed Negroes and the ways in which they could aid the Union cause; members of the commission were Robert Dale Owen, James McKaye, and Samuel Gridley Howe. (Frank A. Flower, *Edwin McMasters Stanton*, Akron, Ohio, 1905.)

It is apparent from later letters to Oliver Johnson (November 22, 1863 [micro.], and April 28, 1864) that James M. W. Yerrinton was occupied with reporting in New York City and did not go to New Orleans.

5. Frederick William Chesson (1833–1888), who was born in Rochester and married Amelia Thompson, George's daughter, edited the London *Dial* until 1863, when he became a writer and then coeditor for the London *Morning Star*. He was largely responsible for the organization of the London Emancipation Society and served as secretary, while Thompson served as chairman, of its steering committee.

Chesson is credited with initiating and managing the London testimonial breakfast honoring Garrison on June 29, 1867. He was the author of a number of books pertaining to British colonial affairs. (Christine Bolt, *The Anti-Slavery Movement and Reconstruction: A Study in Anglo-American Co-operation, 1833–1877,* London and New York, 1969, pp. 13, 49, 51; Frederic Boase, *Modern English Biography,* Truro [England], 1908, IV; *Life.*)

59

TO DANIEL RICKETSON

Boston, May 10, 1863.

My dear Ricketson:

Thomas Sims, the freedman of 1863, and returned fugitive of 1851, would like to tell his narrative to the good citizens of New Bedford, on Sunday evening next, 17th inst., if a hall or meeting-house can be procured.[1] There might be a small admission fee, or a collection in free meeting, to defray expenses, and give him some pecuniary assistance. He tells his story in a manner that cannot fail to interest.

I shall be absent all this week in New York; but if you will consult with a few friends, and inform *Mr.* [Robert F.]*Wallcut* whether Sims had better come or not, it will be doing an act of kindness that will be gratefully appreciated.

In much haste, but with the highest regards, I remain,

Yours, to break all fetters,

Wm. Lloyd Garrison.

Daniel Ricketson.

ALS: Papers of Daniel Ricketson and Family, Old Dartmouth Historical Society Whaling Museum, New Bedford, Massachusetts.

Daniel Ricketson (1813–1898), a Quaker, was born, lived, and died in New Bedford, where he had sufficient means to dedicate his life to what interested him. A convivial man, he had a large circle of friends, ranging from Henry David Thoreau to George William Curtis. He was active in various reform movements, including abolition; he also wrote an anecdotal *History of New Bedford* (1858) and several volumes of minor verse. One of the poems in *The Autumn Sheaf* (1869), dated 1845, is called "William Lloyd Garrison" and begins, "Brave Spirit! the great multitude of men / But little comprehend thee. . . ." (Letter to the editor from Richard C. Kugler, director, Old Dartmouth Historical Society Whaling Museum, June 16, 1975; Anna and Walton Ricketson, eds., *Daniel Ricketson and His Friends,* Boston, 1902.)

1. Thomas Sims (born c. 1828), a bricklayer by trade, was a fugitive slave who had arrived in Boston on March 7, 1851, where he stayed at a black seamen's boarding-house. On April 4 he was apprehended, and neither extensive legal efforts by Charles Sumner, Richard Henry Dana, and Samuel E. Sewall nor an abortive plan for escape were sufficient to prevent his being sent back to his master, James Potter of Chatham, Ga., under heavy guard early on the morning of April 12. He spent

twelve years in the South, mostly in Vicksburg, Miss., before escaping again and re-turning to Boston. There in his first public speech, the first week of May 1863, with his wife and child on the platform with him, he told an audience of a thousand people about his twelve years of servitude. The meeting was also the occasion for remarks by Wendell Phillips and Garrison. Phillips commented on the great changes for the better that had occurred in Massachusetts since 1851. Garrison reminded the audi-ence that the Fugitive Slave Law was still in effect and that the safety of Sims in Boston was owing not to principles of justice and freedom but to "the rebellious po-sition of his late master." (*The Liberator*, April 11 and 18, 1851; March 26, April 2, 9, 16, 23, 30, 1852; May 15, 1863; Benjamin Quarles, *Black Abolitionists*, New York, 1969, pp. 206–207.)

Whether Sims spoke in New Bedford on May 17 is uncertain, since no report of his lecture has been found in either the Boston or the New Bedford newspapers.

---

6 0

TO HELEN E. GARRISON

New York, May 14, 1863.

Dear Wife:

I do not know how the mercury actually stood in Boston on Mon-day, but I am sure it seemed to be of a July temperature in the cars from Boston to this city. Every body was in "the melting mood," every one dust-covered, and immensely relieved on getting through, and resorting to a bath as quickly as possible. Our anti-slavery company was never so small before, with reference to Anniversary Week. It consisted of Edmund Quincy, John T. Sar-geant, and myself—Phillips having preceded us in the night train, in order to be fresh for his Cooper Institute speech, Monday eve-ning.[1] At Worcester, Mr. May and his mother joined us, and these were all the recognized abolitionists in that long and crowded train.[2] What then?

> "It must be that the Kingdom's coming,
> And the year of jubilo"—[3]

and our distinctive movement is nearly swallowed up in the great revolution in Northern sentiment which has been going on against slavery and slavedom since the bombardment of Sumter. Usually, the number of clergymen has been large and conspicuous, going on to attend their several anniversaries meetings; but, this time, I did not see a single one in all the crowd! Of course, there must have been a few; but, if so, they were no longer distinguishable, for the "white chokers," the token of clerical sanctity, had evidently gone "to the receptacle of things lost on earth."

Phillips's meeting at the Institute, Monday evening, was a splendid one, and he acquitted himself in a way to gather fresh laurels from his brow. His speech was reported in full in the Tribune of Tuesday morning.[4] At the conclusion of it, I was loudly called for, but held back. Then calls were made for Horace Greeley, who came forward and made a few remarks in his queer-toned voice and a very awkward manner.[5] The cries were renewed for me, and I said a few words, the applause being general and very marked.[6] When I first entered the hall, and was conducted to a seat on the platform by the side of Major Opdyke, the audience broke out in repeated bursts of applause.[7] What a change in popular sentiment and feeling from the old mobocratic, pro-slavery times! And, re-member, this was a meeting called by the Sixteenth Republican Ward Association![8] In the course of his speech, Phillips made a sharp reference to Charles Sumner's dereliction in securing the elevation of that despiser of the negro race, Col. Stevenson, to a Brigadier General.[9] It took the audience by surprise, but there was no hiss; on the contrary, the censure was applauded as the facts were stated.

Our opening session at Dr. Cheever's Church was attended by a thronged house, and in all respects a great success. As the Tribune of yesterday contained a very full report of the proceedings, you can judge of the spirit of the occasion by a perusal of it.[10] Our evening meeting at the Cooper Institute was also an excellent one—Theo-dore Tilton making the opening speech, (a very good one,) and Phillips following in one of his finest efforts—Henry B. Stanton con-cluding the meeting in an impromptu, racy and eloquent speech, after the olden time.[11]

Our business meetings were interesting, though small. There was a general expression of sentiment, that the Society must not be dissolved until slavery is extinct. Frederick Douglass ventured to show himself, and participated in the discussions, which created some little friction. In view of his ungrateful and treacherous course towards our Society, his assurance seemed to me excessive.[12] "Confidence is a plant of slow growth," and in his case will be par-ticularly so with me.[13] Still, I admire and wonder at his ability.

Yesterday morning, I took breakfast at Mrs. Stanton's, in 45th street, along with Theodore and Angelina Weld, Susan B. Anthony, Phillips, John T. Sargeant, and other friends.[14] It was a very pleas-ant occasion—all the more seeing at the table seven children, from 21 years downward, five boys and two girls, and all fine looking, well-behaved and promising.[15]

Last evening, I went to take tea with Mrs. Underhill, formerly Miss Fox, the medium,) in company with Mr. Sargent, where we had divers spiritual manifestations—communications from John Brown, Isaac T. Hopper, my mother—&c.[16] Isaac and Amy Post, of Rochester, were also present.[17]

The weather has been rainy, as usual, and very warm, with a good deal of thunder and lightning. I have not yet found time to call upon any one, except Rev. Mr. Frothingham.[18] Of course, I have met with a good many friends at the meetings, interchanged a few inquiries, and then separated—among these, Anna Percy, Tommy Benson,[19] Mattie Griffith, &c., but none of the [Edward] Anthonys from Brooklyn. To-morrow I intend visiting a number.

The carbuncle upon John Hopper's neck has almost cost him his life, and still has a frightful look, though he considers himself almost well. He has given me several photographs for Franky. I miss the little deformed boy, Bobby, very much.[20] Little Willie[21] has no idea of his death, as he did not see him when he was dead, and supposes he has gone somewhere to live in a beautiful clime where he is very happy.

The first session of the Convention of Loyal Women was held, this morning, at Dr. Cheever's Church.[22] Lucy Stone was President, Mrs. Wright of Auburn, and Mrs. Coleman of Rochester, Secretaries.[23] Speeches were made by Mrs. Weld, Mrs. Stanton, &c., but hardly any of the speakers were heard for lack of voice, and, on the whole, the meeting was almost a dead failure—resolving itself, in fact, into a Woman's Rights Convention. It has not been wisely got up. It will hold another session in the Cooper Institute, this evening.

Mr. and Mrs. [Cornelius] Bramhall desire me to go to Orange, and spend the Sunday with them; but it is now my purpose to leave here, with John T. Sargent, on Saturday morning, and shall hope to be with you and the children at the tea-table that evening.

Our friend, Henry C. Wright, expects to be with you in the morning, as he leaves for Boston this afternoon. I am glad to see him looking so well and hearty.

I hope Mr. [Parker] Pillsbury's health is improving, but shall not be surprised if he breaks down utterly.

I am feeling very well, and trust the jaunt will aid me in the way of better health.

With a husband's and a father's love, I remain,

Yours, by indissoluble bonds,

W. L. G.

☞ Tell George he may copy from the Standard the speeches of Rev. Mr. Sloane and Robert Purvis, for the [. . .].[24]

ALS: Garrison Papers, Boston Public Library; partly printed in *Life*, IV, 78–79.

1. John Turner Sargent (1809–1877), whose name Garrison spells variously, was a Congregational minister in Boston and after 1865 the president of the Massachusetts Anti-Slavery Society. He was married first to Charlotte Sophia White (1816–1854) and then to Mary Elizabeth Fiske (1827–1904) of New Orleans. With Charlotte he had four sons and two daughters: Christiana Keadie (1839–1914), who remained unmarried, and Elizabeth Stone White Gray (born in 1844 and still alive in 1923), who married William Edmund Dickinson in 1867, subsequently moving to Wisconsin. Sargent had one son by his second marriage. (*Life;* Boston city directory, 1860; Emma W. and C. W. Sargent, compilers, *Epes Sargent of Gloucester and his Descendants,* Boston, 1923, pp. 162–166.)

2. Mary Goddard May (1787–1882) was the mother of Garrison's close friend and associate Samuel May, Jr. (*Life.*)

3. Not identified, though the allusion to various passages in Leviticus 25 and 27 is clear.

4. Wendell Phillips' speech of May 11 was indeed reported fully in the New York *Tribune* on the following day. He urged that the American people be united during the national crisis and that public opinion should impel the government to a position of strong leadership in the crucial conflict.

5. Horace Greeley (1811–1872) arrived in New York in 1831 from his home in Erie, Pa. He soon became a partner in a printing firm and a writer for several of the city's periodicals. In 1841 he founded the New York *Tribune,* which became the finest paper in New York and by the time of the Civil War the most influential paper in America. By temperament and conviction a reformer, Greeley dedicated himself to abolition, the free-soil movement, and universal emancipation. In 1872 he ran a disastrously unsuccessful campaign as the Liberal Republican presidential condidate against the incumbent Ulysses S. Grant.

6. In the New York *Tribune,* May 12, Garrison's brief sppech was summarized; he cautioned against compromise and urged prosecution of the war until slavery was abolished.

7. George Opdyke (1805–1880), wealthy New York merchant and proprietor of the first extensive clothing factory in the city in 1832, was an antislavery Republican who had been active in politics since the Free-Soil convention at Buffalo in 1848. He had served in the New York assembly in 1859 and was elected mayor of the city in 1862. He was to be most severely tested in that post during the draft riots of July 1863. He also published *Treatise on Political Economy* (1851) and *Report on the Currency* (1858), which established him as an economist of the school opposed to John Stuart Mill.

8. The Sixteenth Ward Republican Association, which was known as the "banner ward for Radical Republicanism," encompassed approximately the area now known as Chelsea, with a population of 45,182. In 1863 William C. Russell was the president of the association and H. C. Parke the chairman of its lecture committee. (*Manual of the Corporation of the City of New York,* 1863; New York *Times,* May 11, 1863; New York *Daily Tribune,* May 12, 1863.)

9. Thomas Greely Stevenson (1836–1864) of Boston had been a member of the state militia as a young man and had become a colonel in the federal army shortly after the beginning of the Civil War. Garrison's objection to Stevenson arose from the colonel's opposition to the use of former slaves as soldiers in the Union army. In 1863, with the support of Massachusetts senators Charles Sumner and Henry Wilson, Stevenson was promoted to brigadier general. In 1864 he was killed at the Battle of Spotsylvania.

10. The New York *Tribune* of May 13 printed a seven-column report of the meeting, including various resolutions condemning slavery and advocating strong military action as well as immediate and complete emancipation. Speeches by James R. W. Sloane, Robert Purvis, and Theodore D. Weld were printed in full; those by

Wendell Phillips, Theodore Tilton, and Henry B. Stanton were summarized. The issue for May 14 printed a report of the business meeting and also a brief speech by Garrison.

11. Henry Brewster Stanton (1805–1887) had a long and distinguished career as a lawyer, abolitionist, and journalist. A follower of Garrison's until the late 1830s, when the two men differed regarding the relevance of political action to effect abolition, Stanton became active in political circles, helping to draft the platform for the Free-Soil party in 1848 and to found the Republican party in 1855. In 1840 Stanton married Elizabeth Cady (see n. 14). After the Civil War he followed the career of journalist, working first for the New York *Tribune* and then for the *Sun*.

12. Garrison's distrust of Douglass began in 1847, owing to what he considered Douglass' insufficient concern for his (Garrison's) ill health during the western tour and especially to his resentment over the black abolitionist's decision to reject Garrison's advice by founding the *North Star*. Disagreements between the two men became evident as Douglass, under the influence of New York abolitionists like Gerrit Smith and William Goodell, repudiated the doctrines of nonresistance and moral suasion, accepting instead the necessity for political action. The opposition between the two abolitionists became overt during the early 1850s, and in 1853 Garrison went so far as to cast aspersions on the rectitude of Douglass' family life. Bitter feelings were assuaged and friendly relations reestablished by the 1870s. At Garrison's funeral Douglass reaffirmed his respect and admiration for Garrison's accomplishment. (For an expression of Garrison's feeling toward Douglass, see his letter to Samuel J. May, September 28, 1860, *Letters,* IV, 694, n. 2; for a summary of the controversy between Douglass and Garrison see Philip S. Foner, *The Life and Writings of Frederick Douglass,* New York, 1950, II, 48–66; for evidence of reestablished relations between the two men see FJG, December 10, 1872.)

13. A maxim that can be traced back to Ovid but which was given famous statement in a speech by William Pitt, later First Earl of Chatham, before the House of Commons, January 14, 1766.

14. Elizabeth Cady Stanton (1815–1902), a graduate of the seminary of Emma Willard in Troy, N.Y., was a delegate to the World's Anti-Slavery Convention in London in 1840, where she came under the lasting influence of Lucretia Mott. Subsequently she dedicated her life not only to abolition but especially to woman's rights. It was she who was the guiding spirit of the famous convention in Seneca Falls, N.Y., in 1848, the cornerstone of the woman's rights movement. For this movement she and Susan B. Anthony worked for the rest of their lives. She was coeditor of the first four volumes of the massive *History of Woman Suffrage* (see Susan B. Anthony, below).

Angelina Grimké Weld (1805–1879) was the daughter of an aristocratic slaveholding family in Charleston, S.C. By the mid 1830s she and her sister Sarah (1792–1873) had denounced slavery and moved north. After Angelina's marriage to Theodore D. Weld in 1838, Sarah joined the couple on a farm in Belleville, N.J. After raising three children, the Welds and Sarah Grimké founded the Belleville School in 1851. Some years later they ran another school at the cooperative community at Eagleswood. During the war the family moved to Perth Amboy, N.J., and subsequently to West Newton, Mass.

Susan Brownell Anthony (1820–1906) was the daughter of a farmer turned businessman, who ran a cotton mill first in Adams, Mass., and then in the Hudson Valley near Albany, N.Y. It was her association with workers in her father's mills that prompted a lifelong interest in labor reform. It was also at her father's house that she met many of the leading reformers of the day, including, in addition to Garrison, Phillips, Pillsbury, and Douglass. She was active in the causes of temperance and abolition before dedicating herself, along with her closest associate, Elizabeth Cady Stanton, to the cause of woman's rights. From the convention at Seneca Falls in 1848 until the end of her life she agitated for the equality of the sexes. During the war she and Mrs. Stanton organized the Women's Loyal National League, and in 1866 the American Equal Rights Association. In 1868 she founded and became publisher of the *Revolution*, with Mrs. Stanton and Pillsbury as editors. This paper, together with the National Woman Suffrage Association, organized a year later, agitated for improved working conditions as well as for woman's suffrage, assigning to the latter a higher priority than to Negro male suffrage. Miss Anthony, Elizabeth Cady Stanton, and Matilda Joslyn Gage edited the first three volumes of the *History of Woman Suffrage* (1881–1886). They were joined by Ida Husted Harper, author of the *Life of Susan B. Anthony* (1898–1908), in the editing of volume IV. Mrs. Harper also completed the history by editing volumes V and VI (1922).

15. The seven children of Henry B. and Elizabeth Cady Stanton were Daniel (1842–1891); Henry (born 1844); Gerrit (born 1845); Theodore (1851–1925), an author and journalist who became the Berlin correspondent for the New York *Tribune;* Margaret (born 1852); Harriot Stanton Blatch (1854–1940), a militant woman's rights activist and Socialist party candidate for the United States Senate in 1926; and Robert (born 1859). (Alma Lutz, *Created Equal: A Biography of Elizabeth Cady Stanton,* New York, 1940.)

16. Mrs. Ann Leah Fox Underhill (1814–1891) practiced as a medium in New York City and guided her younger sisters, Margaret and Kate Fox, to wide public attention as spiritualists.

Frances (Fanny) Lloyd Garrison (1776–1823), the wife of Abijah Garrison, was a strong-minded and high-principled woman who greatly influenced her son William. Deserted by her husband in 1808, she supported herself and her three surviving children by becoming a nurse. Her two sons were compelled by circumstance to learn a trade early in life; the girl, like two other daughters before her, died young. Although Fanny had been born with a rugged constitution, the shock of her husband's desertion and the hardships that followed undermined her health and contributed to her comparatively early death.

17. Isaac Post (1798–1872), originally a farmer and for thirty years in the drug business in Rochester, N.Y., was an abolitionist especially active in the Underground Railroad. In 1848 Margaret Fox had converted him and his wife, Amy, to spiritualism.

18. Octavius Brooks Frothingham (1822–1895), after graduating from Harvard Divinity School, became the minister of the North Church in Salem, Mass. In 1855, when his opinions concerning slavery grew too liberal for his parishioners, he left Salem to become minister of the Unitarian society in Jersey City. There he was famous as a liberal Unitarian, the successor, in effect, of Theodore Parker. In 1867 he helped to found and was first president of the Free Religious Association. After 1879, his health having failed, he lived in semi-retirement. Frothingham was the author of many books, including biographies of Theodore Parker and Gerrit Smith.

19. Tommy Benson is presumably Thomas Davis Benson (born 1842), the fifth child of George W. and Catharine S. Benson.

20. Bobby was Robert J. Denyer (c. 1848–1862), an orphan and hunchback whom the Hoppers adopted. When he died of heart disease in October 1862, Octavius B. Frothingham preached at his funeral. (See the letter to Fanny Garrison, September 14, 1862, n. 1[micro.]; *The Liberator,* October 24, 1862; *National Anti-Slavery Standard,* December 6, 1862.)

21. [William] DeWolf Hopper (1858–1935), son of John and Rosa DeWolf Hopper, was to become one of Broadway's most distinguished comic actors. (*Encyclopedia Americana.*)

22. The National Convention of Loyal Women, held May 14, 1863, was dedicated to abolition as well as to woman's rights; from this convention emanated a resolution affirming the government's duty "to recognize the rights of every individual irrespective of color or sex." (*The Liberator,* May 29, 1863; see also *HWS,* II, 50–78.)

23. Martha Coffin Wright (1806–1875), daughter of Anna and Thomas Coffin, originally of Nantucket and the youngest sister of Lucretia Coffin Mott, was very active in the woman's rights movement, but following her sister's example urged that during the war years women work harder to further the cause of abolition. In 1824 she had married Peter Pelham, a captain in the United States Army, and gone with him to his

station in Florida. When Captain Pelham died in 1826, Martha returned to her mother's house in Philadelphia. In the following year she moved to Aurora, N.Y., where in 1829 she married David Wright (1805–1897), a lawyer originally from Philadelphia. Ten years later they settled in Auburn, N.Y. (Anna Davis Hallowell, *James and Lucretia Mott, Life and Letters,* Boston, 1884; *NAW;* see also the letter to Ellen Wright, February 19, 1864, n. 1.)

Lucy Newhall Coleman (born 1817) was a teacher of Negro children in a school in Rochester, N.Y. She was also an active lecturer on abolition and woman's suffrage. After the Civil War she was superintendent of Negro schools in the District of Columbia. (Frederic May Holland, *Frederick Douglass: The Colored Orator,* New York, 1891.)

24. Apparently George Thompson Garrison was at this time employed as a printer for *The Liberator,* since he is listed as a printer at the paper's office (221 Washington Street) in the Boston city directories during this period.

The last word of Garrison's postscript is illegible.

6 1

TO THEODORE TILTON

Boston, June 5, 1863.

Dear Mr. Tilton:

I am very much obliged to you for your kind and confidential letter of the 27th ult.; but I have been too busy with "conventional" and other matters till now, to send you a reply.[1]

Be assured, if I can be of any service to you, during Mr. Beecher's absence abroad, in the manner named by you, it will give me pleasure to do so. Your position is a very responsible one, and it is commendable in you to wish to be aided and strengthened in it; but I have no doubt of your ability, without any external aid, bravely and successfully to discharge the duties thereof.

I am also obliged to you for your kind reference to my son Wendell. As he has no taste for any of the "professions,"—and I am glad of it,—but has scholarly attainments, literary ability, and a deep moral reformatory nature, I am confident his forte will be with his pen, and I should like to see him, somehow, connected with the press, so as to obtain some reasonable compensation for his labors. The Liberator has no circulation that enables me to offer him any thing in the shape of a *quid pro quo,* nor would he be willing to accept it from me if I had. He has never broken to me a syllable on the subject, being singularly unambitious and retiring—too much so for his usefulness. I suppose the Tribune has now more correspondents than it wants; but if an occasional communication from his pen should happen to be acceptable, I have no doubt of the friendly feelings of Mr. [Sydney Howard] Gay and Mr. [George W.]

Smalley to say a good word in his behalf to Mr. [Horace] Greeley. Mr. [Wendell] Phillips suggests that it would be a serviceable thing to Wendell, if he could secure the office of Washington correspondent of one or two prominent journals at the next session of Congress, as it would bring him into direct contact with public men and public affairs, and prove useful to him in many ways.[2]

Of course, I write this in friendly confidence, without Wendell's knowing or suspecting any thing about it.

I have not seen your admirable speech made at the Cooper Institute, at our anti-slavery anniversary, since it was put in tract form. It was not only most opportune, well prepared, and well delivered, but it was the means of eliciting from Phillips a capital speech on the same subject. I deemed it a most elevating and profitable occasion.[3]

I suppose Oliver [Johnson] is at Longwood, attending the Progressive Friends' meeting. What a fine time we had there last year!

Remember me with much esteem to your beloved wife, and believe me

Your attached friend,

Wm. Lloyd Garrison.

Theo. Tilton, Esq.

ALS: William Lloyd Garrison Miscellaneous Manuscripts, New-York Historical Society.

1. Garrison refers to Tilton's letter of May 27, 1863 (Anti-Slavery Letters to Garrison and Others, Boston Public Library), in which Tilton says that he will be in full charge of the New York *Independent* during Henry Ward Beecher's European trip and that he would welcome contributions from Garrison—even paid editorials.

2. Although Wendell Phillips Garrison did not become a Washington correspondent, he did begin work on the New York *Independent*, of which Tilton was then the editor, in January 1864. In July 1865, he became literary editor of the newly formed *Nation*. (Obituary, New York *Times*, March 1, 1907.)

3. Garrison refers to Tilton's speech entitled "The Negro" (Boston, 1863), in which he argued for complete legal equality for the Negro, asserting that "it takes all men to make Man!" In the next speech Phillips commended Tilton and, in effect, made the same argument. (For Tilton's speech see *The Liberator*, May 22, 1863; for Phillips', the issue for May 29.)

6 2

TO GEORGE THOMPSON GARRISON

Boston, June 11, 1863.

Though I could have wished that you had been able understandingly and truly to adopt those principles of peace which are so sacred and divine to my own soul, yet you will bear me witness that I have not laid a straw in your way to prevent your acting up to your own highest convictions of duty; for nothing would be gained, but much lost, to have you violate these. Still, I tenderly hope that you will once more seriously review the whole matter before making the irrevocable decision. . . .

In making up a final judgment, I wish you to look all the peculiar trials in the face that you, in common with all others connected with the colored regiment, will have to encounter. Personally, as my son, you will incur some risks at the hands of the rebels that others will not, if it is known that you are my son. My impression is, that upon the colored regiments the Government means to rely to do the most desperate fighting and occupy the post of imminent danger. Your chance of being broken down by sickness, wounded, maimed, or killed, in the course of such a prolonged campaign, is indeed very great. True, this is not a consideration to weigh heavily against the love of liberty and the promptings of duty; but it makes me tremble in regard to the effect that may be produced upon the health and happiness of your mother, should any serious, especially a fatal, accident befall you. Her affection for you is intense, her anxiety beyond expression. . . .

Printed extract: *Life,* IV, 80–81.

George Thompson Garrison, who had been commissioned a second lieutenant in the 55th Massachusetts Negro regiment, was ordered from Boston late in July. The regiment, composed primarily of the surplus of Negro volunteers who had signed up for the 54th, served as a reinforcement unit for southern operations and was not involved in heavy fighting. On February 21, 1865, the regiment followed central Union forces into Charleston and occupied the city until August 1865, when it was recalled to Boston and disbanded. Both the 54th and the 55th refused to accept discriminatory pay, and consequently served without recompense until July 15, 1864, when the equal pay regulation was enacted. George Garrison served capably; for a brief time in Charleston he even commanded the regiment—perhaps the climactic event of his life. (James M. McPherson, *Marching Toward Freedom: The Negro in the Civil War, 1861–1865,* New York, 1968.)

63

TO HORACE GREELEY

[Boston, June 30, 1863.]

Sir:

By the last arrival from England, it appears that Mr. Mason, Envoy of the Confederate States, had sent to the London *Times* a correspondence between the Rev. Moncure D. Conway and himself—Mr. C. informing Mr. M. that "he is authorized on behalf of the Anti-Slavery people of America, who have sent him to England, to propose that if the Confederate States will immediately commence the work of negro emancipation, the anti-slavery leaders of the Northern States will at once oppose the prosecution of the war; and since they hold a balance of power, will cause the war to cease by the immediate withdrawal of every kind of supplies from it." It is further added that Mr. Mason very properly asked Mr. Conway to produce his credentials. Mr. Conway replied that he would write to America for them. In closing the correspondence, Mr. Mason remarks that "It will perhaps, interest Abolitionists to learn that they have a delegate here prepared, in their name, to enter into a compromise on the question of slavery."[1]

This correspondence is of so extraordinary and grave a character that I beg permission to state, in *The Tribune,* in behalf of the Abolitionists with whom I am identified, that they have not been guilty of such folly and presumption as to authorize any such proposition to be made to Mr. Mason; nor will they forward any endorsement of it to Mr. Conway, who is in England upon his own responsibility alone, representing the Anti-Slavery cause no further than does every other eloquent and devoted friend of freedom who desires to see the rebellion speedily suppressed, and slavery as speedily abolished.

There are at least three weighty reasons why the Abolitionists could not make any overture of this nature to the Confederate traitors, especially through the infamous author of the Fugitive Slave law.

The first is, that no reliance can be placed upon the word of those who stand before the world black with perfidy and treason, and in the most dreadful sense as *hostes humani generis.*[2] Having long since proved themselves capable of uttering any falsehood, however stupendous, practising any deception, however detestable, and breaking any pledge, however solemnly made, it would be the height of infatuation to suppose them morally capable of carrying out any stipulation for the emancipation of their wretched bond-men.

The second reason is, that as they commenced and are carrying on the war expressly and avowedly to obtain wider scope and stronger safeguards for their cherished slave system—and desire their independence upon no other ground—to approach them with an overture for Immediate Emancipation as the method of terminating the struggle and securing their recognition as an independent Confederacy, is to be lacking in self-respect, and to justify them in resenting it as an insult and a mockery.

The third reason is, that the Federal government has already decreed, "forever," the liberation of all the slaves in the Confederate States, and stands solemnly pledged to enforce that decree in suppressing the rebellion. It is, therefore, not only an act of supererogation, but an imputation upon the government to solicit the traitors to do that, as a means of triumph and to screen themselves from punishment, which has been wisely and constitutionally done by President Lincoln to save the Republic.

Yours, for Universal Freedom, and therefore no compromise with the Confederate States.

WM. LLOYD GARRISON.

Boston, June 30, 1863.

Printed: New York *Tribune*, July 2, 1863; reprinted in the *National Anti-Slavery Standard*, July 11, 1863.

In printing Garrison's letter, Horace Greeley, editor of the paper, commented: "We think Mr. Garrison gives too much importance to Mr. Conway's foolish affair." On the same date, the *Tribune* printed an article from the London *Morning Star* suggesting that Mason had tacitly admitted that the South was determined to preserve slavery.

1. Garrison quotes not from the Conway-Mason correspondence but from a summary of it, which he found in the New York *Tribune*, June 30, 1863, and which originally appeared in the London *Times*. In substance, his quotations are accurate, apart from discrepancies in punctuation and capitalization and the change of a few minor words.

2. "Enemies of the human race."

64

TO SAMUEL J. MAY

Boston, July 5, 1863.

Dear Friend:

Your letter of the 2d inst. makes us all, at home, very glad to learn that you are to visit Boston next week, and that we may have the coveted privilege to extend to you our simple family hospitality during your brief sojourn. Do not hesitate to come directly to 14 Dix Place; and, instead of your going to a hotel the night of your arrival, order the hackman to drive to our house, as I should much prefer to sit up till you come than to have you seek a bed elsewhere. It will be no task for me to do so, as I shall have enough to keep me busy in reading or writing till the arrival of the midnight train.

The 50th anniversary you are coming to celebrate, though it can. not reverse the wheels of time, which turn back for no one's accommodation, may make you all feel young again in recalling to memory the earliest college reminiscences.[1] May it prove a pleasant and profitable commemoration to the surviving members of your Class, who may be permitted to greet each other on the occasion!

Your son George has just made us a call, but, as I was lying down, I did not have the pleasure of seeing him. His aunt Charlotte [G. Coffin], my wife, William, Fanny and Frank entertained him, but were not a little surprised to find him disposed to cry, "Peace, peace," when there is no peace,[2] and can be none, until the rod of the oppressor is broken, and the war-breeding, war-creating system of slavery utterly broken down.

Speaking of peace, I shall publish in the next Liberator a letter addressed to you by our old well-meaning, but not always clearly discriminating friend, Joshua P. Blanchard, in reply to the one you wrote to me on the holding of the annual meeting of the American Anti-Slavery Society at New York, in May last, and which was published with the proceedings of that meeting.[3] He left word at my office, (for I did not see him,) that you desired him to send it to the Liberator, if he thought proper. I do not know whether you will feel disposed to make any reply to it; but, if so, I hope your rejoinder will be such as to justify me in declining to open my columns, at this time, to a protracted discussion with him on the peace question. Mr. Blanchard is one of the number who seem to be fond of disputation for its own sake, and ever disposed to have the last word in a controversy. He is a worthy man, and means well; but, ever since this most unjustifiable and wicked rebellion broke out, his sympathies have been paradoxically given to the side of the Southern Confederacy, and, consequently, in opposition to the course of the Administration. Curious enough, he assumes to find in the Declaration of Independence a full warrant for the rebels to set up an independent form of government! Thus—"All governments derive their just powers from the consent of the governed"—the rebels do not consent to the government of the U.S.—ergo, &c. This is as stupid and monstrous a perversion of the meaning of the language of the Declaration as is the rendering of Christ's injunction, "Take, eat—this is my body"—[4] by the Romish Church, so as to prove the doctrine of transubstantiation. Ardently as my soul yearns for universal peace, and greatly shocking to it as are the horrors of war, I deem this a time when the friends of peace will best subserve their holy cause to wait until the whirlwind, the fire and the earthquake are past, and then "the still small voice"[5] may be understandingly and improvingly heard.

Yesterday, our annual celebration at the Framingham Grove brought together a great concourse of the tried and devoted friends of impartial freedom.[6] Phillips made a scathing rejoinder to Montgomery Blair's speech at Concord, N.H., on the 17th of June.[7]

We all send our warmest love to you and yours.

Faithfully yours,

Wm. Lloyd Garrison.

ALS: Garrison Papers, Boston Public Library.

1. May was to attend the Harvard College anniversary to be held July 16, 1863. Since he graduated in the class of 1817, he was celebrating the fiftieth anniversary of his matriculation.

2. Jeremiah 6:14 and 8:11; possibly Garrison is quoting Patrick Henry, Speech in Virginia Convention, March 23, 1775.

3. Joshua P. Blanchard (1782–1868) was a Boston reformer whose favorite cause was peace, though he had served not only on the executive committee of the American Peace Society but also as secretary of the American Anti-Slavery Society. (*Life;* letter to the editor from Jonathan Prude, researcher, September 1970.) May's letter (dated May 11, 1863, and printed in *The Liberator,* May 29) said that slavery could have been peacefully abolished and war averted had the nation's leaders acted upon moral and religious principles, but that since the conflict was in progress, it was necessary to fight till victory in order to destroy slavery and punish slaveholders. Blanchard's reply (dated June 21, and printed in *The Liberator,* July 10, 1863) refuted May's position, insisting that slavery was not the primary cause of the war. The principles of peace, he said, as well as the United States Constitution, required that the war be terminated and the North be separated from the South.

4. Matthew 26:26; Mark 14:22.

5. I Kings 19:12; also Whittier, "Dear Lord and Father of Mankind," stanza 5.

6. The annual meeting of the Friends of Freedom, held under the auspices of the Massachusetts Anti-Slavery Society at Framingham, celebrated the principle of universal emancipation. Numerous antislavery dignitaries gave speeches. (*The Liberator,* July 3 and 10, 1863.)

7. Montgomery Blair (1813–1883), a graduate of West Point turned lawyer, was a man of many political talents. He rose from the position of mayor of St. Louis to that of judge of the Court of Common Pleas, then to solicitor of the Court of Claims, and finally to postmaster general in the Lincoln cabinet. Although he was a liberal on many issues, his speech to the Sons of the Granite State attacked Wendell Phillips for his views on racial amalgamation, which Blair considered destructive of national laws and traditions. At the Framingham celebration on the fourth Phillips replied, condemning Blair's position as "base pandering to the lowest tier of ignorance," designed to achieve selfish electoral success at the expense of justice and dignity for Negroes. (*The Liberator,* June 26 and July 10, 1863.)

6 5

TO OLIVER JOHNSON

Boston, July 14, 1863.

Dear Johnson:

Enclosed, you will find the notice for the 1st of August celebration at Abington.[1] Also, the disclaimer of [Moncure D.] Conway's mischievous overture to [James M.] Mason, by the Executive Committee of the American Anti-Slavery Society. Both for insertion in this week's Standard.[2] You will see that we have tried to deal with poor Conway as tenderly as possible. The most astonishing thing of it all is, that, in the first sentence of his letter, he tells two falsehoods, in order to assume to be duly empowered to negotiate with Mason! He certainly meant well, but he acted upon the vicious maxim of the Jesuits, that "the end sanctifies the means"[3]—the end being, in this case, to make Mason avow that, not even to ensure independence, will the Confederacy consent to the abolition of slavery. Let us trust it may be all "overruled for Good."

Should you copy that portion of the proceedings of the Framingham celebration, July 4th, which relates to Mason and Conway, (and I think it would be well for you to do so,) please alter where I say of Conway, "he has put himself on his back," by substituting, "he has put himself in a tight place."[4]

We are slowly getting the particulars of the horrible excesses of the mob in your city, whose example is very likely to be imitated in degree at least, in all our great cities.[5] I shall not be surprised to hear that both the Standard and Independent offices have been sacked. To-day, there are symptoms that a riot is brewing in this city; and, should it break out with violence, it would naturally seek to vent its fury upon such as [Wendell] Phillips and myself, and upon our dwellings. The whole North is volcanic.

I have no doubt that all this is understood and provided for at Richmond—that there is a perfect understanding between the leading rebels and the leading copperheads—and that they both mean to conflagrate and shed blood to any extent at the North, rather than to have President Lincoln succeed in putting down the rebellion at the cost of slavery.

My heart bleeds to think of the poor, unoffending colored people of New York, outraged, plundered, murdered by the demons in human shape who now hold mastery over New York. "How long, O Lord, how long?"[6]

How sad the fate of Superintendent Kennedy![7] How honorably he deserves to be remembered for the manner in which he aimed to discharge the responsible duties of his position!

Yours, without wavering,

Wm. Lloyd Garrison.

Oliver Johnson.

ALS: Garrison Papers, Boston Public Library; extract printed in *Life*, IV, 83.

1. Garrison refers to a celebration of the twenty-ninth anniversary of the emancipation of slaves in the British West Indies, at which, in addition to Garrison, Henry Wilson and Theodore D. Weld spoke. (*National Anti-Slavery Standard*, July 25 and August 8, 1863.)

2. Both notices were printed in the *Standard*, July 25, 1863.

3. A classic maxim, of Greek origin, often quoted.

4. The repudiation of Conway's proposal was printed without Garrison's revision in the *Standard*, July 18, 1863.

5. Garrison writes on the second day of the draft riots in New York. By the time the first federal conscription bill was enacted in 1863, New York, with its heterogeneous mix of poverty and wealth, was a crowded and unsanitary city with the highest death rate of any in the United States or Europe. The large immigrant population lived in tenements, as many as six to ten in a room; gentlemen of wealth lived in mansions comparable to the best in London or Paris. Tensions inevitable in such a city became overt following the first public drawing for the draft (one of the most resented provisions of which permitted a wealthy man to avoid service upon the payment of $300). By Monday, July 13, mobs, predominantly but not excusively working-class Irish, gathered in many sections of the city, striking out indiscriminantly at individuals of wealth or authority and especially at blacks regardless of status. They looted stores, burned offices and houses, and committed atrocities. Ill-trained police and incompetently led federal troops could not restore order until 119 lives had been lost.

Garrison was correct in anticipating that the riots would spread, but even in the cities most affected (Boston, Hartford, Newark, and Jersey City), the violence was minor compared with that in New York. News of riots in northern cities was gratefully received in the South as evidence of northern disunity. (Adrian Cook, *The Armies of the Streets: The New York City Draft Riots of 1863*, Lexington, Ky., 1974; for a contemporary account see *The Liberator*, July 17, 1863.)

6. A common biblical phrase to be found in approximately this form in such passages as Psalms 6:3.

7. John Kennedy, superintendent of New York police, was repeatedly attacked by a mob on July 13. Beaten unconscious and presumed dead, he was eventually rescued, but he never fully recovered from his injuries. (Irving Werstein, *The Draft Riots, July 1863*, New York, 1957.)

66

TO GEORGE THOMPSON GARRISON

Boston, August 6, 1863

We have all been made very glad, to-day, by the receipt of your pencilled note, dated Hatteras Inlet, July 31st, announcing your safe arrival at Newbern, though a little surprised at your sudden removal with Wild's Brigade, probably to Morris Island. . . .[1]

You may readily suppose that I was very much disappointed in not being able to see you, and give you my parting blessing and a farewell grasp of the hand, when your regiment marched through Boston. Multitudes, with myself, were greatly disappointed that the regiment did not parade on the Common, where we all expected to take our farewell leave. I followed you, however, all the way down to the vessel, hoping to speak to you; but I found myself on the wrong side, and the throng was so great and the marching so continuous that I could not press my way through. After you were all on board, I went with a number of friends to the next wharf below, where we waited more than an hour, hoping to see you off and give you the parting salute. But the rain poured heavily down, and we were all compelled to beat a retreat—keenly regretting that we could not, even from a distance, shout farewell.

Not a day has passed that we have not had you in our liveliest remembrance. I miss you by my side at the table, and at the printing-office, and cannot get reconciled to the separation. Yet I have nothing but praise to give you that you have been faithful to your highest convictions, and taking your life in your hands, are willing to lay it down, even like the brave Col. Shaw and his associates, if need be, in the cause of freedom, and for the suppression of slavery and the rebellion.[2] True, I could have wished you could ascend to what I believe a higher plane of moral heroism and a nobler method of self-sacrifice; but as you are true to yourself, I am glad of your fidelity, and proud of your willingness to run any risk in a cause that is undeniably just and good. I have no fear that you will be found wanting at any time in the trial-hour, or in the discharge of your official duties. . . .

We shall wait for intelligence, from day to day, with the keenest interest—trusting it may be your good fortune to enter that hot-bed of nullification and treason, Charleston, with your colored associates, victorious over all opposition. The fall of that city will give more satisfaction to the entire North than that of any other place, not excepting Richmond itself. I have my doubts whether it will be accomplished for some time. Doubtless the conflict will be long and sanguinary, but in the sequel the city must surrender. . . .[3]

Your mother's thoughts are all about you. God bless you, my boy!

Printed extract: *Life*, IV, 83–84.

1. "Wild's Brigade," sometimes known as "Wild's African Brigade," had been recruited by Edward Augustus Wild (1825–1891), a doctor turned army officer. A na-

tive of Massachusetts and a Harvard graduate, Wild practiced medicine in the Turkish army during the Crimean War and in Brookline subsequently. During the Civil War he rose from captain to brigadier general of volunteers, seeing action in the first battle of Bull Run and being seriously wounded in McClellan's Peninsular campaign and at South Mountain, where he lost an arm. In 1863 he recruited black troops both in Massachusetts and in North Carolina. In September of that year he was transferred briefly to Morris Island on the south side of Charleston harbor, the site of Fort Wagner and Fort Morris, where General Quincy Gillmore had the preceding summer established a military foothold later to be used for attacks on Charleston. Subsequently, General Wild and his brigade served in the vicinity of Norfolk and Portsmouth, did picket duty on the Appomattox River, and, as the war ended, occupied Richmond as part of General Kautz's division. Following the war he became superintendent of a silver mine in Nevada, and he spent his last days in South America. (Ezra J. Warner, *Generals in Blue: Lives of the Union Commanders*, Baton Rouge, La., 1964; E. Milby Burton, *The Siege of Charleston, 1861–1865*, Columbia, S.C., 1970.)

2. Robert Gould Shaw (1837–1863), the son of Garrison's friend Francis George Shaw, commanded the 54th Massachusetts regiment. Despite the skill and courage demonstrated by him and his black troops, Colonel Shaw was killed on July 18, 1863 in the regiment's first major encounter, an attack on Fort Wagner near Charleston. A handsome memorial to Shaw and his regiment by McKim and Augustus Saint-Gaudens was constructed on the Boston Common facing the State House. (James M. McPherson, *Marching Toward Freedom: The Negro in the Civil War, 1861–1865*, New York, 1968.)

3. Garrison's prognosis was accurate. Although under attack by land and sea from 1862 on, Charleston was controlled by Confederate troops until their withdrawal in February 1865. (Burton, *The Siege of Charleston.*)

67

TO AARON M. POWELL

Boston, Oct. 31, 1863.

Dear Aaron;

Your letter of yesterday, enclosing "a certified check for the Maria Marriott legacy—less $25, Government tax"—has safely come to hand.[1] Accept my thanks for what you have done in the matter. I shall, for the present, make a deposit in some safe bank, and take all possible care to see that this sacred legacy of the sainted woman who made it is used in accordance with her wishes. As I told you when here, I do not think it best to announce that I have this money in trust, lest it should subject me to all sorts of annoying appeals, and from parties, perhaps, the least deserving of aid. Of course, in due time, it will be announced in the Liberator and Standard what Maria desired in her Will for the benefit of the suffering colored people.[2]

You truly remark that, in view of her limited means, her bequest was a large and generous one.

Wendell has felt very sorry that he could not get his things ready to join you this week, according to your desire. Yesterday he telegraphed you to that effect. To-day he has received a letter from you, which will enable him to remain at home a few days longer. I believe it is his intention to be with you at Ghent on Thursday afternoon next.

I am both glad and proud that he is disposed to try what he can do in the lecturing-field, to help give the death-blow to slavery.[3] He might have taken up someone of the professions, and no doubt would have succeeded had he chosen to do so; but he has no worldly ambition either for fame or pelf, and loves virtue and truth more than all things else. His moral nature is mature, and he posses a clear vision and a solid understanding. My only anxiety about him [is] as to his voice. He habitually speaks in a low tone in conversation, and will have to exert himself to be distinctly heard in a large hall. But by a little practice he may succeed without any great difficulty. You must cry, (*sub rosa*,) "Louder! louder!" if he fails to speak loud enough, even if he should despairingly reply, "Vere is de vind?"

It was pleasant to have the prompt co-operation of Gerrit Smith offered to us, in carrying on our new movement, in the shape of a donation of $200.

Do not so multiply your meetings as to overtax lungs and strength.

In my mind's eye, I see you all in your dear home, and feel to be with you in spirit. I send the love of our household to you all. We are hoping and expecting to see Lizzie [Powell] in a few days.

Ever truly yours,

Wm. Lloyd Garrison.

A. M. Powell.

ALS: Merrill Collection of Garrison Papers, Wichita State University Library.

1. Maria Marriott (1788–1862), the daughter of Henry Marriott of Claverack, N.Y., and the sister of the better-known Charles Marriott (1782–1843), was a Hicksite Quaker and a dedicated abolitionist. She was also a generous contributor to the American Anti-Slavery Society. The amount of her legacy was $500. (Letter to the editor from Mary L. Thomas, Librarian, Columbia County Historical Society, Kinderhook, N.Y.; obituary, *The Liberator*, June 6, 1862; letter from Aaron M. Powell to Garrison, October 30, 1863, Anti-Slavery Letters to Garrison and Others, Boston Public Library.)
2. Diligent search through files of both *The Liberator* and the *National Anti-Slavery Standard* has not revealed any announcement of the disposition of Miss Marriott's fund.
3. Wendell Phillips Garrison's lecture tour with Powell is mentioned in *The Liberator*, November 6, where his itinerary is given. The itinerary is also printed in the *Standard*, November 7, along with a note under "Personal": "It affords us great

satisfaction to observe that Wendell Phillips Garrison has entered the field as an anti-slavery lecturer. . . ." The purpose of the tour was "to stimulate the people to circulate and sign petitions to Congress for the immediate and total abolition of slavery."

68

TO GERRIT SMITH

Boston, Oct. 31, 1863.

Dear Mr. Smith:

It gave me great pleasure to acknowledge, in last week's Liberator,[1] the receipt of your check for $200, in aid of the movement of the American Anti-Slavery Society, to secure, if possible, the total abolition of slavery throughout our country at the next session of Congress. I need not assure you that the money will be faithfully used for the one specific object which it was given to promote. To that object we shall bend ourselves with zeal and perseverance, seeing as we do in its accomplishment the most effectual, if not the only satisfactory and reliable method to secure national unity, restore peace, and suppress this wickedest of all satanic rebellions. True, that portion of slavery which was exempted from the application of the President's Proclamation of last January is manifestly dissolving "like morning mists before the rising sun,"[2] and must wholly disappear, provided that Proclamation be carried out in every part of Rebeldom; still, with our national affairs so complicated by the war, and with so formidable a division in the political and moral sentiment of the North, we cannot tell what a day may bring forth. Slavery having been recognized, fostered and protected by the General Government, its entire abolition by the Government, in solemn form, would unquestionably be decisive as against all attempts to nullify the Proclamation through new compromises, or to perpetuate a remnant of the slave system. At any rate, a fresh moral agitation of the slavery question cannot fail to be of service to the President, to Congress, and to the Government; for, as yet, the crime of enslaving the negro (aside from the use to be made of him in putting down the rebellion) is not much laid to heart by the people of the North.

I have been somewhat apprehensive lest your repeated declarations of your purpose to make the suppression of the rebellion a *sine qua non*, and not the abolition of slavery, might be injuriously because plausibly misconstrued by the enemies of the Anti-Slavery cause, who also profess to have the same object in view, but who maintain that slavery is to remain intact on the obtainment of peace. Of course, *you* have no doubt that the suppression of the rebellion will be, *ipso facto*, the extinction of slavery; nor have I much doubt that this will be the result. Still, it is not certain; and in a case so momentous, it is desirable, if we can, to "make assurance doubly sure, and take a bond of fate."[3] I fear there is a considerable portion of the Republican party that, in case the rebels should ground their arms, would readily join the Copperheads in making peace on a slaveholding basis, with even some new concessions to the South. Remember that even Horace Greeley doggedly insists that "the President is not *enslaved* by his Proclamation," and may nullify it *ad libitum* if the rebellion can thereby be speedily put down.[4] I fear nothing for the cause of the slave while the war lasts; only when peace is won, and political intrique shall begin its desperate work.

You have already seen that the third Decade of the American Anti-Slavery Society is to be held in Philadelphia, on the 3d and 4th of December. It will be an occasion of thrilling interest.[5] In behalf of the Executive Committee, I not only invite, but warmly urge you and your dear wife to be present on that occasion—an occasion grandly historic. Your presence is greatly desired by us all.

Deep was our regret that we were compelled to abandon our contemplated visit to Peterboro', but we shall hope to be with you another year without fail. Give our kindest remembrances to Mrs. Smith.

Yours, with high regards,

Wm. Lloyd Garrison.

Gerrit Smith.

ALS: Gerrit Smith Collection, Syracuse University Library.

1. October 30, 1863.
2. Not identified.
3. Shakespeare, *Macbeth*, IV, i, 83–84.
4. Although the exact source of the quotation from Greeley has not been found, it is known that at this period the editor of the New York *Tribune* frequently urged Union even at the expense of abolition. In the issue of his paper for March 30, 1863, for instance, he asserted that the President "is nowise fettered by the Proclamation of Freedom." For an exchange of views on the subject between Greeley and Theodore Tilton see the *Tribune*, April 4, 1863.
5. The celebration held in Philadelphia's Concert Hall was suggested at the annual American Anti-Slavery Society meeting in May. Its purpose was "to revive the remembrance of the long thirty years' warfare with the terrible forces of slavery . . . but also to renew . . . the demand for the entire and speedy extinction of slavery in every part of our country." Eleven of the original founders of the society attended, and in contrast to the first meeting, this one was a well-attended and unthreatened celebration. Speakers included Garrison, Henry Ward Beecher, Henry Wilson, Lucretia Mott, and Frederick Douglass. The proceedings were reported in

the *National Anti-Slavery Standard,* December 12, 19, and 26, 1863, and January 2, 1864, as well as in *The Liberator,* December 18 and 25, 1863, and January 1, 1864. The American Anti-Slavery Society published the full proceedings in pamphlet form with an appendix and catalogue of antislavery publications in America from 1750 through 1863. (*Life.*)

---

6 9

TO GEORGE W. JULIAN

Boston, Nov. 12, 1863.

Dear Mr. Julian:

Presuming you will hardly be able to attend the commemorative meeting at Philadelphia, I will only add, that in case of your absence, it would be gratifying to us all to receive a letter from you, to be read on the occasion.[1]

I hope that slavery will receive its death-blow at the hands of the approaching session of Congress, as the only method of securing permanent peace and preserving the unity of the republic.[2] Ever relying upon your liberty-loving co-operation—and deeply sympathizing with you in your recent bereavement[3]—I remain,

Yours, for a speedy jubilee,

Wm. Lloyd Garrison.

Hon. G. W. Julian.

ALS: Giddings-Julian Papers, Library of Congress. This letter is one of a group of autograph notes Garrison wrote on the following printed invitation to the Third Decade commemoration of the American Anti-Slavery Society:

THE THIRD DECADE.
⟦SPECIAL INVITATION.⟧

BOSTON, NOV. 12, 1863.

The AMERICAN ANTI-SLAVERY SOCIETY will commemorate the Thirtieth Anniversary of its formation, on THURSDAY and FRIDAY, Dec. 3 and 4, 1863, at CONCERT HALL, in the City of PHILADELPHIA, commencing at 10 o'clock, A.M., of each day. Its object, as originally announced, and uncompromisingly adhered to for the last thirty years, was and is the immediate and entire abolition of Slavery in the United States, by all those instrumentalities sanctioned by law, humanity, and religion; and thus, "to deliver our land from its deadliest curse, and to wipe out the foulest stain which rests upon our national escutcheon." Its measures were proclaimed to be, and ever have been, "such only as the opposition of moral purity to moral corruption, the destruction of error by the potency of truth, the overthrow of prejudice by the power of love, and THE ABOLITION OF SLAVERY BY THE SPIRIT OF REPENTANCE."

At its approaching celebration, the Society will have the sublime privilege to announce, as the result, primarily, of its disinterested, patriotic, and christian labors,—the emancipation of THREE MILLIONS THREE HUNDRED THOU-

SAND SLAVES, by the fiat of the American Government, on the 1st of January last.

It is not only to revive the remembrance of the long thirty years' warfare with the terrible forces of Slavery, and to acknowledge the hand of a wonder-working Providence in guiding the way of the little Anti-Slavery army through great moral darkness and many perils, that we now invite this meeting, but also to renew, in the name of humanity, of conscience, and of pure and undefiled religion, the demand for the entire and speedy extinction of Slavery in every part of our country.

Your attendance at this Commemorative Meeting, in Philadelphia, on the 3rd and 4th of December next, is respectfully solicited and cordially desired.

In behalf of the Executive Committee,

WILLIAM LLOYD GARRISON,
President

CHARLES C. BURLEIGH, ⎫
WENDELL PHILLIPS, 　⎰ *Secretaries.*

☞ Answers to be addressed to Mr. GARRISON, Boston; or to J. MILLER McKIM, 106, North Tenth Street, Philadelphia.

1. Julian did send a letter, dated November 27, to be read at the meeting. He said that in resorting to force the South had taken an "infernal leap at the nation's throat," making it possible for the North to receive "the remission of its sins through the baptism of fire and blood." In short, "their [the South's] madness has been our salvation." (*The Liberator*, December 25, 1863.)

2. Garrison refers to congressional efforts toward the legal abolition of slavery. Resolutions for an amendment to the Constitution were introduced in December 1863. A final draft passed the Senate on April 8, 1864; after the initial failure on June 15, 1864, to secure a two-thirds majority, it passed the House on January 31, 1865. Following approval by three-fourths of the state legislatures, the Thirteenth Amendment was proclaimed ratified on December 18, 1865.

3. Julian lost his son, Louis Henry (1854–1863), on October 16. (Patrick W. Riddleberger, *George Washington Julian, Radical Republican*, Indiana Historical Collections, 45, [Indianapolis], 1966.)

70

TO ARTHUR TAPPAN

BOSTON, November 12, 1863.

DEAR AND VENERATED SIR:

Thirty-three years seven months ago I was lying in the cell of the city prison in Baltimore, for the crime of exposing and denouncing certain townsmen of mine, whom I detected in carrying on the domestic slavetrade, between that city and New Orleans. Comparatively unknown at that time, and utterly without means to pay the fine and costs of court that were imposed upon me by a slaveholding judge, I might have died within those prison walls, if your sympathizing and philanthropic heart had not prompted you, unsolicited, to send the needed sum for my redemption. It is not for me to trace the consequences of that deed to the cause of the oppressed since that period; but I desire to assure you that my gratitude to you is as fresh and overflowing as it was when I was delivered from my incarceration, and will ever remain so.[1]

It is now more than a score of years since I had the pleasure of seeing you. Time, of course, has been busy with us both in making his impression upon us, although I am considerably younger than yourself. On the 10th of next month I shall complete my fifty-eighth year. I presume you have numbered fourscore years. May God grant us the inexpressibly happy privilege of witnessing a universal jubilee, a horribly wicked rebellion suppressed, and peace and unity secured from sea to sea, before this "mortal shall have put on immortality."[2]

Your ever grateful friend,

WM. LLOYD GARRISON.

ARTHUR TAPPAN, ESQ.

Printed: Lewis Tappan, *The Life of Arthur Tappan* (New York, 1871), pp. 186–187. This letter originally accompanied a printed invitation to attend the Third Decade meeting of the American Anti-Slavery Society. (See the letter to George W. Julian, November 12, 1863, descriptive note.)

Arthur Tappan (1786–1865), born in Northampton, Mass., and originally engaged in business in Boston and Portland, Me., is chiefly associated with New York City, where he established himself as a merchant in the silk-jobbing business as early as 1826. As he accumulated wealth, he contributed generously to virtually all the leading reforms of the period and especially to abolition. He became associated with Garrison in 1830, when he paid the fine that released him from the Baltimore jail. During the following decade he was one of Garrison's most important supporters, though by 1840 he was convinced that Garrison involved himself with too many reforms, and he broke away from the American Anti-Slavery Society to help form the American and Foreign Anti-Slavery Society. By the time of Garrison's letter he was living in retirement in New Haven, Conn. Although invited, Tappan did not attend the meeting to which Garrison refers; his letter of regret was read aloud to the gathering. (See *The Liberator*, December 18, 1863.)

1. Garrison also expressed his gratitude to Tappan directly at the meeting of the American Anti-Slavery Society, December 3–4, 1863. As a result, facts emerged showing that Tappan was not the only would-be benefactor in 1830. Henry Clay, whom Garrison later considered one of the archenemies of abolition, had also been willing to facilitate his release from jail. The new facts reached Garrison obliquely. On December 8, 1863, Abijah W. Thayer of Haverhill, Mass., editor and friend of John Greenleaf Whittier, wrote to Garrison explaining that Tappan was not the only one who sought Garrison's release. Clay, without Garrison's knowledge, had been approached by Whittier and had expressed his willingness to help until he discovered that Tappan had already paid Garrison's fine. The Louisville *Journal* learned from *The Liberator* about Clay's offer to help Garrison and charged both Garrison and Whittier with subsequent ingratitude toward Clay. As Garrison pointed out when he printed portions of the editorial from the Louisville *Journal*, the fact that Clay would have paid the fine had Tappan not paid it first "presents no reason why we should have allowed Mr. Clay to go unrebuked for his subsequent efforts to crush the anti-slavery movement." (All of the pertinent documents involving Whittier, Clay, Thayer, the Louisville *Journal*, and Garrison were printed in *The Liberator*, December 18, 1863, and January 15, 22, March 11, 25, 1864.)

2. I Corinthians 15:54.

7 1

TO JAMES MILLER McKIM

Boston, Nov. 14, 1863.

My dear McKim:

I have been altogether too tardy in returning my thanks for several letters received from you, in regard to the approaching Decade. I am much obliged to you for the various suggestions contained in them, and do not know that I have any to proffer in return. I was, at first, strongly inclined to advocate holding three sessions each day; but, in view of the conclusion to which you and our other Philadelphia friends have come, and also of the extreme brevity of the afternoons in December, I am entirely reconciled to the proposition for only two sessions a day. Nevertheless, I am afraid we shall find it both a difficult and a delicate matter to decide who shall be the speakers among so many as will in all probability be present, each one of whom may desire to be heard. It cannot well be a "free meeting," in our ordinary use of the term.[1] There are certain persons who must have precedence of others. For instance—Wendell Phillips, S. J. May, Lucretia Mott, Mary Grew, Robert Purvis, J. M. McKim, and Beriah Green.[2] I do not know whether the last named will be with us; but should he do so, it will be no more than courteous to ask him to speak, in view of the admirable part he performed at the issuing of the Declaration of Sentiments.[3] Yet I fear he is in a somewhat morbid state of mind relative to the Administration and the Rebellion, and would be more inclined to criminate the former than to denounce the latter.

I trust dear Lucretia Mott, Mary Grew, and Robert Purvis will not fail to speak,—ably representing, as they would, by their sex and complexion, those features of our struggle of which we have all been so jealous and so proud. You must give us your reminiscences, and whatever else may occur to you. At the opening session, it will doubtless be deemed pertinent to have the Declaration of Sentiments read. That task I will perform, adding a supplementary paper, giving a brief sketch of our Anti-Slavery struggle.

Do you know whether Anna Dickinson is to be at home at that time? and, if so, would she be inclined to be among our speakers?

Theodore Tilton tells me he will aim to be present. Whether Parker Pillsbury, or Stephen and Abby Foster, will be with us, I do not know.[4]

Mr. [Samuel] May [Jr.] has sent out a large number of printed invitations to various persons to be at the celebration,—not expecting, however, that many will be able personally to attend. Of course, if our friend Gerrit Smith should be on hand, every one will expect a speech from him. He writes me that he has overworked himself of late, and needs repose.

We have invited Arthur Tappan, but neither Lewis nor Joshua Leavitt.[5]

May we be spared the presence of C. W. Denison![6] But I fear it will suit him to be prominent, if he can, on the occasion. He is a strange compound.

Of the whole number of signers of the Declaration, I believe only one—James F. Otis—ever repudiated its anti-slavery principles and doctrines.[7]

How shall we be able to procure an accurate list of the names of the signers who have died since 1833?

My friend A. H. Love has written to me in regard to giving a lecture in Concert Hall an evening or two preceding the Decade meeting.[8] He will probably show you my reply, as I requested him to obtain your judgment.

Thanks for your proffered hospitality! It is most gratefully accepted. It is doubtful whether Mrs. G. will be able to accompany me, but I shall try to get her consent.

Yours, fraternally,

Wm. Lloyd Garrison.

Our entire household send loving regards to yours.

☞ Should wife not go with me, William diffidently suggests that he would like to share my bed, with your permission.[9] Wendell will also go; he is now absent, lecturing with A. M. Powell.

ALS: Garrison Papers, Boston Public Library.

1. By "free meeting" Garrison refers to the practice of permitting all to speak freely without restriction to a prearranged schedule. In addition to Garrison about twenty-five persons, including all those mentioned in this letter, except Phillips and Green, spoke at the meeting. (*The Liberator,* December 11, 1863.)

2. Beriah Green (1795–1874), originally from Vermont, graduated from Andover Seminary before becoming a minister in Vermont and Maine. Subsequently he became a professor at Western Reserve College in Cleveland and in 1833 president of Oneida Institute at Whitesboro, N.Y. An abolitionist who preached against slavery as early as 1822, he was the president of the convention founding the American Anti-Slavery Society in 1833. At the time of Garrison's letter Green was minister of the abolitionist Congregational Church in Whitesboro.

3. The Declaration of Sentiments was drawn up in 1833 at the founding of the American Anti-Slavery Society. (See *The Liberator,* December 14, 1833; *AWT,* p. 78)

4. Stephen Symonds Foster (1809–1881) of New Hampshire, the husband of Abby Kelley, had dropped out of divinity school to become an outstanding anti-slavery lecturer. He was also active in many other reform movements, such as woman's rights, temperance, peace, and labor.

5. Lewis Tappan (1788–1873), like his older brother, Arthur, was a successful businessman and an influential reformer. Originally associated with the Arthur Tap-

pan firm, he went into business for himself in 1841, retiring in 1849 with the deliberate plan of living off his capital and giving his full energy to abolition and other reforms. As an abolitionist he first followed Garrison, then his brother, Arthur, and the others in the new national organization. In 1855 he broke with the American and Foreign Anti-Slavery Society to associate himself with the newer and more radical organization, the Abolition Society.

Joshua Leavitt (1794–1873), a clergyman, was more generally known as an abolitionist and an editor. He had edited the general reform paper the *Evangelist* (1831–1837) and the *Emancipator* (1837–1848), and finally became the office editor of the New York *Independent* (1848–1873).

6. Charles Wheeler Denison (1812–1881), like the Tappan brothers, was a member of the splinter group that founded the American and Foreign Anti-Slavery Society in 1840. Garrison had found Denison's behavior at meetings offensive as early as 1844 (see his letter to James B. Yerrinton, May 7, 1844, *Letters*, III, 256–257). Denison did not attend the December meeting.

7. James Frederick Otis (c. 1800–1867), lawyer and journalist, repudiated the Declaration of Sentiments of the American Anti-Slavery Society in 1835, as a result of conservative views he acquired during a trip to Virginia. (*The Liberator*, September 19, 1835.)

8. Alfred Henry Love (1830–1913), the son of William Henry and Rachel Evans Love, was a Philadelphia woolen commission merchant. Through his marriage in 1853 to Susan Henry Brown (c. 1830–1913), he became affiliated with the Society of Friends. In 1862 he expressed ardent pacifist views in *An Appeal in Vindication of Peace Principles;* in 1863 he was drafted into the army but refused to serve. He was subsequently indicted but was acquitted because of poor health. When the American Peace Society endorsed the Civil War, he organized a radical peace movement that led to the formation of the Universal Peace Society (later the Universal Peace Union), of which he was president until his death.

9. William Lloyd Garrison, Jr., in fact, rather than Helen E. Garrison, attended the meeting. (*The Liberator*, December 18, 1863.) ·

IV LINCOLN REAPPRAISED: 1864

CRUCIAL MILITARY EVENTS were but a distant prospect in Garrison's letters of 1864. In his letter of May 6 to Oliver Johnson (micro.) he wrote: "A tremendous conflict is now, in all probability, going on between the forces of Grant and those of Lee. I am not particularly sanguine of Grant's success. Any how, Anniversary Week will possess a solemn and thrilling interest." The reference was to a famous, though indecisive, battle. On May 3, Grant, who had for two months been commander-in-chief of the Union armies, crossed the Rapidan River near Fredericksburg, Virginia, and advanced from Chancellorsville toward Spotsylvania Court House, fighting on May 5 and 6 the Battle of the Wilderness. Although he was unable to defeat Lee, he did inflict heavy losses and continue a significant advance. Characteristically, Garrison set into juxtaposition the battle between the commanders and the approaching anniversary meeting of the American Anti-Slavery Society, as though the latter were the more important event, as perhaps it was to a nonresistant who would have liked to ignore the violence around him. On January 13 Garrison wrote a letter in which he showed deeper concern for a potential military event; he asked that his son Frank be excused from military drill at the Boston Latin School.

For Garrison, who was always more concerned with individuals than with battles, the cynosure of 1864 was Abraham Lincoln, his activities and his reelection. Although in the early years of Lincoln's administration Garrison had been critical of the President's moderation, by the early spring of 1864 he had decided to support him for reelection. He wrote to Oliver Johnson on March 14 (micro.), "The best thing that can be done, politically, is to stand by Abraham Lincoln, with all his short-comings." In an editorial in *The Liberator*, March 18, entitled "THE PRESIDENCY" he publicly announced his support, declaring the election of great importance for "the suppression of the rebellion, and the abolition of slavery." He cited his own credentials as a nonpolitical and impartial observer and then stated his conviction that Lincoln must be reelected. "Not that Mr. Lincoln is not open to criticism and censure; we have both criticised and censured him again and again. . . . Nevertheless, there is also much to rejoice over and to be thankful for." Lincoln had "at one blow, severed the chains of three millions three hundred thousand slaves,—thus virtually abolishing the whole slave system . . . as an act dictated alike by patriotism, justice and humanity." Garrison's support of Lincoln was only reinforced by opposition from other reformers—notably Wendell Phillips, Susan B. Anthony, Elizabeth Cady Stanton, and Anna E. Dickinson, who thought General Frémont the better man. It would seem, also, that Garrison became more enthusiastic about the President after interviews with him in June of this year.

About the same date as the interviews (June 7), Francis W. Newman, distinguished English academician, reformer, and brother of John Cardinal Newman, wrote Garrison to remonstrate with him regarding his support of Lincoln and the Civil War. After testifying to Garrison's "immense moral weight," he expressed surprise at that support of Lincoln's policy and of the war, which Newman was no longer disposed to think "a glorious and fruitful war of freedom." Even the Emancipation Proclamation, about which everyone had been so hopeful, had proved hypocritical, since it freed only the slaves in such states as were in rebellion on January 1, 1863, rather than "'the slaves of all the States which *have rebelled.*'" Thereby, through technicalities, the Proclamation excluded several hundreds of thousands of slaves in regions dominated by federal force and in theory freed slaves in other areas not under northern control at all. Also, Newman was indignant at what he considered Lincoln's refusal to face up to moral issues. "Horrible indeed is the augury for your future, when your Chief Magistrate dares not indulge the moralities of his heart, through conscientious tremors at the guilt of violating the wicked laws of conquered rebels! . . . A purer morality *must be enunciated by your Chief Magistrate, and sternly applied,* before you can purge your civil and military administration of virtual traitors."

Always concerned that the British understand the rectitude of his position, Garrison printed Newman's letter in *The Liberator* on July 1, with the brief comment that Newman had in the past "done our government eminent service by his eloquent testimonies in its behalf, . . . but whose vision now seems to be beclouded." Two weeks later Garrison printed a three-column letter in reply to Newman's accusation, in which he answered Newman's argument point by point and in the process expressed fully his views about Lincoln and the effectiveness of his administration. Central to the position expressed in this letter is the following passage, which shows an understanding of the political problems facing the President surprising for a reformer:

His freedom to follow his convictions of duty as an individual is one thing —as the President of the United States, it is limited by the functions of his office; for the people do not elect a President to play the part of reformer or philanthropist, nor to enforce upon the nation his own peculiar ethical or humanitary ideas, without regard to his oath or their will. His primary and all-comprehensive duty is to maintain the Union and execute the Constitution, in good faith . . . without reference to the views of any clique or party in the land. . . . And herein lies the injustice of your criticism upon him. You seem to regard him as occupying a position and wielding powers virtually autocratic. . . .

Speaking of Lincoln more specifically, Garrison continued: "It is my firm conviction that no man has occupied the chair of the Chief Magistracy in America, who has more assiduously or more honestly endeavored to discharge all its duties with a single eye to the welfare of the country, than Mr. Lincoln."

The following week (July 22) Garrison printed a second letter to Newman, in which he continued arguing on specific points. In the meantime, Newman remained unaware of Garrison's two replies because his issues of *The Liberator* for both the fifteenth and the twenty-second were lost in the mail. In *The Liberator* for September 30, however, there appeared another letter from Newman, dated September 1, addressed to the editor of the *English Leader*, who had sent him copies of the two Garrison letters. Newman contended that he did not mean to question Lincoln's honesty but rather his "mean prejudice against color" and his preference for gradual over immediate emancipation. "I see his interpretation of the Constitution is such as to give vast advantage and vitality to the slave system; and from this I feel grave alarm for the future." Again he warned against the possibility of foreign intervention following "any renewal of war." In the editorial comment accompanying the letter, Garrison suggested that Newman recall the state of the nation when Lincoln took office and remember that the Emancipation Proclamation freed more than three-fourths of the slave population, that emancipation had since followed in "Maryland, Western Virginia, Missouri, and the District of Columbia," and that it "is being rapidly consummated in Kentucky and Tennessee, thus terminating the holding of property in man everywhere under the American flag."

On October 14 Newman wrote another letter, which Garrison described as "kind and magnanimous" and was delighted to print on November 4, just before the election. In this letter Newman said: "I ask your pardon if I spoke too abruptly. . . . If I were an American voter, I should unhesitatingly give vote and interest and voice and pen now to Mr. Lincoln, against any candidate who would accept other terms from rebels than unconditional submission. . . . You will, I am sure, not be displeased that I regard the future of the human race now to depend more on the United States than on England."

In his first letter to Newman, Garrison had quoted from a speech Wendell Phillips delivered in Boston in April of 1862, in which Phillips spoke favorably of Lincoln. By 1864, however, Phillips was by no means well-disposed toward the President. In the meantime, friction between Phillips and Garrison that had been smoldering early in the year burst into flame in May at the anniversary meeting of the American Anti-Slavery Society in New York City. At that meeting (referred to in the letter to Helen of May 13 and reported fully in *The Liberator,* May 20 and 27) Phillips spoke of the frightening cost of the continuing war, and he criticized Lincoln and his administration. He lamented that it was Lincoln's policy to reconstruct the Union with as little reference to slavery as possible. Moreover, he regretted that "the Administration has never yet acknowledged the manhood of the negro. . . . The negro is to serve you; you are to fix his wages—what is he worth; if he is insubordinate, there is the Provost Marshall. . . . The negro is a serf, punishable at the will, hireable at the will of the Government. No manhood." He also blamed the administration for having drafted blacks into the army.

Following Phillips' speech, Garrison, who was presiding as president of the society, could not resist "a single remark," and his comments, as reported in *The Liberator,* filled a half-column of print. Granting that more must be done for the Negro, he said, "still, looking at the question broadly, comprehensively, and philosophically, I think the people will ask another question—whether they themselves have been one hair's breadth in advance of Abraham Lincoln?" After the applause subsided, Garrison continued, "For my own part, when I remember the trials through which he has passed, and the perils which have surrounded him . . . when I remember how fearfully pro-slavery was the public sentiment of the

North, . . . when I remember how nearly a majority, even at this hour, is the seditious element of the North, and then remember that Abraham Lincoln has struck the chains from the limbs of more than three millions of slaves (applause) . . . when I remember that we have now nearly reached the culmination of our great struggle for the suppression of the rebellion and its cause, I do not feel disposed, for one, to take this occasion . . . to say anything very harshly against Abraham Lincoln." At this point in his "remark" the applause was "loud and prolonged."

The dispute between Phillips and Garrison continued on the second day of the meeting, when Phillips made the revealing remark that "our work has been taken out of our hands," implying that the war had appropriated the society's rightful goal of freeing the slaves. Then he attacked George Thompson, the English abolitionist who had agreed with Garrison's opinion of Lincoln on the first day of the meeting, and followed by discussing England as a second-rate power. Finally, he focused on Lincoln: "The day of his election I shall consider the end of the Union in my day, or its reconstruction on terms worse than Disunion." When Garrison resumed the platform, he described Phillips' speech as moving from brightness to darkness. He himself proposed to begin and end in brightness. He pointed to "the magnificent spectacle we have been so long desiring to see—a nation struggling to be free! and learning the lesson of impartial justice through divine retribution. The future before us, with liberty, is bright and glorious; and we are to have liberty."

Despite such public display of animosity between the two abolitionists, Garrison was reluctant to admit that there was any irreconcilable difference between them. In *The Liberator* for May 27, for instance, he condemned the Springfield *Republican* for an editorial on the "schism between Phillips and Garrison," saying, "Mr. Phillips is as free to be criticised as he is to criticise; and so are we. Abolitionists are the last persons to make any man their oracle, or to merge their individuality in that of any living being." The opposition between the two men over Lincoln continued at the New England Anti-Slavery Convention in Boston two weeks later, Phillips attacking Lincoln at length, Garrison trying to restrain himself. The convention closed with short speeches from Garrison and Thompson, defending Lincoln.

Some three weeks later the controversy erupted again when Phillips objected to the editorial conduct of the *National Anti-Slavery Standard,* which he considered pro-Lincoln, even after he had led the executive committee governing that paper to an anti-administration position. The issue was brought before a specially convened committee that supported Garrison, agreeing with him that the *Standard* "had been conducted with remarkable fairness and impartiality."[1]

In June Garrison made his first trip to the nation's capital, attending en route the annual meeting of the Progressive Friends at Longwood, Pennsylvania, and the Republican convention that renominated Lincoln in Baltimore. He reached Washington on June 9; that same day Theodore Tilton, editor of the New York *Independent,* introduced him to Lincoln. The President complimented Garrison on looking so young and referred to his recent visit to Baltimore as well as his imprisonment in 1830 in a building no longer standing: "Then, you could not get out of prison; now you cannot get in."[2] At Lincoln's urging, Garrison returned the following day for an hour's private talk. Garrison spoke directly and bluntly about what he considered the mistakes of Lincoln's first term and was much pleased by "the familiar and candid way in which he [the President] unbosomed himself."[3] The trip to Washington left Garrison fully committed to Lincoln's administration. He had been deeply influenced not only by the President himself but also by others he saw, especially Sumner, Wilson, and Stanton.

Also committed to Lincoln's policy was Garrison's friend George Thompson, who landed in Boston on February 6 for his third visit to the United States. During the year Garrison spent a good deal of time with Thompson, arranging his lecture engagements and frequently appearing on the same platform with him. In effect, Thompson had been Garrison's emissary for years. In England he advocated the cause of the North; now in the United States he supported Lincoln and therefore Garrison's point of view against Phillips'. Garrison gave Thompson's visit a maximum of publicity in *The Liberator* and wrote to colleagues about his friend's precarious financial status. He hoped to mount a national testimonial in Thompson's honor, planning to raise some $20,000 for his support. Although some funds were collected—Gerrit Smith contributed $200—the testimonial never materialized. Indeed, its failure was to make Garrison pessimistic about efforts a few years later to raise funds for his own benefit.

Lincoln's reelection, as Garrison made clear in a letter to Oliver Johnson on November 26, had significant repercussions on plans

1. Letter to Oliver Johnson, June 20, 1864.
2. Letter to Helen E. Garrison, June 9, 1864.
3. Letter to Helen E. Garrison, June 11, 1864.

for *The Liberator* and the *National Anti-Slavery Standard* as well as on plans, incidentally, for Garrison's retirement as abolitionist. Had McClellan been elected, the two papers might have profitably merged for another four years. "But," Garrison wrote, "Mr. Lincoln's re-election is certainly the death-warrant of the whole slave system, and indicates that we are very near the day of jubilee. . . . With this cheering prospect before us, it is altogether undesirable to attempt to amalgamate the two papers for so short a period."

So, with Lincoln reelected, with the war in its final stage, with the slaves free, their freedom soon to be guaranteed by an official amendment, Garrison saw his thirty-year mission as abolitionist happily resolved; he could look toward retirement in the near future. In his last extant letter for the year, dated December 13 and addressed to General Benjamin F. Butler, he can be forgiven for the optimism of the statement, "liberty . . . proclaimed throughout all the land to all the inhabitants thereof."

72

TO FRANCIS GARDNER

Boston, Jan. 13, 1864.

Francis Gardner, Esq.

Dear Sir—

My son Frank informs me that, henceforth, the boys connected with the first and second classes in the Latin School are to be subjected to military drill at Boylston Hall, from time to time, as a part of their educational training.[1] I trust the drill is not to be an arbitrary enforcement; but, doubtless, it will meet with general acceptance, and, therefore, exceptional cases may the more readily be allowed. In relation to my son, I very respectfully request and earnestly desire that he may be excused from participating in the drill aforesaid; and this I do on the ground of conscientious scruples on my part, as well as in accordance with his own wishes.[2]

Yours, with high esteem,

Wm. Lloyd Garrison.

ALS: Garrison Papers, Boston Public Library.

1. Boylston Hall, located on the corner of Boylston and Washington streets in Boston, was opened in 1810. Various meetings, concerts and entertainments were held there. Military drill in grammar schools as well as high schools and Latin schools was becoming increasingly common in Boston and in Massachusetts. (*King's*

Handbook of Boston, Cambridge, 1883, pp. 297–298; "Military Drill in Schools," *Christian Examiner*, 76: 232–240, March 1864.)

2. Available sources do not indicate whether Francis Jackson Garrison was excused from military drill.

73

TO HORACE GREELEY

[February 5, 1864]

To the Editor of the Tribune:
SIR:

The telegraphic account of the discussion between Mr. Phillips and myself, at the recent meeting of the Massachusetts Anti-Slavery Society in this city, as published in the Tribune, represents me as saying of Gen. Fremont—"Events have occurred within a year, greatly to diminish my faith in Fremont. Not a word have we heard from him in reference to the proclamation of amnesty. What a glorious opportunity was there lost!"[1] So mischievous a use is likely to be made of this perversion, that you will not only personally oblige me, but perhaps subserve the cause of our common country at this crisis, by inserting in the Tribune what I said upon the Resolution of Mr. Phillips, as given in the official report of the proceedings of the Society.[2]

Yours, for equal and exact justice,

Wm. Lloyd Garrison.

Boston, Feb. 5, 1864.

ALS: Collection of Richard Maass, White Plains, N.Y.; printed in the New York *Tribune*, February 13, 1864.

A full understanding of Garrison's letter requires some historical reconstruction of its context. Garrison refers to the thirty-first annual meeting of the Massachusetts Anti-Slavery Society held at Tremont Temple on January 28 at which Wendell Phillips introduced the following: "Resolved, That, in our opinion, the Government, in its haste, is ready to sacrifice the interest and honor of the North to secure a sham peace; thereby risking the introduction into Congress of a strong confederate minority to embarrass legislation, and leaving the freedmen and the Southern States under the control of the slaveholders. . . . and entailing on the country intestine feuds for another dozen years. . . . " Garrison endeavored to amend the resolution to read that "the Government, in its haste, is *in danger of sacrificing*. . . . " Phillips refused to accept the amendment, and the resolution passed as originally worded.

At the same meeting, in response to Phillips' eulogy of General Frémont, Garrison had said that he "must frankly confess that, while he had been a warm admirer of Frémont, his interest in him had lessened in view of the fact, that in no way had he publicly expressed any satisfaction in regard to the President's Emancipation Proclamation, nor any approval of the act authorizing the enrolment of colored soldiers." When Phillips excused Frémont by saying that the government had forbidden him to speak, Garrison replied: "No! but he has always a right to be magnanimous; and if he may not censure, he may at least loudly approve of those measures which strike at the very roots of the rebellion. What a glorious opportunity he has lost to show himself superior to all personal feelings towards the Government!" (*The Liberator*, February 5, 1864.)

1. The article to which Garrison refers was printed January 30, 1864; Garrison quotes it accurately except for slight differences in punctuation.
2. The *Tribune* printed Garrison's letter on February 13, and also a long account of the exchange between Garrison and Phillips. This version substantially agreed with that printed in *The Liberator*.

74

TO OLIVER JOHNSON

Boston, Feb. 16, 1864.

Dear Johnson:

Yours is just received. You are quite right in regard to what ought to be done with and for George Thompson in your city. Phillips will tell you what our desires are. We wish a reception to be given to G. T. in New York, similar in character to the one that is to be given to him here—i.e., under the auspices of loyal men of standing and character, such as [George] Opdyke, Bryant,[1] &c., who shall invite him to address the citizens in Cooper Institute, and see the whole affair properly attended to, so as to produce the best effect at home and across the Atlantic. Let him be publicly received, not on technical abolition grounds, but expressly for the eminent service he has rendered the country in opposing and exposing the rebellion, and in vigorously and unremittingly supporting President Lincoln and his administration in England. The official invitation here will be issued in the course of two or three days, very respectably signed; and should Gov. Andrew preside at the meeting, as we are sure he will if his health permit, the example will facilitate a similar demonstration with you. Of course, no time should be lost in beating the bush, and catching the birds of loyal respectability; and in engaging the Institute as soon as the time is determined upon for the meeting. Tilton and yourself must initiate the *modus operandi*, as we have done here, while keeping abolitionism, *per se*, in the background.

G. T. lectures in Portland on Thursday evening, 25th inst. On Monday, 29th, he will leave for New York by the land route, and can lecture in the Institute on the next evening, or Wednesday, or Thursday, or Friday evening of that week, as most convenient.

Only, *the same week*, to lecture also in Brooklyn, but not to have the lectures given two evenings consecutively.

It is not material to Mr. Thompson, whether he speaks first in New York or Brooklyn.[2] Mr. Phillips seems to think it best for him to speak first at the Cooper Institute. Of this, you and Tilton can judge. Our friend, Mr. Studley, of Brooklyn, is *very* desirous that he should be heard first there; otherwise, he is afraid the attendance in B. would be very much lessened.[3] As he was so prompt to get the Brooklyn Committee[4] to accept Mr. T. as my substitute, I feel something is due to him and them. True, no positive engagement was made, only an overture. But, should G. T. speak first in Brooklyn, we want, if possible, to have him speak upon invitation of citizens, as in Boston; and both in Brooklyn and New York, as here, to secure for him all that may accrue beyond expenses, in order to help him along pecuniarily. We think he can do better in the prominent cities and towns, by lecturing in this manner, than by receiving the stipend usually offered by Lecturing Associations.

Mr. Studley says that, as the Academy of Music[5] is engaged for some time to come, Mr. Thompson's meeting must be held in Beecher's church; and he expresses the belief and hope that Mr. Beecher will deem it a pleasure to preside on the occasion; or, at least, to give him the welcome greeting.[6] I trust he will do so; if for no other reason than that "one good turn deserves another"; and that turn G. T. rendered H. W. B. on more than one occasion in England. Indeed, had it not been for what G. T. had publicly done for our country, as against the rebellion, prior to B's meetings, no such success could have attended the latter. But I need not enlarge. As soon as you can, let us know what is the programme. I should like to have you and Tilton confer with Mr. Studley, 53 Chamber Street, New York, or 76 Columbia Street, Brooklyn.

Mr. Thompson warmly reciprocates your kind remembrances, and will be glad to grasp your hand.

Yours, ever,

W. L. G.

☞ Wife continues to gain, little by little, and is suffering less pain than hitherto.[7] The Doctor, however, thinks it will be a long time before she will walk again.[8]

ALS: Garrison Papers, Boston Public Library.

1. William Cullen Bryant (1794–1878), having as a young man established himself as a leading American poet, had been with the New York *Evening Post* since 1826, at first as assistant editor, then as part owner, and ultimately as editor. Always an abolitionist, Bryant had changed his affiliation from the Democratic to the Republican party, and by the time of Garrison's letter he was sufficiently radical to question

whether Lincoln should be renominated. He did ultimately support Lincoln, however, and continued to advocate Lincoln's relatively moderate policy of reconstruction after the assassination.

2. George Thompson spoke at Cooper Institute in New York on February 29, giving virtually the same speech he had delivered in Boston on the twenty-third, saying that although British opinion had at times done an injustice to the North, there was now substantial support for the Union, especially from the lower classes. On March 11 he spoke at the Central Union Club of Brooklyn on the same subject, his title being "The Popular Sympathy in England with the Efforts in the United States for the Suppression of the Rebellion and the Liberty of the Slave." On all these occasions the response from the audience was enthusiastic. (*The Liberator*, March 4, 11, and 18, 1864.)

3. Edwin A. Studwell (born 1837), whom Garrison calls Mr. Studley, was connected with a family business in shoes and boots, called Studwell Bros. & West, located at 17 Murray Street in New York City. He was later engaged in real estate enterprises in Tarrytown. He was active in the Society of Friends, publishing between 1866 and 1868 a monthly journal entitled *The Friend;* he was also active in the Republican party and was secretary of the Sumter Club. (Letters to the editor from Esther Katz, researcher, January 21 and February 3, 1973.)

4. Not identified.

5. The Academy of Music opened in Brooklyn Heights in 1861, with a seating capacity of 2,300; it was used for speeches and various kinds of entertainment.

6. Henry Ward Beecher did introduce Thompson, sketching the history of his involvement with emancipation and emphasizing his early support of the North during the Civil War. (*The Liberator*, March 18, 1864.)

7. Helen E. Garrison had suffered a slight stroke in April 1862 and a more serious one on December 29, 1863. Despite various treatments, she never fully regained the use of her limbs. Owing to her inactivity, she grew increasingly obese, by 1866 weighing two hundred pounds. (*Life; AWT.*)

8. Although Helen was to consult many doctors and practitioners of various sorts, her original physician may have been the Dr. Munroe referred to in the letter to Fanny Garrison Villard, May 25, 1866.

75

TO ELLEN WRIGHT

Boston, Feb. 19, 1864.

My dear Ellie:

William has very agreeably surprised me by the announcement, that an *"engagement"* has been entered into between you and him, whereby mutual love has been plighted, and whereof a matrimonial alliance may be expected to follow in due time. Though my personal acquaintance with you is comparatively slight, yet, from what I have seen and from all I hear of you, I have no doubt he has made a very fortunate choice. May yours prove equally fortunate! Of him I need only say, that his character is unsullied, his disposition kind and affectionate, his principles radical and upright, his aims honorable; and his aspirations towards the perfect good. I am sure it will be his delight and study to contribute to your happiness, and to fulfill to the letter the pledge of loving fidelity, through all the trials and vicissitudes of life. You will be not less solicitous to aid and bless him. I give you both my heartfelt benediction. Dear wife, on her sick-bed, adds her own to mine. Fanny and Franky are greatly pleased; and the news will be gratifying to George in his distant camp. Wendell, being absent, will let you know what he thinks of the match, before many days; perhaps he has already done so. Our entire household join in an affectionate ratification of it.

I trust it will prove acceptable to your beloved parents, whom I have long been proud to reckon among my most esteemed friends, and to all your brothers and sisters.[1] The contemplated relation is one of such solemnity in its nature, and of such importance in its consequences, that parents especially may well be excused for feeling the greatest solicitude in regard to its formation. As yours shall know more and more the object of your choice, I trust they will be fully satisfied that he is worthy of their esteem and of your love.

But the essential thing is, that you and William should be thoroughly satisfied with each other, warmed by the same electric flame, and animated by the same spirit. Others must not and cannot choose for us. Love defies all analysis, and baffles all calculation. Its diversity of choice, if it sometimes excites a smile or a feeling of surprise, is essential to the peace and welfare of the world. Criticism, complaint, satire, are unavailing. Love will have its own way; and, generally speaking, its own decisions are instinctively the best.

It seems as if it were only the other day that wife and I were plighting our hearts' affection, and eagerly looking forward to the hour of our being formally united in wedlock. We have been greatly blessed in each other, and in all the dear children that have been given to us. Almost thirty years have come and gone since the twain were made one. May you and William live to celebrate your "golden wedding"!

We all regret that you are not able to pass some time under our roof before your return home.

Carry with you our kindest remembrances to all under the parental roof at Auburn, and the assurances of our liveliest interest in your welfare and happiness.

Yours, tenderly and affectionately,

Wm. Lloyd Garrison.

P.S. Accept the enclosed card photograph. It is the best I have yet been able to procure.

ALS: Garrison Papers, Sophia Smith Collection, Smith College Library.

Ellen Wright (1840–1931) and William Lloyd Garrison, Jr., were married on September 14, 1864. She was the daughter of Martha Coffin and David Wright, both abolitionists and friends of the Garrisons; they are identified in the letter to Helen E. Garrison, May 14, 1863. (Otelia Cromwell, *Lucretia Mott,* Cambridge, Mass., 1958.)

1. Mr. and Mrs. Wright had five children in addition to Ellen: Eliza (1830–1872), a suffragist who married David Munson Osborne and whose son Thomas Mott Osborne became a well-known prison reformer; Matthew Tallman (born 1832); William Pelham (born 1842), who was seriously wounded at the battle of Gettysburg; Frank (1844–1903); and Charles (born 1848), who died in infancy.

At the time of Garrison's letter Frank Wright was an undergraduate at Harvard (class of 1866). He was to become a businessman and to work for various companies in Auburn, N.Y., St. Louis, and Boston. For some years he was a traveling auditor for the American Bell Telephone Company. (*The Eleventh Secretary's Report of the Class of 1866, of Harvard College,* Boston, 1906, pp. 55–57, and other reports in the Harvard archives.)

Ellen also had a half-sister, Mariana Pelham, Mrs. Wright's daughter from her first marriage to Peter Pelham. (Anna Davis Hallowell, *James and Lucretia Mott, Life and Letters,* Boston, 1884; *NAW.*)

---

7 6

TO HENRY WILSON

Boston, Feb. 20, 1864.

Hon. Henry Wilson:

My Dear Friend—

Pardon my delay in answering your kind letter of the 11th inst. Since Mr. Thompson's arrival from England, I have been so occupied with his affairs as to get much behind-hand with my correspondence.

Be assured, I appreciate your friendly spirit and intentions in urging me to visit Washington at this time; and the flattering declaration of the Secretary of War[1], in regard to his wish to see me before he died, is a strong additional inducement to accept your invitation. As my estimable friend, George Thompson, Esq., fully intends visiting Washington by the middle of March, or a few days later, it would be mutually agreeable to us to be travelling companions. Perhaps I may accompany him; but the probability is, that I must remain behind.[2] I shrink from such a journey at this inclement season, in consequence of not yet having fully recovered from my late illness; and though my dear wife is slowly recovering from her

severe paralytic attack, yet, while she continues helpless and confined to her bed, I do not feel justified in leaving her for a number of
days successively. She is quite urgent, however, that I should go to
Washington, in accordance with your desire, and especially in company with Mr. Thompson.

As, therefore, it is quite uncertain when I shall visit Washington,
(though I will try to go there before the session of Congress termi-
nates, if I cannot go soon,) will you do me the favor to give my compliments to Secretary Stanton, and also the accompanying card photograph; and tell him that the interesting reminiscence, respecting
the pecuniary assistance rendered my old coadjutor, Benjamin
Lundy, in starting the "Genius of Universal Emancipation," which
you communicate in your letter, gives me a great deal of pleasure.[3]
It gives me a clue to the interest he has officially manifested in
striking the heaviest blow at the diabolically "peculiar institution,"
by the enrolment of colored soldiers. It runs in the blood.

Here let me say, that I trust the fullest justice will be done to
those soldiers, in regard to their payment; otherwise I am sure
there is trouble ahead. Injustice works disaffection, and can never
prosper. I wish Senator Fessenden could understand that rectitude
is good political economy; and to do the right thing always pays.[4]
He does not seem to have the blood of his venerable and liberty-
loving father running in his veins.[5] His petty calculation of the sum
that will be necessary to pay back dues is worthy only of a trickster.
There can be no *constitutional* distinction between the soldiers of
the government, suffering, bleeding, dying in its defence. As well
proscribe or defraud German, Irish, French or Italian soldiers, as
negroes thus enlisted. Regret and surprise have been privately expressed to me, that you should have moved that the regular payment of these colored patriots should date from January 1, 1864, instead of from the time of their enlistment.[6] No doubt you had
reasons satisfactory to yourself for making such a motion. Could you
briefly state them to me, that harsh criticism may be averted?

A Washington telegram in [James Gordon] Bennett's Herald
states that, on Monday next, President Lincoln will issue a proclamation of universal emancipation.[7] Would to God it were reliable!
It would hallow Washington's birthday to the latest generation. The
country is ready for it—ready for any thing that will strike slavery
out of existence. In the Border States it is a snare and curse to the
government, and directly ministers to the support of the rebellion.
Down with it!

It will be a grand atonement if George Thompson can be allowed
to speak in the hall of the House of Representatives at Washington,

and will help us mightily in the old world among the friends of freedom.[8] On *loyal* grounds, he deserves the compliment.

Yours, very truly,

Wm. Lloyd Garrison.

☞ Please accept the accompanying photograph, and hand to Mr. [Charles] Sumner the one designed for him.

ALS: Grenville H. Norcross Collection, Massachusetts Historical Society.

1. Edwin M. Stanton (1814–1869) spent his early years in Ohio, where he attended Kenyon College for two years, and studied and practiced law, before moving to Pittsburgh in 1847 and to Washington in 1856. In 1860 he was appointed attorney general in the Buchanan administration, and in 1862 secretary of war under Lincoln, later serving under Johnson. He became a leading Radical Republican, and Johnson's attempt to fire him led to impeachment proceedings against the President. In May 1868, when the impeachment failed, the embattled Stanton was finally forced to resign from office. Shortly before his death he was appointed to the United States Supreme Court.

2. As he explains in his letter to Oliver Johnson, March 14, 1864 (micro.), Garrison decided against going to Washington at this time, suggesting that Johnson go instead. In fact, Garrison did not visit Washington until June, when he met Lincoln. (*Life.*)

3. Benjamin Lundy (1789–1839) was the Quaker editor who in 1821 had founded the abolitionist newspaper *Genius of Universal Emancipation.* In 1824 he moved the paper from Ohio to Baltimore and in 1829 persuaded Garrison to become associate editor. During Lundy's absence Garrison attacked Newburyport merchant Francis Todd for his participation in the slave trade. The resulting lawsuits terminated the editorial relationship between the two men and resulted in the paper's being moved to Washington and sporadically to other locations until it ceased publication in 1835. For three years following the demise of the *Genius,* Lundy edited another antislavery paper, the *National Enquirer and Constitutional Advocate of Universal Liberty* (later, under Whittier, to become the *Pennsylvania Freeman*). He published twelve more issues of the *Genius* in Hennepin, Ill., during the last months of his life.

4. William Pitt Fessenden (1806–1869) of Portland, Me., the illegitimate son of Samuel Fessenden, was a Bowdoin graduate at seventeen and a lawyer at twenty-one. In 1854, after preliminary service in the state legislature and in Congress, Fessenden began his long years of service in the Senate. Originally a Whig and then one of the organizers of the Republican party, Fessenden was a moderate abolitionist. In 1861 he became chairman of the Senate Finance Committee and in 1864, upon the retirement of Salmon P. Chase, secretary of the treasury. Although for the most part opposed to Johnson during the Reconstruction period, he did not consider the President to have committed an impeachable offense, and despite harsh partisan criticism he voted against Johnson's guilt at the impeachment trial. (DAB.)

5. Samuel Fessenden (1784–1869), a resident of Portland, Me., was a general in the militia and one of the leading lawyers in the state. He had a brief political career in the state legislature (first in Massachusetts and then, following the separation of Maine in 1820, in the new state), but was more interested in reform than in politics. Under Garrison's influence he became an abolitionist rather than a colonizationist, helping to found the Maine Anti-Slavery Society in 1833 and remaining an active and radical abolitionist throughout his life.

6. Wilson strongly supported the interests of Negro troops despite the recalcitrant attitude of Congress. In February he had reported a joint resolution to redress the inequality of soldiers' pay (for whites $13 per month plus a $3.50 clothing allowance, for blacks $10 per month minus $3 clothing deduction); and he pressed for retroac-

tive payment. Fessenden, supported by a majority of the economy-minded Congress, had disagreed with Wilson. He advocated that equal payment for the two races begin with the passage of the act. Wilson agreed to compromise his position to the extent of setting the date for equal payment at March 1. Senator James Wilson Grimes of Iowa, who favored the equal payment date of January 1, moved to recommend the bill to the military committee. Rather than risk further delay, in March Wilson introduced a new bill, which became the occasion for more debate, owing to a provision for freeing the wives and children of black troops. Finally, in June 1864, the Senate passed legislation providing for general increase of army pay and equal benefits for all soldiers regardless of race. (Ernest McKay, *Henry Wilson: Practical Radical, A Portrait of a Politician,* Port Washington, N.Y., 1971.)

7. Although not labeling the announcement as a telegram, the New York *Herald,* in the issue of February 18, printed, under the heading "Forthcoming Proclamation of Universal Emancipation," the following: "Washington, Feb. 17, 1864, It is understood that on the 22d of February Mr. Lincoln will issue a proclamation of universal emancipation, including the border states."

8. On February 22, 1864, Thompson was invited to appear before a joint session of the Congress. He spoke on April 6, with Lincoln in attendance. He praised the President and brought encouraging messages from English sympathizers with the North. The Civil War was caused, he said, by the institution of slavery and such compromises in the Constitution as had hitherto given it protection. He predicted that the rebellion could be subdued only by the extermination of slavery. (*The Liberator,* March 11 and April 15, 1864.)

7 7

TO JOHN M. FORBES

Boston, March 22, 1864.

J. M. Forbes, Esq.

Dear Sir—

I have just received a letter from my friend, Hon. Gerrit Smith, of Peterboro', N.Y., enclosing a check (payable to your order) for two hundred dollars, in aid of the Testimonial Fund for the benefit of George Thompson, Esq., and as a recognition of the valuable service he has rendered our country and government, in England, since the rebellion broke out. I have handed the check to J. H. Stephenson, Esq., who will convey it to your hands.

I have said to Mr. Stephenson, that in order to give an opportunity broadly for all loyal men to contribute to the proposed Testimonial as they may feel moved, it seems to me not only proper but very desirable—not to say absolutely necessary—that the printed Circular, now circulating privately, should be given to the press, as a matter of general information, with the highly respectable names attached to it. There is nothing in it that calls for prolonged secrecy —nothing that is not honorable to all parties concerned in it. There are very many people who would like to contribute to such a Testimonial, who can be reached in no other way than through the press; and in this manner the Testimonial can be made up in the most speedy and comprehensive way.

In this view of the case Mr. Stephenson agrees with me; but, at his request, I write this note to inquire whether you would object to the circular being printed—for example—in the Liberator and the Anti-Slavery Standard.[1]

The Testimonial is not merely personal in its object—it is of international interest and importance—and, therefore, may properly be made public.

Still, I would like your judgment in regard to it, without taxing your time to write more than a very brief reply.

Thanking you for the friendly interest in Mr. Thompson's case, and highly appreciating all your patriotic and benevolent efforts, I remain,

AL: William Lloyd Garrison Papers, Massachusetts Historical Society; the signature has been cut off the bottom of the sheet on which this letter was written.

John Murray Forbes (1813–1898) was a successful Boston businessman who became a railroad builder and manager. In 1834 he married Sarah Swain Hathaway (1813–1899) of New Bedford, Mass., and they had six children. (Sarah Forbes Hughes, ed., *Letters and Recollections of John Murray Forbes,* Boston, 1900; letters to the editor from H. A. Crosby Forbes, curator, Museum of the American China Trade, Milton, Mass., September 15, 1973, and from Richard C. Kugler, director, Old Dartmouth Historical Society Whaling Museum, New Bedford, June 29, 1973.)

1. The circular was printed in *The Liberator,* April 8, 15, 22, and 29, 1864, and in the *National Anti-Slavery Standard,* April 16, 23, and 30, 1864.

78

TO GERRIT SMITH

Boston, March 29, 1864.

Dear and Esteemed Friend:

It was with a thrill of pleasure that I received your letter, enclosing in the form of a check the generous sum of two hundred dollars in furtherance of the Testimonial to George Thompson, for the eminent service he has rendered our country abroad since the rebellion broke out—to say nothing of his anti-slavery labors in previous years. I shall publish your letter in the next Liberator, trusting and believing so noble an example of liberality will be, in some measure at least, widely imitated.[1] It will be very mortifying indeed, if, under such highly respectable auspices as the Governor of our State [John A. Andrew], the President of the Senate, and the

Speaker of the House of Representatives, the effort or appeal should result in a meagre subscription.[2] The Testimonial, being based on the support of our Government by Mr. Thompson, it is of international rather than personal consequence, and a good deal of interest will be awakened in regard to it on the other side of the Atlantic. Prominent Republicans every where should promptly contribute to it, and, doubtless, many of them would if they could be suitably approached. But with such I have little acquaintance; and I am afraid not much will be obtained outside of direct anti-slavery effort.

For the sake of the good effect in England, I sincerely hope the sum you name—$20,000—will be raised; and it ought to be easily, the appeal being made to all loyal men, and not to abolitionists exclusively.

You express the belief that, should this effort fail of the desired result, it will be owing to the somewhat obscure or indefinite manner in which the circular is drawn up. But the committee[3] having the matter in charge deemed it best not to specify any particular sum of money, but to put it in the shape of a "Testimonial"—presuming that the appointment of Trustees would be seen to imply, not a service of plate to be presented, but money to be invested for the benefit of Mr. Thompson and his family. I wish, however, the circular had been more explicit.

I was delighted to see Mrs. [Elizabeth Smith] Miller at our house during her recent visit to the city, but was very sorry to hear that you are somewhat troubled as to your sleep. Do be very careful as to brain labor, and try to take all the recreation possible.

[Owen] Lovejoy has been suddenly translated. His loss to the cause of freedom will be severely felt.

My dear wife is slowly but surely recuperating. Love to all your precious household. Heaven bless you all!

Yours, with warm esteem,

Wm. Lloyd Garrison.

ALS: William Lloyd Garrison Papers, Massachusetts Historical Society.

1. Smith's letter was printed in *The Liberator*, April 8, 1864.
2. The president of the Senate was Vice President Hannibal Hamlin (1809–1891) of Hampden, Me., who was a lawyer trained in the office of abolitionist Samuel Fessenden. After several terms in the state legislature and three terms as speaker, he was elected to Congress in 1842 and to the Senate in 1848. Largely as a result of his disagreement with the Democratic party's policy regarding slavery, he switched to the Republican party in 1856. In 1861 he became Vice President but was not renominated in 1864. After the Civil War he served briefly as collector of the port of Boston and as president of a railroad before returning to the Senate (1869–1881), where he consistently espoused the Radical Republican point of view.

The Speaker of the House was Schuyler Colfax (1823–1885). Born in New York, he lived most of his life in Indiana, where he served as correspondent of the *Indiana State Journal*, became a proprietor of the *St. Joseph Valley Register*, and engaged in various political activities, eventually organizing the Republican party in Indiana. He served as a member of Congress from 1855 until he became Vice President in 1869. In 1872 his name was implicated in the Crédit Mobilier scandal, which involved reimbursing helpful politicians with stock and dividends from the Union Pacific Railroad. Although he was probably guilty of accepting dividends and agreeing to accept stock, Colfax was not formally censured by Congress.

3. The committee to which Garrison refers consisted of three Bostonians: John M. Forbes, Samuel E. Sewall, and John H. Stephenson.

---

7 9

TO WENDELL PHILLIPS GARRISON

April 14, 1864.

My dear Son:

I very promptly and cheerfully comply with your suggestion to give Mr. and Mrs. Lewis an introductory letter to Mrs. [Ann Leah Fox] Underhill with reference to a "sitting."[1] I hope she will be able to grant the request, and if she is, I am quite sure she will do so. But it is a somewhat delicate matter to ask the privilege for strangers, and therefore I could do no less than to leave it to her convenience and inclination.

Your mother was brought down into the parlor, for the first time, to-day, and has gone through the experiment well. Now that we are likely to have fair weather, she will doubtless recuperate more rapidly, and soon be able to ride out.

Our friend, J. M. McKim, of Philadelphia, has been spending two or three days with us, and goes in this night's train to New York, on his way home. We have enjoyed his visit very much. He desires me to say that he will call at your office to-morrow forenoon, to have a little chit-chat with you and [Theodore] Tilton.

I am much obliged to you for continuing your letters for the Liberator; and I shall ever respect and honor you for any dissent you may make from my opinions as to men and things.[2] Only I trust you will feel constantly anxious to form a true judgment, by an extended scope of vision and a philosophical basis of criticism.

My love for you is unbounded. God keep you.

Your affectionate Father.

☞ Will you or Oliver [Johnson] see that my introductory letter to Mrs. Underhill is put into an envelope, and properly directed?[3]

AL signed "Father": Garrison Papers, Sophia Smith Collection, Smith College Library.

1. John Allen Lewis (1819–1885), from Plymouth, Mass., had been associated with the Boston *Daily Bee* for many years. He was a frequent contributor of articles to *The Nation* on the early history of Massachusetts and on printing. Nothing is known of Mrs. Lewis. (Obituaries, Boston *Transcript,* November 4, and *The Nation,* November 12, 1885.)

2. Although *The Liberator* for this period contains no letters signed by Wendell Phillips Garrison, there is, beginning February 19, 1864, a series of "Letters from New York," signed "M. du Pays," his pseudonym. Many of these letters contain criticism of Lincoln's proclamation of amnesty and other policies and favor the election of Benjamin F. Butler as the next President. (See, for example, the letter dated March 24, which was printed on April 1, 1864.)

3. Garrison's letter to Mrs. Underhill has apparently not been preserved.

8 0

TO GIDEON WELLES

(Private.)

Boston, April 14, 1864.

Hon. Gideon Welles, Secretary of the Navy:—

Sir—

I have just signed, with great readiness and the most thorough conviction of its propriety, a request to you, (in which my friend Wendell Phillips, Esq., as you will perceive, concurs,) in behalf of the Rev. Photius Fisk, one of the Navy Chaplains, who has just been ordered to report himself for duty on board of the U. S. steamer Powhatan—that he may be excused from serving, on account of the broken state of his health, which absolutely disqualifies him from discharging the duties that must devolve upon him in active service.[1] But I wish to say, still further, that his shattered health has manifestly very much weakened his mental powers, so that he is totally unfit to administer spiritual comfort and instruction in any direction whatever. He has broken himself down in the service, though having had something of a respite, and therefore is entitled to the largest indulgence and the kindest consideration possible in such a case. I have known him intimately for several years past, and, consequently, have been cognizant of his mental and physical condition; and at no time have I believed it would be suitable to have him act as Chaplain in any ship, in consequence of his enfeebled condition. I will venture to say, that it would be not only a justifiable but a praiseworthy act to place him on the "retired list." I sincerely hope you will see your way clear to make this arrangement.

Mr. Fisk is loyal to the backbone—in every nerve and muscle—in every drop of blood in his veins. For rebellion and copperheadism he cherishes unutterable abhorrance; and is a devoted and generous friend of the government, whose triumph he is faithfully doing what he can, with his means and testimonies, to secure. Kind, benevolent, singularly sympathetic in all cases of injustice, suffering and oppression, he is ever dispensing his liberality in the most commendable manner, and with good discrimination. He will do incomparably more for the government, acting as he has hitherto done, than it is possible for him to effect on board of any naval vessel. Indeed, I believe he will not long survive, if imperatively required to resume the functions of his office as now summoned.

Pardon me for sending you this letter; but I do so as an act of good will to the government, and of kindness in behalf of a broken-down friend of humanity.

Respectfully yours,

Wm. Lloyd Garrison.

ALS: Merrill Collection of Garrison Papers, Wichita State University Library.

Garrison wrote a shorter, public letter to Welles about Fisk on this same date (micro.).

Gideon Welles (1802–1878) studied law and subsequently became one of the owners and the editor of the Hartford *Times*. Beginning his political career in the Connecticut legislature, he became successively state comptroller, postmaster of Hartford, and chief of the Bureau of Provisions and Clothing for the navy. President Lincoln appointed him secretary of the navy, a post he continued to hold under Andrew Johnson. His administration of the Navy Department was at times criticized, but it is generally agreed today that Welles was direct, honest, and thoroughly competent. Although an early organizer of the Republican party, following the war he returned to the Democratic party, supporting Tilden in the campaign of 1876.

1. Photius Fisk, né Philipangos Kavasales (c. 1807–1890), was born in Greece and later moved to Smyrna, where, after the death of his parents, he was befriended by Photius Fisk, an American missionary whose name he later adopted. Fisk went to the United States to be educated, studied at Amherst College and Auburn Theological Seminary, and became a Congregational minister. After having preached in various New England churches, in 1842 he was appointed chaplain in the navy. Active in the agitation against flogging, he later became an abolitionist and a free-thinker. He retired from the navy in 1864, although his retirement was not offical until 1868, when he was given the rank of captain. Over the years he was generous with the considerable fortune he accumulated; upon his death his estate was bequeathed to the poor of Boston. (Obituary, Boston *Daily Globe*, February 10, 1890; and various papers preserved in his name, Office of Naval Records and Library, National Archives and Records Service, Washington, D.C.)

For some time after the date of this letter, Garrison continued to follow Fisk's career with interest and concern. (In addition to the public letter mentioned above, see the letters to Charles Sumner, April 19, June 26, 1864, and December 14, 1865.)

8 1

TO CHARLES SUMNER

Boston, April 19, 1864.

Dear Mr. Sumner:

Believe me, I am quite as much gratified as though you had conferred a personal benefit upon me, in view of your kind and prompt
action in the case of Rev. Mr. [Photius] Fisk. The same mail that
brought your friendly letter, brought also one from the Secretary of
the Navy [Gideon Welles], very considerately allowing Mr. Fisk to
remain *in statu quo*, for the reasons set forth by Mr. [Wendell] Phillips and myself in our joint letter.[1] We are all very much obliged to
you, and proffer you our heartfelt thanks. Poor Mr. Fisk was entirely overcome by the summons to report himself for duty. His protracted bodily debility has brought on chronic nervousness, with a
good deal of mental feebleness; so that he is, and is likely to be for
the remainder of his life, utterly disqualified to discharge the duties
of a chaplain, and needs to be taken care of, rather than to assume
official responsibility of any kind. I see him frequently, and treat
him with habitual tenderness and sympathy. He has a generous, benevolent nature, and goes to the extent of his means in doing good
to others.

Mr. Welles kindly intimates that, on personal application, Mr.
Fisk may be put upon the retired list. Such an act would be praiseworthy indeed. The application will be made, in due form, immediately.

In a previous letter, you express surprise and regret that a correspondent of the Liberator should have criticised your attempting so
many things in the Senate, touching the slavery question, instead of
concentrating your efforts upon the one all-comprehensive measure for the abolition of the slave system.[2] It was not an unfriendly
criticism; for it was made by one who entertains for you the highest
consideration, and the most grateful appreciation of your long-tried
services. Believing that "the greater includes the less," the only
thought he meant to convey was, the importance of concentrated effort upon the proposition to abolish slavery, instead of looking after
its details. But God bless you for every thing you attempt, whether
by wholesale or in detail, to cripple or exterminate the great abomi-
nation of our land! I do not doubt that you are assiduously endeavoring to leave nothing undone to accomplish this end. Follow

your highest convictions, and you will be fully vindicated in the end.

Your much obliged friend,

Wm. Lloyd Garrison.

P.S. Enclosed you will find Mr. Fisk's application to be put upon the retired list, which please hand or send to the Secretary of the Navy.

ALS: Charles Sumner Papers, Harvard College Library.

1. See the letter to Gideon Welles, April 14, 1864 (micro.).
2. Garrison may refer to the following pasage in "Letters from New York. No. IV," dated March 24 and signed "M. du Pays": "Mr. Sumner is seeking to abolish the inter-State slave-trade. But this, like the repeal of the Fugitive Slave Law, is a waste of energy upon a side issue. No slaves, no trade in slaves; no slaves, no fugitives." (*The Liberator*, April 1, 1864; see also Garrison's letter to Wendell Phillips Garrison, April 14, 1864, n. 2.)

82

TO OLIVER JOHNSON

Boston, April 28, 1864.

Dear Johnson:

In answer to your letter I will say, that I like your proposition to have some suitable hymns printed to be sung at our approaching [American Anti-Slavery Society] anniversary; and as for selecting them, you are *au fait* in such matters, and therefore will need no assistance from me. Perhaps the leader of the choir may have to be consulted as to the metre, &c. If you cannot procure an organist gratuitously, some compensation had better be given rather than not have the music.

[James M. W.] Yerrinton says he will do the reporting for us.

I think it is desirable to have Prof. Day to speak at our morning session, as an omission to have a colored speaker on that occasion, or at the Cooper Institute meeting, might give rise to invidious remarks.[1] It is hardly probable that he would talk on the Constitutional question. My only hesitancy would be on the ground that, if he is with Goodell at this time, he might make a partisan speech against Mr. Lincoln.[2] Is there any other colored speaker to be obtained, adequate for such an occasion? I am not strenuous about having Day.

I thank you for enabling me to correct the blunder as to the true number of our approaching anniversary. It should be the 31st, and not the 30th.[3]

I will try to have the series of Resolutions deliberately prepared.[4] But nothing that I can prepare will suit the opposition party, and they will doubtless urge the adoption of their own, which will be as extravagant and vitriolic as they can venture to make them. However divided the Society may be in judgment concerning Mr. Lincoln and his administration, I hope it will not enter into the arena of politics, to be the partisan of any Presidentail candidate.

I have received from Mrs. [Elizabeth C.] Stanton rather a sharp letter, calling me to account for what I have written about Mr. Lincoln[5] styling him "the golden calf" of the nation, and urging me to help break him in pieces by running up the Fremont flag—inviting me to speak ten minutes at the anniversary of the Women's Loyal National League,[6] with the proviso, "if you are sound on the Presidential question—I could not hear the administration trusted"— and saying of my son Wendell, "he is getting ahead of his father"— &c. All this is idle breath with me. I have just seen another letter from Mrs. Stanton, by which it is evident that she and Susan [B. Anthony] are determined to commit the Women's League to a hot political partisanship of Fremont, if possible, and to the most indiscriminate attack upon Mr. Lincoln. They mean well, but their vision is limited. There will be some sharp personalities, I fear, at our business meetings, but let *us* possess our souls in patience.[7]

It will give me great delight to be with you at our esteemed friends, the [Isaac] Mendenhalls, with dear George Thompson, at the Longwood anniversary.

In New York I shall stop at my friend John Hopper's, as usual. He kindly invites Thompson to accept his hospitality at the same time; but he is engaged at his old place.

As I shall not want to make a speech at our morning session, having to read the Scriptures, Resolutions, Hymn[s,] &c., you may include me with [Wendell] Phillips and Thompson at the Cooper Institute as I do not think they would like to seem to monopolize both meetings. Of course, I should take care to give them the lion's share of time.

I am glad Mr. [Octavius B.] Frothingham is disposed to take a part with us at our morning session.

Faithfully yours,

W. L. G.

☞ When you send your next bundle, tell me whether Hopper lives in 42d or 43d street, and between what avenues.[8]

ALS: Garrison Papers, Boston Public Library.

1. William Howard Day (1825–1900) was a Negro printer who graduated from Oberlin College in 1847. Influential in politics and active in many reforms, he founded a weekly paper, the *Alienated American*, in 1852. For many years he had the reputation of being an effective antislavery lecturer. After the Civil War he was active in the freedmen's associations. (William J. Simmons, *Men of Mark: Eminent, Progressive, and Rising*, 1887; reprint, New York, 1968, pp. 978–984.)

2. William Goodell (1792–1878) was an author, editor, lecturer, and reformer, dedicated not only to temperance and abolition but also to the peace movement. He edited in succession a series of reform papers, including the *Investigator and General Intelligencer* (which eventually became the *Genius of Temperance*), the *Female Advocate*, the *Youth's Temperance Lecturer*, the *Friend of Man*, the *Anti-Slavery Lecturer*, and the *Christian Investigator*. He was a founder of the Liberty party in 1840. Unlike Garrison, he was convinced that slavery could be abolished under the Constitution and within the Union.

3. The meeting in question was held in New York, May 10–11.

4. Although the exact substance of them is unknown, Garrison did in fact introduce seven resolutions. In the discussion that ensued, Stephen S. Foster, Wendell Phillips, and Parker Pillsbury were highly critical of the administration, whereas Garrison defended it. None of the ten resolutions adopted focused on the controversial issue of Lincoln and the effectiveness of his administration. (*The Liberator*, May 20 and 27, 1864; *National Anti-Slavery Standard*, May 14 and 21, 1864.)

5. Garrison refers to his article "The Presidency," which was printed in *The Liberator*, March 18, and in the *Standard*, March 26, 1864. In this article he urged the Republican party to support Lincoln, insisting that any support of Frémont, Butler, or Grant would be merely divisive.

Mrs. Stanton wrote the letter in question on April 22, sending with it a printed notice of the anniversary meeting of the Women's Loyal National League to be held May 12 at the Church of the Puritans. Garrison quotes from the letter correctly. He did not attend the meeting (see the letter to Helen E. Garrison, May 13, 1864).

6. Founded in 1863 and functioning until 1865, the Women's Loyal National League was the first and only women's organization formed for the explicit purpose of influencing political events. Its president was Elizabeth Cady Stanton, and Susan B. Anthony and Charlotte B. Wilbur were secretaries. (*The Liberator*, June 3, 1864; Alma Lutz, *Created Equal: A Biography of Elizabeth Cady Stanton*, New York, 1940, p. 134.)

7. Garrison alludes to Luke 21:19.

8. According to *Trow's New York City Directory*, 1861, John Hopper lived at 96 West Forty-third Street (between Broadway and Sixth Avenue).

---

8 3

TO HELEN E. GARRISON

New York, May 13, 1864.

My dear Wife:

I have just received your letter by the bundle, and read it with a grateful appreciation of your loving spirit in writing it in such a crippled condition. It is more than I wished you to do, and yet all the more gratifying, now that it is done, as it gives me the assurance, under your own hand, that you are getting along comfortably, and that I need not curtail my stay here through apprehension of being specially wanted at home. Thus assured, it is probable I shall not leave this city for Boston until Monday noon by the Shore line, hoping to arrive that night as early as 9 or 10 o'clock.[1] My reason for staying will be, that our dear friends, the [Cornelius] Bramhalls, have committed George Thompson to being with them to-morrow and Sunday at Orange, and that they are lovingly importuante to have me accompany him, with Wendy [Wendell]. They entreat not to be disappointed.

Should to-morrow prove a decidedly stormy day, (the sky is somewhat lowering at this time,) I may conclude to return home by the Shore line to-morrow, as a stormy day at Orange would take away much of the pleasure of the visit; though we should all have a good time within doors, beyond a doubt. Still, I would much prefer to be by your side than any where else; and hardly feel justified to remain longer, even with your consent.

Our two public meetings, at the Cooper Institute and at Dr. [George] Cheever's church, were attended with large and truly respectable and intelligent numbers, and went off with high interest and hearty approval.[2] Thompson acquitted himself admirably on each occasion. [Wendell] Phillips was brilliant and eloquent as usual, but somewhat contradictory in statement, and decidedly opposed to the re-election of Abraham Lincoln. Of course, I briefly expressed my dissent, and gave the reasons why I thought the people would stand by him for another term. The audiences were overwhelming in their approval of my views, though disposed generously to applaud Phillips as far as they could. I trust nothing fell from my lips which was deemed personal or unkind by dear Phillips. He is frank and outspoken in his own sentiments, and will not desire me to be less so. But I did not wish to seem to be in antagonism to himself—for I know that our enemies would like to see us or put us at personal variance—and so I said but very little in reply to two long speeches.

Our business meetings would have been very harmonious, had it not been for Stephen [S. Foster] and Parker [Pillsbury]. We had some plain things said on both sides; but, on the whole, we got along better than I expected, and the Presidential election received no partisan countenance.

Last evening, Thompson and myself took tea at the [Edward] Anthonys with Wendy, and then we three went to Ward Beecher's church, where Thompson made a short and felicitous speech before the Congregational Union.[3]

This evening we spend at Col. [James] McKay[e]'s, where there will be a large circle of friendly people, and we expect to have a good time.

Mary Grew has just left the office, where she has spent most of the forenoon with Thompson, [Theodore] Tilton, [Oliver] Johnson, and myself. She sends you her warmest love, and hopes to see you in or near Boston in all next month. After that time, she goes up in the Adirondack regions, though not to North Elba, where "John Brown's body lies mouldering in the grave."

It will give me great pleasure to see Mary Soules, and to learn a little about the dear ones at Lawrence [Kansas] from her own lips.[4]

I did not attend the meeting of the Women's League, but it was addressed by Phillips, Thompson and others, and went off very satisfactorily.

In life and in death yours,

W. L. G.

☞ My benediction upon the entire household.

ALS: Garrison Papers, Boston Public Library; partly printed in *Life*, IV, 109.

1. The Shore Line was an express train of the Boston and Providence Railroad connecting Boston with New York via Providence, New London, and New Haven. It was said to provide the fastest regularly scheduled service in the United States. (*King's Handbook of Boston*, Cambridge, 1883, p. 40.)

2. The meetings are described in *The Liberator*, May 20 and 27, 1864.

3. The American Congregational Union had been organized in New York in May 1853 to promote Congregational churches by collecting and disseminating information about the history and progress of the sect and by giving financial assistance where needed in the construction of buildings. (Williston Walker, *History of the Congregational Churches in the United States*, New York, 1894, pp. 383–384.)

4. George William Benson (1808–1879), Garrison's brother-in-law, had been successively a Providence wool merchant, the manager of the family farm in Brooklyn, Ct., member of the Northampton (Mass.) Association of Education and Industry, textile merchant, and, during his last years, farmer in the vicinity of Lawrence, Kan. His daughter Mary (born 1843) had been married to William L. Soule of Kansas since 1863. (Letter to Henry E. Benson, August 29, 1831, *Letters* I, 129, n. 1; letter to James H. Garrison, January 1, 1841, *Letters*, III, 5, n. 3; letter to the editor from Jonathan Prude, researcher, September 1970.)

84

TO HELEN E. GARRISON

Hamorton, June 6, 1864.

My Dear Wife:

It is now Monday morning. The throng of guests at this hospitable residence of our friends, the [Isaac] Mendenhalls, have nearly all departed, and in the course of an hour Theodore Tilton and wife and myself will be off for Wilmington and Baltimore, expecting to reach the latter city by 7 o'clock in the evening.[1] From Baltimore I shall go to Washington, making as brief a stay as I can—being desirous, for your sake, to reach home as soon as I can accomplish the object of my visit.

We concluded our series of meetings yesterday—having held seven long consecutive sessions, with crowded audiences throughout. Of course, what with much public speaking, and an infinite amount of "small talk," and visiting here and there, and shaking hands promiscuously, and late hours, and loss of sleep, I am pretty thoroughly used up, yet in very good health and spirits. I have had the kindest and the warmest reception on all hands. No where in the country do I find such friends or meet with such greetings as here. My happiness would have been complete if you could have been with me, restored to the full use of your limbs, and able to endure the delightful fatigues of such a visit. Many regrets have been expressed on account of your illness and absence. In your restoration there is a heartfelt interest, and a heavy load of friendly anxiety will be removed from many minds on hearing of your entire convalescence.

Among others at our meetings has been Anna Dickinson. She made us two speeches—both very acceptable; but the one at the close of our meetings yesterday was the best and most eloquent I have ever heard from her lips. It was upon the condition of women, and the question of their labor. She did not touch upon the Presidential question, either in public or in private, at any time, and I am inclined to think has grown wiser since she was in Boston.[2] She is going on to Baltimore with Tilton and myself, accompanied by the Hutchinsons, (John's family,) who have been with us during our meetings, adding much to the interest of the occasion by their songs.[3] They and Anna expect to hold a meeting together in Baltimore.[4]

My only shrinking from going to Baltimore and Washington is in reference to speech-making, which I shall strenuously aim to avoid, but may be forced to say something. I want to devote my whole time looking about in both cities, and have little desire to see any of the public celebrities. Doubtless, however, I shall have an interview with the President, Secretary Chase, [Edwin M.] Stanton, [Charles] Sumner, [Henry] Wilson, &c.[5] In Baltimore, I am to be hospitably entertained by the son of my old friend John Needles.[6] Friend Needles is out of the city, suffering from a bad fall he received several months ago, but his venerable wife is at home, and she has sent me a very kind letter in reply to my own. My emotions on reaching Baltimore, and going to the old prison after an absence of thirty-four years, will be indescribable.

I wish you could have been with me, so as to have participated in the abundance of strawberries and cream which we have had while here. Our generous-hearted friend, Hannah Cox, if I were to return immediately to Boston, would rejoice to send a generous supply to you and the family.

Did I mention, in my letter of Saturday, that Father Chace and his wife, of Providence, were with us at our meetings?[7] The old gentleman is looking almost as well as he did thirty years ago, and seemed to me as old then as now. Is it a delusion to believe that abolitionists are the best preserved people in the country?

There are many in this region who want to see Fanny. I hope it will be so, next September, she will be able to come to Philadelphia and to Longwood. She must have some recreation, and a long respite from the heavy cares and responsibilities which have devolved upon her since your illness. God be praised for giving us such a child!

How I wish dear Franky was with me! One of these days, he, too, must come here, and see how beautiful it is.

I do not know how the Liberator will get along without me; but I know William will try to do what he can, and perhaps friend [Charles K.] Whipple will kindly give some little additional attention.

Kindest remembrances to Lavinia[8]—boundless love for yourself. Indissolubly your own,

W.L.G.

ALS: Garrison Papers, Boston Public Library.

1. Although Garrison had originally planned to return to Boston on Monday immediately after the meeting of the Progressive Friends at Longwood, Pa., he explained to his wife in a letter dated June 4 (micro.) that he had decided to go on to Baltimore and Washington unless "I get word, before I leave here, that my prompt return is desirable. . . ."

2. Garrison apparently refers to a speech made by Miss Dickinson in Boston on April 27. Although no transcription of the speech can be found in the Boston papers or in the *National Anti-Slavery Standard*, she is supposed to have said "that God had given no great controlling leader for our emergency, because He was determined to educate the people," and to have ridiculed both the appearance and the speech of President Lincoln. She did, however, support Lincoln's candidacy when the Democrats nominated General McClellan. (Letter from Caroline Dall to the Women's Loyal National League, May 1, 1864, printed in *The Liberator*, May 6, 1864; *NAW*.)

3. John Wallace Hutchinson (1821–1908) was a member of the famous quartet founded in 1841 that toured the United States and Europe; he sang baritone and played second violin. In 1855 he and his brothers Asa and Judson went to Minnesota, where they founded the town of Hutchinson. During the war he and members

of his family sang in concerts in aid of the Union cause. John was married to Fannie B. Patch of Lowell, Mass.

4. There is no report in either *The Liberator* or the *Standard* that the meeting was ever held.

5. Salmon Portland Chase (1808–1873) came originally from New Hampshire, but for most of his life was closely associated with the state of Ohio. After practicing law in Cincinnati for some years, he served first as United States senator (1849–1855) and then as governor of Ohio (1855–1859). A strong abolitionist, he did all he could to hinder the spread of slavery into new areas of the Union. He served as Lincoln's secretary of the treasury until 1864, when he resigned to become Chief Justice of the Supreme Court.

6. John Needles (1786–1878), an abolitionist since his early support of Benjamin Lundy, was a Baltimore Quaker and a cabinetmaker by trade. He was married three times: to Eliza Mathews (1793–1840), to Lydia Smith (1797–1848), and to Mary Bowers (died 1879). The son to whom Garrison refers may be John A. Needles, a dry-goods merchant. (*Life;* letters to the editor from Bryce Jacobsen, archivist, Hall of Records, Annapolis, Md., December 5, 1972, and from Nancy G. Boles, curator of manuscripts, Maryland Historical Society, November 6, 1972, citing obituary, Baltimore *Sun,* July 19, 1878.)

7. William Chace (c. 1787–1875), a Providence merchant in wool, leather, and dyewoods, was the father of abolitionist William M. Chace, partner of George W. Benson. Widowed twice, Chace was married at the time of Garrison's letter to Harriet Hall Chace (c. 1797–1875), who was to survive him by six months. (Letter to the editor from John H. Stanley, John Hay Library, Brown University, August 1, 1972.)

8. Not identified.

---

8 5

TO HELEN E. GARRISON

Baltimore, June 8, 1864.

My Dear Wife:

I arrived here in the evening train on Monday, and met with a very kind welcome from the [John] Needles, who were expecting my coming, with George Thompson as my companion. Since then, I have been constantly occupied in seeing the city, which has almost wholly grown out of my recollections. It is ahead of Boston in population and extent, but has not as many good residences or handsome stores. The old jail that I once had the honor and happiness to occupy for a time has been torn down, and a new and handsome prison erected upon its site; so the charm was broken, and it was useless to think of visiting my old cell:—

"High walls and huge the body may confine," &c.[1]

The city is very quiet and very clean; and the general appearance of the people, including the colored people, is creditable.

Yesterday and to-day, I have attended the National Convention for the nomination of President and Vice President of the U.S.[2] It

has been a full one, and its proceedings have been such as to glad-
den my heart, and almost make me fear that I am at home dreaming,
and not in the State of Maryland. Even my friend [Wendell] Phillips would have been highly gratified with the tone and spirit of the
Convention. In the speeches made, every allusion made to slavery
as a curse to be extirpated, and a crime no longer to be tolerated,
has been most enthusiastically responded to; in several instances
the assembly rising to their feet, and giving vent to their feelings in
rousing cheers. The result has been the nomination of Mr. Lincoln
by a unanimous vote, (529,) and of Andy Johnson, of Tennessee, for
the Vice Presidency, by a large majority.[3] It was unanimously voted
that slavery ought to be abolished, the Constitution amended, black
soldiers employed and protected, &c. It was richly worth coming to
the Convention to see and hear what has been said and done. Each
evening there has been a mass meeting held in Monument Square,[4]
addresses made, and the most radical sentiments rapturously applauded, without a single copperhead daring to peep or mutter.
This evening there will be an immense ratification meeting held in
the same Square, with speech-making, &c., &c.

I have been introduced to various members of the Convention—
among them the redoubtable Parson Brownlow, who looks very
sick, and is probably not long for this world.[5] I have made up my
mind not to speak in public, either here or in Washington, though
there is a desire to hear me in both places. To-morrow forenoon,
[Theodore] Tilton, his wife, and myself will be on our way to the
Capital; but how long we shall remain will depend upon circumstances.

I am very well indeed, and find the jaunt, with all its fatigue,
good for me. I shall not be able to give you any minute particulars of
what I have seen and heard until I get home.

P.S. I have just received a letter from you, which was sent to Mr.
[J. Miller] McKim's care at Philadelphia. It seems when you wrote
that you had not received either of the letters I sent to you before
leaving the Mendenhalls; but I trust they came safe to hand. No
wonder you felt disappointed in not getting a line sooner, and I felt
to reproach myself that I allowed any company or meeting affairs to
interfere with sending you a letter promptly. A thousand thanks for
your own kind letter. I was delighted to hear that Mrs. McKim extended her visit a little longer. Every word you wrote was eagerly
devoured, especially the reference to dear George. Heaven bless
and protect you all!

W.L.G.

☞ I hope dear George Thompson is on his feet again. He would have enjoyed the visit greatly.

ALS: Garrison Papers, Boston Public Library; partly printed in *Life*, IV, 113–115.

1. In 1830 Garrison had been imprisoned in the Baltimore jail for forty-nine days (April 17–June 5), owing to his inability to pay the fine charged against him in a libel suit brought by Newburyport shipowner Francis Todd, whom Garrison had condemned in the *Genius of Universal Emancipation* for engaging in the slave trade. Garrison self-righteously enjoyed his confinement, received visitors, wrote letters, and even composed a sonnet, "Freedom of the Mind" (based on Richard Lovelace, "To Althea: From Prison"), which he inscribed on the wall and from which he quotes the first line. (*Letters*, I, 91–107.)
The old prison, constructed in 1801, had become obsolete and had been replaced by a new one, completed in January 1860. (Baltimore *Sun*, January 13, 1860.)
2. The National Union Convention was held at the Front Street Theatre, beginning Tuesday, June 7. During the first evening meeting "there were loud calls for Garrison, who was known to be present, but he did not respond." (*The Liberator*, June 17, 1864.)
3. Andrew Johnson (1808–1875), of an impoverished background and a tailor by trade, was the self-educated politician who rose from congressman (1843–1853), to senator (1857–1862), to military governor of Tennessee (1862–1865), to Vice President (1865), to President (1865–1869). Trying to implement Lincoln's policy of Reconstruction, he found himself entangled in a chronic conflict with a Congress dominated by Radical Republicans. He was impeached by the House of Representatives in 1868, but the Senate failed by one vote to convict him. He remained in office, but without influence.
4. The square in which, between 1815 and 1825, a monument had been erected to those who died defending Fort McHenry during the War of 1812. (Francis F. Beirne, *The Amiable Baltimoreans*, New York, 1951, pp. 91 ff.)
5. William Gannaway Brownlow (1805–1877), once an itinerant Methodist preacher, became the editor in succession of three papers: the *Tennessee Whig* (1838), the Jonesborough *Whig and Independent* (1839–1849), and the Knoxville *Whig* (1849–1861). The last of these papers had become the most influential in the eastern part of the state by the time it was suppressed at the beginning of the Civil War. Always a determined Unionist, Brownlow not only lost his paper but suffered imprisonment for his principles. Following the war, however, he was elected governor of Tennessee and in 1868, United States senator. He was the author of many books and tracts on religious and political subjects. His *Sketches of the Rise, Progress, and Decline of Secession* (1862) had an enormous circulation in the North.

8 6

TO HELEN E. GARRISON

Washington, June 9, 1864.

My Dear Wife:

If I am not dreaming, I am at last in the Capital of the United States. Right from the cars, this forenoon, Judge Bond of Baltimore[1] and [Theodore] Tilton took me up to the White House, and forthwith introduced me to the President, who was receiving a group of persons fresh from the Baltimore Convention, congratulating him on his re-nomination. He received me very heartily, and expressed a desire to see me again, and I expect to do so to-morrow. He referred to my imprisonment in Baltimore thirty-four years ago, and said—"Then, you could not get out of prison; now you cannot get in"—referring playfully to the demolition of the old prison. I was at once surrounded with a larger group of persons than even himself, and introduced to a large number from various parts of the country, many of them of more or less prominence. Leaving the East Chamber, we went to see Secretary [Edwin M.] Stanton, and had a long private interview with him of a most interesting character. I was very much pleased with him, and have no doubt of his thoroughgoing anti-slavery spirit and purpose. But I cannot give particulars.

Secretary [Salmon P.] Chase is out of the city. Neither [William H.] Seward nor [Montgomery] Blair will get a call.

From the White House, we then went to the Capitol, and there found Congress in session. We sent in our cards to [Charles] Sumner and [Henry] Wilson, who instantly came out and insisted on our going upon the floor of the Senate, where we really had no right to be. Sumner conducted me to John P. Hale's chair, which I occupied for some time—Hale not being present.[2] A great number of the Senators were introduced to me, among them were Fessenden, Wade, Wilkinson, Morgan, &c.[3] Quite a sensation was produced by my presence. Sumner and Wilson were exceedingly marked in their attentions.

Tilton and I went afterward to see where we could find a room at the principal hotel to occupy, but our application was in vain. Every hotel is more than full. Fortunately for us, Senator Wilson insisted on our coming to his hotel, (the Washington,) and by his influence got a room for us.[4] We have dined and taken tea with Wilson, who is unremitting in his attentions. To-morrow we shall go to the House of Representatives—to Arlington Heights—&c., &c.[5] I may remain here until Monday, or leave on Saturday, but shall probably not be at home until next week Thursday or Friday. Let nothing be said in the Liberator about this. God bless and preserve you all! Farewell, dearest!

Your loving Husband.

AL signed "Husband": Garrison Papers, Boston Public Library; partly printed in *Life*, IV, 115–116.

1. Hugh Lennox Bond (1828–1893), a graduate of the University of the City of New York, who studied law in Baltimore, was appointed judge of the criminal court there in 1860. A strong Unionist and abolitionist, his liberal and humanitarian decisions were of considerable importance during the Civil War and the Reconstruction

period in conservative Maryland. In 1870 President Grant appointed him to the fourth United States circuit court. In that capacity he was one of those chiefly responsible for breaking the power of the Ku Klux Klan.

2. John Parker Hale (1806–1873) was a New Hampshire lawyer who had had an active political career in his state legislature and as United States district attorney before being elected to Congress in 1842 and to the Senate in 1846. A strong advocate of abolition, he became the Free-Soil party's candidate for President in 1852. On the very date of Garrison's letter, Hale's bid for reelection to the Senate was defeated in the Republican caucus in Concord, N.H., owing to apparent laxity in his conduct as lawyer and senator. In 1865 he was appointed minister to Spain.

3. Benjamin Franklin Wade (1800–1878), Massachusetts-born but a resident of Ohio since his youth, was a successful lawyer turned politician. He rose from the position of prosecuting attorney to membership in the state legislature, and finally, in 1851, to United States senator. As senator he was one of the staunchest Radical Republicans, a man dominated by his deep antislavery convictions. He was the inveterate opponent first of Lincoln and then of Johnson. As president pro tempore of the Senate he would have become President had Johnson been removed by impeachment. Wade returned to the practice of law in Ohio following his retirement from the Senate in 1869.

Morton Smith Wilkinson (1819–1894) was a lawyer born in Skaneateles, N.Y., who later moved west, first to Michigan and then in 1847 to St. Paul, Minn. His political career began there with his election in 1849 to the territorial legislature. In 1859 he was elected to the United States Senate, where he served until 1865. He later served a term in the lower house of Congress (1869–1871).

Edwin Denison Morgan (1811–1883), born in Massachusetts and reared in Connecticut, moved to New York City in 1836, where he became a wealthy merchant and broker. In 1849 he was elected to the city's Board of Assistant Aldermen, becoming its president. Subsequently entering politics, he became a member of the state Senate (where he introduced the bill establishing Central Park), a state commissioner of emigration, one of the founders of the Republican party, and, for two terms, governor of the state. He served in the United States Senate between 1863 and 1869. Twice (in 1865 and 1881) he refused appointment to the cabinet as secretary of the treasury.

4. The Washington House, located at Pennsylvania Avenue and Third Street, was one of the city's leading hotels. (William F. Richstein, *The Stranger's Guide-Book to Washington City and Everybody's Pocket Handy-Book,* Washington, 1864.)

5. When the Union Army, at the outbreak of the Civil War, established fortifications along the Virginia side of the Potomac River opposite Washington, the defense installation on the Custis-Lee plantation was referred to as Arlington Heights. This is the present site of Arlington National Cemetery. (Eleanor Lee Templeman, *Arlington Heritage: Vignettes of a Virginia County,* privately published, 1959, p. 116.)

87

TO HELEN E. GARRISON

Washington, June 10, 1864.
At the White House.

Dear Wife:

I am now at the White House, with [Theodore] Tilton, waiting to have a second interview with the President. He has been receiving, for the last hour, the delegates from the several States that voted for his nomination at the Baltimore Convention. I have no special desire to see him again, except that yesterday he expressed the hope I would call again; for I know he must be bored with callers.

AL: Garrison Papers, Boston Public Library; partly printed in *Life*, IV, 116.
    No fuller version of this fragmentary note has been preserved.

88

TO HELEN E. GARRISON

[Philadelphia,] June 11, 1864.

Dear Wife:

It is now 3 o'clock, P.M. I left Washington this morning, and have just arrived here—very dusty and tired, but in good health and spirits.

Yesterday noon, [Theodore] Tilton and I had an hour's private interview with the President at the White House, and it was a very satisfactory one indeed. There is no mistake about it in regard to Mr. Lincoln's desire to do all that he can see it right and possible for him to do to uproot slavery, and give fair play to the emancipated. I was much pleased with his spirit, and the familiar and candid way in which he unbosomed himself.

Last evening I spent with Solicitor Whiting, (the brother of Anna,) and had a good time.[1]

I shall stay here over Sunday—but have no time to add more.

Love unbounded to you and the children.

Farewell, for a few days!

W.L.G.

ALS: Garrison Papers, Boston Public Library; partly printed in *Life*, IV, 117.
    This letter and the one dated June 13, 1864, to Helen (micro.) are written on the letterhead of the Freedmen's Relief Association, with the address "No. 424 Walnut Street, Philadelphia."

1. William Whiting (1813–1873), a graduate of Harvard College and Law School, was a prominent Boston lawyer and the author of various pamphlets, such as *The War Powers of the President and the Legislative Powers of Congress in Relation to Rebellion, Treason, and Slavery* (1862). Although only obliquely involved in politics, Whiting was solicitor of the War Department between 1862 and 1865. He was also elected to Congress in 1872, but he died before taking office.

Little is known about Anna Maria Whiting, except that she was born to William and Hannah Connant Whiting of Concord, Mass., November 18, 1814, and died in 1867. (Letter to the editor from Marcia E. Moss, reference librarian, Concord Free Public Library, July 19, 1972; see also the letter to Fanny Garrison Villard, February 1, 1867.)

"Eminent Opponents of the Slave Power,"
engraving by John Chester Buttre, 1864

Wendell Phillips in 1861

"'Marching On!'—the Fifty-fifth Massachusetts Colored Regiment Singing John Brown's March in the Streets of Charleston, February 21, 1865," wood engraving,
Harper's Weekly, March 18, 1865

The flag-raising ceremony at Fort Sumter on the anniversary
of the fort's surrender, April 14, 1865

8 9

TO OLIVER JOHNSON

Boston, June 17, 1864.

Dear Johnson:

I have just seen [Wendell] Phillips, and find him greatly excited as to the treatment of the Baltimore and Cleveland Conventions by the Standard, to the disparagement of the latter.[1] He showed me a note he had just written to [William I.] Bowditch, forbidding him, as Treasurer of the American A. S. Society, paying one cent towards the further support of the Standard—pronouncing it a partisan Lincoln sheet! He claims that he has three times committed our Society to his views against the Administration, and therefore the Standard is bound to oppose the re-election of Lincoln! Of course, an earnest conversation, though a brief one, ensued between us, in which I told him he had in every instance compelled a fair and friendly defence of the President by his partisan appeals for Fremont, and his unjust and sweeping accusations.[2] We agreed to call a meeting of the Executive Committee on Monday next, to determine what is to be done; and as P. will doubtless take a bare majority with him, you must be prepared to receive a censure, or a proposition to change the tone of the Standard, or retire from the Editorial Chair. I told Phillips you expressed to me your readiness to leave, if so desired. But you shall promptly know what we decide upon next Monday. I send you this hasty note to apprise you that breakers are ahead. Indeed, I am satisfied that our Society is to be rent asunder, and, therefore, our associated action is soon to terminate.

We are so much divided, that separation or dissolution threatens to be the only alternative; and I prefer the latter.

Ever faithfully yours,

W. L. G.

Handwritten transcription: Garrison Papers, Boston Public Library.

1. Reference is made to "The Platforms," the leading editorial in the *National Anti-Slavery Standard* for June 18, of which Garrison had apparently seen a proof or other prepublication copy. In this editorial Johnson expressed his preference for the convention that nominated Lincoln to the one that nominated Frémont.

2. Phillips' accusations against Linoln and his appeal for John C. Frémont are stated in a letter to Edward Gilbert of New York, dated May 27, 1864, and printed in *The Liberator,* June 3, 1864. "For three years," he writes, "the Administration has lavished money without stint, and drenched the land in blood, and it has not even yet thoroughly and heartily struck the slave system." He praises Frémont for his "earnest and decisive character" and his "clear-sighted statesmanship" as well as his "rare military ability." Frémont, he says, is his first choice for President; Benjamin F. Butler is his second.

9 0

TO OLIVER JOHNSON

Boston, June 20, 1864.

Dear Johnson:

Our Executive Committee meeting has been held, and, knowing you will be anxious to hear what was "the conclusion of the whole matter," I hasten to give you the desired information.

All the members of the Committee were present, except Mr. [Sydney Howard] Gay. [Wendell] Phillips said he had nothing to do in calling it; but charged the Standard with being a partisan Lincoln sheet, relying for evidence upon your animadversions upon the Cleveland Convention in last week's paper.[1]

He declared that if such were to be the character of the paper, he should drop it, and withdraw from the Society. He did not like all of [Edmund] Quincy's leaders, especially the one of last week, but, on the whole, thought he had kept a pretty even balance.[2] He claimed that, on three several occasions, the Am. A. S. Society had by itself, and through its auxiliaries, pronounced against the Administration and Mr. Lincoln as unworthy of confidence or support, anti-slavery wise; and, therefore, the Standard should be governed by its decision. He was not willing to give one farthing to have the paper supported, if favoring the re-election of Mr. Lincoln; but he should wait a little longer to see what its tone might be—&c., &c. His complaint was chiefly against yourself. He was very indignant that you allowed any thing to prevent the appearance of the Fremont Cleveland call in the Standard as soon as it was issued.[3]

Though Mr. [William I.] Bowditch and Mr. [Charles K.] Whipple are anti-Lincoln, no one of the Committee was disposed to take Mr. P's side against the Standard, but the verdict was that it had been conducted with remarkable fairness and impartiality. No wish was expressed to give Mr. Quincy or yourself any instruction or advice as to the future, beyond advising great care not to ever seem to give an undue partiality to Lincoln's nomination, while noting impartially the signs of the times as to both nominations in testing the loyal anti-slavery sentiment of the country. They expressed great confidence in your wisdom and discretion not needlessly to give offence while they agreed in the necessity and duty of your faithfully presenting facts as they may arise, cu[t] where they may.

I received a telegram from you while we were together, and read it to the Committee; but they deemed it unneccessary for you to come to Boston at present.

I fear P. has made up his mind to leave us; but time must determine.[4] He is evidently in a heated state.

Yours, to the end,

W. L. G.

Handwritten transcription: Garrison Papers, Boston Public Library.

1. A reference to the leading editorial in the *National Anti-Slavery Standard,*
June 18 (see the letter to Oliver Johnson, June 17, 1864, n. 1).

2. Since other leading editorials—for instance, those for the issues of June 4 and
June 11 (concerned with the New England Anti-Slavery Convention and with the
nonvoting policy recommended by the American Anti-Slavery Society)—were me-
ticulously neutral regarding the forthcoming election, they were inoffensive even to
Phillips.

3. The call was issued May 6; it was printed in the *Standard* on May 21.

4. In fact, Phillips remained with both the national and the state societies longer
than Garrison, who resigned from the American Anti-Slavery Society in May 1865
and from the Massachusetts society in January 1866.

91

TO CHARLES SUMNER

Boston, June 26, 1864.

Dear Mr. Sumner:

My sojourn in Washington was much too short to enable me to
see you and some others to the extent I desired; but I wish to
express to you my thanks for your very kind attentions, and the
great pleasure I felt on seeing you in your seat in the Senate Chamber—a seat which you have filled with so much personal and historic credit to yourself, and which can have no better successor in
the long hereafter.

The part you have taken in consummating those great congressional measures,—the recognition of the independence of Hayti
and Liberia, the anti-slave trade treaty with Great Britain, the abolition of slavery in the District of Columbia, the consecration of all
the Territories to freedom, the enrolment of negro soldiers for the
suppression of the rebellion, the repeal of the fugitive slave bill,
&c., &c.,—has been as important to the country as honorable to
yourself.[1] A review of your senatorial career must at all times give
you the deepest satisfaction, in that you have constantly endeavored to serve the cause of liberty and to exalt the character of the
republic in every possible way.

You remember the case of our worthy friend, Chaplain Phocious
Fisk, in whose behalf you spoke a kind word to the Secretary of the

Navy, in support of a recommendation signed by Mr. [Wendell] Phillips and myself, some time since, that Mr. Fisk be put upon the retired list of chaplains, in consequence of being hopelessly broken down in health through long service in the navy. Mr. [Gideon] Welles very properly caused a medical investigation to be made at Charlestown as to the condition of Mr. Fisk; the result of which, (just completed,) Mr. F. informs me, is, that he is "physically, mentally and morally disqualified" from longer acting as chaplain. I think he must be mistaken about the term "morally," unless it has been used maliciously on account of his outspoken and uncompromising abolition sentiments; for no immoral charge was made, and I have never heard a word derogatory to his character. On the contrary, I regard him as a very worthy and upright man, animated by noble impulses and desires, and always ready to aid the cause of suffering humanity. As he is pronounced physically broken down, I trust Mr. Welles will feel justified in putting him upon the retired list—assured that Mr. Fisk will use the stipend allowed in such cases in a patriotic and philanthropic manner, to the strengthening of the government against its enemies and the promotion of the common welfare.

When you next see Mr. Welles, will you please renew the suggestion made as to this disposal of Mr. Fisk, if it meet your approbation?

Yours, with warm esteem

Wm. Lloyd Garrison.

Hon. Charles Sumner.

ALS: Charles Sumner Papers, Harvard College Library; extract printed in Edward L. Pierce, ed., *Memoir and Letters of Charles Sumner* (Boston, 1894), IV, 186–187.

1. Garrison lists bills and treaties with which Sumner was concerned between 1862 and 1864. (See the *Congressional Globe*, 37th Cong., 2d sess., II, 1814–1815, III, 2538, 2569, 2596; James F. Rhodes, *History of the United States from the Compromise of 1850 to the McKinley-Bryan Campaign of 1896*, London, 1920, IV, 66–67; *OHAP*, pp. 653, 674–675; *The Liberator*, June 17, 1864.)

92

TO WENDELL PHILLIPS GARRISON

Boston, June 30, 1864.

My dear Wendell:

Your letter, addressed to your mother and myself, announcing your matrimonial engagement, was a surprise to me, if not to her.

Most sincerely do I congratulate you upon the choice you have made, believing it to be in all respects a wise and good one. Lucy [McKim] has always held a high position in my respect and esteem; and now I shall be permitted to love her as a cherished daughter. She is comely in person, and possesses, I think, all those qualities of mind and heart desirable in a wife suited to your taste and wants. She has large self-respect and self-reliance, an amiable disposition, great purity of character, a high ideal standard of goodness, and an affectionate nature. As the daughter of two of my earliest and most beloved friends, to whom I have been attached by the tenderest ties, she will ever have special claims upon my regards. You both kept your secret so well that your announcement is not only exceedingly pleasant, but a charming surprise.

Having said thus much in her praise, I will now say that I think she has done wisely and well in accepting your overtures. I may be blinded by a father's partiality, but I hold you in such high estimation that I should not care to tell you all I feel. From your earliest period of accountability, you have been all that I could have desired as an affectionate, obedient, upright and exemplary child. You have never caused me an anxious thought, nor a single pang of the heart; but, at all times, you have evinced the utmost conscientiousness, the highest integrity, and the most uniform amiability. I am proud of your scholarly proficiency, but incomparably more so of your affectionate disposition and deep moral stability.

Nothing, therefore, remains for me to do but to give you and Lucy my blessing, and to invoke upon you both the benediction of Heaven. May your union be happily consummated in due season, and the results of it prove that you were drawn together by that magnetism of love which binds kindred souls beyond all possibility of separation.

How delighted Ellie,[1] the bosom friend of Lucy, will be to hear of the match! To her, I am sure, nothing could be more desirable. And how pleasant it will be to all the families concerned in it!

Your mother, and William, and Fanny, and Franky, and ere long George, will all express for themselves the pleasure they feel on getting this intelligence. Of course, we shall communicate our satisfaction to Lucy and her parents.

Yours, to bless and approve,

Wm. Lloyd Garrison.

ALS: Garrison Papers, Sophia Smith Collection, Smith College Library.

1. Ellen Wright, who was to marry William Lloyd Garrison, Jr., on September 14, 1864.

9 3

TO LUCY McKIM

Boston, July 11, 1864.

My dear Lucy:

Hitherto, I have esteemed you as the worthy daughter of parents who, for more than a score of years, have stood among the highest on the list of my most cherished friends. Now and henceforth, if Heaven permit, I am to love you as a daughter, through your plighted faith to Wendell, yet to be consummated in wedlock. Though taken by surprise at the intelligence—for how well you and he kept the secret from me in regard to your ripening union!—I am as much delighted as any prospective father-in-law ought to be in such a case. I hope Wendell has said as much to you in my behalf; for I meant to have sent you my approval and blessing at a much earlier date. But since we have been out to Melrose, I have been laboring under a slow fever, which at one time I was apprehensive might assume a typhoidal form. I am now feeling better, though not strong. Happily, dear wife has very much improved by her fortnight's sojourn at M.; so that she is able to go up and down stairs, and walk out doors, far better than she did at home. We shall probably remain at M. ten or twelve days longer. Whether, at the end of that time, we shall go to Newburyport or return to Dix Place, is yet undecided. As a matter of choice, wife would much rather be at home than any where else, especially as an invalid, always fearing she may give some trouble, and preferring to show rather than to receive hospitality. We could not, however, be more delightfully situated than we are at Melrose, in the family of the Sewalls, who have a charming residence attached to a magnificent grove of nearly forty acres, and who sympathize and unite with us in all our views and feelings as old anti-slavery friends and coadjutors.[1]

I believe wife, William and Fanny have already signified to you, by letter, how delighted they are to hear of the engagement. I am quite sure that Wendell has been fortunate in securing your affection; and you have too often heard me speak of him, when I suspected nothing of this kind, to be in doubt as to my estimation of him. He is unspeakably dear to me. Indeed, so are all my children! Take him, and cherish him through all the vicissitudes of life, as flesh of your flesh, and soul of your soul! You will find him ever loving, faithful, pure; and, together, I see not why you may not be as happy as it is given to be, in the blissful state of a true wedlock, and this side of the Spirit-land!

Say to your dear father and mother that I did not suppose they could be nearer to me than formerly; but now we are to be connected by new ties, and in our feelings more closely blended than ever.

Of course, our thoughts are largely absorbed in the approaching nuptials between William and Ellie. I believe theirs is a genuine love-match, and therefore feel assured it will work well for the parties. William is as "happy as a king"—or, still better, as happy as Wendell manifestly is when extolling you to us in his letters, and telling us how he is overflowing with bliss! At one time, I was afraid all my grown up boys would live and die bachelors; but two of them have resolved not to do so, and, should George be spared to return, I trust he will soon follow their good example. As for Franky, see if he do not find a lassie to his taste, in due season! And what of Fanny? Still unengaged; but whoever secures her will get a prize worth having—my word for it. But, you gentlemen, for the present, ask not her hand in marriage!

Yours, lovingly,

Wm. Lloyd Garrison.

☞ The heart's love of our household to all the household at Hilltop.[2]

ALS: Garrison Papers, Sophia Smith Collection, Smith College Library.

1. Samuel Edmund Sewall (1799–1888), a graduate of Phillips Exeter Academy and Harvard (both the college and the law school), was a distinguished Boston lawyer. An active abolitionist, he was among the founders of the Massachusetts Anti-Slavery Society in 1831; he was also the defender of many fugitive slaves. Although the two men were in agreement on most issues, Sewall was more disposed toward political action than Garrison and even served a term in the Massachusetts Senate as a free-soiler. He was also active in the woman suffrage movement. He married twice; first Louisa M. Winslow (1814–1850) and then her younger sister, the poet Harriet Winslow List (see the letter to Helen E. Garrison, May 10, 1865, n. 1). By his first marriage he had two children: Lucy Ellen Winslow, who became a successful Boston physician, and Louisa Winslow. The family lived at first in Roxbury and, after 1848, in Melrose. (Nina Moore Tiffany, *Samuel E. Sewall: A Memoir*, Boston, 1898; David Parsons Holton and Frances Forward Holton, *Winslow Memorial*, New York, 1888, II, 885–886.)

2. Hilltop was the James Miller McKim home at Duy's Street and Cottage Lane, Germantown, Philadelphia. (Charles Moore, *The Life and Times of Charles Follen McKim*, Boston, 1929, p. 9; Philadelphia city directory, 1864.)

94

TO FRANCIS W. NEWMAN

[July 15, 1864.]

DEAR SIR—

For your letter of the 7th ultimo, at once so kindly and so frankly expressed, I beg you to accept my heartfelt thanks; for, believing that you "have no other objects than those sacred interests, Truth and Right," and knowing how zealously you have hitherto espoused the cause of the American Government, as upheld by President Lincoln against the Confederate treason of the South, whatever you may write concerning the terrible trial through which this republic is passing will challenge and deserve my profoundest consideration. "Faithful are the wounds of a friend";[1] and that you are a friend to America and its free institutions, and, consequently, an enemy to the rebellion which, for the horrible purpose of forming a slaveholding empire on this continent, is now filling our land with devastation and blood, you have unmistakably proved by your noble testimonies and acts ever since the war began.

The tone of your letter is to me, however, a matter of surprise;— so unlike, indeed, any thing I have seen from your pen or read from your lips, that I am persuaded it was not spontaneously written, but owes its birth to the promptings of certain ill-balanced, erratic American minds on your side of the Atlantic, whose pretensions to superior vigilance and fidelity in regard to the rights of our colored population, and whose morbid representations respecting President Lincoln and his administration, have evidently affected your imagination and controlled your judgment. Mr. [Moncure D.] Conway's jaundiced views are so literally expressed in your letter, that I shall not do him or you any injustice in attributing its origin to him. And here let me say, that you will not find him a safe counsellor, or a reliable witness on public issues. Impulsive, eccentric, reckless, highly imaginative, and ambitious at this time for "radical" distinction, his flaming zeal is not always according to knowledge; and his vision is too apt to "magnify mole hills into mountains,"[2] and to "give to an inch the importance of a mile,"[3] according to his mood of mind. His extraordinary and unwarrantable correspondence with Mr. [James M.] Mason, wherein he falsely assumed to be duly authorized by "the leading abolitionists of America" to negotiate for the recognition of the independence of the Southern Confederacy, provided it would in some way abolish slavery, (the sole cause of its inception and object of its existence!)

should make our English friends cautious in giving credence to his representations concerning men and things in America, and admonish him that he is not specially competent to call in question the anti-slavery integrity of those whose lives have been devoted to the liberation of the fettered millions on our slavery-cursed soil.[4] However fervent his zeal or praiseworthy his object, the course he is pursuing is well-calculated to damage the American Government abroad, and to help faction and sedition at home.

But, whether correct in my surmises or not concerning the paternity of your letter, I am sorry to see your name appended to it.

Before proceeding to notice its complainings, let me say that I am neither the partisan nor eulogist of President Lincoln, in a political sense. Since his inauguration, I have seen occasion sharply to animadvert upon his course, as well as occasion to praise him. At all times I have endeavored to judge him fairly, according to the possibilities of his situation, and the necessities of the country. In no instance, however, have I censured him for not acting upon the highest abstract principles of justice and humanity, and disregarding his constitutional obligations. His freedom to follow his convictions of duty as an individual is one thing—as the President of the United States, it is limited by the functions of his office; for the people do not elect a President to play the part of reformer or philanthropist, nor to enforce upon the nation his own peculiar ethical or humanitary ideas, without regard to his oath or their will. His primary and all-comprehensive duty is to maintain the Union and execute the Constitution, in good faith, according to the best of his ability, without reference to the views of any clique or party in the land, and for the general welfare. And herein lies the injustice of your criticism upon him. You seem to regard him as occupying a position and wielding powers virtually autocratic; so that he may do just as he pleases—yea, just as though there were no people to consult, no popular sentiment to ascertain, no legal restrictions to bind. In a strain of unmerited sarcasm you say:—

"With your President it is not the treason of the rebels, but your 'military necessity,'—that is, present and galling danger,—which *alone* makes his conscience easy in a deed so rash and desperate as that of giving to his innocent, injured, loyal fellow-citizens [meaning the slaves] their elementary natural rights."

Again you say:—

"Horrible indeed is the augury for your future, when your Chief Magistrate does not *indulge the moralities of his heart,* through conscientious tremors at the guilt of violating the wicked laws of conquered rebels!"

Finally, in reference to the sneering remark of "an eminent person" upon the Emancipation Proclamation of January 1, 1863, that it was an act of "villanous hypocrisy, for the President refused to set free those whom he could, while pretending to set free those whom he could not," you say that you are "now pierced in the heart to discover, that, however envenomed in the phrase, *it was no slander at all, but a terrible truth*"!

This impeachment is of the gravest character. It implies that President Lincoln is a base dissembler, reckless of his moral duties, but anxiously concerned not to incur "the guilt of violating the wicked laws of conquered rebels," and desirous rather to perpetuate than to abolish slavery. I am compelled to say that I regard it as utterly slanderous.

The President was similarly denounced for saying in his letter to Horace Greeley, dated August 22, 1863:—[5]

"My paramount object is to save the Union, and not either to save or destroy slavery. If I could save the Union without freeing any slave, I would do it; if I could save it by freeing all the slaves, I would do it; and if I could do it by freeing some, and leaving others alone, I would also do that. What I do about slavery and the colored race, I do because I believe it helps to save this Union; and what I forbear, I forbear because I do not believe it would help to save the Union. I shall do less whenever I shall believe what I am doing hurts the cause; and I shall do more whenever I believe doing more will help the cause. . . . I have here stated my purpose *according to my views of official duty*; and I INTEND NO MODIFICATION OF MY OFT-REPEATED PERSONAL WISH THAT ALL MEN EVERY WHERE COULD BE FREE."[6]

Now, in similar circumstances, this is precisely what every President, from George Washington to Abraham Lincoln, if true to the trust committed to his hands, would have been bound to say and do. "According to my views of OFFICIAL DUTY"! This is the whole question in a sentence. It is not the evidence of a callous heart or a pro-slavery disposition, but indicates the man of integrity, anxious to know and to do his duty in a time of national calamity, and in the midst of unparalleled official trials and perils. It shows an inflexible determination to maintain the Government, if possible, in fulfilment of his oath of office, and in accordance with the powers (and only the powers) constitutionally within his grasp. Herein he deserves credit, and not reproach. Before the rebellion, he had no right to break the fetter of a single slave in any of the Slave States. After the rebellion, his right to do so was co-extensive with the nature and object of the rebellion, under the war power, and according to "military necessity."

It is my firm conviction that no man has occupied the chair of the Chief Magistracy in America, who has more assiduously or more honestly endeavored to discharge all its duties with a single eye to the welfare of the country, than Mr. Lincoln. And his recent unanimous nomination for reëlection by the National Loyal Convention at Baltimore, (preceded by an equally unanimous nomination by all the loyal States in their legislative or conventional character,) after every effort of his bitter enemies, and of well-meaning but short-sighted friends of the slave, to cause his ejectment, is a splendid tribute of confidence in his honesty, patriotism and ability, and a sufficient answer to all the damaging accusations brought against him, whether by the copperheads on the one hand, or those, who are so acting, under a mistaken idea of duty, as to strengthen and encourage the copperhead movement.

To those who have struggled so long for the total abolition of slavery, and whose desires for the speedy realization of all their aims and aspirations have naturally been of the most ardent character, Mr. Lincoln has seemed exceedingly slow in all his emancipatory measures. For this he has been severely chided, in the *Liberator* and out of it; and, for a time, a pro-slavery purpose was attributed to him, which I am now satisfied was not his animating spirit. It was only a proof of the great circumspection which controlled his acts with reference to the formidable rebellion at the South, and the fearfully divided state of public sentiment at the North, especially on the slavery question. Ever since his inauguration, the country has been violently rent asunder—the Northern soil has been hot with sympathetic sedition—and the possibility of preserving the supremacy of the government and restoring the union of the States is still an open question. Yet what long strides he has taken in the right direction, and never a backward step! What grand and far-reaching anti-slavery measures have been consummated under his Administration! How near he has brought us—if the Government succeed in asserting its rightful supremacy over the rebellious States—to that glad day of jubilee, when not a slave shall be found in all our broad domains to clank his fetters, nor a tyrant to wield his gory lash!

In this connection, let me adduce the testimony of FREDERICK DOUGLASS as to his impression concerning President Lincoln, obtained from a personal interview with him at the White House, and related in a speech delivered last December, in Philadelphia, at the celebration of the thirtieth anniversary of the American Anti-Slavery Society—to wit:—

"Now, you will want to know how I was impressed by him. He impressed me as being just what every one of you have been in the habit of calling him—an honest man. (Applause.) I never met with a man, who, on the first blush, impressed me more entirely with his sincerity, with his devotion to his country, and with his determination to save it at all hazards. (Applause.) He told me (I think he did me more honor than I deserve) that I had made a little speech, somewhere in New York, and it had got into the papers, and among the things I had said was this: That if I were called upon to state what I regarded as the most sad and most disheartening feature in our present political and military situation, it would not be the various disasters experienced by our armies and our navies, on flood and field, but it would be the tardy, hesitating, vacillating policy of the President of the United States; and the President said to me, 'Mr. Douglass, I have been charged with being tardy and the like'; and he went on, and partly admitted that he might seem slow; but he said, 'I am charged with vacillating; but, Mr. Douglass, I do not think that charge can be sustained; *I think it cannot be shown that when I have once taken a position, I have ever retreated from it.*' (Applause.) That I regarded as the most significant point in what he said during our interview. I told him that he had been somewhat slow in proclaiming equal protection to our colored soldiers and prisoners; and he said that the country needed talking up to that point. He hesitated in regard to it, *when he felt that the country was not ready for it.* He knew that the colored man throughout this country was a despised man, a hated man, and that if he at first came out with such a proclamation, *all the hatred which is poured on the head of the negro race would be visited on his administration.* He said that *there was preparatory work needed,* and that that preparatory work had now been done. And he said, 'Remember this, Mr. Douglass; remember that Milliken's Bend, Port Hudson and Fort Wagner are recent events; and that these were necessary to prepare the way for this very proclamation of mine.' *I thought it was reasonable,* and came to the conclusion, that while Abraham Lincoln will go down to posterity not as Abraham the Great, or as Abraham the Wise, or as Abraham the Eloquent, although he is all three, wise, great and eloquent, he will go down to posterity, if the country is saved, as Honest Abraham; (applause;) and going down thus, his name may be written any where in this wide world of ours side by side with that of Washington, without disparaging the latter. (Renewed applause.)"[7]

What could be more ingenuous, or evince a more thoughtful state of mind, on the part of the President, than this frank interchange of views? How clearly it shows his anxiety to do all that he felt could be justifiably and safely done, in the volcanic state of the country, toward the extinction of slavery and the elevation of the colored race! It was neither cowardice nor corruption that led him to pause, hesitate, and carefully weigh the consequences of an untried experiment; it was not that he waited to be "bullied" into concessions to the cause of impartial freedom; nor was it because he was lacking in the feelings of humanity. But when "the elements are melting with fervent heat," and "the earth is moved out of its place"[8]—when to transcend public sentiment so far as to outrage and defy it, is to imperil the existence of the government itself—may not something be charitably allowed for anxious doubt, cautious procedure, and deliberate action? What if the President might have gone faster and farther in grappling with the rebellion and its cause? I, for one, thought he could; he thought otherwise; and it was for him to follow his own convictions, not mine. I may have been mistaken; he may have been more intelligent and accurate as to his possibilities. At the worst, it was wiser to be slow and sure, than premature and rash, in working up to a desirable point. As early as the spring of 1862,—my friend Mr. Phillips being witness,—

"The President said to a leading Republican of New York—'Why don't you hold meetings' (it was two days before that glorious Convention in New York which Carl Schurz made immortal by his great speech)[9]—'Why don't you hold meetings, and *let me feel the mind of the nation?*' 'Sir,' was the reply, 'we are to hold them; we hold one to-morrow.' '*Hold them often; hold many of them; hold as many as possible. You cannot create more anti-slavery feeling than we shall need before we get through this war.*' (Applause.) In other words, the President holds out his hands to the people, and says, 'Am I right?' 'How far may I go?' Answer him. Tell him the ice is thick thus far, and will be thicker an arrow's flight ahead. Tell him that if his message to the Border States leads you to say Amen, a message to the Gulf States that says Liberty will have a tenfold Amen. (Loud applause.) In one sense, *we demand too much of the Government—of the Senate and the Cabinet.* They are the only portions of the government that have definite ideas, but *they are nothing; the masses are everything.* Struggling up to light on all sides are indications of the popular sentiment. *There should be official, grave indications. Leading men, legislative bodies, official corporations,* should speak the will of the North, if it really exist, on this question, *so that the Government may feel able to trust and lean on a well assured public purpose.*" [Speech of Mr. Phillips at the Tremont Temple, April, 1862][10]

Now this was well said and well considered, both by Mr. Phillips and Mr. Lincoln. I see nothing that has since transpired to justify the withdrawal of respect and confidence from the latter by the former, or by any other advocate of the Anti-Slavery cause; on the contrary, the President has been steadily advancing toward the goal of liberty, and perhaps quite as fast as the altered state of the Northern mind would allow him, if not beyond all that could have been reasonably expected of him. For, remember, at that time scarcely one of the numerous measures to which he has given his sanction had been executed, and which will assuredly secure for himself lasting historic renown, and cover his administration with historic glory.

Let us see, then, what has been done. But, first, let me call to your remembrance the appalling circumstances in which President Lincoln succeeded in getting to Washington, to be duly inaugurated as President—the Capital swarming with traitors and assassins—an empty treasury—no army, no navy—the Northern house almost equally divided against itself, and to this hour so divided by sympathy for the Southern rebels as to cause serious apprehension of disastrous outbreaks and bloody conspiracies—the real abolition strength of the country numerically insignificant, and politically speaking, of no importance—prejudice against the negro strong and universal—a general disposition, for a long period subsequently, to avoid the issue with slavery, and to endeavor to restore "the Union as it was," and even worse than it was, with all its pro-slavery compromises—and a sorcery power exerted over the popular mind in regard to constitutional obligations and historical precedents. This was all the moral and political capital Mr. Lincoln had to trade upon for the benefit of the despised and oppressed colored people; yet he has done a vast and truly magnificent business.

Witness the emancipation of more than three millions of slaves by the President's Proclamation of January 1, 1863—a virtual death-blow to the whole slave system! Witness, as a necessary sequence, emancipation in Missouri, Western Virginia, Maryland, the District of Columbia! Witness the entire abolition of slavery in Louisiana and Arkansas! Witness its virtual abolition in Tennessee—leaving only Kentucky to be speedily delivered by the enrolment of her able-bodied slaves as soldiers and freemen, and the consequent liberation of their families! Witness the treaty with Great Britain for the effectual suppression of the foreign slave trade! Witness the consecration of all the vast Territories of the Union to free men, free labor, free institutions! Witness the recognition of the independence of Hayti and Liberia—an act which alone, at any time before the rebellion, would have caused a secession of the Southern States! Witness the abolition of all Fugitive Slave Bills, and the consequent termination of all slave-hunting in the country under governmental sanction—a measure of such signal mercy and beneficence, and so directly striking down the great protective bulwark of the slave system, that its adoption alone would justify popular celebrations and joyful illuminations throughout the country! Witness the abolition of the accursed inter-State slave trade—a trade more revolting and hideous in some of its features than even the foreign! Witness one hundred and thirty thousand colored soldiers, battling against those who would perpetuate their enslavement! Witness the admission of negroes to equal rights in the United States Courts, as parties to suits and as witnesses, even before Judge Taney![11] Witness, finally, the loyal sentiment of the country pledged to the amendment of the Constitution, forever prohibiting slavery in the land! Nor is this all that has been done.

Yours, with the highest esteem,

WM. LLOYD GARRISON.

Printed: *The Liberator,* July 15, 1864; reprinted in the *National Anti-Slavery Standard,* July 23, 1864; partly printed in *Life,* IV, 119.

Francis William Newman (1805–1897), younger brother of John Cardinal Newman, was a distinguished English reformer and academician. In 1840 he became professor of Latin at Manchester New College in York, and in 1846 he was appointed professor at University College, London. Although his major writings were theological, he was interested in innumerable academic fields and contemporary reforms, and he wrote about most of them. The letter to Garrison (dated June 7, 1864, and printed in *The Liberator,* July 1) was an attack on Lincoln and his policies regarding slavery and the South. Garrison's quotations from that letter are accurate.

1. Proverbs 27:6.
2. Garrison refers to the maxim used in English as early as the seventeenth century.
3. Garrison refers to the ancient proverb of Chinese origin.
4. For a full discussion of the controversy between Conway and Mason and Garrison's reaction to it, see the letter to Horace Greeley, June 30, 1863.
5. Garrison's error; the correct date is 1862.
6. A letter by Greeley appeared in the New York *Tribune* under the title "The Prayer of Millions," August 19, 1862, chiding the President for subserviency to slaveholding interests. Garrison's quotation from Lincoln's reply is accurate, although he does add italics and small capitals. (Henry L. Stoddard, *Horace Greeley,* New York, 1946, p. 220; L. D. Ingersoll, *The Life of Horace Greeley,* Chicago, 1873, pp. 404–408; Abraham Lincoln, *Complete Works,* ed. John G. Nicolay and John Hay, 2 vols., New York, 1920.)
7. Garrison quotes from the Douglass speech printed in *The Liberator,* January 29, 1864; except for the omission of a few unnecessary words and the addition of "now" in the sentence ending "that work had now been done," his quotation is accurate.

The three battles mentioned by Lincoln (Milliken's Bend, La., Port Hudson, La., and Fort Wagner, S.C.) were notable for the participation of Negro troops, who fought bravely with heavy losses.
8. II Peter 3:10, adapted; Isaiah 13:13, adapted.
9. Carl Schurz (1829–1906), born near Cologne, was a leader of the abortive German democratic revolution in 1848. In 1852 he immigrated to America, where he became an eminent journalist, an abolitionist, and a friend of Abraham Lincoln. He headed the German-American regiments in the Civil War. In 1869 Schurz was elected the first German-born senator (from Missouri); and in 1877–1881 he served as secretary of the interior, in which office he established a merit promotion system and laid the foundation for today's national parks.

Wendell Phillips was referring to the mass meeting at the Cooper Institute, March 6, 1862, at which Schurz was one of the speakers. Schurz said that although the society of the South had to be reformed following the war, civil rights should not be suppressed. Southerners must be treated fairly and reasonably, and they must be induced to be loyal to the Union "by opening before them new prospects and a new future." (New York *Tribune,* March 7, 1862.)
10. Wendell Phillips' speech was printed in *The Liberator,* April 25, 1862, under the title "Washington and the West." Italics are Garrison's.
11. Roger B. Taney (1777–1864), of an aristocratic Maryland family of planters, had served briefly in the state Senate and as state attorney general before becoming United States attorney general (1831–1833), secretary of the treasury in 1833, and Chief Justice of the Supreme Court in 1835. It was he who wrote the Dred Scott decision in 1857.

9 5

TO FRANCIS W. NEWMAN

[July 22, 1864]

DEAR SIR:—

Not to make my letter to you, in the *Liberator* of last week, too long for convenient perusal, it was somewhat abruptly closed. I desire to look fairly in the face the grievances you specify; though having demonstrated that the most cheering and important anti-slavery measures,—virtually including the total abolition of slavery, and absolutely relieving the government of its old complicity with that foul system of wrong,—have been instituted by President Lincoln and his administration in the prosecution of the war, any minor grievances might be left unnoticed as not affecting the general question at issue.

"The greater includes the less." The abolition of slavery is first in order, and of paramount importance, before we begin to determine the exact political status of those set free. The elective franchise is a conventional, not a natural right; yet, the more it is enjoyed in any community, as a general statement, the better for public safety and administrative justice. It is the boast of England, that no slave can touch her soil without sundering his fetters; yet suffrage is far from being universal among you, for thousands of your laboring poor are deprived of its possession. Nevertheless, you are none the less proud to declare that

> "Slaves cannot breathe in England; if their lungs
> Inhale our air, that moment they are free;
> They touch our country, and their shackles fall."[1]

How is it, then, that—overlooking the great fact, that slavery has been abolished throughout Louisiana—you seek to cast odium upon President Lincoln for not giving the right to vote to the colored population of that State, in the reconstruction of its State government? By what political precedent or administrative policy, in any country, could he have been justified if he had attempted to do this? When was it ever known that liberation from bondage was accompanied by a recognition of political equality? Chattels personal may be instantly translated from the auction block into freemen; but when were they ever taken at the same time to the ballot-box, and invested with all political rights and immunities?According to the laws of development and progress, it is not practicable. To denounce or complain of President Lincoln for not disregarding public sentiment, and not flying in the face of these laws, is hardly just. Besides, I doubt whether he has the constitutional right to decide this matter. Ever since this government was organized, the right of suffrage has been determined by each State in the Union for itself, so that there is no uniformity in regard to it. In some free States, colored citizens are allowed to vote; in others, they are not. It is always a State, never a national matter. In honestly seeking to preserve the Union, it is not for President Lincoln to seek, by a special edict applied to a particular State or locality, to do violence to a universal rule, accepted and acted upon from the beginning till now by the States in their individual sovereignty. Under the war power, he had the constitutional right to emancipate the slaves in every rebel State, and also to insist that, in any plan of reconstruction that might be agreed upon, slavery should be admitted to be dead, beyond power of resurrection. That being accomplished, I question whether he could safely or advantageously—to say the least—enforce a rule, *ab initio*, touching the ballot, which abolishes complexional distinctions; any more than he could safely or advantageously decree that all women (whose title is equally good) should enjoy the electoral right, and help form the State. Nor, if the freed blacks were admitted to the polls by Presidential fiat, do I see any permanent advantage likely to be secured by it; for, submitted to as a necessity at the outset, as soon as the State was organized and left to manage its own affairs, the white population with their superior intelligence, wealth and power, would unquestionably alter the franchise in accordance with their prejudices, and exclude those thus summarily brought to the polls. Coercion would gain nothing. In other words,—as in your own country,—universal suffrage will be hard to win and to hold, without a general preparation of feeling and sentiment. But it will come, both at the South and with you; yet only by a struggle *on the part of the disfranchised,* and a growing conviction of its justice, "in the good time coming."[2] With the abolition of slavery in the South, prejudice or "colorphobia," the natural product of the system, will gradually disappear—as in the case of your West India colonies—and black men will win their way to wealth, distinction, eminence, and official station. I ask only a charitable judgment for President Lincoln respecting this matter, whether in Louisiana or any other State.

Referring to the President, you say:—

"His Proclamation has done immense good; nor will I yield to you in extolling many of his acts. Yet if we had understood the quality of his logic, his *exclusion of morality* from Presidential duties, and his wonderful disowning of all duty towards colored men *not prescribed in the codes of slaveholders,* it would have been impossible to excite enthusiasm for him in an English audience."[3]

Is there not some confusion of mind here? Is the Proclamation destitute of morality? Or do you find it "prescribed in the codes of slaveholders"? And so of the "many other acts" which you are disposed to extol. You do injustice to Mr. Lincoln, and subject him to an unfair impeachment. Be assured, he has tried, to the best of his judgment, faithfully to discharge his constitutional duties, as under solemn oath to God and the people. Granted that he has been sometimes lacking in energy of will, clearness of vision, and power of inspiration: who is complete in all things, and never found wanting? The main thing is, is he honestly and sincerely endeavoring to save the republic, according to the measure of his constitutional power; and has he not done a mighty work for liberty and humanity —unparalleled in any age or nation—since he became President? Because he is guided by what is prescribed in the Constitution, as he understands it, is he to be accused of confessed immorality on his part? Can he act otherwise without being guilty of perfidy? Is it creditable in England for a man to take office, and then do as he pleases, without regard to the conditions imposed upon him?

Again you say—."Mr. Lincoln puts a Southern construction upon the Constitution." Herein you are greatly mistaken, and do him fresh injustice—unintentionally, of course. The only construction Mr. Lincoln puts upon the Constitution is an American one—the same as was put upon it by Washington, Adams, and Jefferson, and the people have always sanctioned.

Again you err in saying—"In old days, the iniquity [slavery] was maintained in Tennessee by local wickedness only. Mr. Lincoln has insisted on upholding it there by Federal guilt."[4] Now, the fact is, before the rebellion, the whole power of this country was constitutionally pledged to maintain slavery in Tennessee, and in every other slave State, if needed, as against a slave insurrection or an exodus of the oppressed. At the present time, in that State, it is a rope of sand,[5] and has only a nominal existence. As elsewhere, its doom is sealed. Here and there, "Northern soldiers" may have been "the vile instruments of the slaveholder," but the cases have been few and far between, incidental and transient, arising more from personal prejudice against the blacks than from official command, and are not likely to be repeated.

Once more you say:—

"Until recently, I have looked on your war with serene satisfaction as a sublime sacrifice for a magnificent future, glorious to you, beneficent to our millions. I have indulged in glowing anticipations, in which I seemed to friends but a wild dreamer. Since I have learned that your President has sanctioned Gen. Banks's ordinances, I begin to fear that I have indeed been a dreamer, and that your enemies here are substantially correct."

Your charge is somewhat indefinite in regard to General Banks's ordinances. One of them is the establishment of common schools—that system which has made New England so prosperous, intelligent and powerful—for the entire colored population under his rule. Surely, you do not mean to condemn that ordinance, or to impeach the President for its enforcement! Please put this great saving measure down to the credit both of Mr. Lincoln and Gen. Banks. It is a tall plume in their caps! Another ordinance is, the total abolition of slavery by Gen. Banks throughout his department, where it was expressly exempted by the President's Emancipation Proclamation of January 1, 1863—thus making it complete throughout the State. Of course, this was done with the sanction of the President, and is an additional plume for himself and the President, of the tallest kind![6]

Finally, you say:—

"If it can be said, 'Garrison does not reprove General Banks's measures,' it will be inferred that they do full justice to the colored race. A great responsibility now rests on you to use your[7] power aright."

Such noble measures as I have referred to deserve no reproof, but rather the warmest commendation. Any measure which is ill-judged and unjust,—such as the ordinance for the cultivation of the plantations—I denounce and condemn.[8] But, at the worst, it is only a temporary shift—for a single year, rapidly expiring—to adjust matters in the midst of a disorganized state of society, where the masters no longer have power to enforce their authority, and where the unemployed and uncoerced are liable to be a burden to the government, or to become vagabonds. It was made needlessly stringent, and is very objectionable in some of its features. It will, however, unquestionably end by its own limitation. Hereafter, its operations will be better known and understood. Gen. Banks has yet to be heard in vindication, or at least explanation of his course in this particular. His two other grand ordinances, already alluded to, will cover a multitude of blunders and mistakes.

As a proof that the colored population within the loyal portion of Louisiana under Gen. Banks's administration regard their altered condition as one calling for enthusiastic public demonstrations, I ask you to read—as I have with pleasure and wonder—the following extracts from a letter which I find in the Philadelphia *Christian*

Recorder, (colored) from JAMES JONES, WARD MASTER in Hospital of the 8th U. S. A., and dated "Camp Parapet, New Orleans, June 19, 1864"[9]:—

Wonderful indeed has been the mighty change in public opinion. Stranger still the change that the feelings and sentiments of the people of the South are daily undergoing in reference to slavery and the colored race. Strange and unlooked-for changes in this direction are daily taking place. Stranger, too, when clothed in the garb of justice and humanity to the colored man, the chief operators in which are Southern slaveholders, in an extreme Southern State. My astonishment is still increased when I behold a State Constitutional Convention, composed of slaveholders, sitting in the slaveholding city of New Orleans,[10] adopting a clause to their Constitution which at once and forever abolishes slavery and involuntary servitude, except it be for crime, within the State of Louisiana—and that, too, without the great and selfish hobby of compensation to owners. This is a triumph indeed, and shows conclusively that Northern arms, under the guidance of the Almighty, have accomplished more than speeches of Northern men in Congress could accomplish. Not only this, but it proves further to me that the Lord has declared, for the last time, that the stain of human slavery must and shall be wiped out. He has made frequent calls to them through the pulpit, the press, and from the halls of Congress. All these they have allowed to pass unheeded, and now they must bow and submit to His holy will; and they themselves are the first instruments in his hands to do what they defied the nations of the earth to do, viz: abolish slavery and declare the slave a man.

Saturday, the 11th, was a day long to be remembered by both white and colored people in the city of New Orleans. This day was set apart by our people for the purpose of giving expression to their feelings and sentiments in reference to the passage of the Emancipation Act. To properly celebrate this great event was a matter of no little interest to them; and, fraught as it was with unknown effects upon the freed men, and placing upon them new and important responsibilities and obligations, it became a matter of double interest to all concerned. Fortunately for themselves and their race, they acquitted themselves honorably. The day was such a one as is only to be seen and enjoyed in the "Sunny South." At an early hour, the people began to pour into the city from the country and surrounding villages. Men, women and children, young and old, those that had ever been free, and those that had just realized the pleasing sensation caused by the falling off of their chains, all were there. For the time being, the plantation, the farm, the workshops, hotels, and all places of labor and amusement, were deserted and forgotten. The people were out to celebrate what to them was a great epoch in the history of their race.

They came by hundreds and thousands; they came with bands playing and banners flying; they came vieing with each other as to who should appear best, and show the highest appreciation for the cause that brought them together. They came in their strength, and as they came their cry was,

"Slavery's Chain is Broken!"

At ten o'clock, A.M., the procession was formed at the Second Baptist Church, which was the place of general rendezvous.[11] From thence they passed through some of the principal streets to Congo Square, the place where the meeting was held.[12]

I cannot be precise in giving your readers the names of the different societies, or their order in the procession. Suffice it to say that religious congregations, Sabbath and day schools, benevolent Societies, Temperance Societies, political and social Clubs, Mechanics' Associations, farmers, and last, though not least, laborers, all had a place in that mighty procession, which as it passed along, headed by the Fourth Louisiana (colored) Cavalry,[13] made even the good men that voted them free almost shudder when they beheld the power and numbers that by their individual and collective aid had been, as it were, brought to life.

The procession arriving at Congo Square, the different delegations were disposed according to programme. The exercises were opened with prayer by the Rev. Mr. Forrest, after which the Rev. Mr. Rodgers, D.D., orator of the day delivered an address replete with historical facts, and plainly showing that the Almighty has called us as a people from under the hand of the hard taskmaster.[14]

It was a masterly effort indeed, and bore on its face the fact that the colored man has a mind, and is capable of thinking and reasoning. The Doctor's address went very far towards convincing the slaveholders that, now that they had opened the door of education to the colored man, they must guard the path to intellectual improvement with a jealous eye, or else they will find a stern and powerful competitor in that same black man, in an intellectual point of view.

The celebration was a complete success. It did honor to all engaged in its arrangements; and our Northern brethren have little to boast of when we contrast behavior and general deportment.

My dear sir, I beg you to take a telescopic rather than a microscopic view of our affairs; and, instead of dwelling upon and magnifying to huge dimensions those incidental errors and outrages which are inevitable in the midst of such an awful civil war, and which are sure to be corrected, fix your gaze upon those sublime and glorious acts of President Lincoln's administration, whereby slavery has received its death warrant, and the haughty Slave Power been laid low in the dust, and still feel justified in looking on this struggle "with serene satisfaction as a sublime sacrifice for a magnificent future."

Accepting your letter as a proof of your personal friendship, and as elicited by a very commendable zeal for the cause of justice and humanity, I remain,

Yours, with a heart full of thanksgiving and joy, and with high regards,

WM. LLOYD GARRISON.

PROF. FRANCIS W. NEWMAN.

Printed: *The Liberator*, July 22, 1864; reprinted in the *National Anti-Slavery Standard*, July 30, 1864; partly printed in Lillie Buffum Chace Wyman and Arthur C.

Wyman, *Elizabeth Buffum Chace 1806–1899: Her Life and Its Environment* (Boston, 1914), I, 260–261, and in *Life*, IV, 123.

1. William Cowper, *The Task*, Book II, lines 40–42. Garrison's quotation is accurate except for the substitution of "Inhale" for "Receive."

2. Garrison quotes the refrain from Charles Mackay, "The Good Time Coming."

3. In various places in this letter Garrison quotes verbatim, adding italics, from Newman's letter to him, dated London, June 7, 1864, which was printed in *The Liberator*, July 1, 1864.

4. In this quotation from the Newman letter Garrison omits after "insisted" the clause "(quite gratuitously, as it has seemed to Europeans)."

5. Garrison uses a phrase of Greek origin.

6. On December 16, 1862, President Lincoln had removed from his command in Louisiana General B. F. Butler since he had accomplished so little in reconstructing that state. He appointed in his place General Nathaniel P. Banks with the clear understanding that Banks constituted the primary authority, even though George F. Shepley, a Butler supporter, remained as military governor. Lincoln instructed Banks to attain "a free State reorganization of Louisiana in the shortest possible time." Despite innumerable ordinances and proclamations and their consistent support by Lincoln, Banks was unable to channel the state's still divided power sufficiently to reorganize the state. He did succeed in sponsoring a general election in which Lincoln moderate Michael Hahn became governor. (J. G. Randall and Richard N. Current, *Lincoln the President*, IV, New York, 1955, pp. 12–19.)

7. Newman used the word "this" instead of "your."

8. General Nathaniel P. Banks had endeavored to keep order in New Orleans with a relatively small force by instituting in 1863 and again in 1864 a labor system that established rigid rules governing working hours and conditions for the freed blacks. Garrison further criticized Banks's policies in letters to Charles E. Norton, January 13, 1865, and to Banks himself, January 21, 1865.

9. Founded in 1847 by the African Methodist Episcopal Church as the *Christian Herald*, this weekly paper was the oldest Negro newspaper in the United States. In 1852 the name was changed to the *Christian Recorder*. The editor in 1864 was John Mifflin Brown (1817–1893). (Peter M. Bergman, *The Chronological History of the Negro in America*, New York, 1969, pp. 107, 188.)

James F. Jones (c. 1840–1864) was a barber by trade, who enlisted in the 14th Rhode Island Colored Heavy Artillery (subsequently the 8th Regiment Colored Heavy Artillery), November 16, 1863. In March 1864 he was assigned as ward master for the regimental hospital at Camp Parapet, La., a fortification constructed by the Confederates and captured by federal troops in 1861. (Letter to the editor from Elmer O. Parker, assistant chief, Old Military Branch, Military Archives Division, National Archives and Records Service, March 26, 1973; Marion Favret Meador, *Jefferson—the Parish of Plenty*, New Orleans, 1967, p. 9.)

10. The convention, which was sponsored by the more radical group among those remaining loyal to the Union, was held in April 1864. The constitution drawn up resembled the earlier one written in 1852, except for the clause abolishing slavery. Although the legislature was empowered to found free schools for Negroes and to give them the vote, it did not do so at this time.

11. The black Second Baptist Church (founded 1849) was located at Melpomene and Freret streets in New Orleans. (*Gardner's New Orleans Directory*, 1861, p. xxii.)

12. Congo Square, later Beauregard Square, was named for Congo Negroes who performed tribal dances there on Sundays. (*Daily Picayune*, October 12, 1879, as quoted in the New Orleans *States*, May 13, 1928.)

13. Probably Jones refers to the 4th U.S. Colored Cavalry, formerly the 1st Regiment Cavalry, Corps d'Afrique, which was organized at New Orleans. (Letter to the editor from Elmer O. Parker, February 12, 1973.)

14. Extensive search has not determined the identity of the Reverend Mr. Forrest and the Reverend Mr. Rodgers.

96

TO SAMUEL J. MAY

Peterboro', Sept. 6, 1864.

Dear friend May:

Fanny and I arrived at the hospitable mansion of our friend Gerrit Smith yesterday afternoon, where we [were] greeted by the entire household in the warmest manner. Gen. John Cochrane, who is on the Fremont ticket, had arrived about an hour in advance of us.[1] We also found Mr. Smith's son at home, somewhat debilitated by what he encountered as a novice in the war at the time of the explosion of the mine before Pittsburg; and a young lady from Kentucky, a Miss Fitzhugh, a niece of Mrs. Smith, and an avowed rebel for the sake of the slave institution, though her mother is a Unionist.[2] Mr. Smith tells Cochrane that he and Fremont, as good patriots, must let the Cleveland nomination slide, and give their hearty support to the nomination of "honest Abe." Cochrane smiles, but is reticent; though Mr. Smith tells me he has no doubt C. will go for Lincoln as against [George B.] McClellan and the Chicago peace (!) platform.[3] It must be apparent, I think, to all but the blindest of the blind, that the Fremont movement has proved an abortion; and the best thing that its nominees and its partisans can do, for themselves and for their country, is to accept what is inevitable, and join the general mass of loyal men in sustaining Mr. Lincoln, and thus save the country from the shame and calamity of a copperhead triumph.

Yesterday before tea, Mr. Smith gave me a ride of several miles, that I might get an idea of "the lay of the land" in this region; and, truly, it is "a goodly country" to behold, wherever the eye turns. The view of Oneida lake, and the extended range of hills beyond, is particularly fine. But you know all about this section, I presume, and I need not go into any details.

In answer to your letter, which was promptly put into my hands, I will state that you may expect us in the Albany morning train that is due in Syracuse at 1 o'clock, *Friday*. We shall remain with you till Monday, and then take the train for Auburn.

Mr. Smith desires me to say, that he is not a subscriber to the Christian Examiner,[4] and shall be happy to read the number referred to by you, if sent to him.

With warmest love to all yours, I remain,

Yours, always,

Wm. Lloyd Garrison.

ALS: Garrison Papers, Boston Public Library.

1. John Cochrane (1813–1898) was a New York City lawyer who served as a Democrat in Congress (1857–1861), supporting the southern point of view on slavery until the Civil War, when he joined the Union army as colonel, subsequently being promoted to brigadier general of volunteers. Never an enthusiastic supporter of Lincoln, he was nominated for Vice President on the Frémont ticket at the Cleveland convention of 1864, though he later campaigned for Lincoln. After the war he became a Liberal Republican and supported the nomination of Greeley in 1872.

2. Greene Smith (born 1842), Gerrit Smith's only surviving son, enlisted in the 14th New York Heavy Artillery, at his father's insistence serving without pay. On July 30, 1864, he saw action before Petersburg, Va. (Garrison mistakenly says "Pittsburg"), in a battle that proved to be one of the Union's most tragic lost opportunities. The 48th Pennsylvania regiment of the 9th Army Corps, which was composed largely of miners, dug a 500-foot tunnel under a Confederate strong point and placed at its end an eight-ton powder mine. The mine was exploded at dawn on July 30, producing a crater 150 feet in diameter (the crater giving the name to the battle that followed). As the crater accumulated a veritable traffic jam of soldiers in gray and in blue, General Burnside and other inept officers issued no orders for the advance that would have cut Lee's army in two and, in all probability, shortened the war. Among those singled out for favorable comment in official Union records was Second Lieutenant Greene Smith, who did his duty and "carried out orders faithfully." (O. B. Frothingham, *Life of Gerrit Smith*, New York, 1878, p. 261; *The War of the Rebellion: A Compilation of the Official Records of the Union and Confederate Armies*, 1st series, Washington, D.C., 1892, XL, part 1, 541–542; and 1893, XLII, part 1, 72.)

Miss Fitzhugh may have been the daughter of Mrs. Smith's brother, James Fitzhugh, who lived for some time in Kentucky. Miss Fitzhugh's mother has not been identified. (Thomas J. C. Williams, *A History of Washington County, Maryland* . . . , Baltimore, 1968, I, 136–140.)

3. McClellan had been nominated on August 29 as the Democratic candidate for President on a platform emphasizing the need for an immediate end to the war.

4. A journal published between 1824 and 1869, which superseded the *Christian Disciple and Theological Review* and was later merged into *Scribner's Monthly* and finally into *Century*. (ULS.)

97

TO HELEN E. GARRISON

Syracuse, Sept. 10, 1864.

Dear Wife:

Yesterday morning we took our leave of the hospitable abode of our Peterboro' friends for this city. During our stay there, all were unremitted in their kind attentions to us, manifestly desirous of making our visit as agreeable as possible. When I go there again, I hope you will be able to accompany me, delivered from your present paralytic infirmity; for great and unfeigned was their regret that you were not in proper condition to be one of our party. It is Gerrit Smith alone who has made Peterboro' famous; for the village itself is utterly insignificant. Besides his own residence, there are only

two or three others in the place that are at all commodious. There is
no ostentation in his manner of living, but every thing is on a liberal
scale, the tables are loaded with well prepared dishes, and a hearty
welcome is given to every guest. No one knows better than he that
"it is more blessed to give than to receive."[1]

We arrived at the depot in this city[2] at 1 o'clock, where we found
our ever attentive and dearly beloved friend, Samuel J. May, awaiting our coming. We drove directly to his house, and were warmly
greeted by Mrs. May and Charlotte Coffin. The former was specially glad to see Fanny, as it was for the first time since the birth of
F. After dinner, Mr. Wilkinson sent his carriage for Fanny, Mr. May
and myself to take a ride, and a charming excursion we had of it.[3]
We made a momentary call at the [Charles B.] Sedgwicks, and in
the evening Mr. S., and his only son and two daughters, called upon
us, and also Mr. and Mrs. Barnes, (who lived in a very beautiful
house opposite,) and we had a very social time.[4]

The weather is perfection itself. This forenoon we have occupied
in a still more extended ride through the city and its environs, in
Mr. Wilkinson's carriage, he very kindly accompanying us, and
making the ride extremely pleasant by the information he communicated on the route. He is very intelligent and agreeable, and from
appearances must be doing a lucrative business. He has purchased
the old but beautiful homestead now occupied by Mr. May—the
house, grove, and eight acres of land, all for a little more than we
gave for our birds' nest at Roxbury.[5] "When this cruel war is over,"[6]
he intends pulling down the old house, and erecting a handsome
edifice. Mr. May is seeking for a dwelling not far from his church,
on account of his difficulty of walking. In other respects he appears
to be in good health.

Fanny is delighted with all that she sees; and the charming scenery and magnificent views around Syracuse have taken her entirely by surprise. Never have I had such opportunities as now to
realize how indescribably fine they are. I know of no inland city
that is so well provided for in this respect.

This evening we shall all take tea at Mr. Wilkinson's. The Sedgwicks and others will be present.

Since dinner, Mr. May has handed me your welcome letter, dated
the 8th inst., announcing that all is going on well with you, and giving those details about home and visitors which are always so interesting when one is abroad. I am glad you are having Mrs. French to
try her healing powers upon you, and trust that the good Quaker
physician, who is said to operate through her, will be able to give
you very material assistance.[7] Let the experiment be fairly made,

and mix as much faith with it as you can; for strong belief has often much to do with surprising cures.

Fanny received your and Franky's joint letter at Peterboro' gladly, and we both wrote to you from that place.

Give our kindest regards to Mr. and Mrs. Thaxter, Miss Cannan, Sarah, Winni, &c., &c.[8] Mr. and Mrs. May and Charlotte Coffin send theirs to you, all deeply regretting that you are not here.

Good bye, dearest one!

W. L. G.

☞ All of your loving sentiments are warmly reciprocated. Blessings on dear Franky.

ALS: Garrison Papers, Boston Public Library.

1. Acts 20:35.

2. The main station being at the corner of West Washington and Franklin streets. (Letter to the editor from Esther Katz, researcher, February 3, 1973.)

3. Alfred Wilkinson (1831–1886), a graduate of Rensselaer Polytechnic Institute and a merchant and banker of Syracuse, had married the Mays' daughter Charlotte (1833–1909) in 1854. (Samuel May, Jr., et al., A Genealogy of the Descendants of John May, Boston, 1878; letter to the editor from Richard N. Wright, president, Onondaga Historical Association, Syracuse, November 6, 1971.)

4. British-born George Barnes (1827–1892) was a prominent Syracuse newspaper proprietor, railroad executive, banker, and manufacturer. From 1852 to 1855 he owned the Syracuse Evening Chronicle and made it the first Republican newspaper outside New York City. He was influential in the consolidation of seven rail lines into the New York Central and Hudson River Railroad Company. Subsequently he helped to organize and administer several large banks in Syracuse. During the Civil War and after he became a prominent steel manufacturer. His wife was Rebecca S. Heermans, whom he married in 1849. (Dwight H. Bruce, Onondaga's Centennial, Gleanings of a Century, Boston, 1896, II, 84–85.)

5. The Garrisons had moved on June 9, 1864, to the house at 125 Highland Street, Roxbury, known as Rockledge, which was to be the family's residence until Garrison's death in 1879.

6. The title of a popular song by C. C. Sawyer.

7. Mrs. French has not been otherwise identified.

8. Daniel Thaxter of Hingham, Mass., and Lucy Scarborough (born 1816) of Brooklyn, Conn., were married in 1850. Thaxter was an optician. (Letters, II, 269, n. 8.)

Miss Cannan, although not listed in pertinent Boston city directories, probably was the Anne Cannan (died 1874) mentioned in The Liberator, August 8, 1862, as a member of the finance committee of the First of August celebration in Abington, Mass. During the late 1840s she was often in company with Eliza Jones Garnaut, the matron of an orphanage, and it is thought that she might have been a nurse. Miss Cannan occasionally visited the Garrison household, providing companionship and assistance to Helen Garrison. (See the letters to Helen E. Garrison, October 10, 1848, Letters, III, 596, n. 1, and September 5, 1853, Letters, IV, 251, n. 15.)

Sarah and Winni were Garrison family servants.

9 8

TO OLIVER JOHNSON

Boston, Nov. 26, 1864.

My dear Johnson:

In communicating to you the conclusion to which I have come, after much anxious thought, respecting the union of the Liberator with the Standard, I regret to think it will cause you great disappointment; yet, as you have been animated by a brotherly regard to my health, welfare and usefulness, and a wish to have nothing done which did not comment itself to my considerate judgment, you will do me the justice to believe that I very gratefully appreciate the efforts you have made to bring about the projected mingling of the two papers. Indeed, your unfailing friendship for more than thrity years—always hearty, but never more so than now—calls for my warmest recognition at all times. That friendship I have tried as heartily to reciprocate; and never have we differed, whether in regard to public affairs or private matters.

I have always esteemed you a sagacious counsellor, and given much weight to your deliberate opinion. Had it not been so, I should hardly have been persuaded to look at any proposition for uniting the Liberator with the Standard; but you were so earnest about it, so obviously satisfied that the change would be greatly to my relief and advantage, as well as beneficial to the cause of freedom and reform generally, and so desirous of having a committee of conference appointed, that I was not unwilling to have the necessary investigation made as to the expediency of the measure. It was certainly desirable, for various reasons, to ascertain how many persons took both papers; and a careful examination of both subscription lists, by Mr. [Samuel] May [Jr.] and Mr. [Charles K.] Whipple, shows the number of such to be considerably fewer than I had supposed—less than four hundred. The actual number of paying subscribers to both papers is under four thousand.

I met the Executive Committee on Friday, to whom the sub-committee made their report. Mr. May, on the whole, was inclined to favor the union; Mr. Whipple was decidedly opposed to it, unless upon the contingency of the stopping of the Liberator. Mr. [Edmund] Quincy was not present; but from the conversation I had with him a few days before, I ascertained that his views were coincident with my own. The other members present were Mr. [William I.] Bowditch, Mr. [John T.] Sargent, and Anne M. Weston.[1] After a full survey of the whole question, I believe the conclusion was pretty unanimous against making the experiment, (even with my consent,) until the next annual meeting of the American Anti-Slavery Society.[2] Your several letters to Mr. May, Mr. Quincy, and myself were duly considered; and they certainly presented the subject in the strongest possible light—though I am confident your calculations were much too sanguine in regard to the financial question.

I will state, very briefly, how the matter lies in my own mind.

1. Had the recent Presidential election resulted in favor of [George B.] McClellan, it would have been regarded as a condemnation of the emancipation policy of Mr. Lincoln; and in all probability we should have had four years of pro-slavery villany and ruffianism to encounter. This would have required a corresponding lease of life of our Society and its organ, and justified—so far as time was concerned—the union about which we have been conferring. But Mr. Lincoln's re-election is certainly the death-warrant of the whole slave system, and indicates that we are very near the day of jubilee. I have no doubt that, among the earliest acts of the approaching session of Congress, the adoption of the contemplated anti-slavery amendment of the Constitution will be successful; in which case the amendment may be so promptly submitted for popular ratification that it may be consummated by the return of our anniversary in May. Should that happen, we shall meet only to disband, and to discontinue the publication of the Standard. With this cheering prospect before us, it is altogether undesirable to attempt to amalgamate the two papers for so short a period; for although it is generously proposed, in that event, to give me the good-will of the joint subscription lists, yet I am persuaded it will be most fitting to let the Standard continue to the end, as it has hitherto been, distinctively the organ of the Society, without change of name.

2. On the whole, I prefer to let the Liberator remain equally distinctive to the end, whether it stop at the close of the present volume, or continue its publication. Should it stop, I shall not object to be a corresponding editor of the Standard, if still desired. But my hope is that its existence may be prolonged.

3. Each paper has its own features and peculiarities; and the continuance of each, for the present, if possible, I think is desirable. The Standard will, of course, be sustained—at least, till next May. What may be the pecuniary condition of the Society at that time remains to be seen. The treasury is now empty, and between now and the Subscription Anniversary probably not a dollar will be put into it; so that a loan must be effected to meet the current expenses till that time. I do not believe—taking my salary into account—that the

union of the two papers would bring any pecuniary relief, but rather increase the burden. It is easy enough to calculate that the great mass of the Liberator subscribers would take the Standard, if I wrote for it; but there is no certainty about it, while the burden of my salary would be inevitable. My conviction is, that many of them would discontinue their subscriptions.

4. I am not insensible to the compliment intended to be conveyed in the assurance, that it is what *I* write that alone interests the readers of the Liberator; but I am not willing to believe, after an editorial experience of thirty-eight years, that, aside from my own lucubrations, I have neither the tact nor the talent to make an interesting journal. This touches me too closely. If the Liberator has been at all effective in the past, it has been owing to its completeness, as a whole, from week to week, and not to what I have written. This is the true value of every journal. My selections have cost me much labor, and they have been made with all possible discrimination as to their interest, ability, and appositeness. The amount of communicated original matter has always been much larger than that of the Standard; and though not always of special interest or value, it has made the Liberator less a transcript, and more readable on that account.

5. The Liberator has an historic position and a moral prestige which would be lost should it be merged in the Standard. True, the loss would be the same should the paper be discontinued, but I shall try to prevent this by increasing the subscription price for the next volume. I confess to a strong desire to keep it along till the amendment of the Constitution is secured, and slavery abolished. It will then have accomplished its Anti-Slavery mission.

6. It is uncertain as to the results of our Subscription Festival, and the unity of the Society in the future.[3] We had, therefore, better defer all action respecting the papers till the May meeting.

It gave me surprise and regret that the project was submitted to the Pennsylvania A. S. Society, in public meeting, though it was all well-intended. It ought not to have been done without my consent, and is the more to be regretted as the union is not to take place. I do not attach much weight to the vote, nearly unanimous as it was— first, because but few copies of the Liberator are taken in Pennsylvania; and, secondly, because I suppose it was generally believed that the proposed change would meet my own wishes.

I think you exaggerate the effect upon my health of the mechanical labor I perform in the office; although, of course, it sometimes causes considerable weariness and prostration. From this I shall aim, in great measure, to exempt myself by being more methodical with the copy, and giving directions to Mr. Yerrinton how to make up the forms.[4] My bodily ailments are bleeding piles and chronic catarrh, and these are equally debilitating, and depressing to the spirits. If I could be cured of these, I should be rejuvenated.

Though you may still feel that the plan you have urged, as to the union of the two papers, is wisest and best, I know you will readily acquiesce in the decision to which I have come; especially as that decision seems to accord with the judgment of the Executive Committee at the present time.

Accept, dear Johnson, a renewal of my grateful acknowledgments for your many kindesses, and the lively interest you have ever evinced in my welfare and happiness. I have not a more attached or a more disinterested friend in the world than your self. And the Anti-Slavery cause has never found a truer advocate or a more faithful laborer than you have been from the hour you espoused it.

Ever faithfully yours,

Wm. Lloyd Garrison.

P.S. I have concluded, on the whole, to raise the price of the Liberator, for the next volume, to $3,50, rather than stop it. It was the unanimous opinion of the Executive Committee, the other day, that hereafter the Standard should be put at $3,00.

ALS: Garrison Papers, Boston Public Library; partly printed in *Life*, IV, 125–126.

1. Anne Warren Weston (1812–1890) was an active member of the Boston Female Anti-Slavery Society and a dependable contributor of poems and articles to the *Liberty Bell*, published by her sister Maria Weston Chapman. She was on the executive committee of the Non-Resistance Society when it was formed in the late 1830s, and it was she who proposed to Garrison a separate nonresistance organ. When Garrison withdrew from the American Anti-Slavery Society in May 1865, Anne Weston did so as well. (*Life;* Weymouth, Mass., Vital Records.)

2. The May meeting of the American Anti-Slavery Society is discussed in letters to Helen E. Garrison, May 10, and Oliver Johnson, May 21, 1865.

3. Funds to support the work of the American Anti-Slavery Society were traditionally raised at the time of the annual meeting. Appeals for funds, along with notices of the meeting, scheduled for January 25, appeared in *The Liberator* in successive issues between December 16 and January 20. In the report of the meeting (*The Liberator*, March 3, 1865) it was announced that a total of $3,300 had been raised.

4. Garrison refers either to James Brown Yerrinton (1800–1866), printer and occasionally editor of *The Liberator* since 1841, or to his son, James Manning Winchell Yerrinton, who has already been identified. (Letter to *The Liberator*, May 9, 1843, *Letters*, III, 158, descriptive note.)

99

TO BENJAMIN F. BUTLER

Boston, Dec. 13, 1864.

Major General Butler,

Sir—

I have just heard, with much surprise and deep regret, that, for some cause or other not known to me, or to any of his friends, Major Thorndike C. Jameson, of the 5th Rhode Island Regiment of Heavy Artillery, has been arrested in your Department, at Fortress Monroe, on his return to his Regiment at Newbern, N.C., and sent to headquarters for trial.[1] It is with great delicacy of feeling, and full consciousness that in such cases it is not for civilians to intermeddle, that I venture to address you in relation to his arrest. Of course, he must stand or fall, according to the nature of the charges and the conclusiveness of the evidence against him. Having known him for many years past—first, as a theological student at Brown University; next, as pastor of a Baptist church in Providence, afterward settled in Melrose in this State, then induced to resume his former pastoral charge in Providence; next, as chaplain of one of the R. I. Regiments earliest in the field; and, finally, as Major of the Regiment with which he is now connected—I cannot believe that he has intentionally done anything criminally incompatible with the spirit, if he has with the letter of the military code, and trust and believe his innocence will be made apparent on an impartial trial. Aside from personal friendship in his case, my sole motive in presuming to address you is to state, that, from an early period, when his standing in the pulpit was thereby imperilled, he openly espoused the Anti-Slavery cause, though not connected with any Anti-Slavery Society, and has always evinced a friendly, sympathetic interest in the welfare of the colored population. Since the Government decided to enrol black as well as white volunteers in the army, Major Jameson has used his influence to induce them to enlist; particularly for some time past in the 1st North Carolina Heavy Artillery, (Colored,) and with encouraging success.[2] In the jealousies and rivalries frequently growing out of such enlistments, and especially aware of the anti-negro feelings which still bias the minds of a portion of the white officers and soldiers, I am apprehensive that Major Jameson may have unfortunately subjected himself to the ill-will and personal dislike of some whose strong hostility to the negro would be gratified to see him cashiered, and who would not be scrupulous in regard to their testimony against him. With your at-

tention drawn to this point, I am confident you will carefully inquire into the *animus* which has led to his impeachment, and
closely scan the evidence that may be adduced to secure his conviction. Beyond this, it would be improper for me to make any suggestion.

Allow me to avail myself of this opportunity to express to you my
high appreciation of your administrative ability, your disinterested
patriotism, and of your noble purpose to extinguish slavery and the
rebellion by the same blow. Had others in high military stations
been animated by your spirit, and energized by your resolute purpose, this bloody war would long ere this have terminated, and liberty been proclaimed throughout all the land to all the inhabitants
thereof.[3]

Very respectfully yours,

Wm. Lloyd Garrison.

P.S. No reply is expected to this letter, and none needed; therefore, in the immense pressure of your multitudinous official duties,
do not occupy a moment of your time in writing one.

ALS: Papers of Benjamin F. Butler, Library of Congress; a rough draft of this letter is
preserved in the Garrison Papers, Boston Public Library. The letter is also printed in
Private and Official Correspondence of Gen. Benjamin F. Butler (privately printed,
1917), V, 424–425.

1. Thorndike Cleaves Jameson (1812–1891), a graduate of Brown University and
a Baptist clergyman, had served as minister of the Third Church in Providence (1840–
1853 and 1858–1861) and of the First Church in Melrose (1855–1858). During the
Civil War he had been chaplain in the 2d Rhode Island Volunteers, and by the time
of the court-martial he was a major with the 5th Rhode Island Heavy Artillery. He
was tried on charges of "fraudulent and dishonest conduct to the prejudice of good
order and military discipline" and of "employing a private soldier as servant and
failing to make the proper deduction from his pay, in violation of the Act of Congress
of July 17th, 1862." Major Jameson was found guilty and sentenced to an $8,000 fine
and three years' imprisonment. Letters from Garrison and other influential people
resulted, on February 11, 1865, in President Lincoln's reopening the case and eventually in a reversal of the verdict, Major Jameson being pardoned and released from
prison. (*Brown University Historical Catalogue, 1764–1894*, Providence, 1895, p.
132; Henry Burrage, comp., *Civil War Records of Brown University*, Providence,
1920, p. 4; Adjutant General's Office, Court Martial Orders Nos. 24 and 149, Department of Virginia, February 2 and March 17, 1865; letters to the editor from Elmer O.
Parker, Military Archives Division, National Archives and Record Service, Washington, D.C., October 12, 1971, and from Carolyn H. Sung, researcher, November 30,
1971.)

2. This regiment, which was later designated the 14th Regiment U.S. Colored
Heavy Artillery, was organized at New Bern and Morehead City, N.C., on March
1864. According to one contemporary account, Major Jameson observed "exact military discipline . . . tempered by the kindest regard for the comfort and well-being
of the soldiers, whose intellectual and moral as well as physical condition were evidently made the subjects of Major Jameson's peculiar care." The regiment was mustered out in December 1865. (Frederick H. Dyer, *A Compendium of the War of the
Rebellion*, N.Y., 1959, I, 199, 247; "Letter from Newbern," signed "A. G.," July 7,
1864, *The Liberator*, July 22.)

3. Leviticus 25:10.

V JUBILEE AND DISSENSION: 1865

THE CONTROVERSY BETWEEN Phillips and Garrison continued unabated in 1865. On January 21, Garrison wrote a letter to General Nathaniel P. Banks soliciting information about his administration of New Orleans in 1863–1864, which had been under attack by Phillips, asking him specific questions and quoting from one of Phillips' speeches. General Banks replied promptly in a letter dated January 30, which filled more than four columns in *The Liberator* for February 24. He described in considerable and convincing detail the condition of destitute blacks in and around New Orleans who, owing to technical loopholes, had not been covered by the Emancipation Proclamation, and what he had done to help them. Most of Phillips' basic charges he denied categorically. He admitted that he had permitted only white men to vote in the election he supervised, but said that he had had no power to do otherwise, since the President and other federal officers and departments had required that he form a government consistent with the state constitution, which provided "that the basis of political power should be the '*white male citizens* of the State.'" He defended the system of using provost marshals as entrepreneurs in the labor system he devised, on the grounds that any marshals who proved dishonest could be eliminated at once by transfer to other duties.

Although Garrison printed Banks's long letter without comment and apparently never explained the extent to which he was convinced by his argument, the general was a welcome ally in the conflict with Phillips. Garrison's sons in their biography write that their father investigated the labor system instigated by General Banks in Louisiana, and that Phillips' allegations "subsequently appeared . . . altogether unjust and exaggerated."[1]

In the early months of the year Garrison had further contact with

1. *Life*, IV, 124.

Lincoln, writing two letters to the President and receiving one in reply. Garrison's letter of inquiry about the unacknowledged gift of a painting contributed by a group of Boston ladies brought a succinct and charming reply from the busy President. Lincoln's inaugural address, which Garrison reprinted in full in *The Liberator,* March 10, he called "without a parallel for brevity, and also for the contrite spirit and reverent recognition of the chastising hand of Divine Providence for our great national sin of slavery. It will inspire fresh confidence in the integrity and firmness of the President touching that hateful system, and deepen the popular feeling as to the duty and necessity of utterly abolishing it in the present struggle."

April, the month following the inaugural address, proved both exciting and cruel. Events unfolded in succession, as though propelled by a tightly coiled spring. On the seventh Garrison was in New York City, the first stop en route to Charleston for the ceremonial raising of the flag over Fort Sumter. There he received from Secretary Edwin M. Stanton a telegram informing him that his son George would be granted a furlough to be with his father in Charleston. On the eighth he and George Thompson, along with many distinguished representatives from church, state, press, and business, sailed on the *Arago.* Also among the guests were Major General Robert Anderson, who had commanded Fort Sumter in 1861, and Henry Ward Beecher, principal speaker at the ceremony to follow. On the ninth Lee surrendered to Grant at Appomattox. On the eleventh the ship arrived at Charleston and continued on to Savannah before circling back to Charleston, where it arrived on the fourteenth, just as Lee's surrender was being officially reported. Shouts of joy reverberated from ship to ship in the crowded harbor, as the important visitors were ferried out to the fort, its ruined walls silent after the long war. The visitors mounted the citadel and found their way down into the inner bowl of the fortress. It was the fifth anniversary of the surrender of the fort to Confederate forces.

The ragged flag of 1861 opened to the breeze as General Anderson and a dozen others pulled on the halyard. "'When the flag reached the apex, the whole bay thundered with such a volley of cannon from ship and shore, that one might imagine the old battle of the Monitors renewed again. . . .'"[2] Even Henry Ward Beecher's speech was an anticlimax. That evening, unknown to the celebrants in Charleston, Lincoln attended Ford's Theatre in

2. A letter, signed "T. L. C.," dated Brooklyn, April 20, reprinted from the New York *Evangelist, The Liberator,* May 5, 1865.

Washington and was shot by John Wilkes Booth. The next morning
Garrison stood in front of St. Michael's Church, listening to the
127th Regiment march down Meeting Street, playing "John
Brown's Body"; and later he looked at the marble slab over Calhoun's grave and said: "Down into a deeper grave than this slavery
has gone, and for it there is no resurrection."[3] The same day Garrison, along with others, spoke to a mass meeting of some ten thousand freedmen and visited his son George's regiment, the 55th
Massachusetts, three miles outside of town. Everywhere there was
adulation, as though Garrison alone had wrought the wonder of
emancipation.

That evening, when most of the visitors sailed north on the *Arago*
toward New York, Garrison remained behind with Beecher and
Wilson and sailed south, planning to visit Beaufort, Savannah, and
St. Augustine. They were going ashore at Beaufort when a telegram
arrived for Henry Wilson. Beecher joked as the messenger walked
to the senator's cabin. A moment later Wilson was on deck: "Good
God! the President is killed!" The ship spun 180 degrees and
headed north. Garrison feared the possibility of "a concerted uprising of all the seditious forces in the North for a desperate *coup
d'état* at the Capital, in conjunction with the Southern traitors."[4]

Garrison's full appraisal of Lincoln came in a speech in Providence on June 1 (reported in *The Liberator,* July 7). He said of the
martyred President that he had "absolute faith in the people, sound
judgment, ready tact, abiding cheerfulness, inflexible perseverance, large common sense, strong powers of reasoning, incorrupt-
ible integrity, and unalloyed patriotism."

Even the death of the leader could not erase from Garrison's
mind the memory of the trip to Charleston, with images of war won
and slaves freed. He was convinced that his life's work was complete, that new times called for new methods, that antislavery societies and periodicals were no longer relevant, that he should retire as an active abolitionist. A significant group of abolitionists led
by Phillips—Radical Republicans by political persuasion—disagreed with him. In May at the anniversary meeting of the American
Anti-Slavery Society Phillips spoke first, in general terms. Then
came Garrison, introduced by George Thompson. Garrison spoke
humorously, complaining that Jefferson Davis had a price of
$100,000 on his head, whereas no more than $5,000 had ever been

3. Reported by the Reverend A. P. Putnam, "Abolitionists in Charleston," *The
Liberator,* May 12, 1865.
4. Garrison, "The Verdict of the People," New York *Independent,* March 29,
1866.

offered for his own. Then he approached the crucial issue, expressing gratitude that "the guns of the American Anti-Slavery Society . . . are spiked, because slavery is abolished." Later in the
meeting the dispute ricocheted between Garrison and Phillips,
Henry C. Wright supporting the former and Charles L. Remond,
the latter. On the final vote for discontinuance of the society Garrison lost by 118 to 48. He was nominated once more as president,
but when he refused to serve, Phillips became his successor. And
so, ironically, Garrison's retirement established the power of Wendell Phillips, his friend turned adversary.

The differences between Phillips and Garrison over the disband-
ing of the national society dramatized what had become an essential distinction between the old associates. Although Garrison had
early been involved with many reforms and had been regarded as a
universal reformer, by 1865 he thought of himself as an abolitionist
with a primary and attainable goal. In contrast, Phillips had entered
reform as an abolitionist and become a professional agitator, a radical. As Irving H. Bartlett put it, Wendell Phillips "knew that the
radical in America could never retire."[5] The break between the two
men can also be interpreted on a broader, more philosophical level
as the familiar dichotomy between moral suasion (Garrison) and political activism (Phillips).

Although he lacked the power to disband the society, Garrison
was in full control of *The Liberator*. By October 1864 he was considering its future course. Oliver Johnson wanted it to merge with
the paper he was editing, the *National Anti-Slavery Standard*, official organ of the American Anti-Slavery Society; but that possibility
had been rejected within a month. Garrison's final decision about
the disposition of his paper was announced in the issue of March
24, 1865; it would cease publication in December.

During its last year, in spite of an increased subscription price,
The Liberator was running a substantial deficit. Hoping to improve
his financial position, Garrison embarked at the end of October on a
five-week lecture tour of the West. He spoke five or six times a
week on the topic "The Past, Present and Future of our Country" in
many western towns and cities, including Cleveland, Detroit,
Springfield, and Chicago. At an average fee of $50 he accumulated
total receipts of some $1,400. But he found that his broad topic and
his merely financial motivation prevented his developing the enthusiasm displayed on earlier lecture tours. On the whole, the trip

5. Bartlett, "The Persistence of Wendell Phillips," *The Antislavery Vanguard*,
ed. Martin Duberman (Princeton, 1965), p. 120.

proved burdensome and debilitating. For the reader, however, the letters he wrote during November and the first week of December are interesting for their many images of the growing West—"a mighty theatre for enterprise, labor, business of every kind . . . [,] a vast empire in process of rapid development. . . ."[6]

For Garrison 1865 was bittersweet. It was the year of jubilee, but also the year of Lincoln's assassination. It was the year for total emancipation (a resolution to Congress in February and ratification of the Thirteenth Amendment in December). But it was also the year for agonies of reconstruction under the Johnson administration. It was the year for the symbolic discontinuation of *The Liberator*, its goal having been accomplished. But it was also the year for Garrison's separation from the American Anti-Slavery Society, and for the elevation to power as its new president of his rival Wendell Phillips. It was the year of climactic resolution and of disappointing frustration—the year, moreover, when, like Othello, Garrison was suddenly aware that his "occupation's gone."

6. Letter to Helen E. Garrison, November 10, 1865.

1 0 0

TO CHARLES ELIOT NORTON

Boston, Jan. 13, 1865.

Dear Mr. Norton:

Be assured, I feel highly gratified and honored by your complimentary letter, inviting me to contribute an article to the pages of the next number of the North American Review, in relation to the somewhat complicated state of affairs in Louisiana concerning the labor-system instituted—only *pro tempore*, of course—by General Banks, the reconstruction policy, and the future of the emancipated blacks.[1] The subject is vast, and presents manifold aspects; and it is certainly one which has awakened much anxiety and interest in my mind. It is not, perhaps, difficult to decide, *per se*, what absolute justice demands in this case; but only as to the possiblities of statesmanship in a comparatively chaotic state of society. While I am solicitous to maintain, uncompromisingly, all the principles I have advocated for the last thirty years, I am equally anxious to be entirely just to all men and all parties, in connection with the new order of things.

I dare not give you an absolute promise to prepare the article you suggest—for two reasons: First, I am not confident that I could write it, even to my own satisfaction, for such a work as your now peerless Review: and, secondly, with the various lecturing engagements I have on my hands, in addition to my editorial duties, I am apprehensive that I shall not be able to command the time necessary to do justice to the subject. Thanking you for your generous overture, all I dare promise is, that I will make the attempt to do what you propose, within the time specified; and if I succeed, you shall be duly apprised of the fact.[2]

It is probable, however, that you wish no uncertainty about the matter. If so, you will, doubtless, readily find some one else who will prepare a much better article than I can, and not run any risk of disappointing you. In that case, please consider me wholly discharged.

It is very pleasurable to me to be assured that you write in behalf of my friend Professor Lowell, as well as your own.[3] That the North American Review has fallen into such hands is high and cheering evidence that the cause of freedom and humanity is upward and onward.

Yours, for universal justice,

Wm. Lloyd Garrison.

Prof. C. E. Norton.

ALS: Charles Eliot Norton Papers, Harvard College Library.

Charles Eliot Norton (1827–1908) was one of the most versatile of nineteenth-century American men of letters. After graduating from Harvard and traveling extensively abroad, Norton spent several years in the East India trade. Beginning in 1855, he followed a literary career: writing books about his travels, writing articles for *The Atlantic Monthly,* editing many volumes of letters, and, with the collaboration of James Russell Lowell, editing the *North American Review,* founding *The Nation* in 1865, and writing several books of art history. Between 1873 and 1897 he was a professor at Harvard.

1. The *North American Review* (1815–1939), at first a quarterly and then a monthly, was a journal of literature, criticism, and history. Founded in Boston, the *Review* moved in 1878 to New York, where it became concerned with the latest social and political movements.

Garrison had expressed disapproval of some of Banks's policies in his letter to Francis W. Newman, July 22, 1864, and was to give his views to Banks himself in the letter dated January 21, 1865.

2. A search of the issues of the *North American Review* for 1865 does not yield Garrison's article.

3. James Russell Lowell (1819–1891), a graduate of both the college and the law school at Harvard, was a noted man of letters as well as an active abolitionist. A prolific poet, essayist, critic, and journalist, he was also for many years Smith Professor at Harvard and an editor of extraordinary range, being associated successively with the *Pioneer,* the *Pennsylvania Freeman,* the *National Anti-Slavery Standard, The Atlantic Monthly,* and the *North American Review.* Probably no American of his day published so many and such varied works of poetry and prose. His later years were spent in part as minister first to Spain and then to England.

101

TO JOHN A. ANDREW

Boston, Jan. 17, 1865.

Gov. Andrew:

Dear Sir—

The bearer of this is my much esteemed friend, Mrs. Jameson, daughter of the late George A. Otis, Esq. of this city, and wife of Major Thorndike C. Jameson, of the 5th Rhode Island Regt. of Heavy Artillery.[1] She wishes to confer with you in regard to the case of her husband, who is under arrest by General [Benjamin F.] Butler at Fortress Monroe, and was for several weeks deprived of all knowledge of the charges alleged against him; and whose trial is yet to come off. Why she submits the case to your notice, she will explain. Without at all going into it, I will only say, that I have known Mr. Jameson for many years—first, as a theological student at Brown University; next, as an acceptable pastor of a Baptist church in Providence, afterward settled at Melrose in this State; and then induced to resume his former pastoral charge in Providence; next, as chaplain of one of the Rhode Island regiments earliest in the field; and, finally, as Major of the regiment with which he is now connected;—and at all times the friend of the colored race, in the pulpit and out of it, and among the most loyal and patriotic in the land in support of the government, and for the suppression of the rebellion. I believe him to be the victim of mean and selfish accusers, and doubt not his innocence will be substantiated upon his trial, in spite of the "hard swearing" of unprincipled men.

Wishing him a good deliverance, and deeply sympathizing with his anxious wife and daughter, I remain,

Yours, with high regards,

Wm. Lloyd Garrison.

ALS: Executive Department Letters 1853–1893, Massachusetts State Library; a handwritten transcription is preserved in the Records of the Judge Advocate General's Office, National Archives.

1. Lucinda Lawrence Otis Jameson has been identified in the letter to Wendell Phillips Garrison, August 1, 1862. Her father, George Alexander Otis (1781–1863), was a Boston merchant and broker known chiefly to posterity for his translation of a history of the American Revolution by Guiseppe Guglielmo Botta, an Italian political exile living in France. (Letter to the editor from Ruth Bell, researcher, October 18, 1971.)

1 0 2

TO NATHANIEL P. BANKS

(Private.)

Boston, Jan. 21, 1865.

Major General Banks:
Dear Sir—

I am urged by the Editors of the North American Review to prepare an article on the reconstruction policy inaugurated by yourself for Louisiana, with reference to her admission to the Union; also, in elucidation of your labor policy for the emancipated plantation slaves. This article they wish to obtain for the next number of their Review. I fear I shall not be able to find time to write it, but I shall make the attempt.

Anxious to understand the whole question, with all its difficulties and complications, as accurately as possible, so that I may do full justice to all parties concerned, and to yourself in special, you will greatly oblige me by forwarding to me any statements or documents relating to this subject that may be at your command, so that I may have a reliable basis upon which to proceed. These shall be carefully preserved and returned, should you desire it.

My esteemed friend and co-laborer, Wendell Phillips, having in his numerous speeches and lectures assailed your administration in the severest manner from the time of its inception till now, I have felt obliged, as a matter of justice, both upon the platform and in my editorial columns, to protest against such a sweeping impeachment, and to accord to you much praise for what you had done in various ways for the freedom and elevation of the colored race within your jurisdiction.

But, while I have given you credit for good motives and certain excellent acts, I confess my mind has not been quite clear as to the expediency of all that has been done. Mr. Phillips deems it an outrage that you did not allow any colored citizens to vote at the late elections. To my reply, that you may have felt it necessary to follow popular usage and constitutional prescription in that particular, he answers that these were readily disregarded by you in regard to the admission of *soldiers* to the polls, who, though citizens, were excluded from voting by the old State constitution; and if you could ignore that constitution in the one case, why not in the other?

But it is your freed labor system that he most sharply condemns, and with the greatest effect before popular assemblies. I enclose an extract from his speech at Cooper Institute, on the 27th ult., which you may not have seen.[1] Is it true, as he affirms in the face of your lucid speech at Tremont Temple, that "General Banks has not permitted the black man any element of citizenship or freedom"; that "the negro cannot make a contract—*cannot appeal to a court when injured*"—&c., &c.? Is it true what he says about your conduct in regard to the gallant colored regiment at Port Hudson? What are the exact facts of that case? I have also seen it alleged that the lash is still used as an instrument of punishment—perhaps only as ordered by the Provost Marshal. Is that so? Are any but the old plantation slaves included in your Labor Order? Why could they not be left, like the poor whites, free to follow their own tastes, work where they pleased, for whom they pleased, and on what terms they pleased? Are there not some of the features of serfdom in their present condition? And *why is it necessary to renew the same binding obligations for another year?* Why were they forbidden to visit New Orleans at the close of the year, except by permission of the Provost Marshal in individual cases?[2]

I am sure you will appreciate the motive and object which lead me to send you this letter.

Very truly yours,

Wm. Lloyd Garrison.

☞ What you may think proper to send me shall be a matter strictly between ourselves.

ALS: Nathaniel P. Banks Collection, Illinois State Historical Library.

1. Phillips' speech, which was printed in the New York *Times*, December 28, 1864, did contain the passages Garrison quotes, but ellipses are not indicated.

2. General Banks's reply (dated January 30, 1865) to Garrison's letter was printed in *The Liberator*, February 24. He described the labor system in some detail, denying most of Phillips' allegations and explaining others. He did admit that "some Provost Marshals have been corrupt and cruel." Concerning the vote, he explained that the instructions of the War Department called for political power to rest in the hands of white male citizens.

103

TO JOHN M. FORBES

Boston, Jan. 21, 1865.

Hon. J. M. Forbes:
Dear Sir—

Your letter was duly received, but found me confined to my house by illness, from which I have now nearly recovered.

You express the belief that the President regards me in a light so favorable that, even in regard to the filling of a vacancy in his Cabinet, my opinion would have weight with him! What he thinks of me, I do not know, having heard no word of commendation from his lips, and received none from his pen. Doubtless, if he has read the copy of the Liberator which has been regularly forwarded to him, he has been gratified at my defence of him, occasionally, from the unjust assaults that have been made upon him. But, beyond this, I am not able to throw the weight of a feather into the scale of his judgment, touching any of his appointments, whether high or low.

I cannot, my dear sir, allow you to claim to be more uncompromising than I am as a "reconstructionist," or as it respects "true democracy," or the exercise of the elective franchise. So, if you have no particular influence with the President, I have none. True, I am willing to be recognized by him as "a radical, with a substratum of common sense and practical wisdom," for these belong to genuine radicalism; but as I know you to be characterized by large common sense and much practical wisdom, as well as an earnest reformer, I insist on keeping your good company to the end.

The interest you express in the appointment of Governor Andrew to a place in the Cabinet, is what his rare fitness and eminent services commendingly justify. I heartily endorse all that you say about him, and trust he will be invited by the President to be one of his Cabinet advisers.[1] I am willing to say this, and more, to the President, in a letter which I am to write to him to-day on another subject—as you think it may have some weight; though I am slightly apprehensive that he may consider my reference to the subject as intrusive and uncalled for. The sequel will show.

I regard the question of questions, at this hour, to be the anti-slavery amendment of the Constitution. That is the rod of Moses to swallow all the rods of the magicians.[2] In comparison with this, all the magnificent victories that have been won by Grant, Sherman, Sheridan, and the army, are as dust in the balance.[3] Trusting that nothing will be left undone to secure its passage at the present session of Congress, I remain,

Yours, to break every yoke,[4]

Wm. Lloyd Garrison.

ALS: Garrison Papers, Boston Public Library.

1. Garrison refers to and quotes from Forbes's letter of January 18, 1865 (Anti-Slavery Letters to Garrison and Others, Boston Public Library), in which Forbes says that he has exhausted his own influence with the President and urges Garrison to support Governor John A. Andrew for a position in the new cabinet, any position, though he thinks, "If the Navy Dept. is to be vacant that is easiest for him &

is considered a New England place." Despite the pleas of Forbes and Garrison, Andrew was not appointed, and Gideon Welles remained as secretary of the navy.

2. Garrison could be referring to the rod mentioned frequently in Exodus and in Numbers, though his statement is closer verbally to a passage about the rod of Aaron (Exodus 7:12).

3. William Tecumseh Sherman (1820–1891), of an old New England family, was born in Ohio. Between his graduation from West Point in 1840 and the Civil War, he served in the Mexican War and was a partner in a banking firm in San Francisco. A colonel at the beginning of the Civil War, Sherman saw action in many battles and rose rapidly in rank, assuming command of the Army of Tennessee when Grant relinquished that post to take command of the Western Department. Sherman played a crucial part in the capture of Vicksburg in July 1863 and of Atlanta in September 1864 as well as in the subsequent March to the Sea. Following Grant's inauguration as President in 1869, Sherman became the general commanding the army; he retired in 1883.

Philip Henry Sheridan (1831–1888), a graduate of West Point in 1853, saw service along the Rio Grande and in the northwest prior to the Civil War At the beginning of the war he was shifted so rapidly from one staff position to another in the armies of the West that he developed a strong appetite for action. Such opportunities came in abundance, however, once he had become colonel of the 2d Michigan Cavalry in May 1862. Thereafter he rose within the year to the rank of major general of volunteers. His brilliant victory at Chattanooga a year later (November 23–25) brought him to the attention of Grant, who put him in charge of all cavalry in the Army of the Potomac. In 1864 as commander of the Army of the Shenandoah, he laid waste to the fertile Shenandoah Valley, which had supplied the Confederate war effort. His victory at Five Forks on April 1, 1865, forced the evacuation of Petersburg and began the retreat to Appomattox. Following the war he commanded the Fifth Military District, reconstructing Louisana and Texas. Removed by President Johnson, he was transferred to Missouri. In 1884, following the retirement of Sherman, he became general-in-chief of the army. The year of his death he completed and published his memoirs. (Richard O'Connor, *Sheridan, the Inevitable,* New York, 1953.)

4. An allusion to Isaiah 58:6.

104

TO ABRAHAM LINCOLN

(Private.)

Boston, Jan. 21, 1865.

To Abraham Lincoln, President of the United States:

Sir—

About the first of July, last year, what was deemed by critics and connisseurs, artistically speaking, an admirable painting, was sent by Adams's Express[1] to your address at Washington; accompanied by a letter from me in behalf of the donors, whose contributions to the object in view amounted to upwards of five hundred dollars. This meritorious picture, executed by a most conscientious and excellent artist, was entitled "Watch Night—or, Waiting for the Hour."[2] It represented a group of negro men, women and children waiting with heartfelt emotion and thrilling delight for the midnight hour of December 31, 1862, to pass, and the introduction of that new year which was to make them forever free. Many photographic copies were made of it, and it was by my advice that it was presented to you as the most fitting person in the world to receive it. Among those who subscribed to send it to you were Governor Andrew and a number of our most prominent citizens.

For some cause or other, no acknowledgment has been made, or at least received, of the receipt of the picture, or of my letter, which contained the names of the donors. As my friend Mr. Sumner assured me, on his return from Washington last summer, that he had seen the picture again and again at the White House, all anxiety has been relieved as to its safe arrival, and we are happy to know it is in your possession. But as the money raised to purchase it was collected by ladies who desire that the donors may be officially apprised of its legitimate application, I write in their behalf to say that it would relieve them of much embarrassment if you would be so obliging, either under your own signature or by the hand of one of your secretaries, as to send me a line, stating that the painting aforesaid was duly received by you.[3]

I shall ever remember, with deep satisfaction, the private interview you were so kind as to accord to Mr. Tilton and myself, last June. Having full faith in your integrity of purpose, and inflexible determination to stand by every word and syllable enunciated by you in your emancipation proclamations, come what may, I have frequently had occasion, both in my editorial capacity and as a lecturer, to defend you against the many sweeping accusations that have been brought against you, sometimes even on the anti-slavery platform. God be with you to the end, to strengthen, enlighten, inspire your mind and heart, and render your administration illustrious to all coming ages! God grant that it may be your enviable privilege to announce, ere long, that, by an amendment of the Constitution, slavery is forever abolished in the United States!

It is not my wish or purpose to meddle with any of your appointments; but you will pardon me if I respectfully suggest that, in any reconstruction of your Cabinet, New England, for her intelligence, wealth, enterprise—her mechanical, manufacturing and commercial power—her glowing and unswerving loyalty—is worthy to be represented in it. And as Mr. [William Pitt] Fessenden is soon to vacate the situation he holds as Secretary of the Treasury, I believe if Gov. Andrew, of this State, should be appointed his successor, he would bring to the place whatever of ability, industry, integrity, vigilance and efficiency it so imperatively requires. He is truly "a host in himself."[4]

Yours, to break every yoke,[5]

Wm. Lloyd Garrison.

ALS: Robert Todd Lincoln Collection of the Papers of Abraham Lincoln, Library of Congress.

1. A Boston firm, founded by Alvin Adams in 1840 for parcel post delivery, which gradually extended its business to other eastern cities. (Alvin F. Harlow, *Old Waybills*, New York, 1934.)

2. The painting (correctly entitled "Watch Meeting, Waiting for the Hour, Dec. 31st. 1862"), which is used as an illustration in this volume, was by William Tolman Carlton (1816–1888). The artist is known to have specialized in portraits and genre pictures; he exhibited at the Boston Athenaeum as early as 1836 and at the American Art-Union in New York in 1850. Although the subsequent history of the painting in question is obscure, it was recently owned by the Hirschl and Adler Galleries in New York and has now been returned to the White House. (George C. Groce and David H. Wallace, *New-York Historical Society Dictionary of Artists in America, 1564–1860*, New Haven, 1957; letters to the editor from Carol J. Heinsius, office 'of the curator, The White House, October 19, 1971, and from Stuart P. Feld, director, Hirschl and Adler Galleries, November 20, 1971 and September 15, 1977.)

3. For information about Lincoln's reply to Garrison's letter, see Garrison to Lincoln, February 13, 1865.

4. Garrison's quotation would seem to be ultimately an allusion to Homer, perhaps by way of Pope's translation of the *Iliad*, III, 293.

5. An allusion to Isaiah 58:6.

105

TO ABRAHAM LINCOLN

Boston, Feb. 13, 1865.

Dear Mr. President:

Your kind and very satisfactory letter, in reply to mine, acknowledging the receipt of Mr. [William T.] Carleton's painting, "The Watch-Night, or Waiting for the Hour," is received, putting me in possession of what I shall value very highly—namely, your autograph.[1] I felt very reluctant to trouble you about the matter; for I known that you must be not only overwhelmed, but almost literally crushed, by the multitudinous matters constantly pressing upon you; and, as I told you last June, my astonishment is that you are above ground. Happily, you are blessed with an elastic and a cheerful spirit; and may you be inspiringly sustained to the end! May you be of those, who, divinely strengthened and guided, are enabled to run, and not be weary; to walk, and not faint![2] God save you, and bless you abundantly! As an instrument in his hands, you have done a mighty work for the freedom of millions who have so long pined in bondage in our land—nay, for the freedom of all mankind. I have the utmost faith in the benevolence of your heart, the purity of your motives, and the integrity of your spirit. This I do not hesitate to avow at all times. I am sure you will consent to no compromise that will leave a slave in his fetters. It is slavery that has brought this dreadful war upon us; and only through liberty will Heaven vouchsafe to our distracted and bleeding country peace. Vast and solemn are your responsibilities; and you need and deserve whatever of comfort, encouragement and support can be given to you.

Pardon me for intruding upon your attention a moment longer. I have just seen, with sorrow and dismay, an announcement that Major Thorndike C. Jameson, connected with a Heavy Artillery Regiment of Rhode Island, has just been sentenced, by court martial, to be dishonorably dismissed from the service, to pay a fine of $8000, and to be imprisoned at hard labor in Norfolk for a period of three years![3] It is a terrible sentence; but if he is guilty to the extent warranting such a fate, then the cry must be for mercy, as far only as it may be safely granted. I have known Major Jameson for several years—first, as a theological student at Brown University; next, as pastor of a Baptist church in Providence; next, as pastor of a similar church in Melrose, near Boston; next, as pastor of his old church in Providence; next, as one of the first chaplains connected with the Rhode Island regiments; and, finally, as Major of Heavy Artillery. He has always been the special friend of the colored people, bond and free; and none more zealous than he in raising colored regiments. I have always esteemed and respected him—his wife being among my most attached friends, and a daughter of the late George A. Otis, Esq. of Boston, the translator of Botta's works. I cannot believe that he is really guilty of the frauds alleged against him; and yet it is possible he may have fallen by the pressure of temptation. But most respectfully and tenderly would I beg you to look into his case, and see that he is not sacrificed to personal malice, or on account of his anti-slavery principles and sentiments. My fear is, that he is the victim of an artful conspiracy, or of some bad men. His suffering and estimable wife has gone to Washington to lay the case before you; and I am confident that you will try to temper judgment with mercy.

Yours, with the highest esteem,

Wm. Lloyd Garrison.

Abraham Lincoln, Pres. U. S.

ALS: John G. Nicolay Papers, Library of Congress.

1. Lincoln's reply to Garrison (McClellan Lincoln Collection, Brown University Library) was printed in *The Liberator*, February 17, 1865, with minor changes in punctuation to clarify the meaning, as follows:

EXECUTIVE MANSION
WASHINGTON, 7th February, 1865.
MY DEAR MR. GARRISON:
I have your kind letter of the 21st of January, and can only beg that you will pardon the seeming neglect occasioned by my constant engagements. When I received the spirited and admirable painting, "Waiting for the Hour," I directed my Secretary not to acknowledge its arrival at once, perferring to make my personal acknowledgment of the thoughtful kindness of the donors; and waiting for some leisure hour, I have committed the discourtesy of not replying at all.
I hope you will believe that my thanks, though late, are most cordial, and I request that you will convey them to those associated with you in this flattering and generous gift.
I am very truly,
Your friend and servant,
A. Lincoln.
WM. LLOYD GARRISON, ESQ.

2. An allusion to Isaiah 40:31.
3. See the letters to Benjamin F. Butler, December 13, 1864, and John A. Andrew, January 17, 1865.

106

TO HOWARD M. JENKINS

Boston, Feb. 28, 1865.

Dear Sir:

I am very much obliged to you for your friendly letter, cordially approving my editorial course, in these trying and anomalous times, with particular reference to public men and to President Lincoln's administration.—Ever since the rebellion broke out, I have specially felt anxious to avoid harsh judgment and hasty impeachment of those in power, knowing how full of perplexity and trial has been their situation; yet I feel that, throughout, I have never been more anxious or more vigilant in behalf of my clients—the millions in bondage—or more deeply impressed with the importance and duty of keeping the anti-slavery standard erect. It is consoling to me to know that, though I have differed, and still differ, from some of my co-laborers, this difference has not at all related to the principles or the objects we cherish, but only as to our judgment of men and measures. If misled in this at any time, still I would prefer to be many times over-charitable than once unjustly censorious.

You can easily imagine that my gladness of mind is very great in view of the entire abolition of slavery, through the Constitutional Amendment; but it is for my country, for the liberated bondmen and their posterity, for those who have been slaveholders and their descendants, for the cause of freedom throughout the world, I am glad, and not with any feelings of personal exultation. Of course, I do not believe the abolition of slavery is "the end of the law for righteousness,"[1] but it is a long stride towards the overthrow of despotism throughout the globe.

Yours for the jubilee,

Wm. Lloyd Garrison.

H. M. Jenkins.

P.S. It will give me much pleasure to lecture in Norristown at some future time.[2]

ALS: Friends Historical Library, Swarthmore College.

Howard M. Jenkins (1842–1902) was one of the proprietors of the Norristown (Pa.) *Republican* and subsequently editor of the Norristown *Herald.* In 1866 he was to move to Wilmington, Del., where he was one of the founders of the *Daily Commerical.* (M. Auge, *Lives of the Eminent Dead and Biographical Notices of Prominent Living Citizens of Montgomery County, Pa.*, Norristown, 1879, p. 559.)

1. Romans 10:4.

2. Garrison did lecture in Norristown on June 12, 1865. (See the letter to Helen E. Garrison, June 11, 1865 [micro.].)

107

TO CHARLES KING WHIPPLE

Boston, March 13, 1865.

Dear friend Whipple:

Your note, requesting me (by desire of Mr. [Wendell] Phillips) to give an affirmative or negative vote upon certain propositions touching the disbursement of a portion of the Hovey Fund, furnishes me an occasion to say, (what I intended to communicate some time ago,) that I desire to have my official connection with the Hovey Committee terminated; so that neither upon the propositions named by you, nor upon any others in the future, do I wish to be consulted or to give my vote. It is evident that we are too widely disagreed, on various matters, to render it pleasant or desirable for me to continue my membership, as I wish to avoid, as far as possible, all disputation and controversy; and I therefore leave a vacancy to be filled or not, as the Committee may choose.

This step I feel bound to take as a matter of self-respect. For when the Committee so act as to impeach my fidelity to that cause which has been dearer to me than "father or mother, or wife or children, or houses or lands,"[1] during the larger portion of my earthly life, and to that race for whose redemption I have been willing to suffer the loss of all things, and pronounce against the Liberator as undeserving of a free circulation, as hitherto, (by a donation from the Hovey Fund,) it seems to me I owe it to them, as well as to myself, to withdraw—not with any feelings of unkindness to any one, but on the score of self-respect and propriety. As they make a difference of opinion about public men and measures as though it were a violation of principle, I have no other alternative than to protest against such treatment as narrow and proscriptive, and to take my leave.

With no reference to the pecuniary view of the case, I confess that I have felt the virtual refusal of the Committee to pay for the hundred copies of the Liberator sent on the "free list" to individuals and societies, during the last year, (in accordance with an old usage, which for the two previous years had been assumed by the Committee, and which it was believed they would be disposed to continue,) more severely than a blow in the face. In view of all the circumstances, and of our intimate and long-tried relations to each other, I must regard the withholding of the usual payment for those hundred copies as not only a very singular procedure, but a severe imputation upon my anti-slavery integrity; and it has imposed upon me a pecuniary burden which the Committee well know I am not able easily to bear, and which would not have been incurred if I had dreamed of any such revulsion of feeling and action on their part. (Of course, I mean the majority.)

The Committee may, if they choose, avail themselves of the technical fact, that they did not formally vote to sustain the "free list" for another year; and, therefore, that there is no claim upon them. None legally, I admit; but this is not the issue. What other motive, except to pronounce sentence of condemnation upon the Liberator, (and, of course, upon myself,) and to make the continuance of the paper still more problematical, could have induced the Committee to refuse to provide for the "free list," as heretofore? They knew that the hundred copies had been regularly sent, and that it was taken for granted the Committee would be as willing last year, as they had been the two previous years, to foot the bill, in order to "help the cause along." Their funds were not exhausted, but waiting to be disbursed. They have a right to act as they think best; and so have I to judge of their action.

Regretting this division, I remain,
Very truly yours,

Wm. Lloyd Garrison.

C. K. Whipple.

ALS: National Park Service, Morristown National Historic Park, Morristown, New Jersey.
This letter provides substantially all the information available about Garrison's controversy with the Hovey Committee.
1. An allusion to Matthew 19:29.

108

TO JACOB HORTON

Boston, March 17, 1865.

* * * * * * * * * *

All the kind feelings you express, I heartily reciprocate. At no time have I ever forgotten "the days of auld lang syne", or the many pleasant incidents connected with them, as pertaining to you both. Be assured, the friendship which was so early formed between us will be a part of my existence, here & hereafter. The peculiar circumstances which conspired to keep me for so many years from my native-place, necessarily prevented our seeing each other, except at remote periods; and so the charm of frequent social intercourse was unavoidably broken. Henceforth, during our earthly pilgrimage, I trust our interviews will not be, "like angels' visits, few and far between,"[1] but reciprocal and comparatively frequent.

The remembrance of my recent visit to Newburyport, and the generous and handsome reception which was accorded to me by the citizens, for dear Liberty's sake, will carry with it a delightful aroma while memory lasts. After so many years of misapprehension, and opposition to my course, it fills me with deep satisfaction —into which, I am sure, nothing merely personal enters—to be thus publicly assured of an entire change of feeling and sentiment, in regard to my labors in behalf of the enslaved millions in our country, on their part.

I wish you could have seen me mounted on the Charleston slave auction-block, on Thursday evening of last week, in Music Hall, in the presence of a magnificent audience, carried away with enthusiasm, and giving me their long protracted cheers and plaudits![2] I attended a similar meeting, for a similar purpose, at Lowell on Wednesday evening last, and, on taking the block, was greeted with the strongest demonstrations of applause, prolonged and repeated as though there were to be no end to them.[3] What a revolution!

My dear wife continues in good health, although much crippled by her paralytic condition. We shall probably go to Providence in the course of a fortnight, to procure some medical aid which promises to be beneficial. We may remain there several weeks, though I shall be in Boston at least half of the time.

All our children are well. We have not had a letter from our son George since he entered Charleston with the 55th Mass. Reg't, singing the John Brown Song, and cheering for Abraham Lincoln and John A. Andrew.[4] What a bitter pill the haughty, conquered Carolinians have had to swallow!

Accept our household love.

Yours, with all my heart,

Wm. Lloyd Garrison.

Handwritten transcription of an extract: Garrison Papers, Boston Public Library; extracts printed in *Life*, IV, 131, 135.

Jacob Horton (c. 1797–1876) was the husband of Garrison's old friend Harriet Farnham of Newburyport. Garrison's parents rented rooms from Martha Farnham, Harriet's mother, and it was in her house that Garrison was born.

1. Thomas Campbell, *Pleasures of Hope*, Part II, line 337.

2. At the Music Hall on March 9 the steps from the slave market in Charleston, S.C., had been presented to the Eleventh Ward Freedmen's Aid Society. When Garrison spoke, he was given a thunderous ovation as "hundreds of white handkerchiefs" waved. (*The Liberator*, March 17, 1865.)

3. On March 15 the same slave steps were transported to Lowell, Mass., for similar speeches by Charles C. Coffin, Edward W. Kinsley, Garrison, and George Thompson. The Lowell *Courier Citizen* reported the next day that, although Kinsley's speech (on education for the freedmen) was the most appropriate, Garrison's was the most eloquent. He "congratulated the country on the destruction of the accursed institution of slavery, and contrasted the state of public opinion now with what it was when he commenced the publication of his *Liberator* in Boston."

4. Many John Brown songs were composed during the Civil War. The most widely known, "John Brown's Body," although usually associated with John Brown of Harpers Ferry, was probably composed by the soldiers in the 12th Massachusetts Volunteer Infantry about one Sergeant John Brown of Boston, who was drowned while crossing the Rappahannock River in 1862. (Boyd B. Stutler, "John Brown's Body," *Civil War History*, 4:251–260, September 1958.)

109

TO HELEN E. GARRISON

New York, April 7, 1865.

My dear Wife:

George Thompson joined me at the Old Colony Depot, and our train arrived at Newport about 9 o'clock in the evening, when we embarked on board of the Empire State for this city.[1] The night was stormy, the ocean rough, we had a head wind and sea, and did not arrive till 10 o'clock this morning. Several of the passengers were sea-sick; and I should have been if I had not immediately gone to my state-room, and taken to my berth, where I rested till morning, having had a very comfortable night of it. And so did Thompson. On arriving at the pier, we found Wendell waiting for us, where he had been three long hours! I felt very sorry that he should have been put to so much trouble and discomfort, as it was wholly unnecessary; but his filial affection is strong, and he made light of his long detention, as you may naturally suppose he would.

From the boat we proceeded to the Independent office,[2] where we found [Theodore] Tilton and Dr. [Joshua] Leavitt, both of whom are going to Fort Sumter—Tilton with us, and the Dr. by a private conveyance. After getting a late breakfast, we went to the office, where our names were enrolled and our tickets for the Arago furnished us; but the steamer will not leave until to-morrow (Saturday) noon.[3] As the weather continues unpleasant, I am not sorry for the delay; trusting that we shall have a fair day to-morrow.

I have just received a telegram from Secretary Stanton, at Washington, as follows:—

"Washington, April 7, 1865.

The Adjutant General has been directed to give Captain Garrison a furlough while you are at Charleston.[4] I hope Mr. Thompson accompanies you. A formal invitation was forwarded to him to your care, by mail, and a duplicate will be sent to Fortress Monroe, where I expect to join your party.

Edwin M. Stanton."

Isn't that handsome and delightful as concerning our dear son? I do not know whether the Secretary supposes George to be a Captain, or whether he intends this as a promotion—probably the former, as it is probable no promotion is made, in such subordinate offices, until there is a vacancy. Anyhow, will not George be happy to be with me while I am there?

I have just had a short but pleasant interview with our dear Samuel J. May, who returns to Syracuse this afternoon, having been to Brooklyn to attend the Unitarian Convention.[5] He says Charlotte Coffin will return to Boston the last of this month; or he may have said, next month—I am not quite sure which. It is his intention to be at our anniversary here in May.

I have also seen our friend, William H. Fish, who, with Mr. May, inquired specially after your welfare, and also after that of the household.

I shall stop with Wendell to-night, and so will Mr. Thompson.

Every body who knows of my going to Fort Sumter is delighted, milita[ry] men and all. Nothing more satisfies me that slavery is annihilated beyond any hope of resurrection than the deference, kindness and congratulation extended to me by those who are the unerring representatives of public opinion. The American Anti-Slavery Society may reasonably conclude that its mission is ended.

Intelligence is this moment received—though it is not official— that Gen. Lee has surrendered with the remainder of his shattered army.[6] If this be so, the rebellion is indeed crushed, and slavery along with it.

I shall rejoice when I am once more by your side, and with the dear ones at home. I only separate myself, for a time, because I believe I can best aid the cause of liberty and peace by so doing. Be careful of yourself while I am gone, and take as much exercise as you can well bear. My heart's love to William and Ellie, to Fanny and Frank.

Your most affectionate husband,

W. L. G.

ALS: Garrison Papers, Boston Public Library; extract printed in *Life*, IV, 137.

1. The Old Colony Railroad, which had been running between Boston and Plymouth since 1845, had in 1862, after two mergers, extended its operations and become the Old Colony and Newport Railroad Company; its current terminal was on Kneeland Street. (Walter Muir Whitehill, *Boston, A Topographical History*, Cambridge, Mass., 1959, pp. 102–103.)

The Fall River Line connected the Old Colony Railroad with New York by supplying service by steamship from Newport; the *Empire State*, a steamer of the beam engine type, had been one of the vessels on this line since 1848. (William M. Lytle, *Merchant Steam Vessels of the United States, 1807–1868*, Mystic, Conn., 1952, p. 58; John H. Morrison, *History of American Steam Navigation*, New York, 1903, p. 310)

2. At 5 Beekman Street.

3. The *Arago* was a vessel owned by the New York and Havre Steam Navigation Company and used as a transatlantic mail carrier until the outbreak of the Civil War.

4. Edward D. Townsend (1817–1893), a native of Boston and graduate of the military academy at West Point, had since 1862 been adjutant general, a post he filled efficiently for many years. He ordered the collecting of war papers, which were later published as *The War of the Rebellion: Official Records* (Washington, D.C., 1880–1901).

Stanton was mistaken as to George T. Garrison's rank at this time; however, he was promoted to captain on July 28, 1865. (*Record of the Service of the Fifty-fifth Regiment of Massachusetts Volunteer Infantry*, Cambridge, Mass., 1868.)

5. The first annual national convention of the Unitarian Church, with 400 delegates attending, met at the Athenaeum in Brooklyn, April 5–6. (For a full report, see the New York *Times*, April 6 and 7, 1865.)

6. Robert Edward Lee (1807–1870), son of Revolutionary officer "Light-Horse Harry" Lee, graduated from West Point in 1829. His already brilliant prospects were augmented by his marriage in 1831 to Mary Ann Randolph Custis, great-grand-

daughter of Martha Washington. After serving in various military capacities as engineer and officer, he became superintendent at West Point (1852–1855). In 1859 he commanded the soldiers who suppressed John Brown's raid at Harpers Ferry. On the outbreak of the Civil War he declined the field command of the Union army before assuming command of the Army of Northern Virginia and becoming adviser to President Davis. His success in the field despite the odds against him continued from Bull Run to Antietam, Fredericksburg, and Chancellorsville. Following defeat at Gettysburg in July 1863, he continued to fight effectively, though he was on the defensive. Two months before the surrender at Appomattox on April 9, he was appointed commander-in-chief of the Confederate armies. Following the war he became president of Washington College, which after his death was renamed Washington and Lee.

110

TO HELEN E. GARRISON

Sunday Morning, April 9, 1865.

My Dear Wife:

Yesterday, at 12 o'clock, M., the Arago slowly and majestically left the pier on her way down the harbor for Charleston; with a fair wind, a bright sky, and a slight undulation of the waves. There was nothing to be desired in the matter of favorable omens. Up to this hour, every thing has gone with us as though we had the elements under our own control—a splendid sunset last evening—a night so brilliant and entrancing that I did not turn into my berth till a late hour—this day the air is warmer, and as beautiful as it can be—and we have come with so little motion that scarcely any have been seasick, and, for a wonder, I have experienced no trouble whatever on that score. I have been to the table promptly at every meal, and partaken of a variety of dishes with a good relish, and no subsequent disturbance of the stomach. Every thing has been provided on a liberal scale, and we are living as though we were at a first class hotel. When we go round Cape Hatteras, we shall probably be put to a much severer test. We have about eighty invited guests on board, bound to see the flag raised at Sumter. Among these are Judge Swain, of the U. S. Supreme Court; Judge Kelley, of Philadelphia; Lieut. Governor Anderson, (brother of the General,) of Ohio; General Anderson and a portion of his family; Rev. Henry Ward Beecher, with his wife and children; Rev. Dr. Storrs, of Brooklyn, who is to perform the religious services this forenoon; Professor Davies, of West Point, and other Professors; Rev. Mr. Scovell, son-in-law of Mr. Beecher, with his wife; Senator [Henry] Wilson; General Dix, and Gen. Doubleday; several merchants; and others whom I [am] unable to identify by name or profession.[1] All on board have been very courteous and attentive to George Thompson and

myself, and they are manifestly pleased that we are on board. I have
had several talks with Gen. Anderson, and he is particularly gratified that we are of the company. He is a very amiable and modest
man, and looks and reminds me more of John Brown than any one I
have seen. He seems to be quite religious in his spirit, and re-
verently recognizes the hand of God in all the wonderful events
which have taken place.

The New York Times, Tribune and Herald have their reporters
on board. Mr. Smith, editor of the Chicago Tribune, is his own reporter.[2]

There is no stiffness of manners. Every one is ready for conversational interchange; and though we are heterogeneous in the professions and pursuits of life, yet there is entire harmony on the slavery question. Secretary [Edwin M.] Stanton has evidently made his
selections with care.

Sunday, 6 P.M.

We have passed Cape Henry, and [are] going up to Fortress
Monroe, where we shall arrive in the course of another hour. How
long we shall remain there, we cannot tell; probably not more than
an hour or two. Several additional guests are to come on board,
among them Secretary Stanton, if he can leave his post.

It is now somewhat cloudy, and looks like rain.

Dear Thompson and I have a state-room together. He is very kind
and attentive to me, bringing me my coffee before I leave my berth
in the morning, as he rises earlier, and assiduous to do all in his
power to make the jaunt pleasant to me.

As all has gone well with us thus far, I trust it will to the end. But
my thoughts are more with you and the dear ones at home than at
Fort Sumter, saving that the prospect of our seeing George brings
him before me continually. Will it not be a joyful surprise to him to
meet me and Mr. Thompson?

How long we shall be gone is uncertain. Nobody seems to know.
Something will depend upon the instructions given by Secretary
Stanton.

All the love that one heart can hold divide among William and
Ellie, Fanny and Frank; taking for your share at least as much as
language can express. Kind remembrances to Mary.[3]

Your loving husband,

W. L. G.

ALS: Garrison Papers, Boston Public Library; partly printed in *Life*, IV, 137–139.

1. Noah Haynes Swayne (1804–1884), whose name Garrison misspells, was originally from Virginia but moved to Ohio because of his antislavery convictions. After
many years in Columbus, practicing law and serving in the state legislature and on

several commissions, in 1862 he was appointed to the United States Supreme Court, a position he was to hold for nineteen years.

William Darrah Kelley (1814–1890), a lawyer, was appointed prosecutor of the pleas and a judge of the Court of Common Pleas in his native Philadelphia before being elected to Congress in 1860, where he remained for fourteen terms, advocating abolition and later high tariffs.

Charles Anderson (1814–1895) was an Ohio lawyer, who had been a member of the state legislature before being elected lieutenant governor in 1863. Upon the death of the incumbent on August 29, 1865, he became governor of Ohio. (*Biographical Dictionary of America.*)

Robert Anderson (1805–1871), a distinguished career soldier, was in command of Fort Sumter at the outbreak of the Civil War and defended his post bravely until forced to surrender. Later appointed brigadier general, he served in Kentucky until ill health obliged him to retire from active duty in 1863. In 1865 he was brevetted major general of volunteers; his mission aboard the *Arago* was to proceed to Charleston and to raise the flag again over Fort Sumter.

Eunice Bullard Beecher (1812–1897) had married Henry Ward Beecher in 1837; she bore him ten children. Mrs. Beecher was a person of distinction in her own right; she wrote for various periodicals and published collections of her articles in book form. (Paxton Hibben, *Henry Ward Beecher: An American Portrait,* New York, 1927; obituary, New York *Times,* March 9, 1897.)

Richard Salter Storrs, Jr. (1821–1900) had a brief legal career before studying at Andover Theological Seminary and becoming the minister of the Church of the Pilgrims in Brooklyn. Between 1848 and 1861 he was one of the editors of the New York *Independent;* late in life he served as president of the American Board of Commissioners for Foreign Missions.

Charles Davies (1798–1876), a West Point graduate in the class of 1815, was professor of mathematics there between 1816 and 1837. He also taught at Trinity College in Hartford and between 1857 and 1865 at Columbia College in New York City. (*The Centennial of the United States Military Academy at West Point, New York,* Washington, D.C., 1904; *Biographical Register of the Officers and Graduates of the U.S. Military Academy at West Point, New York,* Boston, 1891.)

Samuel Scoville (1834–1902), whose name Garrison misspells, was a graduate of Union Theological Seminary and the minister of the Congregational church in Norwich, N.Y., where he was to remain until 1879. Thereafter he had pastorates in New York, New Jersey, and Connecticut. He had married Harriet Eliza Beecher in 1861. (*1903 Congregational Year-Book.*)

John Adams Dix (1798–1879), soldier, lawyer, and politician, was greatly interested in international affairs, free-soil principles, and abolition. He is best remembered as secretary of the treasury under President Buchanan, to which office Dix brought unusual ability and unflinching integrity. At the beginning of the Civil War President Lincoln made him a major general; after the war he served as minister to France. In 1872, although a Democrat, he was asked to run as a Republican for mayor of New York, against Horace Greeley, whom he defeated.

Abner Doubleday (1819–1893) was a West Point graduate who had fought in the Mexican War and the war against the Seminoles in Florida. Stationed at Fort Sumter in 1861, he is supposed to have aimed the first shot fired by Union troops in response to the Confederate attack. He fought in many of the major battles of the war and rose to the rank of major general of volunteers. Among other distinctions General Doubleday is given credit for inventing the game of baseball.

2. Henry Martyn Smith (1830–1895), originally from New Bedford, Mass., and an Amherst graduate, had a distinguished journalistic career both in Chicago and in the East. In Chicago he worked for the *Journal* and the *Republican* and was an editor of the *Tribune.* In his last years Smith returned to the East, where he edited the Brooklyn *Union* and the *New England Home Journal,* and in 1884 was elected to the Massachusetts legislature.

The Chicago *Tribune* had been founded in 1847, with John L. Scripps as its first editor, though Joseph Medill (1823–1899), the publisher, was the figure most closely associated with the paper's history. The *Tribune* was a Republican journal that strongly supported Lincoln and the war effort. (Philip Kinsley, *The Chicago Tribune, Its First Hundred Years*, Chicago, 1945, pp. xiii, 5; A. T. Andreas, *History of Chicago*, Chicago, 1885, II, 498; letter to the editor from J. Richard Phillips, archivist, Amherst College, November 30, 1971.)

3. Probably a servant.

111

TO HELEN E. GARRISON

Charleston, S. C., April 15, 1865.

My dear Wife:

We had a fine passage from Fortress Monroe to Hilton Head, where we arrived on Tuesday night. I experienced no sea sickness of any account, and therefore enjoyed the trip exceedingly. We had a beautiful moon with us all the way each night, and at times the scene was magical. Our good friends, Mr. and Mrs. Severance, Mr. Pillsbury, (brother of Parker,) Mr. Dodge, and a number of others were there, to give me a warm welcome to the shores of Carolina.[1] The next day we went in the steamer Delaware[2] to Savannah, and passed by Fort Pulaski[3] and many other objects of interest, and saw the remains of the formidable obstructions placed in the Savannah river to keep our war vessels at bay. We found carriages waiting for us on our arrival, and went through the principal streets of Savannah, which is a city of mingled gentility and squalor, but entirely dead in regard to all business affairs. Thursday evening we left Hilton Head in the Arago for Charleston, where we arrived at daybreak, outside of the bar. At 11 we left for Fort Sumter, and got there a little after 12. A large concourse present. The exercises of the highest interest. [Henry Ward] Beecher's discourse a good one. The enthusiasm immense. Every thing went off grandly. Have no time for particulars, as I expected to return home this evening in the Arago, but have concluded to remain one week longer, and go again to Savannah and Florida, along with Henry Ward Beecher and family, Tilton, George Thompson, Henry Wilson, &c., &c. Shall probably go to Richmond before getting home. So, be entirely easy about me.[4]

To-day, we have had three thousand colored people turned out to greet us, and a great procession to escort us, with a band of music, through the principal streets, all the way raising shouts to make the welkin ring! Also, a long procession of girls and boys. We have had a magnificent meeting in Zion's church[5]—thousands present—which was powerfully addressed by Judge [William D.] Kelly, George Thompson, Theo. Tilton, Henry Wilson, and also by myself. My reception was beyond all description enthusiastic, and my feelings were unutterable.

As for our dear George, I have not yet seen him, but expect to in the course of a few hours. He returned with his company last evening, from the interior, with 1200 slaves, now freemen.[6] I understand he is in good health, and long to embrace him for your sake and mine. When I get back, I shall have a volume of interesting things to communicate to you and the children. God preserve and bless you all!—I can add no more, for the boat leaves immediately.

Ever your loving husband,

W. L. G.

ALS: Garrison Papers, Boston Public Library; partly printed in *Life*, IV, 139–140.

1. Theodoric C. Severance (1814–1892) moved from Ohio to Boston in 1855 to become the cashier of the Bank of the Republic. In 1862 he moved to South Carolina, where he was a special agent of the Treasury Department and acted as collector of customs at Beaufort. His wife was Caroline M. Severance (1820–1914), an ardent advocate of woman suffrage and one of the founders in Boston of the New England Woman's Club. In 1875 the Severances moved to California, where she continued her woman's club activities. (Letters to the editor from Ruth Bell, researcher, November 18, 1971, and September 30, 1972; obituary, New York *Times*, November 11, 1914.)

Gilbert Pillsbury (1813–1893) was the brother of abolitionist Parker Pillsbury. After graduating from Dartmouth, he taught in various Massachusetts schools and served as state senator. In 1863 he was employed by the federal government as an agent for freedmen in Hilton Head, S.C. Subsequently he moved to Charleston and served as its first mayor (1868–1871) during the Reconstruction period. He later retired to North Abington, Mass. (*General Catalogue for Dartmouth College and the Associated Schools 1769–1910*, Hanover, N.H., 1910–1911, p. 261; Leander W. Cogswell, *History of the Town of Henniker*, Concord, N.H., 1880, pp. 687–688.)

James George Dodge (1813–1904) had been a leading figure in a religious colony in Weathersfield, Ill. He was the author of various religious tracts published in Texas. In the last years of the Civil War he was superintendent of the freedmen employed on the government plantations in Hilton Head, S.C. (Obituary, Boston *Transcript,* March 19, 1904.)

2. Not certainly identified, since fifteen steam vessels by that name were built in the United States between 1813 and 1865. (William M. Lytle, *Merchant Steam Vessels of the United States, 1807–1868*, Mystic, Conn., 1952.)

3. Now a national monument, located near Savannah and named for the Revolutionary hero Casimir Pulaski.

4. Garrison's anticipated trip was abruptly terminated on the evening of April 15, when his group steamed as far south as Beaufort and were about to go ashore. A telegram came for Senator Wilson announcing the President's assassination and death. In a matter of minutes the ship was headed north. (*The Liberator,* May 26, 1865.)

5. A large Presbyterian church on Calhoun Street, designed by Edward C. Jones and David Lopez and built in 1859. (Beatrice St. Julien Ravenel, *Architects of Charleston*, Charleston, S.C., 1945, pp. 214–215.)

6. A search of Civil War records has not revealed the nature of the mission of George Thompson Garrison's company.

112

TO HELEN E. GARRISON

New York, May 10, 1865.

Dear Wife:

Among those who came from Boston with me were Edmund Quincy, Deborah Weston, Sarah Southwick, Mrs. Sewall, Mr. and Mrs. Goodrich, Mr. and Mrs. John T. Sargent, Mr. and Mrs. [Samuel] May, [Jr.] Mrs. Brigham, Mrs. Judge Russell, Mr. and Mrs. Draper, &c.[1] Mr. [George] Thompson had to remain behind to attend to some business, but arrived here at a seasonable hour yesterday morning.

We had, yesterday, our invariable accompaniment to our anniversary, a dismal, pouring, north-easterly rain-storm, making every thing look and every body feel exceedingly uncomfortable. Nevertheless, we had a crowded meeting at Dr. [George B.] Cheever's church, made up of the best elements of brain and heart, and all the proceedings were very satisfactory and harmonious. [Wendell] Phillips was the first speaker, and dwelt, as usual, upon the necessity and importance of securing the ballot for the negro at the South. Nobody dissented from him, and he said nothing touching any of our differences. Mrs. Frances E. Harper made an excellent speech, which received great applause.[2] Mr. Thompson spoke very briefly, and I also made a short speech.

At the close of the meeting, I was surrounded by a throng of beloved friends from all sections of the country, making eager inquiries about your health, and proffering all sorts of congratulations as to the cheering aspects of our cause.

We had our first business meeting yesterday afternoon, with a considerable attendance of the members and friends of the Society. I offered a resolution, setting forth the expediency of dissolving the Society; and Phillips offered another in favor of continuing it. My remarks were brief, but decisive as to the convictions of my own mind. Remond made, as usual, a querulous, fault-finding talk; going, of course, with Phillips, and reflecting upon myself and others.[3] Aaron M. Powell made a long and somewhat uncertain speech as to the best course to be pursued. He was followed by Phillips at considerable length, who resorted to that special pleading which he knows so well how to use when occasion requires, and evidently carried a majority with him. I presume, when the vote is taken, it will be decided in favor of continuing the Society— perhaps by a vote of two to one—and I presume Phillips will be my successor as President. So be it. I regard the whole thing as ridiculous; and I am quite sure that this determination to go on is not the result of any conviction as to the need of continuing the Society, but arises from personal pique and an ulterior purpose, so far as certain persons are pursued. We shall, doubtless, have a warm discussion to-day, and I shall rejoice when it is all over.

Last evening, the National Freedmen's Association had a large meeting at the Cooper Institute, which was addressed by Judge [Hugh L.] Bond, of Baltimore, John Jay, Esq., Frederick Douglass, George Thompson, and myself.[4] The meeting was a very interesting one, and all the speakers elicited much applause.

I saw our Wendell in the audience, though George did not, but had no chance to speak to him. He met us at the depot on our arrival, since which he has been too busy to see us.

Mrs. Hopper received us with the old accustomed warmth and hospitality; and every thing is the same at the house as it used to be, excepting the presence of dear, kind-hearted, noble John Hopper. Mr. Thompson is now with us.

Say to Ellie that it gave me great delight to meet with her father and mother [Mr. and Mrs. David Wright] yesterday, and that I am expecting to go with them to Boston, (or at least with her mother—it is not quite so certain about her father,) on Friday morning. So, be prepared for us at tea-time.

George is enjoying himself very much, and sends his loving regards to you all.

Adieu, dearest!

W. L. G.

☞ There has been great disappointment felt and expressed, because Fanny is not here.

ALS: Garrison Papers, Boston Public Library.

1. Deborah Weston (born 1814), daughter of Warren Weston and sister of Maria Weston Chapman, was active in abolition and other reforms. (Zephaniah W. Pease, ed., *The Diary of Samuel Rodman, 1821–1859,* New Bedford, Mass., 1927, p. 269.)

Sarah Hussey Southwick (1821–1896), the daughter of Joseph and Thankful Hussey Southwick, was an active abolitionist, serving as treasurer of the Boston Female Anti-Slavery Society in 1842, when her mother was president. She was the author of *Reminiscences of Early Anti-Slavery Days,* published in 1893. (Letters to the editor from Ruth Bell, researcher, January 20, February 12, and April 27, 1972, and from Margaret S. Urann, corresponding secretary, Wellesley Historical Society, July 14, 1972.)

Harriet Winslow Sewall (1819–1889), who was married first to abolitionist Charles List (c. 1817–1856) and then, in 1857, to Samuel Sewall, had been for many years an active philanthropist, abolitionist, and woman's rights leader. Her sister Louisa (died 1850) had been Sewall's first wife. In addition to being engaged in social reform, Mrs. Sewall also edited the letters of her friend Lydia Maria Child (1883) and published a volume of poetry (1889).

Although the Goodriches have not been identified with certainty, Goodrich may be Boston resident John Z. Goodrich (1804–1885), a man of far-ranging interests and accomplishments. A lawyer by training, he had founded the *Berkshire Journal* in 1831, run a woolen mill, been elected twice to Congress as a Whig, become a Republican, and served as chairman of that party's national committee. In 1860 he became lieutenant governor of Massachusetts and in 1861 collector of the port of Boston, a position he held at the time of Garrison's letter. (Obituary, Boston *Transcript*, April 20, 1885.)

Dora Taylor Brigham (1820–1907) was the daughter of Edward T. Taylor, a clergyman who founded the Seaman's Bethel in Boston, and Deborah Davis Millet Taylor. Dora Taylor married Dr. Augustine Taft in 1839, and their house was used as a station on the Underground Railroad during the war. Following Taft's death she married Levi Brigham, a friend of Garrison. (Obituary, Boston *Transcript*, July 29, 1907.)

Little is known about Mrs. Thomas Russell except that she was the former Mary Ellen Taylor, the sister of Mrs. Brigham.

Ebenezer (or Eben) D. Draper (1813–1887) was born in Weston, Mass. With his brother George he was one of the founders of the Hopedale Community. He helped to establish the New England Safe Company, one of the largest manufacturing firms in the area, but the business eventually failed. He was a friend of Garrison and active in many of the same reforms, including abolition, temperance, and woman's rights. Draper was married twice—in 1834 to Anna Thwing (1814–1870) and in 1872 to Mrs. Mary Boynton. (Obituary, Boston *Transcript*, October 19, 1887; Thomas Waln-Morgan Draper, *The Drapers in America*, New York, 1892, pp. 108–109.)

2. Frances Ellen Watkins Harper (1825–1911), born in Baltimore to free black parents, taught school in Ohio and in York, Pa. She became a lecturer for the Maine Anti-Slavery Society in 1854 and was active in the Underground Railroad. In 1860 she married Fenton Harper of Cincinnati. After the war she lectured extensively in the southern states. (Samuel Sillen, "Mrs. Chapman and Mrs. Harper," *Masses and Mainstream*, 8:56–63, February 1955; William Still, *The Underground Railroad*, Philadelphia, 1879, pp. 755–780.)

3. Charles Lenox Remond (1810–1873) was born in Salem, Mass., to free black parents, John and Nancy Remond. John Remond was a hairdresser. As a young man Charles established a reputation as an eloquent lecturer and is credited with being the first Negro to speak in public on abolition. In 1838 he became an agent of the Massachusetts Anti-Slavery Society. Two years later he accompanied Garrison as a delegate from the American Anti-Slavery Society to the World's Anti-Slavery Convention in London. He remained abroad for nineteen months, lecturing in England and Ireland. Although in the 1840s and 1850s he was a less spectacular figure than Frederick Douglass, Remond continued active in abolitionist circles. During the war he was recruiting officer for the 54th Massachusetts Infantry. In his later years he was employed as a clerk in the Boston custom house. (Benjamin Quarles, *Black Abolitionists*, New York, 1969.)

4. Garrison refers to the National Freedmen's Relief Association, with membership concentrated in New York, Connecticut, Maine, and New Hampshire. The organization had been founded in February 1862 and was to be combined later in 1865 with other such groups and to function until 1869 as the American Freedmen's Aid Commission. (Julius H. Parmelee, "Freedmen's Aid Societies, 1861–1871," *Negro Education, A Study of the Private and Higher Schools for Colored People in the United States*, 1917; reprint New York, 1969, I, 268–295.)

John Jay (1817–1894), grandson of the Chief Justice, was a graduate of Columbia University. Educated as a lawyer, he practiced in New York City for some twenty years before engaging full time in public service and reform. He worked for Irish relief, was the legal counsel in many fugitive slave cases, opposed the extension of slavery in the territories, helped organize the Republican party in his state, urged the enlistment of blacks in the army, helped organize freedmen's agencies, and worked for the Thirteenth Amendment. After the war he became minister to Austria (1869–1874). He defended public schools in the controversy with parochial schools. He was also a distinguished and much-published historian.

113

TO OLIVER JOHNSON

Boston, May 21, 1865.

Dear Johnson:

I am obliged to you for your letter. Your valediction in the last Standard is written with precision, dignity, and the force of truth.[1] You need not have desired to have me by your side in preparing it. Your own quick instinct, clear insight and ready ability are always equal to the exigency of the hour. I regret that I shall not be able to print your farewell until the Liberator of June 2d. The proceedings of the Business Meetings will occupy two or three numbers of the Liberator, as we are limited as to the quantity of our Brevier[2] type.

I am glad to see Mr. May's letter. It is frank, manly, and right to the point. But it (with your article) will certainly "raise a breeze" in a certain quarter, and you must both be prepared for sharp replications in the Standard.[3]

Mr. May's resolution of thanks to Mr. Quincy and yourself for your long and invaluable services in conducting the Standard, which was sent to Coventry by a very doubtful vote, and through unquestionable misapprehension, will doubtless be adopted by the late Executive Committee, and forwarded to you both. I feel indignant, but even more grieved than indignant, at the suppression of that resolution by a "side wind" at the business meeting. But you need not have any doubt as to the verdict of all unbiassed minds in your case.[4]

I think Mr. May makes a telling point against the new *regime* in regard to using the money now in the treasury of the American A. S. Society, raised as it was by ladies who would assuredly never have gone forward to collect a dollar of it, had they anticipated such an overturn in the management of the Society. I am curious to see how the objection will be met by the Standard.

You announce that Mr. Pillsbury is to be your successor. This is just what I anticipated. Of one thing we may be sure—the tone of the paper will be any thing but jubilant in regard to the state of our good cause.[5] Nevertheless, the heavens are bright, and all its omens cheering.

Does not our friend A. M. Powell owe it to the Society to explain how it happened that the very object of making a roll was defeated by his omission to check the names of those who voted, *pro* and *con?* It was an unaccountable blunder—for, knowing Aaron as I do, I cannot suppose it was an intentional act on his part. What was he thinking about?

How will you have your letters directed hereafter?

Faithfully and always yours,

Wm. Lloyd Garrison.

P.S. My dear wife went to Providence on Friday, to be placed under the treatment of Dr. Joseph Dow, 72 High Street.[6] She will probably remain there two or three months.[7]

ALS: Garrison Papers, Boston Public Library.

1. In his valedictory statement as editor of the *National Anti-Slavery Standard*, printed May 20, Johnson not only defended his own editorial position but also supported Garrison in the controversy with Phillips, favoring the dissolution of the American Anti-Slavery Society. (See also *The Liberator*, June 2, 1865.)

2. Eight point.

3. In his letter (dated May 12, 1865, and printed in *The Liberator*, May 20) Samuel May, Jr., recommended that the $2,200 that had been raised by the Subscription Anniversary and that remained in the treasury of the American Anti-Slavery Society be distributed among the late executive committee of the society, "to be appropriated by them as they shall judge best in aid of the Anti-Slavery cause." He also criticized the appointment of Parker Pillsbury as editor of the *Standard*.

4. Although Garrison's meaning is clear, precisely what happened at the business meeting that rejected the resolution is not known.

5. Parker Pillsbury and George W. Smalley served only briefly as coeditors of the paper, both resigning in 1866. Pillsbury's departure followed a disagreement with Phillips over woman suffrage. Aaron M. Powell, assisted by Phillips, became the next editor. (James M. McPherson, *The Struggle for Equality*, Princeton, 1964, p. 438.)

6. Joseph Dow (1819–1880), born in Maine, worked in the leather business in Woburn, Mass. In 1859 he moved to Providence, where, despite a lack of formal training, he practiced as a "medical electrician" until his death. (Letter to the editor from Nathaniel N. Shipton, manuscript curator, Rhode Island Historical Society, December 15, 1971.)

7. Helen Garrison remained in Providence somewhat more than two months; she returned home the end of July. (Letter from Helen E. Garrison to WLG, July 25, 1865, Merrill Collection of Garrison Papers, Wichita State University Library.)

114

TO WENDELL PHILLIPS GARRISON

Boston, May 25, 1865.

My Dear Son:

I will lose no time in answering your letter, just received on my return from a charming excursion to Lynn, Nahant and Swampscot with William, Ellie, and her mother [Mrs. David Wright].

I am truly glad to hear that an effort is making to raise a pecuniary testimonial for my long tried and strongly attached friend Mr. Johnson, who deserves to receive a much larger sum than that named by you.[1] I must be allowed to contribute my mite, without a refusal, and will do so. If I can induce any others to do likewise, I will gladly make the attempt. Perhaps I had better not write to Edward Harris, unless nothing shall be heard from him in reply to the application already made.[2] I have no doubt that he will very cheerfully make a donation.

Please say to Theodore [Tilton], that, as I shall refer to Oliver's labors in the Anti-Slavery cause, and his withdrawal from the Standard, in the next Liberator, I see no reason why I should not state that he is deserving of a testimonial, and that any who may wish to contribute to it may send their money either to Theodore or myself.[3] If T. thinks this will not be best, let me know, and I will be guided by his judgment. But it seems to me the suggestion will do no harm.

George did not write to any of us before he sailed, nor have you apprized us as to the day of his departure, or the vessel in which he sailed.

I see it stated in the Boston Journal that the 54th and 55th regiments are to be speedily mustered out of service. If this be so, George will soon return to us. But my conviction is, that those two regiments will be kept in South Carolina as a necessity, until their term of enlistment ends.[4]

I learn that George has engaged to carry on a correspondence with A. A. during his absence.[5] I know, by personal experience and observation, how such an arrangement is apt to terminate; and so conclude that there will be a more lasting engagement arising from it. If so, we shall assuredly be well satisfied as a family, I think. But it will be best to let the matter shape itself, and give no publicity among friends as to the fact of correspondence—for the present.

Last Wednesday evening, I was called into the parlor by Fanny, and was taken by surprise by the announcement of Mr. Villard and herself that they had plighted their love to each other, and, as in duty bound, they wished me to give my fatherly sanction to the procedure![6] Of course, I had understood that, between them, there was a growing interest, which, on better acquaintance, and at some future day, might end in such an engagement; but this was so sudden as to be at least momentarily startling. My love for Fanny is so strong, and my estimate of her so high, that I have not been willing to entertain the thought of her cleaving to another in this manner. My acquaintance with Mr. Villard was next to nothing; he was of German birth, and I had no knowledge of or reference given me to his relatives abroad; and though, relying upon your better acquaintance and positive appreciation of him, I had no doubt whatever as to his uprightness and manly honor, yet the whole affair was so sudden, and upon the face of it so hasty and impulsive, that I hardly knew what to say. However, what could I do but to tenderly acquiesce, with the hope that they fully understood and appreciated each other, and all would go well with them. They seem to be inexpressibly happy, and his whole behavior has been very honorable.

I am gratified to know that my course at New York was in accordance with your feelings and judgment.

Ever your admiring father,

W. L. G.

☞ What of "The Nation," and your connection with it?[7] Write to mother when you can, and direct your letters to Dr. Joseph Dow, 72 High Street, Providence.

ALS: Garrison Papers, Sophia Smith Collection, Smith College Library.

1. Various sources, including the Oliver Johnson letters at the Boston Public Library, indicate that the Johnson testimonial had no success.

2. Edward Harris (1801–1872), a prominent banker and businessman, operated the Harris Woolen Company, a textile manufacturing firm in Woonsocket, R.I. For many years he had been an active philanthropist and abolitionist. In 1859, for instance, he contributed $100 to the family of John Brown.

3. Although Johnson's valedictory and various farewell messages in the *National Anti-Slavery Standard* were reprinted in *The Liberator*, May 26 and June 2, 1865, they did not contain editorial comment by Garrison.

4. George Thompson Garrison was released from service in August 1865, when his regiment, the 55th Massachusetts, was disbanded. (See the letter to George Thompson Garrison, June 11, 1863.) The 54th Massachusetts regiment was mustered out in August at Mount Pleasant, S.C., and disbanded at Boston in September 1865. (Thomas Wentworth Higginson, *Massachusetts in the Army and Navy During the War of 1861–65*, Boston, 1896, I, 298.)

5. Garrison refers to Anne Keene Anthony (born 1839), daughter of John Gould Anthony, a naturalist and the brother of Charlotte Benson's husband, Henry Anthony. She was to marry George Thompson Garrison on October 1, 1873. (Charles L. Anthony, *Genealogy of the Anthony Family from 1495 to 1904*, Sterling, Ill., 1904.)

6. Henry Villard (1835–1900) was born Ferdinand Heinrich Gustav Hilgard to a

distinguished Bavarian family. His father was Gustav Leonhard Hilgard, a member of the Supreme Court of Bavaria. Henry Villard's republican sentiments, which were shared by two of his father's brothers, resulted in the termination of his education, begun at the universities in Munich and Würzburg, his immigration to the United States in 1853, and his change of name. After shifting from one minor job to another, in 1858 Villard became a journalist. He was first a correspondent for a German-American newspaper in New York, then for the Cincinnati *Commercial,* then for the *Daily Missouri Democrat* in St. Louis, and finally for the New York *Tribune* and the New York *Herald.* He covered such outstanding news stories as the gold rush in Colorado and Lincoln's campaign and election; subsequently, traveling with the Union armies, he reported various crucial events of the Civil War. On January 3, 1866, he married Fanny Garrison. In 1868 he became involved with civil service reform, serving as secretary of the American Social Science Association in Boston. This post provided him with information that made it possible for him to launch his most lucrative career as railroad financier. After a series of maneuvers, including the raising from friends and associates of a "blind pool" of some $20,000,000, he purchased a series of railroad properties and by 1881 became president of the Northern Pacific Railroad. In the same year he acquired the controlling interest in the New York *Evening Post.* Although he was forced to relinquish control of the Northern Pacific in 1884, other interests, especially public utilities (he founded the Edison General Electric Company in 1889), made him a wealthy man.

7. *The Nation* first appeared July 6, 1865, with an emphatic statement to the public that the journal would seek the elevation of freedmen, discuss public affairs, and be a critic of art and literature. Wendell Phillips Garrison served first as the journal's literary editor; in 1881, when *The Nation* was acquired by Henry Villard's New York *Evening Post,* Wendell Garrison became the editor. Under his leadership the journal became less polemical and more scholarly. (Alan P. Grimes, *The Political Liberalism of the New York* Nation, *1865–1932,* Chapel Hill, N.C., 1953.)

---

1 1 5

TO GEORGE TRASK

BOSTON, May 27, 1865.

DEAR MR. TRASK—

Though my engagements are such as will prevent my being at your Anti-Tobacco meeting next week, yet I beg you to be assured that, from the time you commenced your labors to drive the use of that noxious weed and injurious narcotic from society till now, you have had my hearty sympathy and best wishes.[1] I have admired your perseverance, tact, fidelity, moral courage, good sense, and manifest disinterestedness; and am as sure that you have not labored in vain as I am that

> "Though seed lie buried long in dust,
> It shan't deceive the hope."[2]

notwithstanding the results, as yet, may not appear very encouraging. "Whether they will hear, or whether they will forbear," yea, even though it is certain that "they will not hear," yet "thou shalt speak all my words unto them," is the message from Heaven to every reformer, and every witness in the cause of purity and righteousness.[3] That message you have faithfully heeded, neither intimidated by the ridicule of scoffers, nor disheartened by the indifference of those who ought to have given you the cheering word and the helping hand.

I have read your handsomely printed and skilfully prepared tracts with great interest and satisfaction, and wish they might be put into the hands of every one addicted to the use of tobacco in any form.[4] Yet, so inveterate is the habit when established, but few of this class, whether snuffers, chewers or smokers, can probably be reclaimed; and, therefore, it is even more important that your testimonies, facts and appeals, on this subject, should be read and pondered by those who have not yet defiled themselves, but are liable to be led astray by an all-prevailing vicious custom.

It is a constant source of surprise and regret to me to find many, who claim to be in the ranks of reform and progress, and who are really doing good service in their special field of labor, completely enslaved to the hurtful and disgusting use of tobacco; so that all appeals to them on the score of consistency, virtue and exemplary conduct are utterly in vain. This is to be palpably deficient in symmetry of character, and certainly impairs their moral influence while professing to be anxious for the redemption of a groaning world. They are the least excusable of all who give themselves up to the control of so reprehensible a habit.

Desiring to be put down in the catalogue of those who regard the common use of tobacco as offensive to purity and an intolerable nuisance, I remain,

Yours, to "taste not, touch not, handle not"[5] the unclean thing,

WM. LLOYD GARRISON.

REV. GEORGE TRASK.

Printed: *The Liberator*, June 9, 1865.

George Trask (1798–1875), a Congregational clergyman who had graduated from Bowdoin College and Andover Theological Seminary, was active in many reforms, including abolition, peace, and temperance; he also agitated with special vehemence against the use of tobacco.

1. At the annual meeting of the American Anti-Tobacco Society held in Boston at the Melodeon on May 29, Trask read Garrison's letter, which was "loudly applauded." (*The Liberator*, June 9, 1865.)

2. Not identified.

3. Garrison's biblical quotations can be found in several books, as, for example, Ezekiel 2:5, 7 and I Corinthians 14:21.

4. Although it is not known to what specific tracts Garrison refers, there is at least one extant collection, published after Trask's death: *Temperance and Anti-Tobacco*

Tracts (Boston, n.d.). Trask was also the author of *Thoughts and Stories on Tobacco for American Lads; or, Uncle Toby's Anti-Tobacco Advice to His Nephew Billy Bruce* (Boston, 1852).
    5. Colossians 2:21.

116

TO OLIVER JOHNSON

Boston, May 28, 1865.

My dear Johnson:

Your two letters are before me, stating that my mislaid letter to you has not yet been found, and therefore is probably "gone to the tomb of the Capulets."[1] I cannot see how Mr. [George W.] Smalley could have even accidentally blundered in opening that letter, for it was very plainly directed, and he is not ignorant of my handwriting. And its mysterious disappearance serves to increase the suspicion, (perhaps an unjust one,) that, to serve a purpose, there has been a designed suppression of it. When I had dropped it into the Post Office, it occurred to me (too late, of course) that you had made a request in the Standard to have letters for you addressed to your place of residence. Still, I supposed you would go to the Anti-Slavery Office, (as, doubtless, for some time, in spite of your request or in ignorance of it, letters will be sent to you there,) and get it without risk or delay.

Had you received it, you would have been relieved of all anxiety of mind as to my judgment respecting your farewell address to the readers of the Standard. I deem it so candid and just, so well considered and expressed, that, had I been at your side after you had completed it, I should have had nothing to offer by way of change or addition. Your caution is large and your vision clear, so that you very seldom err even in phraseology in stating or defending your case when wrongfully impeached.

I copied, in the last number of the Liberator, the first and last portion of your exposition and farewell, because it was impossible for me to find room for any thing more, not even for a brief editorial about it.[2] But the entire exposition itself is already in type for the next number, when I shall refer to it.

You have a right to feel deeply injured and aggrieved at the treatment you have received at the hands of W. P. [Wendell Phillips], and the charges he has made against the Standard. I can account for his feeling piqued that the Standard did not countenance the Fremont movement; but not for the personal ill-will and discourtesy he has shown towards you—for you have always been prompt to publish the most eulogistic notices of himself in your exchange papers, as well as all his speeches, and ever shown a kind and forbearing spirit. But it is gratifying to learn, (a fact that I could have had no doubt about,) that you are receiving letters from various parts of the country, all testifying to your fidelity and impartiality in conducting the Standard, and to the value of your self-denying labors in the cause. You have nothing to regret, nothing to modify, nothing to recall, but much to be proud of.

I write in great haste, as I have yet to prepare my address on Mr. Lincoln, to be delivered at Providence on Thursday next.[3] My mind is in a state of collapse, the excitement of the tragedy is over, every thing has been said that need be about Mr. Lincoln, and I expect to have nothing worth listening to. So, don't come to Providence as a listener. Should it turn out to be something better than I now anticipate, perhaps I will deliver it at Longwood, or else at Newtown, where I am to speak the succeeding week.

You may expect Thompson and myself Wednesday morning, next week.

The editorials in Friday's Standard are evidently W. P's. The total silence observed about the withdrawal of yourself and [Edmund] Quincy is neither magnanimous nor respectful.[4]

Ever faithfully yours,

W. L. G.

ALS: Garrison Papers, Boston Public Library.

1. The misplaced letter is Garrison's of May 21, 1865. The quotation is from Edmund Burke, letter to Matthew Smith, May 1750.

2. Although Garrison printed only excerpts from Johnson's statement in the issue of May 26, he did follow his plan to print "the entire exposition" in the issue of June 2.

3. Garrison delivered his eulogy of Lincoln to the Union League at Providence on June 1. For the full text of the speech see *The Liberator*, July 7, 1865.

4. Editorials on several topics appeared in the *National Anti-Slavery Standard* for May 26. Garrison apparently refers to the one headed "Salutation," in which the continuation of the American Anti-Slavery Society is urged in statements like the following: "As in all its past life, the Society rises superior to form and routine, changing its point of attack as the shifting need of the battle demands. . . . Again we change front to fight the battle of Suffrage, seeing that today the ballot-box is the only real charter of emancipation."

1 1 7

TO LYDIA MARIA CHILD

Boston, July 10, 1865.

Dear Mrs. Child:

On returning from Providence, (where I have been spending a few days with my wife, who is there for electrical treatment for her paralysis, and already with beneficial results,) I find a letter from you, making certain inquiries about the escape of William and Ellen Craft from slavery.[1] The best answer I can make to these is to send you their own account of their escape, as published by them in 1860, in London.[2] You will not find it so minute as you desire, but it will answer your purpose, I presume. You will see that they did not belong to the same master, and that Ellen's master was her own father. They say nothing about their ages. My estimate is, that he was about 25, and she a little younger. They arrived in Boston about the last of January, 1849, and remained here nearly two years.

I am glad you are writing something for the Freedmen's Book.[3] Every thing from your pen is read with the deepest interest and the highest satisfaction by multitudes; and your position, therefore, as a writer, is one of commanding influence. You have long since done a great work in the cause of freedom and humanity; and the millions who are now rejoicing that their fetters are broken have reason to bless your name, and look upon you as among their foremost deliverers.

Slavery being abolished, and the rebellion at last suddenly suppressed, we are now in an anomalous and very complex condition, and the work of reconstruction is beset with many difficulties and dangers. But I believe we shall come out right in the end. Of course, much of the old slaveholding spirit remains, and it will try to be as insolent and cruel as possible, especially towards its former victims. It would be miraculous were it otherwise. But this cannot last long. Every thing must gravitate towards freedom and free institutions by an irresistible law. In the mean time, let there be no relaxation of vigilance or labor on the part of the friends of the colored race.

All the household unite in sending kindest regards to you and Mr. Child.[4]

Your much attached friend,

Wm. Lloyd Garrison.

ALS: Alexander C. Washburn Collection, Massachusetts Historical Society.

1. The famous fugitive slaves William Craft (c. 1826–1900) and his wife Ellen (1828–c. 1897) were originally from Georgia. Craft's master was Ira H. Taylor, who was probably the cashier of the bank in Macon owned by James C. Smith, Ellen Craft's father and also her master. She had been given to the Smiths' daughter, Mrs. Robert Collins, as a wedding present, since Mrs. Smith was embarrassed that the slave girl was so light-skinned as to be frequently taken for a member of the family. The Crafts had escaped from slavery about 1848, when Ellen disguised herself as a planter and, accompanied by her "slave" William, went to Philadelphia. The owners attempted unsuccessfully to capture William and Ellen under the Fugitive Slave Law of 1850. The Crafts moved to England, where they lived until 1869, when they returned to the United States and bought a plantation near Savannah. (William Still, *The Underground Railroad*, Philadelphia, 1879, pp. 368–377; William Craft, *Running a Thousand Miles for Freedom; or, the Escape of William and Ellen Craft from Slavery*, 1860; reprint with a preface by Florence B. Freedman, New York, 1969; 1880 U.S. Census, Bryan County, Ga. *NAW.*)

2. Garrison refers to Craft's *Running a Thousand Miles for Freedom.*

3. Mrs. Child was in the process of compiling and publishing at her own expense an anthology of selections from the works of prominent blacks, designed to be read by former slaves. (*NAW.*)

4. David Lee Child (1794–1874), a Harvard graduate, was a lawyer by training, although he spent most of his time as an editor and reformer. In 1828 he was elected to the Massachusetts legislature, edited the *Massachusetts Journal*, and married Lydia Maria Francis. From the early 1830s on, he was an active abolitionist. Between 1843 and 1844 he assisted his wife in editing the *National Anti-Slavery Standard* in New York. Child became connected with the beet sugar industry in the late 1830s, but the factory he built in Northampton, Mass., failed in 1844. Child had fewer associations with Garrison in the 1860s than he did in earlier years.

118

TO HELEN E. GARRISON

Roxbury, July 23, 1865.

Dear Wife:

Frank and I were promptly at the Roxbury depot,[1] yesterday afternoon, at 6 o'clock, to receive Fanny and Harry [Villard] on their arrival. They reported having had a pleasant time in Providence, with thanks to brother Henry, Charlotte,[2] and others, for their kind attentions. They also reported you as still improving, though your poor paralyzed arm continues as much disabled as ever. I trust the Doctor's hopefulness as to its ultimate recovery will be realized; but this only time can determine.

Thursday afternoon Dr. Mann came, according to appointment, and extracted five of my teeth.[3] Only two of them caused me much pain. The eye tooth was very strong and firm, and required a good deal of pulling to get it out. I also had one or two remaining roots to be taken out. Of course, I went through it all without wincing, discarding ether and chloroform. Dr. Mann, as soon as the bleeding ceased, proceeded to take a plaster impression of the gums; the next forenoon, he brought out a set of teeth to see how they fitted before putting them upon a permanent plate; and yesterday he brought them all completed, and they now adorn my mouth, looking so natural that no one would suspect they are artificial. My lacerated gums are still somewhat tender, so that I cannot eat without pain; but I find no difficulty in articulating, so that I shall have no occasion to practise aside, as you considerately suggest in your letter. I am heartily glad the operation is over, and feel sure that I am the gainer by it. In the course of three or four months my gums will shrink so as to require a new plate. How agreeably surprised and fortunate I am to get supplied with so little delay!

Thus equipped, I shall be able to go to Providence on Friday to bring you home, if you desire it. But Mr. Villard proposes taking Fanny and Ella [Ellen Wright Garrison] with him to Newport on Wednesday, and then returning in season on Friday from Newport to accompany you to Boston. I will come, nevertheless, if that is your wish. Whether I come or act by proxy, I will see that Dr. [Joseph] Dow's bill is promptly settled. Remember, *Friday* is to be the day, as it will exactly complete the week.

We have now with us Emma Mott, Maria Hopper, Willie Davis,[4] Frank Wright, and Charles McKim, so that all our beds are occupied. Emma's sister is expected in a few days.[5] A young lady[6] of Ella's acquaintance has been spending a few days with us. Our chances for company will not be lessened by our residence in Roxbury. Of course, the young folks in special must be visited.

Anne W. Weston has written a very kind and congratulatory letter on learning of the engagement between Harry and Fanny, and invites us all to come down and spend a day with them next week.

I saw Abby K. Foster at the Anti-Slavery Office a few days ago, and had a pleasant interview with her—she being in a tender state of mind, and rejoicing to hear of Fanny's engagement, Wendell's prospective marriage, and your improving condition.

William and Ella, Emma and Maria, Harry and Fanny have just gone on a ride to Milton Hill, and to make a call on Mr. Pierce and lady.[7]

Only think of my being made an honorary member of the Phi Beta Kappa at Cambridge![8] "The world moves."[9]

All send their loving regards to you, and kind remembrances to the beloved ones at P.

Your loving

W. L. G.

☞ The report that the 55th Regt. is to be discharged is not confirmed, and I understand is premature.

ALS: Garrison Papers, Boston Public Library.

1. This depot had been the terminal of the Boston and Providence Railroad since it began service June 11, 1835. The railroad provided transportation to New York City via Long Island Sound. (Justin Winsor, ed., *The Memorial History of Boston, 1630–1880*, Boston, 1881, IV, 129–130.)

2. Charlotte Benson Anthony (1803–1886) was the sister of Helen Benson Garrison and the wife of Henry Anthony (1802–1879), whom she married in 1826. The couple had seven children, five of whom lived beyond infancy: Mary Gould (1829–1888), who married William C. Townsend in 1853; Sarah Benson (1832–1895), who married James Tillinghast in 1857; George Henry (born 1835); Joseph Bowen (born 1837), who married Josephine A. Jackson; and Frederick Eugene (born 1840), who married Julia Perkins Adie. (Charles L. Anthony, *Genealogy of the Anthony Family from 1495 to 1904*, Sterling, Ill., 1904.)

3. Dr. Daniel Mann, a resident of Sterling, Mass., had his dental practice in Boston. He was married to Maria Dimock; their son Birney (1847–1903) was a classmate of Frank Garrison at the Boston Latin School, and the two boys became close friends. (Letter to the editor from Mrs. George Otis Tapley, curator, Sterling Historical Society, Sterling, Mass., June 21, 1973; see also *Letters*, IV, 457.)

4. Emma [Emily] Mott (born 1848) was the daughter of Thomas and Mariana Pelham Mott. In 1874 she was to marry George R. Shaw. (Thomas C. Cornell, *Adam and Ann Mott: Their Ancestors and Their Descendants*, Poughkeepsie, N.Y., 1890.)

Maria Hopper (born 1845 and still living in 1890) was the unmarried daughter of Edward and Ann Mott Hopper. (Cornell, *Adam and Ann Mott.*)

William M. Davis (1850–1934) was the son of Edward M. and Maria Mott Davis. He became a geologist and for a time assisted Professor Nathaniel S. Shaler of Harvard and the Lawrence Scientific School; he wrote several books and pamphlets on physical geography. Davis married Ellen Bliss Warner of Springfield, Ill., in 1879, and they had three sons. (Cornell, *Adam and Ann Mott.*)

5. Garrison probably refers either to Maria Mott (previously identified) or to Isabel Mott (born 1846), the eldest of the Thomas Mott children. (Cornell, *Adam and Ann Mott.*)

6. Unidentified.

7. Edward Lillie Pierce (1829–1897) was a graduate of Brown University and Harvard Law School. He was active in politics, becoming a Republican in the late 1850s and attending the party's national convention in 1860. During the war he enlisted as a private; in 1866 he was sent by Secretary Chase to Port Royal, S.C., to supervise freed slaves in the cultivation of cotton. He served as collector of internal revenue at Boston (1864–1866), district attorney of Norfolk and Plymouth counties, and member of the Massachusetts legislature (1875, 1876, and 1897). He is perhaps best known as the author of the official four-volume biography of Charles Sumner. Pierce's wife was Elizabeth H. Kingsbury (died 1880) of Providence, R.I., who bore him six children. (Obituary, Boston *Evening Transcript*, September 7, 1897.)

8. This academic honorary society, the earliest Greek-letter society, was originally a social fraternity, founded at the College of William and Mary in 1776.

Although no record has been found of the meeting at which Garrison's award was made, it is known that Dr. Henry I. Bowditch was instrumental in securing the award for him. Garrison's name does appear in all the Phi Beta Kappa records, including the 1941 general directory. (*Life*; letter to the editor from Kenneth M. Greene, secretary, Phi Beta Kappa United Chapters, Washington, D.C., June 24, 1975.)

9. Garrison alludes to a statement attributed to Galileo.

119

TO HENRY VILLARD

Roxbury, August 10, 1865.

My dear Henry:

Henceforth, in addressing you, in view of the near relationship about to be formed between us by your plighted love to my darling Fanny, you will allow me to dispense with the formal "Mr.," and to call you simply by your Christian name.

As, to-day, you are to take your leave of us for some time, I feel moved to say a few words to you in writing, expressive of my feelings towards you personally, and with reference to your contemplated matrimonial alliance.

I sincerely hope that I have not, by word or manner, since your "engagement," led you to suspect that I did not trustfully approve of it. If I was not particularly demonstrative in the expression of my feelings when the announcement of it was made, or if I seemed to be somewhat reserved and serious, you will not wonder at it if you will place yourself in my situation. For you will recollect with what suddenness the engagement was made; that Fanny had had but a very slight acquaintance with you, and I still less; that the relation thus entered into, when consummated by wedlock, is the most solemn and momentous of all the relations of life, and is fruitful of more bliss or misery than any other, according to the nature of the choice; that, while I had supposed that, sooner or later, my beloved daughter (how beloved, I have no words to express) would be likely to unite her destiny with another, I did not wish to entertain the thought of such an event or such a separation; and that it was not simply natural, but a clear parental duty, on my part, to desire to know something of the antecedents and character of the individual asking her hand in marriage. Of course, you labored under the embarrassment of being a native of another country—of having your relatives on the other side of the Atlantic, and therefore unable easily to introduce them, or to have them visited. As the case stands, you came to us with no letters of recommendation, no certificates of character, no approval of those related to you by the ties of consanguinity—an absolute stranger, "solitary and alone"—on your own merits, as they might be discovered on personal acquaintance. Hence, you will readily allow that some caution and anxiety would be pardonable in me, until I had had opportunities to form my own judgment of your integrity and uprightness.

Those opportunities having been enjoyed, let me say, then—

once for all—that I am thoroughly satisfied that Fanny has made a wise and fortunate choice; that you possess an affectionate, generous and noble nature; that your intentions are in the highest degree honorable, and your aims pure and exalted; that you have an innate abhorrence of all hypocrisies and shams, and carry your heart in your hand, "like an open book"; that your love for Fanny is equalled only by her love for you; that you have alike a large brain and a large heart, and will be sure to employ both in the service of freedom and humanity; and that, as a family, we may at all times safely rely upon your affectionate regard and friendly interest.

Having thus frankly spoken as a father, I need not be reminded that your own beloved sire and cherished relatives will quite as naturally be anxious to know something of the character and qualities of the one to whom you have sacredly plighted your affections.[1] You, at least, appear to have no doubt on that score; and though I may be partial in my judgment, I am free to say that I do not think you could have made a better choice. In personal looks and attractions she is certainly not lacking; but outward beauty is of little account, and frequently evanescent. To her comely appearance Fanny adds the most virtuous qualities and the best traits of character. She is without guile; the embodiment of affection and fidelity; intensely strong in her nature, yet pure in her instincts and quick in her perceptions; ingenuous, confiding, and full of sweet simplicity; generous-hearted, sympathetic, and thoroughly disinterested in whatever she undertakes; of a most equable and amiable disposition; self-poised and self-balanced to a remarkable degree; neat and simple in her habits, and without any taste for fashion or frivolity; bright in her understanding, sure in her moral intuitions, noble in her aspirations, and progressive in her spirit;—in short, she is about all that I can desire her to be, and such as few parents have had the blessing to reckon among their children.

In wedding her, you will take her for what she is—quite a portionless bride. For though I should rejoice to bestow upon her an independent amount of means, yet a life consecrated to philanthropy, and especially to the task of breaking the fetters of four millions of slaves in my hitherto guilty country, (a task happily consummated at last, under God,) has left me, at sixty years of age, without any pecuniary accumulation. But she will never be a burden to you while her health lasts; and in case adversity overtake you, she will help you to meet it with resolute purpose and a brave spirit. Whatever means you may at any time possess to minister to her taste or comfort, be assured that you will best suit her wishes by avoiding whatever is extravagant or showy, and consulting only what is needed on the score of usefulness, beauty, and adaptation—all with a due regard to economical considerations.

I could add much more, for my heart is overflowing with emotion; but this would be superfluous. Let me only say, that both my dear wife and I desire that you and Fanny will select the time for your marriage, whether it be soon or late, that you may deem best. We will not venture to suggest any particular period for your guidance. Whatever decision you may make will receive our hearty approval. Only we hope you will conclude to spend at least the first year under our roof, should your business arrangements permit you to remain in this section of the country. We can accommodate you without any inconvenience, giving you the liberty of the house as to your visiting friends—&c., &c.

In all that I have written, my dear wife cordially concurs.

Yours, most confidingly,

Wm. Lloyd Garrison.

Henry Villard, Esq.

P.S Let the preservation of your health be the first object of your consideration while you are absent from us; and if you find that your neuralgic complaint is getting worse, hasten back to Rock-Ledge, where you will sure to find a warm welcome and good nursing.

ALS: Villard Papers, Harvard College Library.

1. Gustav Leonhard Hilgard (1807–1867), father of Henry Villard (born Ferdinand Heinrich Gustav Hilgard), was a man of considerable distinction in Bavaria, where he was a justice of the Supreme Court. Father and son disagreed politically and socially but were reconciled by 1855. (*Memoirs of Henry Villard, Journalist and Financier 1835–1900*, Boston and New York, 1904, I, 1–8, 35.)

120

TO JAMES MILLER McKIM

Boston, Sept. 11, 1865.

My dear McKim:

Some days ago, I received a letter from Rev, Mr. Shipherd, of Chicago,[1] stating that "at a Convention of gentlemen, *representing the leading Freedmen's Aid Societies of the East and West,* and the late Sanitary and Christian Commissions, held in the city of New York on Thursday, August 24th, it was resolved, after a free and satisfactory interchange of sentiment, to proceed to the organization of a National Freedmen's Aid Commission"; informing me that I had been elected a Vice President of the same; and requesting me to be present, on Friday next, 15th inst., at 9 o'clock, A.M., at the first meeting of the Board of Managers, at the Rooms of the American Freedmen's Aid Union, 67 Nassau Street, New York."[2] To this letter I replied that I deemed it an honor to be connected with such a Commission, and would endeavor to attend the meeting aforesaid.

But I took it for granted that "the leading Freedmen's Aid Societies of the East and West" had been officially and authoritatively represented on the occasion of the formation of the Commission, and that such formation was in accordance with their wishes. This, certainly, was not the case in regard to the New England Freedmen's Aid Society; as I ascertained on Thursday evening last, at a meeting of the Society, where the Rev. Mr. Lowe, who was present unofficially at the New York meeting which formed the Commission, gave a minute account of all that transpired at that meeting, and of the part he took in it.[3] Rev. John Parkman, who also was at the meeting with Mr. Lowe in New York, was not present with us to give us his version of the matter.[4] But, after hearing Mr. Lowe's statements, the surprise was general that the Commission should have been organized at such an informal meeting, where no credentials were presented, probably none held from any Society, and certainly none called for; and the vote was unanimous in dissenting from such a procedure. A committee, consisting of Mr. Lowe, Mr. Philbrick, and myself, was appointed to correspond with other Freedmen's Societies, (Philadelphia, Baltimore, &c.,) in regard to the Commission, and to express the views of the N. E. F. A. Society in regard to it.[5]

At that time, none of the proceedings had been sent for approval from New York to the Society; but, on Saturday, an uncertified copy of the same was received, and also an announcement of the special meeting to be held on Friday morning next in New York. A special meeting of the Society, therefore, will be held on Wednesday evening next, to see what further action to take in the premises.

It is not understood how the Commission is called for by any exigencies connected with the Freedmen's cause. What is to become of the American Freedmen's Aid *Society?* Is it willing to be merged in the other, or in an Eastern branch of the Commission? Why not first have delegates from the various Societies already in the field appointed to meet in conference and duly empowered to act, before assuming their readiness to accept the Commission as their head? I do not think the N. E. F. A. Society will feel disposed to send any of its officers or members to the New York meeting on Friday; and it is not probable that I shall be present. Yet there is an earnest desire

here to have the utmost harmony preserved between all those societies and individuals that are laboring in the Freedmen's cause.

Your attached friend,

Wm. Lloyd Garrison.

J. M. McKim.

ALS: Garrison Papers, Boston Public Library.

1. Jacob Rudd Shipherd (1836–1905), a graduate of Oberlin College, was a Congregational minister who had left his pastorate in Chicago in 1864 to become secretary of the North Western Freedmen's Aid Commission in that city. In 1869 he left
the ministry to engage in banking and later in real estate. In 1877 he moved to New
York City, where he specialized in Long Island and railroad properties. Receiving a
law degree from the University of the City of New York in 1878, he spent his remaining years practicing law. He was also the compiler of *A History of the Oberlin-Wel-
lington Rescue,* New York, 1859. (Chicago city directory, 1864; letter to the editor,
citing *Necrological Record of Alumni, 1904–1905,* from Virginia Harris, head reference librarian, Oberlin College Library, August 30, 1972.)

2. As Garrison's letter implies, a myriad of organizations had been trying to aid
the freedmen both charitably and educationally. Among these were the American
Missionary Association (founded in 1846), which by 1865 had 250 teachers and missionaries throughout the South and Southwest; the United States Sanitary Commission (created in June 1861), which employed as many as 500 agents by 1865; and the
United States Christian Commission (formed in November 1861), which was supported primarily by funds contributed by churches and private persons. Societies
specifically designed to aid the freedmen included the National Freedmen's Relief
Association in New York (founded in 1862) and similar organizations in the other
northern states. Indeed, by 1865 most of the major northern cities had such societies
as well. This plethora of organizations caused a serious overlapping of jurisdiction
and activities and a wasteful competition in fund-raising.

Efforts to unify and coordinate the societies were begun in the spring of 1865,
with the organization of the American Freedmen's Aid Commission (subsequently
divided into an eastern and a western department), which Garrison sometimes calls
the National Freedmen's Aid Commission or the American Freedmen's Aid Society.
The national organization was founded in August, and the meeting held on September 19 resolved disputes over representation and authority, so that the new commission was able to coordinate local societies and improve the life of freedmen everywhere. (Willie Lee Rose, *Rehearsal for Reconstruction: The Port Royal Experiment,*
New York, 1964; Paul S. Peirce, *The Freedmen's Bureau, a Chapter in the History of
Reconstruction,* State University of Iowa Studies in Sociology, Economics, Politics,
and History, 3, No. 1, Iowa City, 1904; Charles J. Stillé, *History of the United States
Sanitary Commission,* Philadelphia, 1866; Lemuel Moss, *Annals of the United
States Christian Commission,* Philadelphia, 1868.)

3. Charles Lowe (1828–1874), originally from Portsmouth, N.H., and a Harvard
graduate, had held pastorites in Unitarian churches in New Bedford, Salem, and Somerville, Mass., before becoming an army chaplain and working on behalf of freedmen's aid. After the war he became executive secretary of the American Unitarian
Association and editor of the *Unitarian Review and Religious Magazine.*

4. John Parkman (1813–1883) was a Unitarian minister who had served in Green-
field, Mass. (1837–1839), Dover, N.H. (1840–1849), and New Brighton, N.Y. (1852–
1858). Subsequently he lived in Boston and is listed in Boston directories until 1881,
although he is not known to have had a church there. (Letter to the editor from
Nancy Sahli, researcher, August 19, 1972.)

5. Edward S. Philbrick (1827–1889), the son of Garrison's friend and supporter

Samuel Philbrick and a graduate of Harvard, was a civil engineer for the Boston and Albany Railroad and later a consulting engineer for the construction of bridges. He was prominent in Brookline affairs and served as selectman and on the water board. (Obituary, Boston *Transcript*, February 14, 1889; *Life*.)

The New England Freedmen's Aid Society, organized in 1862, was originally called the Boston Educational Commission. The society sent 180 teachers to the South in 1866. (Peirce, *The Freedmen's Bureau;* James E. Sefton, *The United States Army and Reconstruction, 1865–1877*, Baton Rouge, 1967.)

121

TO HENRY VILLARD

Boston, Sept. 12, 1865.

My dear Harry:

I have for some time been owing you a letter, and I proceed to discharge that obligation, in accordance with the apostolic injunction, "Pay what thou owest."[1]

First of all, let me say that your letter, in reply to the one I put into your hands on leaving us, was read by me and my dear wife with more than satisfaction—with delight. It was throughly ingenuous, manly, straight-forward—all that we could possibly desire.

Next, let me thank you for your kind and affectionate letter to wife, which had a truly filial ring to it, and which touched her maternal nature to the quick. To whatever extent she can help to supply to you the place of your venerated mother,[2] she will do so gladly —the only drawback being her crippled condition; a condition which further electric treatment and time may yet happily change, so as to allow a comparatively free use of her limbs. That it will be your delight to show us both the affection of a son, we have no doubt.

Your friendly suggestion, in your letter to Fanny, in regard to my writing a history of the Anti-Slavery struggle, will be a matter of consideration when the publication of the Liberator shall have terminated. My connection with that struggle has been so intimate and peculiar, that I do not see how I could write such a history without, on the one hand, seeming egotistical; or, on the other, by studied omission, "leaving Hamlet out of the play."[3] But I will entertain your proposition so far as to see, in due time, whether it will be feasible; and, if so, in what shape.[4]

My Western lecturing tour, as agreed upon some months since, has suddenly "come to grief" by the bankruptcy of the firm at Indianapolis with whom my engagement was made; at least, so writes Bayard Taylor to me in his own case, who had made a similar engagement.[5] Nevertheless, it is my purpose to occupy October and

November in lecturing, "on my own hook," all along from Albany to St. Louis, should circumstances seem to favor.

Ever since your absence, the weather (with scarcely any variation) has been very sultry and depressing. I have had a slow fever hanging about me, which has kept me from all physical and mental effort; and I am not yet rid of it. Consequently, I have done nothing towards preparing any lectures for my contemplated Western tour. In truth, I am utterly at a loss what subjects to treat upon, and wait and long for mental and bodily invigoration. You are very kind to offer to do what you can, by your acquaintance with the press, to facilitate my lecturing course; but it will not be necessary to tax you to any extent in that direction.

For the last week we have been hourly expecting the arrival of the Mass. 55th Colored Regiment from Charleston, but we get no tidings of it. In his last letter, George said we might look for him from the 6th to the 10th inst. There is no doubt, however, that the Regiment is to be speedily mustered out of service. Doubtless, George will be here by the time you return to Roxbury, to give you, with us all, a loving greeting.

Of course, Fanny keeps you posted as to all our home incidents.

The punctuality and frequency of your correspondence with each other, (to say nothing of the ardent contents of the letters,) remind dear wife and me of the days of our courtship, so that we seem to be living them over again. We feel sure that you and Fanny were born for each other.

Most affectionately yours,

Wm. Lloyd Garrison.

Henry Villard, Esq.

☞ Wendell writes to his mother, this morning, that he and Lucy [McKim] will be married somewhere from the 18th to the 21st of December. You and Fanny will select your own time, *ad libitum.*[6] All send their love.

ALS: Garrison Papers, Boston Public Library.

1. Matthew 18:28, adapted.

2. Henry Villard's mother, Katherine Antonia Elisabeth Pfeiffer (1811–1859), daughter of Franz Moritz Joseph Pfeiffer, married Gustav Leonhard Hilgard on June 11, 1833. (*Memoirs of Henry Villard, Journalist and Financier, 1835–1900*, Boston and New York, 1904.)

3. A possible reference to Sir Walter Scott, *The Talisman*, "Introduction," in which he mentions the "play-bill which is said to have announced the tragedy of Hamlet, the character of the Prince of Denmark being left out."

4. Although Garrison did seriously entertain Henry Villard's suggestion, which was subsequently supported by a formal offer from Ticknor and Fields, the project was never completed. (See Garrison's letter to Ellen Wright Garrison, March 23, 1866, n. 2.)

5. Little information is available about the bankrupt lecture agency in Indianapolis, though Bayard Taylor's letter to Garrison, August 30, 1865 (Anti-Slavery Letters to Garrison and Others, Boston Public Library), gives the name Patterson & Co. We have not, however, been able to trace any lecture or travel agency of that name in Indianapolis. At any rate, Garrison did make a full western lecture tour between November and the first week of December 1865. (Letters to the editor from Nancy Sahli, researcher, August 19, 1972, and Joan Gerlach, assistant librarian, Indiana Historical Society, September 6, 1972.)

6. Wendell and Lucy were married December 6, 1865; Henry and Fanny were married January 3, 1866.

122

TO JAMES MILLER McKIM

Boston, Sept. 14, 1865.

My dear McKim:

Your letter, in answer to mine respecting the Freedmen's Commission, is received.

Last evening there was a special meeting of the N. E. Freedmen's Aid Society, at their Rooms, to consider the proposition to recognize the Commission as the head of the Freedmen's movement, having its Eastern and Western wings. It was a long session, and all present expressed their views on the subject. The conclusion arrived at was the unanimous adoption of a Resolution that, as at present advised, the Society saw serious objections to such a movement; and deputing Rev. Charles Lowe, Edward S. Philbrick and myself to represent the Society, and state its views, at the meeting of the "Union," to be held simultaneously with that of the Board of Managers of the Commission, in New York, on Friday forenoon; 15th inst. The Secretary [Jacob R. Shipherd] has doubtless sent you the Resolution, to-day, by mail.

Neither Mr. Lowe nor Mr. Philbrick was present when the delegates were chosen; and on conferring with them since, they say that imperative business engagements render it impracticable for them to be at the New York meeting. Independent of your solicitation for my presence, I had a desire to be with you on the occasion, that there might be the fullest interchange of opinion on a matter of such importance; but I am not feeling well, and therefore shrink from the fatigue of such a sultry journey. Moreover, as William is absent on a visit to Auburn, N. Y., I do not like to be away from home, on wife's account, as her helpless condition makes her more timid than ever when there is "no man about the house." And, finally, as the views expressed by the members of the Society were unanimous for non-concurrence, no room was left for any thing beyond this. Hence, I send you this hasty epistle as a substitute for my presence.

The objections to the Commission were—that it was not formed with the knowledge of the Society, nor was any one present duly appointed to act authoritatively in its behalf; that at the New York meeting no one presented nor was asked to present any credentials from existing Freedmen's Aid Societies, but it was expressly voted that it should be regarded as informal and incomplete, and then it was afterwards improperly announced to the country that the Commission had been duly organized, Gen. Howard[1] himself being given to understand that such was the fact; that there seemed to be no exigency requiring such an organization, the Eastern and Western associations moving harmoniously each in its own sphere; that the Commission would absorb, in salaries, so much money as in all probability would deter thoughtful people from contributing to it, and leave little to be expended for the Freedmen's cause; and, finally, as Mr. Olmsted had positively declined acting as Secretary, no one could be found qualified to fill the situation, at all equal to himself.[2] No objection was made to Bishop Simpson;[3] and there was no disposition to call in question the motives or aims of those who organized the Commission, they being known to be truly desirous of having the best plans and the most efficient measures adopted for the furtherance of the good cause.

With this entire unity of feeling on the part of the N. E. F. A. Society, and the fact that Mr. Olmsted is not disposed to accept the Secretaryship—and understanding that Judge [Hugh L.] Bond and the Freedmen's friends in Baltimore take a similar view of this new project—my conviction is that it will be wise for the Commission not to attempt to go forward until the need of it is felt and called for by the existing Freedmen's Aid Societies.[4]

Your faithful co-worker,

Wm. Lloyd Garrison.

☞ I will confer with you hereafter in regard to my contemplated lecturing tour at the West. What you write about longing for rest, though still willing to toil, touches me tenderly.

ALS: Garrison Papers, Boston Public Library.

1. Oliver Otis Howard (1830–1909), born in Maine, was a graduate of Bowdoin College and West Point, where he subsequently taught mathematics. In June 1861 he became a colonel in the 3d Maine regiment, rising eventually to the rank of major general and seeing service in many major battles. In May 1865 the President appointed him commissioner of the recently organized Bureau of Refugees, Freedmen, and Abandoned Lands, otherwise known as the Freedmen's Bureau. Although

an honest humanitarian, Howard was frequently criticized for being gullible and a poor administrator. Despite his limitations, however, his success continued. In 1869 he became president of Howard University, which he had helped to found. In the 1870s he served on commissions dealing with the Indians, in 1880 be became superintendent of West Point, and in 1886 he was appointed commander of the Division of the East. He was also the author of many biographies.

2. Frederick Law Olmsted (1822–1903), the first distinguished American landscape architect, had acquired during his youth a lasting interest in agriculture and travel. For a time he farmed in Connecticut and attended lectures on agriculture. In 1852 a long conversation with Garrison kindled in him a desire to travel in the South. He wrote letters based on his experiences for the New York *Times;* subsequently he published three books—*A Journey in the Seaboard Slave States* (1856), *A Journey through Texas* (1857), and *A Journey in the Back Country* (1860)—which were ultimately condensed under the title *The Cotton Kingdom* (2 vols., 1861). Following his appointment in 1858 as the chief architect of Central Park in New York City, he acquired many commissions, including the one that resulted in Boston's "emerald necklace" of parks and preserves linking the Common and the Public Garden with the outlying countryside. (Laura Wood Roper, *FLO: A Biography of Frederick Law Olmsted,* Baltimore, 1973.)

3. Matthew Simpson (1811–1884), an indigent and largely self-educated boy, became a prominent religious leader and educator. He was a Methodist minister in Ohio and later in Pittsburgh, as well as professor of natural sciences at Allegheny College. In 1839 he became president of Indiana Asbury (now De Pauw) University, and he later refused the presidency of Northwestern and Wesleyan universities. In 1848 he was elected editor of the *Western Christian Advocate* and in 1852 was made a bishop. In short, he became the most prominent and influential Methodist of his time. He was not without political influence, acting as adviser to Secretaries Stanton and Chase as well as to President Lincoln. He also wrote several books on theological subjects.

4. Ultimately Jacob R. Shipherd became secretary of the American Freedmen's Aid Commission. (See the letter to James Miller McKim, September 11, 1865, n. 1; *The Liberator,* December 1, 1865.)

---

1 2 3

TO EDWIN M. STANTON

Boston, Sept. 15, 1865.

Hon. Edwin M. Stanton:

Dear Sir—

Allow me to congratulate you on your arrival in Boston, which, whether styled "the city of notions," "the Athens of America," or, more pretentiously, "the hub of the universe,"[1] is certainly second to no other on the score of intelligence, patriotism, and love of freedom.

Apprehensive that either your engagements pro tem, or my own, may prevent my seeing you before you leave the city, I avail myself of this method to express to you, renewedly, my grateful appreciation of your great kindness, and I will add moral courage, as well as marked respect for my labors to secure universal emancipation in our slavery-cursed land, in extending to me an invitation to be one of the privileged company to witness the raising of the American flag at Fort Sumter, by General [Robert] Anderson, in April last—an occasion ever to be memorable in our national history as symbolizing the sure triumph of Liberty and Right over the rampant "powers of darkness."[2]

Selecting the witnesses of this sublime spectacle, in behalf of the government, from elements that before the rebellion were incongruous and discordant, both as to their political feelings and their views of slavery and abolitionism, you must naturally have felt some anxiety in regard to the manner in which they would meet each other—and whether it would be possible for them to be oblivious to past differences, and to "mingle into one like kindred drops."[3] It must, therefore, have been exceedingly gratifying to you to know that your representative design and magnanimous spirit were both warmly appreciated and fully reciprocated by them all; and that there was a perfect blending of thought, feeling and sentiment on the occasion, created by one common concern for the safety of the country, the effectual suppression of the rebellion, and the extinction of that terrible system of oppression out of which all our national dangers, divisions and bloody conflicts have sprung. Towards my honored English coadjutor, George Thompson, Esq. and myself, there was no lack of courtesy, kindness or attention on the part of any; but, on the contrary, all expressed their gratification that we were of the party—deeming it specially fitting that the Anti-Slavery sentiment of our country and of Christendom should be thus represented, in regard to a struggle which vitally pertained to the cause of freedom and humanity throughout the world. How deep was the general regret, however, that you were not able to be with us!

I have to thank you, moreover, in behalf of all my family, for your unsolicited kindness and generous consideration in allowing my son, Capt. George T. Garrison, of the Massachusetts 55th Regiment, a furlough of thirty days to visit home at that time,—a privilege which he had not enjoyed nor asked for since he entered the service in June, 1863. It was an act specially appreciated by my dear wife, in her paralytic condition; for when George left us, she was in good health, and in her helplessness yearned to embrace him before the expiration of his term of service, lest she might never again be permitted to see him in the flesh.

Finally, I have to thank you for several photographic views of

Fort Sumter, taken at the time of the celebration, with excellent skill and judgment. I shall very carefully preserve them.

As my appreciation of your character and patriotic labors, I send you a copy of the Liberator of the 1st inst., in which see two articles pertaining to yourself.[4]

Yours, for universal freedom,

Wm. Lloyd Garrison.

ALS: Edwin M. Stanton Papers, Library of Congress.

1. No source has been found for the first two descriptions of Boston; the last may be an adaptation of a line from Oliver Wendell Holmes, *The Autocrat of the Breakfast-Table*, VI.

2. Garrison's quotation is probably biblical and could refer either to Luke 22:53 or Colossians 1:13.

3. William Cowper, *The Task*, Book II, "The Timepiece," line 19.

4. Two articles highly complimentary to Stanton (one of them reprinted from the Boston *Traveller*) were printed in *The Liberator*, September 1, 1865.

124

TO JAMES MILLER McKIM

Boston, Oct. 1, 1865.

My dear McKim:

I have just returned from my visit to Vergennes, Vt., where I addressed an immense gathering at the Agricultural Fair, and at the close was greeted with three rousing cheers, having been serenaded by a brass band the previous evening.[1] Surely, the abolitionists are up, and their old persecutors, the haughty slaveholders, are down.

Your letter is before me, apprising me of an adjourned meeting of the Managers of the Freedmen's Commission in Philadelphia, on the 11th inst., and urging me to prepare an address to the public, to be laid before the Board on that occasion.[2] I really do not know how to command time to write the address; and yet, in the absence of Bishop Simpson, will try to do so.

Then, you also urge me to attend the meeting aforesaid; and, moreover, to be one of the speakers at a public meeting in your city, to inaugurate the movement.[3] Now, I want to be with you on each occasion, and mean to do so if I can; but I have got to have some new teeth, and to get used to them, in the mean time; and, therefore, may not be in a condition to make a public speech. I shall try to find my dentist [Dr. Daniel Mann] to-morrow, and to get him to expedite matters as fast as possible. You see my good will; so that if I fail to be with you, you will understand the reason.

I am sorry to hear that Wendell [Garrison] has been ill, but trust he is recovering.

We are all well at home. I have no time to add more, as the mail closes within a few minutes.

Your loving co-worker,

Wm. Lloyd Garrison.

J. M. McKim.

ALS: Garrison Papers, Boston Public Library.

1. Garrison spoke at the Ninth Annual Champlain Valley Agricultural Fair, September 28, on Reconstruction and the need for continuing Union forces in the South. He also described his April visit to Charleston, S.C. (*The Liberator*, October 13, 1865.)

2. At the meeting of the American Freedmen's Aid Commission in Philadelphia a committee consisting of Garrison, Bishop Matthew Simpson, and John M. Walden was appointed to prepare an address to the public. The address, which was printed in *The Liberator*, December 1, 1865, reviewed the purpose and activities of the commission and appealed for contributions.

3. Garrison did speak at the meeting in Philadelphia on October 11, commending the purposes for which the commission was organized and urging the development of its proposed programs. (*The Liberator*, October 27, 1865.)

125

TO HENRY C. WRIGHT

Boston, Oct. 2, 1865.

Dear Henry:

George brought along with him from Charleston a colored orphan boy, about 14 years of age, for whom he is desirous of procuring a good home.[1] Very opportunely, I have just received a letter from S. Waterhouse, at Ellsworth, Me., in which he wishes me to procure for him precisely such a lad as John is.[2] Mr. W. refers me to you, and to Mr. [Andrew T.] Foss, to certify as to his character and reliableness. Please briefly state what you know of him and his family, and what is his employment. Of course, I do not doubt his trustworthiness; but as he refers to you, and as we feel desirous to do well by the lad, I thought it would be prudent to state the case to you.

I have not seen Franky since his return home from Gloucester, but have no doubt he had a very gratifying time of it, and must have felt greatly obliged to you and others for kind attentions.

I got back from my visit to Vergennes on Saturday evening. The trip was unspeakably pleasant. At the agricultural fair I addressed an immense concourse of people, and was greeted with three rousing cheers at the conclusion. I was also serenaded by a brass band from Jericho the evening previous. Rev. E. H. Chapin made a very eloquent address on the same occasion, and was warmly applauded.[3] I was entertained by the Mayor of the city, G. W. Grandey.[4]

Our dear friend Rowland T. Robinson, of Ferrisburgh, at the close of the exhibition, carried me home to his residence, where I received the kindest welcome;[5] and the next evening lectured to a full audience in the Methodist church at North Ferrisburgh.[6]

I am thinking of going west in the course of a fortnight, to be gone till about the 1st of December. Next week they want me to be one of the speakers at the opening meeting of the Freedmen's Aid Commission, and I intend doing so, if practicable.

The aspect of things at the South is somewhat portentous. If the rebel States, "reconstructed" so as to leave the colored people at the mercy of the savage whites, are suddenly admitted into the Union, there will assuredly be a terrible state of affairs, perhaps leading to a war of extermination. I begin to feel more and more uneasy about the President [Andrew Johnson].

Ever faithfully yours,

Wm. Lloyd Garrison.

Henry C. Wright.

ALS: Garrison Papers, Boston Public Library; extract printed in *Life,* IV, 165.

1. Not identified.

2. Although S. Waterhouse has not been certainly indentified, he could be the attorney Samuel Waterhouse. (Albert H. Davis, *History of Ellsworth, Maine,* Lewiston, Me., 1927.)

3. Edwin Hubbell Chapin (1814–1880) was a minister who began his pastoral career at the Independent Christian Church in Richmond, Va.; he later moved to the Universalist Church in Charlestown, Mass., and ultimately to the Fourth Universalist Society in New York City. (See the letter to Robert Purvis, April 9, 1854, *Letters,* IV, 297, n. 2.)

4. George W. Grandey (1813–1893) of Vergennes, Vt., was a successful lawyer and state politician. In 1846–1847 he was county superintendent of schools; later he became superintendent in Vergennes and served for twenty-four years. For thirteen years he was a member of the Vermont General Assembly; between 1854 and 1870 he was speaker of the House. He was chairman of the state's electoral college in 1868 and delegate at large to the Republican convention in Philadelphia in 1872. Grandey held other positions as well, including court auditor, national bank examiner, mayor of Vergennes, postmaster, and justice of the peace; for twenty-five years he was president of the Addison County Bar Association. (Letter to the editor from Lois C. Noonan, librarian, Bixby Memorial Free Library, Vergennes, Vt., June 11, 1975, with information compiled by Jessie Neill Sievert, great-grandniece of Grandey, Vergennes, Vt.)

5. Rowland T. Robinson was a Quaker farmer in North Ferrisburgh, Vt. He was one of the organizers of the Vermont Anti-Slavery Society in 1834, and he served in the short-lived Vermont Peace Society between 1837 and 1838. He and his wife Rachel Gilpin (1799–1862) used their house as a station on the Underground Railroad. (David M. Ludlum, *Social Ferment in Vermont 1791–1850*, New York, 1939; Hiram Carleton, *Genealogical and Family History of the State of Vermont*, New York, 1903, II, 103.)

6. The North Ferrisburgh Methodist Church was founded in 1838. In 1846, owing to a dispute over slavery, some of the members left to form their own congregation; many of them returned, however, after the Civil War. (Letter to the editor from Reidun D. Nuquist, assistant librarian, Vermont Historical Society, July 27, 1972.)

126

TO HENRY MILES

Boston, Oct. 8, 1865.

Dear Friend:

I was glad to receive your letter, announcing that the meeting I addressed at North Ferrisburgh had proved satisfactory to those attending it, and that the prospect as to the formation of a Freedmen's Aid Society looks encouraging.[1]

You desire to know where the contributions of the Society had better be sent.

Hitherto, the various Freedmen's associations have acted without a head, and, consequently, without that concert and unity so desirable in regard to a work of such colossal magnitude. Recently, therefore, they have approved of the formation of a national head, to be called the American Freedmen's Aid Commission, having comprehensively two branches or wings—an Eastern and a Western one. All auxiliary or co-operative societies at the East are expected to send their contributions of money or clothing to Boston, to the care of the New England Freedmen's Aid Society. Those at the West will send theirs to Chicago. Both branches will duly acknowledge all their receipts, and also make returns to the Parent Society.

I send you, by this mail, the September number of "The Freedmen's Record," which is the organ of the New England F. A. Society, and contains its Constitution, list of officers, directions as to where donations are to be sent, and other interesting intelligence.[2]

Remembering my visit to Vermont with unalloyed pleasure— hoping your projected association will prove a success, and bring a united support for its furtherance—and thanking you most heartily for arranging the meeting at North Ferrisburgh, I remain,

Yours, with much esteem,

Wm. Lloyd Garrison.

Henry Miles.

ALS: Henry Miles Papers, Duke University Library.

Henry Miles (born c. 1796 and still living in 1870), originally from England, was a Quaker farmer in the vicinity of Monkton, Vt. He was the author of an essay, "The Society of Friends in Addison and Chittenden Counties," which was published in 1867 in the *Vermont Historical Gazetteer*. (Letter to the editor from Vivian Bryan, law and documents librarian, State of Vermont Department of Libraries, August 2, 1972.)

1. The Burlington (Vt.) *Daily Free Press*, October 5, 1865, reported that the Freedmen's Aid Association of Ferrisburgh had been formed as an auxiliary of the American Freedmen's Aid Commission.

2. The *Freedmen's Record* (formerly the *Freedmen's Journal*) was published between February 1865 and April 1874 in order to convey information about the southern freedmen, their condition, and the progress of their cause. (*ULS;* letter to the editor from Nancy Sahli, researcher, August 19, 1972.)

127

TO ELIZABETH PEASE NICHOL

Boston, Oct. 9, 1865.

My Dear Friend:

I was thrilled with delight on receiving the letter you sent by your son-in-law, Prof. Nichol, not only for the kind expressions and remembrances contained in it, but because it was brought by himself; leading me to hope that I should have the pleasure of entertaining him hospitably under my roof, showing him some attentions, and communing with him on many topics.[1] But when he first came to Boston, I was unfortunately absent from the city; and since then, he has been so circumstanced as to be unable to see me, except for a very brief interview. I had made arrangements to meet him at the station this evening, on his arrival from New York, and to take him to my residence to spend the night with me, which was all the time he could afford before leaving for England; but I am suddenly summoned to leave in the evening train for Philadelphia, to attend an important preliminary meeting of the American Freedmen's Aid Commission, and so shall not have the pleasure of seeing him again. This I very deeply regret. He impresses me most favorably, and I doubt not he has all others whose acquaintance he has made. He is so well pleased with what he has seen in America, that he thinks of returning again, with a view to lecturing on various subjects. I trust he will not fail doing so.

A quarter of a century has passed away, my dear friend, since we became acquainted with each other, through our common interest in the cause of the fettered slave; and how warm and true has been your friendship for me, how generous your aid to me personally, how untiring your co-operation, throughout that long period! That friendship I have reciprocated in spirit to the fullest extent. I long to see you at Huntley Lodge,[2] and pray Heaven it may be my privilege to do so in the course of next summer. Should we thus be permitted to meet, how much, pertaining to what is past, present and future, we shall have to talk over!

Suddenly called to Philadelphia, it is impossible for me to write you a long epistle, as I fully intended to do. Let me renew the assurance of my profound regard for your character, and heartfelt gratitude for all that you have done for me and mine.

A word as to my family may not be uninteresting to you. My beloved wife still continues disabled by her paralysis, though her general health is excellent, and she is looking quite as fair and young as she did when she was stricken down more than a year and a half ago. Her left arm is useless, and her left knee stiff; yet she is able to go up and down stairs alone, and to walk a considerable distance. During the summer she has been trying the electric battery with decidedly beneficial effect; and her physician is sanguine that she will yet recover the full use of her limbs. I am sorry that I dare not entertain any such hope.

My son Wendell is to be married to Lucy McKim, the only daughter of my beloved coadjutor J. Miller McKim, of Philadelphia, in December. Fanny, "sole daughter of my house and heart,"[3] is to be married in January to a German gentleman, (though thoroughly Americanised by several years' residence in this country,) named Henry Villard, possessing admirable qualities. They will make a visit to Germany next summer, via England, and I shall try to accompany them. His father [Gustav L. Hilgard] is Chief Justice at Munich.

My oldest son George has safely returned from the war. Franky is still pursuing his studies for admission into Harvard College. William has recently entered into the wool trade. We are all well.

The Liberator is now on its last quarter. It will be, on many accounts, hard for me to discontinue its publication; yet, for weighty reasons, I think it best to do so. On the 1st of January next, therefore, I expect to be free from all newspaper responsibility. What I shall do after that time, I do not yet know; but, doubtless, the way will be opened to me in due season. The cause of the freedmen will probably demand and receive my special advocacy for some time to come. Their cause is yet to experience many severe trials, and to excite great hostility at the South; but it must be vindicated at all hazards.

In closing the publication of the Liberator, I shall be able truthfully to say, (and I am not sorry for it as a test of my sincerity,) that it leaves me without a farthing laid up for my family derived from its subscription list, and aside from some generous donations made from time to time for our support—without which the paper could not have been continued. Though the pioneer sheet, and advocating the noblest cause in the world, and allowing all sides impartially a hearing, its subscription list has always been inadequate to meet the expenses involved in its publication. But a good Providence has stood by me from the beginning to the end, and thirty-five volumes will soon have been completed without the failure of a single number to make its regular appearance. My heart overflows with gratitude to the Giver of all good as I review the past, and I bless and praise his holy name. I have not trusted him in vain, for his promises have all been redeemed.

I am gratified to learn that you intend, ultimately, to make so generous and useful a disposition of the whole series of volumes in your possession.[4] They will certainly be valuable for historic reference hereafter in regard to our memorable and unequalled struggle.

The missing numbers you desire to complete your file shall be furnished, if practicable.

I am more than gratified, even delighted, to receive your photograph, and congratulate you that time has dealt so gently with you. Only think of it! It will be twenty five years since we saw each other, next summer!

Pray give my special love and tender remembrances to dear Eliza Wigham, and to the family.[5] They have been so true, so faithful, and so long consecrated to the anti-slavery cause, that my esteem for them is unbounded.

Dear George Thompson is residing in Boston, and will doubtless take this opportunity to send you a message of love. His match business is not yet remunerative, but he has done and will do well pecuniarily in the lecturing field.

Accept our household love. Adieu!

Wm. Lloyd Garrison.

ALS: Garrison Papers, Boston Public Library; a handwritten transcription of an extract is also preserved in the same collection.

1. John Nichol (1833–1894), the son of John Pringle Nichol by his first marriage, was in fact Mrs. Nichol's stepson. By the time of Garrison's letter Nichol had graduated from the universities of Glasgow and Oxford and been appointed to the new

chair of English language and literature at Glasgow, a post he was to hold until he resigned in 1889. He became a distinguished scholar and a minor man of letters.

2. Her residence in Edinburgh, where Garrison was to visit her in 1867. (*Life.*)

3. George Gordon, Lord Byron, *Childe Harold*, III, 1.

4. Mrs. Nichol intended her volumes of *The Liberator* to go to the library of the British Museum, which has the only complete set of the paper in England. (Anna M. Stoddart, *Elizabeth Pease Nichol*, London, 1899, p. 255; letter to the editor from Marjorie Simpson, information service, British Museum Library, August 7, 1973.)

5. Eliza Wigham is identified in the letter to Elizabeth Pease Nichol, April 10, 1863. Eliza's father, John Wigham (not to be confused with John Wigham, Jr. [1782– 1862], his cousin), had married Jane Smeal (died 1888), sister of William Smeal, of Glasgow, in 1840. After John Wigham's death in 1864, Jane Smeal Wigham and Eliza continued to live at 5 South Gray Street, Newington, Edinburgh, the Wigham home since 1819 and a social center for Friends, reformers, and students. Other family members included Eliza's sister Mary, who married Joshua Edmundson of Dublin, and her brothers, John, who was associated with his brother-in-law Edmundson's business in Dublin, and Henry, who also settled in Dublin. (Letter to the editor from A. Baillie, senior assistant, National Library of Scotland, Edinburgh, August 22, 1973, including photocopies of several pages from *A Brief Memorial to Eliza Wigham*. Although no date is given, the memorial was probably published shortly after her death in 1899.)

128

TO HELEN E. GARRISON

Thursday Morning, Oct. 12, 1865.

Dear Wife:

I have not had a moment to myself, since we parted, to sit down and pencil a letter to you till now; nor can I send you a long one, for I am to be immediately engrossed in the business of our Freedmen's Commission.

You will remember, perhaps, that our friend Mr. [James Miller] McKim, on leaving us last week, eulogized travelling by night in a sleeping-car as a perfect luxury.[1]Doubtless it may be so to one who becomes oblivious through unbroken sleep; but I found it so disagreeable that I shall not be in a hurry to try the experiment again. Lying down, I found the hearing much more sensitive to the rattle and roar of the train, and the constant oscillation of the car made the sensation very much like that experienced in a vessel at sea. Throughout the long night, (I "retired to rest" (!) at 9 o'clock,) I may have occasionally dozed for a few moments, but I had no sleep, and was glad to reach New York by six o'clock. Consulting Franky's plainly written direction where to find Mr. McKim, (34th street, East of 4th Avenue, No. 134,) and knowing that he would be waiting for me to take breakfast together, I took my valise, shawl and umbrella, and walked from 27th to 34th street, but found no 134; and so, concluding that it must be 24th street instead of 34th, I went

there, found 134, but not my friend, as he did not board there.—
(His boarding-place is 18th street, No. 134.) Despairing of finding
him, I took a horse-car, and went down to a restaurant in the Times'
building,[2] near the offices of the Independent and The Nation, and
took breakfast; then went to the office of The Nation, and after waiting an hour had the pleasure of embracing Wendell, who had been
detained by the boat later than usual. Soon after, McKim came in,
and stated that he was going to Philadelphia in the 10 o'clock train,
and wished me to accompany him. Wendell went down to the
depot with us. Of course, we had but little time for conversation beyond mutual inquiries as to Brooklyn and Rockledge. He was looking and feeling as well as usual.

On our way to Philadelphia we were detained nearly two hours,
in consequence of the disabling, first, of one engine—next, of another. On arriving in the city, McKim went to the Freedmen's
Rooms, and I to Germantown. Both Mrs. McKim and Lucy were absent, and did not return till late tea-time, not expecting us till the 10
o'clock night train. However, I told the colored girl who I was, and
got her to show me to my chamber, where I washed and rested a
little—feeling very empty about the stomach, not having had any
dinner, nor any opportunity to procure food. At tea-time McKim got
home, and wife and daughter soon after; and, of course, a very
pleasant time we had of it. You are always the first inquired after
wherever I go, and any encouraging word I can say in regard to
your improvement gives manifest pleasure. Say not, dearest, that it
is because you are my wife. All who know you love and esteem you
for your own good qualities; and they see and understand how
faithfully you have met your responsibilities as a wife and mother.

I believe the wedding-day for Wendell and Lucy is now fixed for
the 6th or 7th of December. It will be more convenient for me to
have the ceremony take place than at the close of the month, and,
therefore, I am glad of the alteration of time.

I shall bring you some of Mrs. McKim's nice sweet corn, which
she says you will know how to cook. At each meal we have had the
fresh sweet corn gathered from the garden, in the eating of which
you would have revelled. It is equal to anything Providence can
grow.

Yesterday we had two sessions of our Commission, and found
ourselves to be very united in spirit, and in the resolutions and testimonies we adopted. Bishop [Matthew] Simpson was with us
throughout. I am very much pleased with him—a sensible, modest,
straight-forward man. We are to have another meeting this forenoon.

Last evening we had a splendid meeting of four thousand persons at the Academy of Music, multitudes being unable to gain admission.[3] Addresses were made by Bishop McIlvaine, Bishop Simpson, Rev. Dr. Bellows, Rev. Henry Ward Beecher, and myself.[4] I was driven into a corner as to time, being the last speaker, and made a failure of it, I am quite sure. I never do half as well on a platform with others, as I do if I have a meeting entirely to myself. The meeting, as a whole, was a great success.

This afternoon I am going with the McKims to James and Lucretia Mott's, to take tea, and spend the evening. I saw Lucretia last evening at the meeting. She was looking very saintly, and as growing more and more fit for her heavenly translation. I expect to have a very pleasant time.

It has been bright weather ever since I left. I hope you have had some additional rain; but it is all right, whether it rain or shine.

A father's love to the dear children. A husband's love to you. Wherever I go, I carry you in the core of my heart. Adieu!

Yours, endlessly,

Wm. Lloyd Garrison.

ALS: Garrison Papers, Boston Public Library.

1. Although improvised sleeping cars were introduced on American railroads as early as 1836–1837, it was not until 1865, when George M. Pullman built "the Pioneer," a specially equipped car with upper and lower berths, that sleeping cars became popular. They were first used on a transcontinental journey in 1870. (*Dictionary of American History.*)

2. Garrison refers to the New York *Times* Building, an elegant five-story structure with plate-glass windows, marble floors, paneling, and frescoes, which had been finished in 1858 at the apex of the triangle formed by Park Row and Nassau and Beekman streets. (Meyer Berger, *The Story of the New York TIMES, 1851–1951,* New York, 1951.)

3. Four thousand people attended the meeting at the Academy of Music, held to inaugurate the American Freedmen's Aid Commission. Garrison spoke of the changes of the past fifteen years and urged the commission to go forward with its proposed plans. (*The Liberator,* October 20 and 27, 1865.)

4. Charles Pettit McIlvaine (1799–1873), originally from New Jersey and educated at both the college and theological school at Princeton, had been the minister of a series of parishes on the East Coast before 1831, when he was elected Episcopal bishop of Ohio and ex officio president of Kenyon College. Although an Episcopalian, he was also an evangelist and engaged in a number of tractarian controversies. He was the author of many books and pamphlets, including *The Evidences of Christianity in Their External Division* (1832) and *Oxford Divinity Compared with that of the Romish and Anglican Churches* (1841). He ventured into politics to the extent of unofficially representing President Lincoln in England in 1861.

Henry Whitney Bellows (1814–1882), a graduate of Harvard College and Divinity School, was for most of his life associated with New York City, where he became minister of the First Unitarian Church when he was twenty-four. A convivial man (he was, in fact, a founder of the New York Century, Union League, and Harvard clubs), he was a brilliant conversationalist and preacher as well as the author of various sermons and books. He was also involved in reformatory activities: he established Antioch College at Yellow Springs, Ohio; he reorganized his own Unitarian fellowship, founding the National Conference of Unitarian Churches in 1865; and he edited the *Christian Examiner* (1866–1877), emphasizing especially civil service reform.

129

TO JAMES MILLER McKIM

Rockledge, Oct. 15, 1865.

My dear McKim:

The passage from New York to Groton was made in good time, though the night was stormy, and I passed a very comfortable night in my state-room. I arrived home at 7 this morning, taking the household somewhat by surprise, and finding all well.

I deem it proper to submit to you, for your consideration and advice, what I find here in regard to my announced lecturing tour to the West.[1] (1) An invitation to lecture before the Ladies' City Mission Society at St. Louis, at $100.[2] (2) Another to lecture at Kansas City, Mo. (3) Another to lecture at Indianapolis. (4) Another to lecture at Vineland, N.J. (5) Another to lecture before the Allegheny Literary Society of Allegheny College, Meadville, Pa.[3] (6) Another to lecture before the Cleveland Library Association.[4] (7) Another to lecture before the Toledo Library Association.[5] (8) Another to lecture before the Young Men's Association at Chicago.[6] (9) Another to lecture at Warren, Ohio. (10) Another to lecture before the Encore Club at Quincy, Ill.[7] (11) Another (from S. J. May) to lecture at Syracuse—Mr. May promising to arrange for several other lectures in other places. (12) Another to lecture at Penn Yan.[8] (13) Another to lecture at Easton, Pa. (14) Another to Akron, Ohio—pledging one hundred dollars and expenses. (15) Another to lecture at Pittsburgh, one or more times. (16) Another to lecture at New Bedford. (17) Another to lecture at Ipswich, Mass. (18) Another to lecture at Princeton, Illinois. (19) Another to lecture at Richmond, Ill. Every mail is bringing similar overtures, and nearly all in consequence of the newspaper announcement of my intention to go West. You see, therefore, the dilemma in which I am placed by that announcement. Do not consider me unstable when I ask you what I ought to do in these circumstances. It is true, we agreed at New York as to our Maine and other meetings, and to consider the Western tour abandoned; but is it too late to recall that agreement, (as it has not been made public,) expecially if I attend the meeting at *Portland?*[9]

I find my pecuniary necessities such as to require me to do the best I can, pecuniarily, for some time to come, in the way of lecturing. Should I engage for the Freedmen's Commission, I should not feel it right to receive as much pay as I can probably get by lecturing independently, and *ad libitum;* and, therefore, in view of the stress laid upon me by the Liberator, in order to carry it through, I beg you to see Wendell [Garrison], (and Theodore [Tilton] and Oliver [Johnson] if you think best,) and confer as to the course I ought to pursue. You need no assurance from me as to the importance I attach to the Freedmen's educational cause, and of my profound and heartfelt interest in it; but I wish you to bear in mind that, even if I should go West, I should carry that cause with me, and support it (incidentally at least) both in public and in private, and so give it, perhaps, a considerable impulse. After the Liberator is off my hands, and the new year comes in, I shall then be absolutely free to work with and for the Commission—in England, if I go there, or at home, if I do not.

If such publicity had not been given to my going West by the leading journals of the country, and such interest awakened in it, every thing could be easily settled. Now, what shall I do, my dear friend? The case is in your hands. Turn it well over in your mind, and let me hear from you speedily. I will send no replies to the Western letters until I get your answer.

Your ever attached friend,

Wm. Lloyd Garrison.

J. Miller McKim.

ALS: Garrison Papers, Boston Public Library.

1. On his lecture tour to the West, Garrison spoke from four to six times a week for fees ranging from $25 to $100, with total receipts of $1,400. Among the places mentioned in this letter, he was able to speak at the following: Pittsburgh and Meadville, Pa.; Akron, Cleveland, and Warren, Ohio; Indianapolis and Richmond, Ind.; Chicago, Princeton, and Quincy, Ill.; and Syracuse, N.Y. In each place he apparently repeated the same lecture, "The Past, Present and Future of Our Country," urging local newspapers not to give a full report or transcription, since he planned to discuss the same topics elsewhere. In this speech he began with autobiographical recollections, recounting how he set out on his career as abolitionist facing brickbats and rotten eggs in Massachusetts and ended it "nearly smothered in flowers" in South Carolina. He went on to deny that abolitionists were responsible for the war, to attack Jefferson Davis, who, he said, deserved to be hanged, and to condemn Copperheads as followers of Satan. He pronounced the abolition of slavery the turning point in American history, and he predicted that the elimination of prejudice against blacks would be the inevitable accompaniment of equal civil and educational rights. At times his humor delighted the audience, as in Chicago when he discussed a southern traitor named Toombs ("Hark from the Toombs a doleful sound"). (Chicago *Tribune,* November 17, 1865; *AWT,* p. 302.)

2. Garrison probably refers to the Ladies Union Aid Society, which he may have confused with the City Mission House in the same city. (St. Louis city directories, 1864, 1865, 1866.)

3. The Allegheny Literary Society was founded on December 27, 1833. (Letter to the editor from Ann Winter, assistant librarian, Crawford County Historical Society, Meadville, Pa., July 13, 1973.)

4. The Cleveland Library Association (founded February 1848), a private library with reading rooms open to the public, sponsored lectures during the winter season. (Cleveland city directory, 1857–1859.)

5. Garrison probably refers to the Young Men's Association, a private library that sponsored lectures during the winter. (Toledo city directory, 1860.)

6. The Young Men's Association of Chicago (later called the Chicago Library Association) was a private subscription library, founded in 1841 and incorporated in 1851, that sponsored lectures. This organization apparently ceased to function after the fire of 1871. (A. T. Andreas, *A History of Chicago*, Chicago, 1884.)

7. The Encore Club has not been further identified.

8. Penn Yan (the name derived from "Pennsylvania Yankee," most of the early settlers being from Pennsylvania) is located in the Finger Lakes district of New York state, at the head of Keuka Lake and near Lake Seneca.

9. Garrison consulted with McKim about the meetings in Maine because of the latter's position as corresponding secretary of the eastern department of the Freedmen's Aid Commission, Garrison himself being first vice president. In fact, he did make both trips, leaving with McKim for Maine on October 24 (six days before his western trip); they visited Portland on October 24 and 26 and Bangor on the twenty-fifth. Garrison's speeches stressed the importance of immediately extending the rights of citizenship and education to the freedmen and of assisting them financially. In each city the speeches were followed by private meetings with prominent local citizens for the purpose of helping to organize local freedmen's societies. (*The Liberator*, November 3, 1865.)

130

TO MARIA WESTON CHAPMAN

Syracuse, Oct. 31, 1865.

Dear Mrs. Chapman:

I have just arrived here on my way to the West, and lose no time in doing what I tried to get time to do in person before leaving Boston—namely, to thank you, with an overflowing heart, and also your good son Henry, for your joint contribution of the generous sum of two hundred dollars in aid of the Liberator, and as a token of personal regard.[1] Your own kindness has been repeatedly shown in this manner, and therefore my indebtedness to you is of an accumulative nature. In other ways, by words of counsel and of cheer, how much I have been indebted to you, during a period of twenty-six years, I should find it difficult to express. Your friendship has been proved through every scene of adversity and trial, of combat and danger, and from it I have derived strength and inspiration. Be assured of my perpetual gratitude, even if I do not indulge in a multiplicity of words in thanking you.

In making your joint donation, I am sure it will be peculiarly gratifying to you and Henry to know that it could not have come at a more opportune period; for the increasing expenses of printing the Liberator for the past and present year,—much outrunning its enhanced subscription-price,—have largely exceeded its receipts; so that it has nothing to fall back upon, to complete the present volume, and therefore it is that I am absent from my post, when I am most desirous of being at it, in order to procure the means to enable me to print the additional numbers to the end of the year. I shall not regret that thirty-five years of editorial labor in the cause of the oppressed will leave me without a farthing derived from the subscription list of the Liberator.

But at no time, however severe the pinch or dark the hour, have I seen even a temporary failure of the prediction, "Trust in the Lord, and do good, and verily thou shalt be fed."[2]Most wonderfully have my needs been supplied, when I knew not where to turn, or how to continue the publication of the Liberator; all the more so as I have never asked a human being for assistance to enable me to prosecute my anti-slavery labors, or for any other purpose.[3] Surely, I have been led in a way that I knew not, and the mercies of God have never failed me. I have been kept from destitution, my dear wife and children have had what they needed for their comfort, and troops of kind and generous friends have volunteered to assist to the end of the conflict. Every thing we now have is of their giving, (all of it as unexpected as it has been impromptu,) and nothing derived from the income of the paper.

You will pardon this reference to the manner in which I have been led and sustained. It is to you, my dear and faithful friend, and to such as you, that I owe, under a gracious Providence, the continuance of my labors to "undo the heavy burdens, and to let the oppressed go free."[4] Now it is given to us to rejoice together in the fruition of our hopes and the fulfilment of our desires. It is not a triumph of persons but of principles, and we rejoice and give thanks, not as partisans or victors, but for our dear country's sake, and the cause of freedom and humanity throughout the world.

Whatever remains to be done to complete the sublime victory which has been achieved, and to secure to the freed people all that justice demands, I am sure we shall aim to do, "in the spirit of love and a sound mind."

Your grateful and attached friend

Wm. Lloyd Garrison

Mrs. Maria W. Chapman.

P.S. Please remember me affectionately and gratefully to Mary, and to all at Weymouth.[5] Will you increase my obligations by writing something for the Liberator while I am absent?[6]

☞ My son Wendell is to be married on the 7th of December and Fanny probably about the 7th of January.—December 10th will complete my 60th year.

Handwritten transcription: Garrison Papers, Boston Public Library.

1. Henry Grafton Chapman (1833–1883), son of Henry G. and Maria Weston Chapman, attended Boston Latin School and Heidelberg University. In 1855 he went to China as an officer on a merchant ship. The same year he began his career as a stockbroker with the firm of Ward, Campbell, and Company in New York City. By 1873 he was president of the New York Stock Exchange. He married Eleanor Jay (died 1921), and one of their children was John Jay Chapman, essayist, poet, and the author of a biography of Garrison. (M. A. DeWolfe Howe, *John Jay Chapman and His Letters,* Boston, 1937; Melvin H. Bernstein, *John Jay Chapman,* New York, 1964.)

2. Garrison telescopes Psalms 37:3.

3. The attitude toward finances Garrison expresses in this letter is typical, though one might question his statement "I have never asked a human being for assistance. . . ." It is true that he avoided directly asking for gifts, but he repeatedly sought loans not only for *The Liberator* but also to cover personal expenses, and it is not clear whether he paid back all the loans. Since during his early years as editor of *The Liberator,* Garrison was in chronic financial difficulty, in 1839 a committee of his friends (including Francis Jackson, Edmund Quincy, and William Bassett) assumed the debts of the paper and began supervising its finances. During the years 1839 to 1842, Garrison received loans from Francis Jackson, Samuel Philbrick, and George W. Benson to cover household expenses and the medical and funeral costs of his brother. Despite a trust fund of $2,289.79 set up for Garrison in 1849 and increasing fees from lectures, Garrison's unstable financial condition continued until the successful national testimonial in his honor in 1866–1867. (*AWT,* pp. 147, 181, 252; for a full statement about the testimonial see Introduction VI, "Retirement and Financial Security: 1866.")

4. Isaiah 58:6.

5. Mary Gray Chapman (c. 1798–1874), sister-in-law of Maria W. Chapman, was also active in the antislavery cause. (*Life.*)

6. A search of issues of *The Liberator* during Garrison's lecture tour (those for October 20–December 15, 1865) reveals no letters or articles by Mrs. Chapman.

131

TO HELEN E. GARRISON

Syracuse, Oct. 31, 1865.

Dear Wife:

I arrived at the dismal depot in this place, this morning, at 6 o'clock, in the midst of a cold, blustering rain-storm—the mud in some of the streets being almost knee-deep. Mr. Wise,[1] of Auburn, accompanied me as far as Albany, and then went to the Delavan House to find lodgings for the night.[2] I would gladly have done so too, but I did not dare hold over, not knowing whether a meeting had been advertised for me or not, this evening. I found Mr. Wise a very pleasant and intelligent gentleman, and we talked so much that the distance was measurably forgotten. Col. Tappan[3] left us at the Worcester junction. How the young boys grow up into Captains, Colonels, Generals, and the like! And the young girls, how they will grow up to be married! And the old folks, (of course, you and I are not in that category,) how they will persist in growing older and older!

I waited at the depot a full hour after my arrival, (walking backward and forward "like one distraught," the aspect of things looking grim and desperate,) before taking a hack for Mr. May's; and then I arrived before any of the family were up, excepting the servant-girl. I was in a state of bodily collapse, and my spirits quite flabby-dabby. Soon Mr. May made his appearance, and was equally delighted and surprised to see me. He was not expecting me till the noon train. I was immensely relieved in mind on finding that, in consequence of his absence to New York, and the political excitement of the State election, no meeting had been advertised for me.[4] Mr. May has a bad cough, which has troubled him a good deal for a month past, and which allows him scarcely any rest during the night. Charlotte's is a good deal better. (I did not forget the letter entrusted to me by Aunt Charlotte [Coffin].) The kindest inquiries were made after you and the children. I found Joseph and his young wife here, making a wedding-visit.[5] She is very pleasant and good-looking. They have had nothing but dismal weather since they have been here. "The course of true love," &c.[6]

To-day Mr. May attends a wedding and a funeral within three hours of each other. That is literally "from gay to *grave*."[7] But each event is as wisely ordered as the other.

Tell Franky I find a letter here from Mr. Caughey, at Erie, addressed to Mr. May, saying that their principal hall is pre-engaged for another purpose on Friday evening, and wishing to know if I cannot name some other evening not far distant, so as to ensure a good attendance.[8] If not, then they will take me for that evening, rather than not have a taste of my quality. I have just sent a telegram to him to postpone the lecture indefinitely. It will give me rest.

My travelling expenses will undoubtedly make a considerable hole in my receipts. At the Pittsfield depot they charged me thirty cents for two dough-nuts and a small cup of coffee. Think of ten cents a piece for dough-nuts! The hack-driver charged me one dollar to bring me up from the depot to Mr. May's house, though fifty cents should have amply sufficed. But he outfaced me, and said it was the regular price. "And that's the way the money goes."[9]

If Franky has the last Independent, (it was left on the dining-table,) I wish him to cut out Mrs. Child's letter on the first page, and hand it to Mr. [James B.] Yerrinton for insertion in the Liberator, next outside.[10]

After all, I came away, leaving my photographs. Enough for two stamps may be sent to me, in an envelope, at Detroit, Chicago, and Pittsburgh.

I did not take a sleeping-car at Albany, and had a hard night of it in getting through.

Your loving but jaded

W. L. G.

P.S. This evening I expect to see the Sedgwicks.—Let this week's Liberator be sent to me at Akron, Ohio.—I saw John and Lydia Spooner on the way to Springfield in the cars, she looking superbly.[11]

☞ Tell William to take twenty-six dollars from my Freedmen's fund, ⟦my travelling expenses to and from Bangor,⟧ if he needs it to meet my bills.

☞ A father's love and blessing to all the household of children.

ALS: Garrison Papers, Boston Public Library.

1. Not identified.

2. The Delavan House was a large hotel built on Broadway, Steuben, Montgomery, and Columbia streets in 1844; it was constructed in part on the site of the house of General Peter Gansevoort. Edward C. Delavan (1793–1871), who built and owned the hotel was a wealthy wine merchant turned temperance reformer. (Cuyler Reynolds, compiler, *Albany Chronicles: A History of the City Arranged Chronologically,* Albany, 1906, p. 557; George A. Worth, *Random Recollections of Albany from 1800 to 1808,* Albany, 1866, p. 45.)

3. Not identified.

4. There had been a Democratic convention in Albany on September 9 and a Union Republican convention in Syracuse on the twentieth, the latter having been somewhat disturbed by the question of Negro suffrage; and there had been various contests for state offices; but the political excitement in the state was hardly unusual. (DeAlva Stanwood Alexander, *A Political History of the State of New York,* New York, 1909.)

5. Joseph May and Harriet C. Johnson (born 1833), daughter of Philip C. and Mary K. Johnson and sister of artist Jonathan Eastman Johnson, were married in New York City on October 24 by Joseph's father, Samuel J. May. (Samuel May, Jr., et al., *A Genealogy of the Descendants of John May,* Boston, 1878; *The Liberator,* November 3, 1865.)

6. Shakespeare, *A Midsummer Night's Dream,* I, i, 134.

7. Alexander Pope, *Essay on Man,* Epistle IV, line 380.

8. Andrew Harvey Caughey (1827–1924) was educated at Erie Academy, Pa., studied law, and was admitted to the bar in 1851. He had a varied career as editor, teacher, principal of Erie Academy, and professor at Lafayette College, before studying for the ministry and becoming pastor of a Presbyterian church in Kingsville, Ohio.

Garrison in fact spoke at the First Universalist Church on November 3. (Letter to the editor from George S. Brewer, secretary, Erie County Historical Society, June 27, 1973.)

9. From the popular London ballad of the 1850s, "Pop Goes the Weasel," attributed to W. R. Mandale.

10. Lydia Maria Child's letter to Theodore Tilton, which attacks slaveholders and President Johnson, was printed in the *Independent*, October 26, and in *The Liberator*, November 10, 1865.

11. John Adams Spooner and Lydia Sylvester Spooner (died 1867) were the son and daughter-in-law of Bourne Spooner; see the letter to Helen E. Garrison, June 7, 1867, n. 3 for his identification. (William T. Davis, *Ancient Landmarks of Plymouth*, Boston, 1883, p. 249; FJG, June 3, 1867; obituary, *National Anti-Slavery Standard*, June 1, 1867.)

132

TO HELEN E. GARRISON

Syracuse, Nov. 1, 1865.

Dear Wife:

I remained in the house all day yesterday, as the walking was execrable and the weather stormy, but I got well rested, and this morning feel in very good trim. The day promises to be pleasant. I shall not go to Lockport until the morning. I have not yet done any thing toward jotting down points for my lecture, but shall do so in the course of the day; though I greatly fear my lecture will be a disappointment to those who hear it. I am always conscious of speaking less fluently, and less satisfactorily to myself, when I am speaking for pay than when I am not. Most happy shall I be when my tour is ended, and I am once more by your side, and under our household roof, where I would always be as a matter of choice. In the mean time, try to keep yourself very cheerful, and comfort yourself with the hope that I may be doing some little service in the cause of God and humanity, as well as procuring the means of subsistence. You have sustained yourself, thus far, in your crippled condition as a paralytic, with admirable resignation and patience; and I trust you will allow no feelings of sadness to depress you, but rather strive to look on the bright side. Your general health is so good that there is at least some ground for hope for the restoration of your limbs to their natural action; especially by a further use of the battery, under the appliance of Dr. [Joseph] Dow, if, on a renewed examination of your case, he shall express the same confidence in regard to it that he has done hitherto. But we will talk the matter over at length on my return.

As I have had no lecturing to do here, and shall not have at Erie and some other places originally laid down in my programme, I shall have less of a load to carry,—sufficiently heavy, nevertheless,—though my receipts will be proportionably less.

My travelling expenses will be much larger than I at first anticipated, but I shall get through as economically as possible.

After my bills are paid at home with what I may send to William from time to time, I want Fanny to be supplied to the extent of her needs, if possible, knowing that she will endeavor to buy nothing unnecessarily expensive or useless. I only regret I have not thousands to give her as testimony of my love, and as her marriage dower. Fortunately, Harry is abundantly able to provide for her as a wife, and will take delight in seeing that, as such, she lacks nothing conducive to rational enjoyment. It will be her duty to see that, in the excess of his generous desires, he does not spend his money too freely. Even "riches take to themselves wings, and flee away,"[1] and economy and forethought in the manner of living are virtues to be cherished, though for the hour we abound in prosperity.

I shall feel quite uneasy about the Liberator during my absence. Perhaps it may not be convenient for Mr. [Charles K.] Whipple to keep a general supervision over it, or he may be called out of the city. I hope [James M.] Winchell [Yerrinton] will be able to assist his father [James B. Yerrinton] in reading proof, &c., so that the typographical and other blunders may not be annoyingly multitudinous. Tell William, George and Franky to watch the papers, and see what may come, from day to day, desirable for insertion in the Liberator.

Should you wish to drop me a line on receipt of this, it may be sent to me at Cleveland, Ohio.

I am having a very pleasant time here with Mr. May, and Alfred and Charlotte, and the children,[2] and Joseph [May] and his bride [Harriet Johnson May]. They all send kind remembrances to you.

Carrying you all at home in my heart, I remain, dear wife,
Your ever faithful

W. L. G.

ALS: Garrison Papers, Boston Public Library.

1. Proverbs 23:5, adapted.
2. At the time of Garrison's letter four Wilkinson children had been born: Alfred (1858), Marion (1861), Josephine (1862), and Louisa Forman (1864); eventually there were nine children. (Samuel May, Jr., et al., *A Genealogy of the Descendants of John May*, Boston, 1878.)

133

TO HELEN E. GARRISON

Lockport, Nov. 2, 1865.

Dear Wife:

Last evening I went with Mr. [Samuel J.] May to spend it with the [Charles B.] Sedgwicks, and had a very pleasant time indeed— quite a number being present. We returned home at 11 o'clock, and at that time the moon and the stars were shining brilliantly. About midnight, the whole scene suddenly changed, and the heaviest storm of the season set in with immense violence, a perfect equinoctial gale. It blew so in the morning, that I at first came to the conclusion that I should have to remain, and give Lockport the goby. But I got down to the depot just in season to take the train, not having a minute to spare. It was a very dismal ride all the way to this place, and the weather looked very forbidding for an evening meeting. It, however, soon cleared up. I went to the hotel, dined, and "booked" myself, and waited for somebody to call upon me. But neither Mr. Helmer nor Mr. Gaskins was visible.[1] At tea-time a substitute for the former came, and stated that Mr. Helmer had been called away; that Mr. Gaskins had handed me over to Mr. H., and I was not to speak before the Young Men's Christian Association;[2] that the attendance would be very slim, almost a total failure, in consequence of the absorbing interest taken in the State election; that the Republicans were feeling shy of me, lest a friendly recognition by them should be turned against them by the Copperheads—&c., &c.

I have just returned from the meeting. There were a hundred or more present, chiefly females. The price of tickets was 30 cents— another drawback upon the attendance. The platform was far off from the audience, and the comparative emptiness of the house made every thing look cold and cheerless. I was occasionally applauded, but, to myself, my effort was very near a dead failure.

Under the circumstances, it is hardly probable that I shall get enough to pay my expenses. Nobody seems to be responsible, and, instead of realizing $75, I shall probably not get $20. Indeed, I know not what to ask, for the receipts will only cover expense of the hall, advertising, &c. The whole thing is a muddle and a failure. How could I speak with any zeal or interest thus situated? Nobody has called upon me; nobody spoke to me after the lecture; and I never was in a place so entirely devoid of interest and attraction. I shall leave it in the morning gladly. To-morrow evening I am to lecture in Erie; but I fear it will prove another flash in the pan, for the principal hall is occupied, and the people are all by the ears in regard to their pending election. My expenses will be much larger, and my receipts much smaller, than I calculated before starting. Lecturing is not to my taste.

Mr. May's cough gives me some anxiety for him. Every night it troubles him by its violence, being long protracted. He says it is the hardest he has ever had.

If it is possible, he will be very happy to unite Harry and Fanny in the bonds of wedlock. But I doubt, in view of his cough, whether he will be able safely to go to Boston for that purpose in January.

William can use $26 of the Freedmen's funds, for family expenses—that being the amount of my expenses to Maine with [James Miller] McKim. Perhaps I mentioned this in a previous letter.

I hope to have a line from you some where on my journey, and to learn that all is going on well at home. My thoughts, dear wife, are with you continually, and you draw strongly upon my sympathetic feelings. I shall be most happy to get back to Rockledge.

With love to all the dear children,

Ever tenderly yours,

W. L. G.

ALS: Garrison Papers, Boston Public Library.

1. The identity of Mr. Helmer is uncertain, although there were two doctors by that name (Josiah H. and A. M.) in Lockport at this time. (Letter to the editor from Charles H. Boyer, curator, Niagara County Historical Society, Lockport, N.Y., January 21, 1975.)

Mr. Gaskins remains unidentified. Since Garrison often mistakes names, it is possible Mr. Gaskins was actually Mr. Gaskill and that the man in question was Joshua Gaskill, a lawyer, or, less probably, Jedediah Gaskill, a dentist. There was a Thomas Gaskin in politics in Niagara Falls during the 1890s. (Letter to the editor from Charles H. Boyer, January 21, 1975.)

2. The Lockport YMCA was founded in 1861.

134

TO HELEN E. GARRISON

Meadville, Pa., Nov. 5, 1865.

Dear Wife:

When I was in Syracuse, Mr. [Samuel J.] May received a letter from Erie, stating that they could not get their public hall on Friday evening, and only a small meeting in a Universalist church, located at one side of the town, could be expected, and wishing to know if I could not give them some other evening. I telegraphed back to postpone the matter indefinitely; but, at Lockport, I received a telegram from them, stating that they would expect me to lecture in Erie, nevertheless, on Friday evening, though under adverse circumstances. On arriving at Erie, I found that I had left my trunk and valise at Buffalo, and therefore could have no change of clothes or linen! I was laboring under the delusion, (though having the checks in my pocket,) that my baggage had been checked from Lockport to Erie, instead of to Buffalo, and so gave myself no thought about it, though I had more than three hours of leisure on my hands at Buffalo. No telegraphing to Buffalo could avail me anything, for the checks must be sent back before the baggage would be delivered up. My only chance of getting it is at Cleveland, on Wednesday, as it can not overtake me on my present circuitous route. Here is a fix. I have had to buy me a shirt and some collars, to get me decently through this place, Warren and Akron, in the way of linen. Should I miss getting my things at Cleveland, I shall be in a straight indeed, as I shall be moving in advance all the time.

At Erie, I was hospitably entertained by Mr. Catlin, formerly editor of the True American, and gave my lecture to a small but select and respectable audience in the little Universalist church.[1] As the meeting was suddenly extemporised, and not in the regular course of lectures, the receipts were small. They paid me $25, and the same amount at Lockport—making one hundred dollars less than our original calculation. I expect this sort of luck in almost every place, and, therefore, my journey will prove far less remunerative than I had hoped. There is no help for it. Where the number present is hardly enough to cover the expense of hall and advertising, to exact $75 is altogether too trying for me; especially as all the parties are greatly disappointed at the result, and more expecially as I know my lecture is a very dull one, and not improved by its repetition.

I arrived here yesterday forenoon in an earlier train than was expected by those who invited me, and took a room at the hotel and had dinner; when I was called upon by Joshua Douglass, Esq., a prominent lawyer in this place, who kindly invited me to stay with him.[2] I accordingly paid my hotel bill, ($1.50,) and am now in his family, where I am very comfortably located, and receiving every attention. They are Unitarians. Mrs. D. is a very sensible lady, and a decided reformer. They have my lithographic likeness (the same as the one in our parlor) hanging upon the wall. I am lucky in making their acquaintance.

Lieutenant George Thompson Garrison,
between 1863 and 1865

William Lloyd Garrison, Jr.,
about 1863

Wendell Phillips Garrison,
1861

Garrison and
Fanny Garrison Villard,
about 1866

Francis Jackson Garrison, 1863

Helen E. Garrison,
about 1865

"Rockledge," 125 Highland Street, Roxbury

Last evening, I lectured to a small audience, in a hall dimly lighted, and never was more stupid in my manner, or more unsatisfactory in my talk. It was a dark stormy evening, alternately raining and snowing and, consequently, the walking very bad; for the mud is of the worst kind. I felt my effort to have been a dead failure, and no one said any thing to the contrary. The truth is, my lecture is crude and disjointed, and I have no time to recast it. It will cause general disappointment, I am quite certain; and that is the reason why I feel so about exacting $75, coupled with the knowledge that it must be paid by one or two individuals, owing to the slim attendance. What they will pay me here, I do not yet know. But I know that few places can afford to pay that price, even for the most popular lecturer. I am more and more disinclined to public speaking; and it always worries and annoys me when I speak for pay. How I long to get home!

To-day (Sunday,) the ground is covered with snow, and the air is filled with the swiftly falling flakes indicating an old-fashioned storm.

Tell William I received his letter and telegram in regard to Warren, Toledo, &c. A few minutes before, I had received a telegram from Warren, saying they would expect me to-morrow evening. Doubtless there will be a slim attendance there, on account of the state of the roads and streets. The next evening I am to be in Akron, and the next in Cleveland.

It is formidable to think of more than a month's absence from home from this date. Consider me by your side at all hours in spirit.

Nothing takes the life out of me in lecturing so much as to have a scattered audience remote from the platform, and a badly lighted hall, making "darkness visible."[3] It is strange that better arrangements are not made for giving a cheerful light on the occasion.

I got acquainted with Senator Lowrie, at Erie, a man of large wealth, a most radical abolitionist, and reminding me alike of Gerrit Smith and Charles Sumner, both in his looks and manners.[4]

I trust all is going well with you. If, for any good reason, I ought to be at home, let me know, and I will countermand the lectures in other places. With a heart brimming over with love for you and the dear ones, I remain,

Always and ever your own

W. L. G.

ALS: Garrison Papers, Boston Public Library.

1. The *True American*, a reform paper specializing in abolition and temperance, was published in Erie, Pa., between 1853 and 1861 or 1862. Henry Catlin, about

whom little is known, was the editor and proprietor of the paper by 1856. Garrison's lecture was apparently given in the First Universalist Church, which was built in 1844 and remained standing until late in the century. (*Nelson's Biographical Directory and Historical Reference Book of Erie County, Pa.*, Erie, 1896, p. 176; letter to the editor from George S. Brewer, secretary, Erie County Historical Society, June 27, 1973.)

2. Joshua Douglas, Jr. (1829–1906), whose name Garrison misspells, was born in Riga, N.Y., and died in Minot, Mass. He was a prominent Meadville lawyer and Republican. His second wife was Lavantia Densmore Douglas (1827–1899), whom he had married in 1853. (Letter to the editor from Ann Winter, assistant librarian, Crawford County Historical Society, Meadville, Pa., July 13, 1973.)

3. John Milton, *Paradise Lost*, I, 63.

4. Walter Lowrie (1784–1868), reared on his father's farm in Butler County, Pa., became prominent in state and then in national politics, rising from the state House and Senate to the United States Senate. He had been active for many years in the Presbyterian church, serving as secretary of the Board of Foreign Missions (formerly the Western Foreign Missionary Society) between 1836 and 1868.

135

TO HELEN E. GARRISON

Cleveland, Nov. 9, 1865.

Dear Wife:

I was greatly relieved in mind on receiving here a letter from you and Franky, informing me that all is going on well with you in the loved home circle. As often as you can intercept me with a line, without too great fatigue, do so.

At Warren there was a fair audience to hear me, but it would have been doubled but for the execrably muddy state of the streets. Judge Sutliffe, one of the signers of the Declaration of Sentiments, was indefatigable in his attentions to me while there.[1] He has a large brain, and an uncommonly clear and profound mind. He boards at the hotel,[2] being a bachelor.

At Akron I had a large gathering, and my lecture was evidently well received. I stopped at the Empire Hotel,[3] a large and well-conducted house, and was handsomely entertained by Mr. Brown, the landlord, whose estimable wife is the daughter of the late Judge Leicester King, of Warren, who was an eminent, and much respected, and early friend and advocate of the anti-slavery cause, and also one of the early patrons of the Liberator.[4] My hotel bill was settled by the Lecturing Committee, in addition to paying me $100. To-day I have sent a check to William, to the amount of $300, to be used as wanted, especially in getting our darling Fanny properly provided for her coming wedding-day. I should like to have her settle Mr. Endicott's bill out of it, as it was rather a delicate matter for me to ask him to give me an unlimited credit.[5]

Last evening I lectured to a crowded and most respectable audience, and was well received. I have sent William the Leader's notice of my address, and also an attack upon me by the Copperhead sheet here, the Plain-Dealer.[6]

I am stopping at the Weddell House, which is an immense affair, and conducted in an admirable manner.[7] Of course, the tables being loaded with every kind of food and fruit, the board is high. I was in hopes of receiving the hospitality of some who know me here; but it is naturally taken for granted that a professional lecturer will prefer to be at a hotel, where he can be freely called upon without interfering with domestic arrangements.

I have seen here Judge Spalding, an old anti-slavery coadjutor and a member of the next Congress—Prof. Thome—Mr. Coles, editor of the *Leader*—Mr. Peixotte, a bright and acute young man on the Lecturing Committee—Mr. Jacob Heaton, an old stanch friend, of Salem in this State—and several others.[8] Particularly have I been delighted to see my old and beloved friend Thomas Jones, and family, who so kindly took care of me while I was so desperately ill here nineteen or twenty years ago.[9] He and his wife are looking exceedingly well for their years, though he is somewhat lamed by his rheumatism. They have eleven children living, and nearly all married. He very kindly gave me a ride about the city this afternoon. It has doubled in size and population since I was here twelve years ago. Some of its avenues are of magnificent length and breadth—particularly Euclid and Prospect. It has the largest depot in process of building that I have yet seen in the country.

I am glad to hear that Harry is to be with you on Thanksgiving Day. It will be some compensation for my absence. But how I wish I could then be at home! I shall be in spirit, assuredly.

I am still receiving applications to lecture as I go along, but, of course, I cannot accept them.

Tell dear Franky I am greatly obliged to him for writing to me, and sending me the photographic cards. In the morning I start for Detroit. Angels guard you all! Good night!

W. L. G.

N. B. On going down into the parlor, to-day, at 2 o'clock, who should I see, sitting "solitary and alone," but dear George Thompson! The meeting was most unexpected to us both. He arrived in the city at 10 o'clock, this forenoon, expecting to go right on in the train for Buffalo and Syracuse, but lost the connection by a few minutes. He had come all the way from Pittsburgh, where he had given two lectures.[10] All the hours he was waiting below stairs, I was in my room, neither aware of the proximity of the other till I discovered him! We took dinner together, and he left for Buffalo in the 3.20 P.M. He was looking very well in the face, and feeling better in spirits than when he left Boston, though he misses a travelling companion, as I do. He has as many applications to lecture as he wants, and will do exceedingly well this winter, pecuniarily, should his strength hold out.

I would be glad to write something *en route* for the Liberator; but I am so constantly on the move in the cars, or so occupied in seeing people wherever I stop, that it is as much as I can do to find time to send you these almost illegible scrawls.

Thompson has promised to meet me at Pittsburgh on the 2d of December, where there is to be held a large Freedmen's Aid meeting.[11] Mr. [James Miller] McKim also intends being there at that time.

By the time I reach Philadelphia for the wedding on Dec. 6th, I shall probably be in a collapsed state of mind and body. But I shall try to be careful, though the temptation to lecture over-long is very powerful, in my anxiety to meet the many points that present themselves.

Remember me to Katy and Winnie. Frank may give my salute to the cat. Hope dear Ellie [Ellen Wright Garrison] is relieved of her neuralgia.

P.S. Fortunately, I found my trunk and valise safe at the Express Office here on my arrival, as sent from Buffalo.

ALS: Garrison Papers, Boston Public Library.

1. Milton Sutliff (1806–1878) had been an active abolitionist for many years, having, as Garrison says, signed the Declaration of Sentiments when the American Anti-Slavery Society was founded in 1833. A distinguished Ohio lawyer and politician, he had been active in 1848 in the Free-Soil party and in 1850 had been elected state senator. Seven years later he became a member of the Ohio Supreme Court. (Letter to the editor from Georgia R. Kightlinger, corresponding secretary, Trumbull County Historical Society, Warren, Ohio, July 4, 1973.)

2. Either the Gaskill House or the American House. (Letter to the editor from Georgia R. Kightlinger, July 4, 1973.)

3. The Empire House, located on Market Street between Howard and Main streets. (C. S. Williams, compiler, *Williams' Akron, Wooster and Cuyahoga Falls Directory*, Akron, 1859–60.)

4. Charles Brown (1814–1880), from Westmoreland, Vt., at one time a dealer in horses and cattle, was an elder in the Disciple Church. In 1842 he had married Julia A. King (born 1817). During the war he served as a private in the 125th Regiment. (Letter to the editor from Georgia R. Kightlinger, October 3, 1973.)

Leicester King (1789–1856), from Suffield, Conn., was one of the leading merchants of Warren, Ohio. He married Julia Ann Huntington October 12, 1814. Active in state politics, he was a promoter of the Pennsylvania-Ohio Canal, a member of the state legislature from 1833 through 1839, and the abolitionist candidate for governor in 1842 and for President in 1847. Between 1840 and 1842 he was a justice of the Ohio Supreme Court. (*Weld-Grimké Letters.*)

5. William Endicott, Jr. (1826–1914), from a distinguished Massachusetts family, was a graduate of Williams College, with an honorary master of arts degree from Harvard. He was a senior partner in the dry goods firm of C. F. Hovey & Company. For twenty-seven years president of the New England Trust Company, he held offices in various western railroads. (Obituary, Boston *Transcript,* November 7, 1914.)

6. Garrison refers to two Cleveland newspapers. The *Leader,* formed in 1854 by the merger of the *True Democrat* and the *Forest City,* was of free-soil and Whig persuasion; it supported Lincoln and the Republican party. The *Plain Dealer,* founded in 1842, was a Democratic paper, supporting Douglas, McClellan, and other members of the party. (Sidney Kobre, *Development of American Journalism,* Dubuque, Ia., 1969; Archer E. Shaw, *The Plain Dealer, One Hundred Years in Cleveland,* New York, 1942.)

7. The Weddell House, a fashionable Cleveland hotel erected in 1847, was one of the leading hotels in the West. (*The Western Reserve, the Story of New Connecticut in Ohio,* Indianapolis, 1949.)

8. Rufus Paine Spalding (1798–1886), a Yale graduate and a practicing lawyer, had served as associate justice of the Ohio Supreme Court, 1849–1852. He was a Republican member of Congress from 1863 to 1869. (*Biographical Directory of the American Congress, 1774–1971.*)

James Armstrong Thome (1813–1873), born in Augusta, Ky., was one of the antislavery rebels at Lane Theological Seminary; he subsequently graduated from Oberlin in 1836. He became an agent of the American Anti-Slavery Society and toured the British West Indies to observe the effects of emancipation there. After a decade as professor at Oberlin College (1838–1848), he became the minister of the First Congregational Church in Cleveland, a post he held for twenty-three years. Following the Civil War, on behalf of American freedmen he went on a mission to England and Scotland sponsored by the American Missionary Association. The final year of his life he was called to the ministry of a church in Chattanooga, Tenn. (*In Memoriam, Rev. J. A. Thome,* Cleveland, 1873.)

Edwin Cowles (1825–1890), whose name Garrison misspells, had been a resident of Cleveland since childhood. A printer by trade, his association with several printing firms included a partnership with T. H. Smead (1844–1853) and later with Joseph Medill and John C. Vaughn. Medill, Cowles & Company published a free-soil paper that became in 1854 the Cleveland *Leader,* of which Cowles shortly became owner and editor. In 1861 Lincoln appointed him postmaster of Cleveland. He was a determined Republican and supporter of Grant, Blaine, Hayes, and Garfield.

Benjamin Franklin Peixotto (1834–1890), whose name Garrison spells incorrectly, who was born in New York City, moved early in life to Cleveland, where he became of the editors of the *Plain Dealer* and a supporter of Stephen A. Douglas. For many years he was active in the Independent Order of B'nai B'rith, becoming grand master in 1863. In 1867 he moved to San Francisco to practice law. In 1870 President Grant appointed him consul to Bucharest, where he labored effectively for six years to oppose Rumanian anti-Semitism. He subsequently served as consul to Lyons, France. In 1886 he founded a Jewish periodical, *The Menorah, A Monthly Magazine.*

Jacob Heaton (1809–1888) was a dry goods merchant of Salem, Ohio, who had been a teacher and was active in developing the public school system. He was an abolitionist whose house was a station on the Underground Railroad. A member of the Free-Soil party, he was a delegate to the Pittsburgh convention in 1852. During the early days of the Civil War he became commissary of subsistence in the army. Following the war he formed an insurance agency in Salem. (Salem *News,* March 21, 1964.)

Garrison probably refers to Thomas Jones, the father of John Percival Jones, the future senator from Nevada. He and his wife, Mary Ann, emigrated from Herefordshire, England, to Cleveland, where he became a marble cutter. An abolitionist, he served as treasurer of Cleveland's Liberty Club in 1844. (See the letter to Helen E. Garrison, September 18, 1847, *Letters*, III, 528.)

10. Under the auspices of the Tennyson Club, George Thompson delivered two speeches, "From London to Calcutta" and "The Signs of the Times," on November 6 and 7 at the Masonic Hall in Pittsburgh. (Letter to the editor from Ruth Salisbury, assistant director and librarian, Historical Society of Western Pennsylvania, Pittsburgh, May 30, 1974.)

11. The Freedmen's Aid Commission of Western Pennsylvania held its anniversary meeting on December 2, 1865, at Lafayette Hall. Both Garrison and Thompson, as well as Hugh L. Bond of Baltimore, John R. Shipherd of Washington, D.C., and C. G. Hussey of Pittsburgh, spoke. (Pittsburgh *Daily Commercial*, November 30, 1865.)

136

TO HELEN E. GARRISON

Toledo, Nov. 10, 1865.

Dear Wife:

I left Cleveland this morning at 8 o'clock, (paying ten dollars for two days' board at the hotel,) and have just arrived at this place—1, P.M. As the train for Detroit does not leave till 3, I will pencil a few lines upon my knees for your perusal, though nothing has occurred to communicate since I wrote to you last night.

I should like to have lectured here, as it is a flourishing city of twelve thousand inhabitants; and yet, had they been able to arrange for a lecture this evening, I should be in a poor condition to deliver it; for my stomach is out of order, and I am suffering from colic pa[in]s. Last night I slept but very little, in consequence. I know not to what to attribute the producing cause, but think it must be owing to eating some poor ice-cream at dinner. I must fast to-day.

We are due at Detroit at 6 o'clock this evening. My lecture to-morrow evening is to be for the benefit of a colored association. Perhaps arrangements will be made for me to speak on Sunday evening, though I have advised to the contrary.

My dear friends, Dr. Owens and Thomas Chandler, (brother of the lamented Elizabeth M.,) of Adrian, have sent me the kindest invitation to share their hospitality on visiting that place on Monday next.[1] Also, friend Comstock, an old Liberator subscriber.[2] It will be very tantalizing to see them only a few hours, as on Tuesday morning I go to Hillsdale. I wish I had two or three spare days to spend with them.

You will remember that when I was last in Detroit, I could procure neither hall nor meeting-house in which to deliver an anti-slavery address. As my lecture there to-morrow evening will not be one of a regular course, I do not anticipate a large audience —probably more colored than whites.

The weather is a little raw, yet mild for the season. No snow is to be seen in any direction; yet every day makes its fall the more certain. I am content with bare ground.

The West is a mighty theatre for enterprise, labor, business of every kind. It is a vast empire in process of rapid development, and its capacity for growth and prosperity seems boundless. Every thing is in the gristle, but a solid and gigantic growth is sure. Our East is fossilized in contrast. We have gone to seed. Still, it is pleasant to see finished towns and villages, with repose and comfort.

You need not feel any concern about me. When I get to Detroit, I will get some hot drops or pain-killer, and trust I shall feel bright to-morrow.

Always your devoted and loving

W. L. G.

P.S. I wonder our friend Mr. [Wendell] Phillips did not feel like speaking at Lady [Mrs. George A.] Otis' funeral. It makes me the more regret at being absent.

☞ Detroit, 6 P.M. Just arrived much exhausted, and find to my dismay that my lecture is advertised for this evening, and another for to-morrow evening. Am doubtful whether my colic pains will enable me to get through the lecture.

*

11 P.M. Had a small and select but highly appreciative audience; among them Mr. Howard, U. S. Senator, & wife.[3] Spoke for two hours! Do not feel the worse for it. Was introduced to quite a number of ladies and gentlemen. Senator H. said he would call on me to-morrow. Was glad to see Giles B. Stebbins and his wife at the meeting.[4]

*

Nov. 11 Did not sleep much last night. Purchased a bottle of Davis's Pain-Killer, and feel better for taking it.[5] Have been with a friend, Mr. Myers, to see Rev. Dr. Durfee, with reference to the Freedmen's Aid Commission, & had a pleasant interview.[6] The meeting this evening will probably be better attended than that of last evening. Am to take tea, this evening, with the widow of the late William Buffum, of R. Island, a brother of Arnold.[7]

ALS: Garrison Papers, Boston Public Library.

　　1. Woodland Owen (born in 1819 and still living in 1879), whose name Garrison misspells, was an English dentist who emigrated to Rochester, N.Y., in 1842; by

1848 he had set up practice in Adrian, Mich. By the early 1850s he was active in the antislavery cause; many prominent abolitionists, including Henry C. Wright, Stephen and Abby Kelley Foster, and J. W. Walker stayed at his house. (See letter to Helen E. Garrison, October 10, 1853, *Letters,* IV, 266, n. 13.)

Thomas Chandler (1806–1881) was a Delaware farmer who moved to Adrian in 1830 with his sister Elizabeth M. Chandler (1807–1834). Both Chandlers were Garrisonian abolitionists, and Thomas was one of the founders of the Michigan Anti-Slavery Society in 1836. Miss Chandler was known for her antislavery verse, much of which was published in the *Genius of Universal Emancipation* and *The Liberator.* In 1836 Benjamin Lundy edited a posthumous volume of her verse, as well as a volume of her essays. (*NAW.*)

2. Garrison refers to Edwin Comstock, son of the Addison J. Comstock who founded the town of Adrian in 1828. (Mrs. Frank P. Dodge, "Landmarks of Lenawee County," Michigan Pioneer and Historical Society *Historical Collections,* 38:478–491, 1912.)

3. Jacob Merritt Howard (1805–1871), who was born in Bennington County, Vt., was graduated from Williams College in 1830. He practiced law in Detroit and served in Congress (1841–1843). Subsequently he became a Republican member of the Senate (1862–1871). As a senator Howard favored radical reconstruction; he drafted the first clause of the Thirteenth Amendment. In 1835 he married Catherine A. Shaw (died 1866).

4. Giles Badger Stebbins (1817–1900), whom Garrison first met at the Northampton Association of Education and Industry, apparently moved to Detroit in 1863. An abolitionist lecturer of some reputation, he toured with Abby Kelley and Stephen S. Foster in 1845. He was the author of a number of pamphlets and articles concerned with abolition, free trade, religion, and industrial education. His wife was the daughter of Benjamin and Sarah D. Fish of Rochester, N.Y., but remains otherwise unidentified. (Giles B. Stebbins, *Upward Steps of Seventy Years,* New York, 1890.)

5. The painkiller had been devised as a universal remedy in 1840 and patented in 1845 by Perry Davis (1791–1862), a shoemaker turned licensed minister, of Taunton, Mass. Owing to the business skill of Davis' son, Edmund (1824–1880), the medicine became very popular; it was even marketed on an international scale by Christian missionaries. That Perry Davis was a generous supporter of the Baptist church and a temperance advocate is ironic, considering the high alcoholic content of his patent medicine. (Stewart H. Holbrook, *The Golden Age of Quackery,* New York, 1959.)

6. Mr. Myers has not been identified, and no minister named Durfee has been found in Detroit. A Dr. Calvin Durfee, who had been a minister in Brooklyn, Ohio, in the 1850s, was at the time of Garrison's letter a resident of Williamstown, Mass., but there is no evidence that he was in the Middle West at this time. (*The Congregational Year-Book,* Boston, 1880.)

7. Ann L. Sheldon Buffum, American-born daughter of English parents, had been married to cotton manufacturer William Buffum (died 1865) of Smithfield, R.I. William was the brother of the better-known Arnold (1782–1859), a hatter turned abolitionist. He was the first president of the New England Anti-Slavery Society in 1832, a founder of the American Anti-Slavery Society in 1833, and a successful lecturer for the cause. He also founded in Fall River, Mass., experimental schools based on educational theories he had discovered on a trip to Europe. (David Buffum, *The Buffum Family in Rhode Island,* Newport, R.I., 1890, p. 18; Lillie Buffum Chace Wyman and Arthur Crawford Wyman, *Elizabeth Buffum Chace 1806–1899, Her Life and Its Environment,* Boston, 1914; *Two Quaker Sisters, From the Original Diaries of Elizabeth Buffum Chace and Lucy Buffum Lovell,* with introduction by Malcolm R. Lovell, New York, 1937, p. 39.)

1 3 7

TO HELEN E. GARRISON

Adrian, Nov. 13, 1865.

Dear Wife:

I arrived here yesterday afternoon from Detroit, and received warm greetings at the depot from my old friends Dr. [Woodland] Owen, Thomas Chandler, Jacob Walton, Edwin Comstock, Samuel Hayball, and others.[1] Last evening we had the best and largest audience I have addressed since I left home, all the seats in the spacious and beautiful church of Rev. Mr. Powell[2] being filled, and the aisles occupied with chairs and settees. I spoke for two hours, feeling in the right mood, and held the unbroken attention of all present to to the close. My Cleveland audience was a large one, but not equal to the one last night; and I had the intellectual and moral elements of the city and its surroundings present.

I am stopping with Dr. Owen, who has built him a handsome residence since I was here, in a charming locality. His wife is one of the brightest and pleasantest of women.[3] I had hoped to see her venerable mother—a very remarkable woman, in her way, with whom I was delighted when I was here twelve years ago—but she is a hundred miles away with one of her children, lying hopelessly ill, and Mrs. Owen leaves to-morrow to see the closing scene.[4]

Great was my joy to receive, at the hands of Rev. Mr. Powell, a letter from you, and another from William, in the same envelope. Yours was dated the 7th, and his the 8th inst. All the little details of home matters you send me are just what I want to get. I feel so happy to be assured of your own health, and that every thing goes along smoothly with you. As for dear Ellie, she has my warmest sympathies for her suffering condition, with her terrible neuralgic attacks, and trust her contemplated visit to Philadelphia will be such a change of atmosphere as to relieve her entirely. I hope she will be able so to arrange her visit as to be there at Wendell's and Lucy's marriage, as her presence on that occasion would be peculiarly gratifying to them.

My visit to Detroit did not nett me a penny. I lectured on Friday and Saturday evenings to three hundred persons—one hundred and fifty each evening, out of a population of sixty thousand people. But, fortunately, they were highly respectable, intelligent, and influential, and much gratified with my lectures. On Sunday evening, a considerable company met me at the Russell House,[5] to talk about the Freedmen's cause, and the interview will, no doubt, help to give a fresh impetus to that cause. I dined, that day, with Mr. Delany, a young married man, a nephew of Cyrus McNeally and wife, of Ohio, old anti-slavery friends; and in the evening took tea with the estimable widow of the late William Buffum, of Rhode Island, (brother of Arnold,) and their daughter.[6] On Saturday, I called on the leading Orthodox clergyman, Rev. Dr. Duffield, and had a pleasant interview, chiefly with reference to the Freedmen's Aid Commission, of which he is a member.[7] The next day I received a letter of introduction to him, through the mail, of our Mr. [James Miller] McKim at New York.

On Sunday afternoon, I addressed the colored Sabbath School in the Baptist church of which Rev. Mr. Chase, an excellent white man, is the pastor.[8] One of the scholars was ninety years of age. At the close of the meeting, she came forward, and gave me her benediction.

I received $25 for my two lectures at Detroit—paid $14 at the hotel, $5.50 to get from Cleveland to Detroit; and the same to get me back to that place would, as you see, leave me nothing. The hotel bills average $5 a day, (with fire,) to say nothing of the expense of railway travelling. But I blame no one at Detroit, in view of all the circumstances. Artemus Ward lectured to an immense audience the same evening—Charles Kean and his wife acted before another—&c.[9] Then, Friday evening is the evening universally reserved for religious weekly meetings; and Saturday evening is no time to get people together.

Mrs. [Giles B.] Stebbins came with me from Detroit to visit the Owens.

I leave this afternoon for Hillsdale, to lecture there this evening. I feel better than I did at Detroit, but necessarily somewhat worn. My voice holds out remarkably in spite of my incessant talking; yet I fear it will utterly give out. The weather for a week has been superb—glorious—the true Indian summer.

Farewell, dearest!

W. L. G.

P.S. I am obliged to Willie [Garrison] for his letter. You are all with me, every step of the way. How I long for home! Yet I am now having a most pleasant time.

ALS: Garrison Papers, Boston Public Library.

1. Jacob Walton (born 1818 and still living in 1887) moved from Buckingham, Pa., to Saline, Mich., in 1834 and to Raisin, Lenawee County, in the same state, in 1851. A farmer by occupation, he was also a politician, serving in 1869–1870 and 1873–1874 as a Republican representative in the state legislature. (*Michigan Biographies . . .*, Lansing, 1924, II, 402.)

Samuel Hayball has not been identified.

2. Not identified.

3. Garrison refers to Jane Parton Illenden (or Illendon) Owen (1822–1902). (John I. Knapp and Richard I. Bonner, *Illustrated History and Biographical Record of Lenawee County, Michigan*, Adrian, Mich., 1903.)

4. Sarah Grant Illenden (1782–1866), who was English by birth, had married Richard Illenden in 1805. The family, including eight children, moved to Pembroke, N.Y., in 1830. At the time of her death Mrs. Illenden was with her son Richard Illenden, II (born 1824), a farmer of Three Rivers, Mich., who was an active abolitionist and the treasurer of the Michigan Anti-Slavery Society. (W. A. Whitney and Richard I. Bonner, *History and Biographical Record of Lenawee County, Michigan*, Adrian, Mich., 1879, pp. 342–345, 503–505.)

5. Detroit's leading hotel, which opened in 1857. (Frank B. Woodford and Arthur M. Woodford, *All Our Yesterdays: A Brief History of Detroit*, Detroit, 1969.)

6. Mr. Delany and the Cyrus McNeallys have not been identified.

The William Buffums had two daughters, Anne Vernon Buffum (born 1825) and Mary Lee Buffum (born 1830); it is not known which daughter was in Michigan at the time of Garrison's visit. (Lillie Buffum Chace Wyman and Arthur Crawford Wyman, *Elizabeth Buffum Chace 1806–1899, Her Life and Its Environment*, Boston, 1914, 321; David Buffum, *The Buffum Family in Rhode Island*, Newport, R.I., 1890, p. 33.)

7. George Duffield (1794–1868) was a brilliant and uncompromising Presbyterian minister. A graduate of the University of Pennsylvania at seventeen, he was ordained as minister of the Presbyterian church in Carlisle, Pa., at twenty-two. From this post he was dismissed in 1835, owing to a controversy over his puritanical principles and especially his theology as expressed in the book *Spiritual Life: or, Regeneration* (1832). After several brief ministries he was called to the Protestant Church (now the First Presbyterian) in Detroit, where he remained for thirty years, becoming one of the leaders in the New School of Presbyterian theology and a prolific publisher of sermons and books on theological subjects.

8. Supply Chase (1800–1887), originally from Guilford, Vt., served in Detroit between 1861 and 1874 as minister of the Second Baptist Church (incorporated in 1839 as the city's first black church). (Letters to the editor from Alice C. Dalligan and Noel Van Gorden, first assistants, Burton Historical Collection, Detroit Public Library, August 11, 1973, and July 8, 1975; Woodford and Woodford, *All Our Yesterdays*, p. 156.)

9. Charles Farrar Browne (Artemus Ward), 1834–1867, of Waterford, Me., became a printer and editor before discovering his bent as humorist. While still in his teens, Browne went west, eventually settling in Cleveland, where he worked for the *Plain Dealer*. The success of the whimsical fictions published in that paper under the name Artemus Ward led him to New York City, where he had more abundant opportunities for invention in the pages of *Vanity Fair*. He published several successful books, but his great popular success came through lectures throughout the United States and in England. He died of consumption at the height of his spectacular British lecture tour.

Charles John Kean (1811–1868), the son of English tragedian Edmund Kean, was more popular in the United States than at home. He made his English debut in 1827 and his American in 1830 in *Richard III*. After their marriage in 1842, he and Ellen Tree Kean (1805–1880) appeared repeatedly together in a great variety of plays. They gave their farewell performances in Shakespearean and classical tragedies at New York's Broadway Theatre in 1865.

138

TO HELEN E. GARRISON

La Porte, Nov. 16, 1865.

Dear Wife:

Before leaving Adrian, I had a ride through the place and its suburbs with Rev. Mr. Powell, (who constantly reminded me of Theodore Tilton,) and Dr. [Woodland] Owen and his wife, and Mrs. [Giles B.] Stebbins. The weather was mild and beautiful, and we all enjoyed ourselves exceedingly. My visit there, though all too brief, was pleasant indeed.

At Hillsdale, I was invited by President Fairfield, of the flourishing college there, (some four or five hundred students, young men and young women,) to stop with him; but as I had to get up at 5 o'clock the next morning, to take the train for this place, I did not like to disturb the family.[1] I therefore took tea with him, and found him a very social and genial spirit; and after the delivery of my lecture, I went to the hotel, and took a bed—the landlord saying that if I would give him a card photograph of myself, he would consider his bill squared.[2] I did so readily, and much to his satisfaction, though probably nothing but my notoriety led him to desire the picture. I had a large number of the students to hear me at Hillsdale, and spoke two long hours, to my dismay when I looked at my watch. But the attention of the audience was fixed and unbroken from beginning to end, and they frequently applauded the sentiments; though my lecture is too serious, as a whole, to make loud applause either proper or desirable. Hillsdale is a handsomely located village of some three or four thousand inhabitants, and full of promise as to its future growth—as, indeed, most of these Western towns are.

I arrived here a good deal jaded, and somewhat hoarse, yesterday forenoon, and was cordially met at the depot by Rev. Mr. Ash, Rev. Mr. Noyes, L. Crane, Esq., and other gentlemen, but went at once to the hotel to get a little rest.[3] After dinner, Mr. Noyes took me to see their new school-house, which is nearly completed, and which is almost equal in size and architectural taste to any one we have in Boston. On ascending to the cupola, an immense and very charming view of the place and country was obtained, though, in consequence of the level character of the land as far as the eye could reach, presenting little that was picturesque, except three small but beautifully clear lakes, from each of which small boats can pass to the other through a narrow passage, or by being lifted across a few feet of land.[4] Mr. Crane, Rev. Mr. Ash, Mr. James Craig,[5] (who had come from Lima over a hundred and twenty miles to hear me lecture, an old subscriber to the Liberator,) and myself road for two hours through and around La Porte, its Lakes, &c., and nothing could be more enjoyable of the kind. The day was the finest of the fine, like summer itself in June. The Indian summer has been in all its glory for a week past, and still continues.

The large hall,[6] last evening, was filled with the "cream" of the place, notwithstanding the tickets were fifty cents, and again I was tempted to speak two hours long, unwittingly, but it was apparently no trial of their endurance, for they seemed deeply interested throughout, and it was impossible for better attention to have been given. Some four or five went out not long after I had begun, but they were doubtless copperheads, as this place is barely loyal in the matter of parties. I am quite sore about the lungs and very hoarse this morning, and in no condition to speak this evening at Chicago, as I regret to know I must, according to an announcement in the Chicago papers. I wanted to be in the best trim when I spoke there. But I am glad to see it stated that I shall only speak to night there, and so shall have nearly four days in which to recuperate before I lecture at Princeton. Still, there is little rest for me— there being so many to see, and to talk with. If I can only get through without breaking down, how fortunate I shall be!—for I have undertaken to carry a very heavy load, in my wish to get something to keep our pot boiling.

I should like to have Franky pay Seaver what is due for my photographs—three dozen, according to my reckoning.

At Chicago, I shall make another remittance to William, out of which let him settle with Curtis for Franky's clothes and my own.[7] I distribute his business circular as I go along. There are not so many sheep in this region as elsewhere.

I have been requested to lecture at Jacksonville on Thursday evening, 23d inst., and have promised to do so if Mr. Herndon has not made an appointment for me that evening at Springfield.[8] I shall know definitely about it, either at Chicago or Quincy.

How generous and opportune was our friend M. G. Chapman's gift to Fanny! I will thank her for it when I get home, though, of course, Fanny has already done so.

I leave here at 11 o'clock, and expect to be in Chicago at dinner time, where I shall expect to get tidings from home. I trust all is well with you all.

I travel so fast that I do not know what the papers say of me, from place to place, except in a few instances. Enclosed are one or two notices.

A father's love to the children—a husband's to you. Adieu, dearest!

W. L. G.

ALS: Garrison Papers, Boston Public Library.

1. Edmund Burke Fairfield (1821–1904) was a graduate of Oberlin College and Seminary. In 1849 he went to Spring Harbor, Mich., to become president of Free Baptist College, which moved to Hillsdale in 1853 and changed its name to Hillsdale College. During his tenure he was active in state politics, serving as state senator (1857) and as lieutenant governor (1859). In 1875 he became president of the normal school in Indiana, Pa., and the following year chancellor of the University of Nebraska, but resigned in 1882 when his fundamentalist views were challenged by several members of the faculty. During his later years he was minister of two Congregational churches (one in Mansfield, Ohio, the other in Manistee, Mich.) and United States consul to Lyons, France (1889–1893).

2. Probably Garrison stayed at the Smith House, but the landlord has not been identified. (Letter to the editor from Sarah Dimmers, president, Hillsdale County Historical Society, September 15, 1973.)

3. Garrison mentions three community leaders who were active in founding a town library. J. P. Ash, minister of the Baptist Church, was the corresponding secretary of the library; George C. Noyes, a Presbyterian minister, took the initiative in founding it; and L. Crane, a Unitarian, became its president. (Letter to the editor from Madeline G. Kinney, curator, La Porte County Historical Museum, La Porte, Ind., January 11, 1974.)

4. The La Porte area includes several beautiful lakes, which provided quantities of clear ice for the Chicago market.

5. Not identified.

6. Huntsman Hall, built in 1854 and destroyed by fire in the 1870s. (Letter to the editor from Madeline G. Kinney, January 11, 1974.)

7. John Curtis, Jr., is listed in various Boston directories, beginning in 1842 and ending in 1888, as being in the clothing business. In 1853 he was associated with G. P. Atkins and in 1877 with Walter Brooks & Company.

8. William Henry Herndon (1818–1891) of Illinois had been an abolitionist since the 1830s. In 1844 he became the junior law partner of Lincoln, doubtless having some influence on Lincoln's knowledge of and perhaps his attitude toward the antislavery movement. Although Herndon himself had a modest political career as mayor of Springfield and as state bank examiner, he is remembered by posterity chiefly for collecting anecdotes about his famous partner and for publishing the three-volume *Herndon's Lincoln: The True Story of a Great Life* (1889), source of the romantic story of Lincoln and Ann Rutledge.

139

TO HELEN E. GARRISON

Chicago, Nov. 17, 1865.

Dear Wife:

I arrived here yesterday (a thousand miles from home!) at 1 o'clock, expecting to see some one at the depot to receive me; but I was disappointed, and not a little taken aback. However, I drove to 247 Michigan Avenue, not knowing whether the name of the gentleman who invited me to his house before I left Boston was Paine or Freer. So, when the young man who opened the door for me was cautiously asked by me who lived there, he replied, "Freer"— which, of course, made my perplexed mind freer, and settled the name of my entertainer. Mr. Freer and his wife were formerly of Port Byron, N.Y.; but, for thirty years past have resided here, bringing up a family of eight children, who are all at home, and living in handsome style on the most desirable avenue in the city, fronting the glorious Lake Michigan, which from my window presents as boundless a sea-view as the Atlantic ocean.[1] They are old and thorough abolitionists, and disposed to do every thing in their power to make my visit here agreeable. He is a quiet, thoughtful, sensible man, and I am glad to make his acquaintance.

Laboring under great bodily debility, and being very hoarse, I trembled, on going to the hall last evening, lest I should fail to make myself heard, or even should utterly break down; but I spoke for nearly two hours, (you see how incorrigible I am!) holding the audience—the largest I have yet had, and highly intelligent and respectable—in rapt attention, broken by applause, throughout. At the close, the platform was thronged with persons, of both sexes, eager to take my hand and be introduced to me—among them several of the clergy of the city. It was some time before I could get through with the introductions. The persons were chiefly from New England. Among them were Mr. and Mrs. Doggett, (with whom I am to stop Saturday and Sunday,) and Mrs. Currier, the medium, the particular friend of Dr. Dow and his wife, who is recently from Maine.[2] Also, a son of my old friend, George W. Stacy, of Milford, who is a clerk at the Madison House.[3] Also, Rev. Mr. Hammond and wife, who have just made me a visit here.[4] She is the sister of the lamented Owen Lovejoy. He was a student at Oneida Institute more than thirty years ago, under Beriah Green and John Frost, and an abolitionist from the start.[5]

I have also had a call from James Long, Esq.,[6] an old settler and a firm abolitionist, who recalled his acquaintance with me as long ago as 1829, when he met me and Whittier at Rev. Mr. Collyer's in Boston.[7] He is a much esteemed citizen.

Chicago outruns my highest anticipations. With a great deal that is embryotic, rough, unfinished, cheaply built, it contains edifices which, in point of size, architectural taste, and magnificence, will compare favorably with the finest in Boston, New York or Philadelphia. It has a population nearly as large as that of Boston; yet, when I commenced the Liberator, Chicago had scarcely a house or an inhabitant, and gave no sign of ever having an existence in the future! Most of the palatial residences have been erected by those who came here without any pecuniary means. I am overwhelmed with astonishment when I see what has been done in so short a time.

Though I requested the reporters of the daily presses here to give only a very brief abstract of my lecture last night, they (the Republican, Tribune, and Times) publish all its salient points—the Copperhead sheet, the Times, making a very full report—much to my confusion; for as all those papers have a wide and extended circulation in this western region, I shall be repeating to audiences, for the remainder of my trip, what they (or at least very many of them) will have previously read; and so it will be trite indeed.[8] It is too bad to be served in this manner, especially after you have requested not to be reported at length, and when it is known that the lecture is to be substantially repeated in other places. But there is no help for it now.

I was glad to be introduced to the audience by Rev. Robert Collyer, who has recently returned from Europe, and who is to dine with me to-day, and with whom I am to take tea to-morrow evening.[9] He urges me to occupy his desk on Sunday, but I must resolutely decline, much as I should like to gratify him. My hoarseness is of that kind that will probably cleave to me during the remainder of my tour, as I am kept talking incessantly; and the weight of my lecturing is yet to come upon me.

The weather still continues perfectly glorious, and as mild as summer. Every day I am looking for a sudden and violent change. Chicago must be a very undesirable place in cold, wet, stormy weather, its location is so low and flat, notwithstanding it has been graded several feet high. I trust it will remain fair until I leave it. To-morrow I shall particularly devote to seeing it. It has some very wide and fine avenues, but not quite equal to those in Detroit. Every thing at the West is on a huge and generous scale.

My heart bounded on finding here, awaiting my arrival, a letter from you—another from Fanny (for which special thanks for special reasons—tell her I agree with her as to her view of the matter)—another from William—another from Franky—and another from Wendell. Was I not a happy father and husband?

I am relieved to hear that the Liberator affairs are managed without any difficulty. I wonder how back payments are coming in. No doubt Mr. [Robert F.] Wallcut will try to do his best to collect what is due. No doubt a considerable amount will be lost.

If Henry C. Wright calls again, give him my affectionate regards, and tell him I am frequently meeting with those who kindly inquire after him.

Wendell apprises me that the wedding day is definitely fixed for December 6th. That will be the day, I think, on which the Declaration of Anti-Slavery Sentiments was duly signed in that city thirty-two years before. How deeply do I regret that you will not be able to be with us on the occasion.

Give my loving regards to Charlotte Coffin, Mr. and Mrs. [Daniel] Thaxter, Mrs. [Thorndike] Jameson, Georgina,[10] &c., &c.

Ever thine,

W. L. G.

P.S. If dear Harry is with you, tell him I have seen and been welcomed by Mr. White[11] and others of the Tribune.

ALS: Garrison Papers, Boston Public Library.

1. Lemuel Covell Paine Freer (1813–1892) and his wife, Esther Wickes Marble Freer (died c. 1875), settled in Chicago in 1836, where Freer became both a lawyer and a master in chancery, as well as a conscientious abolitionist. During the period of rapidly rising land values, he specialized in real estate law and amassed a considerable fortune, becoming one of Chicago's leading citizens. In 1878 he married Antoinette Whitlock. (Paul Gilbert and Charles Lee Bryson, *Chicago and Its Makers*, Chicago, 1929, p. 619.)

2. Garrison probably refers to William E. Doggett (1820–1876) and his wife, Kate Newell Doggett (c. 1828–c. 1884). Doggett was a merchant in dry goods and foodstuffs, and vice president of the Merchants' Savings, Loan and Trust Company and of the Chicago Mercantile Association. He was a supporter of the Chicago Christian Union, which was founded to aid young men unemployed as a result of the fire of 1871, and was one of the sponsors of the Inter-State Industrial Exposition in 1873. Mrs. Doggett was elected to the the Academy of Science in 1869; in November of the same year she served as a delegate from the National Woman Suffrage Association to the Frauen Konferenz in Berlin. She wrote for the *Agitator,* the woman's rights newspaper, and was also one of the founders of the fashionable Fortnightly Club in 1873. Mrs. Doggett translated into English Charles Blanc's *The Grammar of Painting and Engraving* (Paris, 1867). (Louise Bessie Pierce, *A History of Chicago*, New York, 1957; Samuel Bradlee Doggett, *A History of the Doggett-Daggett Family*, Boston, 1884, pp. 505–506; *National Union Catalog, Pre–1956 Imprints;* Chicago city directory, 1864.)

Extensive search has not revealed the identity of Mrs. Currier.

Dr. Dow's wife was Eliza F. Dow (c. 1819–1880). At her death she left a thirteen-year-old daughter. (Letter to the editor from Nathaniel N. Shipton, manuscript curator, Rhode Island Historical Society, December 15, 1971.)

3. Theodore E. Stacy has not been further identified.

The Matteson House (misspelled by Garrison "Madison House") was a five-story brick hotel opened in 1851 on the northwest corner of Randolph and Dearborn streets. After being destroyed in the fire of 1871, it was rebuilt at another location and continued until the 1880s to be one of the best hotels in Chicago. (A. T. Andreas, *History of Chicago*, Chicago, 1884; Pierce, *A History of Chicago*.)

4. Henry Laurens Hammond (1815–1893) was a well-known Chicago Congregational minister and theologian; he married Elizabeth Gordon Pattee Lovejoy (born 1815). (Edward Magdol, *Owen Lovejoy: Abolitionist in Congress*, New Brunswick, N.J., 1967; letter to the the editor from Neal J. Ney, assistant reference librarian, Chicago Historical Society, June 27, 1973.)

5. Oneida Institute (organized in 1827 and incorporated in 1829) was a manual labor school in Whitesboro, N.Y., founded to educate young men intending to enter the ministry. It became a controversial center for revivalist reform and received national publicity for the radical abolitionist views of such men as Beriah Green, who was president between 1833 and 1843 (the year the institute was discontinued), and John Frost (1783–1842), supporter of Charles Grandison Finney and one of the institute's founders. Frost was a delegate to the founding convention of the American Anti-Slavery Society in 1833 and was an officer of the American Society for Promoting the Observance of the Seventh Covenant. (Louis Filler, *The Crusade Against Slavery, 1830–1860*, New York, 1960; Robert S. Fletcher, *A History of Oberlin College*, 2 vols., Oberlin, Ohio, 1943; *National Union Catalog, Pre–1956 Imprints*.)

6. Not further identified.

7. William R. Collier (1771–1843), whose name Garrison misspells, was the Baptist minister and publisher of the *National Philanthropist*, whom Garrison had known when Collier was the editor of that paper. Subsequently he edited the *American Manufacturer* and ran a boarding house, where John Greenleaf Whittier boarded while he worked for the paper. (*Life.*)

8. Of the three papers mentioned by Garrison only the *Tribune* has been previously identified. The Chicago *Republican* (published between 1865 and 1872) was a protectionist Republican paper. The Chicago *Times* was published between 1854 and 1895; it later merged with the *Herald* to become the Chicago *Times-Herald* and subsequently the Chicago *Herald and Examiner*. Consistently opposed editorially to the Chicago *Tribune*, the *Times* was staunchly Democratic. After a long summary and quotations, this paper characterized Garrison's speech in the issue for November 17, 1865, as a "rehashing of a large number of dull platitudes and stale nothings, which in the present day had lost their applicability and force." (Andreas, *History of Chicago*; Phillip Kinsley, *The Chicago Tribune, Its First Hundred Years*, 3 vols., New York, 1943–1948.)

9. Robert Collyer (1823–1912) emigrated from England in 1850. He became a lay Methodist preacher and later a Unitarian, moving to Chicago in 1859 to become minister-at-large at the First Unitarian Church and then minister of the Unity Church on the North Side. He was also an active abolitionist. Collyer remained in Chicago until 1879, refusing calls to a number of leading churches in Boston, Brooklyn, and New York City, though he ultimately moved to the Church of the Messiah in New York. He was a distinguished lecturer and the author of several books.

10. Georgina may have been Mary Amy Georgina Otis (1823–1908), an unmarried daughter of Lucinda Smith and George Alexander Otis. (William A. Otis, compiler, *A Genealogical and Historical Memoir of the Otis Family in America*, Chicago, 1924.)

11. Horace White (1834–1916) became city editor of the Chicago *Evening Journal* soon after graduating from Beloit College. In 1854 he moved from that post to become correspondent for the Chicago *Tribune*, for which he reported the Lincoln-Douglas debates. During the war he was that paper's Washington correspondent, and with his good friend Henry Villard and others he organized a news agency competitive with the Associated Press. Following the war he became editor of the Chicago *Tribune*, a post he held until 1874. In 1877 he became associated with

Villard in various railroad operations. When Villard purchased *The Nation* and the New York *Evening Post* in 1881, White, Carl Schurz, and Edwin L. Godkin were recruited to develop and run them. In 1899 White became editor of the *Evening Post*. In addition to being a journalist and an executive, White was a distinguished Greek scholar and economist; his *Money and Banking, Illustrated by American History* (1895) remained a popular textbook into the 1930s.

140

TO JAMES MILLER McKIM

Chicago, Nov. 17, 1865.

My dear McKim:

I received your letter addressed to me at Detroit, enclosing an introductory note to Rev. Dr. Duffield. I had previously called upon him, and spent a pleasant hour with him; but I sent him your note, with a line, as it contained a friendly reference to Mrs. D.[1]

I spoke twice in Detroit to small but very intelligent and respectable audiences. The evenings (Friday and Saturday) proved very inauspicious, as I did not lecture for any Society, and particularly as I had to compete (in addition to the weekly religious meetings) with "Artemus Ward," and Charles Kean and his wife, the actors. I only received enough to pay travelling expenses, but I trust my lecture concerning the Freedmen's cause will give it a fresh impulse in that city. I had a private and satisfactory meeting on the subject, at the Russell House, of some estimable men and women, (among them Mr. and Mrs. Leggett, Mrs. Papineau, &c.) who were much interested in my statements.[2]

I have just received another letter from you here, in regard to Pittsburgh, and the projected union of the Christian Commission with the Freedmen's Aid Commission.[3] I think that union desirable.

Levi Coffin and Mr. Walden have just called upon me, from Cincinnati.[4] Levi is on his way to the West, and Walden thinks of returning back to C. in the morning. They are here for a conference with the Freedmen's Committee, to which I am not invited.[5]

I am to lecture in Cincinnati on Thursday and Friday evenings, Nov. 30th and Dec. 1st. I shall leave in the Friday night (10 o'clock) train for Pittsburgh, arriving there Saturday morning, so as to be able to attend the Freedmen's meeting that evening, in case it is strongly preferred to have it that evening rather than on Sunday evening.[6] But, "other things being equal," I should, of course, much prefer Sunday evening, because I shall in all probability be exceedingly exhausted by incessant travelling and continual lecturing and talking. Will you let the friends there, having the matter in charge, know that they are at liberty to select either Saturday or Sunday evening, as they may deem most advisable? I can get some rest on my arrival Saturday. It seems to me that Sunday evening would insure a fuller attendance, as Saturday is a busy closing of the week's affairs. But the Pittsburgh friends will know what is best for that latitude.

I am very glad that George Thompson is to be with us on the occasion. I met him unexpectedly at the Weddell House in Cleveland, and he told me of what was contemplated, as he had just come from Pittsburgh, on his way to Buffalo and Syracuse.

I addressed a large and very intelligent and respectable audience here last evening, and, though laboring under severe hoarseness and great bodily debility, was well received by the audience. All the morning papers, contrary to my wishes, report my lecture so fully (the Copperhead sheet, the *Times,* almost *verbatim,*) that, as they circulate far and wide, it will be shorn of its interest to many who will come to hear me. It is not fair play.

I shall not leave here till Monday morning, when I go to Princeton.

The day is rapidly approaching for our beloved children to unite their destiny in the sacred bonds of wedlock. I trust and believe it will prove a most felicitous and perfect union.

Ever affectionately yours,

W. L. G.

P.S. Have you read the report of the speeches in the *Standard,* made at the meeting of the Penn. A. S. Society?[7] They are the bluest of the blue.[8] How one-sided it all is!

☞ Of course, I should prefer to avoid the night ride from Cincinnati to Pittsburgh if Sunday evening will answer the purpose for the meeting.

ALS: Garrison Papers, Boston Public Library.

1. Isabella Graham Bethune Duffield (1799–1871) was the daughter of Richard and Joanna Graham Bethune, both natives of Scotland, the sister of George Washington Bethune, and the wife of George Duffield. Mrs. Duffield was president of the Ladies' Soldiers' Aid Society and was active during the Civil War in forwarding hospital supplies to Union forces. (Silas Farmer, *History of Detroit and Wayne County and Early Michigan,* Detroit, 1890, pp. 310, 660; letter to the editor from Alice C. Dalligan, assistant, Burton Historical Collection, Detroit Public Library, August 11, 1973.)

2. Garrison probably refers to Augustus Wright Leggett (1816–1885) and his wife (1815–1900), a socially prominent couple who had moved to Detroit from Clintonville, Mich., in 1864. (Letter to the editor from Alice C. Dalligan, August 11, 1973.)

Perhaps Garrison refers to Mrs. Seth L. Papineau of Detroit, who is known to have been a benefactor of Harper Hospital. (Farmer, *History of Detroit,* p. 659.)

3. McKim was instrumental in the movement to unify the various aid societies.

4. Levi Coffin (1789–1877) was a birthright Quaker who had grown up on a farm in North Carolina and moved to Newport, Wayne County, Ind., in 1826, where he was the proprietor of a store. His house in Newport was one of the most active stations on the Underground Railroad. He also participated in the free-labor movement, running for a time in Cincinnati a wholesale outlet for the sale of goods produced without the taint of slave labor. After 1862 he devoted all his time and energy to the cause of the freedmen, his efforts extending as far as England, where he helped to found a freedmen's aid society.

John Morgan Walden (1831–1914) was born in Ohio to a family of Virginian background. After trying several occupations, including carpentry and teaching, he became a Methodist minister and eventually the pastor of the York Street Church in Cincinnati. During the Civil War he was active in the freedmen's cause. He worked first for the Ladies' Home Mission, later becoming corresponding secretary of the Western Freedmen's Aid Commission and the Methodist Freedmen's Aid Society. In 1867 he became presiding elder of the Methodist church (East Cincinnati District) and in 1884 was elected bishop.

5. Garrison probably refers to a meeting of the branch of the American Freedmen's Aid Commission, of which John M. Walden was secretary.

6. For a description of the meeting, which was held on Saturday, December 2, see Garrison's letter to Helen E. Garrison, December 3, 1865.

7. The twenty-ninth annual meeting of the Pennsylvania Anti-Slavery Society was held at West Chester, Pa., on October 26, 1865. A resolution calling for the dissolution of the society was debated and soundly rejected. Wendell Phillips, assisted by Mary Grew, Parker Pillsbury, Robert Purvis, and others, dominated the session and prevailed against Garrison, who thought that an antislavery society was anomalous since slavery had been abolished. Garrison's anger at the proceedings was hardly assuaged by the unanimous adoption of a resolution praising his dedicated commitment to abolition. (*National Anti-Slavery Standard,* November 4 and 11, 1865.)

8. Possibly Garrison refers to the conservative views of the members who spoke against his resolution for dissolution of the society.

141

TO HELEN E. GARRISON

Princeton, Nov. 21, 1865.

Dear Wife:

I arrived here yesterday, at 2 P.M., and found the place to be a village of about three thousand inhabitants, with a fine court-house, but few very noticeable residences.[1] Soon after my arrival at the hotel, I was called upon by several of the citizens—among them a brother of William Cullen Bryant, the poet, who very kindly accompanied me to see the widow of the lamented Owen Lovejoy and her family, who lived about a mile from the hotel.[2] The call was necessarily a brief one, but I was impressed by the solid character and intelligence of Mrs. Lovejoy. There are nine children, of whom three are boys. Four of the daughters were present, and admirable specimens of well-developed girlhood they were.

Last evening, considering the size of the village, I had a large audience, very intelligent, who listened to me for two hours with unbroken interest and warm approval. I was very hoarse, but happily feel no worse for it this morning. Quite a number of leading citizens came to give me their hands and their thanks at the close of my lecture—among them Mr. and Mrs. Bliss, formerly of Pawtucket, R.I., (she a daughter of Ray Potter,) Dr. Ferris, formerly of Providence, and an old democratic pro-slavery opponent of Thomas Davis, but now a thorough anti-slavery man—&c.,&c.[3]

This morning until the present noon, my room has been filled with persons to see me—Mr. J. H. Bryant and his brother included.[4] I am kept talking incessantly, and my throat needs to be lined with brass and my lungs to be made of steel. It is a hard and trying predicament to be placed in. It will be almost a miracle if I get through without being thoroughly prostrated as at Cleveland some years ago.

I leave here in an hour for Galesburg, to wheeze through my lecture as best I may. Then off for Quincy to do the same thing to-morrow evening—and so evening after evening till I break down—perhaps.

Tell Franky, in sending me my photographs to Pittsburgh, (about which I wrote to William,) they had better be divided, perhaps, into two packages. I wish him to pay Seaver all that is due.

Fanny must have a first-rate likeness taken when she is twenty-one. I will see about it on my return.

I am glad to find, on my tour, a general conviction of loyal men that the true method to deal with the South is to hold her firmly by the strong arm of the General Government until she can be safely admitted by the adoption of free institutions. No matter what their Constitutions may be as States, they must not now be allowed to set up house-keeping for themselves, any more than the lunatics in Bedlam.

Time goes slowly with me, incessantly occupied as I am. Happy shall I be to embrace you and the dear ones once more.

Lovingly yours,

W. L. G.

ALS: Garrison Papers, Boston Public Library.

1. The courthouse at Princeton, Ill., had been completed on the site of an earlier structure in 1860; it was a two-story, gabled brick building with a central tower. (Let-

ter to the editor from Mrs. Melvin Dant, Bureau County Historical Society, Princeton, August 5, 1973.)

2. John Howard Bryant (1807–1902) was the energetic and pioneering younger brother of William Cullen Bryant. In 1832 John Bryant had settled, originally as a squatter, on land slightly south of Princeton, Ill. Chiefly occupied as a farmer, he also built bridges and roads, manufactured bricks, edited a local paper, and helped found the first township high school in Illinois. He was active in politics, moving from the Democratic, to the Free-Soil, to the Republican parties before becoming a Liberal Republican and ultimately returning to the Democratic party. He was an active abolitionist, especially in the Undergound Railroad movement. In addition, he had some literary ability and published a volume of poems in 1855, as well as *Life and Poems* in 1894.

Eunice Storrs Denham Lovejoy (1809–1899) had reared two families. She had three children by her first husband (Butler Denham, died 1841): Lucy Storrs (1837–1907), Mary B. (1840–1905), and Elizabeth S. (1842–1925). By her second husband, Owen Lovejoy (died 1864), she had six more: Sarah Moody (1844–1881), Owen Glendower (1846–1900), Ida Taylor (1848–1909), Sophia Mappa (1849–1933), Elijah Parish (1850–1931), and Charles Perkins (1852–1914). A tenth child, Owen Glendower (1845–1846), had died in infancy. The Lovejoy home was a principal stop on the Underground Railroad. (Letter to the editor from Mrs. Melvin Dant, August 5, 1973; Edward Magdol, *Owen Lovejoy: Abolitionist in Congress*, New Brunswick, N.J., 1967, pp. 37–40.)

3. Perhaps Garrison refers to Zenos Bliss (1835–1905) and his wife (born 1843), who lived at Buda, some fifteen miles southwest of Princeton. The Blisses were prominent in their community; Bliss was a veteran of the Civil War. (Letter to the editor from Mrs. Melvin Dant, August 5, 1973.)

Ray Potter (1795–1858) was a free-will Baptist minister in Pawtucket, R.I., who had been one of the founders of the American Anti-Slavery Society in 1833 and a loyal Garrisonian abolitionist. He was much admired by Garrison until the early months of 1837, when he confessed to illicit sexual relations with a member of his parish. Repercussions from the scandal resulted in his resignation as minister, his exile from the state, and eventually his imprisonment under an archaic statute. Later in life he became a businessman. (*The Liberator*, February 25, 1837; *Admonitions from "the Depths of Earth," or the Fall of Ray Potter in Twenty-Four Letters: Written by Himself to his Brother, Nicholas G. Potter*, Pawtucket, R.I., 1838.)

Dr. Ferris was probably Peter W. Ferris (born c. 1800), a dentist in Princeton. A clerk of the town council in 1863, he was at one time principal of a grade school. (Letter to the editor from Mrs. Melvin Dant, August 5, 1973.)

4. Since John H. Bryant had at this time two brothers in the Princeton area, it is uncertain whether Garrison refers to Austin (1793–1866) or Arthur (1803–1883). (Charles H. Brown, *William Cullen Bryant*, New York, 1971, pp. 34, 475.)

142

TO HELEN E. GARRISON

Springfield, Nov. 24, 1865.

Dear Wife:

I have just arrived here, and am under the roof of my friend Mr. [William H.] Herndon, who has put into my hands welcome letters from you and dear Franky, by which I am relieved of all anxiety as to home matters. In your crippled state, you must not fatigue yourself in writing to me, glad as I am to get your letters, with their home intelligence.

My last letter, I believe, was written to you at Princeton. On Tuesday, I went to Galesburg, and had a fine audience, and was much pleased with the place. On Wednesday evening, I lectured in Quincy to another highly respectable and numerous audience. The town is on a high bluff on the Mississippi river, and one of the finest and most business-like in the State. I was most hospitably entertained by John K. Van Doorn, Esq., who, for thirty years, has been a staunch abolitionist, and looked all manner of perils in the face in sheltering and succoring multitudes of fugitive slaves; for, in times past, Quincy was almost as pro-slavery and mobocratic as any part of the South.[1] He gave me an extended ride around the town, and thus enabled me to see its position and development. I was introduced to a considerable number of the leading citizens, (among them ex-Governor Wood, who has a palatial residence of the first class,) and treated with marked courtesy and respect.[2] Before the rebellion, I could not have spoken there without exciting mob violence.

Yesterday, I came to Jacksonville, a place I had not down in my lecturing programme; but I was fortunately able to address the people in the handsomest hall I have yet seen in the State, that will seat fifteen hundred persons.[3] Although the meeting was got up hurriedly, and there was but very little time to give notice of the lecture, I had a large audience, the very *élite* of the place,—the President, (Sturtevant,) Professors and students of the College, a strong array of young ladies from two or three large seminaries, judges, lawyers, physicians, merchants, clergymen, &c.[4] At the close of my lecture, I was warmly congratulated by many, and the platform was crowded with persons eager to take me by the hand. I had a protracted hand-shaking with the young ladies of the seminaries, or colleges as they are called, who filed before me in regular procession. Am I not in danger of getting spoiled? Of course, you will not be jealous!

I had to leave Quincy before three o'clock in the morning, in order to reach Jacksonville in season; which was the only time I have yet had to start at an unseasonable hour.

Take it as a whole, beauty of location, neatness of appearance, and cosy and handsome residences, Jacksonville is the handsomest town I have seen on my western tour. It has a large infusion of the New England element, and also of Kentucky and Missouri settlers, and before the war was bitterly copperhead in its politics. It has an immense and handsome State asylum for the insane, another for the deaf and dumb, and a retreat for idiots, and is well provided with colleges and schools.[5] It also abounds with trees, shrubbery, and gardens. I was indebted to a young student for an extended ride through and around the town. I stopped at a hotel kept by a Kentuckian, Col. Dunlap, but he "don't know how to keep a hotel." Every thing was done in a lazy, slip-shod manner.[6]

I am now suffering from a violent and sudden attack of opthalmia in my right eye, which is prevalent at the West this season, and which makes reading and writing very painful. I ought to be confined to a dark room for some time, as it may prove very troublesome in the future. It makes the eye look as well as feel badly. I fear it may necessitate my recalling some of my appointments. Dr. Reed, a homoeopathic physician at Jacksonville, kindly supplied my with Arnica, Mercurious, &c., without charge, by the use of which I may get relieved.[7] I checked my trunk at Quincy for this place, but on arriving here cannot find it. There is another depot here, and possibly it may be there; but I fear it has been left at some way station.

I am to lecture here to-morrow (Saturday) evening, and on Sunday evening take the night train for Lafayette.

Loving remembrances to the dear household—to Harry, if at home —to Daniel and Lucy [Thaxter], the Bradfords,[8] Miss Cannan, &c.

Ever Yours,

W. L. G.

P.S. Give Franky a father's thanks for his letters to me. I have seen but one number of the Liberator since I left. Tell Franky I intend leaving Cincinnati in the Friday evening train, Dec. 1st, so as to reach Pittsburgh Saturday morning.

☞ Am pleased to hear that dear Fanny is getting some wedding presents.

☞ I shall send to Wendell a hundred dollars, $50 for him, and $50 for Lucy, to be spent in purchasing such presents with it as he shall deem best.

ALS: Garrison Papers, Boston Public Library.

1. John K. Van Doorn (1814–1875) of Quincy, Ill., had been dealing in lumber since 1852. During the war he became United States commissary in charge of distribution of food to the destitute in his state, many of whom were refugees from Missouri. (*The History of Adams County, Illinois*, Chicago, 1879, p. 705.)

2. John Wood (1798–1880) emigrated in 1819 from New York state to Illinois. In 1822 he built a cabin in what was to become Quincy. During the remainder of his long life he was intimately involved with major projects affecting the city he founded as well as the state. Between 1834 and 1840 he was a town trustee; he served often as alderman and seven times as mayor. From 1850 to 1854 he was a member of the state Senate; in 1856 he became lieutenant governor, and in 1859,

governor. Early in the Civil War he became quarter master general of Illinois; in 1864 he was made colonel of the 137th volunteers. From his first days in the state he was a consistent abolitionist.

3. Garrison probably refers to Strawn's Opera House, which was built on the public square in 1861 by cattlebroker and businessman Jacob Strawn. This auditorium, which was popular with artists and lecturers, was considered the finest in Illinois, outside of those in Chicago. (Clarence P. McClelland, "Jacob Strawn and John T. Alexander, Central Illinois Stockmen," *Journal of the Illinois State Historical Society,* 34:195, June 1941.)

4. Julian Monson Sturtevant (1805–1886), a graduate of both the college and the divinity school at Yale, was associated with Illinois College during most of his life— as tutor (1828–1830), as professor of mathematics, natural philosophy, and astronomy (1831–1844), as president as well as professor of mental and moral philosophy (1844–1876), and, finally, as professor of mental science and government (1876–1886).

Illinois College, one of the oldest in the central section of the country, had been founded as a Presbyterian institution in 1829 by the Reverend John Millot Ellis of the American Home Missionary Society and the so-called Yale Band (a group of seven Yale men dedicated to college education in the Middle West). Also situated in Jacksonville were the Jacksonville Female Academy (founded in 1830) and the Illinois Conference Female Academy (chartered in 1847).

5. Garrison refers to the State Central Hospital for the Insane (functioning since 1851), the State School for the Deaf (oldest of Illinois charitable institutions, founded in 1839 and functioning since 1845), and the State School for the Blind (founded in 1849).

6. James Dunlap (1802–1879) was born in Kentucky but had settled in Jacksonville, Ill., in 1830, where until 1838 he ran a general store. Thereafter he went into the railroad business and was largely responsible for building the first railroad in the state (completed in 1845). He was also a successful farmer and stock dealer and active in the real estate business. In 1856 he built Dunlap House, the leading hotel in the area. In 1861 Lincoln appointed him chief quartermaster of the 13th Army Corps. Married to Elizabeth Freeman since 1824, he was the father of eleven children. (*Atlas Map of Morgan County, Illinois,* Davenport, Ia., 1872, p. 46; obituary, Jacksonville *Daily Journal,* July 9, 1879.)

7. Maro McLean Reed (1801–1877), the son of a distinguished Connecticut physician, graduated from Yale College and from the medical school at Pittsfield, Mass., before practicing in Hartford (1825–1830). Following his marriage to Elizabeth Lathrop in 1830, he moved west and settled in Jacksonville, Ill. After a quarter of a century as a conventional physician, he adopted homeopathic principles, under which he practiced until his death. In addition to being a physician, Reed was an active reformer, dedicated to both temperance and abolition; it was, in fact, the existence of slavery in Missouri that caused him to prefer Jacksonville over St. Louis for his home. (Jacksonville *Daily Journal,* April 15, 1915.)

8. Information about the Bradford family is, at best, scanty. Sarah Whitwell Tyler Bradford was married to John Bradford and died on April 5, 1866, at the age of eighty. The Bradfords had a son and two daughters, Rebecca, who died in December 1877, in Paris, and Sarah. (Letter to the editor from Gary Bell, researcher, February 20, 1974.)

143

TO WENDELL PHILLIPS GARRISON

Springfield, (Ill.) Nov. 25, 1865.

My Dear Son:

I am now in the capital of Illinois, which is a bustling, thriving town of seventeen thousand inhabitants, and was formerly the residence of Mr. Lincoln. I am to speak this evening in the Representatives' Chamber, a privilege which has been extended only to Mr. Lincoln, S. A. Douglass, and one or two others.[1] I have been introduced to Governor Oglesby, and other prominent citizens, and been very courteously received here as every where else.[2] The hall is not a large one, but my audience will doubtless be very intelligent and select. I am a good deal worn by much speaking, and quite hoarse. The load I have undertaken to carry is a heavy one, and I shall be extremely fortunate if I do not break down under it. My right eye is badly affected by an attack of opthalmia, which is quite prevalent at the West at this time, but is somewhat better than a day or two ago, when it was almost closed. The weather for more than a fortnight has been uninterruptedly fair, and perfectly glorious.

I am stopping with William H. Herndon, Esq., Mr. Lincoln's late law partner, and bosom friend for many years. He is preparing a Life of Mr. Lincoln, which will be unique as going into the private characteristics and social traits of Mr. L.[3]

To-morrow (Sunday) evening, I shall take the train for Lafayette, Indiana, where I am to lecture on Monday evening; then on Tuesday evening at Indianapolis, Wednesday evening at Richmond, and Thursday and Friday evenings at Cincinnati. Friday night I take the train for Pittsburgh, to address a Freedmen's meeting on Saturday evening. On the succeeding Monday evening I shall give my last lecture on this tour in P., then hurry down to Philadelphia to be at the wedding ceremony on the 6th.

I enclose a draft for one hundred dollars to your order—fifty to be spent by you, and fifty for Lucy, in buying whatever may suit your taste and hers to that extent. I am not particular, of course, about the exact division of that sum, but do not refuse to use it all. My regret is, that I have not thousands to offer you, whom I love so much. I have already realized a thousand dollars on this tour—my expenses not exceeding one hundred and fifty dollars. If I am able to fulfil my other appointments, I shall make three or four hundred more. My lecture here is impromptu on my part, and not before any association, and therefore will not be paying like the rest.

I have kept your mother pretty frequently informed as to my movements, deeming it best to send my letters to her; indeed, finding no time to send any to any body else; and at home they have kept me posted as to what has taken place in Boston and the family circle. I got three letters from your mother, and one from Franky, here. All seems to be going on well.

I have received one letter from you, for which accept my thanks.

I have seen only one number of "The Nation" since I left. I am anxious to know what its prospects of permanence are.

Give my love to Mr. and Mrs. McKim, dear Lucy, the [Edward] Anthonys, Oliver Johnson, [Theodore] Tilton, &c. &c.

Your affectionate father,

Wm. Lloyd Garrison.

W. P. Garrison.

ALS: Garrison Papers, Boston Public Library.

1. Stephen Arnold Douglas (1813–1861), whose name Garrison misspells, was a prominent Illinois Democrat and lawyer. In 1843 he began his long career in Congress, where he served first in the House and then in the Senate. He is especially remembered for securing the passage of the Kansas-Nebraska bill, for presidential aspirations in 1852 and 1856, and for his debates with Lincoln during his successful senatorial campaign of 1858. Although in 1860 he ran opposite Lincoln as the Democratic candidate, he consistently supported the President in the early days of his administration.

2. Richard James Oglesby (1824–1899), originally from Kentucky, became a lawyer who practiced successfully in several Illinois towns. He saw service in both the Mexican and Civil wars, rising to the rank of major general. In 1864, 1872, and 1884 he was elected governor of Illinois, though he resigned in 1872 to serve in the United States Senate.

3. Although his extensive materials were earlier used in other biographies, *Herndon's Lincoln: The True Story of a Great Life* was not published until 1889.

144

TO HELEN E. GARRISON

Lafayette, (Ind.) Nov. 27, 1865.

Dear Wife:

I have just arrived here from Springfield, having ridden all night long, and feeling a good deal fatigued for lack of sleep. I am hospitably entertained by Hon. Cyrus Ball, Cashier of the Union National Bank, whom I found kindly waiting for me, with Mr. Joseph White, (by whom I was invited to lecture here,) at the depot at an early hour on my arrival.[1] His wife is a very pleasant and social lady.[2]

They live in a handsome style, and will see that all my needs are cared for.

My right eye is much improved in appearance, the opthalmia gradually lessening. I am also better of my hoarseness, though not in good speaking order. I have yet a heavy consecutive load to carry. First, I am to lecture here this evening; to-morrow evening at Indianapolis; Wednesday evening at Richmond; Thursday and Friday evenings at Cincinnati; Saturday and Monday evenings at Pittsburgh. It is too great a strain, but I must try to go through with it.

I found here a letter from William, enclosing one from Mr. Travelli at Pittsburgh, and another from William R. Hooper at Washington.[3] I have written to the former that I shall leave Cincinnati, at the close of my Friday evening lecture, in the night train for Pittsburgh, and so shall be able to attend the Freedmen's Aid meeting there on Saturday evening. I shall have to decline the invitation to Washington, as I must hurry home from Philadelphia; and yet there is to be a special and very important meeting of the American Freedmen's Aid Commission at Washington, Dec. 13th, and a public meeting in its behalf in the Hall of the House of Representatives, at both of which I am expected to be present, and which I should like very much to attend.[4] But I must decline doing so. The Liberator demands my return.

For three weeks the weather has been uninterruptedly bright and glorious. I never have had such luck before, and no sign of a change yet.

They have here no decent hall for a lecture, but a very fine and spacious one is in process of completion.[5] I do not anticipate much of an attendance, as I do not speak in behalf of any association.

I enjoyed myself at Springfield highly.—Mr. [William H.] Herndon and his wife were very kind and attentive, and I was introduced to a number of prominent citizens, including Gov. [Richard J.] Oglesby. My meeting there, on Saturday evening, in the Representatives' Chamber, numbered only two hundred persons, but they were the cream of the cream of the city— the Governor and his Staff, military officers of various grades, lawyers, merchants, ministers, &c. My lecture elicited much applause, and though two hours' long, (incorrigible man!) riveted their close attention from beginning to end. I took tea, on Saturday evening, with Rev. Mr. Hale, a Presbyterian minister, a most amiable man and warm abolitionist, who resembles Adin Ballou in his looks, voice and manner almost like a twin brother.[6] To reciprocate his courtesy, I went with Mr. Herndon to hear him preach yesterday forenoon. In the afternoon I walked out to Oak Ridge cemetery with Mr. H., where the remains of Mr. Lincoln lie entombed.[7] It is a most charming place, and quite equal, if not superior, in its natural features, to Mount Auburn.[8] There are but few monuments as yet. There was quite a throng of visitors, and many carriages, and a good many colored persons. What multitudes will yet visit that spot in the course of time! The place selected for Mr. Lincoln's monument is admirably chosen, but it will be a good while before the monument is erected. Sufficient funds have not been received by a good deal.

Calling at the house of the keeper of the grounds, (who was absent,) I recorded my name in a huge volume already numbering thousands of names, and purchased several card photographs. The good wife voluntarily went with us to Mr. Lincoln's tomb, unlocked the door, and let us see the coffin, draped and festooned. Until within a week, the tomb has been constantly guarded by soldiers. The coffin is to be removed to a new tomb very shortly, above ground, instead of inside of a bank.

Mr. Herndon, as the bosom friend and law partner of Mr. Lincoln for many years, has told me many interesting facts and anecdotes about him—all going to raise him still more highly in my estimation.

I am rejoiced to hear that Harry has been able to visit Rockledge, and no doubt the pleasure was mutual all round. Ask Fanny if it was not exquisite in her own case. God bless them both, and you and our loving household!

Ever yours,

W. L. G.

ALS: Garrison Papers, Boston Public Library.

1. 1. Cyrus Ball (1804–1893) was the self-educated son of an Ohio farmer. Having tried several occupations (farming, teaching, merchandising) before being admitted to the bar in 1828, and then serving for five years as justice of the peace, in 1840 he was elected associate judge for his district. He was active in many businesses, including dry goods, the Lafayette Artificial Gas Company, railroads, and the Union National Bank, which was founded in 1865 and liquidated in 1875. (R. P. DeHart, *Past and Present of Tippecanoe County, Indiana,* Indianapolis, 1909).

Joseph White has not been identified.

2. Rebecca Gordon Ball (1816–1900) was Cyrus Ball's second wife, whom he married in 1838, and by whom he had five children. Mrs. Ball was described as a woman of "rare intellect and fine judgment," and she earned a local reputation as a poet. (DeHart, *Past and Present.*)

3. Mr. Travelli has not been identified.

William R. Hooper was a minor clerk in the post office department, and also, apparently, an agent who arranged lectures in Washington. (Andrew Boyd, compiler, *Boyd's Washington and Georgetown Directory* . . . , Washington, 1865, p. 230.)

4. Doubtless Garrison refers to an executive session preceding the public meeting on the evening of December 13, at which there may have been discussion of the

need for a stronger Freedmen's Bureau as well as for the merger of the American Freedmen's Aid Commission and the American Union Commission. A large crowd attended the meeting, including Chief Justice Salmon P. Chase; Schuyler Colfax, Speaker of the House; William Dennison, postmaster general; James Harlan, secretary of the interior; and Gideon Welles, secretary of the navy. The Chief Justice presided, and the major address was delivered by Henry Ward Beecher, who argued eloquently for Negro and female suffrage, saying, "Politics will always be barbarous until men and women give their votes together. Woman is the great civilizer, and when woman stops at home and man goes abroad, the man begins to be animal." (Washington *Evening Star*, December 14, 1865.)

5. Garrison refers to Spencer Hall, the upper floors of which had been gutted by fire in the early 1860s and were being reconstructed. (Letter to the editor from Mildred Paarlberg, curator of collections, Tippecanoe County Historical Association, Lafayette, Ind., May 10, 1974.)

6. Albert Hale (1799–1891), pastor of the Second Presbyterian Church of Springfield, Ill., between 1839 and 1867, was a liberal-minded reformer, being both an abolitionist and an opponent of the Mexican War. With other graduates of the Yale Divinity School, Hale founded the Illinois College at Jacksonville, Monticello Female Seminary, and other educational institutions. ("Historical Notes," *Journal of Illinois State Historical Society*, 26:170, 1933; Russell F. Thrapp, "Early Religious Beginnings in Illinois," *Journal of Illinois State Historical Society*, 4:309, 1911; the Rev. G. S. F. Savage, "Pioneer Congregational Ministers in Illinois," *Journal of the Illinois State Historical Society*, 3:81, 1910.)

Adin Ballou (1803–1890) was the Universalist minister and reformer who founded the first of the Utopian communities, Hopedale (near Milford, Mass.), in 1841.

7. Lincoln's body had been placed in a vault on May 4, 1865, in the Oak Ridge Cemetery, founded in 1856. What Garrison saw was a temporary vault and monument; the final installation was not completed until 1874. (Caroline R. Heath, editor and compiler, *Four Days in May: Lincoln Returns to Springfield*, Springfield, 1965; Kate Brainerd Rogers, "The Name of Lincoln," *Journal of the Illinois State Historical Society*, 7:60–69, 1914; Paul M. Angle, *"Here I Have Lived": A History of Lincoln's Springfield, 1821–1865*, New Brunswick, N.J., 1935, pp. 179–180.)

8. Mount Auburn Cemetery, consecrated in 1831 and located on the border between Cambridge and Watertown, Mass., was founded by the Massachusetts Horticultural Society as the first garden cemetery in the United States. (Nathaniel B. Shurtleff, *A Topical and Historical Description of Boston*, Boston, 1871; A. C. Lyons, *Invitation to Boston*, New York, 1947.)

145

TO WILLIAM H. HERNDON

Lafayette, Nov. 27, 1865.

My dear Mr. Herndon:

I arrived here this morning at 6 o'clock, and found waiting for me thus early my friends James Howe, Esq. and Hon. Cyrus Ball, Cashier of the National Bank.[1] I am partaking of the hospitality of the latter. Of course, I am a good deal fatigued, having closed my eyes scarcely for a moment during my long night's ride.

To my surprise and dismay—and, doubtless, to your own, also, in regard to their mysterious disappearance—I find in my outside pocket the accompanying legal documents, which I must have unwittingly taken from your table, supposing they were a packet belonging to me. "All's well that ends well"—so that I hope you will find every thing right at last.

I have had a considerable number of the leading citizens dining with me to-day, and a very pleasant interview with them.

I am just getting ready to go to the meeting, and so have no time to fill my sheet. I am, and shall continue to be, full of pleasant remembrances in regard to my visit to Springfield. What an afternoon we spent yesterday at Oak Ridge cemetery, where lies all that is mortal of our great national martyr in the cause of liberty and his country! My indebtedness to you for your unwearied kindness and attention, and also to your amiable wife, is large, and will always be gratefully remembered.

With my kindest regards to her, and to all the children, I remain,[2] Your attached friend,

Wm. Lloyd Garrison.

Hon. Wm. H. Herndon.

ALS: William Lloyd Garrison Collection, Chicago Historical Society; a handwritten transcription is preserved in the Herndon-Weik Collection, Library of Congress.

1. James Howe (1806–1886), a native of Plattsburg, N.Y., was the founder in 1831 of the New York *Spirit of the Times* (later *Wilkes Spirit of the Times*), and had employed Horace Greeley as a compositor. In 1841 Howe moved to Lafayette, Ind., where he founded the Lafayette *Daily American* and became the proprietor of the Lafayette Hotel. In 1859 he became city clerk and in 1878 he was elected justice of the peace. By his wife Hannah Wilstach (died 1889) he was the father of five surviving children. (Letter to the editor from Mildred Paarlberg, curator of collections, Tippecanoe County Historical Association, Lafayette, Ind., May 10, 1974.)

2. Herndon's second wife, whom he married in 1862, was the former Anna Miles (born c. 1836) of Petersburg, Ill.; their only child to date was Nina Belle, born the year of Garrison's letter. By his first wife, the former Mary J. Maxcy, Herndon had six children: Nathaniel J. (born 1841), Annie M. (born 1843), Beverly P. (born 1845), Elizabeth R. (born 1849), Leigh W. (born 1852), and Mary F. (born 1856). (David Donald, *Lincoln's Herndon*, New York, 1948.)

146

TO HELEN E. GARRISON

Cincinnati, Dec. 1, 1865.

Dear Wife:

On arriving, at tea-time, at Richmond from Indianapolis on Wednesday evening, I was met at the depot by Major Isaac Kinley, who recognized me at once by Grozelier's portrait of me, which he has hanging up in his parlor, and who carried me in his buggy to his very pleasant residence, where I was warmly welcome by his wife, who used to keep a studio in Boston, and who has her parlor filled with her own productions, which indicate a good deal of artistic talent.[1] She used to attend Theodore Parker's meeting, and had seen me frequently before. I found with her Mrs. Josephine Griffing, just from Washington, endeavoring to get supplies for the destitute freed women and children in that city.[2] Major Kinley is of Quaker parentage, and commanded a regiment largely made up of Quaker young men, and himself badly wounded in the thigh at Stone River.[3] He is a very pleasant, energetic, intelligent man, and went into the struggle solely for the cause of universal emancipation. I was made to feel at home at once. My evening meeting was well attended by the best people, among them a number of Friends, notwithstanding the weather was rainy and unpropitious. The next morning, (yesterday,) before leaving for this city, Mrs. Kinley gave me a drive all about Richmond and its suburbs, which I highly enjoyed, as the place is admirably located, and one of the neatest and handsomest cities I have seen at the West. On going to the depot, $75—the price of my lecture—was put into my hands in handsome national currency. Inconsiderately, I put the roll of bills into the outside breastpocket of my overcoat. On going to purchase my ticket, I stepped aside from the crowd, and took from the roll a five dollar bill to pay my fare here, and returned the remaining $70 to the same pocket. I must have been observed by some sharp-sighted thief; for in a few minutes I found my $70 gone, and, of course, expect never to see the money again. It is a large loss for me, especially at this time when I so much need money in winding up my Liberator affairs, to say nothing of the future. In how many ways that sum might have been advantageously used! There would be some satisfaction if I knew it would be spent for a good purpose; but it will go for rum, profligacy, and kindred vices. It is the first money I ever lost in this way, and I shall endeavor to see that it is the last.

I enclose a draft for $300, to William's order, which he will add to what he has already received.

I was happy to find here a letter from you, and another from William—or, rather, two from you—giving assurance that all is going well with you at the dear home, and also interesting home details.

I am glad to hear of the pleasant time enjoyed by Harry and Fanny, and that he impresses you more and more as one worthy to espouse our darling daughter. I am abundantly satisfied that the

match will prove a fortunate one. I hope to meet them in Philadelphia, with William and Ellie, on Wednesday next.

I lectured here last evening to a moderate sized audience, though
a very respectable one, and received every evidence of pleasing
and interesting them throughout. The evening was rainy.

This evening I am to lecture in behalf of the Freedmen's cause,
and at the close to take the night train for Pittsburgh, where I expect
to arrive to-morrow at dinner-time. I shall be in a used up conditon
to speak there to-morrow evening, but they are urgent to have me
speak on the occasion—George Thompson is to be with me. Love
to George, William, Fanny, Frank, Charlotte Coffin, Mr. and Mrs.
[Daniel] Thaxter. My regards to Katy and Winnie.

Ever thine,

W. L. G.

☞ I shall aim to get home on Saturday evening next week, at 5 or
6 o'clock, in the day train from New York. Speed the day!

ALS: Garrison Papers, Boston Public Library.

1. Isaac Kinley (born in 1821 and still living in 1906) came from Quaker stock in
Randolph County, Ind. After teaching school briefly he read law and was eventually
admitted to the bar. Active in state politics, he had served in the 1850s as surveyor of
Henry County and as state senator, being especially concerned with educational
matters. His first wife had died in 1854; in 1859 he married Jeanne Adams. On the
outbreak of the Civil War he was commissioned as a captain and was subsequently
promoted to major, resigning after being wounded at Murfreesboro in December
1862. Following the war he moved to Wayne County; he was elected state senator
from that county and served from 1866 to 1870. Thereafter, he moved to California.
(Wayne County, Ind., marriage records, Book G, p. 505; George Hazzard, *History of
Henry County, Indiana, 1822–1906*, New Castle, Ind., 1906.)

Leopold Grozelier's portrait of Garrison, based upon a daguerreotype by Lorenzo
G. Chase, was a lithograph executed in Boston and published by William C. Nell on
May 5, 1854. (Francis Jackson Garrison and Wendell Phillips Garrison, compilers,
The Words of Garrison, Boston, 1905, pp. 115–116. This source incorrectly gives the
name as Louis rather than Leopold Grozelier. See Harry T. Peters, *America on
Stone: The Other Printmakers to the American People*, New York, 1931, p. 200 and
plates.)

2. Josephine Sophie White Griffing (1814–1872) was born in Hebron, Conn., and
moved in 1842 with her husband, Charles Stockman Spooner Griffing, to Ohio,
where the couple became active abolitionists. Their home was a station on the Underground Railroad. After 1848 Mrs. Griffing divided her time between abolition
and the woman's rights movement. Going to Washington in 1863, she agitated for
federal assistance for the freedmen and was influential in setting up various bureaus
for their aid. She and her daughter Emma were agents of the National Freedmen's
Relief Association. After the war Mrs. Griffing became corresponding secretary of
the National Woman Suffrage Association. (*NAW*.)

3. The Battle of Stones River, or the Battle of Murfreesboro as it is more often
called, was a series of skirmishes and assaults between Union troops under General
William S. Rosecrans and Confederate troops under General Braxton Bragg from
December 31, 1862 to January 2, 1863. The Confederates ultimately retreated, with
heavy losses on both sides. (Mark M. Boatner, *The Civil War Dictionary*, New York,
1959.)

147

TO HELEN E. GARRISON

Pittsburgh, Sunday, Dec. 3, 1865.

Dear Wife:

My second lecture in Cincinnati was delivered on Friday evening to a small audience, in behalf of the Freedmen's cause—the attendance showing little interest in that cause, and less in me; and I think I never acquitted myself so poorly on any occasion. This was mainly owing to my uncertainty whether I had not made a number of the same points, and used the same illustrations, in my lecture the previous evening; and so I made a confused and poor talk of it, (so it seemed to me, and to the audience also, I think, though I do not know,) and was glad enough when it was over. I do not "take" to Cincinnati at all, and do not think I shall be in a hurry again to visit it. Its proximity to the Kentucky shore has necessarily contaminated it with contempt for the negro; and though it is loyal, it is very badly infected with colorphobia. The price of tickets, 50 cents, had much to do in making a small audience; for if the doors had been thrown wide open, few care any thing about the condition or wants of the freedmen. There was not half enough received to pay for the hall, posters, advertising, &c.; leaving me, of course, nothing, though I was paid for the other lecture.

I attended a meeting of the Freedmen's Aid Committee in the afternoon.[1] A good deal of clothing and money has been received from England, but very little obtained in Cincinnati.

After my lecture, I took the train for Pittsburgh, at 10 o'clock at night, and rode until yesterday afternoon, more than seventeen hours—the longest consecutive ride I ever had by rail in my life—and found myself pretty essentially used up on my arrival here. I drove directly to the residence of Dr. E. H. Irish,[2] (a Quaker family,) where I was hospitably received, and where I found dear George Thompson, but not Mr. [James Miller] McKim as I expected, who writes me that he cannot be present, being busy with home affairs at this time.

Last evening we had a free meeting in behalf of the Freedmen's cause, which brought together a fair audience, one highly respectable too, and speeches were made by Rev. Mr. [Jacob R.] Shipherd, Judge [Hugh L.] Bond, George Thompson, and myself—not separating till half past 10 o'clock. It was a live meeting, and all the speeches were received by the assembly with warm approval. Thompson spoke very eloquently and feelingly, making the closing speech. He is to give a lecture here on Tuesday evening. Mine comes off to-morrow evening—then for the midnight train on my way to Philadelphia, to see that union of hands and destinies in which we are so deeply interested. It is hard that you cannot be present on the occasion; but you will be in spirit, with your motherly and wifely nature, if you cannot be in body.

I am still smarting in mind about the seventy dollars which a pick-pocket relieved me of at Richmond, Indiana—thinking in how many gratifying ways I might have spent the money. But regrets are vain.

Last evening I mailed a letter for you here, which I wrote at Cincinnati, and meant to have mailed there. I sent it to William's address,[3] as it contained a draft for three hundred dollars. It will need his signature, and George will have to preserve it carefully till William's return. If Fanny needs more money, let her have it. Tell Franky to take what spending money he wants. I wish you to buy for yourself what you or the family may need.

Tell Franky that I received my photographs all safe, with his letter. I was glad to learn that our terraced banks had been attended to, and also the tree.

Mary-Ann [Johnson] will deeply feel the loss of her mother; but to the latter the transition must prove a blessing.[4]

Only a few days more, and, God willing, I shall be by your side, and with all the dear household.

Forever your own

W. L. G.

ALS: Garrison Papers, Boston Public Library.

1. Established in 1863 following a split with the American Contraband Relief Association, the Western Freedmen's Aid Commission provided clothing, medical care, and education to refugees in Cincinnati as well as to southern freedmen. As Garrison implies, a large part of the commission's funds was obtained from England. (Joseph E. Holliday, "Freedmen's Aid Societies in Cincinnati, 1862–1870," *Cincinnati Historical Society Bulletin*, 22:169–185, July 1964.)

2. Elisha H. Irish (born before 1832, died 1866), son of William Beckford Irish of Philadelphia and Lydia Cadwallader, was an attorney and one-time state senator. (Letter to the editor from Ruth Salisbury, assistant director and archivist, Historical Society of Western Pennsylvania, June 11, 1974.)

3. Bailey, Jenkins and Garrison, 164 Congress Street, Boston. (Boston city directory, 1866.)

4. Little is known about Mrs. Broughton White (died 1865) except that she was the wife of a Congregational minister in New Hampshire. (Letter to the editor from Laura P. Abbott, librarian, Vermont Historical Society, Montpelier, June 18, 1974.)

148

TO SAMUEL J. MAY

Roxbury, Dec. 10, 1865.

My Beloved Friend:

Your very kind and affectionate letter of the 19th ult. reached me at Springfield, Illinois, as directed, and was read with great pleasure and interest. I was much gratified to hear that Mr. [George] Thompson succeeded so well with his lecture in your church, and that it elicited so much approval.[1] I parted from him at Pittsburgh, Pa., on Monday night last, where he was to lecture the next evening. I found him in better physical condition than I expected, though somewhat debilitated. During January and February, he is engaged to lecture almost every evening consecutively; and this makes me tremble for his safety. It is a far heavier load than he ought to attempt to carry, especially in view of the inclemency of those two months, the fatigue of constant travelling, the number of people to see and converse with privately—&c., &c. But he is always ready to comply with friendly or professional overtures, if possible, and especially to lose no opportunity to secure pecuniary aid for his family,—all the more as his match enterprise gives no promise, at present, of paying success. Should he be able to carry out his lecturing programme, he will probably realize over two thousand dollars, above all expenses. This will prove a most seasonable relief.

You were not only very considerate, but exceedingly kind, to get my limbs and life insured for the time and in the manner designated by you; and in presenting to me the policy as a token of your personal regard and attachment, you have added to the number of my numerous obligations to you. I will accept it thankfully, because not to do so would give you pain, and to do so will augment the sum of your happiness; yet, knowing how limited are your means, how many thrust themselves upon you for assistance, and how over-generous you are, I shrink from having you taxed on my account, even to the smallest extent. I will endeavor to look after the policy, from year to year, as you suggest.

Fortunately, I have returned home, after six weeks' absence and an extended tour, without any mishap. I was able to keep every engagement, and did not miss a single train. Most of the time I was very hoarse, and feared I should utterly break down, as there was no end to private talking in addition to the exhaustion of almost continuous public lecturing. At Quincy I had a severe attack of opthalmia in my right eye, which lasted me several days, with much inflammation; but by skilful homœpathic treatment I got over it much sooner than could have been reasonably expected. The disease is quite prevalent at the West this season.

On Tuesday I came from Pittsburgh to Philadelphia, and on Wednesday had the unalloyed satisfaction of seeing my cherished son Wendell united in the holy bands of wedlock to Lucy, the beloved daughter of my early friend and coadjutor, J. Miller McKim. The day was brilliant—the number of persons gathered to witness the ceremony in Dr. [William Henry] Furness's church large and very select, whose congratulations were abundant—and the statement on the part of Dr. Furness, of the nature, obligations, cares, sorrows, joys and felicities of the wedded state, in a true union, was most felicitously and comprehensively stated.[2] After the marriage services, we had an elegant entertainment served up at Mr. and Mrs. Denis's,[3] in the city, for the relatives and a few friends; and in the afternoon the wedded couple took the train for New York, where they were enabled to have quickly a Thanksgiving Day, (on Thursday,) in accordance with their own feelings as well as in compliance with the President's Proclamation.[4] They will board in New York at least during the winter. In Lucy, wife and I have gained another daughter, and Mr. and Mrs. McKim in Wendell a son. It is one of those too rare matches in which no room is left for anxiety or doubt as to the fitness and felicity of the alliance.

Speaking of wedlock, I am reminded of the near approach of the day for our darling Fanny to be united to her chosen one. Supposing you could legally "tie the knot," I mentioned to you, when at Syracuse, how pleasant it would be to us to have you perform the act for Harry and Fanny, as you did for wife and me; but I learn this cannot be by the laws of this State, and so we must employ another —probably it would be our neighbor, Dr. Putnam.[5] Though it would be exceedingly gratifying to have you present as a beloved friend, yet, as you cannot do the very thing needed to be done on the occasion, we could neither ask nor expect you to take so long a journey, at so inclement a period as it might prove, merely to witness the ceremony; therefore, we must "take the will for the deed." Besides, were it otherwise, in view of your cough and the very delicate state of your health, (which will need very careful nursing all through the winter,) we should not be willing to consent to your running any such risk, even though you were feeling considerably better.

If the record is reliable, sixty years ago, to-day, I was ushered into this breathing world; and so am now celebrating my sixtieth birthday with my family. It is a period of life that I once regarded as aged, and even venerable; but what is aged and venerable seems, now, considerably beyond me. It is so with you, I presume, though you lead me by a number of years—(I shall try to keep as near you as time will permit.) Where is the magic line that perceptibly indicates we have parted with infancy, boyhood, manhood, and become positively aged? In spirit, certainly, I still feel very young; nevertheless, I must cherish no delusion about my state. I am sixty years old. Well, I would not be any younger; for that could be only by reversing the laws of nature, and what but evil could grow out of such reversal?

My Western trip exceeded my anticipations. I return to find all well at home. Charlotte [Coffin] is with us, and sends loving regards to you all. So do we as a family. Remember me to the [Charles B.] Sedgwicks.

Ever admiringly yours,

Wm. Lloyd Garrison.

Rev. S. J. May.

ALS: Garrison Papers, Boston Public Library.

1. May's letter, which was printed in *The Liberator,* November 24, 1865, described Thompson's lecture, "The Past, the Present and the Future of these United States." May said that Thompson blamed many major American problems on the compromise regarding slavery found in the Constitution.

May's church, the Church of the Messiah (organized in 1838), by 1843 was located on Lock Street (now North State) at Burnet Avenue, Syracuse. After being destroyed by a windstorm in 1852, the building was restored and served until 1885. Samuel J. May was pastor from 1845 to 1867. (Letter to the editor from Richard N. Wright, president, Onondaga Historical Association, Syracuse, N.Y., July 24, 1973.)

2. The Unitarian Church of Philadelphia, of which William Henry Furness was minister between 1825 and 1875, had been constructed at Tenth and Locust streets in 1828; the new building, by Frank Furness, was not constructed until 1884. Following the retirement of William Furness in 1876 Joseph May, son of Samuel J. May, became the minister. (Joseph Jackson, *Encyclopedia of Philadelphia,* Harrisburg, 1933; J. Thomas Scharf and Thompson Westcott, *History of Philadelphia, 1609–1884,*Philadelphia, 1884.)

3. Garrison apparently refers to Fred Dennis, who was, during the late 1860s, owner and editor of the Auburn (N.Y.) *Morning News.* His wife was Anne McKim Dennis (died 1893), the niece and adopted daughter of the J. Miller McKims. In 1891, she married Wendell Phillips Garrison. (Charles Moore, *The Life and Times of Charles Follen McKim,* Boston and New York, 1929.)

4. President Johnson designated Thursday, December 7, "to be observed in all places of religious worship as a day of National Thanksgiving for the great mercies of God to our nation during the year now closing." (*The Liberator,* November 24, 1865.)

5. George Putnam (1807–1878), a graduate of the college and the divinity school at Harvard, was the minister of the First Church of Roxbury between 1830 and 1878. He was chosen a Fellow of the Harvard Corporation in 1852; the following year he

was a member of the convention to revise the state constitution. During the Civil War he was a consistent supporter of President Lincoln. He served a term in the state legislature (1869–1870). Putnam had been married to Elizabeth Ware (1808–1866) since 1831, and the Putnams, with their six children, lived near the Garrisons. (Eben Putnam, *A History of the Putnam Family in England and America,* Salem, Mass., 1891, VII, 74–77.)

149

TO HENRY VILLARD

Roxbury, Dec. 10, 1865.

Dear Harry:

Home again, after an absence of six weeks, having travelled thousands of miles, delivered a score of lectures, seen an immense number of people, entered at least the portals of the far West, gazed wonderingly at the seemingly interminable prairies till my very spectacles ached, "done" Detroit, Chicago, Springfield, Quincy, Cincinnati, Pittsburgh, and many other places comparatively near or remote, satisfied all comers that I have neither horns nor hoofs, satisfactorily interchanged views with a great number of representative men on the state of the nation, grown more convinced than ever that "this is a great country," lost no appointment and no railway connection, experienced no mishap, (except having my pocket picked of seventy dollars at Richmond, Ind.) and returned in as good mental and physical a condition as when I went away.

On Wednesday, the wedding of Wendell and Lucy came off according to the programme, in Rev. Dr. Furness's church at Philadelphia, in the presence of a large assembly of the very best people in that city and vicinity. The day was mild and brilliant, and all the omens auspicious. Our gratification would have been enhanced, if you had been with us; but we knew how imperative your presence was at Washington.[1] As Fanny has doubtless written to you a minute account of the affair, I need not add another word, excepting that I am very happy Wendell has secured so estimable a wife, and Lucy so faultless a husband. They shall have our benediction.

At Chicago, I had the pleasure of seeing Mr. [Horace] White at the Tribune office, but only for a few minutes. The Tribune gave me a handsome introductory notice, and quite as full a report of my lecture as I desired. The city interested me prodigiously. Its growth, in so short a period, is a matter of profound astonishment. Who shall venture to predict its future without seeming beside himself? With Lake Michigan, looking like another Atlantic ocean, the steamers and sailing vessels upon its broad bosom, and the commercial bustle every where visible, it seemed as though I must be in a city on the seaboard, instead of a thousand miles in the interior away from Boston.

Accept my thanks for your efforts to secure a lecture from me at Washington, about this time, through the agency of William R. Hooper, Esq. I was obliged to return home from Philadelphia, and here I must remain until the close of the year—only three numbers of the Liberator to be published to complete the period of its existence. Whether I shall be able to visit Washington before the final adjournment of Congress is problematical. I shall have two powerful inducements to do so when you and Fanny are located there. But how shall I spare my daughter at all? Or how will her dependent mother do without her presence?

The wedding-day is coming on apace. I am glad to hear that you intend being with us on Christmas day, anticipating the joyous alliance of hearts and hands, which is to come off, I understand, on Wednesday, January 3. I have just written to my beloved friend, Rev. Samuel J. May, of Syracuse, N.Y., that his presence will not be expected, as, by the laws of this Commonwealth, he cannot legally perform the marriage service in your case. Our neighbor, Rev. Dr. [George] Putnam, will doubtless be specially gratified to "tie the knot," and thus considerable trouble and expense can be saved. Your expenses will be sufficiently onerous, be as economical as you can. Remember, Fanny is one who has been brought up in simple habits, and needs no gifts nor display to satisfy her of your love, or to gratify her taste.

Do not feel obliged to answer this hasty note, as you are overtaxed in writing already, and we shall hear from you *via* Fanny.

Yours, with the warmest regards,

Wm. Lloyd Garrison.

Henry Villard, Esq.

P.S. William and Ellie are in Germantown. Wife and the children desire to be lovingly remembered. Be careful of your health.

ALS: Garrison Papers, Boston Public Library.

1. Henry Villard had in the fall become the Washington correspondent for the Chicago *Tribune*. December 1865 was a critical political period in Washington, with President Johnson and Congress beginning to diverge over Reconstruction policy. (*Memoirs of Henry Villard, Journalist and Financier, 1835–1900*, Boston and New York, 1904; J. G. Randall and David Donald, *The Civil War and Reconstruction*, Lexington, Mass., 1969.)

150

TO WENDELL PHILLIPS GARRISON

Roxbury, Dec. 14, 1865.

My dear Wendell:

Accept my grateful acknowledgments for your filial epistle on my becoming "a sexagenarian," in the completion of my sixtieth year on the 10th of this month. It gives me joy to receive this tribute of your affection and gratitude, because it emanates from a heart that was never guilty of insincerity. I reciprocate your loving expressions to the full. As, in the order of time and in the course of nature, I must decrease and you increase, my prayer is that you may exceed me in all things wherein I may have been of any benefit to my fellow-men, especially to the sacred cause of liberty, which, in its utmost scope, comprehends all things concerning human destiny. You have commenced a career of public usefulness, which, if no casualty occur, may cover a period of half a century. Though you may never be called to antagonize with the powers of darkness, organized in a colossal system of oppression, as I have done; yet you will find no lack of wrong and outrage to expose, of craft and imposture to unmask, of downtrodden helplessness and innocence to defend. The best way to be good is to try to do good to others. The surest method of growing in knowledge and in grace is to find a real cross, to which shall be added in due time a crown. Whoever espouses the side of right is victorious, whether on the scaffold or in the midst of consuming fire. I know you will be ready for every good word and work.

Being in very good mental and bodily condition, it is difficult for me to realize that I am sixty years old. It is a period that I once regarded as aged and venerable; but, somehow, it does not appear so now! Indulge me in this pleasing hallucination. I shall be old "one of these days," beyond a peradventure, if I live long enough. Till then, let us talk of agitation and reform.

Sunday was a day of family greetings; and unspeakably pleasant was it for me to be once more at home. I found your mother in as comfortable a condition as when I left her for the West. Would that I had the power or the means instantaneously to restore to her the use of her paralyzed limbs! Let us hope that something may yet be found for her entire restoration.

I hope to see you to-morrow, and may do so before this receives your perusal. I leave for New York this afternoon, via Providence and Groton, to attend a conference respecting a proposed union of

the American Freedmen's Aid Commission with another association. I shall aim to return home to-morrow afternoon; but, of course,
must not fail to see my beloved daughter Lucy, at your rooms in
Tenth Street. I invoke all heavenly blessings upon you both.

Your ever loving father,

Wm. Lloyd Garrison.

Wendell P. Garrison.

ALS: Garrison Papers, Boston Public Library.

151

TO CHARLES SUMNER

Boston, Dec. 14, 1865.

Dear Mr. Sumner:

At the request of Rev. Photius Fiske, of this city, a chaplain in the
U.S. Navy, I send you the accompanying document, relative to a recent cowardly and brutal assault upon him by Commander Matthias
C. Marin, of the U.S. Navy, which he respectfully and urgently desires you to put into the hands of the Secretary of the Navy for his
grave consideration.[1] Said Marin, I understand, has on another occasion been court-martialled and punished for intemperance, brutality, and other misdemeanors, and is unquestionably a disgrace to
his profession. He ought to be called to account for thus outraging a
navy chaplain, who is in poor physical condition, alike unable and
unwilling to return blow for blow, and whose character is without
reproach. No doubt Secretary Welles will investigate the case.

I have just returned from an extended tour to the West, as far as
the Mississippi river, addressing numerous audiences of high respectability, and seeing many representative men in various places.
I have found but one opinion, whether the test was made publicly
or privately, in regard to that *questis vexata*, "Reconstruction"; and
that is, that not one of the revolted States should be admitted into
the Union without being put under a longer probation. No matter
what may be the promises made, or the constitution presented: it is
not a question of words or of parchment but of the actual spirit, design and condition of the South. In the nature of things, by the laws
of the human mind, she is not and cannot for a long time be loyal,
but is still rebellious though subjugated, and as treasonable as ever
though wearing the mask of submission. Nothing is left her, by way
of revenge or evil device, but to get back to the Union without

delay, so as to exercise absolute legislative and municipal authority over all who dwell on her soil, especially her landless, homeless, penniless freedmen, and all from the North who are endeavoring to give light and knowledge to that ill-used and fearfully wronged class. To secure this admission, she will move "hell from beneath," and whatever is hellish in the land. She is an old covenant-breaker, rotten with perfidy, and still demonized by her old slave system. It is idle for us to rely upon any promises or pledges she may make. Security is to be found only in *keeping her out*—time and events must determine how long—and subject to the direct and omnipresent power of the U. S. Government, which *must not be withdrawn.*

Thanks for your prompt action and untiring vigilance in this matter, in the series of resolutions presented by you to the Senate. Thanks also to your colleague, Mr. [Henry] Wilson, for his co-operative efforts in the same direction.

Yours, for impartial liberty,

Wm. Lloyd Garrison.

Hon. Charles Sumner.

ALS: Charles Sumner Papers, Harvard College Library.

1. Matthias C. Marin (died 1895) rose steadily in rank from midshipman (1832), to lieutenant (1844), to commander (1861); he retired as captain in 1864. Fisk's complaint against Marin for assault was dismissed by Secretary Gideon Welles in a letter to Fisk dated January 25, 1866, suggesting that "in the absence of evidence to corroborate your own testimony, which the Court might not regard as conclusive proof, the result of a trial would perhaps not be satisfactory to you, nor be of benefit in any respect." There is no record that Marin was ever court-martialed. (Letters sent to officers by the Secretary of the Navy, Office of Naval Records and Library, National Archives, Washington, D.C.; *List of Officers of the U.S. Navy and of the Marine Corps, 1775–1900,* New York, 1901; letter to the editor from Harry Schwartz, Navy and Old Army Branch, Military Archives Division, National Archives, Washington, D.C., October 17, 1974.)

152

TO OLIVER JOHNSON

Boston, Dec. 23, 1865.

Dear Oliver:

Only one more number of the Liberator, and "Othello's occupation's gone"![1] As among my earliest, most attached, and most valued friends and coadjutors—as one who has been repeatedly entrusted with the editorial care of the paper—and having so recently closed your connection with the Anti-Slavery Standard—perhaps it would be gratifying to you to send me a congratulatory and farewell letter for insertion next week.[2] If so, it would be still more gratifying to me to publish it,—bating and omitting all personal panegyric. I merely make the suggestion, as your modesty may hold you back where your desire is strong. Possibly you may not be able to find a leisure hour to do this; but if you can, I am sure you will. I cannot find room for a long letter, of course, for I shall be crowded for room; but one from half a column to a column in length will do. I must receive it by Wednesday morning, at the latest—Tuesday morning would be more convenient still. I am sorry it did not occur to me to make this suggestion to you when I saw you the other day —an interview altogether too brief, but my time was very limited.

How much, dear Oliver, I have owed you in the past for your steadfast friendship, your sound judgment, your clear vision, your hopeful spirit, your hearty co-operation, and your many acts of brotherly kindness! If in any way, or to any extent, I have been of any service to you, I shall rejoice.

I write in haste. Give my warmest regards to Mary Anne. Also, to dear Theodore, who shall *not* be excluded from the last number of the Liberator, if he feels "moved in spirit" to send a brief farewell![3]

Ever your faithful friend,

Wm. Lloyd Garrison.

Oliver Johnson.

ALS: Garrison Papers, Boston Public Library.

1. Shakespeare, *Othello*, III, iii, 357.

2. Johnson's letter, which praised Garrison for his contribution to the movement and approved of the termination of the paper now that slavery had been abolished, was printed in *The Liberator*, December 29, 1865.

3. Theodore Tilton's brief letter hailing *The Liberator* as "Prophet and Apostle," like Johnson's, was printed in the last issue of the paper, December 29, 1865.

VI RETIREMENT AND
FINANCIAL SECURITY: 1866

ALTHOUGH 1866, the first year of his retirement, was frustrating for Garrison in a number of ways, it was also the year that brought him prospects of financial security.

Despite a friendly and grateful letter to Wendell Phillips on January 1, the relationship between the two men deteriorated further that same month. At the meeting of the Massachusetts Anti-Slavery Society late in January, they clashed over the discontinuation of that society, just as they had in December over the national organization. And the outcome was the same: Phillips prevailed by a majority vote. On February 3 Garrison wrote a blunt letter to the *Independent,* attacking Phillips and defending himself. On the fifteenth he continued the attack in a letter to *The Nation,* inveighing against Phillips' opinions as expressed in recent and earlier speeches. In a letter to James Miller McKim, February 11 (micro.), Garrison pronounced "the breach now, doubtless, . . . past healing."

About the middle of February Garrison left Boston for his second and last visit to Washington, speaking in Philadelphia on the way. Although the trip was primarily for the purpose of visiting his daughter, he also gave two public speeches, at the Union League Hall and to the black congregation of Dr. Henry Highland Garnet. He arrived in the city in the midst of political events that were exciting in themselves and influential on his future position. On February 19 he was in the visitors' gallery when President Johnson's message vetoing the extension of the Freedmen's Bureau bill was presented to Congress. The bill had been designed to extend indefinitely the life of the Freedmen's Bureau, which had been established during the last months of Lincoln's administration with the provision that it should expire one year after the end of the war.

The new measure was calculated to furnish former slaves, in such states as had not yet been reconstructed, with necessary relief, with educational facilities, and with the protection of civil rights. It was in the area of civil rights that the bill came into most extensive debate, for cases involving discrimination were to be tried by military courts, and infractions to be punished by fine and/or imprisonment. Of the veto Garrison said in his letter to Theodore Tilton of March 8: "What the veto intends to put down, it will in essence and substance put up—that is, the cause of impartial justice and universal liberty. It will rejoice none but the brutal contemptuous enemies of the hapless negro race."

More unexpected and more shocking to Garrison than the veto was the performance he witnessed in front of the White House: President Johnson's "indecent and incendiary harangue to the motley crowd that gathered . . . on the 22nd inst."[1] Garrison's evaluation of this speech was consistent with the point of view expressed in the *National Anti-Slavery Standard* for March 3, where the President was described as speaking "in a loud and excited tone, gritting his teeth, and accompanying his words with violent gesticulations; denouncing the majority of Congress in unmeasured terms, indulging in vulgar attacks against persons he called by name." More conservative papers, however, reacted more favorably. The New York *Times* said on February 23: "It will be seen that he indulges in no roundabout phrases in dealing with those whom he believes to be seeking the destruction of the Union; nor does any consideration of official dignity and etiquette deter him from meeting in the most direct and open manner their implied menaces and denunciations." The following day the *Times* concluded that the speech was "an honest, impulsive, impassioned declaration of his unalterable determination to stand by the Constitution."

Garrison was considerably influenced by what he had observed in Washington—positively by both Sumner and Wilson and negatively by Johnson and Seward. When, late in February, he spoke at the Academy of Music in Brooklyn, he sounded less like a Lincoln moderate than a Radical Republican. The *Standard* commented on March 3: "If Wendell Phillips chastises Andrew Johnson with whips, Garrison laid on with thongs of twisted scorpions." In that speech Garrison also said that the freedmen must become complete citizens "with the right to own land, to inherit and bequeath property, to be justly remunerated for their labor, to sue and be sued, to

1. Letter to Theodore Tilton, March 8, 1866.

testify in all courts, to be represented and vote for representation as do the whites."

Given the altercation with Phillips and the exciting Washington experience, Garrison's retirement as editor and abolitionist showed promise of a high level of activity. On March 20, however, he fell while running to catch a train and seriously injured the right arm and shoulder that had been hurt less painfully by a similar fall in February. He was treated unsuccessfully by a series of doctors and remained in considerable pain during the rest of the year.

Garrison's ill health during 1866 provided for him a convenient excuse to avoid writing the history of the antislavery movement that he had undertaken in March to do for Ticknor and Fields. Although late in the summer (the first volume having been scheduled for publication in October) the publisher was advertising the book as about to be printed, Garrison had, in fact, not written a page. He was full of excuses about his defective memory and his being too close to the events he was to evaluate. But the essential fact was that he was not a scholar and historian but a man of action and a publicist.

Ill health intensified Garrison's financial predicament during 1866. His finances had always been uncertain, if not precarious, and now that he had no salary or other regular income he was thrown back on lecturing for his livelihood—except that the pain throbbing in his injured right arm and shoulder made effective speaking difficult. Fortunately for his well-being, his friends, especially Samuel J. May, George Thompson, Edmund Quincy, and Samuel May, Jr., had been concerned about Garrison's finances. In October 1865 Samuel J. May had given Garrison an insurance policy that paid medical bills during his current illness. On October 16 Quincy discussed his finances in a letter to Irish abolitionist Richard Davis Webb, saying that "there should be a testimonial raised sufficient to put him at ease for the rest of his life."[2] The real decision to raise funds was made early in 1866, with a goal set of $50,000. On April 18 a formal meeting was held at the home of Henry I. Bowditch to launch the drive, or, as it was put in nineteenth-century terms, "to consider the propriety of a National Testimonial to WM. LLOYD GARRISON."[3] At the meeting Governor John A. Andrew called Garrison "the prophetic leader of a great movement," who had worked for abolition virtually without remuneration for thirty-five years. "It would be," he said, "only an act of

2. Anti-Slavery Letters to Garrison and Others, Boston Public Library.
3. Unpublished records of the testimonial, Merrill Collection of Garrison Papers, Wichita State University Library.

justice, on the part of the country, to take care that the remaining days of this true and brave friend of humanity should be set free from anxiety and care, so far as the possession of a fair competency could do this." A standing committee of seven was selected, including the governor, Samuel E. Sewall, and Edmund Quincy, with Samuel May, Jr., as the secretary and paid agent.

Several meetings were held during a two-week period before Garrison discovered the project. His first response was that he was grateful for the effort, but not optimistic about its success, in light of the failure of fund-raising efforts on behalf of George Thompson and of John Brown's family. Garrison underestimated the effectiveness of the well-organized and hard-working committees. Carrying a letter of introduction, May called on prominent men not only in Boston, but in New York, Philadelphia, and Washington. Eighty-five distinguished men, including two cabinet members, eleven governors and ex-governors, seventeen senators, fourteen congressmen, thirty-five businessmen, and six prominent literary men, signed a statement that was printed in a circular announcing the drive. This circular, along with letters from Chief Justice Salmon P. Chase and Senator Charles Sumner, was sent to one thousand potential contributors, and it was subsequently printed in newspapers throughout the country. Moreover, May recruited local agents in many sections of the country.

The most substantial contributions were recorded during the spring and early summer. The largest donation was from Elizabeth Pease Nichol of Edinburgh, who gave £100 ($688.89). Small contributions from poor people accumulated during the summer and fall and into the following year. A high percentage of the gifts came from New England and the Atlantic seaboard, but there were sporadic contributions from farther west (New York state, Ohio, Michigan, Indiana, Illinois, and California), from southern states (Virginia and South Carolina), and from Great Britain. The total amount raised was $35,275.99, of which after deduction of expenses, a net of $33,010.23 remained for Garrison.[4] No contribution was made to the testimonial by Wendell Phillips, but Garrison in a letter of January 1 expressed his gratitude for "generous pecuniary aid" in the past. Although Garrison did not receive formal possession of the fund until March 1868, he was paid interest on the amount collected, and in the spring of 1866 the mortgage of $3,000 was paid on his house.

4. Unless otherwise specified, the source of information about the national testimonial is *AWT*, pp. 309–311.

Other events of importance to Garrison in 1866 included the birth of his first grandchild, the celebration of the first anniversary of the raising of the flag at Fort Sumter, visits to family and friends (even hymn singing with the McKims), and a spiritual séance. All of these he was able to enjoy despite the quarrel with Phillips and his ill health. He must also have enjoyed contemplating the prospect of financial security in the years to come.

153

TO WENDELL PHILLIPS

Roxbury, Jan. 1, 1866. ⟩

My dear Phillips:

I am so unwell, to-day, as to make an effort to write even a brief note burdensome; yet I cannot allow the new year to come in without sending you and your dear wife all the good wishes and congratulations which it so pleasantly evokes. May it prove to you both the most enjoyable year in your earthly pilgrimage, thus far.

I also wish to renew to you the expressions of my gratitude for your numerous acts of kindness, and the generous pecuniary aid you have rendered to me and mine, through so many years of personal friendship and anti-slavery co-operation. You have helped greatly to render it possible for me to prosecute my labors, and also to drive "the wolf want" from my door, by instrumentally securing for me, and those dependant upon me, a comfortable home. The expense of my son Wendell, to you, covering his entire collegiate course, alone made a large bill of indebtedness on my part. You have helped to shape his destiny; and I trust you will never have occasion, by any act of his, to regret what you have done in his behalf. Though, like his father, he is not wont to deal profusely in thanks, you may be assured that your liberality and kindness will ever be most gratefully appreciated by him.

Though, my dear P., you and I have differed somewhat in our judgment of the bearing of events and the action of public men upon that cause which has been equally dear to our hearts, yet it is my comfort and solace to know that in our principles, our desires, and our claims for equal and exact justice to the colored race as to the white, we blend together as fully now as ever. May our friendship be as perpetual as sun, moon and stars, but without their occasional obscuration!

I intended and desired to write a long letter to you, especially in view of the termination of the Liberator, and the abolition of slavery throughout the land; but I am obliged to forbear, on account of bodily languor and debility.

With my still *admiring* regards to your dear and noble Ann, and hoping we shall have the pleasure of seeing you at our beloved Fanny's wedding at 12 o'clock, M., on Wednesday next, I remain,

Your affectionate and grateful friend,

Wm. Lloyd Garrison.

Wendell Phillips, Esq.

ALS: Typographic Collection, Columbia University Libraries.

154

TO JAMES B. YERRINTON

Boston, Jan. 1, 1866.

My dear and faithful friend Yerrinton:

In offering you the good wishes and heartfelt congratulations which the advent of another year naturally prompts, I confess that these are mingled with feelings of sadness in view of the fact that, to-day, we part company in reference to the Liberator, after your connection with it as its printer for a quarter of a century. The primary object and sublime mission of the paper having been consummated, its existence fitly covers the entire period of the struggle, and ends with it. Hence the separation between us to which I refer: but, though only relating to business, and not to that friendship which we formed so closely more than thirty years ago, yet the little printing-office has daily brought us together, and enabled us to know each other as intimately as it is possible, in every phase of human thought and feeling. I wish to improve this opportunity to testify to the unfailing good temper and kindness of spirit and manner which you have manifested amidst all the annoyances and perplexities connected with type-setting, bad proof, illegible manuscript, &c., &c. Never has there been a sharp or hasty word between us. Your disposition is so good that mine must have been crabbed indeed at any time to have caused a ripple upon the surface of our feelings toward each other. Blessed with good health, you have been always at your post,—not even indulging, for once, in that occasional recreation which seems to be almost indispensable to the recuperation of mind and body. Such assiduity and steadiness I have never known, and call for special recognition. But your work on the Liberator has not been a mere mechanical performance. You have mingled with it the liveliest interest in the welfare of the paper, in the principles it has inculcated, in the humane and god-like object it has aimed to achieve, and in whatever has related to my personal safety and success. You were an abolitionist from the start, and never hesitated to show your colors or define your position; hence you have a right to rejoice in this year of jubilee as one of the little band whose testimonies and labors have, by the blessing of God, resulted in breaking every yoke and letting the oppressed go free.[1] For many a year it was any thing but reputable to be even the printer of the Liberator; but that reproach is now wiped out, and in the future will make your memory honored.

Accept the accompanying trifle[2] as but the very slightest token of my esteem and friendship. I deeply regret my pecuniary inability to send more, but you know my situation. Be assured that, if it were in my power, nothing would give me more pleasure than to liberate you from type-setting for the remainder of your days. May it be yours still to welcome and enjoy many a new year. God bless you!

Ever faithfully yours,

Wm. Lloyd Garrison.

J. B. Yerrinton.

Typed transcription: Garrison Papers, Boston Public Library; partly printed in *Life*, IV, 169, n. 2.

1. An allusion to Isaiah 58:6.
2. According to a notation in the hand of Francis Jackson Garrison at the bottom of the second page of the letter, this "trifle" was $50.

155

TO FANNY GARRISON VILLARD

Rockledge, Jan. 7, 1866.

My dear Fanny:

As yet, we have not had sufficient time at home to miss you as far away, with no expectation of returning for several months; besides, the company of Henry[1] and aunt Charlotte [Anthony] till yesterday afternoon, and that of our dear daughter Lucy till now, has served to fill that vacancy which we shall assuredly feel more and more. Nothing special has occurred since you left. We hear nothing but expressions of delight on the part of those who attended the wedding. All the decorations in the parlor remain as when the eventful ceremony was performed; but as the weather, for the last three days, has been of Arctic severity, (this morning the mercury ranging four degrees below zero,) none of our friends have called to see us, and, consequently, our floral exhibition is in vain. It will be removed to-morrow, though I fear some of the plants will be injured by the cold.

The letters that you and Harry so thoughtfully and so promptly wrote to us from Worcester gave us great pleasure in their perusal. May the joys of your honeymoon be perennial! I know how Harry is feeling, even without the description he gives in his letter; for have I not had my first week of marriage, with all its thronging emotions and delights? But I have this advantage—that I have added to that week more than thirty-one years, and so have had "lengthened sweetness long drawn out,"[2] and an accumulation of bliss which he is yet to realize. At the end of thirty-one years, let him report himself, and compare notes! If in the flesh, I shall then be in my ninety-second year; and my testimony will then be, as it is now, that "it is not good for the man to be alone"[3]—neither for the woman. The novelty of your new relation will soon pass away, and with it much of the excitement attending it; but your love for each other will deepen and strengthen with years. Of this I have no doubt. Yet I find it hard to give you up; for my parental affection for you has been, and through all vicissitudes will continue to be, inexpressibly great. I know, by your strong love for me and your dear mother, you will try to be as near us as you can in locality, and to sojourn with us as often as circumstances will permit. I shall cherish the hope that, ultimately, you and Harry will make Rockledge or its vicinity your chosen residence.

Your mother is specially anxious about you this terrifically cold weather. She says you ought to be more warmly clad as to your underclothes, and that you must be careful of unnecessary exposure. Remember the homely adage—"An ounce of prevention is worth a pound of cure."[4]

Hepza[5] came back on Friday, punctual to her promise. She is very quiet and retiring, and seems desirous to be useful in house matters, as well as serviceable to your crippled mother.

What say you to having a generous piece of Mrs. Fayerweather's wedding-cake sent to you, leaving the balance with us for distribution among the many friends who were disappointed in not seeing, or tasting, or taking home, anything of the kind?[6] At home we are unanimous in thinking this will be a judicious and gratifying disposal of it. But it shall be as you and Harry wish about it.

Lucy returns to New York in the morning, via Springfield. I shall accompany her as far as East Brookfield. In the evening I am to lecture at North Brookfield. On Tuesday evening I am to speak in New Bedford, and to be the guest of ex-Governor Clifford, who went with me in the Arago to Fort Sumter.[7]

We are sorry indeed to part with Lucy. She has brightened our house since you left by her presence. Tell Wendell she has won the esteem of all who have seen her. Salute Harry with a kiss for me, and another for your mother.

Adieu, darling!

Your loving Father.

AL signed "Father": Villard Papers, Harvard College Library.

1. Presumably the reference is to the son, not the father.
2. John Milton, "L'Allegro," line 140, misquoted ("lengthened" for "linked").
3. Genesis 2:18, adapted.
4. While the idea dates back to ancient times, T. C. Haliburton (Sam Slick) recorded the phrase in *Wise Saws* (1843).
5. An unidentified servant.
6. The baker of the cake was Sarah Harris Fayerweather (c. 1814–c. 1870) who, in 1831, had been the first black girl to be enrolled in Prudence Crandall's ill-fated school in Canterbury, Conn. (Samuel J. May, *Some Recollections of Our Antislavery Conflict*, Boston, 1869, p. 41; letter to the editor from Ruth Bell, researcher, March 27, 1972.)
7. John Henry Clifford (1809–1876) was a prominent New Bedford lawyer who had been district attorney for southern Massachusetts (1839–1849) as well as attorney general of the state (1849–1853). In 1850 he became famous for his prosecution of Harvard professor John White Webster for the murder of Dr. George Parkman. In 1853 he became governor of the state, serving for one term before being reappointed attorney general. During the Civil War he supported Lincoln's policies, and he also served in the Massachusetts Senate. In 1867 he became president of the Boston and Providence Railroad, a position he held until his death.

156

TO SARAH SALISBURY TAPPAN

BOSTON, January 25, 1866.

MY DEAR MISS TAPPAN:

Your very kind letter enclosing a photograph of your revered father, gives me inexpressible pleasure.[1] This likeness better reveals his features to my recollection than the one he had the kindness to send me, though that is highly prized. Be assured I shall carefully preserve them both in my collection of portraits of friends, the most cherished and beloved—not merely because he was my liberator from the Baltimore prison in 1830,[2] and among my earliest coadjutors in the then persecuted but now triumphant cause of the downtrodden slave, but for his Christian graces and virtues, making his character illustrious and proving his love for God by his love for man without regard to complexion, race, or clime.

He was the embodiment of integrity and justice, of world-wide philanthropy and genuine piety, of true modesty and utter self-abnegation. He had a solid understanding, a great conscience, and a warm heart. No man was ever more faithful to his convictions of duty, lead where it might, through the flood or through the fire.

At all times "ready to be offered" in the service of God, and the cause of suffering humanity, he was serene in the midst of fiery trials and imminent perils, being crucified to "that fear of man which bringeth a snare," and having his life "hid with Christ in God."[3]

There are many forms of martyrdom besides being literally burnt to ashes, requiring as much courage and fortitude, and as great a heart and will, as the stake. Some of the most trying of these he had to confront for a long period in the rabid pro-slavery city of New York, but who ever knew him to shrink from the cross? He could neither be appalled by mob violence nor seduced by worldly interest. As a merchant naturally desiring customers, and a wide market, and having an immense business at stake, he had the most powerful temptation to avoid an espousal of so unpopular a cause as that of abolition, but in the spirit of his Master, he said, "Get thee behind me, Satan."[4] Though not so conspicuously identified with the anti-slavery struggle for some years past as formerly, his interest in it never lessened; and now that the nation has decreed universal emancipation, I doubt not that he is cognizant of the glorious event, and with the liberated millions rendering praise and thanksgiving to God.

Where or what I should have been without his benevolent interposition to release me from my Baltimore imprisonment, it is in vain for me to conjecture. My deep indebtedness I shall never forget.

Your much obliged friend,

WM. LLOYD GARRISON.

Printed: Lewis Tappan, *The Life of Arthur Tappan* (New York, 1871), pp. 399–400.

Miss Tappan is no doubt Sarah Salisbury Tappan (1819–1896), the only unmarried one of the Tappans' five surviving daughters. (Daniel Langdon Tappan, *Tappan-Toppan Genealogy* . . ., Arlington, Mass., 1915.)

1. Arthur Tappan had died on July 23, 1865.
2. See *Letters*, I, 92–93, n. 1; and the letter to Arthur Tappan, November 12, 1863, descriptive note.
3. II Timothy 4:6; Proverbs 29:25, adapted; Colossians 3:3.
4. The reference is to either Matthew 16:23, Mark 8:33, or Luke 4:8.

157

TO FANNY GARRISON VILLARD

Boston, Jan. 27, 1866.

My Darling:

Another long and pleasant letter was received from you to-day. In getting through with your varied correspondence since your arrival in Washington,—writing letters of acknowledgments for favors received, &c.—you must have had a severe task. Speaking of favors—we erred in supposing the wedding cake from Salem was a gift from Mrs. Putnam,[1] for in her note she expressly stated that it was her sister Susan[2] who made and sent it. As soon as I ascertained the mistake, I wrote a letter to Susan, thanking her in your name for her kind and generous gift, and sending her your card photograph. I am afraid, however, that you may have sent a letter of thanks to Mrs. Putnam, supposing the cake to have come from her. If you have, it may be a somewhat difficult thing to straighten the matter out satisfactorily to all parties.

On Wednesday,[3] the American Anti-Slavery Society held two meetings (forenoon and afternoon) in the Melodeon,[4] preparatory to the Subscription Festival at Music Hall in the evening. Of course, I attended neither of them. The audiences in the day-time were small, and the chief speakers Mr. [Wendell] Phillips, Mr. and Mrs. [Stephen S.] Foster, and Theodore Tilton. Phillips and Tilton also made speeches in the evening; though they had a sharp encounter in the discussions at the Melodeon. Music Hall was about half filled. What was the amount of money raised, I have not heard. No doubt every string was pulled in order to make it at least equal to last year's.[5]

On Thursday forenoon the annual meeting of the Massachusetts Anti-Slavery Society was held at the Melodeon; on which occasion Mr. [Edmund] Quincy made his valedictory address as President of the Society—laying before the meeting the vote of the Board of Managers, recommending the dissolution of the Society in consequence of the abolition of slavery throughout the republic. I gave a brief exposition of my own views, in favor of dissolution; and was followed by Mr. Phillips in a long and labored speech, full of special pleading and unjust imputations upon his old associates. Several others participated in the discussion. The vote in favor of discontinuing the Society was only about one to three, and Mr. Phillips succeeded in carrying his point. He outfaced Mr. [William H.] Seward and the nation in plumply denying that slavery was abolished; and said that, if it were so, we could not tell how soon it might be re-established; ergo, the necessity for continuing the Society! Of course, as the whole thing is a farce, I care nothing for it.

I hope sometime next month to have the joy and delight to see you and Harry in Washington; for I shall endeavor to make my arrangements so that, after lecturing in Philadelphia, I can proceed to the Capital. Something may occur, however, to prevent it; yet I shall hope not to be foiled visiting you, either in February or March.

It is pleasant to know that every thing goes on joyously under your own roof. The various receptions you have attended do not appear to have raised your ideas of Washington society; but I am quite sure your analysis of it is entirely correct.

I have good reason to believe that what General [Nathaniel] Banks said to you about me was a sincere expression of feeling, long entertained.

Do not feel that you must answer every letter from Rockledge separately; for, in writing to one, you wrote to us all.

Adieu! darling!

Your Loving Father.

P.S. Your mother is writing to you to-day, and no doubt will tell you all about the visits of Anne Morrill, Mrs. [Theodoric] Severance, Mrs. [Samuel B.] Chase of Valley Falls, Mrs. Jarvis,[6] &c. Love to Harry.

AL signed "Father": Garrison Papers, Boston Public Library.

1. Caroline R. Putnam, widow of Joseph, was probably the daughter of John and Nancy Lenox Remond, Negro caterers in Salem, Mass., and the sister of Charles Lenox Remond. She was a hairwork manufacturer with a place of business listed in Salem directories at various locations on Essex Street. (Letter to the editor from Dorothy M. Potter, librarian, Essex Institute, May 4, 1972.)

2. Not otherwise identified.

3. January 24.

4. The Melodeon, built in 1836 as the Lion Theatre, had been a concert and lecture hall since 1839. (William W. Clapp, "The Drama in Boston," in Justin Winsor, *The Memorial History of Boston*, Boston, 1881, IV, 371.)

5. According to a report in the *National Anti-Slavery Standard*, March 3, the total raised was $2,834.70—"not as large as in the past but larger than we had reason to expect."

6. Anne (or Annie) Morrill (c. 1843–1867) was the daughter of Dr. Alpheus Morrill (1808–1874) of Concord, N.H., and his second wife, Eliza Ann Cate, whom he married in 1838. In July 1866 Annie married Josiah Grahme Bellows (died 1906). Less than a year later she died after giving birth to twins. (Obituary, Boston *Post*, April 9, 1867; Ezra S. Stearns, ed., *Genealogical and Family History of New Hampshire*, New York, 1908, II, 717.)

Mrs. Jarvis may have been Almira Jarvis (1804–1884), the wife of Dr. Edward Jarvis of Dorchester, Mass. (Letter to the editor from Ruth Bell, researcher, April 1, 1972.)

158

TO HARRIET BEECHER STOWE

[January 1866]

DEAR MRS. STOWE:

For your very appreciative and congratulatory letter on the "marvellous work of the Lord,"[1] which the Liberator marks as finished, I proffer you my heartfelt thanks, and join with you in a song of thanksgiving to Him, who, by a mighty hand and an outstretched arm has set free the captive millions in our land.

The instrumentalities which the God of the oppressed has used for the overthrow of the slave system, have been as multifarious and extraordinary as that system has been brutal and iniquitous. Every thing that has been done, whether to break the yoke or to rivet it more strongly, has been needed to bring about the great result. The very madness of the South has worked as effectively anti-slavery-wise as the most strenuous efforts of the abolitionists.

The outlawry of all Northern men of known hostility to slavery—the numberless pro-slavery mobs and lynchings, her defiant and awful defence of the traffic in human flesh, her increasing rigor and cruelties towards the slaves, and finally her horrible treason and rebellion to secure her independence as a vast slaveholding empire, through all time, all mightily helped to defeat her impious purpose and to hasten the year of jubilee. Thus it is that

> God moves in a mysterious way,
> His wonders to perform;
> He plants his footsteps in the sea,
> And rides upon the storm.[2]

And who but God is to be glorified?

Printed extract: Harriet Beecher Stowe, *Men of Our Times* (Hartford, Conn., 1868), p. 211. It seems likely that Garrison's letter was written in January, inasmuch as he is answering her congratulatory letter of January 2, 1866 (Anti-Slavery Letters to Garrison and Others, Boston Public Library).

Harriet Beecher Stowe (1811–1896), the daughter of Lyman Beecher and sister of Henry Ward Beecher, married Calvin E. Stowe in 1836. In 1851–52 she published one of the most famous and influential novels of the nineteenth century, *Uncle Tom's Cabin*. She also wrote a second antislavery novel, *Dred, a Tale of the Great Dismal Swamp* (1856), as well as various works of fiction with New England settings. Her fame and popularity were somewhat diminished in England by her publication of *Lady Byron Vindicated* (1870), which referred to Byron's relations with his sister as incestuous.

1. A quotation from Mrs. Stowe's letter.
2. William Cowper, *Olney Hymns*, "Light Shining Out of Darkness."

159

TO THEODORE TILTON

[Boston, February 3, 1866.]

DEAR MR. TILTON:—

I thank you for your voluntary correction, in the last number of *The Independent*, of a gross misstatement of my position, by the New York *Times*, in regard to the cause of the liberated bondmen at the South. It is not true that I "hold that the abolition of the odious slave system renders further agitation in behalf of the black man, distinctively, an unmixed evil to the race themselves." No such preposterous sentiment has ever been recorded by my pen, or uttered by my voice. I believe exactly the contrary to what the *Times* alleges, and expect to act in accordance with that belief either until full and complete justice is in all things meted out to colored citizenship as it is to white, or until my earthly pilgrimage is ended.[1]

But I am not greatly surprised at this willful misrepresentation, or unintentional blunder (as the case may be), on the part of the *Times* —seeing that there are some with whom I have been long associated in the anti-slavery struggle who lose no opportunity to give currency to the same aspersion; doing what in them lies to make it popularly believed that I have lost my interest in that still most deeply injured race, whose cause I have so long espoused in the face of peril, outlawry, and death; and that I am now for leaving them to their fate, with only homeless, penniless, landless freedom! If, for example, any one will read the speech of Mr. [Wendell] Phillips, made at the recent anniversary of the Massachusetts Anti-Slavery Society in Boston, and published in the *Anti-Slavery Standard* of this week, he will find—*i.e.*, if language means anything—all those who deem it a matter of good sense and propriety to dissolve the Anti-Slavery Society now that slavery has been abolished by the fiat of the nation, virtually branded as recreant to their principles and professions as Abolitionists; though in nothing pertaining to the claims of the emancipated do they differ from him. "*Et tu, Brute?*"[2] I know that, on making this criticism upon his speech at the time, some in the audience who went with him cried out, "No, no!"—but there is the speech in print, as revised and corrected for the press by Mr. Phillips; and against this paradoxical denial I place its direct impeachment of our zeal, perseverance, and fidelity. Allow me to quote a passage or two from it:

"I have watched the speeches, I have watched the journals, I have watched the printed declarations of that party which went off last May, and with the exception of a few articles, which I could count on the fingers of one hand, I affirm, with all respect and *in fidelity to the slave,* that that party has not made itself heard and felt by the American public in behalf of suffrage for the black man before the Southern States are admitted to the Union; and on the President's real position, so far as I know, no person has sufficient evidence to settle what is their real opinion on those two momentous questions. * * * I have seen their weekly journal—⟦meaning the *Liberator* ⟧—I have watched its labors; I know the one or two cases that can be named against me; but in eight months, during the most critical period of the history of the American Republic, I affirm, with all respect and no unkindness, that those lips have been substantially silent. * * * I do not believe that the men who go off from us, numbering perhaps the majority, and *bearing down your banner,* will be heard of by you as you have heard of them in times past, in the front rank, day by day, week by week, reported out of spite in every opposition journal, sneered at by every Conservative Republican, denounced as factious by every adherent of the President. *You will never hear of them;* you have not heard of them lately. * * * When at the bidding ⟦bidding!⟧ of my friend, Mr. Garrison, you pull down this Massachusetts Anti-Slavery flag, the members of the Republican party will fold their arms and say, 'The Abolitionists say the work is done ⟦the very falsehood of the *Times* ⟧—we can go home. *They say the President is right* (!)—that the Administration can be trusted; that Congress is on guard; *we can devote ourselves to making money,"* etc., etc.[3]

I do not propose, at this time, to take any notice of these insinuations and aspersions beyond entering an emphatic denial of them, and remarking that, when they fall, from such lips, with such emphasis, the *Times* is not to be very severely dealt with for asserting that, as an "old, well-tried assailant of slavery," I "have declared that continued agitation can work only evil." If Mr. Phillips really believes what he says, it is difficult to perceive what "possible respect" he can entertain for me, or those whom he associates with me. The *Liberator,* "for the past eight months," has been before its readers and the public, and they know whether the trumpet has given an uncertain sound or not, in regard to the matter of reconstruction or suffrage. If I had the *cacoethes scribendi*[4] as Mr. Phillips has the *cacoethes loquendi*—as much fondness for writing as he has for speech-making—doubtless, he would have been able to find more articles of the kind he was in search of.

But, not content with making these disparaging charges against his old associates, Mr. Phillips, with swollen self-complacency, proclaims: "If anything has been done by the anti-slavery body on the question of suffrage before reconstruction, it has been done by the men whom they left behind. * * * It is only because *I, and such as I*, stand at the door, and keep Wade Hampton[5] out to-day, that Yankee teachers are permitted to live and labor in the Southern States—to distribute even cheap food and cheap books."

To all this exhibition of personal antagonism and egotistical assumption, it will suffice to make one more quotation as an offset: "Now, they have as much right to their course as I have to mine; *their judgment is as likely to be correct as mine.* I allow for this honest difference of opinion. *I have no right to criticize.*" No right to criticize indeed! Certainly not to indulge in unmerited sarcasm and inexcusable misrepresentation. If we, who dissent from some of his sayings and doings, are as "likely to be correct" as himself, and it is only "an honest difference of opinion," how is he warranted in striking such an attitude, and in making so grave and vital an arraignment?

All that I assume—all that those who agree with me assume—is that, slavery being constitutionally abolished and prohibited, the work of agitating for its overthrow is ended. There is no need of any more anti-slavery journals, anti-slavery lectures, anti-slavery speeches, anti-slavery tracts, or anti-slavery contributions. All these are happily obsolete. But the work of educating, elevating, protecting, and vindicating the emancipated millions, in regard to all possible rights and immunities, is not done; *it is only just begun;* and in the great philanthropic, patriotic, and Christian work I, and those opprobriously associated with me by Mr. Phillips, take as deep and absorbing an interest, and expect to participate as earnestly as himself. I make no boast of what I have done, or what I intend to do; but the multitudinous audiences I addressed in public, and the numerous leading citizens with whom I conferred in private, during my extended tour at the West, in October and November last, can judge whether the imputations thus thrown are merited or not.

Yours, for the rights of all men,

WM. LLOYD GARRISON.

BOSTON, Feb. 3d, 1866.

Printed: *Independent*, February 8, 1866.

1. Tilton's "voluntary correction" appeared in the *Independent*, January 25, 1866, under the heading "Personal," as follows:

Misuse of a Good Man's Name
The New York *Times* seeks to justify its hostility to the Radical Republicans in Congress, and to the measures they propose, by an appeal to the example of Garrison and his friends, as follows:

"Life-long friends of the slave, like William Lloyd Garrison, retired from the arena of strife when the destruction of slavery was accomplished. They hold that the abolition of the odious institution renders further agitation in behalf of the black race, distinctively, an unmixed evil to the race themselves; and, with a promptitude that does them honor these, the old, well-tried assailants of slavery, have declared that continued agitation can work only evil."

This is a misuse of a noble man's name, for which there is no apology in anything that he has said or done. Mr. Garrison does indeed hold that, as slavery is abolished by a decree of the American people, recorded in the fundamental law, there is no longer any need of *anti*-slavery societies or newspapers —that such societies are in fact an anachronism. But he is at the same time in favor of suffrage for the negro, and of such agitation as may be found necessary to secure it. The attempt of the *Times*, itself behind the name of Garrison is alike unwarrantable and preposterous. It can earn the right to plead *that* name as an authority only by such fidelity to the cause of impartial liberty as it has never yet exhibited.

2. Shakespeare, *Julius Caesar*, III, i, 77.

3. Garrison quotes accurately (with a few minor changes, including the addition of italics) from Phillips' speech as printed in the *National Anti-Slavery Standard*, February 2, 1866.

4. Juvenal, *Satires*, vii, 51.

5. Phillips refers to Wade Hampton (1818–1902), the South Carolina planter and general who, though he had not favored secession, supported wholeheartedly the southern cause—both in the field of battle and financially. Following the war (in 1877) he was to become governor of his state and later United States senator.

160

TO OLIVER JOHNSON

Roxbury, Feb. 11, 1866.

My dear Johnson:

After heartily thanking you for your letter, (and also, through you, Theodore [Tilton] for his,) allow me to request, if you do not happen to be otherwise engaged, that you will come after tea on Wednesday evening next, and spend an hour or two with me in social chit-chat at Wendell's boarding-house, 155 East 10th street. Of course, in this invitation I include Mary-Ann. It would give me great pleasure to see Theodore, also, at the same time; but his living in Brooklyn makes it reasonably out of the question. I will not fail to see him, however, on my return from Washington.

I mean to improve the kind and generous overture, contained in both your letters, to write for the Independent—with this proviso, that what I shall send must be as freely abridged, or omitted wholly, as though the author were unknown. Remember this.

No credit was given to the London Daily News (in which it appeared editorially) for the handsome notice of me and the Liberator in the article copied by the Independent.[1] I presume the omission was unintentional. If so, might it not be well to let the readers of the Independent know from what source it came? No doubt Miss [Harriet] Martineau wrote the article.[2]

I feel inexpressibly sad at the breach which has taken place in the Anti-Slavery ranks, especially with W. P. [Wendell Phillips.] I presume my letter about him in the Independent will be taken by him as a mortal affront, as it was certainly sharp and pointed. But I can stand anything but an imputation upon my fidelity to the colored race; and I know not why he should be allowed to hold us all up to view as hauling down our flag, and beating a retreat, without being strongly rebuked for it. Perhaps he will as sharply respond to my letter in the next Independent.

Hastily, but affectionately yours,

Wm. Lloyd Garrison.

Oliver Johnson.

ALS: Garrison Papers, Boston Public Library.

1. The London *Daily News* was founded in 1846 by Charles Dickens as a forum for his ideas on social reform, but he remained with the paper only briefly. The editor in 1866 was Thomas Walker.

2. Harriet Martineau (1802–1876), sister of James Martineau, was an energetic reformer and one of the most varied and prolific of English writers. The daughter of a once-successful Norwich manufacturer who lost his property before his early death, she was obliged to support herself from her writings, most successful of which were her moralistic tales and the books concerned with travel. Her trip to the United States (1834–1836), during which she supported the abolitionists so vehemently that she risked physical danger, provided her with the material for two books: *Society in America* (1837) and *A Retrospect of Western Travel* (1838). In 1839 she published what she considered her finest work, the novel *Deerbrook*. Over the years she wrote innumerable magazine articles on a variety of topics. On the occasion of the publication of the last issue of *The Liberator* she wrote an article about Garrison (see the *Independent*, February 8, 1866). Extolling him as "the Moses of the colored race," she summarized Garrison's contribution to the cause of abolition, concluding: "He said he would be heard; he was heard effectually; and now he proposes to be silent. It is to be hoped that we shall not for such a reason forget him. History certainly will not; and if she relates that before the second American revolution the nation had so sunk that the world taunted it with having no great men, she will add that this was a mistake, for there was one great man—the second printer's journeyman who did a great work for his country—William Lloyd Garrison."

161

TO GEORGE W. JULIAN

Boston, Feb. 11, 1866.

Hon. G. W. Julian:

Dear Sir—

I am very much obliged to you for sending me a printed copy of your terse, well reasoned, and admirably expressed speech on Suffrage in the District of Columbia, delivered in the U. S. House of Representatives on the 16th ult.[1] Of course, I cordially approve its spirit, its object, its premises and conclusions. All honor to you, and the noble band in both Houses, who are resolved to make no compromise that shall leave the colored population of the District and the still rebellious South without the possession of all those rights and immunities which belong to citizenship! The House has since acted upon the question of Suffrage in the District in a manner that will give historic reputation to this session, if it do not recede from its position. May the Senate be as strong in the same direction!

I trust Congress will not readmit any one of the late rebel States into the Union. They are still as full of the spirit of revolt as ever, and are not to be trusted in any promises they may make for the future. The Government is solemnly bound to be omnipresent, omniscient, and omnipotent in every part of the South for a long time to come; as a speedy withdrawal of its presence and power from that demonized section will in all probability be followed by the most frightful consequences.

The President is evidently sincere as to his convictions about the best policy to be pursued; but as that policy is warmly approved by the rebels on the one hand, and the copperheads on the other, it is strange that he does not see his error.

You need not respond to this, as I hope to be in Washington next Saturday, and to spend several days in the city.

Yours, with high regards,

Wm. Lloyd Garrison.

ALS: Giddings-Julian Papers, Library of Congress.

1. Julian's speech was reported in the *National Anti-Slavery Standard,* January 20, 1866. He urged the giving of the suffrage to the 20,000 black citizens in the District of Columbia, in order to make them friends.

162

TO CHARLES SUMNER

Boston, Feb. 11, 1866.

Hon. Charles Sumner:

My Dear Friend—

Be assured, I am an attentive reader of all your sayings, and a close observer of all your doings, on the floor of the Senate, in vindicating the rights of our common humanity, and devising measures to give sure protection and absolute justice to the millions you have been so largely instrumental in bringing out of the Southern house of bondage. I have perused your eloquent and unanswerable speech on the Suffrage question, and need not say that it contains the noblest sentiments, to which all the faculties and powers which God has given me thrillingly respond.[1] It will, doubtless, be more efficacious out of the Senate than in it, as it will help to educate the popular mind up to the point of abolishing all complexional distinctions before the law, North and South.

While those distinctions are so broadly drawn at the North,—as witness the political disfranchisement of their colored inhabitants by three-fourths of all the free States,—it is not possible, I fear, to m⌐ke the franchise universal at the South on this very account. But what may be done is one thing; what ought to be done is quite another, and certainly the very thing to be urged until the nation is prepared to grant it. Your speech, based as it is upon absolute justice and eternal right, is an admirable elementary treatise; and I trust will have the widest circulation.

What assiduity and perseverance, what courage and determination, what devotion and inflexible purpose you have shown, through fiery trials and at the risk of martyrdom, "in season and out of season,"[2] to effect the downfall of the atrocious slave system, and thereby elevate and save the republic! If, to this extent, the year of jubilee has come, you have done much towards ushering it in, and have a right to be specially glad and grateful that Heaven has been pleased to make you so potential an instrumentality in bringing about its beneficent designs.

I know there is a mighty work yet remaining to be done, and that at the South the powers of hell are still strong and defiant, resolved upon doing whatever evil is possible, in the spirit of diabolical malignity. But, "fore-warned, fore-armed." By the help of God, we will overcome the devices of the enemy, nor abate aught of heart or hope in any struggle we may yet be called to pass through. Let the friends of impartial freedom present an undaunted front, remember the wonderful victories already achieved, and thank God and take courage.

I have much that I would like to say to you on paper, but I am now pressed for time. Next Saturday, however, I expect to be in Washington, and to remain there eight or ten days; so I shall hope to have the pleasure of an interview with you.

Yours, uncompromisingly for the right,

Wm. Lloyd Garrison.

ALS: Charles Sumner Papers, Harvard College Library.

1. Garrison refers to Sumner's speech "The Equal Rights of All," which he gave in the Senate on February 6 and 7. He spoke against the proposed Blaine amendment, which provided that "whenever the elective franchise shall be denied or abridged in any State on account of race or color, all persons therein shall be excluded from the basis of representation." Sumner argued that the Constitution guarantees the right of all tax-paying citizens to representation and that the states should not be given the power to deny this right on the basis of race or color. He said that the ballot is peacemaker, reconciler, schoolmaster, and protector. "The promises of the Fathers must be sacredly fulfilled. This is the commanding rule, superseding all other rules. This is the great victory of the war,—perhaps the greatest. It is nothing less than the emancipation of the Constitution itself." (Charles Sumner, *Complete Works*, Boston, 1900, XIII, 113–269; *National Anti-Slavery Standard*, February 17, 1866.)

Mrs. Frances D. Gage, describing the Senate chamber while Sumner was speaking, said that the galleries were overflowing with people who listened with "a silence that was almost more than silence." (*Standard*, February 17.)

2. II Timothy 4:2.

163

TO FANNY GARRISON VILLARD

Boston, Feb. 11, 1866.

My dear Fanny:

How difficult it is to get over an old habit! I am writing this at Rockledge, and yet you see this is dated *Boston*. It is so, unconsciously so, with almost every letter I write.

To-day at home; a week from to-day I hope to be, with Franky, in the Capital, having a *capital* time with you and Harry. We shall probably remain with you until Monday morning, 24th inst. which will give us ample time to see all that we shall care to see at Washington, though we shall be sorry indeed to be separated from the wedded pair. I have no wish for parties or entertainments, but desire as much quietude and *abandon* in moving about as practicable. Of course, there are some of our public men—such as Sumner,

[Henry] Wilson, [Benjamin F.] Wade, [George W.] Julien, [William D.] Kelley, Stevens,[1] &c.—whom I shall aim to see; but these I can find any day in their places, or at their boarding-places. Do not go to the trouble and expense of inviting a numerous company on my account. You know my habits and tastes in regard to such matters.

As the time draws near for our leaving home, your mother naturally feels as if she could not be left behind; nor should she be, were it not for her crippled and helpless condition. But she will derive great satisfaction from the thought that we are with you, and that we shall soon report to her the various pleasant things attending our visit.

Wendell wants Franky to abide with him awhile, (in Lucy's absence,) on his way back, and to bring his books, and study *ad libitum*. So, while the same proposition is made by you, and gratefully appreciated by F., we had better return together.

Your mother will miss us both, during our absence; but Hepza and Ella [Ellen W. Garrison] will do all they can to fill the vacancies; and no doubt dear, good Charlotte Coffin will be happy, as usual, to be her companion, and remain till I get home.

I shall send Harry, by this mail, (perhaps you have already seen it,) the last number of the Independent, in which you will find a letter from me, under my own signature, somewhat sharply taking W. P. [Wendell Phillips] to account for his disparaging and invidious speech in Boston, last month.[2] It is inexpressibly painful to my feelings to have this breach occur, but the responsibility rests with him. We shall probably never meet again as of old. Whether he will reply to my letter, through the Independent, remains to be seen.[3] It was somewhat hurriedly written; and I would modify or omit one or two descriptive epithets in it, if I were to write it over again. They will be likely to sting to the quick.

Mr. Sumner's last speech was as able and eloquent as it was elaborate and exhaustive.[4] Of course, I second the motion for all that he demands for the colored race; but such a speech is really much more for popular effect than adapted to Congress, which can only go as far in the matter of suffrage as the people will tolerate. How far that is, is quite problematical.

We have had very steady cold weather for some time past; but, to-day, Nature is in her melting mood—the mercury ranging at 40°. Your poor mother is closely imprisoned, in consequence of so much ice, and will rejoice indeed when "the time for the singing of birds has come,"[5] that she may be able to tread the earth once more and take an occasional ride. She is, nevertheless, looking exceedingly well.

The title of my coming lecture in Philadelphia is, *"Liberty* Victorious"—not the *South*.⁶ It will not at all please those who are morbidly inclined.

Franky received a letter from you yesterday, and probably will answer it to-day.

In consequence of the reference to W. P. in this letter, you had better burn it after you and H. have perused it.

Remember, we hope to be with you on Saturday, in the regular morning train from Philadelphia.

All send loving regards to you and Harry.

Your affectionate Father.

☞ In the Independent you will see a very handsome notice of me and the Liberator from the London Daily News, though the credit was accidentally omitted. I have no doubt Harriet Martineau wrote it.

AL signed "Father": Garrison Papers, Boston Public Library.

1. Thaddeus Stevens (1792–1868), a native of Danville, Vt., who had settled in 1816 in Gettysburg, Pa., was elected to the state legislature in 1833 and to Congress in 1848. Long an abolitionist, Stevens became a leading free-soiler. During the Lincoln administration he served as chairman of the Ways and Means Committee. His was among the most radical and aggressive voices in Congress, both on the conduct of the Civil War and on the policy regarding Reconstruction. At the time of Garrison's visit to Washington, Stevens was belligerently supporting the Freedmen's Bureau bill, which Johnson was to veto, though it later passed in revised form.

2. See the letter to Theodore Tilton, February 3, 1866.

3. A search through issues of the *Independent* subsequent to February 8, 1866, when Garrison's letter appeared, reveals no reply from Phillips.

4. For Sumner's speech, see the letter to Charles Sumner, February 11, 1866.

5. Song of Solomon 2:12, adapted.

6. Garrison spoke in the Concert Hall in Philadelphia on February 15, under the auspices of the Social, Civil, and Statistical Association of the Colored People of Pennsylvania. His title, according to the report in the *National Anti-Slavery Standard*, was "Liberty Triumphant," and he spoke in far milder terms than in the speech in Brooklyn (see the letter to Fanny Garrison Villard, March 3, 1866, n. 3). He was not even particularly critical of President Johnson. (*Standard*, March 3, 1866.)

164

TO EDWIN L. GODKIN

[February 15, 1866.]

TO THE EDITOR OF THE NATION:

Your vindication last week of the conduct of THE NATION against the gratuitous arraignment of Mr. Wendell Phillips was convincing and ample.¹ Had you chosen, however, to enquire why he essayed to play the champion for Mr. [Charles] Sumner on this particular occasion, and, of all men, to stigmatize you as a "heartless and unfair critic" of that philanthropic senator, you might easily have removed from Mr. Phillips every vestige of an excuse for assuming either office. For, in the first place, while *he* regards and publicly brands President Johnson as virtually a traitor to his country, who deserves immediate impeachment and trial, Mr. Sumner declared, when seeking to justify his epithet of "whitewashing:" *I have no reflection to make on the patriotism or the truth of the President of the United States.* Never in public or in private have I made any such reflection, and I do not begin now."[2] And this, surely, Mr. Phillips must regard quite as bad as "whitewashing," and to the taste like wormwood!

But the *sang-froid* of this novel partizanship is quite refreshing in view of Mr. Phillips's severe, not to say savage, assault upon Mr. Sumner in the spring of 1863, when he exclaimed:

"Peel off Seward, peel off Halleck, peel off Blair, *peel off Sumner* —yes, *Massachusetts senators as well as others.* No, I will not say peel off our Massachusetts senators; but I will say their recent action has *very materially lessened my confidence in their intelligence and fidelity.* I will tell you why. When the government called on New England for a negro regiment, and we went from county to county, urging the blacks to enlist, one Massachusetts colonel [[Thomas G.] Stevenson], dared to say, down in South Carolina, in the face of the enemy, that he had rather be whipped without negroes than conquer at their side—a Massachusetts colonel, in that hour of emergency and critical issue.[3] His case within twenty days went before the Senate of the United States, and the very week that his apology was filed in the War Office at Washington, *Massachusetts senators begged their reluctant brothers to make him a brigadier general.* Yes, Massachusetts senators, thoroughly informed and *put upon their guard, against the repeated remonstrance of their fellow-senators,* INSISTED *on rewarding the mutineer!*"[4]

Again:

"Thus we see high-handed defiance of the Government's policy enter the Senate as a colonel and come out a brigadier. Sigel, Fremont, Butler, Hamilton, Phelps, and a host of others idle, yet *a negro-hater promoted on a plea of necessity to get good officers! When Mr. Sumner let personal feelings lead him to such a step,* HE BETRAYED THE NEGRO."

Again:

"*Massachusetts senators reward the mutineer* TO CONCILIATE HUNKER TREASON."[5]

This aggravated statement and damnatory criticism Mr. Phillips was not satisfied with rehearsing to public audiences in various cities, but he was careful to make them a portion of the last speech contained in the volume of his "Speeches, Lectures, and Letters" published the same year,[6] and thus designedly to send them down to posterity, aspersing the motives, impeaching the integrity, and blackening the conduct of Messrs. Sumner and Wilson, who had done and suffered more in the anti-slavery cause than any other two public men in the land, and whose illustrious career, as well as upright character, should have shielded them from such a merciless attack. This was all the more wanton and inexcusable because Mr. Sumner, we are told, and also others whose testimony was unimpeachable, minutely laid before Mr. Phillips all the facts in the case, placing an almost totally different aspect upon it, and relieving "the Massachusetts senators" of all suspicion of intentional wrong-doing in the appointment of Col. Stevenson, who, however betrayed in a moment of excitement to say, in a private conversation, what Mr. Phillips imputes to him, promptly forwarded to the War Department his humble apology, as Mr. Phillips admits; and who laid down his life in the service of his country in the spirit of a brave soldier and a true patriot. In relation to Mr. Sumner in special, is this to be a "heartless and unfair critic"—or how shall it be characterized? When, on a certain occasion, at an anti-slavery celebration, Mr. Phillips contemptuously said of Henry Wilson in his speech, "I could make a better senator out of the sweepings of a bar-room caucus,"[7] because Mr. Wilson had said or done something displeasing to him, was this a just appreciation of one who, by his inherent energy and manly character, had succeeded in exchanging a cobbler's shop for the Senate Chamber of the United States, and to whose indomitable zeal and tireless industry, accompanied by sound discretion and admirable tact, the cause of freedom, in its broadest signification, owes its most important legislative triumphs?

Instances like these might be multiplied by any one who should take the pains to search Mr. Phillips's later speeches for them, or should simply recall that in his phraseology Mr. Lincoln was once "the slave-hound of Illinois,"[8] and a certain Massachusetts major-general "a strolling mountebank."[9] It is one thing to be a comprehensive statesman; another to be an eloquent rhetorician. Mr. Phillips not infrequently mistakes sweeping condemnation for courageous censure, a lover of paradox for a bold enunciation of the truth, and extravagance of impeachment for fidelity to the claims of the oppressed. This habit is growing upon him in proportion to the lack of provocation; while he is still listened to for his oratorical ability, his criticisms are daily becoming less valuable and less regarded.

AN ABOLITIONIST.

Printed: *The Nation*, February 15, 1866.

Although this letter, which is printed under the title "An Impartial Critic," is not signed by Garrison, it is included here because of the attribution to him in the index to *The Nation* (Daniel C. Haskell, compiler, New York, 1951) and because in style and content it is not inconsistent with what Garrison would have written at this period.

Edwin Lawrence Godkin (1831–1902), born in Ireland, came to the United States in 1856. In 1865 he and James Miller McKim established *The Nation*, dedicating it to the cause of freedom. With Godkin as editor the journal became a distinguished weekly concerned not only with reform but with literature, art, and public affairs. In 1881 *The Nation* was sold to the New York *Evening Post* (owned by Henry Villard), Godkin becoming editor of the paper and Wendell Phillips Garrison editor of the magazine.

1. Garrison is responding to an editorial, "Wendell Phillips as a Whipper-In," (*The Nation*, February 8), in which that journal defends itself against Phillips' charge that its policy was "timid, vacillating, and non-committal."

2. Garrison quotes from Sumner's speech, "Remarks in the Senate, on a Message of President Johnson on the Condition of the Southern States," December 19, 1865, adding his own italics. (Charles Sumner, *Complete Works*, Boston, 1900, XIII, 51.)

3. See Garrison's letter to Helen E. Garrison, May 14, 1863, n. 9.

4. Garrison's quotations from Phillips are accurate except for the addition of italics and capitals. (Wendell Phillips, *Speeches, Lectures and Letters*, 1st ser., Boston, 1863, p. 559.)

5. Phillips, *Speeches*, p. 561.

6. That is, 1863.

7. Diligent search has failed to find this quotation in the speeches of Phillips.

8. Garrison refers to Phillips' brief comment about Lincoln printed in *The Liberator*, June 22, 1860.

9. The reference is to Nathaniel P. Banks, who was so described in Phillips' speech, "The South Victorious," at the opening of the Fraternity course of lectures at the Music Hall, Boston, October 17, 1865. (*National Anti-Slavery Standard*, October 28, 1865; see also his speech at the annual meeting of the Massachusetts Anti-Slavery Society, January 29, 1863, *The Liberator*, February 13, 1863; and Garrison's letter to Banks, January 21, 1865.)

165

TO HELEN E. GARRISON

Philadelphia, Feb. 16, 1866.

Dear Wife:

The inevitable north-easterly rain which has for so many years successively met me on my arrival in New York did not fail me on Wednesday evening. Franky having written you the particulars of our visit to Mrs. [Augustus] Savin, &c., I need not go over the same ground. Thursday morning, the weather had suddenly changed to a cutting severity, and, in consequence of a window being broken in our car, our ride to Philadelphia was not particularly comfortable. We arrived at 2 o'clock, and were soon at the house of our devoted friend, Alfred H. Love, in 6th Street, uncle Henry [Anthony] taking quarters at the Continental Hotel.[1] The mercury continued falling through the day, but the night was clear and brilliant. I had a large audience (at least two thousand) in the evening at Concert Hall, and occupied about an hour and a half in the delivery of my lecture. I felt in very good trim, though I did not go to bed at New York until 2 o'clock in the morning. My voice was clear and full throughout, and I think none failed to hear me in the spacious hall. The lecture in several passages was warmly applauded, and well received as a whole, though some of its criticisms must have been keenly felt by some of the Anti-Slavery friends present, who take a morbid view of things. Of this class, however, the larger portion staid away— among them Robert Purvis, who has become entirely estranged; saying to Alfred, one day, that when the Liberator came to hand, he threw it from him, as far as possible, with feelings of disgust! Only think of it! This is a specimen of evil work wrought by—I need not say whom. Dear Lucretia Mott was present, as kind and sweet as ever, notwithstanding our difference of judgment on some points. I also had on the platform Rachel Moore, the noted female preacher, who dined with me at Alfred's.[2] She is living at Germantown; and Henry, Franky and I are going to take tea, and spend the evening at her house, along with Mrs. [James Miller] McKim and Lucy. We three are going to Hilltop this afternoon. Mrs. McKim was at my lecture, and Franky escorted her to the residence of Anna Dennis.

Frank and I had a good night's sleep, and feel in prime condition this morning. It is very cold indeed, but a glorious day, and no doubt will be very comfortable as to temperature by noon. We shall roam about the city this forenoon, look at paintings and pictures, and see whatever happens to turn up.

A number of inquiries were made about you last evening at the hall, by various friends. You are always remembered. In the morning, at 9.15, we are off for Washington.

Ever your own

W. L. G.

ALS: Garrison Papers, Boston Public Library.

1. The Continental Hotel, which was designed by John McArthur, Jr., was located at the corner of Ninth and Chestnut streets. At the time it opened on February 16, 1860, it was the largest hotel in the country and one of the most luxurious. (Ellis Paxson Oberholtzer, *Philadelphia, a History of the City and its People*, Philadelphia, 1911, II, 357.)

2. Rachel Wilson Moore, a Hicksite Friend living in Poughkeepsie, N.Y., had in 1856 become the second wife of John Wilson Moore. In 1867 she published *Journal of Rachel Wilson Moore Kept during a Tour to the West Indies and South America in 1863–1864.* (Letter to the editor from Elizabeth Tritle, Quaker Collection, Haverford College Library, September 18, 1972.)

166

TO WENDELL PHILLIPS GARRISON

Washington, Feb. 22, 1866.

Dear Wendell:

Thanks for your two letters, and the suggestions contained in them. It is out of the question, however, to try to persuade me to give an off-hand lecture at Brooklyn, with reference to matters and things in Washington—the President's Veto, &c.[1] So, have my theme announced as "Liberty Victorious." Of course, I shall say something about what I have seen and heard here, before concluding my lecture; but I wish to have no special announcement made on that point. Trust me as to the testimony I shall give.

I have come here at a very interesting and opportune period. This is a live Congress, and every day is big with events of national importance. I have heard several very radical speeches in the Senate —one by Senator Yates, "flat-footed" in favor of universal ⟦male⟧ suffrage;[2] another by Senator Wade, on his proposed amendment of the Constitution, allowing no man to be re-elected to the office of President of the United States—a very bold speech in its utterance;[3] and a third by Senator Trumbull, distinguished for logical power and vigor of treatment, pulverizing the President's Veto, and showing him to have falsified all its provisions and purposes. I have also listened to the reading of a speech by that Kentucky factionist, Garret Davis, in support of the Veto.[4] The copperhead strength is very weak, in intellect and numbers, in both houses of Congress.

Last evening, I called with Harry at Secretary Stanton's residence, but he and his wife[5] had gone out to spend the evening.

This forenoon I had a brief interview with General [Oliver O.] Howard, who is, of course, full of uncertainty as to what is to be the duration or power of the Bureau; but he told me that he had an interview with the President yesterday, who gave him to understand that he should speedily announce, by proclamation, that the war has ended and peace been restored; and that the Bureau would continue until a year from that date, according to the terms of the Bill constituting the Bureau. He is not, however, to be depended on, especially as all Rebeldom and Copperdom are so warmly espousing his course. To-morrow promises to be a very lively day in the Senate, on the subject. Senator Wilson is to introduce another Bill, providing for the continuance of the Bureau two years from May next, with enlarged powers; but if it pass, the President will doubtless Veto it, as in the former instance.[6]

To-day, (22d,) Washington is all astir. The day is superb as to the weather—like an April day in Boston—and Pennsylvania Avenue is thronged by all sorts of people. An immense mass of secessionists and copperheads are holding a meeting at the Theatre,[7] to sustain the recreant President; and I understand he is to address them! I am sure the bottomless pit is equally jubilant.

I have just come, with Franky, from the Capitol, where a most fitting and eloquent eulogium has been bestowed upon the character and services of the late Henry Winter Davis by Senator Cresswell of Maryland.[8] The hall of the House was crowded in every part. The Judges of the Supreme Court were present—the leading military men—dignitaries of all kinds—Senators and Representatives, &c. I got in after the oration began, and was standing back near the door, when Speaker Colfax got his eye upon me, and instantly sent a messenger to conduct me to a seat near to Secretary Stanton, Judge [Salmon P.] Chase, and other notables. After the services, I spoke to Stanton, who expressed great regret that he was not at home last evening, and said he would not be absent again if I would call. I was introduced to a large number of Senators, Representatives, and persons from various parts of the country, and warmly received.

To-morrow evening I am to lecture in the Union League Hall— hold four hundred—as all the others are engaged.[9] On Sunday evening I expect to address the colored people in one of their churches.[10]

Your ever affectionate

Father.

P.S. This forenoon, Harry hired a barouche, and gave Fanny, Frank and myself a ride to Georgetown heights. Harry is a great sufferer from his neuralgic attacks. Fanny is in prime condition. All send special love to you and Lucy.

☞ To think of Henry Ward Beecher eulogizing the President and his Veto![11]

AL signed "Father": Garrison Papers, Boston Public Library; partly printed in *Life*, IV, 176–177.

1. President Johnson had vetoed the bill to extend the Freedmen's Bureau on February 19, returning it to the Senate on the twenty-second with a message explaining that, although he agreed basically with the purpose of the bill to secure fundamental rights for the freedmen, he felt that it attempted to do so by unconstitutional means that would be damaging to other public rights. (For the text of the President's speech see Edward McPherson, *The Political History of the United States of America during the Period of Reconstruction*, Washington, 1871, pp. 68–72. For comment on the entire situation see Kenneth M. Stampp, *The Era of Reconstruction, 1865–1877*, New York, 1966, pp. 130–136.)

2. Richard Yates (1815–1873), a lawyer from Jacksonville, Ill., held a variety of public offices: member of the state legislature (1842–1846; 1848–1850), member of Congress (1851–1855), governor of the state (1861–1865), and United States senator (1865–1871). A moderate abolitionist, he was a consistent supporter of Lincoln and his policies and expressed his approval of the administration by the ardor with which he raised troops. During the period of Reconstruction he favored harsh measures against the South and voted for President Johnson's impeachment.

Garrison refers to the same speech by Yates as that mentioned in his letter to Helen E. Garrison, February 19, 1866, n. 7 (micro.). Concerning suffrage for women, Yates argued as follows: "Woman is excluded by the inevitable improprieties of the case. The ballot is in politics what the bayonet is in war. Those only who wield the sword are, by universal consent of both ancient and modern civilization, supposed capable of wielding the ballot." (*Congressional Globe*, 39th Cong., 1st sess., Appendix, pp. 98–105.)

3. Senator Benjamin Franklin Wade had introduced a joint resolution proposing that the Constitution be amended to limit the President to one four-year term. He also attacked President Johnson for being so lenient with the South, accusing him of wanting to return to the Union rebellious states "unwashed and red with the blood of their country men." (*Congressional Globe*, 39th Cong., 1st sess., Part I, pp. 931–933.)

4. Lyman Trumbull (1813–1896), an Illinois lawyer, held a series of state offices (legislator, secretary of state, justice of the supreme court) before serving in the United States Senate (1855–1873). During the Civil War he was both Lincoln's supporter and his critic, being determined to limit and control the power of the executive. In 1864 and 1866 respectively, Trumbull sponsored resolutions that eventually evolved into the thirteenth and the fourteenth amendments. During the Reconstruction period he soon became critical of Johnson and his vetoes and seemed for a time to agree with the Radical Republicans. Eventually, however, his moderate and constitutional principles prevailed, and he helped to prevent Johnson's conviction during the impeachment proceedings.

Garret Davis (1801–1872), a lawyer in Kentucky since 1823, had served in the state legislature (1833–1835), in Congress (1839–1847), and in the Senate (1861–1869). During the early years of the Civil War he was a strong unionist, even proposing that confiscation of property be the punishment for aiding the rebellion; but by 1864 his views had modified and he was severely critical of Lincoln's policies.

The speeches of Trumbull and Davis to which Garrison refers were in fact delivered in reverse order, Trumbull's being in answer to Davis'. Davis had said that southern whites were destined to be the proprietors and blacks the cultivators of the land and "that mutual confidence and good will are essential to the welfare of both races." Extending the powers of the Freedmen's Bureau, he thought, was unconstitutional, would require too much money, and would establish military despotism; in short, it would make impossible the good relations between the races so essential to the country. Trumbull, on the other hand, expressed surprise at the President's veto, denying that an extension of the Freedmen's Bureau under the War Department would result in despotism. Indeed, he said, the bill established military jurisdiction only in the absence of civil courts to protect freed Negroes. (*Congressional Globe*, 39th Cong., 1st sess., Part I, pp. 933–942.)

5. Ellen M. Hutchinson Stanton (died 1873) had married Edwin M. Stanton, as his second wife, in 1856.

6. Senator Henry Wilson introduced the Freedmen's Bureau bill a second time on February 21, but since it failed to get a two-thirds majority, the President's veto remained in force. (McPherson, *Political History,* p. 74.)

7. Grover's Theatre (now the National Theatre) at 1321 E Street, N.W., built in 1835, with a capacity of 2,500. (Letter to the editor from Carolyn H. Sung, researcher, March 30, 1972.)

8. Henry Winter Davis (1817–1865) was a conservative Maryland lawyer who was first elected to Congress in 1855, where he became a leader of the Know-Nothing party. In the years preceding and during the Civil War he took a strong unionist stand, vigorously opposing the secession of his state. But gradually—partly owing to Lincoln's not appointing him to his cabinet—he became unalterably opposed to administration policies. He had such power in the House of Representatives that he persuaded his fellow members to support his plans for Reconstruction rather than Lincoln's. Although Davis and Lincoln were temporarily reconciled before the election, following the assassination, Davis opposed Johnson's plans just as he had opposed Lincoln's. Davis' career was abruptly terminated by death from pneumonia.

John Angel James Creswell (1828–1891), whose name Garrison misspells, was another Maryland lawyer turned politician. His public career began in 1861 with his election to the state legislature; in 1863 he was elected to Congress and in 1865 to the Senate. In 1869 President Grant appointed him postmaster general; he resigned in 1874 to concentrate on private business.

9. Garrison mistakes the name of the place where he spoke; it was actually called "Union League Rooms." The same mistake appears in *Life,* IV, 178. (Letter to the editor from Carolyn H. Sung, researcher, March 30, 1972.)

10. Garrison spoke on February 25 at the Fifteenth Street Presbyterian Church, where Henry Highland Garnet was pastor. (See the letter to Theodore Tilton, March 8, 1866.)

11. Beecher had spoken at the Academy of Music in Brooklyn on February 20, approving the President's veto and rebuking the zeal of partisans who were ignorant of the operation of social and economic laws. He said that the freedmen must be protected, but not at the expense of the Constitution. (*National Anti-Slavery Standard,* March 3, 1866.)

167

TO FANNY GARRISON VILLARD

Roxbury, March 3, 1866.

My dear Fanny:

Home again, safe and sound. It seems, nevertheless, as if I could step into your house, or go from there to the Capitol, as easily as I can go from Rockledge to the Norfolk House.[1] Knowing where and how you are situated, the distance between us will hereafter seem greatly abridged. In imagination, I shall on taking my meals seem to be at the table with you and Harry, and Mr. and Mrs. Lander, and to be served by Sarah in the most attentive way.[2] Franky will write you to-morrow, and doubtless give you the particulars of our journey home. We met uncle Henry [Anthony] in New York, and we all returned together on Thursday.

My lecture in the Academy of Music, on Tuesday evening, drew out a large audience, and the closing part of it about President Johnson excited a great sensation, and elicited immense applause, mingled with some copperhead hisses. What I said was quite impromptu, but I am more and more convinced that Pres. Johnson will attempt a *coup d'etat* against Congress by the time summer is upon us.[3] He will do it "constitutionally," and to "preserve the Union," and to put down Northern "conspirators"! The elements of violence are gathering for the onslaught. Tell Harry his 15,000 loyal men in Washington will all be wanted![4]

I found your mother looking fair and fresh, and waiting to hear all about her children at W. There is nothing new to write about; and as the mail closes in a few minutes, I am obliged to close abruptly.

With parental love to you and Harry, and kindest regards to Mr. and Mrs. Lander, I remain,

Your fond father,

W. L. G.

ALS: Garrison Papers, Boston Public Library.

1. Norfolk House was a small boarding hotel that had opened in Roxbury in 1825. (Justin Winsor, *The Memorial History of Boston*, Boston, 1881, III, 576.)

2. Although his wife is not mentioned in any of the sources, "Mr. Lander" is probably William W. Lander (c. 1844–1876), and the Landers probably lived in the same Washington boardinghouse as the Villards. Lander was born in Salem, Mass., where he had little formal education owing to his father's failure in the India trade. In 1861 he went to Washington as secretary to Charles Sumner. In the fall of the same year he became a captain in the commissary department. During the Civil War he rose to the rank of major and saw service in various capacities; he also continued to do secretarial work for Senator Sumner when he was stationed near Washington. In 1866 he became collector of internal revenue in North Carolina. Two years later he resigned after having some difficulties with President Johnson and returned to Salem, where he was appointed postmaster, a post he lost in 1870. In 1873 he moved to Denver, Col., where he became assistant postmaster. (Obituaries, Denver *Daily Times*, October 11, New York *Times*, October 15, 1876; see also the letter from Francis Jackson Garrison to Fanny Garrison Villard, September 27, 1866, William Lloyd Garrison Papers, Massachusetts Historical Society, where Lander is mentioned as a radical who is likely to be decapitated by "His Accidency.")

Aside from the fact that she was a servant, Sarah has not been identified.

3. Garrison lectured in the Academy of Music in Brooklyn, N.Y., on February 26 (a week after Johnson's veto of the Freedmen's Bureau bill), giving much the same speech he was later to deliver in other cities. He attacked Johnson for his opposition to Congress: "I would have [Congress] wipe out from the slate all that he has done in the matter of reconstruction, and begin the work anew, as alone constitutionally empowered to inaugurate and perfect it. . . . I deny the right of President Johnson . . . to do anything more in rebeldom than to hold it with a firm military grasp until Congress shall determine when, how, and where elections shall be held, who shall be allowed to vote, and what shall be the necessary conditions precedent to the readmission to the Union of the late self-styled Confederate States. Those States are

still treasonable in spirit, in language, and in purpose, and lack nothing but the power and the opportunity to induce them to try the bloody game of secession over again. They do not know . . . what it is to be loyal or truly American—only Southern—bitterly, arrogantly Southern, hence they are in no sense qualified to have the reins of government in their own hands, but must be held under guardianship until free institutions are firmly rooted in their soil."

Garrison's prediction that the President would by summer attempt a coup against Congress was not substantiated. Though relations between Johnson and Congress steadily deteriorated, power was shifting to Congress, which was able to sustain many bills over his veto, and the elections of 1866 proved victorious for the Republicans. (Garrison's speech was printed in the *National Anti-Slavery Standard,* March 10, 1866, and it was reported in other papers, including the New York *Times,* February 28, 1866; Eric L. McKitrick, *Andrew Johnson and Reconstruction,* Chicago, 1960.)

4. Garrison probably refers to veterans of the Civil War who were loyal to the Union—who were, in other words, Radical Republicans. These men were to meet in a series of conventions during the summer of 1866, including one in Pittsburgh with 15,000 "Loyal Soldiers." (See the letter from Francis Jackson Garrison to Fanny Garrison Villard, September 27, 1866, William Lloyd Garrison Papers, Massachusetts Historical Society; also Ellis P. Oberholtzer, *A History of the United States Since the Civil War,* New York, 1926, I, 395–396.)

168

TO THEODORE TILTON

[March 8, 1866.]

To the Editor of the Independent:

I have just returned home from a ten days' visit in Washington—a visit made without the slightest reference to public affairs, but solely to enjoy a little recreation with some who are endeared to me by the ties of consanguinity and relationship.[1] It was not my design or wish, therefore, to deliver any lecture while there; but, being very strongly importuned, I consented to do so, and, accordingly, addressed a very respectable and intelligent audience in the Union League hall.[2] This was far from being either commodious, or tastefully furnished; but no larger hall could be obtained, except on condition of excluding all colored persons! Applications were made to procure some one of the churches, but in vain; even the Unitarian church was peremptorily refused.

By invitation of Rev. Dr. Garnet (colored),[3] I addressed a crowded assembly of all complexions in his church, on Sunday evening last, and at the close of the services was warmly clasped by the hand by nearly all present. It was an occasion not soon to pass from memory.

My visit was at a singularly opportune and momentous period. Two events occurred which not only greatly excited Washington, but have since shaken the republic to its foundations—namely, the veto of the Freedmen's Bureau bill by President Johnson, and his indecent and incendiary harangue to the motley crowd that gathered in front of the White House on the 22d inst.

I happened to be in the Senate when action was taken upon the veto by that enlightened body, after an elaborate, most eloquent, and irrefutable reply to its sophistry and mendacity by Senator [Lyman] Trumbull—a reply of which there should be millions of copies circulated broadcast. Owing to the defection of three or four, on the loyal side, who had previously voted for it, the bill was lost for the lack of only two votes to make the required two-thirds.[4] While the vote was being taken,

"There was silence deep as death;"[5]

but when the result was announced, in one portion of the galleries there burst forth such boisterous applause as to indicate exactly where the secession and copperhead spirits had congregated in order to commence that subterranean jubilation which is now coming up from every quarter of the land. True, there were some expressions of disapprobation in other parts of the galleries; but the great body of loyal spectators, though greatly surprised and pained, kept their feelings in abeyance, and observed the proprieties of the place. For myself, I felt no perturbation of mind; for I never saw more clearly how assuredly this seeming triumph of the enemy would, ere long, confirm anew the truth of the scriptural declaration, "He taketh the cunning in their own craftiness, and the counsels of the froward he carries headlong."[6] It is only when such great issues are not presented and met, through universal degeneracy, that there is good reason for anxiety and alarm. But when there is wide-spread, all-pervading excitement in regard to a righteous cause, no rebuff, whether given by perfidy or power, need be greatly feared, though always to be deplored. As God lives, what the veto intends to put down, it will in essence and substance put up—that is, the cause of impartial justice and universal liberty. It will rejoice none but the brutal and contemptuous enemies of the hapless negro race; it will intimidate none but the cowardly and time-serving. It will do more to promote agitation, excite discussion, and advance the lines of the armies of freedom than a million of dollars contributed expressly for that purpose. No thanks to the author of it: "he meaneth not so in his heart."[7] Let him look out for the tenth wave that is coming![8]

The veto itself requires no dissection here. Its objections to the Freedmen's Bureau bill are manifestly hollow, because they are based on a gross falsification of the provisions of the bill. Take, for example, the assertion that it establishes military jurisdiction over all parts of the United States containing refugees and freedmen, whereas it simply extends that jurisdiction over the officers and employés of the Bureau. Again, instead of the bill being intended to feed, clothe, and educate "four millions of freedmen," only ninety thousand have required any aid of the Bureau; and, instead of having exclusive reference to freedmen, it equally concerns the poor white refugees of the South who need succor—seventeen thousand five hundred of these having been fed by the Bureau in Tennessee alone, to seven thousand five hundred of a different complexion. Again, the Bureau is authorized by the bill to interfere for the administration of impartial justice only where "freedmen and refugees are discriminated against by local law, custom, or prejudice;" so that it is only for the South to abolish all such unjust discrimination to render the Bureau alike powerless and unnecessary. Again, the bill is to remain in force "until otherwise provided by law," and therefore can be modified or repealed just like any other law of the land. Instead of increasing the pecuniary burdens of the government, it has already saved many millions of dollars, and, if not hampered, will save many millions more. Finally, it is evident that the President declines the additional trust reposed in his hands by the bill, not because he is unwilling to wield extraordinary power (for he is now attempting to play the despot over Congress in the matter of reconstruction, which really is none of his business), but solely on account of his unwillingness to extend that protection to the freedmen of the South which they so much need against their old tyrannical masters and rebel enemies. His hallucination of mind about his being the Moses of the liberated slaves savors strongly of lunacy.

While, a few days previous to the veto being sent to Congress, there was some anxiety as to what disposition the President would make of the [bill], nevertheless, it was generally believed [that] he would affix his signature to it; [or at] the worst, return it with some technical objections that might be easily obviated; so that it came, at last, almost "like hail [out of a] clear sky." There was nothing like consternation, but only unfeigned surprise, intense regret, and deep solemnity of mind. It was, in fact, the announcement by the President that he had gone over to the enemy, burned the bridge behind him, and was determined either to have his own usurping way, or run the risk of a fresh civil war, with all its awful consequences. It was a direct intimation to Congress that in vain would be its projected legislation for the temporary government of the South; for he would veto every measure of that kind, and by his patronage rely on preventing a two-thirds vote defeating his purpose. It was sublime to see with what dignity, firmness, and courage Congress met the shock. True, three or four members of the Senate, who in the first instance voted for the bill, went for the veto; but these trimmers must be handed over to their constituents, to be dealt with as justice demands.

The conduct of the President, in sending such a veto, was all the more inexcusable, inasmuch as it is unquestionably true that he had the bill submitted to him some days previous, and all its provisions scrutinized, without a word of disapprobation on his part![9] Lieutenant-General Grant also very carefully examined it, and gave it his approval—merely suggesting that he thought all the appointments had better be from the army, for certain cogent reasons which he stated.[10] Thus doubly fortified, Senator Trumbull felt confident that no breach would follow, and was as much astounded at the appearance of the veto as though the capitol had been shaken to its foundations by an earthquake. His speech in review and refutation of the veto was alone worth going to Washington from Boston to hear —so clear in its analysis, so powerful in its logic, so crushing in its application![11] Both in manner and matter, it was all that could be desired. Millions of copies of his speech should be circulated through the land.

The anniversary of Washington's birthday was celebrated by commemorative services in the House of Representatives, in reference to the lamented death of that most gifted and undaunted champion of liberty in Maryland, HENRY WINTER DAVIS—

> "One blast upon whose bugle-horn
> Was worth a thousand men."[12]

There was a good assembly present, made up of the most patriotic elements in Washington; and the oration delivered by the Hon. Mr. [John A. J.] Cresswell, the successor of Mr. Davis in the Senate, was in all respects worthy of the occasion and its subject.

Another observance (?) of the day was by a motley gathering of rebels and rebel sympathizers at Grover's theater, who, after being harangued by certain well-known demagogues, marched in procession to the White House, and were there addressed at considerable length by President Johnson, in a speech which, for its bitterness of tone and malevolence of spirit, there are no words to describe. I meant to have made a critical review of it this week; but this letter is already sufficiently long, and the verdict of the nation has already been pronounced.

Yours, for a new struggle for freedom and equality,

W. L. G.

Printed: *Independent,* March 8, 1866.

Theodore Tilton was editor of the *Independent* at this time.

1. Garrison was in Washington by February 17 and back in Roxbury by March 1; he gave a lecture on the twenty-sixth in Brooklyn, N.Y., on his way home.

2. Garrison's speech was reported in the Washington *Evening Star,* February 23, 1866.

3. Henry Highland Garnet (1815–1882) was an escaped slave who had been educated at Oneida Institute before becoming a part-time preacher and lecturer for the American Anti-Slavery Society. His fame as a black abolitionist declined after 1843, when he delivered an ill-timed speech before a convention of free Negroes in Buffalo, urging slaves to murder their masters. Thereafter he served as pastor in a series of churches in New York City and state, and after 1864 at the Fifteenth Street Presbyterian Church in Washington. In 1881 he became the United States minister to Liberia, where he died a few weeks after taking his post.

4. The following senators voted for the passage of the Freedmen's Bureau bill on January 25 and voted against overriding the President's veto on February 21: James Dixon (Conn.), James R. Doolittle (Wis.), Edwin D. Morgan (N.Y.), Daniel S. Norton (Minn.), William M. Stewart (Nev.), and Peter G. Van Winkle (W. Va.). Waitman T. Willey (W. Va.) had apparently been absent on January 25 but voted on February 21 to sustain the veto. (Edward McPherson, *The Political History of the United States of America during the Period of Reconstruction,* Washington, D.C., 1871, p. 74.)

5. Thomas Campbell, "Battle of the Baltic," stanza 2, line 7.

6. Job 5:13, adapted.

7. Isaiah 10:7, adapted.

8. Garrison refers to the common belief that every tenth wave is larger than the nine preceding it.

9. Senator Trumbull, who had tried to write the Freedmen's Bureau bill in such a way as to make it acceptable both to Johnson and to Radical Republicans, read the bill to the President—perhaps during the period of its debate in the Senate (January 11–25)—and assumed that he found it satisfactory. (Eric McKitrick, *Andrew Johnson and Reconstruction,* Chicago, 1960, p. 12; George F. Milton, *The Age of Hate: Andrew Johnson and the Radicals,* New York, 1930, pp. 284–285.)

10. Although no document is known to the editor supporting Garrison's statement about Grant's study and approval of the draft of the Freedmen's Bureau bill, Grant had returned to Washington from his tour of the southern states begun November 27, and in his report to the President of December 18 he approved the continuation of the Freedmen's Bureau: "In some form," he said, "the Freedmen's Bureau is an absolute necessity until civil law is established and enforced, securing to the freedmen their rights and full protection." In this report Grant also suggested that coordination of the efforts of the bureau and the army would be improved by regarding every officer on duty with troops in the southern states as an agent of the Freedmen's Bureau, and by having all orders from the head of the bureau sent through department commanders. (McPherson, *Political History,* pp. 67–68.)

11. This is the same speech by Trumbull described in the letter to Wendell Phillips Garrison, February 22, 1866: see also n. 4 of that letter

12. Sir Walter Scott, *The Lady of the Lake,* Canto VI, stanza 18, lines 27–28. Garrison changes "his" to "whose" and "were" to "was."

169

TO IRA STEWARD

BOSTON, March 20, 1866.

DEAR SIR:

I have read with interest the printed appeal "to the Workingmen and Women of Massachusetts, and their Friends," signed by yourself and Messrs. John McCombe and James W. Simpson as a Committee appointed at the State Convention of the Eight-Hour League of Massachusetts to procure "contributions in aid of the movement having for its object a reduction of the hours of labor for the overworked of this country."[1] The same principle which has led me to abhor and oppose the unequalled oppression of the black laborers of the South, instinctively leads me to feel an interest in whatever is proposed to be done to improve the condition and abridge the toil of the white laborers of the North—or, rather, of all overtasked working classes, without regard to complexion or race—and more equitably to adjust the relations between capital and labor.

Of course, the change you are seeking to effect, in regard to the number of hours to be exacted as constituting a day's labor, will meet with more or less opposition as injurious and unattainable. For there never has been a reformatory measure proposed, on an extended scale, that has not subjected its advocates to the charge of mawkish philanthropy, visionary scheming, social disorganization, or raving fanaticism. It has always been denounced as uncalled-for, inexpedient, destructive; and everything evil has been predicted of it in case it should be carried. This is not in every instance owing to a selfish or hardened nature, but often arises from lack of reflection or investigation—a disposition to be contented with things as they are—a morbid distaste for what is opprobriously called "agitation," —an unfeigned apprehension of terrible consequences, (which are solely in the imagination,) while there is no vision to see the disastrous tendencies of what is so tenaciously adhered to. There is such a thing as being "penny wise and pound foolish;"[2] and this is seen wherever capital is arrayed against labor, or where employers are intent only upon their own gains, and care little or nothing for the condition of the employed.

Between capital and labor there is no necessary antagonism. Where they are the most closely allied in a common effort or a common interest, there will invariably be found the best pecuniary results. Aside from the drones in society, we are all employers and employed—*i.e.*, while we work for others, we expect others to work for us. Whenever the laborer purchases a hat, or coat, or a pair of boots, or a loaf of bread, he is to that extent a capitalist, employing another to furnish a specific article for him. This dependence is mutual and universal; hence, the more it is recognized and regarded, the more intelligent, happy, virtuous and prosperous will be a community.

Wealth, accumulated at the expense of the moral and intellectual development of the working classes, is built upon a sandy foundation, and in due time ends disastrously.

In order that this development may be secured, they should have whatever leisure from toil is necessary to effect it, aside from obstacles which, for the time being, may be insurmountable. The general welfare is bound up in it.

Though the law of supply and demand is inexorable, yet it is neither rigorous nor unjust in its natural operation. It relates to the good of all, and that is the largest prosperity and the soundest political economy. If the hands are to be employed, the head is to be enlightened and the heart improved. For this there must be allowed a reasonable amount of time. How many hours of physical toil a day, as a general rule, may be most profitably occupied with this end in view remains to be tested, and perhaps in the present state of things cannot be abstractly determined; but I am firm in the conviction that eight hours a day will better promote bodily health, inspire industry, develop genius, stimulate enterprise, augment pecuniary gain, and subserve the cause of morality, than any extension of time beyond that limit. My reasons for this conviction I do not propose to state in this letter; the only object of which is to indicate that your movement has my warm approval, and to express the hope that the very moderate sum your League is endeavoring to obtain to carry it on will be readily contributed by those who are animated by a human and philanthropic spirit, or who intelligently understand the laws of political economy. To this end I enclose my mite, and wish I could make it many times larger.[3] This I could not consistently do if I did not believe that, in the prosecution of its noble enterprise, the League will give no countenance to the spirit of complexional caste in regard to any of the working classes.

Yours, for that justice which ensures prosperity,

WM. LLOYD GARRISON.

TO IRA STEWARD.

Printed: Boston *Daily Evening Voice*, May 2, 1866.

Ira Steward (1831–1883) was apprenticed as a machinist at Providence, R.I., under the system requiring a twelve-hour working day. After a few months he began to agitate for shorter hours. In 1863, at the Boston convention of the International

Union of Machinists and Blacksmiths, he was responsible for the first resolution to demand a law limiting the working day to eight hours. In the years to follow he worked assiduously for this cause, by appearing before the Massachusetts legislature, by lecturing, and by writing articles for labor papers (among them the Boston *Daily Evening Voice*, in which Garrison's letter was printed). He became president of both the National Ten-Hour League and the Boston Eight-Hour League. In 1869, with the aid of Wendell Phillips, he established the Massachusetts Bureau of Labor Statistics. Working through this organization and with the assistance of his wife, Mary B. Steward, he also helped to improve working conditions for women and children. By 1867 several state legislatures had passed eight-hour laws; but when the labor movement relinquished political for economic action, Steward's influence waned.

1. Although the Grand Eight-Hour League of Massachusetts seems to have been a largely ineffectual organization, it held many meetings, circulated petitions, and wrote frequently to legislators. One of its favored projects, the establishment of a free hall for workingmen and workingwomen, was not accomplished. The League was more active in the early seventies than at the time of Garrison's letter.

The decision to appeal for $5,000 in contributions, to which Garrison refers, had been made at the state convention of the league in Boston, February 7, 1866. Garrison was among the first to be solicited, but his reply was not published until May, perhaps in order that it might be included in the *Daily Evening Voice* along with favorable letters from Gerrit Smith and Dioclesian (Dio) Lewis. Garrison's letter to Steward is his only known contact with the labor movement in the 1860s. (Letter to the editor from Hilda Armour, researcher, July 18, 1975; Boston *Daily Evening Voice*, February 8, April 28, and May 2, 1866.)

John McCombe and James W. Simpson, whose signatures accompanied Steward's on both the printed circular which Garrison mentions and the fuller statement to be found in the *Daily Evening Voice*, April 28, have not been further identified.

2. Garrison uses the maxim common in English since the Renaissance.

3. How much Garrison contributed is not known.

170

TO ELLEN WRIGHT GARRISON

Roxbury, March 23, 1866.

My dear Ellie:

Do not conclude in consequence of my silence since I left Auburn, that you are either forgotten or unappreciated; but you know my procrastinating habits in regard to all epistolary matters, and must let me off as forgivingly as possible.

I commiserate you in regard to the bad luck you must have had, since you left Rockledge, concerning the weather. A letter just received from William states, (it is written at Cadiz, [Ohio]) that he has not yet found a fair day out West, and that he has had a tough time of it in the matter of travelling. The evening was cold and unpleasant when I lectured at Syracuse, but the audience was larger than could have been reasonably anticipated, and highly respectable and intelligent.[1] I had a very pleasant time with my dear S. J. May, and, like old veterans, we fought all our old battles over again.

I was particularly pleased with my visit to Oneida, which is a very pretty and thriving village. The hall suited me exactly, and the audience was large and warmly appreciative. The gentleman who had charge of the lecture, and extended to me the most elegant hospitality, Mr. Homer Devereaux, President of the National Bank, was so pleased, and said all the audience were so gratified, that he insisted on my promising to give another lecture there next winter.[2]

I have lectured only once since—at Rockville, a manufacturing village in Connecticut, and one of the most thriving, handsome, beautiful and romantic places I have ever seen. I was very hospitably entertained by J. N. Stickney, Esq., whose home was very similiar to ours at Rockledge in many of its features.[3]

I am now "on my ears"—still hesitating what to decide upon in regard to my future occupation. The proposition of Ticknor & Fields[4] still remains unaccepted, through my fears that I shall not be able to write such a work as will sell, or as the vastness and importance of the Anti-Slavery struggle demand. But this week I am resolved to "screw my courage up to the sticking point,"[5] and give a definite answer—probably in the affirmative.

You remember the severe fall I had in Charles Street, some weeks ago, on going to take tea with Mr. and Mrs. Fields.[6] Four or five days ago, I had the misfortune to be thrown in the same violent manner at Grantville,[7] in my hurry to catch the train for Boston, and I have been suffering ever since, especially in my right shoulder and arm which give me a great deal of pain, as though I may have possibly fractured the bone. As yet, I have had no surgical examination, though I may be compelled to resort to it.

Every thing goes on at home as quietly as usual. To-day we have aunt Charlotte [Anthony], and uncle Henry [Anthony], and Sarah Tillinghast, and Julia Randall, from Providence, with us, who intend remaining a day or two.[8]

Fanny continues to write frequently, and still finds much enjoyment in Washington, though looking forward with eagerness and delight to her visit home about the middle of April. She will remain with us only about a fortnight.

I regretted, bad as the weather was, to have had so brief a visit at Auburn, but I enjoyed it very much, and "hope to come again."

Didn't my lecture in the Academy of Music at Brooklyn make a sensation throughout Rebeldom and Copperdom![9]

Wife and Franky join in loving remembrances to you and your

dear parents. We miss you continually, and shall rejoice to see you and William once more in the family circle.

Nothing special is received from Wendell or Lucy.

Rejoicing that you are my daughter-in-law, and that William is so happily mated, I remain,

Ever affectionately yours,

Wm. Lloyd Garrison.

ALS: Garrison Papers, Sophia Smith Collection, Smith College Library.

1. Garrison's lecture "On the State of our Country and What We Owe the Freedmen," which he had also delivered in Washington, Philadelphia, Brooklyn, New York, and Boston, was given on March 8; it strongly denounced President Johnson. Garrison spoke in Shakespeare Hall, an auditorium occupying the third and fourth floors of the Bastable Arcade Building on Warren Street at the east end of Hanover Square. The structure was built between 1862 and 1863 and was destroyed by fire in 1891; the site is now occupied by the State Tower Building. (Syracuse *Journal,* March 6, 1866; letter to the editor from Richard N. Wright, president, Onondaga Historical Society, April 2, 1972.)

2. Horace (not Homer) Devereaux (sometimes spelled "Devereux") was not only the first president of the First National Bank, which had been founded October 1, 1864, but the president of Oneida village. (Mrs. L. M. Hammond, *History of Madison County, State of New York,* Syracuse, 1872, p. 531; John E. Smith, ed., *Our County and Its People,* Boston, 1899, p. 297.)

3. John Newton Stickney (1818–1893), a native of Vassalborough, Me., who had settled in Rockville in 1845, was a banker, businessman, and ardent Methodist. (Letter to the editor from T. R. Harlow, director, Connecticut Historical Society, March 28, 1972.)

4. The publishing firm of Ticknor and Fields was owned by William Davis Ticknor (1810–1864) and James Thomas Fields (1817–1881). Ticknor, the senior partner, had been a publisher and bookseller since 1832. Fields became his junior partner in 1838, and the firm assumed its familiar name in 1854. Ticknor and Fields published *The Atlantic Monthly* and the works of many of the leading writers of the day.

5. Shakespeare, *Macbeth,* I, vii, 60, adapted.

6. Annie Adams Fields (1834–1915) was a woman of great beauty and a prominent hostess, whose salon on Charles Street included many of the most distinguished American and English authors of the period. She was herself a well-known writer and editor, having published many volumes of letters, biography, and poetry.

7. Garrison means Granville, Mass., twenty miles southwest of Springfield.

8. Sarah Benson Tillinghast (1832–1895) was the daughter of Charlotte Benson and Henry Anthony. In 1857 she married James M. Tillinghast. (Charles L. Anthony, *Genealogy of the Anthony Family from 1495 to 1904,* Sterling, Ill., 1904.)

Julia Randall (born 1828) was the daughter of Eliza Thurber (born 1793), first cousin of Helen Garrison's mother, and Dexter Randall, a Providence lawyer and politician, whom Eliza married in 1813. Apparently a spinster, Miss Randall was a close friend of the Garrisons, whom she often visited; on occasion she nursed Helen through illness and served as a companion. (Frank Alfred Randall, *Randall and Allied Families,* Chicago, 1943, pp. 102–103; Mary Benns, *The Thurber Family,* unpublished manuscript in possession of the Rhode Island Historical Society, 1942, p. 8.)

9. For an account of Garrison's lecture see the letter to Fanny Garrison Villard, March 3, 1866.

171

TO WENDELL PHILLIPS GARRISON

Roxbury, March 25, 1866.

My dear Wendell:

It is a long, long time since I attempted any thing in the way of rhyme. I now send you four Sonnets for the *Nation*.[1] If, for any reason, (and none need be rendered to me,) they shall not be accepted, you may hand them to [Theodore] Tilton or [Oliver] Johnson, and see if they will "pass muster" for the *Independent*.

For a week past I have been *hors du combat*, owing to another severe fall I have had, while violently running to catch the train at the Grantville depot for Boston. I tripped, and went headlong, precisely as I did some weeks ago in Charles Street—striking heavily on my right shoulder and arm, and also right collar bone, which have given me constant pain ever since. I have had no surgical examination, but may yet require it. I am pretty sure there is no dislocation, but there may be a fracture of the bone.

Of course, all use of the pen is at present a painful effort.

I was out at Grantville, making a call upon the [Joseph] Southwicks. Mr. S. is in a very enfeebled condition with dropsy of the heart, and cannot long survive.

I am still at a loss to know what to attempt in the way of steady employment. When doing nothing, my candle must necessarily burn at both ends, and in the middle, the price of family living is so enormous. The lecturing season is now over. My last lecture was given week before last at Rockville, a very picturesque manufacturing village in Connecticut, twenty-five miles from Hartford towards Providence. Previously, I had been to Auburn, Syracuse, and Oneida,—receiving in each place $50, in all $200, exclusive of travelling expenses. I have no engagement on hand, but think some of preparing a special lecture on President Johnson, to be delivered in the Tremont Temple or Melodeon, on Fast Day evening, on my own hook,[2] but may not feel able to do it.[3]

I have not yet seen or written to Mr. [James T.] Fields about his proposition to me to write the history of the Anti-Slavery struggle. Fanny, in her letters, chides me sharply for my delay, and perhaps you will do the same. Be merciful! It is a matter requiring the gravest deliberation before I actually commit myself one way or another. I confess, I do not feel competent to the mighty task, and fear I shall make a failure of it if I try. To-morrow I shall aim to have an interview with Mr. Fields, and will report progress.

Aunt Charlotte [Anthony] and Julia Randall are with us from Providence. Sarah Tillinghast has also been with us. We are all in usual health. Fanny names the 15th of April as the time for getting home. William and Ellie expect to be back about the 4th of April. We envy you, at least your summer residence, in Llewellyn Park at Orange. With many kisses for dear Lucy, and a benediction upon you both, I remain, hastily, (as Mrs. Dall has just come in,)[4]

Your loving Father.

AL signed "Father": Garrison Papers, Boston Public Library; extract printed in *Life*, IV, 179.

1. Garrison's four "Sonnets for the Times" were printed in the *Independent*, March 29, 1866.
2. "On Fast Day evening, on my own hook" is written in Garrison's hand between the last two lines of the paragraph. Presumably he intended the two phrases to be inserted after "Melodeon."
3. Garrison apparently did not lecture on Fast Day, for there is no mention of such a lecture in the Boston *Transcript* for April 6, 1866, the date on which other such lectures were reported.
4. Caroline Wells Healey Dall (1822–1912), daughter of a successful Boston merchant and wife of Charles H. A. Dall, Unitarian minister and missionary to Calcutta, was a leading figure in the woman's rights movement of the 1860s and 1870s.

172

TO JAMES MILLER McKIM

Roxbury, March 31, 1866.

My dear McKim:

Your letter, and one previous from Wendell of a similar import, were duly received. It is entirely out of the question—my going to the West on the mission you suggest—for two reasons:—

First—Ten days ago, I had a very violent headlong fall at Grantville, (the second one within a few weeks,) which did me more harm than to have either dislocated or broken a bone; for it so injured and strained the muscles of my right arm, especially at the shoulder, affecting also the collar bone, that I have been in constant pain ever since, and nothing that I have tried of liniments, &c. has given me the slightest relief. My right hand is also stiff in the joints, making it painful for me to use the pen. I shall probably feel the injury for some time, and doubt if it will ever be repaired to the full extent. Instead of going to Chicago, therefore, I am off directly for Providence, to put myself under Dr. [Joseph] Dow for electrical treatment, where I expect to remain a week or ten days—perhaps longer—according to the success of the treatment. If you have occasion to write to me again, direct to me at Providence, care of Henry Anthony, Esq., 9 Benevolent Street.

It is as I expected it would be. The Western Freedmen's Aid Commission are not willing to affiliate with the American Commission as newly organized.[1] Three weeks ago, I received a letter from R. S. Rust, Cor. Sec. of the W. F. A. Commission, enclosing a series of resolutions adopted by the Board, giving several reasons why they cannot become auxiliary to the American Union, and stating that they deem it expedient to adhere to the basis already adopted in their legal character, and labor as heretofore exclusively for the benefit of the freedmen.[2] Levi Coffin and Thomas Kennedy both endorse Rust's letter.[3]

I have not yet answered the letter. Perhaps you have received a similar one.

I cannot go West for another reason. I have agreed with Ticknor & Fields to write a history of the Anti-Slavery struggle, and must consecrate this whole year to the completion of the work—or, rather, the first volume by October—600 pages large octavo.

I would add more, but must run to take the train for Providence.

Affectionately yours,

Wm. Lloyd Garrison.

J. M. McKim.

ALS: James Miller McKim Papers, New York Public Library.

1. The Western Freedmen's Aid Commission had been formed in Cincinnati, January 19, 1863. In February 1866 the American Freedmen's Aid Commission, of which both Garrison and McKim were officers, had been combined with the American Union Commission to form the American Freedmen's Union Commission, which it was thought could cooperate more efficiently with the federal Freedmen's Bureau than could two separate organizations. (See the second annual report of the Western Freedmen's Aid Commission, Cincinnati, 1865; New York *Times*, February 12, 1866; Willie Lee Rose, *Rehearsal for Reconstruction: The Port Royal Experiment*, New York, 1964.)

2. Richard Sutton Rust (1815–1906), born in Ipswich, Mass., and a graduate of Wesleyan University, had been president of Wilberforce University (1859–1863) and of Wesleyan Female College in Cincinnati (1863–1865). He was currently corresponding secretary of the Western Freedmen's Aid Commission, although later in 1866, after the various local societies combined to form the American Freedmen's Union Commission, he became discontented with that organization and helped organize the Freedmen's Aid Society of the Methodist Episcopal Church at Cincinnati.

3. Little is known of Thomas Kennedy except that in 1865 he was secretary of the board of directors of the Western Freedmen's Aid Commission and a member of several of its committees. (Letter to the editor from Frances Forman, reference librarian, Cincinnati Historical Society, April 25, 1972.)

173

TO WENDELL PHILLIPS GARRISON

Providence, April 10, 1866.

My dear Wendell:

A year ago, to-day, I was on board of the Arago, on my way to Fort Sumter with Major-General [Robert] Anderson and party. How many startling and far-reaching events have been crowded into that brief space! How sad and shocking was the assassination of President Lincoln! And how sad and shocking to have such a perfidious successor as President Johnson! Who can tell what another year will bring forth? We have a strong loyal Congress, it is true, to interpose as a breakwater against Executive usurpation while it remains in session; but what may not such an unscrupulous betrayer of the party that elected him, as Andrew Johnson, do when that body adjourns, and he has nothing to fear from its presence or legislation? You have rejoiced with me, and with millions of others, in the passage of the Civil Rights Bill over his Veto by Congress. The lines are now broadly drawn.

It is now ten days since I came here to see what Dr. [Joseph] Dow could so with his electrical apparatus for the sprains in my right shoulder and arm. He has experimented daily, but thus far without any effect, though he is sanguine that he can relieve me in a few days more. I am not. My pains are sharp and constant every day, and every hour of the day, and all through the night. No doubt rheumatic inflammation has "set in," which will somewhat complicate the case. Being thus disabled, it is only with considerable anguish that I can write a brief epistle like this; and, therefore, I am compelled to forego letter-writing almost wholly, excepting to your mother, with whom I keep up a daily correspondence—Frederick Anthony taking mine to her every morning, and bringing one from her every evening. But for this, I should have tried to send an article or two for *The Nation*, as I ought, before the present volume is concluded, to do something in that line, so as to redeem the promise made in the Prospectus.

I believe you have been informed that, verbally, I have agreed with Ticknor & Fields to write a history of the Anti-Slavery movement, in two volumes of six hundred pages, large octavo—the first to be ready for sale by next Christmas, if possible; the other in the course of next year. They offer me favorable terms, and pecuniary advances while I am preparing the work; but calculate upon a larger sale than I do—at least 25,000 copies in this country, to say nothing of England. When I return home, we shall have an agreement in writing.

I would have left Providence to-day, and been with you to-morrow, to attend an important meeting of the Managers of the American Freedmen's Commission, were it not for my crippled condition. Please tell Mr. [James Miller] McKim that he will greatly oblige me by stating the cause of my absence to the meeting.

Could I do so, I would also attend a celebration of the anniversary of the flag-raising at Fort Sumter which is to be held in Brooklyn next Saturday, and to which I have been invited.

Charlotte and Henry [Anthony] are enjoying themselves highly at Washington with Harry and Fanny. They will return in about a week, bringing Fanny along with them—the darling. Harry has been quite unwell, and is evidently in a bad way. [Theodore] Tilton told him that what he needs is "a constitutional amendment."

Your mother gets along pretty well, though she says her foot is somewhat swollen, and her left arm growing more stiff. She will have to come to Providence to receive treatment by and by.

How are you getting along? Letters are too infrequent between us, but I know you must be busy to wearisomeness with your office duties; and I need no written assurance of your affection or remembrance, as I am sure you need nothing of the kind from me.

With overflowing love to dear Lucy, I remain,

Ever your loving Father,

W. L. G.

ALS: Garrison Papers, Boston Public Library.

174

TO EDWIN A. STUDWELL

Providence, April 13, 1866.

Edwin A. Studwell, Esq.

My Dear Friend—

It is fortunate that the spirit has a locomotive power beyond that of the body, as it is only in that way I shall be able to be at your commemorative gathering to-morrow.[1]

The occasion cannot fail to be one of thrilling interest, especially to such of your company as were privileged to be at Fort Sumter on the 14th of April, 1865, to witness the re-raising of that flag, which, when it was struck down by traitorous hands, was stained, alas!

with the blood of four millions of slaves driven to unrequited toil beneath its folds, but which, when again unfurled to the breeze on the same battlements, was the glorious symbol of universal emancipation! You will vividly recall the scenes of that great historic day— the brilliancy of the weather, the gorgeous appearance of the numerous vessels decorated with their multitudinous rainbow colored flags, the mighty host of spectators congregated within the shattered walls of Sumter, the impressive ceremonies that followed, the stirring speech of the eloquent orator of the day, the shouts that made the welkin ring as the national ensign was run up to the utmost height of the lofty flag-staff, the thunderous discharge of cannon, first from the Fort and then promptly responded to by a hundred pieces from the adjacent batteries, and, finally, the heartfelt congratulations everywhere given and reciprocated upon this signal triumph of loyalty over treason, of liberty over slavery, of right over wrong. You will also remember what the visit to Charleston revealed as to the utter humilation of that haughty but subjugated city—the terrible destruction effected, on the right hand and on the left, by the shells thrown into the city, and still more by the conflagration (the work of Confederate hands) which swept away the finest portions of it; the profound solemnity created in every mind, as though traversing the streets of ancient Nineveh or Babylon; the absence of all signs of business and commerce, of municipal authority and neighborly intercourse, of permanent residence and home-born population, except on the part of the rejoicing freedmen. These and many other reminiscences attending the outward and homeward voyage will throng the memory, and make your celebration one of deep emotion.

What mighty events have since transpired to affect our national destiny and electrify the civilized world! In all time, whose death ever so affected the sensibility or so excited the reverence of the nations of the earth as that of the murdered Lincoln? What expressions of sympathy, of condolence, of horror, of personal appreciation, poured in from every quarter of the globe! How unparalleled the lamentation in our own country, in view of the awful tragedy! And why was all this? Not because a foul murder had been committed, nor because the victim was the President of the United States, but, incomparably beyond all other considerations, because Abraham Lincoln sundered at a blow the chains of more than three millions of chattel slaves, and thereby sent the accursed slave system reeling to the dust!—and because he fell a martyr in the cause of our common humanity and of universal freedom!

What high hopes were entertained of the patriotism, loyalty, and executive trustworthiness of his successor! Yet how have these been blasted! Andrew Johnson might have placed his name high on the roll of the illustrious and world-renowned benefactors of the human race; but, by his evil and treacherous course, his usurping and despotic policy in the interests of those who are still rebels in spirit and purpose, his perfidy as their *soi-disant* "Moses" toward the liberated bondmen of the South, he seems bent upon sending his name down to posterity along with those of Benedict Arnold and Judas Iscariot. For what is the meaning of the jubilant shouts heard throughout Rebeldom, and vociferously responded to by the entire body of Northern Copperheads, in view of his liberty-crushing vetoes, but that he is on their side and acting in accordance with their wishes, and therefore false to his oath of office, and recreant to all that is sacred in justice and precious in liberty? Allow me, therefore, to offer you the following cold water sentiment:

The speedy impeachment and removal of Andrew Johnson from the office he dishonors and betrays!

Yours, for the execution of justice,

Wm. Lloyd Garrison.

ALS: A. Conger Goodyear Collection, Yale University Library; also printed in *The Friend*, May 1866.

1. This letter was sent to Studwell as secretary of the Sumter Club on the occasion of its anniversary dinner in Brooklyn, N.Y.

175

TO SAMUEL MAY, JR.

Roxbury, May 7, 1866.

Dear Mr. May:

Your very kind and considerate letter,—enclosing a check for $500 in my behalf on account of the Testimonial fund, and also the names of those obtained to the appeal,—was safely put into my hands, and read with heartfelt emotions of gratitude towards yourself personally, and those who desire to show their appreciation of my past Anti-Slavery labors generally, by making my declining years free from pecuniary anxiety and embarrassment.[1] The whole affair is an utter surprise to me. No such Testimonial had I dreamed of,—feeling that I had always been amply compensated by a gracious Providence, whether in regard to spiritual or material comfort, for whatever of obloquy and ostracism I may have encountered, or peril incurred, or toil performed, during the long and trying struggle for the abolition of slavery in our land. Nor could I possibly accept it on the score of special personal merit; for very many others have labored not less devotedly and untiringly, (yourself among the number,) to "break every yoke and let the oppressed go free";[2] and we have all been richly rewarded in the consciousness of well-doing, and the liberation from chains and slavery of the hapless millions who challenged our sympathy and aid. It is not its *personal* application that is peculiarly agreeable to my feelings, but because it will be a handsome vindication of the Anti-Slavery movement as such, and of the Abolitionists as a body, from the cruel aspersions to which they were constantly subjected for a period of more than thirty years—a vindication by Congressional Senators and Representatives from twenty-one States, Governors, college professors, judges, lawyers, merchants, and other prominent members of society—headed by the Chief Justice of the United States [Salmon P. Chase]. On that ground the Testimonial will prove of historical significance and value, and give a new illustration of the fact that

> "———ever the right comes uppermost,
> And ever is justice done."[3]

On examining the list of names appended to the appeal, I am truly astonished at the success attending your efforts to obtain them. Six years ago, you could not have secured, probably, one tenth of the number. What a marvellous change in feeling, sentiment, and appreciation has been wrought towards us in that brief period! And it is most gratifying to know, from your lips, that no importunity was needed to induce any one to subscribe his name; for you found a very willing mind in every instance.

My dear friend, I feel sure that to you I am mainly indebted for the conception of this Testimonial, and doubtless shall be for its completion, as far as that may be practicable. My ever faithful coadjutor, Edmund Quincy, has also seconded it with a hearty good will, I am equally certain. My indebtedness to you both, therefore, already large through numerous kindnesses extended to me through all the years of our mighty conflict since we first joined hands, will be greatly augmented; and it will never be forgotten by me while aught of memory is left.

How much of the generous sum named in the appeal can be obtained remains to be seen. I shall be neither disappointed nor mortified if it shall prove a comparative failure; for I know full well how, in other cases where there seemed to be no lack of good-will or liberal purpose, it has proved an up-hill work to obtain any considerable donations. The most direct personal application is needed to secure the desired amount.

Not needing, at present, the check you enclosed, and not wishing to receive any thing from the fund in its present state, I have returned the check to Mr. [William] Endicott [Jr.].

Your grateful friend,

Wm. Lloyd Garrison.

Rev. Samuel May, Jr.

ALS: Garrison Papers, Boston Public Library.

1. For detailed information about the national testimonial in honor of Garrison see Introduction VI, "Retirement and Financial Security: 1866."
2. Isaiah 58:6, adapted.
3. Not identified.

176

TO FANNY GARRISON VILLARD

Roxbury, May 25, 1866.

My dear Fanny:

You are so constant in your epistolary favors that you not only deserve but get the unanimous thanks of the household. Gratifying, however, as it is to hear from you so frequently, we should be sorry to have you overtaxed in your desire to please us. That I do not write to you or Harry oftener is because my arm and shoulder are as full of anguish as ever; ten weeks having elapsed without bringing the slightest relief, day or night. Dr. Munroe has manipulated the arm a few times, and thinks he is gaining upon it; but I do not, as yet, "see it."[1] I have tried a variety of liniments, and Dr. Geist has given me several homœopathic powders; but nothing comes of these in the shape of relief.[2] My nervous symptom is a good deal unstrung, and I am able to achieve nothing from week to week.

Dr. Munroe was here yesterday, and spent two hours in manipulating your mother's paralyzed limbs, and promised to come this afternoon. He is very unreliable as to his appointments, but is really interested in your mother's case, and says he means to give it his special attention, believing he will in the end be successful. I am glad your mother has a growing confidence in his skill, knowledge, and method of cure. God grant it may be given him to restore her limbs to their normal condition! Would not our joy and gratitude be unbounded? Emancipated from her present crippled state, how much she and I would enjoy in social visits, pleasant excursions, and hospitable interchanges! Let up hope for the best, while being resigned to whatever may be the will of Heaven.

I am immensely relieved to hear of your speedy recovery from the illness which prostrated you. Be all the more careful as the summer heat increases.

You write gaily about our family prospects, the proposed testimonial to me, &c. I have no belief that any thing like the sum named will be raised, and caution you not to be (as I shall not be) disappointed should it not amount to more than ten thousand dollars. That, indeed, would be a very handsome gift, and far beyond my deserts. Still, if no more should be realized, it would somewhat "take the bloom from the peach," in view of the sum publicly proposed. Dear George Thompson (who deserves a pension from both England and America) did not get one thousand dollars on his "loyal testimonial". The failure was owing mainly, I think, to a lack of direct personal application. It is surprising how little pecuniary aid can be obtained through printed circulars and letters.

The Perkins's estate is still in the market. I wish it were possible for us, as a family, to get possession of it.[3] Mr. P. asks fifteen thousand dollars for it, but would perhaps take a thousand less. I think it would be a good investment of a portion of the funds now being raised for my benefit. It would make a charming abode for Harry and you, or William and Ellie, besides removing all difficulty about a right of way for us.

Charlotte Coffin stayed with us yesterday and last night. She will leave for Syracuse in a few days, to be gone for at least three months. Your mother will miss her exceedingly.

We hear nothing from Hepza. She is at Lynn, and may come to us at any hour.

Next week is anniversary week in Boston. I do not intend taking any part in any of the meetings, and, should Hepza come, may slip off to Providence till they are over.

Ellie is expecting her mother next Tuesday evening.

We all deem William fortunate in regard to his partnership.

Franky has a bad cold, with sore throat.

Ever most lovingly yours,

W. L. G.

☞ I am trying a new rheumatic and neuralgic remedy for my shoulder.

Our household love to dear Harry. When are you coming home?

☞ I have just ordered H. C. Phillips, of Philadelphia, to send you some card photographs.[4] I will pay him.

ALS: Garrison Papers, Boston Public Library.

1. Possibly Garrison refers to William F. Munroe (1840–1875), who served in the Civil War as acting assistant surgeon, United States Army, and who afterward practiced in Pepperell, Mass. A physician of the same name is listed in the Boston directory for 1866, at 109 Mt. Vernon Street. Another doctor, William H. Munroe of 63 Beach Street, is listed in the same directory. (Thomas Francis Harrington and James Gregory Mumford, *The Harvard Medical School, A History, Narrative and Documentary 1782–1905*, New York and Chicago, 1905; letter to the editor from Nancy Sahli, researcher, July 1, 1972.)

2. Christian F. Geist (1806–1872) was a German homeopathic physician who had been trained under Dr. Wohlleben in his native country. Immigrating to the United States in 1835, he settled first in Allentown, Mass., and then in Boston, where between 1840 and 1843 he studied under Dr. Robert Wesselhoeft. He practiced most of his life in Boston. (William Harvey King, *History of Homœopathy*, New York and Chicago, 1905, I.)

3. Garrison may refer to the property of Benjamin Perkins (c. 1797–1870), who is listed in Boston city directories as treasurer of the Home Missionary Society. Although his property has not been located with certainty, it may be that which was owned by William Lloyd Garrison, Jr., in 1873 and was situated just behind the Garrisons' property. (Letter to the editor from Nancy Sahli, researcher, August 19, 1972.)

4. Philadelphia city directories list Henry C. Phillips as a photographer with a shop at Ninth and Chestnut streets.

177

TO WENDELL PHILLIPS GARRISON

Roxbury, June 14, 1866.

Dear Wendell:

Only think of it! Your father is at last a grandfather! The expected advent came this morning at half past 4 o'clock, and Ellie presented William and the household with a dear little babe, plump and "cunning looking," the first of a long line of descendants may it prove— mother and child doing extremely well. The babe is a girl, and is already named Agnes.[1] Every thing went off in the best possible manner, and we are all relieved of anxiety as to the event. I know you and Lucy will be delighted to hear the news, and therefore lose no time in communicating it. Ellie has been remarkably well for the last three or four months, and taken a great deal of out-door exercise, even up to yesterday. It has proved favorable to an easy accouchement, and unquestionably to the healthy condition of the child.

Dr. (Miss) Lackshefka (English—I always forget how she spells her name)[2] officiated on the occasion—the quickness of delivery not allowing time to bring Dr. [Christian F.] Geist in season from Boston, as originally designed. I am very glad it so happened.

It is very fortunate and gratifying that Ellie's mother [Mrs. David Wright] is with her. She has an excellent nurse.

For the past two days, Dr. [Daniel] Mann has been with us, completing a set of teeth for me. I am now satisfactorily equipped.

I gain very slowly as to my arm and shoulder, and may have to suffer a good while longer. Possibly, if we ever get clear, settled, warm summer weather, it may bring me very considerable relief. I have already lost three months, not having been able to achieve anything during that time. It is a serious matter as to my finances—with the enormous expenses of living, the employment of various doctors, and doing nothing to secure any remuneration.

Mrs. Hallowell luckily came from Medford soon after breakfast, and is spending the day with Ellie—delighted, of course, with the new comer.[3]

Your mother is well, excepting her crippled state, and contrives to get through a large amount of light reading, and to write many letters, in the course of a week; not being able to get out much, with the weather so unsettled and rainy. She does not get as much manipulation at the hands of Dr. Munroe as she expected or desires, in consequence of his having so many patients to attend to.

Franky, I am sorry to say, has had a bad cough for the last three weeks, and expectorates a surprising amount of mucus matter. He is very weak, feverish, and somewhat emaciated, so that we are all a good deal alarmed about him. It is really a critical period in his life, and he must throw his classics to the dogs for the present as a matter of self-preservation. I do not see any chance for him to go through his examination at Cambridge next month, unless he recuperates in a surprising manner; and we all seriously question whether he will be well enough to make it safe for him to enter college at the next term. His health is far more to be consulted than his education at Harvard. He has been under Dr. Geist's care for a week past, but as yet makes no gain. He has lost his spirits very much though he exhibits no despondency—only abiding seriousness. We have not expressed our fears to him any farther than to make him understand that he must no longer pursue his studies. He needs out-door exercise, and a gymnastic course of treatment.

I enclose the latest card photograph of Fanny. We all think it is decidedly the best one she has had taken.

With loving regards to Lucy and her parents, I remain,

　　　　　　　　　　　　　　　　Your affectionate Father.

AL signed "Father": Garrison Papers, Sophia Smith Collection, Smith College Library.

1. Agnes Garrison (1866–1950), who never married, lived in the Boston area but spent her later years in Wianno, Mass. She died in Santa Barbara, Calif. (Obituary, Boston *Herald*, April 1, 1950.)

2. Marie Zakrzewska (1829–1902) was born in Berlin, where she studied midwifery, graduating from the Charité hospital in 1851. Moving to the United States in 1853, she graduated from Western Reserve Medical College in 1856. Three years later she accepted a post at New England Female Medical College in Boston. In that city in 1863 she founded the New England Hospital for Women and Children, where she was an attending physician until 1887, and thereafter until her retirement in 1899 an advisory physician. (*NAW.*)

3. Anna Coffin Davis Hallowell (1838–1913), the daughter of Edward M. Davis and Anna Mott, the eldest child of James and Lucretia Mott, had been the wife of abolitionist Richard Price Hallowell since 1859. She was the author of *James and Lucretia Mott, Life and Letters* (1884). (*Friends' Intelligencer*, March 15, 1913.)

178

TO FANNY GARRISON VILLARD

Roxbury, July 6, 1866.

Dear Fanny:

I avail myself of the last opportunity to send you and Harry my benediction, and your mother's. I might supplicate the Divine Power to watch over and protect you, grant you a safe and rapid passage across the Atlantic, make your European visit equally serviceable and delightful, and ultimately return you to us, to find us in a better condition as to health than when you left us. But I deem this quite unnecessary, because I see no cause to distrust the watchful guardianship or the loving-kindness of Him "whose tender mercies are over all the works of his hand," and "who doeth all things well."[1] Much as I love you, I would have no supernatural or abnormal intervention for your special benefit. I shall not, therefore, plead for a fair wind, a smooth sea, or a succession of charming days to the end of your voyage; but only hope that you may be so fortunate as to be thus favored.

You are soon to be among a people "of a strange speech,"[2] and with manners and customs widely differing from those in which you have been educated. No doubt some of them may appear to you ridiculous and preposterous; nevertheless, avoid the appearance of eccentricity, and learn to conform except in those cases where virtue is to be vindicated, a high morality exemplified, and principle adhered to, cost what it may. Consent to nothing that you conscientiously believe to be wrong; and at the same time endeavor to enlarge and broaden your understanding so as to keep your conscience in a healthy condition, so as to avoid being morbid on the one hand, and hypercritical on the other. Shun disputation as such; and when called upon to defend what you regard as truth and duty, be earnest without undue excitement, and positive without dogmatism. You will have much to learn, and may also be able to instruct, by way of reciprocity.

Do not allow yourself to be drawn into any expensive, foolish, or unseemly custom as to dress, but set an example of good taste and laudable sobriety. Your danger will be considerable in this direction, because you are liable to be petted, and brought into gay society.

Almost all Americans become more or less corrupted by a residence abroad, and inclined to class distinctions among the people. Give no countenance to the spirit of caste, or to aristocratical assumptions. Be at least as radical when you return as when you left us.

Regard me as with you always. If any unexpected calamity or sorrow occur, send to me for any needed advice or aid. But I am sure that in Harry you will find one who will leave nothing undone to make you contented and happy.

Should you reach Munich, and see Harry's father [Gustav L. Hilgard] and relatives, assure them of my earnest desire to make their personal acquaintance, and tell them I am proud of my German son-in-law.

Mrs. [Dora] Brigham kindly stayed with your mother till near the time of your return.[3] I am glad your mother not only makes no lamentation over your departure, but takes pleasure and solace in thinking what you are to see and enjoy abroad. She meant to have written you a parting word, but she is now getting her rubbing by Mrs. Smith, and will be too much exhausted to put pen to paper afterward.[4] Besides, the mercury ranges over 90 in the shade.

I forgot to get for you a bottle of camphor. Take a small one along with you.

Doubtless, Mr. [James Miller] McKim and Lucy will see you depart in the steamer. Give them my loving remembrances. Tell them Wendell is enjoying his visit. He has gone to-day to Lynn and Beverly.

Adieu, my darling!

W. L. G.

P.S. Ellie passed a comfortable night, and is looking a little better this morning, though very pale and weak. Franky will leave us to-morrow on his pedestrian excursion.[5]

☞ Tell Harry I shall rely on a faithful translation of my letter to his father.

ALS: Garrison Papers, Boston Public Library.
1. Psalms 145:9 and Mark 7:38, adapted.
2. Ezekiel 3:5 and 6.
3. Thus in manuscript; Garrison's meaning is obscure.
4. Mrs. Smith has not been identified.
5. Frank kept a detailed diary of his "pedestrian excursion," which began in Providence on July 9 and took him and his friends through Massachusetts, New York, Vermont, and New Hampshire. He left the group on July 25 at Lake George and went to West Randolph, Vt., to spend two and a half weeks with Mr. and Mrs. James Hutchinson, Jr.; on August 17 he returned home. (Francis Jackson Garrison, manuscript tramp journal, July 9–August 17, 1866, Merrill Collection of Garrison Papers, Wichita State University Library. Frank began the journal during the outing but did not complete his account of the trip until 1868.)

179

TO FANNY GARRISON VILLARD

Rockledge, July 19, 1866.

Dear Fanny:

It is a fortnight, to-day, since you bade us farewell. How you have measured time, while on the trackless deep, I expect to hear in due season; I trust not by any rule known to me, during such a billowy journey, have you kept your reckoning—for the days seem very, very long, and the nights almost interminable. A little sea-sickness is doubtless good for the system, but a good deal of it is—purgatory. Luckily, whatever other discomforts you may have experienced, you and Harry have escaped what is called our heated term. If June was cold and shivering, July has shown more than a tropical fervor. Day after day the mercury has ranged above 90 in the shade— sometimes 100, and over—with no cool intervening day or night. Very many fatal cases of sun-stroke in Boston, New York, and other cities, have already been recorded. You will experience no such hot weather abroad—at least, not in England, where I trust you are now safely landed.

The latest news from Europe indicates the war between Prussia and Austria to be virtually ended—almost as soon as begun!—by Austria being "driven to the wall,"[1] and calling for the interposition of Louis Napoleon.[2] As no great principles of freedom and equality *for the people* are involved in the struggle, may it be brought to a speedy close! Whether the Italians will like the transfer of Venitia to the French Emperor better than to remain under Austrian control, remains to be seen.[3]

Peace restored, you will have no difficulty in going directly to Munich. Should any thing occur to prevent this, our friends, the

Bradfords, (Sarah and Rebecca,) are hoping it may be agreeable to you to be with or near them at Montauban, near the Pyrenees. They told me, on leaving, that they should try to see you in Paris.

Since you left, the finest and wealthiest portion of Portland [Me.] has been reduced to ashes—twelve thousand people rendered houseless, and property destroyed to the enormous amount of from twelve to fifteen millions of dollars![4] So destructive a fire—considering the size of the city—has never before occurred in this country. Relief is pouring in from every quarter.

General Jim Lane is dead and buried, though he lingered several days after his suicidal act.[5]

Boston has been patriotically excited to a high degree, for a few days past, by the presence of General [William T.] Sherman. I did not attempt to see him. He is now in Hanover, N. H., attending the Dartmouth college exercises in company with Chief Justice [Salmon P.] Chase. His speeches have been commendably brief, and non-committal on public matters.

Franky is enjoying his pedestrian excursion highly.[6] In his last letter, dated "In camp between two fine ponds, four miles from Palmer depot, and five miles from Ware village, Mass.," he says— "I find in the Boston Journal a very interesting letter from Munich, written by Dr. Winslow, who lived in the Kittredge house[7] the first winter we were in Roxbury.[8] I shall save it. His daughter[9] was a schoolmate of Fanny, and is now at Munich with him." He further adds—"I am in good trim, and think I shall stand the walking as well as any." He will be absent until September, but no doubt he will find ways and means to send you now and then a letter.

I have been to the Pavilion,[10] in Boston, about a dozen times, to be treated by Mr. Nelson by "the laying on of hands" for my injured arm; but I have received no relief whatever, and have even suffered more than less.[11] So, I am going to cease making any more applications, and to leave nature to operate unmolested—taking what recreation I can, and trying to build up my system by exercise and diet. Hence, I shall go to Orange this afternoon, to spend some ten days with Wendell and Lucy; from which place I will duly report progress. I am satisfied my shoulder-bone is cracked, and the chances are that it may give me an indefinite amount of pain and suffering.

I have just called upon our dear and venerated friend, Miss Henrietta Sargeant, and received a warm welcome. She asked a great many questions about you and Harry, and all the family—did not know that you had sailed for Europe, nor that I was a grandfather—and was much interested in the news. She has given a hundred dollars to aid the Portland sufferers, as well as clothing, and is always doing good. She looks aged and very feeble, though she said nothing of herself. She desired to be most lovingly remembered to you, and to have her regards and congratulations given to Mr. Villard.

I saw Mrs. Chapman and Mary [G. Chapman], a few days since, and they made kind and special inquiries about you both.

Dear Ellie, after having been a great sufferer and had a narrow escape, is now fairly convalescent, and, with care, will soon be about the house.[12] The babe is five weeks' old to-day, and weighs ten pounds. She promises well as to her looks.

Congress has promptly passed the new Freedmen's Bureau bill over another veto of President Johnson.[13] He has fully gone over to the enemy.

William has been unwell for a day or two, but is at his store to-day. The wool business is stagnant. No sales.

Love to dear Harry. Adieu, darling!

Your affectionate Father.

AL signed "Father": Garrison Papers, Boston Public Library.

1. An expression of sixteenth-century origin.

2. Charles Louis Napoleon Bonaparte (1808–1873), after a frustrating youth during which he and his family were exiled from France, made two unsuccessful attempts to seize power (1836 and 1840). In 1848 he was elected president and in 1852 was proclaimed Emperor Napoleon III. In April 1866 he had negotiated a Franco-Prussian alliance; but he was too weak to prevent Prussia from becoming the dominant European power following the Seven Weeks War, in which Prussia defeated the alliance of Austria, Bavaria, Hanover, and other German states.

3. Within a year after the defeat of Austria, which had controlled Venice, the city was in fact incorporated into United Italy.

4. A fire which started in a shop on July 5 was spread by a gale from the south until it had destroyed almost the entire business district of the city. (New York *Times,* July 6 and 10; *The Nation,* July 12, 1866.)

5. James Henry Lane (1814–1866), born and bred in frontier country, was by training a lawyer but by preference a soldier. He served as a colonel in the Mexican War before becoming lieutenant governor of Indiana (1849–1853) and member of Congress (1853–1855). In 1855 he moved to Kansas, where he worked to organize antislavery forces in the territory, his military activities against proslavery residents prefiguring those of John Brown. He also worked assiduously to secure the admission of Kansas as a state, and in 1861 he became the first United States senator from Kansas. A strong supporter of President Lincoln, he was appointed in June 1861 brigadier general of volunteers, becoming the recruiting commissioner for Kansas. By January 1863 he had recruited one of the first black regiments to join the Union army. Although as a radical he had wielded enormous influence both in Kansas and in Washington, after the war he became so conservative as to support President Johnson's veto of the Civil Rights bill—an action that made him very unpopular in his state. A series of pressures, including those caused by allegations of questionable financial dealings so depressed Lane that on July 1, 1866, he shot himself; he died ten days later.

6. For a description of Francis Jackson Garrison's walking tour, see the letter to Fanny Garrison Villard, July 6, 1866, n. 5.

Frank's letter (some eight pages long) to which Garrison refers was written to Helen E. Garrison on Sunday, July 15, as the young man rested after several days of strenuous hiking. (Francis Jackson Garrison, manuscript tramp journal, July 9–August 17, 1866, Merrill Collection of Garrison Papers, Wichita State University Library; for a description of the tour see also the Vergennes *Vermonter*, August 10, and a reprint in the Boston *Traveller*, August 13, 1866. In this article, entitled "Collegians Afloat," special mention is made of "Frank Garrison [son of Wm. Lloyd Garrison].")

7. Charles Frederick Winslow (1811–1877) graduated from Harvard Medical School in 1834. He was the author of several books on geology, cosmography, and physics. His letter entitled "Glance at the Bavarians and Some of their Institutions" appeared in the Boston *Daily Journal*, July 10 and 13, 1866. (*Harvard University Quinquennial Catalogue of the Officers and Graduates, 1636–1930*, Cambridge, Mass., 1930, p. 857; *Catalog of Books by Library of Congress Printed Cards*, Ann Arbor, Mich., 1946, CLXIV, 428.)

The Kittredge house was probably either the large property at 155 Highland Street owned by S. F. Kittredge or the one on Highland Avenue, near the Garrisons' house, owned by Alvah Kittredge. (Griffith Morgan Hopkins, *Combined Atlas of the County of Suffolk, Massachusetts*, Philadelphia, 1873, II, 59, 69.)

8. The winter of 1864.

9. Not further identified.

10. The Pavilion was a hotel at 57 Tremont Street. (Boston city directory, 1866.)

11. George S. Nelson, magnetic physician, is listed in the Boston city directory as living and working at 57 Tremont Street.

12. Although the birth of Agnes Garrison on June 14 seemed perfectly normal, Ellie had a difficult time for a month thereafter. Family letters do not specify the nature of her illness. (See the letter from Helen E. Garrison to Fanny Garrison Villard, July 17, 1866, Merrill Collection of Garrison Papers, Wichita State University Library.)

13. The same month as Garrison's letter, Congress had passed an extension of the Freedmen's Bureau bill over the President's veto.

180

TO HELEN E. GARRISON

Orange, N.J., July 23, 1866.

Dear Wife:

Saturday the weather was lowering, with occasional showers, and somewhat chilly, making it undesirable to go out even for a ramble in the Park; so I staid within doors, and gave myself to an examination of books, particularly poetical effusions, to conversation, and to rest—if there be any rest connected with ceaseless pain, for my arm was (as it continues to be) as troublesome as ever. Mr. [James Miller] McKim, in consequence of his cough—which is, indeed, a serious one—did not go to the city, but remained in his chamber the most of the day. My old anti-slavery friend, Mr. William Green, spent the evening with us, and we passed a pleasant hour together.[1] He was one of the signers of the Anti-Slavery Declaration of Sentiments at Philadelphia in 1833, being at that time a merchant in New York, and was one of the most reliable "spokes in the wheel." He afterwards retired from business, and removed from New York to Hartford. For the last seven years he has been a resident in the Park, and is a near neighbor of Mr. McKim, having one of the finest residences and most delightful situations in the Park. Yesterday he left to be gone a week, much to his regret and mine.

The weather continued to be somewhat overcast yesterday, cool, and threatening rain, until noon, when the sun asserted his kingly supremacy, and made a brilliant demonstration. In the forenoon, Wendell and I took a long stroll through the romantic windings which are here found in every direction, making a high ascension, and getting extended and charming views through the openings. We had a feast of mulberries, which we picked as we rambled.

After dinner, from 4 to 6 o'clock, Wendell, Lucy, and I went to ride through the Park and beyond it, going to the top of Eagle Rock, driving quite to the edge, where one of the most extensive and beautiful views presents itself to the eye—in some of its aspects reminding of the view presented from Mount Holyoke.[2] The ascent to the Rock is by a broad avenue, just completed, very gently graded, and making a right royal road. We made no calls by the way, as our object was to see nature, not men or women.

The more I see of the Park, the more I am delighted with it. My first impressions were so strong, and my feelings so enthusiastic, that I was afraid I should experience some abatement of my admiration; but not so. In extent it is about as large as the great Central Park at New York, but with features far more romantic and unique. A residence here, however, would be much too solitary for you, and so I shall make no proposition to leave Rockledge to take up our abode here. There are beautiful homes scattered through the Park, but the addition of a hundred others would add greatly to its social enjoyment, leaving ample scope for lawns, groves, and family seclusion. The price of land is now two thousand dollars an acre: it was once forty dollars on the average.

Last evening, Lucy indulged me by playing a number of good old psalm tunes on the piano, and we had some family singing. Charley [McKim] has a capital voice, of great compass, and may yet distinguish himself as a singer. He accompanies Lucy, as she plays on the piano, with his castanets, and is very skilful in the use of them. He is a dear good, handsome, affectionate boy—as sweet in spirit and appearance as a new blown rose.

How is grandpa's baby? Kiss it for me, and give its mother another in my behalf. Kindest regards to dear Mrs. [David] Wright and Julia [Randall]. Love to William. Any news from Franky?

Hurriedly, your own loving husband,

W. L. G.

ALS: Garrison Papers, Boston Public Library.

1. William Green (1796–1881), originally in the hardware business, became the proprietor of a rolling and smelting plant at Boonton, N.J., where he developed a cooperative system permitting the employees to share in the profits. Long active in the antislavery cause, Green had been one of the founders of the American Anti-Slavery Society in 1833, serving as its first treasurer. He had also been active from the early years in the New York Anti-Slavery Society. Green was among the first to purchase a building site in Llewellyn Park. (*Life;* obituary, New York *Times,* October 23, 1881.)

2. Eagle Rock, the highest point in Llewellyn Park, commanded a view north and south from Tarrytown to Sandy Hook. (*National Anti-Slavery Standard,* June 11, 1864; see also Jane B. Davies, "Llewellyn Park in West Orange, New Jersey," *Antiques,* 107, No. 1: 142–158, January 1975.)

181

TO HELEN E. GARRISON

Orange, July 28, 1866.

Dear Wife:

Not having written to you for a few days past, I must give you a few particulars as to the manner in which I have been spending my time.

On Tuesday last, I went to New York to report myself to Dr. Dunham, according to agreement, but needed no additional powders, as I had not used up those he had given me at first.[1] I have not, however, received any perceptible benefit, as my arm still remains as incorrigible as ever.

In the afternoon I went up the North River some thirty miles to a beautiful little village called Nyack, to spend the night, in company with Theodore Tilton and his wife, and Mrs. Bradshaw of Brooklyn, an intimate friend of theirs, and a very pleasant and intelligent lady.[2] We all went by special invitation of Rev. L. D. Mansfield, Principal of the Rockland Female Institute—a very popular and admirable school for young ladies.[3] The sail up the river in a spacious and handsomely arranged steamer was indescribably enjoyable, as the weather was brilliant, and the views on both sides of the river quite enchanting. There was a large number of passengers on board, particularly of ladies and children. On the way, while talking with Theodore on deck, I observed to him that over our heads there was a supply of life-preservers, in case of an emergency; but had scarcely uttered the words before the alarming cry was raised, "The boat is on fire!"—and the smell of burning wood became very strong, in confirmation thereof. For a few moments there was great and general consternation, some of the ladies fainting; but, happily, it was quickly announced that the fire was extinguished, and the danger over. A few moments more, and the vessel might have been wrapped in flames; in which case, situated as we were at the time, very few of the passengers would have escaped with their lives; for I think the life-preservers would not have done much for the women and children.

On arriving at Nyack about 5 o'clock, we were met at the landing by Mr. Mansfield, with his carriage and a span of spirited horses, and first driven three miles up the river to Hook Mountain, an extended elevation resembling Arthur's Seat[4] at Edinburgh, Scotland, a lion couchant—then driven back to the Institute, which occupies an elevated point near the village, is palatial in size and appearance, and commands a most varied, extensive, and magnificent landscape. After tea, we had a boat-ride upon the Hudson for an hour or two, several others joining our party, the river being very placid, and the moon shining gloriously. It was an evening and an excursion long to be most pleasantly remembered.

The next morning, Mr. Mansfield took us in his carriage across the ferry to Tarrytown, (the river being three miles wide,) and drove us down the river on the east side to Irvington, to the late residence of Washington Irving—a charming and romantic retreat on the banks of the Hudson. The house is two hundred years old, somewhat modernized, and a curious structure on the whole, and occupied by Irving's nieces.[5] An adjacent estate is owned by Moses H. Grinnell, of New York; and as we drove through the grounds, I felt as if I were on some English nobleman's domains, so extensive and lovely were the lawns, so grand the trees, so rich the shrubbery, and so picturesque the views.[6] The house was a first-class one, and the whole estate of great pecuniary value. But such possessions do not make happiness.

Driving back to Tarrytown, (palatial residences to be seen in every direction,) we took the cars for New York—on arriving in the city went to Mrs. [Augustus] Savins, (with whom Tilton is now boarding,) and was warmly welcomed by her—next, went and took tea with Mr. Bailey, a merchant residing opposite Gramercy Park,[7] Tilton accompanying me, and enjoyed a tremendous thunder storm —eating some huckleberries and milk which proved stale and unwholesome, so as to be wholly indigestible. The next morning I was quite sick for several hours, and vomited freely. Tilton called in a homœopathic physician, who gave me some powders; and in the afternoon I was enabled to get down to Wendell's office,[8] and go back to Orange, and have since felt quite recovered.

Yesterday I called to see Mrs. Bramhall for the first time, and had a pleasant chat with her and Marcia;[9] and to-morrow am to dine and take tea with them, Wendell and Lucy to be also at the latter.

I am having a very pleasant time indeed. Thanks for your letters. Shall be sorry not to see dear Mrs. [David] Wright, Ellie, and the babe before my return home. I shall hope to see you on Thursday morning next. Love to all as one. All send loving regards.

Ever your own

W. L. G.

ALS: Garrison Papers, Boston Public Library.

1. Doubtless Garrison refers to Carroll Dunham (1828–1877), president of the American Institute of Homeopathy and dean of the New York Homeopathic Medical College, who lived at 68 East Twelfth Street in New York City. (Obituary, New York *Times*, February 2, 1877.)

2. Martha Bradshaw, wife of Andrew Bradshaw, a flour merchant, taught Sunday school at the Beecher church in Brooklyn and was one of the Tiltons' best friends. She was made a deaconess of the Plymouth Church in 1869 and testified at the Tilton-Beecher trial in 1875. (Paxton Hibben, *Henry Ward Beecher: an American Portrait*, New York, 1927, p. 238; letter to the editor from Esther Katz, researcher, November 13, 1972.)

3. Leroy D. Mansfield (1820–1900), a graduate of Union College and a minister, taught at Brooklyn Polytechnic Institute until 1858, when he became principal of Rockland Female Institute, which had opened as a school for young ladies in 1856. During the summer the institute was used as a resort under the name Tappan Zee House, with Mansfield and his brother Charles as proprietors. (Mrs. S. S. Colt, ed., *The Tourist's Guide through the Empire State*, Albany, 1871, pp. 34–36.)

4. A basaltic hill overlooking the city, from which King Arthur is said to have watched his men defeat the Picts.

5. Washington Irving (1783–1859), journalist and man of letters, spent his last thirteen years like an eighteenth-century English squire at his beloved Sunnyside, surrounded by six unmarried nieces. At the time of Garrison's letter the surviving nieces would have been Catharine Ann (1816–1911), Sarah (1817–1900), and Mary Elizabeth Irving (1820–1868). (Stanley T. Williams, *The Life of Washington Irving*, New York, 1935, II; Pierre M. Irving, *The Life and Letters of Washington Irving*, New York, 1864, IV.)

6. Moses Hicks Grinnell (1803–1877) had for many years been engaged in shipping and international trade. His firm, Grinnell, Minturn & Company, was one of the most extensive and successful in New York. Grinnell was also active in banking and insurance and was president of the chamber of commerce between 1843 and 1848. He served as a member of Congress (1839–1841) and as collector of the port of New York (1869–1870). With his enormous wealth he was always generous, contributing, often anonymously, to many private and public charities. His second wife was Julia Irving, a niece of Washington Irving.

7. Garrison probably refers to Isaac H. Bailey (1819–1899) of 23 Gramercy Place, a leather and hide merchant, whose firm was Bailey and Weisel of 87 Gold Street,

New York. He was both an ardent abolitionist and a staunch Republican. (Obituary, New York *Tribune*, March 25, 1899.)

Gramercy Park is located between Third and Fourth avenues and Eighteenth and Twenty-third streets. Beginning in 1831, it had been developed by real estate promoter Samuel B. Ruggles as an exclusive residential area, owners of property being furnished with golden keys for entrance to the private park. (*New York City Guide*, compiled by the Federal Writers' Project of the Works Progress Administration, New York, 1939.)

8. At 3 Park Place.

9. Not identified, although she may have been a daughter of Cornelius and Ann Bramhall. See the letter to Fanny Garrison, September 25, 1862.

182

TO FANNY GARRISON VILLARD

Roxbury, Nov. 2, 1866.

My dear Fanny:

Your last letter, dated I believe not far from Heidelberg, (we have sent it to Providence, so I cannot now refer to it,) gave us all uncommon pleasure because it contained a description of your visit to Harry's birth-place, and of his relatives and friends whom you had met, and by all of whom you had been received so kindly. That visit must have been peculiarly gratifying to you. I can imagine how anxious you must have felt in regard to the impression you would make upon his relatives in special, though we have had no misgivings about it at home. If you have been gratified and charmed with those now so closely related to you, Harry writes that they have been not less so with you. (*En passant*—your mother was pleased and thankful for the few lines he so kindly penned for her perusal.) I am sure you will strive to do every thing in your power to make yourself useful as well as agreeable to them. As for the dear invalid aunt at Heidelberg, whose excellent photograph it is always a pleasure to look at, we feel under special obligations to her for her affectionate reception of you, and hope that, ere this, she has been quite restored to health. And as for the noble, generous, attentive brother-in-law Richard, he seems to have thoroughly won your esteem by his worth and kind attentions.[1] As he desires to perfect himself in English, and you in German, you can happily aid each other, and thus become all the better acquainted. I trust you will commend yourself to Harry's father at Munich as satisfactorily as you have done to Richard and the aunt, as it will add to our joy to be assured that he thinks Harry has been fortunate in his choice of a wife, even if she is "a foreigner," and "of a strange speech."[2] By the by, it seems you are really learning to speak and understand German with considerable facility and accuracy. Tell Harry if he was not inclined to speak German to you in America, he must be equally disinclined to speak English in Germany, so as to help you all he can in your German education!

Ere this, if all has gone well with him, Franky and you and Harry must have had a glad embrace. I had hardly dropped my letter to Franky into the post-office last Friday, before the afternoon paper announced the safe arrival of the Bremen[3] at Southampton that day, in just thirteen days from New York—the exact time I calculated for the voyage before F. started. I wait to hear whether he left the steamer at Bremen on the 15th day, according to "Saunty's" prediction.[4] When I told Saunty, a day or two since, that we had just received a letter from you, she immediately added that you had made a most favorable impression upon your German acquaintances— thus confirming what Harry had averred about it. I shall try to get information concerning your movements, from time to time, of Saunty or Mrs. Wyman,[5] "in advance of the mail," and shall report accordingly. O, what a thrill of pleasure we experienced to get news of Franky's arrival at Southampton, almost simultaneously, by means of the Atlantic cable—or, rather, by apparent time, five or six hours before he got there! A letter from him is doubtless on the way to us, and we shall confidently look for it in the course of another week.

We are enjoying the society of our dear Lucy very much, and on Wednesday next Wendell will join us to spend a week with us. Both are in good health, and as happy as though they were married yesterday. Isn't that your case and Harry's? Tell him that we are most deeply affected by his unwearied efforts to make your visit abroad all that is possible of delight and enjoyment. He is proving himself to be a lover and husband indeed. Have I not tried to do the same with regard to your beloved mother? Should you make as good wife as she has done, and you can hardly make a better if you try ever so much, he will have found in you a real prize! There, now!

Percy[6] has just dropped in to invite Lucy to go with Mr. and Mrs. Thaxter and herself to see the celebrated Ristori,[7] this evening, in the character of Judith. She will accept the invitation. The French actress is winning universal applause. I shall try to see her once.

Mr. Jenkins's only child is at the point of death with diptheria.[8] The loss of this dear boy will be a terribly severe one to the father.

In the wool business there is nothing doing. The stagnation for the last six months has been almost total. Poor William feels quite blue, as he thinks there are no signs, scarcely any hopes of any improvement for a long time to come.

Charley McKim has just come in from Cambridge to see Lucy, looking as fresh and rosy as one of your fairest German young ladies. He sends his loving regards to you and Harry and Frank.

Our darling Agnes is a premium baby! She is wholly Garrison and Benson in her features and disposition, and therefore must be handsome and good-natured! There's no mistake—she's A 1.

Every thing is now quiet in public affairs, except in Maryland. December will probably bring "the tug of war."[9]

I am very glad that you saw my esteemed friend, Mr. Vickers, at Heidelberg, and his German wife.[10] You knew him here, I believe.

A legion of blessings upon you, and Harry, and Frank, from

Your doating Father.

AL signed "Father": Villard Papers, Harvard College Library.

1. Henry Villard's invalid aunt was Anna-Maria Pfeiffer (1809–1872), the sister of Katharina Antonia Elisabeth Pfeiffer Hilgard, Henry's mother. Richard Popp was the widower of Henry's sister, Anna Dorothea Friedrike Hilgard (1834–1864). He and Henry had first met at a summer riding school. (Henry Villard, *Jugend Erinnerungen, 1835–1853,* New York, 1902; FJG, April 18, 1872.)

Henry's parents have already been identified. The remaining members of the Hilgard (Villard) family were his sister, Emma Ottilie Friedrike Hilgard (born 1837), and her husband, Robert V. Xylander (1830–1905), a Bavarian major general, who served from 1874 to 1884 in the Berlin war office. (Villard, *Jugend Erinnerungen;* Anton Bettelheim, ed., *Biographisches Jahrbuch und Deutscher Nekrolog,* Berlin, 1907, X, 276.)

2. Garrison seems to allude to Ephesians 2:19 and Ezekiel 3:5, 6.

3. The *Bremen* was a North German Lloyd passenger steamer that made her maiden voyage to New York in 1858. (David Budlong Tyler, *Steam Conquers the Atlantic,* New York and London, 1939; Georg Bessell, *Norddeutscher Lloyd, Geschichte einer bremischen Reederei,* Bremen, 1958.)

4. Saunty was the nickname of a Mrs. Peabody, evidently a clairvoyant, who has eluded identification. (Letter from Ellen Wright Garrison to Martha Coffin Wright, May 9, 1867, Garrison Papers, Sophia Smith Collection, Smith College Library.)

5. Mrs. Wyman has not been identified.

6. Garrison probably refers to Percy E. Scarborough (born 1843), who was the daughter of Theodore and Caroline Simmons Scarborough and apparently the niece of Mrs. Daniel Thaxter, the former Lucy Scarborough. (Letter to the editor from Carol Hagglund, researcher, June 6, 1971.)

7. Adelaide Ristori (1822–1906) was a celebrated Italian (not French) actress, who was making the first of four visits to the United States. She was appearing in Boston in Paolo Giacometti's historical tragedy *Judith,* which had been published in an English translation in New York the year of Ristori's visit. (Boston *Daily Evening Transcript,* November 2, 1866.)

8. Charles E. Jenkins (1817–1882), from Scituate, Mass., was a Boston wool merchant and the partner of William Lloyd Garrison, Jr., until 1871. He was at one time vice president of the Massachusetts Charitable Mechanic Association and served on the Boston Board of Aldermen during 1870–1871, the latter year as chairman. His wife was Nancy W. Jenkins, and Charles Jenkins, Jr. (c. 1860–1866), was their only

son. (Scituate vital records; Boston city directories; obituaries, Boston *Daily Evening Transcript,* November 12, 1866, and August 12, 1882.)

9. Garrison refers to the elections for the Fortieth Congress, which in the country at large were overwhelmingly won by the Radicals. In Maryland, however, where they did not win, the Radicals attempted to rig the election by imprisoning the duly chosen election commissioners. The conservatives then appealed to President John-son to prevent insurrection, and he arranged with the secretary of war to have forces in readiness if necessary. Since the conservatives won the election, there was no rioting and no need to use force. (George Fort Milton, *The Age of Hate: Andrew Johnson and the Radicals,* New York, 1930.)

10. Not identified.

183

TO FANNY GARRISON VILLARD

Roxbury, Nov. 30, 1866.

My dear Fanny:

Accept our thanks for the handsome presents intended for us by you and Harry, in advance of their arrival. The China tea-sett we shall highly prize, and hope to transmit them to our children un-broken.

Yesterday was our annual State festival—Thanksgiving. It was also made national by proclamation of the President. How we missed you all from our family circle! It subtracted not a little from the enjoyment of the day, especially as neither your mother nor I felt in good bodily trim—I suffering a good deal of pain from my arm, (which threatens to trouble me all winter,) and she still feeling the disturbing effects of the medicine she has been taking, in con-nection with her magnetic treatment. For the first time, almost, since we were married, we had neither relative, friend nor stranger to dine with us. Our turkey weighed fifteen pounds, and was as tender as it was huge, and very nicely cooked withal. The plum-pudding was of generous dimensions, and exactly to our taste. Katy, by the aid of our friend Mrs. [Daniel] Thaxter, had great success with her squash, apple and mince pies, some of which we gave to John Murray, Mrs. Madden,[1] &c. Oranges, apples and nuts, of vari-ous kinds, furnished a good evening treat. The turkey alone cost five dollars!

In the forenoon I went to hear Dr. [George] Putnam preach, and he gave an admirable discourse in merited laudation of Massachu-setts as the focal point of the world's civilization—to the extent of her territory, "the glory of all lands,"[2] on the score of universal edu-cation, thrift, industry, enterprise, all-pervading competence, aggregated wealth, superior intelligence, active charity, world-wide philanthropy, enlightened piety, her devotion to the cause of liberty, her reformatory tendencies, and her lofty patriotism. In all that concerns the general welfare, her million and a half of people are better fed, better clad, better housed, and better governed, than any similar number to be found in any other part of the globe. All this was claimed in no vain or boastful spirit, but simply as the result of her common school system, in connection with free speech, a free press, and free institutions. For little could be attributed to her soil, which was comparatively rocky and sterile; or to her climate, which was harsh and rude. She was pre-eminent for her brains, and because she held to the development of brains. On returning home, I sent Dr. P. a note of thanks for his discourse, telling him I experienced only one drawback while listening to him, and that was the darkened state of his meeting-house, which made every thing look almost sepulchral, and which would prevent my hearing him frequently, even though he combined the love of a John, the zeal of a Peter, and the eloquence of a Paul!

You say in your last letter, (Nov. 1,) that Frank appears to be lacking in *vim*. It will be very difficult for him to overcome his habitual *vis inertiæ*,—as he has never given himself to labor or exercise; but he must make resolute and persistent efforts to do so. We are glad to hear that he is about taking some lessons in horse-back riding. Although he is bodily weak for his years, he has a good frame naturally, and he can doubtless acquire a good deal of muscular vigor by systematic effort. This is a matter of far more importance to him, at this critical period of his life, than the acquisition of any amount of German or French. You and Harry must see that he makes it paramount. Not that I am indifferent to his obtaining some knowledge of the German language, especially now that he has German relatives and is in Germany; but this is of little importance, compared with a good physical development.

Talking with Dr. Putnam, a few evenings since, he said that Munich had the reputation of being an unhealthy city—bleak and cold in the winter, and abounding in fever in the summer. This was afterwards confirmed by our neighbor, Dr. Zack,[3] who earnestly conjures me not to allow Frank (with his pulmonary tendencies) to remain in Munich longer than February, and then to send him either to Vevey or Zurich—the former place being the more desirable. Of this you and Harry must judge.

Early in this month, William sent Harry one thousand dollars, in five-twenties, to be used to defray Frank's expenses as he may need. Of this transmission, William forgot to apprise Harry at the time. Let us know if the bonds were received.

As I had no wish that Frank should go to College against his inclinations, so I have none that he should remain abroad until Harry and you return unless he desires to do so. Let him understand that I give him *carte blanche* to remain, or to come back at any time within the year, according to his own convictions (united with your judgments) as to what would be best in his case. In case he should have a return of his cough, as he had it in the Spring, probably it will be prudent to send him to Vevey or Zurich for recuperation. Give him his mother's blessing—and mine—and the love of us all.

It is a comfort to know that you have a photographic view of Rockledge to look at from day to day.

Congress commences its session on Monday next. There does not appear to be any great curiosity to know what the President will say in his message. He will not be impeached, it is pretty certain, owing to the timidity of the Republicans.

Our grand-baby continues to be the delight of our home. Ellie is a good, loving mother.

Farewell!

Your fond Father.

P.S. Our compliments to Harry's father, aunt, sister, &c. The weather is warm as June.

AL signed "Father": Garrison Papers, Boston Public Library.

1. John Murray (1809–1866) seems to have been a handyman in Roxbury; he was evidently highly regarded by its residents. (Letter to Francis Jackson Garrison, December 28, 1866 [micro.].)

Mrs. Madden is mentioned in Frank's diary as a washerwoman. She has not been otherwise identified. (FJG, April 9, 1870.)

2. Ezekiel 20:6 or 15.

3. A reference to Dr. Marie Zakrzewska, who is identified in the letter to Wendell Phillips Garrison, June 14, 1866.

184

TO FRANCIS JACKSON GARRISON

Roxbury, Dec. 7, 1866.

My dear Frank:

As the last letter received from Fanny was dated Nov. 7, it follows that some ten days longer than usual have transpired since we heard from our loved absent ones. This hiatus has seemed almost a whole year's flight to your daily expectant mother, and added something to a depression of spirits which she has felt for a fortnight past —mainly, owing, however, to her system being so thoroughly "stirred up" from the course of magnetic treatment which she is trying, and from which we are hoping for favorable results. In spite of her self-abnegation and habitual patience, she is feeling the absence of yourself and Fanny more and more as "an aching void," and this is not for her good; but as soon as we can procure for her a congenial companion and nurse, (and we are not without hopes that Miss Wiggin will consent to stay with us through the winter,) she will doubtless have her mind diverted, and become more cheerful.[1] As there is a steamer on the way from Halifax to Boston, it is possible that, by to-night or at the latest by to-morrow morning, we shall receive tidings from you. Indeed, I shall confidently expect to see Mr. Vickers on her arrival. But as the foreign mail closes this afternoon, I do not deem it best to lose it, in order to announce the receipt of a letter from you or Fanny. Moreover, it may happen that none will come to hand.

On Monday afternoon, I went to Mrs. Peabody, in company with our friends Mr. and Mrs. Ashby of Newburyport, their neice Miss Putnam of Brookline, Miss Wiggin, Mr. [George] Thompson and Mrs. [Dora] Brigham, to have a "sitting."[2] We had a very pleasant time, and the Ashbys had some very satisfactory tests. On going to the house, I mentally said, "Charley, if you can indicate your presence this afternoon in some way, do so."[3] So, as our circle was about breaking up, and I had obtained nothing, I pleasantly inquired, "Am I to get no test?" Instantly the medium said, turning to me, "Charley is here, and he reports having seen Franky only three hours ago; says he is in better health than when he left home—that he thinks a great deal of his brother-in-law—that he is having a tip-top time—that he sends his love to his mother, and to all at home— that his father has always been indulgent to him, and he hopes will be lenient if, with so many things to see, he shall not at first diligently give himself to the study of the languages—that some of the German food rather sticks a little in going down"—&c., &c. Mrs. Peabody knew nothing of Charley, and asked me who he was. I told "Saunty" what Dr. Zack [Marie Zakrzewska] had reported about the unhealthiness of Munich, and she made very light of it; said we need not have any uneasiness on your account, and that she would keep us advised as to your physical condition. She said, moreover, that you were occasionally querying in your mind, whether Saunty had communicated to us anything respecting you or Fanny. I asked her whether your mother's impression, that you were homesick, was correct. She said, no; that you did indeed think often of home, and somewhat missed its daily love influences and surroundings, but that, nevertheless, you were satisfied that your foreign sojourn would be all for the best—a sojourn which she declared (as she had done before) would be more serviceable to you than going to college.

Harry, doubtless, will have a good laugh over this message, so far as the "spirits" are concerned; but he will certainly find in it nothing to object to. I record it simply as an incident that may interest you; and if you can confirm any portion of it, let me hear from you.

On Wednesday, I called upon my esteemed and venerable friend, Deacon Samuel May, to give him my congratulations upon the completion of his ninetieth year, with none of his faculties seriously impaired, and in very comfortable health.[4] I expressed the hope that he might be permitted to see his hundredth anniversary, under the same favorable circumstances. If we are made for immortality, however, and death is nothing more than transition or a new birth, it is of comparatively little consequence how long we sojourn here below. "That life is long which answers life's great end."[5]

On the 10th inst. I shall have completed my sixty-first year. As the average length of human existence is less than forty years for a generation, I have transcended the ordinary limit by more than one third; and so must at all times be "prepared for the flight, and ready [to] be gone."[6] Not that I feel in the least the pressure of years but, according to the laws of nature, which are neither to be evaded or countermanded, my summons may now come without surprise at any moment. With dear little Agnes upon my shoulder, I feel as if thirty years had been removed from the count; for all my children have been borne by me in a similar manner, and the illusion is almost like a continuance of the series. She continues to grow finely, and is sunbeam and star to us all.

Congress has convened, and the President delivered his message.[7] It is subdued and measured in its tone, though still stubbornly bent on the policy of reconstruction marked out by its upstart author. It is manifest, already, that Congress is bent on carrying out its own programme, conscious that the people will expect nothing less, and perhaps will insist on something more. The popular feeling is cheering.

Dr. John S. Rock died a few days ago. He was an able man, both as a writer and a speaker, and has made his name historical by having been the first colored lawyer ever allowed to practise in the Supreme Court of the United States.

Henry Vincent, the eloquent English lecturer, gave a very

spirited and stirring address on the relations of England to America during the rebellion, before the Mercantile Library Association on Wednesday evening.[8] It was so well received that they have arranged for another lecture from him in Music Hall on Monday evening next—subject, Oliver Cromwell.[9] His visit to this country will help to subserve the cause of international peace and amity.

We should like to know, when you or Fanny write again, whether Harry goes by the name of Villard or Hilgard in Munich.[10] If by the former, how was the change explained or received by his relatives and acquaintances? If by the latter, is it not placing him in an awkward position to address letters to him as Henry Villard?

I leave to your mother the task (not a heavy one) of giving you such home and neighborhood incidents as may interest you both.

The season continues remarkably mild and pleasant. We are not without any snow or ice, and to-day is as soft and charming as any one in May.

I am still improving, though not without a good deal of pain in my shoulder. As soon as we can get some one to be with your mother, I shall sit down in earnest to see what I can do with my pen.

The wool business still continues paralyzed, with no bright prospects in the near future. If William feels a little blue and uneasy, he is to be excused. I am surprised that he is half as cheerful. But this is owing very much to the serenity of his partners.

Count upon my "indulgence" to any extent, so far as making your health an object of paramount consideration over the languages.

I have nothing further to communicate respecting the "Testimonial." I saw Mr. [Samuel] May [Jr.] the other day, but he said nothing of its progress. If any considerable addition had been made, I think he would have mentioned it. It will probably "hang fire" at fifteen or twenty thousand dollars. Whatever the sum, in view of my disabled condition for the past ten months, (wherein I have spent thousands with no income but my policy insurance,) it will indeed prove exceedingly opportune, and save me from great embarrassment and distress of mind. I am not apprised how long the Committee intend to keep the Testimonial open to subscription.

Our household affairs move along very smoothly. Katy and our girl Bridget[11] get along like sisters, and both are very kind to your mother, and also to the baby.

A few days ago, we had another photographic picture taken of Rockledge. The "negative" looked very good, but no impression has yet been sent for my examination. The artist also took a stereoscopic view of the place. I will hereafter enclose a copy, if it shall prove satisfactory. I wish I could send you one of the large size; but yours will answer.

The colored people of Providence have invited me to participate in their celebration of New Year's Day and the Emancipation Proclamation. I shall try to do so, but have declined to make any positive engagement.[12]

George Thompson lectured to a rather dull and cold audience, at Fitchburg, last Sunday evening. Mr. [James Miller] McKim wishes him to go to Chicago, along with Judge [Hugh L.] Bond of Baltimore, to attend a Freedmen's meeting. He is yet undecided about going.[13] In the Spring he will probably return to England.

Give our most friendly and respectful salutations to all our German relatives at Munich. Your mother, in special, deeply sympathizes with the good aunt in her affliction, of whom Fanny speaks in such admiring and affectionate terms. We hope she is greatly improved in regard to her lameness. How gratified Fanny must be to have a sister [Emma Hilgard Xylander] by her side! Harry's father [Gustav L. Hilgard] we remember with the regard due to his years, station, and relationship. Are you yet able to ask for bread and butter in German? I send a father's blessing to you all.

W.L.G.

ALS: Garrison Papers, Boston Public Library.

1. Miss Wiggin may be Mary Wiggin, a matron at the Massachusetts General Hospital, who, since she was unable to work, was spending the winter with the Garrisons. (Letter to the editor from Nancy Sahli, researcher, July 1, 1972.)

2. William Ashby (1787–1881) and Ann Babcock Ashby (1797–1883), his second wife, were residents of Newburyport, Mass. The Ashbys seem to be historically significant only as sponsors of the annual laurel picnics begun in the 1850s, which many abolitionists attended. (Letter to the editor from Wilhelmina Violet Lunt, curator, Historical Society of Old Newbury, Newburyport, Mass., May 3, 1972; see also the letter to Helen E. Garrison, June 25, 1865, n. 2 [micro.]; and John B. Pickard, *The Letters of John Greenleaf Whittier*, Cambridge, Mass., and London, 1975, III, 157.)

Miss Putnam has not been identified.

3. Garrison refers to his son, Charles Follen Garrison (1842–1849). See *Letters*, III 618–622.

4. Samuel May (1776–1870), father of Samuel May, Jr., was a prominent Boston manufacturer of hardware and of cotton and woolen goods. A Unitarian, he served as deacon of the Hollis Street Church; he was also a member of Theodore Parker's Twenty-Eighth Congregational Society. In association with Samuel Gridley Howe he established the Massachusetts Asylum for the Blind and was an officer of the Boston Dispensary. May was one of the original proprietors of the Boston Athenaeum.

Samuel May's wife was the former Mary Goddard (1787–1882), an early supporter of temperance, abolition, and woman's rights. (Samuel May, et al., *A Genealogy of the Descendants of John May*, Boston, 1878, pp. 15–16.)

5. Edward Young, *Night Thoughts*, "Night V," line 773.

6. Isaac Watts, "To the Memory of the Rev. Thomas George," *Horae Lyricae*, Book I, 250. Garrison substitutes "prepared" for "dressed."

7. President Johnson's message was transmitted to Congress on December 4, 1866. It expressed disappointment at the failure of Congress to seat loyal members from southern states. He said, in part: "The interests of the nation are best to be promoted by the revival of fraternal relations, the complete obliteration of our past differences, and the reinauguration of all pursuits of peace. . . . Let us endeavor to preserve harmony between the coordinate departments of our Government, that

each in its proper sphere may cordially cooperate with the other in securing the maintenance of the Constitution, the preservation of the Union, and the perpetuity of our free institutions." (Edward McPherson, *The Political History of the United States of America during the Period of Reconstruction*, Washington, D.C., 1871, pp. 143–147.)

8. Henry Vincent (1813–1878) had become well-known as one of the chief advocates of the Chartist movement, which during the late 1830s and the 1840s had attempted to reform electoral practices in order to extend the suffrage to a larger percentage of the working class. Along with Joseph Sturge, Vincent had founded the Complete Suffrage Union. After his active political agitation ended, he continued as a public lecturer both in England and in the United States.

The Mercantile Library Association, located at the corner of Summer and Hawley streets, was founded in 1820 for the purpose of improving "young men engaged in mercantile pursuits." In addition to traditional library services the association sponsored lectures and subsidized courses in such subjects as foreign languages, bookkeeping, and navigation. (*Sketches and Business Directory of Boston and Its Vicinity for 1860 and 1861*, Boston, 1860, pp. 90–92; see also the letter to Wendell Phillips, November 27, 1853, *Letters*, IV, 280, n. 2.)

9. Oliver Cromwell (1599–1658), the Puritan leader and Lord Protector of England, 1653–1658.

10. By 1873 Henry Villard was going by the name of "Hilgard-Villard" in Germany and contemplating officially changing his name back to Hilgard. Although it is uncertain what name he used in his native country in 1866, by that date his relationship with his father had greatly improved; and, in fact, he was at the bedside when Gustav Hilgard died in 1867. (*Memoirs of Henry Villard, Journalist and Financier, 1835–1900*, Boston and New York, 1904, II, 269; see also the letter from Fanny Garrison Villard to Francis Jackson Garrison, November 11, 1873, Villard Papers, Harvard College Library.)

11. Not identified.

12. Apparently Garrison did not go to Providence, since his letters around the first of the year are all dated from Roxbury and do not mention the trip.

13. Thompson did not go to Chicago. (See the letter to James Miller McKim, December 31, 1866, [micro.].)

VII HONORS AND AWARDS: 1867

FOR GARRISON the year 1867 began and ended on the theme of impeachment. Early in the year he composed an article on the subject, published in the *Independent* on January 10. Citing his own speech at the Brooklyn Academy of Music in February 1866, he said that he had been urging the impeachment of President Johnson, whom he considered "obstinate . . . , unprincipled, and as self-conceited as he has proved himself perfidious." If he is not liable to impeachment, "then the phrase 'high crimes and misdemeanors' becomes a mockery, and he may act the part of factionist and usurper to any extent with impunity. But the President of the United States is as amenable to trial and conviction for betraying his trust as the humblest official in the land, and should be as readily brought to the tribunal of justice." He regretted that "no patriot has yet ventured to stand up in the House of Representatives and demand his impeachment and removal from office." In fact, on January 7, virtually at the same time Garrison was writing these words, Congressman James M. Ashley of Ohio introduced a resolution of impeachment, and the House Judiciary Committee was charged to investigate allegations against the President. The committee reported back to Congress in June 1867 that there was no evidence of "high crimes and misdemeanors." In July the committee was given new instructions, and on November 20 it recommended impeachment. This conclusion was officially reported to the House on December 2, and the vote for impeachment was defeated on December 7. Garrison wrote to Oliver Johnson on December 11, grateful to those members of Congress who voted in the affirmative, and determined that "the Presidential bully and usurper" be impeached. Garrison was to follow the impeachment trial the following spring with great interest.

One of the central figures in the Johnson administration, Secretary of State William H. Seward, a man who had in the 1850s been considered a strong political proponent of abolition, aroused Garrison's ire at this time even more than did Johnson. Although Seward is generally respected by posterity as an exceptionally effective politician, he offended Garrison by his conciliatory policy toward the South and by his support of Johnson's vetoes (he was the author of several of the presidential messages concerning them). In the *Independent* on February 21 Garrison compared Seward and Johnson, concluding that Seward "is by far the more guilty of the two; he has sinned against light never vouchsafed to the half-civilized Tennessean; he has become recreant to principles which the former never professed. In all the loyal ranks there is now 'none so poor as to do him reverence.'"

On the local level Garrison was confronted with other problems. He, Wendell Phillips, and others were trustees under the abolition bequest of philanthropist Francis Jackson, who had died in 1861. Urging that the bequest be used to further black suffrage, Phillips recommended that the board contribute the funds to the American Anti-Slavery Society and its organ, the *National Anti-Slavery Standard,* which advocated Negro suffrage. Although Garrison firmly believed that blacks should vote, he considered their need for education of prior importance, and so he recommended that the trustees support the freedmen's societies in their agitation for Negro education. Despite this conviction, however, Garrison was the one to propose a compromise, which was accepted by the trustees in January 1867—that the funds be divided between the two uses. When on March 2 Congress passed the basic Reconstruction Act, providing that reconstituted state governments must be based on suffrage that included blacks, Garrison changed his mind. Reasoning that black suffrage had, in effect, been established by the act, he insisted that the entire bequest be used toward education. The master in chancery to whom the Supreme Court of Massachusetts referred the case agreed with Garrison's position and ordered the fund so appropriated. When a majority of the trustees refused to comply, the court reconstituted the board; and eventually (in 1870) the money was contributed to the New England branch of the Freedmen's Union Commission.[1] Seldom has a petty controversy involved at such length and so vehemently the minds and spirits of so many able and honorable men.

But 1867 was hardly the year Garrison remembered for its problems. Rather, it was the year of honors and rewards. It was the year when the success of the fund-raising testimonial was assured, and it

1. *Life*, IV, 237–238; see also FJG, April 20, May 5, 1870.

was the year for an honorific trip abroad. In the spring Garrison was named by the American Freedmen's Union Commission as a delegate to an antislavery conference in Paris. It seemed an appropriate time for a trip to Europe: he could be with his daughter and son-in-law and his son Frank; he could also escape the pressures at home and perhaps recover his health. Moreover, the success of the testimonial made the trip feasible financially. Accompanied by George Thompson, Garrison sailed from Boston for Liverpool on May 8. In many ways this trip proved to be one of the most exciting and satisfying experiences of Garrison's life. The excitement began with the sailing of the *Cuba*. Many of Garrison's friends and associates joined him aboard for a bon voyage celebration; others came by private tug to see the ship off. Among this group was Edmund Quincy, who reported that a stranger unaccountably with them turned to him and said, "What's all this fuss about?" Quincy replied, "Why, don't you know? It's all for Garrison, he's cock of the walk now!"[2]

The letters Garrison wrote during his European tour, most of them addressed to his wife, are self-explanatory and need little comment here. Certainly, Garrison found himself the center of attention almost everywhere, and he thrived on the adulation, especially at public ceremonials like the breakfast in his honor at St. James's Hall in London on June 29. At this function there were several speakers, including John Bright and John Stuart Mill. The chairman, the Duke of Argyll, heartily congratulated Garrison on his contributions to emancipation in the United States, "the greatest cause which in ancient or in modern times, has been pleaded at the bar of the moral judgment of mankind." Garrison spoke exuberantly to a responsive audience. He urged continued peace and forbearance, so that England and the United States "may lead the world to freedom and glory."

The antislavery conference that provided the rationale for Garrison's trip was held in Salle Herz, 48 rue de la Victoire, for two days (August 26 and 27), with Edouard Laboulaye, president of the French Emancipation Society, presiding. The delegation appointed by the American Freedmen's Union Commission consisted of three persons—Garrison, William Cullen Bryant, and C. G. Hammond of Chicago. With the assistance of several others, including Salmon P. Chase, James Miller McKim, and Francis George Shaw, the committee had prepared a report that supplied a history of emancipation in the United States and described the present condition of the freedmen as well as the efforts being made to help

2. *AWT*, p. 317.

them. Garrison spoke to the convention on the second day, apologizing for his ignorance of the French language and expressing his "abiding faith in the feasibility of a universal language" to help ameliorate prejudice and hatred between nations. Garrison said that the United States had at the time of its formation committed the "fatal error" of protecting instead of prohibiting slavery. He admitted that during the recent Civil War public opinion in the North had been hostile to emancipation, accepting abolition "only as a military necessity to suppress the rebellion." He also confessed that he was disappointed in the Emancipation Proclamation, which gave the blacks "nothing more than homeless, houseless, landless, pennyless freedom. Though ceasing to be chattels, they were not clothed with citizenship." Garrison also condemned the Black Codes of the South, and President Johnson as "the unworthy successor of the lamented Lincoln." He did, however, praise the Second French Republic for abolishing slavery in its colonies. He concluded his remarks to the assembled delegates as follows: "However divided we may be in our religious or political sentiments, as against Slavery and the Slave Trade we are one in spirit, one in faith, one in the assurance of ultimate victory."[3]

Garrison's European trip in 1867 was propitious: it withdrew him from nagging troubles at home and gave him time to see in clearer perspective the accomplishments—both personal and professional—of his four decades of dedication to human freedom.

3. *Special Report of the Anti-Slavery Conference Held in Paris on the Twenty-Sixth and Twenty-Seventh August 1867* (London, 1869). For a report of Garrison's speech, see pp. 32–38.

185

TO JAMES RUSSELL LOWELL

Roxbury, Jan. 1, 1867.

Dear Mr. Lowell:

I am very much obliged for your kind note of the 29th ult., and for the expression of your hearty sympathy and friendship.[1] Of course, I am highly gratified to receive the good opinion of so noble a champion of freedom and reform as John Bright of England, in regard to my Anti-Slavery career. I have been thinking of writing him a letter, applauding him for all that he is saying and doing in behalf of the disfranchised millions in England, and proffering him my profound respect for his character. This will give me a good opportunity to do so, in acknowledging this expression of his personal regard. Overwhelmed as he must be by pecuniary solicitations at home, I shrink from his contributing a farthing to the "Testimonial," and appreciate his £5 just as much as though it were £500.

As to the "Testimonial" itself, as designed by the estimable Committee that started it, I have had faith in its pecuniary success only to a limited extent; not because of a lack of generous feeling, but because such movements generally end in disappointment, especially if they have any reference to philanthropy and reform. Witness, for example, the abortive attempt to procure funds in substantial aid of the destitute family of John Brown. Witness a similar failure with reference to our nation's friend and benefactor, the disinterested and eloquent George Thompson of England—though the appeal was made under the signatures of the Governor of the Commonwealth, the President of the Massachusetts Senate, the Speaker of the House, prominent Boston merchants, &c.[2] I believe less than eight hundred dollars were realized; though this discreditable amount was largely owing to a neglect of setting in motion the right agencies, and not because as many thousands might not just as easily have been raised, if diligent and proper application had been made.

I have had no wish or occasion to inquire into the success of the "Testimonial"; yet I am not ignorant of the fact that its consummation has proved an uphill work, and that a very large proportion of it remains to be obtained, owing to many unforeseen and unavoidable drawbacks. But, whether it succeed in whole or in part, I make no claim to any part of it, and my gratitude will be none the less. My reward has already been ample in seeing the horrible slave system overthrown, and the millions in whose service the larger portion of my life has been spent set free from their galling fetters.

More than millions of dollars do I value the fact,—a fact still to me almost incredible, so astonishing is the change in popular sentiment that has been wrought,—that what I so long attempted for the enslaved, and for my beloved native land, (attempted under what obloquy, and through what peril and persecution!) has at last received a generous and an honorable recognition from the representative men of the nation, under their own signatures—among them the Chief Justice of the United States [Salmon P. Chase], the Senators and Representatives from twenty-one of the loyal States, judges, lawyers, divines, merchants, collegiate professors, and the most eminent in American literature! That God should have so graciously permitted me to live to receive such a mark of appreciation and regard, and to witness such a revolution!

Your own honored name, I believe, is on the list. This was no surprise, though it was a special gratification to me; for, at an early period, you flung all worldly considerations and the chance of literary reputation and success to the winds, and unhesitatingly allied yourself to the hated band of abolitionists; nobly daring to be "in the right with two or three"[3] as against the vast majority of the nation, and the powers of darkness. The service you rendered to the Anti-Slavery cause was valuable beyond computation.

Congratulating you upon the ascendency of freedom in our land, and wishing you "a happy new year," I remain, dear sir,

Very admiringly yours,

Wm. Lloyd Garrison.

Professor J. R. Lowell.

ALS: Burnett Collection of James Russell Lowell Papers, Harvard College Library.

1. In his letter (Lowell Papers, University of Rochester Library), Lowell quotes from a letter written by John Bright to accompany his contribution of £5 to the Garrison testimonial. Bright warmly praises Garrison, both as a man and as an abolitionist.

2. The unsuccessful campaign to raise funds to support John Brown's family can be traced in the pages of *The Liberator* during the last two months of 1859 and throughout 1860 (see the issues for November 25, December 2, 16, 23, 1859, and January 13, February 10, September 21, and November 30, 1860). The fund-raising began at a meeting at Tremont Temple on November 19; among the speakers were Wendell Phillips, Governor John A. Andrew, and even Ralph Waldo Emerson, who contributed $50 at once. Other meetings followed, but only insignificant funds accumulated. (For an interesting glimpse of John Brown's widow, by this time in Red Bluff, Calif. see the *National Anti-Slavery Standard,* November 24, 1866.)

For a description of the unsuccessful attempt to raise funds in support of George Thompson, see the letter to Oliver Johnson, March 10, 1863.

3. Lowell, "Stanzas on Freedom," last line.

186

TO FRANCIS JACKSON GARRISON

Roxbury, Jan. 18, 1867.

My dear Frank:

Your last letter, dated 25th ult., was of great interest to us in all its details, especially relating to the Christmas festival, and the handsome and numerous gifts so kindly and generously presented to you and Fanny by Harry, his sister [Emma Xylander], aunt [Anna-Maria Pfeiffer], father [Gustav L. Hilgard], and the two brothers-in-law, Richard [Popp] and Robert [Xylander]. For such marked regards for you both, by our German relatives, we as a family feel very

grateful, and beg to have conveyed to them our heartfelt acknowledgments for their manifold kindnesses, and the affectionate manner in which they have taken you both to their hearts. Your recipro-
cation of their esteem and friendship, so warmly expressed in your
letters, appears to be fully equal in kind. We feel sure the more they
know you and Fanny, the more they will be satisfied with the marriage relation thus unexpectedly established; as the more we see
and know of Harry, the higher grows our appreciation of him. We
can readily conceive that, when they first heard of Harry's engagement and marriage, they must have felt a good deal of solicitude as
to the choice he had made, and partly so on account of Fanny's
American parentage and origin; for very few are wholly delivered
from national prejudice and partiality. Moreover, though they may
have had no doubt that Harry had chosen exactly to his own taste,
yet they may have naturally had some apprehension that his wife
might not prove agreeable to them. On both sides there appears to
be the utmost satisfaction; and, surely, this is matter for thanksgiving. Neither you nor Fanny will spare any pains still further to commend yourselves to their regard. Try to be serviceable in every
way, and be specially attentive to Harry's father and the dear invalid aunt. Sister Emma appears to have smitten you deeply with
the pale beauty of her face, the sweet cadences of her voice, and her
unceasing kindness. We are charmed with your description of her;
but regret to hear that she is such a sufferer bodily, and so deficient
in the quantity and quality of her blood. "Is there no balm in Gi-
lead? Is there no physician there?"[1] Alas! that ancient interrogation
is as applicable in our day as when it was first uttered, and to every
place alike. "We all do fade as a leaf,"[2] and the stamp of mortality is
upon us all.

> "The pomp of heraldry, the boast of power,
>   And all that beauty, all that wealth e'er gave,
> Await alike *the inevitable hour:*
>   The paths of glory lead but to the grave."[3]

So be it. They who would have it otherwise presume to be wiser
and better than the infinite Creator of all things. The Divine Power
that we trust to-day, may be safely trusted forever.

According to your description of Emma, she evidently needs that
nutrition which makes good blood. Fresh air, attention to diet, regular but not excessive exercise, and less mental activity, will undoubtedly do for her far more than medicine. If you could contrive
to send me a small lock of her hair, and also one of aunt's, I will see

what kind of a diagnosis of their case Mrs. Rockwood,[4] a good healing medium, will make, without her knowing anything of the parties.

"Saunty" does not always succeed in her descriptions of your doings, as you show. Be assured, I accept nothing as true, in that direction, until it is proved. Still, there can be no reasonable doubt
that sometimes events are foreseen, and correctly described, both
by persons in the body and out of the body. But infallibility belongs
only to Him who sees the end from the beginning, and is from everlasting to everlasting.

Speaking of "Saunty," (I have not seen Mrs. Peabody since your
letter was received,) it reminds me that there have been recently
some extraordinary "spirit manifestations" at Mrs. [Dora] Brigham's
house; such as bells ringing over the heads of the circle, floating
in the air, and dropping upon the table; a spirit hand seen to extinguish the light; spirit hands touching the hands or garments of all
present; pocket-books taken out of pockets, the money abstracted,
and then returned; watches removed in the same manner; the contents of one table conveyed by an invisible power from end of the
parlor to another; the bosoms of ladies partially unbuttoned, and
articles thrust therein, and taken therefrom, powerful rappings
on the table and floor; ladies' head-dresses and finger-rings removed and interchanged; an alabaster-box put into the hands of one
of the ladies, filled with silver coins; the handkerchiefs of all present strongly scented with various perfumes; a message communicated in writing apparently with a piece of blue chalk; the table
marked with the same on its surface and underneath; the same substance drawn across Mr. [George] Thompson's cheek and mouth;
ladies' hair taken down and tied in various ways; sticks of candy extracted from the pocket of one of the company, and thrust into the
mouths of two of the number; a basket, containing artificial oranges
and lemons emptied, and its contents distributed around the circle,
and the basket successively put upon the head of every one present
in a grotesque manner; striking and tickling of persons by spirit
hands—&c.,&c. The medium was a little chubby girl,[5] about twelve
years old, as simple and ingenuous as possible, belonging to East
Cambridge. Though these things were done in the dark, from time
to time as the light was put out, yet as the company was select and
above all deception, and many of these things were done at the
same moment with amazing rapidity, (so that more than ninety
matches were lit during the performances,) there is no accounting
for them on any hypothesis of trick or collusion. Mr. Thompson has

written a full account of all that transpired on the occasion. Several of the most surprising things I have not stated. But, enough!

I have written two articles for the *Independent,* which have been published, strongly urging the duty and importance of impeaching and removing Andrew Johnson from the office he disgraces.[6] The question has been referred to the Judiciary Committee, and they are giving it their most serious consideration.[7] I am inclined to think they will report favorably; and, if so, that the House will make an impeachment in due form. But it is scarcely to be expected that two-thirds of the Senate will be found to concur. Without the President is deposed, I do not see how any plan of reconstruction by Congress can be made available.

As Fanny will doubtless have occasion to make some purchases on her own private account, either in the way of gratifying her taste or of making presents, I desire her to use some of the funds entrusted to Harry on your general account,—to the extent of a hundred dollars, if needed. Not that Harry is not ready to supply her generously with all that she may require, but that I may have the pleasure of making what may pass for a Christmas or New Year's gift. Tell her she must *not* hesitate to accept it.

Though we at home (no great judges, to be sure) thought she played very creditably on the piano, it is gratifying to be assured that she is still making scientific proficiency. I hope she will strive to attain the highest point of excellence in that direction, both as to style and sentiment. While she devotes herself chiefly to the more intricate kinds of music, you can pay special attention to what is simply lyrical; and I rather think by due application, you will be able to play even more than the half dozen pieces you promise your mother on your return.

I am glad to hear of the physical exercise you are taking; but I would rather you would take more of it, and study less. Still, I can easily conceive of your anxiety to communicate in German with your relatives; for, with your strong social nature, it must be very trying to you to continue almost dumb in their presence. *I* should feel quite unhappy to be thus shut up. To think that neither Harry's father nor you have ventured to interchange a word with each other! I am very sorry that he cannot know my dear boy by actual conversation. But Harry and Fanny must assist you as interpreters. It is very kind in the aunt and sister Emma to try to help you along in the language.

Your account of Richard and Robert, and of their kind attentions to Fanny and yourself, is very gratifying. How brotherly!

Your mother is looking and feeling quite well. We shall follow up the treatment she is receiving.

The baby [Agnes Garrison] flourishes. The brothers and Ellie send love to you and Fanny and Harry. Heaven protect you all!

Your loving Father.

P.S. Yesterday morning, it began snowing very gently, and continued all through the day and night with increasing violence— mercury nearly at zero. Roads obstructed in every direction, and no doubt many sad disasters will be reported. The snow-drifts are enormous. No such storm has happened for many years.

☞ Mother has told you how highly we admire and prize the beautiful tea-sett sent by Harry.

☞ Your account of your German student companion was quite touching.[8] Good for Harry!

AL signed "Father": Garrison Papers, Boston Public Library.

1. Jeremiah 8:22.
2. Isaiah 64:6.
3. Thomas Gray, "Elegy Written in a Country Churchyard," stanza 9, slightly misquoted.
4. Not identified.
5. Not identified.
6. The two articles, entitled "Impeachment of the President" and "The Duties of the Hour," appeared in the *Independent*, January 10 and 17, 1867.
7. The House Judiciary Committee (consisting of James Wilson, chairman, Francis Thomas, D. Morris, R. E. Trowbridge, George S. Boutwell, Thomas Williams, Burton C. Cook, and William Lawrence) was charged to investigate allegations of high crimes and misdemeanors brought against President Johnson in the resolution of Congressman James M. Ashley on January 7, 1867. The committee reported on March 3, conveying the results of its investigation and urging that further inquiry be made by a committee formed under the new Congress. (*National Anti-Slavery Standard*, March 9, 1867.)
8. Garrison refers to the German student named Metzger, whom Henry Villard had selected as a companion for Francis Jackson Garrison. They spent much time together in Munich, walking, sightseeing, and visiting museums. Young Garrison tells how he introduced Metzger to ice cream and how Metzger took him to the Hofbrauhaus, an activity one is not certain his father would have approved. (FJG, January 5, 18, 1867.)

187

TO SAMUEL MAY, JR.

Roxbury, Jan. 24, 1867

Dear friend May:

Your letter of yesterday is just received. It seems you had at least a small share of the obstruction and annoyance which the late heavy and far-reaching storm so unexpectedly brought to so many people. You must have felt somewhat anxious about your wife and daughter, and a good deal relieved on reaching home to find that they had experienced no special discomfort.

I am in perfect agreement with you as to the best manner of using the bequest of our ever cherished friend, Francis Jackson. Regretting that you will not be able to attend the meeting on Monday forenoon, I shall aim to be present, to give my voice and vote for making the New England Freedmen's Commission the medium through which wisely and beneficially to spend the sum that may be awarded to us as Trustees by the Court. At this moment, I forget who the Trustees are, besides yourself, Mr [Wendell] Phillips, Mr [Charles K.] Whipple and myself.[1] Unquestionably, Mr Phillips will advise that the bequest be given to the American Anti-Slavery Society for the support of the Standard, and the agitation of the Suffrage question; and it is not unlikely that he will get a majority of the Trustees to side with him. In that case, I think it may be well for us who are in a minority to let the Court and the Master in Chancery[2] know what view we take of the question. As for the Suffrage movement, it is now every where discussed, and almost universally approved among the loyal people of the country, and will doubtless be duly cared for by Congress; so that, anxious as I am to see universal suffrage established, I perceive no special reason why the funds left by Mr Jackson should be used in that direction. But the freedmen are perishing for lack of knowledge, and need a hundred teachers and schools where now they have but one. It grieves and astonishes me that W. P. and his party are so utterly indifferent to the education of the freedmen.

I am very sorry you took so much trouble to explain how you happened to make no reference, when I saw you, to the very slight token of my esteem and indebtedness which it gave me so much pleasure to offer you. I thought nothing about it, and certainly wished for no special recognition of it. But I did very much regret that George was so thoughtless as to put you to the trouble of getting the package to your father's house. It had been at the store since the new year came in, and I had intended to see it duly sent; but it happened that I did not go into the city for several days, and thus the mistake and the delay occurred.

This is the evening for the "Subscription Anniversary" to continue the operations of the old Society. Many who have been in the habit of contributing to it will probably do so this year from force of habit. Some others will make a strain to swell the subscriptions to the usual amount, and some "radical" Republican aid (not given in other days) may be added. But I do not believe the pecuniary success will be large.

To-morrow is the anniversary of the Massachusetts Anti-Slavery Society. I need not say that I shall not attend any of the meetings.

Last evening, I heard Gen. Butler on the impeachment of the President.[3] Music Hall was well filled, but the General was too long in reaching the question of impeachment, and the lecture, on the whole, lacked directness and fire.

Your attached friend,

W.L.G.

Rev. Samuel May, Jr
Leicester,
Mass.

P.S. To-morrow I propose letting Dr Bigelow, of Boston, examine my injured arm, which still causes me unceasing pain.[4]

Wife sends her love with mine to you all.

Handwritten transcription: Garrison Papers, Boston Public Library.

1. The additional trustees were William I. Bowditch, Edmund Jackson, and Edmund Quincy.

2. John Codman (c. 1808–1879) of 4 Court Street and 23 West Cedar Street. (Boston *Vital Statistics* and city directory, 1867.)

3. General Benjamin F. Butler was one of the leading Radical Republicans in Congress, invariably taking an extreme stand on the impeachment of Johnson and on Reconstruction. Butler's speech, which was primarily concerned with impeachment, was briefly reported in the Boston *Evening Transcript*, January 24, 1867.

4. Henry Jacob Bigelow (1818–1890), the son of a distinguished physician, was one of the most prominent American surgeons of his day. He is credited with many surgical innovations and with having first published information about the use of ether.

188

TO OLIVER JOHNSON

Roxbury, Jan. 25, 1867.

My dear Johnson:

I am much obliged to you for sending me the approving extract from Theodore [Tilton]'s letter: it is all that can be reasonably asked or desired. I shall be entirely at ease in my mind about writing for the Independent, if you and Theodore will not allow me to crowd others out, and will be sure to publish only such articles of mine as may be deemed worth it, without any regard to personal consideration. Moreover, I have such an appreciation of your critical judgment, it will oblige me if you will at any time change one word or phrase for another where the sentiment will not be changed or impaired. And this recalls what I wrote yesterday in regard to the epithet "devilish trick."[1] That is the old blunt Miltonic way of using words descriptively; but in our day the term "devilish" is so flippantly used,—as e.g. "devilish good," "devilish bad," "devilish smart," &c., &c.,—it has perhaps ceased to be forcible. I suggested "fiendish" in its stead. Perhaps "scurry," or "scurrilous," or "knavish," would be preferable to either. Decide for me.[2]

Theodore must have had a good time and done a good work for freedom and humanity (as well as met with large pecuniary success) by his numerous lectures at the West. He will be lucky indeed if he returns home without any injury to his lungs or general health. Fortunately, he speaks naturally and with almost conversational ease, and therefore will not be so likely to break down, though his appointments are almost fearfully numerous and consecutive. His exposure of Crosby at Chicago, in regard to the exclusion of Mrs. Jones and Mrs. De Mortie from the Opera House, was as nobly characteristic as his decision was triumphant.[3]

Last evening the "Subscription Festival" came off as usual, but with what result I have not heard.[4] To-day is the annual meeting of the Massachusetts A. S. Society. Of course, I shall not be present.

Yesterday forenoon, Mr. [Wendell] Phillips appeared before the Legislative Committee to whom was referred the Constitutional Amendment, and argued against its adoption as "a swindle," notwithstanding its unanimous adoption by fifteen loyal States, with the exception of the Copperhead members.[5] I do not think the Massachusetts Legislature will be disposed to follow his advice, though he may influence some votes. I have regretted that Theodore has seconded P's opposition to that Amendment to the full extent, and with the same sweeping impeachment of Congress. Can that be "a swindle," which Rebels and Copperheads abhor and oppose?

Ever faithfully yours,

W.L.G.

ALS: Garrison Papers, Boston Public Library.

1. Garrison alludes to John Milton, *Paradise Lost*, IV, lines 393–394.

2. Garrison had submitted to the *Independent* four rather pedestrian sonnets (printed January 31, 1867). In this letter he is discussing the phrasing of a line in the second sonnet; Johnson selected from the alternates proposed by Garrison the word "fiendish."

3. Uranus H. Crosby (1830–c. 1871) moved from Massachusetts to Chicago in 1850 to work in a distillery, ultimately accumulating a considerable fortune. In 1865 he opened Crosby's Opera House, an ornate five-story building in the Italian style, which contained, in addition to the auditorium, offices, stores, studios, and an art gallery. (A. T. Andreas, *History of Chicago*, Chicago, 1885, II, 601–606; *Edwards' Chicago Business Directory*, Chicago, 1866–1867.)

In his lecture at the Opera House in Chicago, Tilton told what he knew about prejudice against Mrs. John Jones of 218 Third Avenue, the "wife of a well-known, wealthy, and public spirited citizen of Chicago." He said that Mrs. Jones had written him explaining that she and Mrs. DeMortie (see below) had been refused tickets for his lecture unless they sat in a "proscribed" section of the auditorium. When Tilton called at the box office to challenge such prejudice against blacks, he was told that the ticket seller was merely following "the orders of the manager of the Opera House." Then Tilton appealed to Edwin Lee Brown, president of the Young Men's Association under whose auspices Tilton was to speak. Brown was indignant at the prejudice and gave the offended ladies, through Tilton, complimentary tickets for the best seats in the house. (*Independent*, January 14, 1867.)

Louise DeMortie (c. 1833–1867) was born in Norfolk, Va., and educated in Boston, where she became a professional poetry reader in 1862. Subsequently she moved to New Orleans, where she established an orphanage for children of freed slaves, which she maintained by lecturing in many northern cities. She died in New Orleans during a yellow fever epidemic. (Obituary, *National Anti-Slavery Standard*, October 26, 1867.)

4. The thirty-third Anti-Slavery Subscription Festival in the Music Hall apparently attracted fewer people than the celebration of the previous year, though the funds raised were at least as high. (*Standard*, February 2, 1867.)

5. Wendell Phillips argued before the Massachusetts Joint Committee on Federal Relations that the Fourteenth Amendment had become virtually obsolete, owing to the changes in the condition of the country since its passage by Congress. In fact, the amendment was even silent on the problems associated with Reconstruction. Although the committee reported against ratification, the vote in both the state Senate and the House favored the amendment by an overwhelming majority. (Edward McPherson, *The Political History of the United States of America during the Period of Reconstruction*, Washington, D.C., 1871, p. 194.)

189

TO FANNY GARRISON VILLARD

Roxbury, Feb. 1, 1867.

My dear Fanny:

Our latest intelligence from Munich is your letter, dated Jan. 2. You will see, therefore, that no letter has since been received from Frank, though one was due several days ago, and in all probability will be received to-morrow, as there is a Liverpool steamer now on her passage from Halifax to Boston. Of home matters and incidents, (nothing new or specially interesting, however,) I suppose your mother has fully treated in her letter; for what she writes to you, from week to week, she is not willing that I should read, (so sensitive is she in the matter of composition,) while she is eager to read every word I write. That is hardly fair; but, if at any time I happen to repeat what she has already reported, you will by this be able to understand how it comes to pass.

I have, at last, had my arm and shoulder examined by Dr. [Henry

J.] Bigelow, the most eminent surgeon in Boston. He finds no dislocation or fracture, and confirms what Dr. Cotting originally said, that recovery is mainly a matter of time.[1] He prescribes certain local applications, which I am now trying—the shoulder still being very painful. I am a good deal relieved in mind to have his decided opinion that I shall not be permanently crippled.

I write an article every other week for the New York Independent; and that is all that I accomplish. I have not ventured yet to deliver a lecture, and had to get George Thompson to supply my place last week before the Lyceum at Worcester. Next Friday evening, I am booked for a lecture at Woonsocket, but shall probably have to let Mr. Thompson speak in my stead.[2] I am also down for a lecture in the Academy of Music at Brooklyn, N.Y., on the 26th inst., and trust I shall be able by that time to deliver it.[3] It was in that building, a year ago, that I gave my last public address. How much pain and misery I have since been called to endure!

The Annual Subscription Anniversary for the benefit of the Anti-Slavery Standard was held last week at the Music Hall, but the attendance was slim, and the receipts probably small. Phillips was the only speaker on the occasion. The next day, the annual meeting of the Massachusetts A. S. Society was held at the Mercantile Hall in Summer street.[4] It had three sessions, at all of which I was assailed and held up as recreant to the cause by S. S. Foster and Dr. Knox, and defended by James N. Buffum, J. T. Everett, Mrs. F. W. Harper, &c.[5] J. T. Sargent spoke of my sword as being sheathed, but exulted that the "blazing scimetar" of Wendell Phillips was wielded with such effect as to make any remembrance of me almost obsolete! Phillips heard all these attacks, and received all this adulation, without saying a word. How altered!

At last, the Court has decided upon the points raised in regard to the legality of Francis Jackson's will—affirming the anti-slavery bequest, but disallowing what was given to the woman's rights cause. We, the Trustees, had a meeting at Edmund Jackson's[6] on Monday forenoon, to see how far we could agree as to the disposal of the bequest, provided the Court should see fit to accept our decision. The whole amount coming to us is $9,200. It was finally compromised so as to propose giving to the American A. S. Society $4,200, and $5,000 to the Freedmen's Education Society.[7] I hope the Court will decide to give the much larger portion of it to the latter object.

New Year's day, I sent "The Wounded Scout," with a handsome bracket, (costing $25 in all,) to J. B. Smith as a token of our esteem, and our appreciation of his kindness and generosity in making such a handsome entertainment at your wedding for nothing.[8]

William has made some sales in wool since my last, but business continues dull. If the tariff bill should pass, (and this seems doubtful,) things may take a turn for the better.[9]

I have just received a pleasant letter, giving the particulars of Wendell's attempt to keep "bachelor's hall" while she [Lucy McKim Garrison] and her father and mother made a visit to Philadelphia. She found every thing at the Park in prime order.

Ellie was going to the Concert this afternoon, but has a severe neuralgic attack in the head, (after the manner of Harry,) and feels miserably; otherwise, she desires me to say, she should have written to you by this conveyance. She sends her loving regards to you all.

I met Mr. Frank Sanborn in Boston this forenoon.[10] He gave me sad intelligence—namely, that our esteemed friend, Miss Anne Whiting, was lying at the point of death [with an] ovarian tumor, with dropsy, at the residence of her sister, Mrs. Barker.[11] We shall deplore her loss.

We have had a very severe January, with a vast amount of snow. To-day it is thawing like Spring—yesterday the mercury was below zero!

With all conceivable love to you, and Harry, and Frank, and regards to all the relatives, I remain, in gallopping haste, as the mail closes directly,

Your ever admiring Father.

AL signed "Father": Garrison Papers, Boston Public Library.

1. Benjamin Eddy Cotting (1812–1897), with degrees from both the college and the medical school of Harvard, was a distinguished Boston physician with a considerable reputation as a surgeon. He was a founder of the Obstetrical Society of Boston in 1861 and of the Roxbury Medical Improvement Society in 1866; for many years he was active in the Massachusetts Medical Society. (Thomas Cushing, *Memorials of the Class of 1834 of Harvard*, Boston, 1884, pp. 57 ff; Walter L. Burrage, *History of the Massachusetts Medical Society, 1781–1922*, privately printed, 1923.)

2. Garrison spoke at Woonsocket on Tuesday, February 12, as the second lecturer in the Philomathean course; he urged the impeachment of Andrew Johnson and the postponement of Reconstruction until the southerners were thoroughly loyal. (*Woonsocket Patriot and Rhode Island Register*, February 15, 1867.)

3. Garrison did speak at the Brooklyn Academy; for his own description of the speech see the letter to Helen E. Garrison, February 28, 1867.

4. The meeting of the Massachusetts Anti-Slavery Society took place on January 25 in the second-floor auditorium of the Mercantile Library Association; the criticism and support of Garrison were reported in the *National Anti-Slavery Standard*, February 2, 1867. (R. L. Midgley, *Sights in Boston and Suburbs, or Guide to the Stranger*, Boston and Cambridge, 1857.)

5. Thomas Knox was a Boston physician who, according to the city directory, was located in 1867 at 87 Cedar Street. During the war he was an army surgeon. Dr. Knox's attack upon Garrison was less extensive than it might have been had not President John T. Sargent interceded by recognizing Mrs. Frances E. W. Harper, who

spoke favorably of Garrison's past achievements. While Knox was in South Carolina, he investigated irregularities in the distribution of clothing intended for poor blacks and published a book entitled *Startling Revelations from the Department of South Carolina, an Exposé of the so-called National Freedmen's Relief Association* (1864). (*Standard,* February 2, 1867; letter to the editor from Hilda Armour, researcher, November 18, 1975.)

James Needham Buffum (1807–1887), a carpenter and builder, was the operator of the first steam-powered planing mill in Lynn, Mass. Twice he was elected mayor of that city. For many years he had been a zealous abolitionist and a friend of Garrison. He was also a debating club member, and he served as vice president of the Friends of Social Reform, a Fourier organization in which Garrison's brother-in-law George Benson had been active. (Letter to the editor from Harold S. Walker, associate director, Lynn Historical Society, June 21, 1972; *Letters,* II, 311, III, 138.)

Joshua Titus Everett (1806–1897) was apparently a lawyer by profession, although he was known primarily as a reformer. For many years he served as president of the Worcester County North Division Anti-Slavery Society. Long a friend to Garrisonian abolitionists, he supported Garrison's right to follow his own convictions in withdrawing from the antislavery society. (Letter to the editor from Edith M. Maynard, librarian, Worcester Historical Society, October 27, 1970; *Standard,* February 2, 1867; *Letters,* II, 576.)

6. Edmund Jackson (1795–1875), brother of Francis Jackson, was a prosperous businessman and a generous contributor to the cause of abolition. He sided with Phillips in the disposal of his brother's estate, preferring that the major portion of the bequest be used for the American Anti-Slavery Society rather than for the education of the freedmen. (*Letters,* I, 165, n. 5.)

7. No doubt Garrison refers to the educational wing of the New England Freedmen's Union Commission, which was in itself an amalgam of various organizations. Such associations had gone through so many changes of name that it was difficult for Garrison and his contemporaries to use the names with precision.

8. Sculptor John Rogers' group, "The Wounded Scout, a Friend in the Swamp," was patented in 1864. It was made of painted plaster, cast from a bronze master model; it is now owned by the New-York Historical Society. An estimated sixteen to twenty copies are believed to be in existence today. (For more information about Rogers and his work see the letter to him, March 17, 1869; David H. Wallace, *John Rogers, the People's Sculptor,* Middletown, Conn., 1967, p. 211.)

Joshua Bean Smith (1813–1879) was a waiter turned caterer who had lived in Boston since 1836. While he was head waiter at the Mount Washington House in South Boston, he became a good friend of Charles Sumner, who, with other friends, donated funds to help him start a catering business. He was an active abolitionist and during the Civil War a successful recruiter of black soldiers. Made a Mason in 1867, he was the first black member of the Grand Lodge of Massachusetts. Between 1873 and 1874 he was a member of the Massachusetts legislature and served as chairman of the Committee on Federal Relations. (Obituary, Boston *Post,* July 7, 1879; see also the letter to Joshua B. Smith, March 23, 1855, *Letters,* IV, 334, descriptive note.)

9. The tariff bill in question, which passed the Senate on March 3, represented a compromise between the wool-growing and the wool-manufacturing interests; it taxed raw and processed imported wool. (New York *Times,* March 4, 1867.)

10. Franklin Benjamin Sanborn (1831–1917), a graduate of Phillips Exeter and Harvard, settled in Concord, Mass., where he became a notable radical reformer and abolitionist. He was the friend and later the editor and biographer of Thoreau, Emerson, Hawthorne, John Brown, and others. For a time he edited the *Commonwealth* and the Springfield *Republican* (1868–1872).

11. Louisa Jane Whiting Barker (born 1820) was the daughter of William and Hannah Connant Whiting of Concord; she married clergyman Stephen Barker of Leominster, Mass., in 1858. During the war she and her husband visited many

military hospitals; she also lectured to promote the Sanitary Commission's attempts to improve living conditions among front-line troops. (Letters to the editor from Marcia E. Moss, reference librarian, Concord Free Public Library, July 3 and 19, 1972.)

190

TO FANNY GARRISON VILLARD

Roxbury, Feb. 19, 1867.

My dear Fanny:

On Sunday morning, William went into Boston, and rejoiced us on his return by bringing a letter from you, dated at the close of last month, which we eagerly perused.

It seems you and Frank have had a taste of fashionable life at Munich, in the matter of balls, parties, operas, &c. A mere taste will be all that either of you will care to have; for there is little of real profit or pleasure to be found in the routine of worldliness. Operas, however, are not to be classed with fashionable balls; yet you know my taste does not run in that direction. We all should have liked to take a peep at Frank in his ball costume. In borrowing a hat for the occasion, he showed his economical training. Take care, darling, not to lose your native simplicity in regard to manners and dress, and vindicate your womanhood by high aims.

Poor Harry still continues to be afflicted with his terrible headaches. I believe they are largely occasioned by his eating his food so rapidly, in such large pieces, and never using his teeth in mastication. I wish it were possible for him (and is it not?) to make the experiment of slow eating, and not mixing at one meal too many things together.

Your mother has twice had her feelings wounded—(her disease makes her peculiarly sensitive)—first, by what Frank wrote respecting her urging you to remember certain persons in the way of presents; and second, by what you wrote to her about my loss of sleep in acting continually as her guardian and nurse. She cannot recollect that she has spoken of any presents, except in a single instance; and it grieves her to think she should be deemed thoughtless about my health. I do not know who wrote to you on the subject, except that I did not; probably it was William. Your suggestions to your mother were all considerately made and kindly meant, and there was much truth in them as to my need of unbroken sleep. But I have not suffered so much for loss of sleep, in relation to your mother, as I should have done if I had not been such a sufferer from my wounded shoulder and arm that I could not sleep. Please make no further reference to this or any other matter that may indicate forgetfulness on her part. You know she is thoroughly unselfish and unexacting even in her crippled condition, and at all times means to be delicate and considerate in her suggestions.

Concerning presents to anybody, do not give them a moment's consideration, I mean for any on this side of the Atlantic. It is proper that both you and Frank should make suitable presents to your German relatives and attendants; but do not tax Harry for anything of the kind. Use Frank's money *ad libitum,* and without hesitation, as you wish to make gifts or particular purchases for yourself.

Frank writes that you are thinking of all going to Paris about the 20th of March. Let us know when we are to cease directing our letters to Munich; and when we send them to Paris, whether to send them in care of the American Consulate, as formerly.

I am a good deal concerned about the expense that will be thrown upon Harry in the matter of boarding, &c. at Paris, on account of the enormous rise in prices growing out of the vast influx of population from all parts of the world to see the "Exposition."[1] I know you will study to economise for him as much as possible, and be content with very simple lodgings. Shun what is fashionable there as far as practicable. "A penny saved is a penny earned."[2] Harry, you know, is generous to a fault, and needs to be kept in check. He will find, more and more, that the expenses of married life, if one moves in a genteel sphere, are very different from those of single life.

Tell Frank I do not wish him to pinch himself in the way of economy, but freely to buy what he needs.

Dearest, I am strongly thinking of going to England with George Thompson in May, and from thence to Paris in June, when there is to be a World's International Anti-Slavery Convention.[3] I cannot now say whether it is probable I shall go, and therefore you must not calculate upon seeing me, as though it were "a fixed fact." The greatest drawback will be the helplessness and loneliness of your dear mother, though she will never express a word of discouragement. If I can hire Julia Randall to remain with her during my absence, I shall feel justified in going, as in that case your mother will feel reconciled to my doing so. I shall write to Julia in a few days about it.

How great would by my *fatherly* joy to embrace Harry, and yourself, and Frank in the French capital! I should wish to make a hurried trip to Switzerland, and then return to England, visiting its principal cities, and returning home by the first of September. More about this in another letter.

A copy of the Boston Daily Advertiser will be sent to you, containing a list of the names of contributors to my Testimonial fund.[4] The whole amount thus far received and acknowledged is full twenty-one thousand dollars—not quite half the sum originally named, but double what I supposed at the outset would be realized. It is not likely much more will be added to it; but it will come at a very opportune period, as my last year's expenses were upwards of three thousand dollars, with scarcely a dollar's income. The amount received from England is about seventeen hundred dollars, included in the sum total. Among the English contributors were John Bright, J. Stuart Mill, Wm. E. Forster, M. P., &c.[5] Very few of the abolitionists at home have contributed anything, nor did I wish them to do so. Only one colored man is among the contributors—William Still, of Philadelphia—and he has generously given one hundred dollars.[6]

Last week I lectured in Woonsocket. It was the first time for the last eleven months. I was a good deal exhausted at the close. On Tuesday evening next [February 26, 1867] I am to lecture at the Academy of Music in Brooklyn, N.Y., when I hope to see Wendell, and the next day shall probably go out with him to the Park. They are all well there.

Theodore Tilton has lectured more than a hundred times, at the West, and made a good thing of it pecuniarily.

It is yet doubtful whether President Johnson will be impeached; but if he is, the trial will not come off till the next Congress, which will be convened forthwith.

Mary Townsend will be gratified to know that you have received her letter.[7] Send her one in return if you can.

Alfred H. Love and his wife made us a call on Sunday. She is to remain in Boston a week, and will probably spend an afternoon with us before she returns. She is very *lov*-able.

I was examined, the other day, by Dr. Sweet, the natural bonesetter.[8] He says confidently that I broke the rim of the socket, through which the arm bone was driven; and that, if I had at first had the arm and shoulder splintered and kept in the right position, a cure could have been effected in the course of a month. It is too late now, and I shall always suffer more or less from the injury, especially in all sudden changes of the weather.

William went yesterday to Lewiston, Me., on business. He will probably get home to night. The wool business continues very dull.

The Swasey family are talking of boarding where Harry did, at Mrs. Appleton's in Highland Street.[9]

We look every day at the photographic card sent us by Frank, containing the fine public buildings in Munich.

Our household regards to Harry's father, aunt, sister, and brothers-in-law.

Hastily,

your ever loving Father.

AL signed "Father": Villard Papers, Harvard College Library.

1. The international exposition had opened April 1, 1867, on approximately the present site of the Eiffel Tower. The United States exhibit was the eighth largest in size. (Eugene Rimmel, *Recollections of the Paris Exposition of 1867*, Philadelphia, 1868.)

2. Garrison uses the English maxim dating back to the seventeenth century.

3. Garrison had been appointed to represent the American Freedmen and Union Commission at the World's Anti-Slavery Conference, the other American delegates being William Cullen Bryant and C. G. Hammond, both already in Europe. (*National Anti-Slavery Standard*, March 9, 1867.)

4. The Boston *Daily Advertiser* (founded in 1812) was the first successful daily paper in New England. Established as a mercantile paper, it evolved into a Whig publication that strongly supported Daniel Webster and later Lincoln and also specialized in literary and art criticism. It was purchased by the Hearst company in 1917. (Mott.)

5. John Stuart Mill (1806–1873), son of James Mill, was the brilliant English Utilitarian philospher and politician. In 1823 he founded the Utilitarian Society, which met regularly until 1826. In 1825 he edited Jeremy Bentham's *Treatise upon Evidence*. Over the years to follow he demonstrated that he was one of the most prolific of philosophers by publishing at frequent intervals distinguished works on philosophical and political subjects. A partial list is the following: *A System of Logic* (1843), *Principles of Political Economy* (1848), *On Liberty* (1859), *Utilitarianism* (1861), *Examination of Sir William Hamilton's Philosophy* (1865), and *Subjection of Women* (1869). For many years Mill was a clerk in East India House, but in 1865 he was elected a member of Parliament for Westminster, a post he held for three years.

William Edward Forster (1818–1886) was born to a prosperous Quaker family but subsequently became a member of the Church of England. Entering Parliament in 1865, he assumed prominence in the debates over the Civil War in the United States, becoming in 1868 undersecretary for the colonies. He sponsored many liberal reforms concerned with poverty, the condition of Ireland, and education. He was responsible for many of the early efforts to establish a national system of education in England.

6. William Still (1821–1902) was the black leader whose own experience as the child of fugitive slaves persuaded him to dedicate his life to helping his race. Born in New Jersey, he settled in Philadelphia in 1844, where he was employed as a clerk by the Pennsylvania Society for the Abolition of Slavery. His house became an important station on the Underground Railroad; it is estimated that more than ninety percent of the slaves escaping through Philadelphia between 1851 and 1861 stopped there. Following the war he served on the Freedmen's Aid Commission and agitated, often successfully, against racial discrimination. In 1872 he published *The Underground Railroad*.

7. Mary Gould Anthony Townsend (1829–1888), the daughter of Charlotte Benson and Henry Anthony, married bank cashier William Comstock Townsend (c.

1825–1882) in 1853; in 1868 Townsend was to secure the agency of the National Life Insurance Company for Rhode Island. The family lived at 59 Brown Street, Providence. (Charles L. Anthony, *Genealogy of the Anthony Family from 1495 to 1904*, Sterling, Ill., 1904; Rhode Island census of 1865; FJG, November 30, 1868.)

8. Stephen Sweet (1798–1874) of Franklin, Conn., was the son, grandson, and great-grandson of "natural bone setters." In 1843 he had treated Helen Garrison's dislocated elbow. (Letter to the editor from Elizabeth B. Knox, secretary and curator, New London County Historical Society, Conn., January 10, 1970.)

9. Garrison refers to the family of Lucy Richardson (1825–1905) and Isaac Nathaniel Swasey (1820–1874). Born in Waltham, Mass., Swasey settled in New York City, where he became a coffee importer and wholesaler. In April 1867 the Swaseys were to take a house in Cedar Street near the Garrison residence in Roxbury. They were close friends of the Garrisons. (*Letters*, IV, 323, n. 3; letter from Helen E. Garrison to Fanny Garrison Villard, April 15, 1867, Merrill Collection of Garrison Papers, Wichita State University Library.)

Mrs. Appleton has not been further identified.

191

TO HELEN E. GARRISON

New York, Feb. 28, 1867.

Dear Wife:

As Wendell has written to William since my arrival, you have heard that I got here in due time. I have been so occupied till now as to be unable to sit down, and scribble even the briefest epistle to you.

I was fortunate in getting a seat in the cars at Boston just as I wanted, being a single one, and therefore having it all to myself till I got to New York. I did not once rise up from it during the whole journey. I was also fortunate in not seeing any one in the cars that I knew, or that appeared to know me; for I had not finished my lecture by a dozen pages, but these I was able to complete with the pencil on the way, for copying afterward. All this portion was in reference to the impeachment of the President, and I was enabled to satisfy my own mind on that subject.

I found Wendell waiting for me at the depot on my arrival, and we went immediately over to Hoboken, and took the train for Orange, where we arrived about half past 7, receiving an affectionate greeting from Lucy and Mr. and Mrs. [James Miller] McKim. Tuesday morning I returned to New York, and called to see A. M. Powell at the Standard office; then went to the Freedmen's Commission Room,[1] then to the office of the Nation, and from thence over to Brooklyn to attend the funeral of Mrs. Oakford, (Mrs. Anthony's daughter,) the services being conducted by Rev. Mr. Chadwick and Rev. Mr. Putnam, Unitarian ministers.[2] There was a pretty large attendance, and the occasion was made very impressive. Beautiful tributes were paid to her character. She looked greatly emaciated, but still very pleasant, like one in a tranquil sleep. I did not see any of the Anthonys, and have since had no time to call there. Wendell was one of the pall-bearers, and accompanied the remains to Greenwood Cemetery.[3] I went to Mr. [Edwin A.] Studwell's, and there finished writing out my lecture before tea.

The attendance at the Academy of Music was only moderate in size, but better than I feared, and larger than that which assembled to hear Ward Beecher or Mrs. [Elizabeth Cady] Stanton. (Mrs. Stanton's lecture, by the way, was very able, and gave great satisfaction to all who heard it.) I was in good voice, and was heard without difficulty by all present. My lecture occupied an hour and a quarter, and was listened to with unbroken attention from beginning to end.[4] The New York Herald had five reporters present, and my lecture was very fully printed in that paper, though it was mangled a good deal in some parts in the reporting of it.[5] The Tribune sent over no reporter. In this I was disappointed; as I had hoped to have my entire lecture, from my manuscript, given to the public through that medium. The Standard, however, will publish it in full next week.

Wednesday I was trying to get a good photograph taken at Lewis's, in New York, but failed as usual.[6]

I forgot to state that Wendell heard my lecture, and took a bed with me at Mr. Studwell's.

Yesterday I took dinner at Dr. Taylor's, with Powell, and saw my pet, Abby Hutchinson Patton, and Dr. Rogers and his wife, of Worcester.[7] At that hour, a little babe of Dr. Taylor was lying dead in the house.

After dinner, I went to Orange with Wendell and Mr. McKim. Several of the neighbors came in in the evening—Mr. and Mrs. [Cornelius] Bramhall, Mr. and Mrs. Lane and her sister, Mr. Green, &c.—and we spent a very pleasant time together till near midnight.[8]

This afternoon I am going to Yonkers, to spend the night with friend Barney.[9] To-morrow forenoon I am to be at Brady's for a photograph.[10] I shall calculate to take the Shore Line at noon for Providence, and spend the night at Charlotte[Anthony]'s—and hope to be with you and the dear ones by tea-time Saturday evening. How I have missed the baby[!]

All send their loving regards.

Your ever loving

W. L. G.

ALS: Garrison Papers, Boston Public Library.

1. Located at 69 Nassau Street. (Letter to the editor from Esther Katz, researcher, December 6, 1973.)

2. Helen M. Oakford (1835–1867) was the daughter of Edward and Helen Hastings Grieve Anthony. In 1857 she married New York broker John D. Oakford; the family lived at 36 Livingston Street in Brooklyn. The Oakford children were Edward G., Charles, and Helen. (Charles G. Anthony, *Genealogy of the Anthony Family from 1495 to 1904*, Sterling, Ill., 1904; letter to the editor from John H. Lindenbusch, executive director, Long Island Historical Society, September 12, 1972.)

John White Chadwick (1840–1904) from Marblehead, Mass., attended the State Normal School at Bridgewater, Phillips Exeter Academy, and Harvard Divinity School, from which he graduated in 1864. Shortly thereafter he became the minister of the Second Unitarian Church of Brooklyn, where for the remainder of his life he distinguished himself as preacher, lecturer, and man of letters. He was the author of many books on religious and scientific subjects and was also a popular poet.

Alfred Porter Putnam (1827–1906) had been the minister of the First Unitarian Congregational Church (or Church of the Saviour) since September 1864. Under his guidance the church was active in establishing missions and religious associations. (Henry R. Stiles, *The Civil, Political, Professional and Ecclesiastical History . . . of the City of Brooklyn, New York, from 1683 to 1884*, New York, 1884, II, 1086–1087; *National Union Catalogue, Pre–1956 Imprints.*)

3. Greenwood Cemetery was established as the Brooklyn counterpart of Mount Auburn Cemetery in Cambridge, Mass. In its rural setting, 478 acres in all, are buried such famous New Yorkers as Horace Greeley, Henry Ward Beecher, and DeWitt Clinton. (Charles Lockwood, "Greenwood, Fashionable Cemetery with a View . . . ," *Smithsonian*, 7, No. 1: 56–63, April 1976.)

4. Garrison's speech, with one exception the first given after almost a year of ill health, was the third in the Fraternity Course of Lectures at the Brooklyn Academy of Music. Entitled "Our National Situation," it celebrated the achievements of former slaves despite the cruelties of the frustrated southern whites. The great questions of the hour, Garrison said, related to Reconstruction and citizenship, that is, the establishment of free institutions throughout the country. He also called for the impeachment and deposition of President Andrew Johnson. The *National Anti-Slavery Standard*, under the editorship of Aaron M. Powell with substantial control by Wendell Phillips, disagreed with Garrison's basic optimism, asserting that "the Slave Power of the South" was not yet crushed, there was still much to be done, and that Congress had been greatly remiss, but conceded that Garrison's delivery had been good and his demand for Johnson's impeachment eloquent. Powell's comments indicated the widening disagreement over postwar tactics between the loyal Garrisonians and those who had chosen to remain with the American Anti-Slavery Society under Wendell Phillips' leadership. (*Standard*, March 9, 1867.)

5. Garrison must have been reveling in his return to the podium, for, although his speech was substantially "mangled" by the New York *Herald*, he reacted mildly to the omissions, misquotations, and permutations evident when the *Herald*'s report is compared with that in the *Standard*. It should be noted, however, that the *Standard* coverage was printed with the benefit of Garrison's written copy. (New York *Herald*, February 27, 1867; *Standard*, March 9, 1867.)

6. Richard A. Lewis, who lived in Brooklyn, owned R. A. Lewis' Celebrated Photographic Gallery, established in 1839 and located at 160 Chatham Street in Manhattan. Lewis probably died between 1885 and 1889. (New York City directories; letter to the editor from Esther Katz, researcher, October 31, 1973.)

7. Dr. Taylor cannot be certainly identified. In Brooklyn directories two physicians are listed: Edward G. Taylor, 268 (later at 338) Hudson Avenue, and John T. Taylor, a surgeon of Flushing Avenue at the corner of Ryerson. (Letter to the editor from Esther Katz, April 26, 1974.)

Efforts to identify Dr. and Mrs. Rogers have failed.

8. The first city directory for Orange, N.J., published in 1870, lists two residents of Llewellyn Park named Lane: William, who dealt in boots, and Isaac Remsen, whose business was insurance; they were both listed as living at Clarendon Place and were probably father and son. No other information is available.

Probably Garrison refers to William Green; see the letter to Helen E. Garrison, July 23, 1866, n. 1.

9. Nathaniel Barney (1792–1869), a native of Nantucket, was an importer and manufacturer of whale oil products. He was a lifelong abolitionist. His last years were spent in Yonkers, N.Y. (Obituary, *Standard,* September 18, 1869; *Letters,* III, 272.)

10. Mathew B. Brady (1823–1896) excelled as a daguerreotypist in the early 1840s and as a photographer in the mid-1850s, winning national and international prizes for his work. He established a studio in New York City, first at Fulton Street and Broadway, and by the time of Garrison's letter farther uptown at 785 Broadway; Brady lived at 108 East Twenty-second Street. During the Civil War he and a group of assistants became famous for photographs of camp and battle scenes. A poor businessman, Brady lost money during the war and in the panic of 1873. He spent his last years in Washington, little known and impoverished. Brady published several volumes of his photographs, but no Garrison likeness has been found.

192

TO SAMUEL MAY, JR.

(Private.)

Roxbury, April 5, 1867.

My Dear Friend:

I duly received your note, in relation to the case of our faithful co-laborer, George Thompson. When I alluded to the desirableness of his returning home to his family, and especially the propriety of his being a representative champion of the colored race at the approaching Anti-Slavery Conference in Paris, I had no thought of taxing your kindness, or Mr [Samuel E.] Sewall's, in his behalf. You have had a delicate and laborious task in trying to complete the "Testimonial," as far as practicable; and I should deem it quite an outrage, at least very unreasonable, to ask you to start another subscription, even to facilitate the object I have alluded to. Dear, generous Mr Sewall, too, is constantly appealed to for donations of one kind and another, and ought to have some rest. My embarrassment about G. T. has been, that those who have helped the "Testimonial" are principally such as I could have applied to in his case, were it not that I am thus precluded from doing so by personal considerations; and, certainly, *you* ought not to be put to even the slightest trouble about it. At the same time, in view of the recent death of his oldest and only son, and his long absence from his family, it is due to appearances that he should return home this spring.[1]

Nothing but his pecuniary situation has kept him here so long; so that, in fact, he has remained in the U.S. as a matter of necessity rather than of choice. But he would almost sooner die than make his case known even to those who would take a friendly interest in it. From what I can find out, he would gladly go over with me, if he could be relieved of the expense of the trip to and from England;— say, $400. I say *from* England; because, unless he can find something to do that will afford him the means of livelihood when he gets home, he will have to return next fall, again to enter the lecturing field at the West. If, therefore, enough can be procured to pay his passage home, I shall feel justified, by various weighty considerations, to pay his passage back to Boston, rather than to leave him behind. Dear Lucretia Mott has raised one hundred dollars for him, and hoped to have raised another hundred, but she has been very ill, and much concern is felt lest it may prove her last sickness. I spoke to Mr McKim about the matter when I saw him a few weeks ago, and he promised to do what he could; but nothing has yet come of it, to my knowledge. Nevertheless, I have taken the responsibility of securing a passage for G. T. on board of the Cunard steamship Cuba, which sails from Boston on the 8th of May, and in which I have engaged my own.[2] You know I thought of going over in the Great Eastern,[3] from New York, on the 16th of May; but she has altered her time to the 28th of May, I have concluded to sail from Boston on the 8th—the next Cunarder not leaving Boston till the 22d. Mr Thompson knows what I have done, and will make his arrangements accordingly, though ignorant of the *modus operandi.*

I do not know how efficient G. W. Light would prove in soliciting subscriptions; but I believe he is an old canvasser, and therefore ought to be "familiar with the ropes."[4] I think, moreover, his esteem for Mr Thompson would prompt him to do his best.

I thank you for sending me the Circular of the London New Broad Street Committee, relating to the Paris Conference, as I had not seen it before.[5] If one was sent to me from London, it never came to hand.

As I am officially authorized to represent the American Freedmen's Aid Commission at Paris, I shall need no such paper as you kindly suggest. Should Mary Grew go [to] the Conference, the same question will arise as came up before the World's A. S. Conference in London in 1840; but I think she could not be excluded.[6]

I spoke to you about Miss Estlin's coming to America the present year.[7] Mr McKim writes me that it is now very doubtful whether she makes the visit. She will not come till the fall, any how.

Your attached friend

W. L. G.

Rev. Samuel May, Jr
Leicester
Mass.

P.S. Tell your dear wife that if she will go to Paris, &c. I will most gladly do every thing in my power to make the visit agreeable. So will Fanny, and Mr Villard, and Frank.

Handwritten transcription: Garrison Papers, Boston Public Library.

1. In 1831 George Thompson married Anne Erskine Spry (died 1878), daughter of Richard Spry, a minister connected with the household of the Countess of Huntingdon. She is supposed to have been considerably above her husband's station, and she may have been at least partly responsible for his chronic financial difficulties. Mrs. Thompson had a sister in Baltimore whom she visited during the Thompsons' trip to the United States in 1834–1835. (Letter to the editor from C. Duncan Rice, Yale University, December 26, 1970; *Letters*, I, 549; FJG, May 3, 1878.)

The Thompsons had six children: Louisa (born c. 1832), who accompanied her parents to the United States in 1834, and who married Frederick A. Nosworthy; Amelia (born c. 1833), who also came to America as an infant in 1834, and who married Frederick W. Chesson; Herbert (1835–1867), born while his parents were in the United States; William Lloyd Garrison (1836–c. 1851), called Garrison or Garry; Edith (born c. 1840), still living with her parents in 1867; and Elizabeth (1845–1847). Garrison characterized the Thompson children as lacking in animation and resembling their mother rather than their father. "The children," he wrote to Helen E. Garrison, August 13, 1846, "are not handsome, but remarkably quiet—far too much so, for me—and very studious." (Letter to the editor from C. Duncan Rice, December 26, 1970; *Letters*, I, 549–550, II, 117, and III, 364, 368, 475.)

2. The *Cuba*, built in Glasgow in 1865 by Tod and MacGregor, exemplified a new design in steamships: by eliminating the paddle wheels, the designers were able to construct passenger accommodations amidships. (Frank E. Dodman, *Ships of the Cunard Line*, London, 1955.)

3. Notable in nautical history for her enormous size (692 feet long and 19,000 tons), the *Great Eastern*, which had been in service since 1858, was for more than forty years the largest ship afloat. She was designed by I. K. Brunel with many advanced features, including a double bottom, tubular deck, and steam steering gear. Despite her extraordinary features, the giant vessel proved an economic disaster on the Liverpool to New York run. (F. Lawrence Babcock, *Spanning the Atlantic*, New York, 1931, p. 122.)

4. George Washington Light (1809–1868), who was born in Portland, Me., to John and Nancy Light, was the Boston publisher and sometime poet whose literary collection, *The Boston Book* (1841), included Garrison's best known poem, "The Free Mind." Light edited and published the *Essayist: A Young Man's Magazine* (1831–1833) and the bimonthly *Young American's Magazine of Self-improvement* (1847). He also published a collection of his own poems in 1851. Since he died in the McLean Asylum in Somerville, Mass., in 1868, it seems unlikely that he was recruited to solicit funds for George Thompson. (*National Union Catalog, Pre–1956 Imprints; Life.*)

5. The London New Broad Street Committee was the executive body of the anti-Garrisonian British and Foreign Anti-Slavery Society, which had its headquarters at 27 New Broad Street. Later in the month the international antislavery convention was postponed until August. (*National Anti-Slavery Standard*, April 20, 1867.)

6. In fact, Mary Grew did not attend the Paris convention.

7. Mary Anne Estlin (1820–1902), the only daughter of Margaret Bagehot and John Bishop Estlin, was a prominent British abolitionist who had long been active in the Bristol and Clifton Ladies' Anti-Slavery Society. She and the society were Garrisonian in orientation and independent of the British and Foreign Anti-Slavery Society. Miss Estlin was to visit the United States in 1868 in company with Richard D.

Webb. She died at her home, 36 Upper Belgrave Road, Clifton, and obituary notices were printed in the London *Inquirer*, November 22 and 29, 1902. (Letters to the editor from Elizabeth Ralph, city archivist, Bristol Archives Office, February 11, 1971, and John Creasey, deputy librarian, Dr. Williams's Library, London, March 5, 1975.)

193

TO LUCRETIA MOTT

Roxbury, April 8, 1867.

Lucretia Mott:

My dear and revered Friend—

In common with a great many others who are strongly attached to you, and whose estimate of the beauty and perfectness of your character no language can express, I have been greatly concerned to hear of your serious indisposition for some time past, and painfully apprehensive that it might have a fatal result; but a letter from our beloved Ellie to William, received to-day, brings us the cheering intelligence that you are decidedly better, with a fair prospect of soon being restored to your usual state of health. Though you are about eleven years older than I am, if my reckoning be not at fault, I feel a strong desire that you should remain in the body until the time for my departure has also come, that I may go hand in hand with you to the Spirit world. Indeed, so great a company of beloved ones have already gone before—so many are vanishing on the right hand and on the left—that I feel more and more prepared for that great change which in due time comes to all, and ready for the translation. Yet I desire the prolongation of your valuable life, if it be the will of Heaven, because it affords such an example of active sympathy with suffering humanity in all its multiform phases, such an exhibition of goodness of heart, benevolence of spirit, moral heroism in the investigation and assertion of truth, complete womanhood in the relation of wife and mother, marked ability and usefulness as a public religious preacher, reverence for the will of the Heavenly Father as revealed to your own understanding, and total consecration of all your faculties and powers to the service of righteousness in its widest and most practical application. Perhaps it will never be given you to know how many you have blessed and aided by your counsel and sympathy, your liberality and co-operation, your testimony and example; but the number is very great, and constantly augmenting. To come into your presence is always to be the better for it; your company is ever edifying and pleasurable;

and, associated with your dearly beloved husband, who is indeed worthy of you, your home—to borrow the language of Dr. Watts— seems "like a little heaven below."[1] Accept this as from the core of my heart, with no wish or intention to burn incense, or indulge in mere compliment.

William reminds me that you and James will celebrate the fifty-fourth anniversary of your marriage on Wednesday next. I should like to be one of the circle at Roadside on that day, but circumstances forbid.[2] I hope, however, that this letter will arrive seasonably, bearing my congratulations to you both, and my fervent wishes that you may be permitted to renew this celebration for a series of years to come, with no drawback of sickness or calamity. You will have your children, and your children's children, and affectionate relatives, and admiring friends to felicitate you on this rare attainment beyond the "golden" era, and to give you their united benediction. I am glad it so happens that your cherished sister [Martha Coffin Wright] from Auburn is with you, and also Ellie, whose absence with darling grand-daughter Agnes makes a serious void in our household, and for whose return we are looking almost impatiently.

On the 8th of May, in company with my dear friend and co-laborer George Thompson, I expect to sail from Boston for Liverpool, to make a final visit to English friends, to visit the Paris Exposition, to attend the approaching World's Anti-Slavery Conference in that city, and to embrace my darling Fanny and Frank on my arrival. I trust the voyage may prove beneficial to my health, for I have been a good deal broken since my unfortunate headlong falls last year, and write this with a feverish brain and hand. Heaven bless you for what you have lately done to help George Thompson pecuniarily, so as to enable him to see his wife and children after so long a separation!

Your loving friend,

Wm. Lloyd Garrison.

P.S. The health of my dear Helen is now remarkably improved, and she is looking young, and fresh, and fair. She endorses all I have said about you, and unites with me in affectionate regards to all the household at Roadside.

ALS: Friends Historical Library, Swarthmore College; also printed in Anna Davis Hallowell, *James and Lucretia Mott, Life and Letters* (Boston, 1884), pp. 421–423.

1. Garrison refers to Isaac Watts (1674–1748), the nonconformist teacher and theologian who is remembered chiefly for his hymns. Garrison quotes from "For the Lord's Day Evening."

2. Roadside, the Motts' home since 1857, was located about eight miles from

Philadelphia on the Old York Road opposite Oak Farm, where Edward M. Davis and Thomas Mott lived with their families. The house was removed in 1911, and today the site is part of a residential development. (Homer T. Rosenberger, "Montgomery County's Greatest Lady: Lucretia Mott," Historical Society of Montgomery County *Bulletin*, 6:131, April 1948.)

194

TO FRANCIS JACKSON GARRISON

Roxbury, April 16, 1867.

My dear Frank:

In your last, you mentioned that Harry was writing a letter to William, but it has not yet come to hand. We expected to have heard from one of you to-day, but may do so to-morrow, as a steamer has arrived at New York from England.

I have to announce to you another death—that of Major George L. Stearns, who died at New York last week, of lung fever, after five days' illness.[1] It was measurably owing to his Emigrant Aid Society that Kansas was saved from Border Ruffianism. He was John Brown's right hand man, so far as pecuniary assistance was concerned. He was foremost in enlisting colored soldiers, and did a large business in that line in Tennessee. He was full of loyalty and liberty, and labored efficiently throughout the rebellion. He scattered tens of thousands of copies of "The Right Way," every week, gratuitously; and largely at his own expense. With some peculiarities of character and temperament, his sympathies were strong and active for the poor and oppressed of every race and color; and no citizen will be found to fill his place for many a year.

The time is fast hastening when I am to say good-bye to your mother, the boys, Ellie and the babe [Agnes Garrison], and a host of cherished friends. It will be hard to leave, and yet the prospect of embracing Harry, Fanny and yourself will break the force of the shock, and be a source of unspeakable joy. O, may all still go well with you! And, in due time, may we all be permitted to return to Rockledge, there to hold a jubilee meeting, with nothing to mar the pleasure of the occasion. Should your mother continue as well as she now is, I shall leave her without any anxiety; for she is looking and feeling better than at any time since she was stricken down. There is no danger about her leg; and under the manipulations of Miss Andrew,[2] she is constantly improving, losing what is morbid about her system, and growing more and more compact.

Miss [Mary] Wiggins leaves us to-day, after a visit of four months.

She has been an invalid, more or less, all that time, and so has not been able to do any more for your mother than to pass the time with her; but this has been a real service, as she has helped to keep your mother in excellent spirits by her liveliness and humor. We shall miss her.

Oliver and Mary-Ann Johnson came yesterday. She will remain several weeks—he a few days. We have received no further word from Julia Randall concerning her father's illness[3]; but she will doubtless be able to be with your mother a part of the time.

In mentioning Major Stearns's death, I forgot to mention that Mr. Thompson and I attended his funeral at Medford. The services were conducted by Rev. Mr. Towne and Rev. Samuel Longfellow, and appropriate tributes were bestowed by Ralph Waldo Emerson and Prof. Parsons.[4] I was feeling too unwell to speak on the occasion, though invited to do so.

Last evening, the Tremont Temple was thronged by the friends of temperance to give an ovation to Hon. Henry Wilson, who was enthusiastically received, and who made a strong and effective speech in favor of the law of prohibition, and against the license system, which so many wine-bibbers and rum-sellers are seeking to substitute for the former.[5]

Black has taken the best photograph of me that I have had taken.[6] I shall bring some copies with me.

My portrait, by Billings, (a little larger than life,) is nearly completed, and is pronounced by the friends who have seen it as the best that has yet been painted of me. It is to be placed in the Mechanics Hall at Worcester.[7]

Some of the colored people have purchased a beautiful timepiece for me, which will be presented in a few days, I presume. Mr. [Samuel] May [Jr.] informs me that the Test[i]monial will be ready for presentation by the 1st of May. I know not what the whole amount will be—perhaps $25,000. Love and benediction to Harry and Fanny.

W. L. G.

P.S. Every thing in the matter of reconstruction at the South is getting along swimmingly.

My kindest regards to Mr. and Mrs. [John A.] Lewis.

ALS: Garrison Papers, Boston Public Library.

1. George Luther Stearns (1809–1867), a prominent Boston businessman and reformer, was an abolitionist politician who supported presidential candidate James G. Birney in 1840. Stearns's second marriage in 1843 to Mary Elizabeth Preston, a niece of Lydia Maria Child, doubtless further stimulated his antislavery activities. He was a financial supporter of the Free-Soil party in 1848 and helped Charles

Sumner gain a Senate seat in 1851. Later he supported John Brown, contributing funds for the defense of Kansas against the Border Ruffians and helping to purchase a farm for the Brown family at North Elba, N.Y. Stearns was also chairman of the Massachusetts State Kansas Committee backing Brown in his raid at Harpers Ferry. (Garrison apparently confuses this committee with the New England Emigrant Aid Society, which had been chartered in 1855 to colonize Kansas with free-soil sympathizers.) During the Civil War Stearns was commissioned major and was a recruiter for black regiments. In 1865 he founded a Radical Republican paper, *The Right Way.* (Oswald Garrison Villard, *John Brown, 1800–1859,* New York, 1943, pp. 274 ff.)

2. Miss Andrew has not been identified.

3. Dexter Randall (c. 1788–1867) was a Providence lawyer with both bachelor's and master's degrees from Brown University. An "old charter Rhode Island Democrat," in the 1840s he opposed Thomas Dorr and the new constitution sponsored by him and his People's party, as is indicated in his pamphlet *Democracy Vindicated and Dorrism Unveiled* (1846). In 1813 he had married Elizabeth Thurber, a cousin of Helen Garrison's mother, by whom he had twelve children, including Julia, the ninth. (Abraham Payne, *Reminiscences of the Rhode Island Bar,* Providence, 1885; *Historical Catalogue of Brown University, 1764–1914,* Providence, 1914; James N. Arnold, *Vital Records of Rhode Island, 1636–1850,* Providence, 1891.)

4. Edward C. Towne (1834–1911), who was born in Goshen, Mass., attended the college and divinity school at Yale before becoming minister of the Unitarian church in Medford, Mass., where he proved too controversial to remain after 1867. Later he was a minister in Manchester and Birmingham, England. Towne was also a writer of some reputation, publishing articles in the Chicago *Examiner* as well as a number of books on miscellaneous topics. (Charles Brooks, *History of the Town of Medford, Massachusetts,* Boston, 1886; Vertical File Material, Unitarian Universalist Association, Boston.)

Samuel Longfellow (1819–1892) was educated at the college and the divinity school at Harvard, where he acquired transcendental beliefs not unlike those of his mentor, Theodore Parker. Although he served as minister in several churches in Massachusetts, New York, and Pennsylvania, his recurring poor health, his radical convictions, and, one suspects, his financial independence resulted in a somewhat sporadic professional life. Longfellow published poetry and hymns; he was also the author of a two-volume life of his brother, Henry Wadsworth Longfellow.

Theophilus Parsons (1797–1882) attended Harvard College, studied law, built a successful practice, and became editor successively of the *United States Literary Gazette,* the Taunton *Free Press,* and the *New England Galaxy,* before beginning his major career as professor at the Harvard Law School. He became famous for his lectures, his anecdotes, and his extensive scholarship, especially his book on contracts, which reached nine editions. After his retirement in 1869 he remained in Cambridge, revising his books and writing essays on religious subjects.

5. Senator Henry Wilson urged that members of temperance societies solicit signatures to temperance pledges in order to counteract the agitation for repeal of the Massachusetts prohibitory laws. He also reported at length on the Congressional Temperance Society, the third such organization to have been formed, the others having disbanded because of intemperance or lack of interest. (Boston *Daily Evening Traveller,* April 16, 1867.)

6. James Wallace Black (died 1893) was a Boston photographer in partnership with John G. Case at 163 and 173 Washington Street. Black made the first successful photographs from a balloon on October 16, 1860, taking shots of Boston from a height of 1,200 feet. (Boston city directory; Beaumont Newhall, *The History of Photography from 1839 to the Present Day,* New York, 1949; Josef Maria Eder, *History of Photography,* New York, 1945.)

7. Edwin T. Billings (1824–1893) studied art in Worcester, Mass. After painting for a time in Alabama, he settled in Boston, where he painted portraits (either from life or copies) of such notable persons as Agassiz, Phillips, Wilson, and Lincoln. His portrait of Garrison still hangs in Mechanics Hall, Worcester, and appears as

the frontispiece to this volume. (Mantle Fielding, *Dictionary of American Painters, Sculptors, and Engravers*, New York, 1965; William Young, ed., *A Dictionary of American Artists, Sculptors, and Engravers: From the Beginnings through the Turn of the Twentieth Century*, Cambridge, Mass., 1968; letter to the editor from William J. Hennessey, curatorial assistant, Worcester Art Museum, August 15, 1973.)

Mechanics Hall, which opened in 1857, contained a library as well as an auditorium with a seating capacity of approximately two thousand. After a recent period of decline and the threat of demolition, the building was restored by the people of Worcester, reopening in 1977. (Letter to the editor from William J. Hennessey, August 15, 1973; *Preservation News*, February 1978.)

195

TO WILLIAM C. NELL

Roxbury, April 23, 1867.

My dear Nell:

I shall be happy to see the delegation of my colored friends on Friday evening next, as designated in your letter just received.[1] Primarily I have no doubt that I am indebted to your strong friendship and warm appreciation of my anti-slavery labors for the presentation that will be made on that occasion. It will be all the more valued on that account; though I shall feel none the less obliged to every one contributing to the testimonial.

Yours, faithfully,

Wm. Lloyd Garrison.

Wm. C. Nell.

ALS: Garrison Papers, Boston Public Library.

William Cooper Nell (1816–1874) was an outstanding Boston Negro, the author of a number of books and pamphlets, including *The Colored Patriots of the American Revolution* (1855). In 1856 Nell sent out an appeal to Boston citizens for aid in establishing Garrison and his family in their own home. In 1861 he became a clerk in the office of John Gorham Palfrey, the postmaster at Boston (see the letter to Helen E. Garrison, September 4, 1867, n. 6), and as such was the first Negro to hold a federal position. ("The Garrison Homestead," December 10, 1856, Anti-Slavery Letters to Garrison and Others, Boston Public Library.)

1. Six men and six women called on Garrison on April 26 to give him an elaborate clock with a bronze grouping that represented History teaching by Example. Garrison spoke appropriately and called for remarks from George Thompson and Oliver Johnson. Cake, ice cream, and lemonade were served in the dining room. (*National Anti-Slavery Standard*, May 4, 1867.)

196

TO JOHN A. KENNEDY

ROXBURY, May 1, 1867.

JOHN A. KENNEDY, ESQ.:

DEAR SIR:

The receipt and perusal of your letter of the twenty-fifth ult. gave me very great pleasure.[1] I thank you for the warm and generous approval of my anti-slavery career contained in it, and rejoice with you in the total abolition of slavery throughout our land. If, as a humble instrumentality in effecting the overthrow of that nefarious system, I have been prominent, it has not been of my seeking; for, at the outset, I expected to follow others, not to lead; and, certainly, I neither sought nor desired conspicuity. Standing for a time alone under the banner of immediate and unconditional emancipation, I naturally excited the special enmity and wrath of the whole country as the "head and front" of abolition offending;[2] and now that the cause once so odious is victorious, and four millions of bondmen have had their fetters broken, it is not very surprising that, in this "era of good feeling,"[3] my labors and merits are immensely overrated. Others have labored more abundantly, encountered more perils, and endured more privations and sufferings; but every one has been indispensable, in his or her place, to bring about the grand and glorious result; and it is not a question of comparison as to who was earliest in the field, or who labored the most efficiently, but one of sympathy for the oppressed, and an earnest desire to see their yoke immediately broken. There should be no boasting on the one hand, nor jealousy on the other. Therefore, while disclaiming any peculiar deserts on my part, I trust the "testimonial," which has been so unexpectedly raised in approval of my anti-slavery career, will not be viewed by any of my co-laborers as invidious, but rather as symbolizing a common triumph and a common vindication.

Be assured, it will not be the particular amount subscribed to the testimonial by any one that will attract my attention or excite my gratitude, but only the evident spirit in which the subscription is made. Of course, I did not know that any application had been made to you by any agent of the very responsible committee having it in charge; but your name alone, with only "the widow's mite"[4] annexed, would give me high satisfaction, knowing your early and steadfast interest in the success of the anti-slavery movement, in connection with the labors of Benjamin Lundy—that persevering and indomitable pioneer, to whom I shall ever be immensely indebted for having been the first to call my attention to the subject of slavery, and to urge me to consecrate my life to the extirpation of that barbarous system. He ought to be far better known and remembered, and I have deeply regretted that, for unknown reasons, his relatives were not willing that I should prepare his biography.

You are quite right in saying that, without the slaveholders' rebellion, we could scarcely have expected such a result within a century or two. Yet that rebellion was simply the product of the moral agitation for the abolition of slavery, and, in fact, its triumphant culmination. Truly,

> "God moves in a mysterious way,
> His wonders to perform;"[5]

and, if ever the cunning were caught in their own craftiness and the counsels of the froward carried headlong, it has been signally illustrated in the fate which has overtaken the haughty "lords of the lash"[6] at the South.

Your handsome recognition of the eminent service rendered by Mr. Helper and his *Impending Crisis* is well merited.[7]

It was in the same cause you almost lost your life, and fell crushed and mangled under the blows of traitorous and pro-slavery ruffians in New-York, while doing official and manly service in the cause of liberty and order.[8]

Very truly yours,

WILLIAM LLOYD GARRISON.

Printed: J. E. Snodgrass, "Benjamin Lundy: A Sketch of His Life and of His Relations with His Disciple and Associate, William Lloyd Garrison," *Northern Monthly Magazine,* 2, No. 5: 514–515 (March 1868). For Garrison's reaction to what Snodgrass has to say about Lundy see his letter to Wendell Phillips Garrison, March 6, 1868 (micro.).

1. In his letter (April 25, 1867, Anti-Slavery Letters to Garrison and Others, Boston Public Library) Kennedy praised both Lundy and Garrison for their contributions to abolition and sent a contribution of $50 to the testimonial fund. He also warmly commended Hinton Rowan Helper for the influence of his *Impending Crisis* (see n. 7). (Unpublished records of the testimonial, Merrill Collection of Garrison Papers, Wichita State University Library.)
2. Shakespeare, *Othello,* I, iii, 80, adapted.
3. A phrase originally applied to the administration of James Monroe.
4. Mark 12:43; Luke 21:2.
5. William Cowper, *Olney Hymns,* "Light Shining Out of Darkness."
6. Not identified.
7. Hinton Rowan Helper (1829–1909), son of a North Carolina farmer of German descent, was a storekeeper until he unsuccessfully joined the Gold Rush in 1850; this experience led to the publication in 1855 of *Land of Gold; Reality vs. Fiction,* which propounded racist views. Two year later he published the controversial and influential antislavery book *The Impending Crisis of the South,* in which he presented a statistical economic argument against slavery. In 1859, with the assistance

of Horace Greeley, he published a compendium of the views expressed in the book, which became a crucial document in electing the Speaker of the House that year: the first Republican candidate, John Sherman of Ohio, endorsed the book and the second and ultimately sucessful candidate, William Pennington of New Jersey, rejected it. More significant than this election, however, was the fact that southerners came to identify Republicanism with Helper's type of abolitionism. During the war Helper served as consul in Buenos Aires, and in 1863 he married an Argentine woman, Marie Louisa Rodriguez. In his last years Helper promoted the Pan American Railroad, the failure of which project left him impoverished. (George M. Fredrickson, ed., *The Impending Crisis of the South, by Hinton Rowan Helper,* Cambridge, Mass., 1968, pp. ix–lxiii; Hugh C. Bailey, *Hinton Rowan Helper: Abolitionist-Racist,* University, Ala., 1965, p. 128.)

8. For information on the 1863 draft riots in New York City and the attack on Kennedy, see the letter to Oliver Johnson, July 14, 1863, nn. 5 and 7.

197

TO SAMUEL MAY, JR.

Roxbury, May 7, 1867.

Dear Mr. May:

I have been duly notified that "the adjourned hearing before the Master in Chancery, under the order of the Supreme Judicial Court in the case of Jackson ex. vs. Phillips et als. will be had at his office, No. 4 Court Street, Boston, on Wednesday, May 15th at 11 o'clock in the forenoon." As I am to embark to-morrow for Europe, it will not, of course, be possible for me to attend the meeting aforesaid. Nevertheless, as one of the Trustees in this case, I respectfully ask to be permitted in this manner to say in brief, what I might otherwise say more at length, in what way I think the anti-slavery legacies conveyed in the Will of Francis Jackson would be applied most in accordance with his wishes, could he be enabled to speak for himself at this time.

The whole amount remaining to be expended I understand to be about nine thousand two hundred dollars. You will recollect that when the matter was submitted to the Trustees, some time ago, in order to obtain their views for the consideration of the Master in Chancery and the Court, it was voted, on my motion, that five thousand dollars should be given to the New England Freedmen's Union Commission, and four thousand two hundred dollars to the Anti-Slavery Standard at New York. I made this motion, as you are aware, not as in accordance with my wish or judgment as to the wisest use of the money, so far as the Standard was concerned, but solely because of the nearly equal division of opinion in the Board of Trustees, and wishing to avoid every appearance of unfairness in the adjustment of this *vexata questio.* You and Mr. [William I.] Bowditch were absent on that occasion, though represented by letter or by proxy. It is proper to state that only Mr. [Charles K.] Whipple and myself audibly voted for my motion; Mr. Edmund Jackson and Mr. [Edmund] Quincy only seemingly acquiescing in it by silence, though in reality not approving it—Mr. Quincy being in favor of appropriating the whole of the legacy to the Freedmen's Commission, and Mr. Jackson in favor of giving one fourth part of it to the Anti-Slavery Standard, and the remainder to the Commission.

Mr. [Wendell] Phillips, at that interview, dwelt upon the importance of securing the ballot for the freedman as paramount to every other consideration, and accordingly argued the expediency and propriety of sustaining the Anti-Slavery Standard because of its advocacy of the suffrage question. All the Trustees were for vindicating the right of the freedmen alike to the ballot and to education; but we were not agreed as to the precise channel through which to make that vindication. Happily, since we met, by the Reconstruction Bill passed by Congress, the Southern freedmen have been put in possession of the elective franchise, and are now voting and even being voted for; and though it is true that in some of the Northern States colored men are denied that right, all the signs of the times indicate that, ere long, this proscriptive policy will be abandoned.

Under these circumstances, I feel released from adhesion to the motion I made as aforesaid, and would advise that no division of Mr. Jackson's bequest be made, but that it be given, without delay, and as a whole, to the New England Freedmen's Union Commission; thoroughly satisfied that it cannot be so surely and efficiently expended for the enlightenment, elevation and freedom of the emancipated bondmen of the South through any other channel or instrumentality. The officers and managers of that Commission are among the most trustworthy citizens in the State.

Very truly yours,

Wm. Lloyd Garrison.

Rev. S. May, Jr.

Handwritten transcription: Garrison Papers, Boston Public Library; printed in the *National Anti-Slavery Standard,* August 24, 1867.

198

TO HELEN E. GARRISON

Afloat, Thursday, 3 P.M. [May 9, 1867.]

Dear Wife:

I have just left my berth, (after lying in it for more than twenty-two hours,) with the steamer rolling uneasily from side to side, and feeling sick at the stomach, to make a desperate attempt to pencil a few lines to you, so as to forward them at Halifax, which port we are expecting to make by 8 o'clock this evening, having had a strong head wind, a rough sea, and plenty of fog, ever since we left Boston.

*   *   *   *

I had written only thus far when I was compelled by sickness to retreat to my berth, where I have been lying till now—8 o'clock, P.M.—after having vomited freely. We have just arrived at Halifax, after a run of thirty-one hours, which is very good time, considering what the wind and weather have been. We shall probably leave here by midnight, or a little earlier.

As William and Ellie must have given you all of the particulars you cared to know respecting what occurred before I left the harbor, it will not be necessary for me to repeat them. The tug-boat was crowded with friends to give dear [George] Thompson and myself a farewell, and to participate in the intended presentation. It was unfortunate that we did not join the party at Long wharf;[1] for then we could have interchanged greetings with them all. Unfortunately, in consequence of the pitiless rainstorm, all was crush and confusion in the saloons and passage-ways of the Cuba, and it was impossible to find those who were looking for us, and we for them. Thompson was more fortunate; as, coming over in the tug, he was enabled to keep with the mass. Knowing that Mr. Waterston was to make the parting address, I kept closely to him—Mr. [Samuel E.] Sewall, Isaac Winslow, and a few others being with us.[2] Finding there could be no reunion of our forces, Mr. Waterston, at the last moment, whispered in my ear the substance of what he was deputed to say—of profound esteem for my character, of high appreciation of what I had done for the freedom of a down-trodden race, and of hearty good wishes for a prosperous voyage and a safe return. To this I replied as briefly, in such words as I could command in such an embarrassed position, and then we separated with a warm grasp of hands. [Mr. W. stated that the Testimonial had reached the full sum of $30,000. Is it not a most substantial token of approval and regard?⟧ I failed to see dear Mr. [Samuel] May[,Jr.], Mr. [Edmund] Quincy, and many of those whom I most desired to see. Fortunately, I was able to grasp the hand of Mrs. [Maria W.] Chapman, Mary Willey,[3] Mrs. [Dora] Brigham, Mr. [William C.] Nell, and a score of others as they passed out of the vessel by an open window in the saloon at which Thompson and myself were standing. Did ever any two men ever have truer or more worthy friends than we have? G. T. was warmly greeted, after the olden time. How the tugboat steamed down the harbor as far as the School Ship,[4] in spite of the drenching rain—(and I grieve to think how many of the ladies must have got perilously wet)—what wavings of hats and handkerchiefs followed to the last moment—how Uncle Sam's cannon thundered their passing salutes from the School Ship and the Revenue Cutter[5]—&c. &c., you already know. The demonstration was affecting and impressive, after all, but it would have been particularly inspiring, and in the highest degree inspiring, if we could all have met on board of the Cuba, as originally planned. Never mind. It may prove for the best; and perhaps when I return a more auspicious greeting may meet me in the harbor, provided the weather and the hour of arrival permit. I owe much to Judge Russell for this demonstration, and for his sake in special regret that his good intentions could not be fully carried out.[6]

Thompson put into my hands a magnificent boquet of roses, lillies of the valley, and other flowers, presented by dear, faithful, enthusiastic Mrs. Brigham, the remembrance of which will carry their perfume with me across the Atlantic, all through my tour, and back to Rockledge. Let her know how happy she made me by its presentation.

I trust Ellie took no cold, and that my darling Agnes will not wholly forget grandpapa. O, how I already miss you all!

It was very fortunate that Mary-Ann [Johnson] did not go with us, for she would have added to her cold. She must be very careful indeed of herself; and if she finds the over-sight of you more than she can safely bear, she must beat a retreat in season. Doubtless, you will shortly see good Charlotte Coffin, and, in a pinch, may be able to secure the companionship of Julia [Randall], at least for a time, now that her father is gone.

Do not fail to keep up constant treatment while I am gone. Should Miss Andrew go to Tiverton, she has done you so much service that I think you had better present her with five or ten dollars, in addition to her professional charge. Employ Miss Houghton afterward, if you like her, as I think you will.[7]

Tell William to remember Mr. [Benjamin] Perkins, as I told Mr.

P. I should send him some money. I think fifteen dollars will answer.

I should like to have forwarded to me such notices of my departure as the newspapers may make. I see Oliver [Johnson] has made a brief but excellent notice of the clock presentation in this week's *Independent*.[8]

Give my thanks to Mrs. Cobb & her sister for their farewell demonstrations.[9]

Let Katy not be troubled for lack of kindling wood. Some had better be bought.

I am feeling very qualmish, though now at the wharf. Love to all as one.

Yours, ever and evermore

AL: Garrison Papers, Boston Public Library.

1. Long Wharf, which was constructed between 1710 and 1721, was the longest wharf in the country; international cargo vessels could dock without assistance. The wharf consisted of a public thoroughfare thirty feet wide and a sixteen-foot-wide space in the middle for docking smaller boats; warehouses were built on it, as well as a battery at the end. (Justin Winsor, *The Memorial History of Boston*, Boston, 1881, II, xx, 440, 496, 502, 504; Walter Muir Whitehill, *Boston: A Topographical History*, Boston, 1959, pp. 20–21.)

2. Robert C. Waterston (1812–1893) had studied at Harvard College before being ordained as a minister in 1839. The following year he married Anna Cabot Lowell Quincy (1812–1899), youngest daughter of Josiah Quincy and sister of Edmund Quincy. Waterston was successively the pastor of several Boston churches, including the Church of the Saviour and the Bedford Street Church. He was also the author of a number of books and pamphlets, including the *Tribute to William Cullen Bryant* (1878.).

Isaac Winslow (1787–1867), originally from Maine, was a retired sea captain and merchant who had introduced whale fishery to France. On retirement he settled first in Danvers, Mass., and subsequently in Philadelphia. (David P. and Frances K. Holton, *Winslow Memorial, Family Records of Winslows and Their Descendants in America* . . . , New York, 1888, II, 885–886.)

3. Mary Willey (1818–1907) of Stoneham, Mass., the daughter of Ephraim and Mary Noble Willey, was active in the antislavery cause. (Letter to the editor from Ruth Bell, researcher, January 7, 1973.)

4. Apparently a training ship docked in the Boston harbor.

5. The revenue cutter was a ship (in 1867, the *Pautuxet*) used by the Boston custom house. (Boston city directory, 1867.)

6. Thomas Russell (1826–1887), a Harvard graduate, was in 1859 appointed a judge of the Superior Court of Boston and in 1866 collector of the port of Boston. In 1869 he became the United States minister to Venezuela. He had for many years been an abolitionist devoted to political action. (Obituary, Boston *Transcript*, February 9, 1887.) Russell participated in the planning of the farewell demonstration for Garrison.

7. Marcia A. Houghton, a member of the Massachusetts Medical Society, was an "electric physician" with an office at 8 Cottage Place. (Boston city directory, 1868.)

8. The article to which Garrison refers appeared in the *Independent*, May 9, 1867. A later article in the same newspaper, May 16, 1867, described the presentation of the Garrison testimonial fund, as well as the departure of the *Cuba*, and in-

cluded the full text of Nell's presentation of the clock and Garrison's response. (See the letter to William C. Nell, April 23, 1867.)

9. Aurelia L. Beattie Cobb (1826–1896), the third daughter of William and Jane Beattie of East Thomaston, Me., married Samuel Crocker Cobb on November 21, 1848. The Cobbs were neighbors of George Putnam as well as of the Garrisons. In 1873 Cobb became mayor of Boston. (James M. Burger, *The Memoir of Samuel Crocker Cobb,* Boston, 1892.)

Mrs. Cobb's sister was probably either Angeline S. Beattie (born 1822), who married John H. McClennan of Boston in 1842, or Jennie C. Beattie (born 1833), who married Gustavus A. Hilton, also of Boston, in 1853. (*Eaton's History of Thomaston, Rockland and South Thomaston,* Rockland, Me., 1972, II, 143–144.)

199

TO HELEN E. GARRISON

At Sea, Thursday, 10 A.M., May 15 [1867].

Dear Wife:

I dropped you a line at Halifax, reporting progress between Boston and that place, which I trust duly reached you. To-day, at noon, will be eight days since we left the wharf at East Boston; and we are now within twenty hours' sail of Queenstown, the port of Cork; so that, if we have no drawback, in the evening Transcript[1] to-morrow you will have the cable announcement of our arrival at Q., getting knowledge of the fact almost as soon as we shall. The distance from Queenstown to Liverpool is 240 miles, which latter port we expect to reach on Saturday morning; thus making the voyage of three thousand miles in less than ten days—a splendid trip as to speed. For twelve hundred miles we were enveloped in a dense and disagreeable fog, excepting just before entering the harbor of Halifax, when the fog fortunately lifted, and gave us time to get fairly out of the harbor, when it again encompassed us with an impenetrable veil. But there was no abatement of our speed. On we rushed, with a full head of steam and all sails set, at the risk of coming in collision with other vessels or encountering some ice-berg; our steam whistle giving out its piercing screams every few minutes, admonishing all comers to beware of contact with us. This precaution, however, can be of very little use; for it is often impracticable to determine from what quarter sounds proceed, and where nothing can be discerned a few yards from the ship, it is a matter of luck, rather than of seamanship, if no disaster follow. It was not only very foggy but very cold, and nothing was done to warm the saloons. I have had reason to be thankful many times that I took my large heavy shawl with me, in spite of G. T[hompson]'s advice to leave it behind, and rely upon his own; for he has needed his all the way. The fifth day out a cold and pelting rain was substituted for the fog, driving all the passengers to close quarters. Indeed, though not suffering from sea-sickness, I have kept to my berth quite three-fourths of my time, having taken my meals in my state-room and retained them all upon my stomach, though feeling occasionally a little giddy and qualmish. This is the only fair morning we have had. The sun is for the first time shining clear, and the ocean in all directions is presenting a brilliant appearance. We are now rushing onward at the rate of full fourteen knots an hour. Yesterday morning we overtook two New York steamships that left four days before we did, and soon run them out of sight; and this morning we have passed another. They, however, are designed to carry freight rather than passengers. Our vessel, the Cuba, is the largest in which I have ever crossed the ocean, being of nearly sixteen hundred tonnage. She is said to be the strongest boat of the Cunard line, and most satisfactory in all her arrangements. I shall aim to return in her if I can. Her captain, Stone, makes no conversation with any of the passengers, or even the officers, and, of course, awakens no personal interest.[2] Why he is thus silent I cannot surmise, unless it is owing to his peculiar temperament, and a lack of conversational powers. He is faithful to his official duties, and that is the main thing. It is wonderful to observe the quietude and precision with which the complicated management of this huge ship, in every department, is conducted. No bawling, no bustle, but every thing moving like clock-work.

We have nearly two hundred passengers on board, and of officers and crew about one hundred and fifty more. The passengers are made up of Yankees, Britishers, Canadians, Southern ex-slaveholding Secessionists, Cubans, Frenchmen, Spaniards, Germans, Italians, &c., &c.; all remarkably courteous to each other, thoroughly well-behaved, and the most quiet and gentlemanly set that I have met with in my seven times' crossing the Atlantic. We have a number of clergymen on board, both of the Established Church and of dissenting denominations, including our colored associate, Bishop Payne, President of Wilberforce University.[3] The religious services, on Sunday, were conducted by a young Scotch Presbyterian clergyman, belonging to Halifax, named Grant—a very pleasant and agreeable companion, who reminds me in his manner of speech of Robert Dale Owen, and whose laugh is precisely like that of E. H. Heywood.[4] He was married the day before he came aboard, and is on a sort of wedding tour to Scotland. His wife has not made her appearance at the table. I did not hear his sermon, but am told it was very practical and acceptable. Rev. Dr. Lothrop, with his wife, is aboard, but we have not yet spoken to each other, nor met face to face.[5] He invariably takes his breakfast in the saloon, after all others have done, making a regular spread of it, like a genuine gourmand. At dinner he has at least two kinds of wine, partaking freely of the same. He spends a large portion of the time in the smoking-room, with a higgledy-piggledy company of smokers, his religious example as a shepherd of the flock ending in smoke. The wife of Rev. O. B. Frothingham is also with us,—a very gentle, intelligent and agreeable lady.[6] Our friends, Mr. and Mrs. Snow, of Fitchburg, are much with Mr. Thompson and myself, and sit with us at the same table; and we enjoy their society very much.[7] Mr. Osgood, of Roxbury, whose residence is in Bartlett street near Shawmut avenue, early introduced himself to me, and has made himself very agreeable in conversation.[8] He has been a great traveller, and for several years resided in San Francisco. He tells me he is on the Standing Committee of Rev. Dr. Putnam's society.[9] We have likewise with us a very courteous gentleman, named Wood, who is in the wool business in Boston, and referred to William as engaged in the same line.[10] Mr. Rand, the printer, related to John Ritchie, with his wife and sister, is also of our general company.[11] It seems that, as an apprentice in the office of the Boston Commercial Gazette,[12] he was obliged to put in type the inflammatory placard which, on the 21st of October, 1835, brought together the mob of "five thousand gentlemen of property and standing," to break up the meeting of the Boston Female Anti-Slavery Society, into whose hands I fell for a time, and from whose vengeance I could find no shelter except in a cell in Leverett street jail. Almost from that moment Mr. Rand has been an abolitionist, as his worthy and stalwart father, Rev. John Rand, was from the beginning.[13]

Sitting opposite me at the table are three German Jews, Louisiana planters, who have lost all their slaves by the rebellion, and who profess to regret their loss chiefly because their slaves, now that they are free, will be unable to take care of themselves! Of these Israelites it cannot be said that they are without guile;[14] nevertheless, they are unobtrusive in manner and very respectful (as indeed all on board are) to Mr. Thompson and myself.

There is far less wine drunk at the table than I have ever known before under similar circumstances and there is not one boisterous associate among us.

The chief employment on board is eating and drinking. First, breakfast at 8 o'clock; lunch at 12; dinner at 4; tea at half past 7; and supper from 9 to 10, if any choose to order it. I have regularly partaken of every meal, except the late supper, and eaten with a vigorous appetite. The tables are loaded with every thing to tempt the appetite, as at a first-class hotel in our great cities; and the amount of flesh, fish and fowl daily consumed, and of fruits, and jellies, and pies, and puddings, and various other dishes disposed of, is really astounding. I really believe more than double the quantity is eaten than would be possible on land, such a sharpener is the ocean air. The cooking is uniformly perfection itself.

Dear Thompson has had no sea-sickness whatever. He has been most attentive to all my needs, and helped me to surmount my ocean trials greatly. Jonathan and David, of old, were not more bound up with each other than we are. I am unspeakably happy that he is with me, and feel to bestow a benediction upon good John Ritchie for enabling him to get home to his family and native land. I believe he has written a long letter to Dora [Brigham], portions of which she will undoubtedly be glad to read in your hearing. You will thus learn some particulars of our voyage which I may have omitted. He has also written a letter to Oliver Johnson, which Mary-Ann will doubtless see when she goes to New York on her way to Longwood.

My arm has troubled me very little since I left. I have not yet tried the voltaic belt around it, reserving that for trial till I get to Paris. I have had, however, the voltaic soles constantly in my boots, and have not had cold feet at any time. I am very desirous that you should make the same experiment, assured that you will derive benefit from it.

I shall not be able to announce our arrival at Queenstown before closing, as all letters must be put into the mail-bag at 6 o'clock this evening, and we shall not arrive at Q. till to-morrow morning. But the cable medium will make this particular item of intelligence unnecessary, and obsolete when this is read by you. I shall write to you at Liverpool, where, arriving Saturday morning, I shall probably remain over till Monday morning, (spending the Sunday at Birkenhead, opposite the city, with G. T., at the residence of his son-in-law, Mr. Nosworthy, who married Louisa)[15]—then off for London, where I shall remain three or four days till I can get a suitable outfit of clothing—then off to Paris. As yet I have—and, until I see the dear ones at Paris, can have—no definite programme as to my future course. But it lies in my mind to remain in Paris two or three weeks—then return to London, and do up my English visiting till about the middle of July—then return to Paris, and go with Harry and the children to Switzerland, possibly to Munich—then come back and visit Scotland and the Highlands with Frank—then off for the Anti-Slavery Conference at Paris—then for home on the first of September. It may be that I cannot well achieve all this in that time; but I shall be guided by your wishes and your condition, and will come either sooner or later as may seem best. Of one thing be assured, that you will not be more happy to see me by your side than I shall to be there, and that you will never be out of my thoughts for a moment. Yet, as a mark of respect, I am somewhat desirous to visit our German relatives at Munich, and to spend a week or ten days in that city, making their better acquaintance, and seeing its objects of curiosity.

I need not say that I shall be as eco[no]mical as possible in regard to my travelling expenses; but these, in the altered state of prices, will be unavoidably twice as heavy as usual; and having Frank with me, the whole will reach a considerable amount. No doubt, in addition to what I brought with me, I shall ultimately need to draw the full sum of five thousand francs of Bowles, Drevet & Co., to whom I have a letter of credit to that amount.[16] I wish William to confer with Mr. [Samuel] May [Jr.] or Mr. [William] Endicott [Jr.], if necessary, in regard to that sum, and the payment of it whenever it shall have been drawn; of which I will seasonably inform him. A part of my expenditure will necessarily be in making presents here and there for favors received, or favors remembered. Besides, Fanny must be remembered, for love's sake.

It is probable that I shall have a public meeting, or reception of some kind, in London; another in Manchester; another in Newcastle; another in Edinburgh; another in Glasgow—&c., &c. It is doubtful whether I shall go to Belfast or Dublin; but I would like Frank to see both cities, if time permits.

Yesterday was the day for a hearing in Boston before the Master in Chancery on Mr. Jackson's Will. I hope to receive the particulars, in due season, either from Mr. May or William.

Let William be sure to send me the Standards containing the proceedings of the anniversary of the American A. S. Society, and whatever may be of interest to me concerning the cause of the freedmen.[17] Also, the Independent regularly.

Mr. Thompson and I can hardly get over our feelings of regret that our friends on board of the tug-boat had to endure "the peltings of the pitiless storm"[18] at our departure. O, how favored, and honored, and blessed we are to have such friends! Tell Dora [Brigham] her bright, smiling countenance and earnest farewell looks will not be forgotten by me or G. T. And so of good Mary Willey.

Mrs. Chapman's kind present of a box of Albert biscuits has proved exceedingly relishable, and been gratefully appreciated. I felt *so* disappointed that I could not see her and dear Mary G. [Chapman] at least a few minutes before leaving! But my eyes were full of tears at such an affectionate demonstration as was made by the choice company thus brought together. Heaven bless them all!

Rockledge, I presume, is beginning to show leaf and blossom, and to put on its robes of beauty. Tell William to make it look as attractive as possible, for the credit of the situation.

Dear baby Agnes! how I am yearning to cover her sweet face with kisses, and to bear her aloft upon my shoulders! Try to keep me in her remembrance by showing her my portrait. ⟦Has [James Wallace] Black's yet been framed? If so, she will best recognize that.⟧

What from dear Wendell and Lucy? Don't I long to see baby Lloyd, and to make him know that he has a loving grandpapa in me?[19]

With the most affectionate remembrances to George, and William and Ellie, and kindest regards to all the dear friends as one, I remain, dearest,

Your fond and faithful

W. L. G.

☞ What of my portrait by [E. T.] Billings? Have you seen it? Has it been noticed by the press?

☞ Special remembrances to my dear and venerated friends, Miss [Henrietta] Sargent and Miss Roby.[20]

ALS: Garrison Papers, Boston Public Library.

1. The Boston *Evening Transcript* (1830–1941), under the editorship of poet Epes Sargent (until 1853) and Daniel M. Haskell (until 1874), had become a leading paper and the organ of Boston culture. (Mott, pp. 217, 291.)

2. Captain Stone has not been otherwise identified.

3. Daniel Alexander Payne (1811–1893), the son of free black parents of Charleston, S.C., was apprenticed at several trades before joining the Methodist Episcopal Church in 1826. In 1829 he opened a school for black children, which flourished until it was forbidden by law in 1834. The following year Payne moved to Pennsylvania, where he studied at the Lutheran Theological Seminary in Gettysburg. Licensed to preach in 1837 and ordained in 1839, his first call was to a church in East Troy, N.Y. In 1840 he moved to Philadelphia, where he again opened a school. For many years he was active in the African Methodist Church, serving as minister of a church in Washington, D.C., and subsequently in Baltimore; by 1852 he had become a bishop. In 1863 he purchased the Methodist liberal arts institution, Wilberforce University; he remained its president for thirteen years. He was the author of numerous biographical and religious works.

4. George Monro Grant (1835–1902), who married Jessie, daughter of William Lawson, in Halifax, was principal of Queen's University at Kingston, Ontario, between 1877 and 1902. He was moderator of the Presbyterian Church in Canada in 1899 and became president of the Royal Society of Canada in 1901. He wrote a number of books, including *Ocean to Ocean* (1873). (Letter to the editor from C. Bruce Fergusson, provincial archivist, Public Archives of Nova Scotia, February 15, 1974.)

Robert Dale Owen (1801–1877) was the son of Robert Owen, with whom he came to the United States from Scotland in 1825 to found an experimental community at

New Harmony, Ind. Although the community failed in two years, Robert Dale Owen soon became interested in another, founded by Frances Wright at Nashoba, near Memphis, Tenn. He traveled with Miss Wright to Europe, where he met William Godwin, Mary Shelley, and other radical reformers. Owen later returned to live in New Harmony. An opponent of organized religion, he worked for a time with a group called the Free Enquirers. He served in the state legislature (1836–1838) and in Congress (1843–1847), where he was instrumental in settling the Oregon boundary dispute with Great Britain (1844) and in establishing the Smithsonian Institution in Washington (1845). He also worked for better public education, property rights for married women, and more liberal divorce laws. An advocate of gradual abolition, he was the author of *The Policy of Emancipation* (1863) and *The Wrong of Slavery* (1864). His other works included *Hints on Public Architecture* (1849); *The Future of the North-West* (1863); a novel, *Beyond the Breakers* (1870); and the autobiographical *Threading My Way* (1874).

E. H. Heywood is identified in the letter to Oliver Johnson, October 7, 1861.

5. Samuel Kirkland Lothrop (1804–1886), a graduate of the college and divinity school at Harvard, served as minister of the Unitarian Church in Dover, N.H. (1829–1834), before becoming pastor of the Brattle Square Church in Boston. Active in civic and cultural affairs, he was a member of the Boston School Committee, the Massachusetts Humane Society, the Society of the Cincinnati, and the Massachusetts Historical Society. Garrison errs in thinking that Lothrop was accompanied by his wife, for she had died in 1859. The lady was his invalid daughter Olivia (1842–1878), who was going abroad for her health. (Obituary, Boston *Transcript*, June 18, 1886; Thornton K. Lothrop, ed., *The Life of Samuel Kirkland Lothrop*, Cambridge, 1888; Andrew Peabody, *Memoir of Rev. Samuel Kirkland Lothrop*, Cambridge, 1887.)

6. Caroline Elizabeth Curtis Frothingham (1825–1906) was the daughter of Caleb and Caroline Matilda Agry Curtis of Boston. (Samuel C. Clarke, *Records of Some Descendants of Wm. Curtis of Roxbury, 1632*, Boston, 1869; manuscript diary of James Herbert Morse, XII, 16, Manuscript Collection, New-York Historical Society.)

7. Benjamin Snow (1813–1892), a prominent citizen of Fitchburg, Mass., was a paper manufacturer, real estate broker, and alderman. His first wife was Mary Boutelle (1819–1851), mother of four of his children, including naturalist and educator Francis Huntington Snow. His second wife, whom he married in 1852, was Margaret Pollock (1830–1912), by whom he had one son, William. Benjamin Snow died in the Worcester Insane Asylum. (Letter to the editor from Eleanora F. West, librarian, Fitchburg Historical Society, November 29, 1973.)

8. John Felt Osgood (1825–1894), a native of Salem, Mass., was a commission merchant with an office at 25 Central Wharf and a residence in Roxbury. (Boston city directory, 1864, 1865; obituary, Boston *Transcript*, August 1, 1894.)

9. George Putnam, who is identified in the letter to Fanny Garrison Villard, November 30, 1866, was pastor of the First Religious Society (Unitarian) in Roxbury. The traditional New England standing committee was similar in function to a board of trustees today. (Letter to the editor from Gary Bell, researcher, March 14, 1974.)

10. Charles Greenleaf Wood (1822–1894) had just retired from the dry-goods jobbing firm of Stone, Wood & Co. and was setting out for eighteen months of foreign travel. He is described in his obituary as a cultivated and public-spirited man. (Obituary, Boston *Transcript*, April 23, 1894.)

11. George Curtis Rand (1819–1878) was a well-known printer. As a young apprentice in 1835, he had worked on the handbill intended to incite the mob against Garrison, but he subsequently became an active abolitionist. In fact, it was he who printed *Uncle Tom's Cabin*, a venture that established him as an abolitionist and enhanced his financial status. In 1850 Rand married the widow of the Reverend John Roper. Her brother Abraham Avery became a member of Rand's firm. (Obituary, Boston *Daily Advertiser*, December 31, 1878.)

Rand's sister, Martha Loring Rand (born 1817), has not been further identified.

(Florence Osgood Rand, *A Genealogy of the Rand Family in the United States,* New York, 1898, p. 77.)

John Ritchie (c. 1837–1919) was the son of Uriah Ritchie and Susan White Rand, sister of George Rand. During the Civil War he was in the quartermaster corps of the 54th Massachusetts Regiment. In 1866 he married his cousin Caroline Poole, after whose death in January 1867 he spent much of his time traveling. In 1876 he married a German woman, Rosa Schoepffer. He was a member of the executive committee of the Anti-Imperial League, as well as a member of the Boston Scientific Society and a fellow of the American Academy. (Obituary, Boston *Evening Transcript,* July 12, 1919; FJG, April 25, 1876.)

12. The Boston *Commercial Gazette,* founded in 1795 as the Boston *Price-Current and Marine Intelligencer,* was later called *Russell's Gazette* and in 1840 combined with the *Independent Chronicle and Boston Patriot,* the *Centinel,* and the *New England and Palladium* to form the *Daily Advertiser.* (Mott, p. 187.)

13. John Rand (1781–1855) was ordained a Baptist minister in Boston in 1806 and did evangelical work in the vicinity of that city. He and his wife, Betsy Babcock of Milton, had thirteen children. (Rand, *Genealogy of the Rand Family.*)

14. Possibly an allusion to John 1:47.

15. Frederick A. Nosworthy (born c. 1827), from Abergele, Wales, was a merchant dealing in dried fruits, with a place of business at 24–26 Mathew Street, Liverpool, and a residence at 12 Caroline Place, Devonshire Road, Claughton, Birkenhead. He was married to Louisa S. Thompson (born c. 1835). Garrison mentions their six children (see the following two letters), but the national census of 1871 lists only five. (Letter to the editor from Brian J. Barnes, director of leisure services, Central Wirral Area Library, Birkenhead, England, July 4, 1974.)

16. Bowles, Drevet & Co. (later, Bowles, Brothers & Co.) had offices at various locations: 12, rue de la Paix, Paris; 449 the Strand, London (opened in 1870); 19 William Street, New York City; and 76 State Street, Boston. (Letter to the editor from Ilana Stern, researcher, December 4, 1975.)

17. The thirty-fourth annual meeting of the American Anti-Slavery Society was held on May 7 at Steinway Hall and on May 8 at Dodworth Hall in New York City. (*National Anti-Slavery Standard,* May 18 and 25, 1867.)

18. Shakespeare, *King Lear,* III, iv, 29, adapted.

19. Lloyd McKim Garrison (1867–1900), despite his early death, became one of the more distinguished of Garrison's progeny. A graduate of Harvard College and Law School, he became a successful New York attorney, a member of the firm of Gould and Wilkie. He was also an accomplished writer of magazine articles and the author of a volume of verse. His office was on Wall Street, his home on Washington Square North. At the end of the Spanish-American War, Garrison was a member of a commission appointed by President McKinley to study the Spanish laws operative in Cuba. While visiting in Lenox, Mass., he died of typhoid fever. He was survived by his wife, the former Alice Kirkham of Hastings-on-Hudson, whom he married in 1896, and by a son and daughter. (Obituary, Boston *Evening Transcript,* October 5, 1900.)

20. Hannah Robie (1784–1872) was the aunt of Samuel E. Sewall. She was born in Halifax, Nova Scotia, where her father, Thomas Robie, had fled during the American Revolution. Although Robie later returned to the United States, Hannah chose to divide her residence between the home of her brother Simon in Halifax and that of her favorite nephew, Samuel Sewall, at Melrose, Mass. (Nina Moore Tiffany, *Samuel E. Sewall: A Memoir,* Boston, 1898.)

2 0 0

TO HELEN E. GARRISON

Liverpool, May 18, 1867.
10 o'clock, A. M.

Dear Wife:

I am able not only to shout, "Land O!" but to announce the safe arrival of the Cuba at this port, at a very early hour in the morning, having made the passage from Boston to Liverpool in the remarkably short time of nine days and a half, including stoppages at Halifax and Queenstown. I am scarcely able to hold my pencil, however, in consequence of vertigo and sickness at the stomach, brought on I know not how. We arrived at Queenstown yesterday morning, and, after leaving some twenty of our one hundred and ninety two passengers, steamed rapidly for Liverpool. The day was bright, the air bracing, and all our invalids were out upon deck. At noon I began to feel a return of the sea-sickness I had between Boston and Halifax, only worse; and, retiring to my berth, did not leave it till the Cuba arrived here, having vomited a good deal, (my stomach being like a vinegar barrel,) and passed a very uneasy night. At 8 o'clock our trunks were inspected by the custom-house officers, and then we were carried by a tug to the dock, where Mr. [George] Thompson and I took a hack, and were brought to the Washington hotel,[1]—Mr. and Mrs. [Benjamin] Snow, and others of our company, also coming to the same place. After writing the first half a dozen lines of this note, I had to take to my bed where I have been lying several hours, and from which I have risen to make a desperate attempt to finish what I have begun, so that it may go by the Scotia this afternoon.[2] I have vomited a good deal, which has given me some relief; but my head is very giddy, and my stomach out of tune. More remains to be ejected from my system before I shall be in proper trim; but there is nothing serious in this attack, and I have no doubt that, after a night's rest on land, I shall feel quite well again.

Mr. and Mrs. Nosworthy (Louisa Thompson) came to see us as soon as we got to the hotel, to invite us to go at once to their house at Birkenhead, a beautiful elevation across the Mersey like Hoboken across the North River from New York, and urging us to remain with them at least till Monday. Of course, Mr. Thompson will go, for his daughter's sake, but it is uncertain whether I shall feel strong enough to accompany him. I shall try to do so, however. Louisa is looking very fresh and bright, and has six children all living, and all born since I last saw her. She has been very kind and sympathetic in my case, and is anxious to get me to her home that she may properly nurse me.

At Queenstown dear Franky intercepted me with a long letter from him, full of congratulations, and giving careful directions about getting to Paris. Another letter was put into my hands here before I left the ship, renewing the directions with all possible explicitness. The children will look for me on Monday evening. Had it not been for this sickness, I should have taken the train this afternoon for London, and to-morrow morning (Sunday) have proceeded to Paris. In that case I should have been only eleven days from Boston to Paris!

My plan now is, to remain here till to-morrow afternoon; then, if I am able, take the train for London with Mr. Thompson—stop at the Charing Cross hotel[3] over night—then proceed alone on Monday morning to Paris, and by 7 o'clock, P. M. hope to embrace our dear ones in their own suite of rooms. The thought of it ought to banish all feelings of sickness, but my stomach and head are in too rebellious a state to be so easily quelled. [Here I have had to stop, and vomit again.]

Franky writes very discouraging accounts about the health of Harry's father [Gustav L. Hilgard], who is in a most morbid condition and confined to his bed, greatly emaciated, believing it to be his last sickness. Harry is daily expecting to be summoned to Munich on that account. He is inclined, under all the circumstances, to let Fanny accompany me in my travels in England, along with Franky. I shall probably remain in Paris till about the middle of June, then return to England for a month, then we shall all go to Switzerland for a time, then return to Paris, &c.

You will receive this with a letter I pencilled for you just before reaching Queenstown.[4]

Ever your own

W. L. G.

☞ Keep up good spirits till my return. Time is rapidly flying.

ALS: Garrison Papers, Boston Public Library.

1. Not identified.

2. The *Scotia,* built in Glasgow in 1863 for the Cunard Company, was the last of the paddle steamers built for the Atlantic service. She was the first ship to cross the ocean in less than nine days. (Henry S. and Harold E. Young, *Bygone Liverpool,* Liverpool, 1913, p. 42.)

3. The Charing Cross Hotel, which was built adjoining the station between 1863 and 1864, survives today, with the addition of several stories.

4. Garrison refers to his letter written at sea, May 15.

2 0 1

TO HELEN E. GARRISON

Paris, May 24, 1867.

Dear Wife:

The date of this letter indicates where I am; but the intelligence has already been communicated to you by Frank in his last epistle. Before saying any thing about Paris, I will commence where I left off in my hastily written note from Liverpool, on Saturday last. On the afternoon of that day, my sea-sickness still continuing with great violence, and my head whirling like a top, I with great difficulty went with Mr. [George] Thompson and Louisa to the residence of Mr. [Frederick A.] Nosworthy at Birkenhead, about three miles from the city, and then immediately to bed, passing a feverish night, but feeling somewhat relieved the next morning. Before I got up, Louisa was on hand with a good cup of tea and some dry toast, which I very much relished, as I had eaten nothing for twenty-four hours, and had vomited at different times most copiously. Every attention was shown me by Mr. Nosworthy as well as by Louisa. They have a fine house, elegantly and tastefully furnished throughout, with statuary, paintings and engravings of real merit, and most charmingly located—as desirable a home as any one could reasonably desire. Of the six children, only the three youngest were at home—all in good condition and very pretty—the boy of two or three years old with round and rosy cheeks, the very image of her mother when she was in Boston in 1834. In the course of the forenoon, we made an excursion through one of the most beautiful parks I have ever seen, perfectly Eden-like; but my head being still giddy and stomach queasy, my enjoyment was consequently somewhat marred. At noon Mr. T. and I crossed the ferry to Liverpool, where we joined our friends Mr. and Mrs. [Benjamin] Snow, (with their son William,) of Fitchburg at the Washington hotel—all dining together, and then starting for London in the Sunday 4 P. M. train.[1] The distance between the two cities is about two hundred miles, and, as the day proved very fine, we all enjoyed the ride exceedingly, it seeming as if we were riding through a vast park, cultivated to the highest degree, and presenting such greenness of grass and foliage, and such wondrous beauty of scenery, as almost constantly to excite exclamations of admiration and delight. We had a first-class carriage all to ourselves. At ten o'clock we reached the London station, and drove immediately to the Charing Cross hotel— a vast pile—where I took leave of dear G. T. As we had eaten heartily on the way of biscuits, cake and oranges, no supper was needed; so I went immediately to bed, but did not get much sleep, my sea-sickness still affecting my head. I took a mutton-chop, two or three slices of dry toast, and a cup of tea for breakfast; which, with my lodging, cost me half a sovereign—about three dollars and a half of our currency! It cost me three sovereigns (including a telegraphic despatch to Harry) for my passage from London to Paris. You see how expensive my tour is likely to prove. I came by railway to Folkstone; then took a steamer for Boulogne across the Channel, (it raining nearly all the way, the passengers being quite unprotected, but, fortunately, the sea not being rough,) and about one o'clock stood for the first time on French soil. On landing, the passengers were in the greatest confusion to know what to do, or where to go to find the railroad station. There seemed to be no official head to direct us; and no one who could or cared to communicate with us in English. Taking my valise in my hand, and leaving my trunk to be lost or found on my arrival here, I walked more than half a mile at a venture, following others who seemed to be equally perplexed, and at last fortunately found the railway station. Even then, all was confusion, and I, with many others, came very near losing the train. I was aided by an English lady, closely resembling Lydia Spooner, who, with her husband, was going to Paris, and who readily spoke French. The time occupied between Boulogne and Paris was a little over four hours—the speed on the English and French railways being considerably faster than on our own. Half the distance the soil was sandy and poor, and prospect unattractive, but the last part of the journey presented a pleasing cultivated aspect, though not comparable to English husbandry or rural beauty. At half past six P. M., I had the inexpressible pleasure of meeting Harry, Fanny and Frank at the depot; and you can imagine the rest. They all looked as though not a day had elapsed since we parted from them. You need give yourself no concern about Fanny; her Munich photograph, for some cause or other does not represent her as she is. I see no change whatever in her; and none in Frank, excepting that he has certainly improved in his health and looks. Everything has gone most happily with them, and Harry and Fanny still appear to be in courtship rather than in a state of matrimony, by the admiration they feel and express for each other. Of course, I enjoy all this highly.

I forgot to state that, on parting with Mr. Thompson, I gave him three sovereigns for his wife, three for his daughter Edith, and three for Amelia, (Mrs. [Frederick] Chesson,) it being the birth-day of the last, as an apology for not bringing with me, or sending by Mr. T., a single American present for any of them; and wishing them to suit their own taste in making their purchases.[2] I have also given Fanny two sovereigns in your name, which gave her much pleasure as coming from her mother.

I wish you could see the suite of rooms that we occupy at the Hotel du pont de l'Europe[3]—they are so curiously yet conveniently grouped, so cosy and snug, with everything new and neat, with not an inch of space to spare, and yet answering our purpose very well, excepting when visitors come. These, however, are fortunately few, because there is no desire on Harry's and Fanny's part to make an acquaintance. In order to shield them and myself, I have kept my being in the city almost a secret; but last evening Col. McKay found me out, through Harry, and spent a couple of hours with us in lively conversation, imparting a good deal of information to me concerning French characteristics, and also the charming places he had visited in Switzerland, where his wife is still residing.[4] He returns to New York on the 4th of June, but expects to come back in August. To-morrow he is to introduce me to M. Laboulaye and M. Cochin.[5] I shall also call soon upon M. Tourgueneff and Count Gasparin;[6] but I shall shun all dinner and other party invitations, and endeavor to keep *incog.* as much as possible.

I called the other evening at the Grand Hotel,[7] (an immense and magnificent structure,) to see Mr. and Mrs. [John A.] Lewis. She is looking uncommonly well; he rather thin and pale. His sight remains about the same. Mrs. Lewis has come to the conclusion, from her experience in shopping, that the French are arrant cheats, and that honesty is a rare virtue here, as well as truthfulness. They will go to Switzerland during the summer, accompanied by Mr. and Mrs. [George] Rand, and Miss Martha Rand, Mr. R.'s sister. Her unexpected arrival has given Mrs. Lewis inexpressible joy, as Miss Rand has been a mother to her from early childhood.

I have not yet seen Mrs. [Eliza Jackson] Eddy, but intend calling upon her in a day or two.[8] Fanny represents her as looking and feeling very poorly.

I have called at Bowles, Drevet & Co's banking rooms, (the great resort of Americans,) and been warmly greeted by the firm.

Arriving here Monday evening, weak, giddy and exhausted, I kept within doors all day Tuesday, in order to get recuperated. Wednesday and Thursday have been devoted to seeing Paris and the Exposition. Of the city itself, I can only say that, in the grandeur of its buildings, the number of magnificent governmental edifices, the number and extent of its avenues, the many beautiful parks, the multitudinous promenades and drives, &c., &c., it is absolutely overwhelming to the senses, and far exceeds my anticipations. It is the central point of the world for all that is splendid, fashionable, sensual, and frivolous; and with its ten thousand showy equipages, and scores of thousands of vehicles, and hundreds of thousands of people in the streets, it presents a spectacle to the eye beyond the power of language fitly to describe. It is "Vanity Fair," on a colossal scale, as described by Bunyan in "Pilgrim's Progress," and full of temptations and allurements to those who think only of present enjoyment, and forget all that relates to immortal life. There are no homes here, in the American sense; and no splendor can atone for the absence of these. This must be Elysium to those who live in their animal nature, and only to eat and drink and dissipate *ad lib.*, but the reverse to the spiritually minded.

I have seen the interior of Notre Dame, a wonderful old cathedral, and also of St. Eustace, another marvellous structure; also the Tuilleries, the Louvre, the Boulevards, &c., &c., &c. Much more remains to be seen, and all my time will be occupied in sight-seeing till I leave for England—about the 14th of June, when Fanny and Frank will accompany me, and return to Paris about the middle of July, to join Harry; then we shall all go to Switzerland—I returning with Frank about the twentieth of August to attend the Anti-Slavery Conference. If I get good news from you,—not otherwise,—I shall remain till the middle of October on this side the Atlantic, so as to see Rome and Florence if possible, and then sail for home from Liverpool, bringing Fanny and Frank with me—Fanny promising to accompany me if I wait till then; otherwise I must return without her.

Henceforth, till otherwise ordered, direct all letters to me or Frank to the care of F. W. Chesson, Esq., Star Office, London, England.[9]

My sheet is full. I long to hear from you and the dear ones at Rockledge. Nothing has come later than when I left. How are the darlings, Agnes and Lloyd? Has Lucy fully recovered? How is the wool business? Who is with you now? All our love to you and the children, and all inquiring friends.

Your own loving

W. L. G.

P.S. Mrs. Eddy has just called in. She is very pleasant, and looking pretty well. She intends sailing for home on the 20th of July. Fanny has gone with her to find a dress-maker.

P.S. Tell William to look closely after the "rocks."[10] In case they are offered for sale, i. e. forced to a sale, he must have some one (apparently not in our interest) to buy them for us, if within a reasonable price. Harry is very anxious about our securing them.

☞ I have spent one day in the Exposition. It is truly a marvellous and colossal affair.

ALS: Garrison Papers, Boston Public Library.

1. William Snow (born 1854) was the only son of Benjamin and Margaret Pollock Snow. Little is known of him except that he eventually moved to New Zealand. (Letter to the editor from Eleanora F. West, librarian, Fitchburg Historical Society, November 23, 1973.)

2. The Thompson children are identified in the letter to Samuel May, Jr., April 5, 1867, n. 2.

3. Henry and Fanny Garrison Villard had engaged rooms on March 12, 1867, in the new Hôtel du pont de l'Europe at 17, rue de Turin. (FJG, March 12, 1867.)

4. Maria Ellery Goodwin McKay (c. 1827–1908), daughter of Frederick Goodwin of Plymouth, Mass., had married Colonel James McKay (spellings vary), as his third wife, in 1853. They had one son, Henry Goodwin McKaye. Maria McKay wrote several volumes of essays, including *The Abbés of Port Royal and Other French Studies* (1892), which contained an introduction by Thomas Wentworth Higginson. (Percy McKaye, *The Life of Steele McKaye, Genius of the Theatre*, New York, 1927, appendix 1, notes 53 and 121; letter to the editor from Kenneth C. Cramer, archivist, Dartmouth College Library, March 11, 1974.)

5. Edouard-René Lefebvre de Laboulaye (1811–1883) was a distinguished writer, professor, and politician. A lawyer by training, he taught at the Collège de France before entering politics as a leading figure in the liberal opposition to the Empire. In 1871 he was elected *député de Paris;* four years later he was elected to the Senate. During the last decade of his life he served as administrator of the Collège de France. He was the author of many articles and books on political and religious subjects. (*La Grande Encyclopédie*, Paris, 1886–1903.)

Pierre-Suzanne-Augustin Cochin (1823–1872), like Laboulaye, was a well-known writer and liberal politician. He was elected to the post of mayor of the tenth arrondissement of Paris in 1853, and later served on the municipal commission of the Seine. His politics were Catholic and liberal. He was a prolific author; his many works include *Abolition de l'Esclavage* (1861) and *Abraham Lincoln* (1869). (*La Grande Encyclopédie*.)

6. Nikolai Ivanovitch Turgenev (1790–1871) was an historian and government employee who in 1813 became Russian commissioner to Baron von Stein, administrator of the German provinces recovered from France after the battle of Leipzig. After returning to Russia, he was implicated in the Decembrist plot in 1825 and condemned to death, but escaped to Paris, where he lived the rest of his life as an expatriate. He was the author of a three-volume work, *La Russie et les Russes* (Paris, 1847). (*La Grande Encyclopédie*.)

Agénor-Etienne, comte de Gasparin (born 1810) was a French Protestant politician and journalist who served as a member of the council in the Ministry of Public Education and then as a deputy for the district of Bastia. He was famous for his many publications, including works on slavery, the penal system, and religious persecution. (*Nouvelle Biographie Générale*, Paris, 1853–1866.)

7. Located next to the Opera House, at 12, Boulevard des Capucines, the Grand Hotel, with more than six hundred rooms, was one of the largest hotels in Paris at the time. (*Baedeker's Paris and Its Environs*, London, 1888.)

8. Eliza Jackson Merriam Eddy (1816–1881) was the daughter of Francis Jackson. Her first husband, Charles D. Merriam, died in 1845, and in 1848 she married James Eddy. (*Life.*)

9. The London *Morning and Evening Star* was founded in 1856, its chief proprietor being Samuel Lucas, the brother-in-law of John Bright. The paper, described as a radical penny paper, found its greatest readership in the London middle classes and served as a liberal competitor to the *Daily News* until 1870, when it was absorbed by the *News*. The *Star* was in 1858 one of the first newspapers to subscribe to the Reuters news agency. From 1864 to 1868 the co-editors were Justin McCarthy and Frederick W. Chesson; in 1868 McCarthy resigned to lecture in the United States; it is not known how Chesson fared in the editorial changes in 1870. The *Star* office was located at Dorset Street and Salisbury Square, E.C., with an advertising agency at 67 Fleet Street and a city correspondent at 21 Threadneedle Street, E.C. (Francis Wil-

liams, *Dangerous Estate: The Anatomy of Newspapers,* New York and London, 1958; *Post Office London Directory for 1867; Life.*)

10. Garrison apparently refers to land adjoining his own residence, Rockledge, on Highland Street in Roxbury. Since the house was constructed on a ledge of rock some feet above the street, the additional property would probably have permitted access from the street behind the house. Because information and maps of real estate transactions for this time and area are scanty, efforts to determine whether the Garrisons acquired the property have been futile, although it is known that various family members did buy nearby land in later years.

202

TO HELEN E. GARRISON

Paris, May 31, 1867.

Dear Wife:

It seems to me scarcely credible that I date my letter in May, so much has been crowded of travelling, novelty and sight-seeing within the last three weeks—i. e., since I left home on the 8th instant I have sailed three thousand miles—seen whatever is visible from a railroad carriage window for a distance of two hundred miles, between Liverpool and London—stopped one night in "the capital city of the world"—taken a long railroad ride from London to Folkstone—crossed the Channel to Boulogne—traversed a wide sweep of French territory from Boulogne to Paris—and seen as much of Paris and its environs, including the Grand Exposition, as the most diligent pains-taking could possibly achieve. It is hard to persuade myself that all this is not the panoramic vision of a dream; for dreams have often a vividness not surpassed by any experience in our waking hours. I have been able to accomplish all the more here, in consequence of Harry's thorough knowledge of whatever in Paris is worth seeing; so, following his directions, it is impossible to go amiss, and no time is lost. I shall not attempt to narrate where I have been, or what I have seen. Whatever is possible of human skill, contrivance, invention, and artistic skill in every branch of human industry, is here to be found, and there is no end to one's admiration and wonder. Especially is this true of the vast and astonishing variety of things to be seen at the Exposition. I have spent several days in wandering through its multitudinous but admirably arranged avenues—(Fanny and Frank always, and Harry often with me)—and the half has not yet been reached. I doubt whether I shall be able to examine the whole of it before leaving for London on the 14th of June. The poorest display is made by our own country; for, excepting half a dozen creditable paintings, and one or two locomotives, and some agricultural implements, there is nothing worth looking at. Indeed, it is useless for the United States to attempt to compete with the old world in anything but our free institutions and the general condition of the people. Ultimately, we shall be able in all things to take perhaps the highest rank.

I wish I could have you with me to take rides through the wonderful avenues of the city and the various extensive parks, that you might see miles of palatial buildings, equipages of every description, and hundreds of thousands of people constantly in the open air, sitting in social groups, or taking their lunch at little round tables, and enjoying themselves in all sorts of ways. The spectacle would be bewildering to you, and in the evening the effect would be nothing short of enchantment.

A teetotaller here is a rare person. Beer and ale and wine are here consumed in large quantities; yet, strange to say, out of the endless throng I have seen, only two have been in a staggering condition.

We have had nothing stronger, of course, at our own little table, than tea and cold water; for Harry is as abstemious as any of us, and has not once indulged in smoking a cigar. He has had one or two attacks of neuralgic headache, but these have been short, and comparatively slight. He is very industrious with his pen, writing letters for the Chicago Tribune; but so few of what he sends are printed, that I should think he would get quite disgusted or discouraged. A letter from his aunt [Anna-Maria Pfeiffer], at Munich, says his father [Gustav L. Hilgard] remains about the same, but as soon as he is able will go to some watering-place for his health. She intimates that Harry must hold himself in constant readiness for a summons home.

Fanny will go with me to England. It is surprising that neither marriage nor a European residence has made the slightest alteration in her personal appearance. She is as youthful as she was under our roof, and in all things apparently the same. Equally is this true of Frank, except that there is a little more down upon his cheeks in the shape of an incipient beard. We are all in excellent health, except that, for some days past, I have been somewhat hoarse. Harry will remain here after we leave, (unless called to Munich,) and on our return will accompany us to Switzerland—say, by the first of August.

I have scarcely seen an American since I came, so as to recognize him. I met Senator Doolittle at Bowles, Drevet & Co., on his way to St. Petersburg, on a governmental mission of some kind.[1] He is a coarse looking man, of the Andy Johnson type; and, recreant as he has proved himself to the cause of freedom in our country, I was not disposed to prolong my accidental interview with him. No doubt he will be flatteringly received by the Russians; for they have a singular liking for Americans, no matter who they are.

Sarah Remond called to see me the other day, but, to my regret, I was absent.[2] Fanny, however, was at home, and learned from her that she had been residing in Florence for some months past. We reciprocated her visit last evening, but was told she had just gone out. A short distance from the house we met Mrs. Putnam and her son, and were warmly greeted by them.[3] I am to see Sarah to-morrow forenoon. She does not fancy Paris, Mrs. Putnam said, and will return to London next week.

I wrote to George Thompson last week, but have got no letter from him as yet. Mr. and Mrs. [Benjamin] Snow (who are with us at this hotel) inform me that, before they left London, he seemed to be very much depressed, and looking and feeling very differently from what he did on shipboard. I fear family matters are at the bottom of this. Probably the death of Herbert [Thompson] has made Mrs. Thompson more querulous and morbid than ever. It is strange he does not answer my letter.

I have been out to Saint Cloud, the Emperor's summer residence, where are beautiful parks, and had a very enjoyable time of it with Fanny and Frank. I have not attempted to see either the Emperor or the Empress, except incidentally on going to the Exposition, when it was announced he would review a regiment of sharpshooters just opposite; but his little boy had to appear as his substitute.[4] The review, in itself, was a mere farce. Nearly all the crowned heads of Europe are soon to be here, including the king of Prussia, with the redoubtable Count Bismark, and several oriental grandees and rulers.[5] Next Sunday is to be signalized by a great horse-race, and in the evening by a magnificent illumination of the garden and waterworks at Versailles. There is no very perceptible difference between Sunday here and any other day, except that it is still more given to amusement and recreation. People observe it as they please—work or play, and they do both. Very few, comparatively, especially of the men, attend church.

We have been made glad by a letter from William, of the 13th inst., and another from Ellie. I am rejoiced to be assured that you are bearing my absence bravely, and getting along hopefully. Keep up your spirits, my dear, to the end, remembering that the time is rapidly passing, and that it will not be long before we may be permitted to rejoice together at Rockledge, having Fanny and Frank with us.

Ever, dearest, your own,

W. L. G.

AL: Garrison Papers, Boston Public Library. Half of the last sheet of this letter consists of a signed note in the hand of Francis Jackson Garrison, who also provided the complimentary close and the initialed signature for his father's letter.

1. James Rood Doolittle (1815–1897) practiced law in Rochester, N.Y., before becoming district attorney in Wyoming County. He entered national politics when he campaigned for James K. Polk in 1844. Subsequently he was a supporter of the Free-Soil party and a Barnburner Democrat. He moved to Racine, Wis., in 1851, becoming judge of the first judicial circuit. In 1856 he joined the Republican party and was elected the next year to the United States Senate, where he served until 1869. He was friend and advisor to Lincoln and an opponent of the impeachment of Andrew Johnson. He spent his last years practicing law in Racine and Chicago.

2. Sister of Charles Lenox Remond, Sarah Parker Remond (born in 1826 and still living in 1887) was one of the most distinguished of black abolitionists. Born and educated in Salem, Mass., she began attending antislavery meetings as a child. As an adult she joined the Salem Female Anti-Slavery Society as well as the Massachusetts and Essex County societies. In 1856 she toured New York and Ohio as agent and lecturer for the American Anti-Slavery Society. Interested also in the woman's rights movement, she attended the national convention in 1858 and the following year went on a mission to England. She remained abroad until after the Civil War, when she lectured on behalf of the freedmen's cause and became active in the London Emancipation Society and the Freedmen's Aid Society of London. She studied medicine in Florence, Italy, between 1866 and 1868 and was certified for "Professional Medical Practice." (*NAW.*)

3. Mrs. Caroline Remond Putnam was the sister of Charles L. and of Sarah P. Remond. As Garrison explains in a letter to Oliver Johnson, March 29, 1869 (micro.), Edmund Quincy Remond, the son of Mrs. Putnam, went by his mother's maiden name.

4. On January 29, 1853, Napoleon III had married Eugénie de Montijo, countess of Teba (c. 1826–1920). Their son was Eugène Louis Jean Joseph (1856–1879). After the fall of the empire in 1870, the family moved to England, where the prince was educated at Woolwich from 1872 until 1875. In 1879 he lost his life in the English expedition against the Zulus in South Africa.

5. William I (1797–1888), a man of military prowess and conservative conviction, had become king of Prussia on the death of his brother in 1861. Even more powerful than the king was Otto Edward Leopold von Bismarck (1815–1898), who became the prime minister of Prussia in 1862, his administration fighting sucessful wars against Denmark in 1862 and against Austria in 1866. In 1867 Bismarck became chancellor of the North German Federation. Following the war with France (1870–1871), which was marked by cooperation between northern and southern German states, he and William I founded the German Reich, of which Bismarck was the first chancellor.

203

TO HELEN E. GARRISON

Paris, June 7, 1867.

Dear Wife:

My letter to you, last week, was broken off very abruptly, even before putting my name or initials to it, in consequence of my being obliged to meet an engagement at that time; so I had to get Frank to finish it for me.

I received a letter from you on Monday, and Fanny one from Ellie, the contents of both being eagerly devoured by us all. The matter of absorbing interest to me, while I am gone, will be the state of your health and spirits; and I want you to keep me truly apprised of your actual condition, so that I may govern myself accordingly. You write that you are feeling very well, and getting along comfortably; and this gives me great relief and pleasure. You do not say whether you have had any change in your treatment; whether Miss Andrews has gone to Tiverton, as she contemplated doing; and if so, whether you intend employing Miss [Marcia A.] Houghton for a time, as an experiment, under Mrs. Snow's direction.[1] I wish you to do nothing which is not entirely agreeable to your feelings and judgment; yet I feel as if the galvanic battery, skilfully applied, in connection with manipulation by the hand, will be an additional force for good in your case. You know how highly I appreciate what Miss Andrews has done for you, and how glad I shall be to enlarge her professional sphere, both for her own sake and that of suffering humanity. I hope to hear, from time to time, that you are still losing in weight and growing more compact, at the same time improving in health, as you have been doing for the past year. Do try to walk as much as you can, and especially to swing your arm with all the will power you can muster. I also want you to improve the beautiful summer to ride out often, no matter about the expense, taking Ellie and darling Agnes, whom I sigh to see, and Mrs. [Mary Ann] Johnson or Julia [Randall], as the case may be, along with you. I take it for granted that Mary Ann is now at Longwood, as this is the week for holding the Progressive Friends' meetings in that place. Such are her sisterly sympathy and kindness, I have no doubt she will most cheerfully return to Rockledge by the first of July, in case she is needed. In the mean time, I trust it will be both agreeable and convenient for Julia to be with you; but if she cannot, then Hepza.

My desire is to return home without any unnecessary prolongation of my visit on this side of the Atlantic; but Harry, and Fanny, and Frank are urgent for me to remain until the middle of October, in order that I may see Switzerland without haste, and perhaps other portions of Europe, certainly including the Rhine, and possibly going to Munich. All this on the supposition that every thing is going on well at home, and no pressing need presents itself for my return at an earlier period. By remaining till that time, I shall have the unspeakable satisfaction of bringing Fanny along with me, unless some unforeseen obstacle prevents, as she cannot leave at an earlier period. Should she return, she would probably remain with us till next Spring, and then come back to Paris or Munich; or perhaps it will be possible for Harry to come over to her, and remain in the United States. Very much will depend, however, in his case, upon the state of his father's [Gustav L. Hilgard], aunt's [Anna-Maria Pfeiffer], and sister's [Emma Xylander] health. Nothing has been heard from them since I last wrote.

My own health is now excellent, and I get so thoroughly tired during the day in going about that I sleep very soundly. My arm gives me no trouble, although not entirely free from pain. I feel confident that I shall return home much improved, both in regard to my mental and my physical condition.

The children are well and happy as usual, and we are all enjoying ourselves to the brim. Fanny is at present troubled with a slight eruption in her face, the effect of the poisonous ivy at Rockledge; but it is simply uncomfortable with its burning sensation, and not at all serious.[2] I am surprised to see how much physical endurance she possesses; for she is quite equal to any of us, not excepting stalwart Harry, in making pedestrian and other excursions. And I again assure you that you need not give yourself any uneasiness about her "changed appearance," in reference to her card photograph; for she has not altered one whit, that I can perceive, since the day of her marriage. You may not like to have her remain quite so stationary!

You can easily imagine how surprised, pained and shocked we were by the intelligence of the death of Lydia Spooner; and we still find it hard to credit the fact. You know how kind and loving she always was to Fanny, and with what affection Fanny has ever regarded her. Lydia was also much attached to our whole family. She was remarkable for her personal beauty and attractions, and, of course, was praised and flattered to a perilous extent; but she never exhibited any vanity, and retained her ingenuousness and self poise in an admirable manner. It was always a pleasure to me to meet her, she was so kind, bright, cheerful, companionable. Poor John must feel the blow heavily; and as for our dear, stricken friends, Mr. and Mrs. Bourne Spooner, they must be overwhelmed by this terrible bereavement.[3] I shall write to them by this mail, expressive of my sympathy and grief at the sad event. Who is next to follow in the circle of our friends and acquaintances? For how the list has been extended within the past year! Truly, there is no certainty of our earthly life at any time.

For the past week we have been as busy as possible in seeing still more of Paris and its suburbs, and the Great Exposition. On Sunday we were at Versailles, and wondered at the magnitude of its domains, were fascinated by its varied attractions, examined its miles of paintings and statuary in the galleries of the palace, rambled in its broad avenues under trees arranged in Gothic shape, and were inexpressibly delighted at the playing of scores of fountains at the same hour, (one of them costing in its erection over three hundred thousand dollars, and over two thousand dollars for every half hour it is in operation,) some ten or fifteen thousand spectators being present. Mr. and Mrs. [Benjamin] Snow, of Fitchburg, (who are stopping at the same hotel with us,) being with us. But Frank, who is now writing to you, will doubtless give you some further particulars of our visit. Also an account of the immense military demonstration made yesterday afternoon at the Bois de Boulogne racecourse,—sixty thousand cavalry, infantry, artillery, &c., &c.,—the Emperor Napoleon [III], the Emperor Alexander of Russia, and the King of Prussia [William I], with various princes and nobles, reviewing them—the procession occupying two hours' time in marching, and each brigade numbering three thousand men.[4] As a spectacle, it was the most gorgeous and the most imposing of any I have ever witnessed, or ever expect to witness.[5] The sun shone clearly out, adding to the brilliancy and effectiveness of the scene. There was no end to the number of vehicles present, and it would be useless to estimate the number of spectators. [It is estimated that half a million of persons were at the horse-race, at the same spot, last Sunday.] Of course, in a moral point of view, this mighty warlike display gave me no pleasure, but rather much pain at seeing such a perversion of human nature in support of usurpation and oppression. As the royal party rode out of the park, they were fired upon by a Pole, who doubtless intended to kill the Emperor of Russia, but he only succeeded in killing the horse of an officer riding by the side of the royal carriage, the pistol bursting in his hand. He was immediately arrested.[6]

I have dined with Madame Coignet and Miss Dowling, who have been at the head of the Freedmen's movement in Paris, and to whom Mr. Shaw, at Staten Island, gave me a letter of introduction.[7] Miss Dowling is an English lady, and acted as my interpreter, though Madame Coignet is able to speak English to some extent. I there met the Editor of the *Journal des Debats*, but as he could not speak English, nothing passed between us.[8] I have also dined with Monsieur Tourgueneff, my Russian admirer, and a nobleman by nature as well as by station—Fanny and Frank being with me, Harry being confined at home by a neuralgic attack. Madame Tourgueneff was suffering from a similar attack, but for our sakes bore up bravely under it until after the sumptuous dinner was over.[9] She is very stout, very fair, and very pleasant in her manners, and was partly educated in Scotland. I have also had a very agreeable interview with the celebrated Professor Laboulaye, who strongly reminded me in his sweet, gentle manners, and in the shape of his head, of the lamented Professor Follen.[10] Even he is not allowed to address a class or assemblage of persons in more than two places in the whole city of Paris! Every thing here is under governmental *espionage* and dictation, and therefore in a volcanic condition, although the volcano is capped for the present.

I have now seen in detail the greater portion of this wonderful city, but not half of the Exposition. A week from to-morrow we shall leave for London (expecting Harry) to be gone probably five or six weeks; then return, and go to Switzerland during the month of August. Until notified to the contrary, let all letters be directed to me to the care of F. W. Chesson, Esq., office of the Morning Star, London.

It is strange that I have not yet received a line or word from Mr. [George] Thompson since I parted from him, though I sent him a letter a fortnight ago. I have written to Mr. Chesson, to inquire into the cause of his silence.

I am glad to hear that you received the letter I wrote to you at Halifax.

Yesterday Frank and I called upon Mrs. [Eliza Jackson] Eddy, but remained only a few minutes, as she was evidently just going out, and as we were in a hurry to go to the Exposition. She was very pleasant and in good spirits, and renewed her statement that she intended to sail for Boston in the China on the 20th of next month.[11]

Fanny returns a "unanimous vote of thanks" to Ellie for her entertaining letter, and will try to reciprocate the favor soon. Ellie, singularly enough, forgot to enclose the card photograph of Agnes; so she must try again. If it is not a good one, I would let Whipple or [James Wallace] Black try to better it.[12] As Agnes will be a year old on the 14th of this month, I hope it will occur to William and Ellie to celebrate the event by having her likeness taken; and so every succeeding year. A few days later, this year, will make no difference, if they have not already anticipated this idea.

We all remembered dear Wendell's birthday on the 4th inst., and wished we could make him hear our good wishes in his behalf. We hope to hear continued good news in regard to Lucy and Lloyd. We constantly bear you all in our hearts and memories.

What a delightful time you all must have had at the visit of our affectionate and attached friends, Dr. Drew and his wife and baby![13] Would there not have been "high times," if I had been present when the two babies were on the floor together, confronting each other in infantile play! A curious coincidence that—their weighing just nineteen and a half pounds each! I hope Agnes will touch twenty when she is one year old. I was much gratified with the kind letter the Dr. sent me from Rockledge, as was Fanny with the one sent by Mrs. Drew.[14] We shall not forget their favors. They appeared to have enjoyed their visit very highly.

It is pleasant to hear of the visit of old friends to the house to see you. Our loving remembrances to dear Mr. [Robert F.] Wallcut and family, Miss Cannan, Mary Willey, Dora [Brigham], &c., &c.

On reperusing your letter I perceive that you are trying electricity, but given by whom, or how often, you do not say. I presume, however, that you are employing Miss Houghton. If so, I hope you are trying Mrs. Snow's preparation for your canker, or whatever the internal humor may be; and be sure to follow her directions strictly, in order to test the experiment fairly and fully. Give me further particulars.

It is possible that our beloved Charlotte Coffin is with you. In that case, receive my congratulations, and give her my benediction.

Give my regards to Dr. Putnam and [. . .] Thwing when you see them.[15] Also to the Simmonses.[16]

I shall be interested to hear from William as to his visit to Ohio, and the state of the wool business.

Tell George time is flying, and he must try to fall in love with some worthy girl, and push the matter, remembering "faint heart never yet won fair lady."[17]

Adieu, my beloved!

W. L. G.

P.S. How are you getting along with Katy and Bridget? If comfortably, give them my remembrances.

ALS: Garrison Papers, Boston Public Library; partly printed in *Life*, IV, 191–192.

1. This Mrs. Snow has not been identified.

2. Since Fanny had not been home for nearly two years, Garrison's meaning here is obscure. In fact, he is referring to what he calls, in a letter to his wife of June 30, 1865 (micro.), "that annual affliction." In reply on July 2 (Merrill Collection of Garrison Papers, Wichita State University Library), Helen suggested that the affliction might be "the affects of the old [poisoned blood] remaining in the system."

3. Bourne Spooner (1790–1870) was a Plymouth businessman long active in the antislavery movement. In 1813 he married Hannah Bartlett (born 1792), and in 1824 he founded the Plymouth Cordage Company, located in an area of North Plymouth called Seaside. Lydia was their daughter-in-law. (Letter to the editor from Vallory Hokanson, assistant secretary, Plymouth Antiquarian Society, February 15, 1972.)

4. Alexander II (1818–1881), eldest son of Nicholas I, became emperor of Russia in 1855. He introduced an epoch of reform marked by the freeing of the serfs, the establishing of law courts modeled on those of France, and the popular election of district councils. He also attempted to establish a new literature and to support the

freedom of the press. In international affairs his reign was not without its successes. The attempted assassination to which Garrison refers, however, augured ill for the future. After many other such attempts, Alexander was killed by terrorists in March 1881 on the streets of St. Petersburg.

Although there were two racetracks in the Bois de Boulogne, Garrison no doubt refers to Longchamps.

5. A report in the New York *Times* for the same date as Garrison's letter confirmed his judgment about the grand review. With its 80,000 infantry and 400,000 spectators, the review was considered to be the most brilliant ever held in Europe.

6. Two reports of the incident in the New York *Times,* June 7, confirm the facts of the attempted assassination as described by Garrison.

7. Clarisse-Josephine Gautier, Mme. Coignet (born 1824), was the author of several works on education, history, philosophy, and sociohistorical subjects, including *De l'enseignement public au point de vue de l'université, de la commune, et de l'Etat* (1856) and *De l'education dans la démocratie* (1883). (*Dictionnaire de Biographie Française.*)

Miss Dowling has not been identified.

Francis George Shaw (1809–1882) was a wealthy Bostonian who had moved to Staten Island in 1846. He married his cousin Sarah Blake Sturgis. Their children were Anna, who married George William Curtis; Josephine, who married Charles Russell Lowell and became a noted philanthropist and reformer; and Robert Gould Shaw, who commanded the 54th Massachusetts regiment and was killed in 1863.

8. *Journal des Débats* was a liberal paper, edited at the time of Garrison's letter by Edouard-François Bertin (1797–1871).

9. Nikolai Ivanovitch Turgenev has been identified in the letter to Helen E. Garrison, May 24, 1867; his wife has not been otherwise identified.

10. Charles Follen (1796–1840) was born in Germany but immigrated to the United States, becoming the first professor of German literature at Harvard University. Both he and his wife, Eliza Lee Cabot Follen, were active in abolition and other reforms. He died in the fire on the steamer *Lexington.*

11. The *China* was built for the Cunard Company in 1862 and saw service on that line until 1880. Historically the ship is of more than routine interest, since it was the first of the Cunard screw steamers, which were much more efficient than the earlier paddle steamers. (Frank E. Dodman, *Ships of the Cunard Line,* London, 1955, pp. 38, 41.)

12. John A. Whipple (1837–1893) was a Boston photographer with a business address at 267 Washington Street and a residence in Cambridge. (Obituary, Boston *Transcript,* June 5, 1893; Boston city directory, 1867.)

13. Garrison refers to Thomas Bradford Drew (1834–1898), a friend of his sons George and Frank, in whose diary he is frequently mentioned. This is the same person to whom Garrison wrote on April 25, 1861 (micro.), thanking him for sending bouquets of mayflowers from Plymouth. Drew was a dentist who began practice in 1852 but disliked the profession and had virtually given it up by 1868. At the time of the present letter he had a wife, Mary, and a small daughter. His diaries, preserved at the Massachusetts Historical Society, record his admiration for Garrison and his interest in the antislavery movement.

14. Francis Jackson Garrison notes the receipt of these letters, which have apparently not been preserved. (FJG, June 3, 1867.)

15. Apparently Garrison refers to Ebenezer Withington Thwing (1806–1883), who owned a variety store in Springfield, Mass. (See *Letters,* IV, 594, n. 2.)

16. George A. Simmons (1808–1884) from Keene, N.H., had developed a method for refining whale oil. His wife was Belinda P. Simmons (died 1891). The family lived next door to the Garrisons at the corner of Highland and Cedar streets. (Obituaries, Boston *Post,* February 28, 1884, and Boston *Evening Transcript,* December 10, 1891.)

17. Cervantes, *Don Quixote,* Part II, Book iii, chapter 10.

204

TO RICHARD D. WEBB

Hotel du pont de l'Europe, 17 Rue de Turin,
Paris, June 9, 1867.

My dear friend Webb:

It was not till some days ago that I received your letter of April last, (sent I believe to the care of Mr. May,) with its fraternal greeting and hospitable overture, anticipatory of my arrival in England. Yesterday Mr. [Frederick W.] Chesson sent me yours of the 19th ultimo, addressed to his care at London, and couched in a similar spirit. Thanking you warmly for both, and fully reciprocating the kind expressions contained in them, I can only say, now, that it is my intention to go to London next Saturday, accompanied by my daughter and son, (Fanny and Frank,) and to remain in England some five or six weeks; then to return to Paris, and go with them to Switzerland till the last week in August, when it will be necessary for me to come back to this city to attend the Anti-Slavery Conference at that time; then to visit the Rhine and various parts of Germany; and then possibly have two or three additional weeks left for England before sailing from Liverpool for Boston, about the middle of October.

It was my calculation when I left home to return on the first of September; but my children so strongly urge me to remain till the 15th of October, in order that I may see something more of Europe, that I have consented to do so, provided I continue to receive good news from Boston in regard to my wife's health and spirits. Moreover, my children promise to accompany me home, if I will prolong the time of my visit here.

It is now twenty-seven years, almost to a day, since I had the pleasure and good fortune to make your acquaintance, and that of our esteemed friend James Haughton, at the World's Anti-Slavery Convention in London, in 1840.[1] How much has grown out of it since that time, bearing upon the Anti-Slavery cause and the abolition of slavery in the United States! It has bound us very closely together in the ties of a pure friendship, through all the changes and vicissitudes of a long protracted and desperate struggle. Happily, we continue to this day, and are permitted to see one of the most marvellous as well as one of the most beneficent displays of Divine Power ever yet witnessed on earth. Our meeting together cannot fail to revive many delightful reminiscences.

At what time I shall visit Dublin, I cannot now determine, nor how many days I can remain when I come. I shall certainly be glad to break bread with you at your table; but as my daughter and son will be with me, I cannot think, for a moment, of quartering ourselves upon you, even for a day. If we could hire a couple of bedrooms *pro tempore*, it would suit us in preference to going to a hotel. I do not think we shall visit any other place in Ireland. I wish to spend as much of our time in Scotland as possible, seeing old friends, the Lake scenery, &c.

It will give me very great pleasure to see at your house, or elsewhere, dear Miss [Mary A.] Estlin, for her own sake, and that of her beloved and lamented father.[2] She has proved herself to be a true friend and a most efficient coadjutor ever since we knew each other. Let me here say, that I was equally surprised and grieved at the tone of a letter she sent last Spring to my friend J. M. McKim, concerning George Thompson, and his return to his native land, after so long, so unpremeditated, and so unavoidable an absence from his family. If I know anybody in the world to the heart's core, it is G. T.; and no one is more wrapt up in my affection, confidence and esteem than himself. Whatever failings he may be thought to possess, as a modest, unselfish, uncomplaining, unobtrusive, yet devoted, eloquent and successful advocate of enslaved and suffering humanity, he commands my gratitude and admiration to the fullest extent. Who, in the final struggle, did so much for the abolition of West India slavery as himself by his irresistible popular appeals? Who but he first grappled with the nefarious Apprenticeship system, and in the face of even Anti-Slavery opposition (in certain quarters) succeeded in bringing it to an end?[3] Was he not equally successful in his onslaught upon that colossal monopoly, the old East India Company?[4] Who labored more disinterestedly or more efficiently for the repeal of the Corn Laws than himself?[5] And who can measure the results of his toils, and sacrifices, and perils in the United States, to break the fetters of the millions now happily delivered from their house of bondage? I know of no living man who has made his life more resplendent in the service of mankind.

Yours, with the highest esteem,

Wm. Lloyd Garrison.

Richard D. Webb.

ALS: Garrison Papers, Boston Public Library.

Richard Davis Webb (1805–1872) was a charming and witty Dublin printer who advocated temperance, abolition, and nonresistance. By birth a Quaker, he left the Society of Friends when it proved too conservative for his activities as reformer. Webb and his wife, Hannah (1809–1862), also an abolitionist, were among Garrison's best British friends. Webb was the author of the *Life and Letters of Captain John Brown* (1861). (*Life; Letters*, II, 684, n. 1.)

1. James Haughton (1795–1873), a Dublin corn and flour merchant, was active in many reforms, such as temperance, peace, education, and the abolition of slavery and of capital punishment. The founder of the Hibernian Anti-Slavery Society in 1837, he was a loyal Garrisonian. (Letter to the editor from C. Duncan Rice, Yale University, June 2, 1970.)

2. John Bishop Estlin (1785–1855), a prominent English ophthalmic surgeon and reformer, had been a strong advocate of abolition, temperance, education for the impoverished, religious toleration, and the suppression of medical frauds.

3. Garrison refers to the provision in the 1833 act abolishing slavery in the British West Indies, by which slaves were bound, under a system of apprenticeship, to work part-time for their masters during a period of seven years.

4. Thompson had been in India as an agent of the British India Society investigating land reform and Indian labor at a time when British affairs in India were under the jurisdiction of the East India Company. During his sojourn there he espoused the cause of the Rajah of Sattara. Thompson's reports were published in the *British Friend* between May 31, 1843, and January 31, 1844. (Letter to the editor from C. Duncan Rice, March 10, 1971.)

5. As a member of the Anti-Corn-Law League, Thompson was associated with Cobden in advocating the elimination of the tax on corn imported from abroad.

205

TO SAMUEL MAY, JR.

Paris, June 11, 1867,
17 Rue de Turin.

My dear friend May:

I have not ceased deeply regretting, since I left home, the great discomfort and exposure to which my unspeakably beloved Anti-Slavery co-workers and warm personal friends were subjected by the violent rain-storm at the time of the sailing of the Cuba; and the unflinching manner in which they went through it all, and the affectionate demonstrations made by them up to the last moment of our final separation, cause a moistening of the eyes as often as I recall the scene. Especially did I regret the impossibility of collecting our company together in the saloon of the Cuba, and carrying out the programme as originally intended by the Committee of Arrangements; but the violence of the rain forced an indiscriminate huddling together of passengers and visitors in utter disregard of relationship and purpose; and, wedged in inextricably, in vain did Mr. [Robert C.] Waterston, and a few other friends who were near us, essay to force a passage through, and to join those who were anxiously waiting for our appearance, though we knew not where to find them. It was a scene of utter confusion, and threw a "wet blanket" upon the perfect enjoyment of the occasion. I felt the most poignant regret that I could not take by the hand, and give the parting adieu to every one who so kindly came to evince their friendship and esteem, especially yourself, the Chapmans and Westons, Judge [Thomas] Russell, and others I need not mention. As to the "Testimonial," Mr. Waterston did all that was possible under the circumstances, in a brief but tender expression of feeling and sentiment toward me on the part of the contributors; to which I could make only a hurried and very inadequate reply.[1] I was very glad that Mr. Thompson was so fortunate as to come in the tug-boat to the Cuba with the great body of the friends, and was sorry indeed that I was not equally fortunate. Nevertheless, the scene was thrilling to us both, as we sailed down the harbor, to see how bravely our friends in that little vessel bore "the peltings of the pitiless storm,"[2] in following after us as long as it was proper; and our hearts beat high with pleasure and gratitude at such a loving demonstration. I fear some of the ladies got badly drenched, but I trust none were made ill by the exposure. God bless them all!

I have now been in Paris three weeks, our voyage across the Atlantic proving an uncommonly swift and smooth one, enabling me to reach this city in eleven days from Boston, besides stopping an entire day in Liverpool. Under the guidance of Mr. Villard, (who is as familiar with Paris as I am with Boston,) I have been enabled to see almost everything that is specially notable in this truly wonderful city; and my organ of marvellousness has had a chance to be largely developed. It is said, on all hands, that, within the last twelve years, Paris has been essentially changed, almost recreated, through the imperial will and magnificent resources of the Emperor; so that there is no city like unto it for the number, breadth and extent of its splendid boulevards and streets, the grandeur and height of its buildings, the multiplicity and beauty of its parks and gardens and galleries of paintings and statuary, all freely opened to the people, who know how to appreciate and enjoy them. It is a city in which pleasure and sensualism, enjoyment and restraint, splendor and display, commingle to the fullest extent, making everything "gay and festive," and at the same time without any collision or disorder. The French people appear to be uniformly sociable, polite and amiable, and the lower classes incomparably better behaved than our own. They seem almost literally to live in the streets, doing almost all their eating out of doors, and knowing nothing of home and its sacredness. Though every body drinks wine or beer, it does not seem to intoxicate as with us, and must have a very small per cent. of alcohol in it; as, out of hundreds of thousands of persons I have seen, only three or four have been visibly intoxicated and not one of these badly so. Of course, I adhere to my total abstinence principles as in the United States, and have not tested the quality of what is here universally drank, even by a single sip. In this I am a *rara avis.*

I have been many times to the Great Exposition but have not yet seen half that may be found within its vast area. It surpasses all power of description.

On Saturday I go to London, to be accompanied by Fanny and Frank, and to remain in England about six weeks; then we shall go to Switzerland, whence I shall return the last week in August to Paris, to attend the Anti-Slavery Conference; then go to the Rhine, to Munich, &c.; expecting to reach home about the 1st of November.

Your affectionate and indebted friend,

Wm. Lloyd Garrison.

P.S. Give my kindest regards to your dear wife and children, and to your revered father and mother, and family.

☞ In case you have occasion to write to me, (and a letter from you would give me great pleasure,) send to the care of F. W. Chesson, office of the Morning Star, London.

☞ My health has very much improved, and my arm gives me no trouble. I have had very pleasant interviews with M. Tourgueneff and M. Laboulaye, and expect to see M. Cochin in a day or two.

☞ Americans here feel very indignant that Horace Greeley should have gone bail for Jefferson Davis.[3] What next?

☞ One reason for my remaining longer than I originally intended is, to have the pleasure of taking Fanny home with me on a visit to her mother.

☞ I continue to hear good news from home concerning dear wife's health and spirits.

ALS: Garrison Papers, Boston Public Library.

1. Robert C. Waterston reported on the success of the national testimonial, saying that $30,000 "had been collected and placed to his credit." (*Life,* IV, 190.)

2. Shakespeare, *King Lear,* III, iv, 29, adapted.

3. Greeley's liberal views and desire for reconciliation between North and South caused him to support the movement for Davis' release and to sign his bond on May 13.

206

TO WILLIAM LLOYD GARRISON, Jr.

Paris, June 14, 1867.

My dear William:

In the morning we (i. e., Fanny, Frank and myself) take the train for London, hoping to arrive there by 9 or 10 o'clock at night; though the route we have selected (via Rouen and Dieppe) is the longest and the most uncertain one, owing to the greater distance across the Channel. But we shall thereby save, collectively, some eighteen or nineteen dollars in gold; and this is a consideration not to be despised in these days of exorbitant prices, even though it may put us to some discomfort for a few additional hours. Mr. [George] Thompson has engaged lodgings for us at 22 Southampton Street, Bloomsbury; but, by the time this reaches you, we shall probably have left London for other parts of the kingdom. Until further advised, however, letters had better be directed to us to the care of F. W. Chesson, office of the Morning Star, London, who will see that they are duly forwarded. As yet, I have no definite programme laid out; but think it not unlikely that we shall go to Scotland about the 1st of July, and remain there a fortnight; say a week in Edinburgh, three or four days in Glasgow, and then make a quick tour of the Highlands. I have received two or three letters from dear Richard D. Webb, warmly expressive of his old and unabated friendship, and insisting upon our accepting his hospitality when we visit Dublin. Possibly we may make that our last visit before returning home, and so go to Cork, and take the Liverpool steamer at Queenstown. We shall endeavor to get back to Paris about the 25th of July; so that after the 10th of July, letters had better be addressed to the care of Bowles, Drevet & Co., 24 Rue de la Paix, Paris, as hitherto.

I have also received two letters from our old friend, William Robson, London, as cordial and affectionate and complimentary as though there had been no difference of opinion between us about the war and the rebellion in America, and offering us his hospitality and all possible attentions during our stay in the city.[1] I have, however, declined all overtures as to quartering ourselves upon any family, not wishing to interfere with family usages in our constant moving about to see "the sights"; and therefore got Mr. Thompson to engage us lodgings, that we might be *ad libitum* in all our goings. Of course, we shall visit Mr. Robson's home, and break bread with him and his wife; and also, as he says he is entirely at leisure, accept now and then his proffered good services in showing us about the great metropolis. It is pleasant indeed to know that he is in such a fraternal state of mind.

Two or three days ago, I wrote a letter to M. Cochin, expressive of my admiration of his character and works in relation to Slavery and the Results of Emancipation, and my desire to have an interview with him, if agreeable, before leaving Paris for London. He immediately wrote a very cordial note in reply, and then drove in his carriage a long distance to our hotel, and sent up to me his card, with the letter. As I happened to be all alone, (Harry, Fanny and Frank having gone out to take a walk,) I could not read his letter, which was written in French; and as the servant who brought me the letter and card could not understand a word of English, I could not make any response; and so M. Cochin had to drive home without seeing me! He left an invitation to have me take breakfast with him the next morning, and Harry at my request went along with me to act as my interpreter. We were very heartily received; but though Cochin, I am assured, can speak very well in English, yet his diffidence was apparently so great about it that he chose to carry on the conversation wholly in French, talking with great fluency and animation, Harry interpreting what he said as he went along. We stopped only twenty or thirty minutes, declining to take the breakfast which we saw spread in another room, though he assured us that his wife (whom we did not see, as she probably expected to see me at breakfast) could speak English readily.[2] Cochin is in the prime of life, has a fine countenance, and in his manners is a finished gentleman, as well as one of the most eminent men in France for his literary and scientific ability. His family descent is old and high.

This forenoon Mr. Chamerovzow, Secretary of the British and Foreign A. S. Society, called to see me, and I am to take tea with him and his family this evening, to confer about the Anti-Slavery Convention here in August.[3] He was very cordial; and stated that his wife is an invalid from paralysis of the left side, precisely as is your mother. I like his appearance and address.

Harry has drawn on you for $800 in gold, at [thirty] days' sight, in my behalf, and on the strength of the letter of credit given to me in Boston by Brevet, Drevet & Co.[4] on their firm here—the 5-20 bond I brought with me remaining untouched for future emergencies. Choose your time for buying the gold within the period named; and, if necessary, consult Mr. [Samuel] May [Jr.] or Mr. [William] Endicott [Jr.]. Don't fail to have the obligation promptly met, I pray you. Good bye!

Your loving father,

W. L. G.

P.S. I am feeling and looking very well, and so are Fanny and Frank. Harry has a touch of his old enemy, the neuralgia. Mrs. [Eliza M.] Eddy called to see us yesterday, in good condition. She has concluded to sail from Liverpool on the 6th of July instead of the 22d. She is going to London in a few days. Mr. and Mrs. [Benjamin] Snow have gone to Switzerland.

☞ Tell your mother I love her dearly—Ellie and Agnes ditto. . Love to George and all inquiring friends.

ALS: Garrison Papers, Boston Public Library; partly printed in *Life*, IV, 192.

1. William Robson (c. 1805–1892), the youngest son of the Robert Robsons of Warrington, was postmaster of the town during the 1840s and 1850s and was active in various reforms, including abolition and temperance. His wife, Margaret, was also an abolitionist. The Garrisons visited the Robson house in London on June 19. (*Letters*, IV, 552, n. 1; FJG, June 19, 1867.)

It is not known how Garrison and Robson differed over the Civil War.

2. Mme. Cochin has not been identified.

3. Louis Alexis Chamerovzow (died c. 1876) was the successor to John Scoble as secretary of the British and Foreign Anti-Slavery Society, which had issued the call to the World's Anti-Slavery Convention in 1840. (See *Letters*, IV, 310, n. 1.)

4. Garrison mistakes the name of Bowles, Drevet & Co.

---

2 0 7

TO RICHARD D. WEBB

(Private.)

Paris, June 14, 1867.

My dear Friend:

I am greatly obliged to you for your frank and explanatory letter in regard to our friends G. T. [George Thompson] and M. E. [Mary A. Estlin]; but I did not mean to put you to the trouble of sending a reply to what I wrote *en passant*, and what, of course, I meant to be between ourselves. My appreciation of Miss E. has been very strong from the time I formed her acquaintance; and the warm eulogy you bestow upon her for her many virtues, and the eminent service she rendered the Anti-Slavery cause for so long a period in the United States, I heartily endorse. I am sure she would not do intentional injustice to any person, living or dead; but I am also as sure that she does not properly appreciate the labors, sacrifices, and real merits of G. T.; though I very well understand why it is some of his habits and peculiarities are not to her taste, and therefore lead her to underestimate his true worth. It was the expression, in her letter to Mr. [J. Miller] McKim, of the hope that G. T. had left England for good, and that he would not return again, that particularly excited my surprise and hurt my feelings; especially in view of the fact that he was in exile from his wife and children as a matter of pecuniary necessity, and in order to procure the means to "keep the wolf from the door."[1] No person better knows the infirmities of G. T. than I do; and he has never found me backward in giving both expostulation and advice. Yet I know how to make a wide margin of allowance for him, without compromising any principle, or lowering the standard of personal character. He has a very susceptible temperament which carries his spirit to starry heights or sinks it to abysmal depths; in moral heroism he is a giant, in self-reliance a child; he craves and needs the sympathies of his friends; and deserves them too, for many reasons; he is, and in his utter unselfishness is always likely to be, poor in this world's goods, and as age is advancing upon him he is liable to fits of depression, not knowing what he had better do, and unwilling to trouble even those in whom he most confides with any of his concerns. Unfitted for business, his thoughts are continually in the interests of mankind; and though not born for a leader, he was born to labor in the broad field of humanity and reform, where he would get but inadequate remuneration, and, consequently, need occasional pecuniary assistance. I know that there is a prevalent idea in England that he is improvident—in other words, that he is "regardless of money," as you say. But I think that injustice is done him in this particular. I have been his guest for weeks at a time; and I have never seen a table set with more habitual frugality. He makes no personal display and indulges in no personal extravagance that I know of, his habits being simple and his wants few, he studiously shunning all fashionable and costly society. In America he has been very economical and saving, so as to be able to make regular remittances for the support of his wife and unmarried daughter [Edith]. He always had a very moderate income in England, yet by his personal conspicuity and position as a philanthropist and reformer was necessarily subjected to incidental expenses that helped to keep his purse quite empty. Where, or when, he has manifested any recklessness in the use of his means,—allowing him any scope for the generosity of his nature,— others may know, but I do not.

The suggestion made by Mr. McKim to Miss E., in regard to employing G. T. to deliver lectures in behalf of the Freedmen's cause in various parts of the Kingdom, was certainly well meant, however useless or impracticable it might be; and it need not have been declined in a manner to wound the sensibility of any one. Mr. McKim sent me Miss E's letter, without note or comment; so I do not know how he felt about it. Of course, G. T. knows nothing of the matter, nor will any thing be said to him on the subject.

As to G. T.'s lecturing appointments in America, he has observed them with commendable fidelity, except in one or two cases, when the miserable state of his health justified the failure. All last fall and winter, he had to abandon the lecturing field on that account, though very desirous of turning every possible penny; thus losing several thousand dollars. I assure you that his mental and physical prostration was so great as to give us all great uneasiness. But enough.

It shall be as you wish concerning our acceptance of the hospitality proffered by you and your son,[2] when we come to Dublin; of which coming you shall be duly apprised. You are irresistable!

In the morning we shall be off for London.

Yours, "through thick and thin,"

Wm. Lloyd Garrison.

R. D. Webb.

☞ Don't bother yourself about replying to this.

ALS: Garrison Papers, Boston Public Library.

1. Garrison uses an expression that can be traced back to fifteenth-century England.

2. Alfred Webb (1834–1908) was a good friend of Garrison's. It was Webb who had accompanied him to have his daguerreotype taken in Dublin in October 1846. Webb was to visit the United States in 1872 and spend some time with the Garrisons at Rockledge. (*Life.*)

---

2 0 8

TO S. ALFRED STEINTHAL

Huntly Lodge,
Edinburgh, July 15, 1867.

Dear Mr. Steinthal:

Thanks for your letter of the 10th inst. The reading of it caused equal amusement, surprise, and regret—the regret having reference to the annoyance caused good Dr. Gottheil[1] by the ludicrous perversion of the term I used, "Fourth of Ju-liars," (not *Jew*-liars,) in my remarks at the Manchester banquet, by such of his people as were not present. I am thus admonished that it is a hazardous thing to indulge in punning! As soon as I received your letter, I sent an explanatory note to Dr. G., showing that, so far from having cast any imputation upon Jewish veracity, I was "an Israelite indeed, in whom there was no guile,"[2] in the matter referred to, and that they were those who professed to be Christians to whom my criticism was applied. I have given him liberty to publish my note in any way he may think best.

I was very sorry that we were deprived of the pleasure of your company at the dinner in Manchester. The reception extended to me was indeed a most hearty and generous one. A similar welcome, in the form of a soiree, was given me at Newcastle-upon-Tyne; and another in this city on Friday evening. A public breakfast is to be given me in Glasgow on Friday or Saturday of this week. Such congratulations, commendations and honors are quite too much for me. Instead of expanding, I am shrivelling all up! In another point of view, however, I feel greatly to rejoice; and that is, the promotion of peace and good will between England and the United States by this interchange of fraternal sentiments.

Proffering my warmest regards to your wife and children, I remain,

Your attached friend,

Wm. Lloyd Garrison.

Rev. S. A. Steinthal.

ALS: Garrison Papers, Boston Public Library. Inasmuch as the manuscript has a number of revisions, it may be a rough draft and not the recipient's copy.

S. Alfred Steinthal (1826–1910) was the son of a German emigrant who had become a British subject. He was trained for the ministry at Manchester New College, thereafter serving as minister at Bridgewater as well as in domestic mission work. In 1852 he married the daughter of the Reverend Franklin Haworth. Since 1864 he had been the Unitarian minister at the Cross Street Church in Manchester. He was active in many reforms, including antivivisection, the establishment of Sunday schools, female suffrage, and temperance. Between 1866 and 1884 he was secretary of the section of the Social Science Association concerned with economy and trade. (Brian Harrison, *Dictionary of British Temperance Biography*, [Coventry] 1973, p. 117.)

1. Gustav Gottheil (1827–1903) was born in a part of Prussia that is now Poland. The product of Jewish schools in Posen, he later attended the universities of Berlin and Bonn, receiving his Ph.D. degree. In 1855 he became assistant rabbi of the Berlin congregation, and in 1861 became rabbi of the Congregation of British Jews in Manchester. After thirteen years in that post he came to New York City to be assistant to Dr. Samuel Adler of Temple Emanuel. Active in community affairs of all sorts, he worked not only for Jewish schools and organizations but also to improve interfaith understanding. He was, for instance, vice president of the Nineteenth Century Club and a leading member of the Unitarian Club. He wrote several books and many articles published in the *North American Review* and the *Unitarian Review*. (Obituary, *Jewish Chronicle*, May 1, 1903.)

2. John 1:47.

2 0 9

TO ELIZABETH PEASE NICHOL

Glasgow, July 23, 1867.

My very dear friend:

We have had a most hospitable reception at the beautiful and romantic residence of A. F. Stoddard, Esq., Bloomfield, Port Glasgow, about 18 miles from this city, on the Clyde, and four miles from Greenock.[1] To-morrow, at 9 o'clock, A. M., we shall take the train for London direct, hoping to arrive safely there by 10, P. M. How long we may remain in London, or whether Frank and I will go to Paris until the last of August, we cannot now decide, because every thing is uncertain about the movements of Mr. Villard, in consequence of the serious illness of his father at Munich. If we get no word from him to the contrary, we all expect to leave for Paris on Monday next. You shall be duly apprised of the decision we may make. In the mean time, all letters for me may be addressed to F. W. Chesson, Star Office, London.

You will have seen, ere this, by the Glasgow papers that have been sent to you, how cordial has been the welcome given to me by the friends of freedom and progress here. Language is too weak to express my feelings in view of the kind and generous treatment which I have everywhere received since I came from Paris. But I cannot and will not appropriate to myself one hundredth part of the laudation which has been so liberally showered upon me.

The address presented to me at the public breakfast on Friday morning was written and read by Rev. Dr. Anderson, and was a very marked expression of his respect for my character and high appreciation of my Anti-Slavery labors.[2] It yet remains for any representative of the American church or clergy to bestow any commendation upon my career, or to speak approvingly of the Anti-Slavery movement. Of course, in view of the past, it is hardly to be expected.

It is very comforting to me, my beloved friend, to think that my visit to this country,—though made for another purpose, that is, for recreation, social visiting, and the restoration of my health,—promises to be productive of good in various unforeseen directions, to encourage and stimulate the work of reform on the broadest scale, and especially to strengthen the ties of amity between England and America. Thanks to you, and to such as you, for opening the way for me to be both seen and heard. Without such co-operation, I could have done little or nothing.

Now that I have been to Huntly Lodge, enjoyed your hospitality, and communed with you on various subjects, and yet have had to leave so soon, the whole seems almost like a pleasant dream. It was very hard to say "farewell" to you, lest it might be forever on earth; but I will cherish the hope that we may meet again before my return to the United States; nay, that you will accompany me thither.

I have had an urgent invitation to visit Bradford, and receive the congratulations of its people in a public manner—W. E. Forster, M. P., being expected to preside.

I have also been invited to attend a mammoth gathering of the National Temperance League, at the Crystal Palace, on the 3rd of September,—as well as meetings at Birmingham and elsewhere.[3]

These invitations I am unable to accept, until my travelling programme on the Continent is decided upon.

It has been very dismal wet weather since we came here. We are going back to London without seeing anything of the Highlands or of the Lake scenery at Windermere, &c., as we cannot wait for fair weather any longer.

Fanny and Frank send you their most affectionate regards. Mine you have had ever since I knew you.

With my benediction, yours,

Wm. Lloyd Garrison.

Elizabeth Pease Nichol.

P.S. A letter has just been received from you, enclosing one sent to you for me. I suppose you received one from Fanny yesterday.

ALS: Garrison Papers, Boston Public Library.

1. Arthur Francis Stoddard (born 1810) was the son of Solomon Stoddard (1771–1860) and Sarah Tappan Stoddard (1771–1852), the sister of Arthur and Lewis Tappan. In 1840 Stoddard married Frances E. Noble (born 1821) of Williamstown, Mass., and the couple had eight children. (Elijah W. Stoddard, *Anthony Stoddard of Boston, Mass., and his Descendants: A Genealogy*, New York, 1865, pp. 83, 86–87; letter to the editor from Anthony J. J. McNeill, local history librarian, Greenock, Scotland, September 26, 1974.)

2. William Anderson (1800–1872), who was born in Kilsyth and educated at Glasgow University, had since 1822 been the minister of the John Street Church, where he had acquired a considerable reputation as a preacher. He was an active reformer. Despite his own low opinion of popery he became a strong supporter of the Catholic Emancipation bill. He also agitated for abolition in the West Indies. (Andrew Aird, *Glimpses of Old Glasgow*, Glasgow, 1894.)

Excerpts from Anderson's address, Garrison's reply, and other details of the public breakfast may be found in the Edinburgh *Scotsman*, July 20, 1867.

3. The National Temperance League was formed in 1856 by the merger of the National Temperance Society and the London Temperance League. Especially active in the league were William Tweedie and John Phillips, honorary secretaries, and Sir Charles Trevelyan, the first president, the latter being succeeded in 1862 by Quaker businessman Samuel Bowly, and the former by Robert Rae as full-time secretary. The league shunned party politics and religious peculiarities and urged total abstinence. (Murray Hyslop, *Lest We Forget: The Rae Memorial Lecture 1931*, London, 1931, pp. 10–11, 15.)

The Crystal Palace, the huge glass and iron edifice designed by Joseph Paxton for the Great Exhibition of 1851, had been built originally on Hyde Park but removed and reconstructed in 1854 on a site just outside the southern boundary of the county of London. The remnant of the building, which was almost totally burned in 1936, was removed in 1940. (Stuart Rossiter, ed., *London*, London, 1965.)

210

TO OLIVER JOHNSON

22 Southampton Street, Bloomsbury, W. C.
London, July 30, 1867.

My dear Johnson:

Ever since the receipt of your welcome letter, I have been intending to send you a reply; but I have been in such a whirl of engagements, and had so many things to attend to, so many notes and epistles to respond to here, so many social and public gatherings to participate in, so many personal calls to make, so many to call upon me, so many "sights" to see, so much travel to go through, &c., &c., that I have been defrauded of a good deal of sleep, as well as very busily occupied. Strange to say, that, notwithstanding all this, my health has very much improved since I left home, so that wherever I go, I am repeatedly told by those whom I met during my visit in 1846, that I do not appear to have grown a day older, and that they "find no change in me" on the score of personal appearance! It is my baldness, however, that looks as young as it is did twenty-one years ago; "only this, and nothing more."[1] Nevertheless, I am really looking and feeling much better than I did when I left home; and if I receive no pull-back, I shall return very generally improved in "the outer man." My right shoulder still feels very tender and sensitive about the socket, but it causes me no acute pain; and I trust will have suffered no permanent injury by my falls.

I was glad to hear that your meetings at Longwood went off so satisfactorily. Where free speech is allowed, there are so many unbalanced and erratic spirits likely to turn up, that it is unavoidably ever a hazardous "running for luck"; for

"License they mean when they cry liberty."[2]

You will see, by the newspapers I have forwarded to you from time to time, in what a cordial and handsome manner I have been received in London, Manchester, Newcastle, Edinburgh and Glasgow. As I have steadily refused to lecture, or to speak at any popular gathering, these breakfasts, tea parties, soirees, &c., have been devised as methods to bring together a considerable number of repre-sentative men and women; but none of them have been of my seek-ing. On the contrary, I have studiously sought to avoid all observation, and, as far as practicable, to "keep in the quiet," seek-ing rest and recreation; yet, in spite of all my precaution, I have had very little of these, but a good deal of excitement and fatigue to en-counter; for I could not well refuse to receive welcome and congrat-ulation in the social, though somewhat public manner in which these have been so generously extended to me. If I had the weak-ness to aim at conspicuity and securing popular applause at this time, there is not a city, town or village in the Kingdom that would not readily give me a most friendly reception; but I am sure you know me too well to suppose that I wish for anything of the kind, and can readily imagine how trying it has been to me (even pro-longed Anti-Slavery martyrdom) to receive such an outpouring of panegyric for my Anti-Slavery labors, though coming from those who mean not to flatter, and whose good opinions any man might be proud of.

We (Fanny, Frank and myself) had a charming time in Edin-burgh, especially under the roof and at the beautiful residence of our dear friend Elizabeth Pease Nichol. You will see that an ex-traordinary mark of respect was paid to me by the Lord Provost and Councillors in formally presenting me with "the freedom of the city," for it is seldom bestowed even upon the highest dignitaries.[3] The last one that received it before me was the Duke of Edinburgh, Prince Alfred;[4] and the one before him was Lord Palmerston.[5] John Hampden had it conferred on him in his day.[6] Some twenty years ago, George Thompson had the same honor vouchsafed to him—a remarkable coincidence in our Anti-Slavery career, considering that I am American by birth. The tea party given by the Ladies' Emancipation Society was a very enjoyable affair, not less than two hundred persons being present.[7] Mrs. Nichol during our stay spared no exertion to show us all that was specially deserving our observation (a great deal) in and around the city, and to make us feel entirely at home.

In Glasgow, also, we had a very warm greeting, and enjoyed the elegant hospitality of Arthur F. Stoddard, Esq., a native of North-ampton, Mass., and a nephew of Arthur Tappan, and once a clerk in his store. Our friends, Andrew Paton and William Smeal, were spe-cially attentive to us.[8] Unfortunately, all the time we remained, the weather was very dismal—cold, foggy, dirty, and the rain falling more or less heavily; so that we were compelled to come back to

London without making the tour of the Highlands. This was a serious disappointment.

We expected to have gone this week to Switzerland, but I have concluded to remain in England until near the time for holding the Anti-Slavery Conference in Paris, the last week in August, and make the Switzerland excursion in September. I shall probably visit Birmingham, Bradford, Leeds, &c., there to receive friendly greetings, and with special reference to promoting subscriptions in behalf of the Freedmen's cause.

I have felt the deepest sympathy for your dear wife in her serious illness at Rockledge, and regret to hear that she has not yet recovered her usual health. It is possible that at this time of writing, she may be at our house giving her good company to Helen. Wherever she is, convey to her my heartfelt appreciation of her intended kindness in the matter of companionship for wife, and hope they both will be able to pass many pleasant days together.

It is not probable, now, that I shall sail for home before the 26th of October; and yet, as Fanny will not be able to accompany [me] as she expected, on account of the illness of Mr. Villard's father [Gustav L. Hilgard], it is possible I may do so in September. Mr. V. arrived here last evening from Paris, in order to consult with us about our future movements.

I send this by the hand of a friend, who leaves immediately. With the warmest remembrances to Theodore [Tilton] and wife, Mrs. [Augustus] Savin, &c., I remain,

Yours, most affectionately,

Wm. Lloyd Garrison

Oliver Johnson.

P.S. The person by whom I expected to send this hastily written letter has suddenly left, but I may be able to get it to him at Queenstown, *en route* to New York.

George Thompson is at present taking a little recreation in the neighborhood of Leeds, at the residence of his cousin, Mr. Donisthorpe.[9] He has been very poorly nearly all the time he has been at home, but writes that he is recuperating. Nevertheless, I take very little encouragement from this; for I think his constitution is much shattered, and that he will never be able vigorously to say, "Richard's himself again."[10] His wife is also a good deal broken, and feels the death of Herbert very keenly. What Mr. T. will do, or thinks of doing, for the future, whether to remain on this side of the Atlantic or to return to the United States, I do not know. Here, even if his health were much better than it is, there seems to be nothing that he can do by way of remunerative employment; and I fear that he could do little in the lecturing field, if he should go back to our country. It is very sad.

I am gratified to learn that the Court at Boston has decided in giving the remainder of Francis Jackson's Anti-Slavery bequest exclusively to the Freedmen's cause, because it seems to me the best disposal of the money.

I now and then see a copy of the *Independent,* and notice the ground that has been taken against it by Rev. Edward H. Beecher and other orthodox clergymen, on the ground that it is not sufficiently sectarian and denominational but I trust there will be no faltering in its "independent" course, and no fettering its free and earnest spirit in the advocacy of truth and duty as revealed day by day.[11] Has a new opposition journal yet been started at the West?

I also, now and then, see a copy of the *Anti-Slavery Standard. The Nation* I do not see at all.

It will give me great joy to turn my face homeward as soon as practicable. My thoughts are continually with my dear crippled wife, and I am anxious to be by her side.

ALS: Garrison Papers, Boston Public Library.

1. Edgar Allan Poe, "The Raven," stanza 1, line 6.

2. John Milton, "On the Detraction Which Followed Upon My Writing Certain Treatises," line 11.

3. The Lord Provost of Edinburgh at this time was William Chambers (1800–1883), who had built up a successful publishing business with his brother Robert. Their firm produced inexpensive and useful tracts and compilations of information, as well as a ten-volume encyclopedia. Chambers visited the United States and published *Things as They Are in America* (1854) and *American Slavery and Colour* (1857). He was chosen Lord Provost in 1865 and held the position for three years. (*Oliver and Boyd's New Edinburgh Almanac and National Repository,* Edinburgh, 1867.)

4. Prince Alfred Ernest Albert (1844–1900), second son of Queen Victoria, who had also been duke of Edinburgh since May 1866, followed a career in the Royal Navy, ultimately rising to the rank of Admiral of the Fleet. In 1862 he had been elected king of Greece, but he refused the throne. (*Burke's Peerage and Baronetage,* London, 1975.)

5. Henry John Temple, third Viscount Palmerston (1784–1865), early a member of Parliament, had been associated with a series of governmental administrations, his reputation having been chiefly established in the Foreign Office as foreign minister. In 1855 he became Prime Minister, an office he held, except for a brief hiatus, until his death.

6. John Hampden (1594–1643) was an Oxford graduate and member of Parliament who became famous through his leadership in the fight to eliminate an ancient tax, the "ship-money," which had traditionally been levied on ports and maritime towns during war. He was impeached in 1642 but eluded arrest. He was killed at the battle of Chalgrove Field in 1643.

7. The Edinburgh Ladies' Emancipation Society (founded in 1833 to promote worldwide abolition) gave the tea for Garrison on July 12. (*Edinburgh Ladies' Emancipation Society, Annual Report,* 1861; FJG, July 12, 1867.)

8. Andrew Paton (1805–1884) was a Glasgow abolitionist and associate of William Smeal. He and his sister Catherine were active supporters of the North during the Civil War. (*Life.*)

William Smeal (1793–1877) was a grocer and leading Glasgow reformer. He was secretary of the Glasgow Emancipation Society throughout its history (1833–1875). Smeal had met Garrison in 1840, and he remained a loyal Garrisonian abolitionist. (B. R. Crick and Miriam Alman, eds., *A Guide to Manuscripts Relating to America in Great Britain and Ireland,* London, 1961, p. 501.)

9. George Edmund Donisthorpe lived at Holly Bank, Moor Allerton, Leeds. He was an industrialist who manufactured machine tops and nails and an inventor who was instrumental in perfecting the combing machine for wool. (Letter to the editor from J. M. Collinson, archivist, Leeds City Council, Department of Leisure Services, December 22, 1975.)

10. Colley Cibber, *Richard III,* V, v, 85.

11. During the last several years there had been a growing disagreement between the Beechers and the *Independent.* In 1863 Henry Ward Beecher had been eased out of the editorial chair, and the paper became more political in its orientation. In 1865 Oliver Johnson had replaced Joshua Leavitt as managing editor, thereby shifting the paper's political bias to the left. The following year Henry Ward Beecher's opposition to the paper increased when he supported his sister, Harriet Beecher Stowe, in another controversy, and the *Independent* suspended regular publication of Beecher's sermons. In December 1867 a group of orthodox clergymen met in Chicago to discuss all the problems involved in the controversy and founded a rival paper, the *Advance.* (Donald D. Housley, *"The Independent*: A Study in Religious and Social Opinion, 1848–1870," dissertation, Pennsylvania State University, 1971; Ann Arbor: University Microfilms, 1972, pp. 154–157.)

Although Edward Beecher (1803–1895), to whose name Garrison mistakenly adds the initial "H," was less involved in the controversy with the *Independent* than his brother, he did attend the meeting in Chicago in 1867. After graduating from Yale and studying at Andover Seminary, he became minister of the Park Street Church in Boston. Four years later Beecher moved to the West, where he became prominent as president of Illinois College in Jacksonville; he later returned to Boston, then moved to Galesburg, Ill., where he served as pastor of the First Congregational Church. As early as 1837, when he was one of the chief defenders of the martyred Elijah P. Lovejoy, he had been an active abolitionist. He was the author of a *Narrative of the Alton Riots* (1837) and of several books on theological topics. He spent his last years in Brooklyn near his brother.

211

TO WILLIAM LLOYD GARRISON, JR.

22 Southampton St., Bloomsbury, July 31, 1867.

Dear William:

It is now a week since we returned from Glasgow to London, having been baffled in our expectations of making a Highland tour in consequence of the unpropitious state of the weather. Scarcely any one is aware that I am again in the city, (for I have kept quite secluded,) and, therefore, the callers upon us have been very few. This has enabled me to get some rest, which I very much needed, though I still feel and look somewhat jaded. Miss [Mary A.] Estlin, of Bristol, was with us nearly all the time from Thursday to Monday, when she returned home. It showed how much she wanted to see us all by coming so far expressly for that purpose. On Sunday forenoon I went to hear Rev. Wm. H. Channing preach at Kensington, she accompanying me, being intimately acquainted with him, as he preached last year at Bristol. He is trying to start a Unitarian church in that quarter of London; but I should think he would be entirely discouraged, as we found him with only a baker's dozen for an audience, in a room no larger than our parlor at Rockledge, with chairs to be occupied at that, and with ordinary looking people.[1] A litany was read and recited as long as that used in the Established Church service, and apparently the same; including a specific recognition of the rightful reign of kings and princes, and complimenting "our gracious Queen Victoria and the Royal Family." Think of this for an American, and especially for one claiming to be a reformer! I did not enjoy the services at all.

To oblige Miss Estlin, Fanny and Frank went with her to hear Mr. Channing, but scarcely found an apology for an audience. He is not adapted to make a popular impression, and it seems to me must fail in his present attempt, after a few months. I went to take tea with Mrs. [George] Thompson, (Mr. T. being at Leeds,) and spent the evening with her and Edith. She is feeling very miserably, and has cause to feel so for reasons which I may not here put to paper, but she has my deepest sympathy, and I am now satisfied that she has not had justice done her in regard to home affairs. The future looks very dark for the family; for it is a very serious question what he can and what he will do for a living. Here nothing [is] open to him whatever; and, for various reasons, it is utterly useless to attempt to raise any sort of testimonial in his behalf, or procure any subscriptions. If he returns to the United States, it is very problematical whether in his disabled and broken condition, he can enter [the] lecturing field to any extent, or to popular acceptance and should he go back, there are grave and weighty reasons why he should take Mrs. Thompson and Edith along with him. I am distressed about them. Of course, this is only for the family.

I took cold at Glasgow, and have had a sore throat and hoarseness ever since, though not badly. Fanny and Frank continue to have excellent health. Harry came to us on Monday evening, and we are now having a pleasant time of it all together. He talks of remaining here a week or ten days, having given up his rooms at Paris, and then going to Munich to see the exact condition of his father, with reference to the future. All send love to all the dear ones at home.

Yours affectionate Father.

(*Special and Private.*)

It is probable that Harry will write you by mail, to-day, as to the financial strait in which he suddenly finds himself plunged.[2] Lest he may fail doing so, I will send you a few lines about it.

It seems that, on going to Paris from Munich in the Spring, Harry wrote to Mr. [Horace] White, of the Chicago Tribune, saying that he could not live in Paris as the correspondent of the Tribune, unless he received at the rate of one hundred dollars a week for his letters. To this proposition he received no reply; and taking it for granted that it was entirely satisfactory, he began to write and send letters with great assiduity and punctuality, and has continued to do so ever since. A considerable number of these have been published, and a considerable number not, so that at times Harry has felt quite discouraged in not knowing what, when, or how much to write; no complaint or suggestion being made by Mr. White on the subject. Harry has, in the mean time, written White at least a dozen times privately, pressing W. to let him know how his dividends and his other financial accounts stood. White has never replied till last Sunday, when a letter is received from him, informing Harry that he does not remember what terms were spoken about as to his Paris letters, but that he has put them at fifty dollars a week, and that Harry has exhausted all his dividends besides that amount, in his drafts upon White! Saying, moreover, that he (White) will be off for recreation until some time in September, and no further calls for money can be attended to till that time! Thus, eight hundred dollars of dividends which Harry supposed remained intact have all been used up, he calculating, all the while, that he was getting his one hundred dollars a week for his letters, and spending accordingly. Whether he will get the additional fifty allowed him ultimately, or before he gets back to Chicago, (an indefinite period, though he would go back immediately if it were not for the serious illness of his father [Gustav L. Hilgard], which renders every thing uncertain as to the time of his continuance on this side of the Atlantic,) remains to be seen. In the meantime, he is placed in a situation of pecuniary embarrassment, with his necessary current expenses and no ready means to draw upon. He tells me that you have advanced for him $200 to pay his life insurance; which sum he was intending to cover by a check to be sent to you at the time he received White's astounding letter. Of course, *you* must not be jeoparded or crippled to this extent; and, therefore, I will assume the responsibility of the $200—you providing for it out of such means of mine as you have, by virtue of your power of attorney. I feel as if I ought to do all that can properly be done in an emergency like this, as it will be a painful and delicate matter for Harry to ask for a loan from his aunt [Anna-Maria Pfeiffer]; and he cannot approach his father at present to make any such appeal, as he is not even allowed to see his father. Harry will remain here a week longer, and then be off for Paris and Munich, unless he hears something from the latter place to the contrary. I have offered to lend him what money he needs, but he thinks he may be able to get along without taking it. In what way I do not see. So that brings me to my own financial situation. In addition to the one thousand dollars in 5–20s I brought with me, I shall draw upon Bowles, Drevet & Co. for the same amount, to the full extent of the letter of credit so honorably and confidingly given me by the firm in Boston, and which you will be sure to see is promptly met by conferring with Mr. [William] Endicott, [Jr.] Mr. [Samuel] May, [Jr.] Mr. [Samuel E.] Sewall, &c., if need be. Whether I shall have to draw upon you for any further sum will depend upon various contingencies. Travelling is very expensive here, even for a single person; but when *three* are to be provided for, you can easily see that a large aggregate is soon run up; and if Harry is to be temporarily helped, the load becomes still heavier.

When I left Paris, I was determined that Fanny's expenses in England should not cost Harry a farthing, first, because I surmised that he was getting straitened as to the wherewithal, but more particularly as I wished to do something more for Fanny than I was able to at the time of her marriage, and because I wished her to see England and some of my English friends, and she could not do so without greatly burdening Harry if he had to meet the expense. She must remain with me until I go to Paris about the 20th of August— probably via Ostend and the Rhine—as Tante [Anna-Maria Pfeiffer] writes that she had better not come to Munich, on account of the nervousness of Harry's father, so that Harry cannot take her along with him. We have now been in Great Britain something over six weeks. Our total expenses, (travelling, boarding, hiring rooms, &c.,) thus far, amount to about $300 in American currency—averaging $50 a week. But about half that time we have received the hospitality of friends in Manchester, Newcastle, Edinburgh, and Glasgow, but for which the sum would have been much greater—say, $600, or $100 a week. It is the travelling such long distances for three of us that costs so much. For instance—from London to Glasgow, via Manchester, Newcastle, Melrose, and Edinburgh, our railroad expenses were £12, or $85 in present American currency; and they were nearly $60 in coming in a straight line back. Postage has been a heavy item, not only upon letters of all kinds, but upon large numbers of newspapers that I have bought and sent to various friends in the U.S., containing accounts of my receptions, &c. There are also incidental expenses continually occurring, which, though small singly, make something of an aggregate. Add, then, to this total amount the expenses of the household at home, the electric treatment of your mother, (which must be continued at all events, so long as she is improved by it,) &c., and the expenses of the present year will prove very great.

When I left home, you know, I thought I should leave for Boston, at Liverpool, about the 1st of September; thinking I should go to Switzerland in July and August. Then came the proposition that I should remain on this side until the last of October, so as to make it practicable for Fanny to go home with me. This appeared to reconcile your mother to my remaining abroad till that time. In consequence of the illness of Harry's father, and the altered state of things, Fanny feels like remaining with Harry, "for better, for worse"; and though it is not certain that she will do so, there is so much doubt about it as to make it a serious question with me, whether I ought to protract my visit here till the 26th of October, or try to get home by the middle of September, for your mother's sake, and with reference to pecuniary matters. I say the 26th of Oct., for that is the time for the sailing of the steamer from Liverpool to Boston, which would best conform to my wishes and plans in case I remain over. A Boston steamer goes from L. every fortnight; consequently, one will sail Oct. 12th. But there is to be a great Temperance gathering in the immense Free Trade Hall at Manchester a week later in the month, and they want to give me a marked farewell on the occasion, as well as to secure my presence and testimony for the Temperance movement.[3] No doubt it would be a stirring occasion, and, "other things being equal," I should like to improve it, which, of course, I could not do if I left before October 26. Besides this, there is to be a mighty Temperance celebration at the Crystal Palace at Sydenham, near London, on the 3rd of Sept., at which my presence is earnestly implored by the Committee of the National Temperance League as a "trump card" to bring together some thirty thousand persons in express trains from various parts of the Kingdom. If I consent to attend it, then I could not sail for Boston (in case I gave up remaining till the 26th Oct.) till the 14th of September; and that would be just the beginning of the equinoctial period, and the voyage would in all probability prove a very rough, though perhaps not at all a perilous one. Now, what I want is, your opinion, and George's, and Wendell's, and your mother's, and Ellie's opinions, as to what I had better do—keeping first in view your mother's condition, and, next, the matter of expense of remaining till the last of October. If I return before that time, I shall not be able to go to Switzerland at all; but that I care comparatively little about, though it would gratify me to see "a little rising ground" in that direction. Look carefully over the whole ground, and do not lose a mail in sending me a reply. Direct it to the care of Bowles, Drevet & Co., at Paris, as usual. Remember me kindly to Mr. Bailey and Mr. [Charles E.] Jenkins, and to all inquiring friends.[4] I trust your business prospects are improving. Kiss Ellie and darling Agnes often in my behalf.

AL signed "Father": Garrison Papers, Boston Public Library.

AL: William Lloyd Garrison Papers, Massachusetts Historical Society.

The opening letter is Garrison's regular correspondence with William; the second is an unsigned private communication. Although the letters are now at two separate depositories, Garrison almost certainly wrote and mailed them together. The private letter has no salutation or closing, probably because Garrison considered it a supplement to the other.

William Lloyd Garrison, Jr., is certainly the recipient of the private communiqué, since Garrison gave him power of attorney, as mentioned in the letter, during his absence (document, May 7, 1867, William Lloyd Garrison Papers, Massachusetts Historical Society). The date of the private letter, July 31, 1867, is confirmed by Garrison's reference to Henry Villard's letter to William of the same date (Villard Papers, Harvard College Library).

1. William Henry Channing (1810–1884), nephew of William Ellery Channing and a graduate of both the college and the divinity school at Harvard, was a restless and peripatetic clergyman and man of letters. He had been the minister of Unitarian and other liberal churches in Boston, New York City, Cincinnati, Washington, D.C., and Rochester. After 1854, except for the war years, he spent most of his life in England, preaching in various churches and writing and editing articles and books. His most important single work was the three-volume *Life of William Ellery Channing* (1848).

The facts regarding Channing's abortive attempt to establish a church and a following in London are obscure. Apparently he became the minister of the Free Christian Church on Newton Street, Kensington, sometime before the end of 1867; his biographer suggests December as the date. At any rate, this, his last parish, was plagued with dwindling numbers, and in about two years it ceased altogether. (Octavius B. Frothingham, *Memoir of William Henry Channing*, Boston, 1886, pp. 344–347.)

2. Henry Villard did write to William describing his financial difficulties and promising to borrow money, once he reached Munich, in order to repay his loan. (Henry Villard to William Lloyd Garrison, Jr., July 31, 1867, Villard Papers, Harvard College Library.) Villard severed his ties with the *Tribune* when he returned to the United States and became secretary of the Social Science Association.

3. The Free Trade Hall, an auditorium in the Italian Palatial style, was built on Peter Street, Manchester, in 1856; it held 6,000 people. Largely destroyed by fire bombs in World War II, the building was reconstructed in 1951. (Karl Baedeker, *Great Britain, Handbook for Travellers*, Leipzig and New York, 1901; L. Russell Muirhead and Stuart Rossiter, eds., *The Blue Guides, England*, London, 1965.)

4. Joseph T. Bailey (1816–1894), wool merchant and senior partner in William Lloyd Garrison, Jr.'s, firm, was born in North Scituate and moved to Boston when he was twenty-five. He served as alderman for several terms, was elected president of the Massachusetts Charitable Mechanic Association, and was also president of the Boylston National Bank. (Obituary, Boston *Post*, August 16, 1894.)

2 1 2

TO HELEN E. GARRISON

Paris, August 12, 1867.

Dear Wife:

On returning from Scotland to London,—Harry deeming it best that we should defer our contemplated visit to Switzerland till September,—it became a matter of grave consideration what to do with the time on our hands before the holding of the Anti-Slavery Conference in Paris. I was strongly desirous of going to Oxford, Warwick, and Stratford-on-Avon, having never seen those places; but the cost of such a trip, even only for ten days or a week, for three of us, including heavy hotel expenses, deterred me from undertaking it, and I deemed it wiser to come directly to this city, as we all did on Saturday, after remaining more than a week almost incog. in London, getting as much bodily rest as possible.

Last Thursday, I called to see William E. Forster, member of Parliament, (Harry accompanying me,) and spent a pleasant half hour with him. On taking our leave, he advised us to be at the House of Commons by 4 o'clock, P.M., saying the great debate on the Reform Bill, as it had been sent down from the House of Lords, would come off that night, and he would try to get us admitted to the galleries. We gladly complied with his suggestion. Between four and five hundred members were present. It was an occasion of historic interest, and the discussion on both sides was marked by great ability. Gladstone and John Bright spoke with more than their wonted eloquence and power, and I deemed myself very fortunate to have heard them in their best trim.[1] No other person who spoke was at all comparable to either of them. As a parliamentary speaker, Gladstone takes the lead; as a popular orator, Bright has no peer. During a brief recess, Mr. Forster took me to the coffee room of the House, and hospitably gave me a supper; introducing me there to Lord Amberly, (the oldest son of Lord John Russell,) who sails this month for a six months' tour in the United States; to the Archbishop of Canterbury, by whose side I afterward sat in the House, in a privileged seat; and to several members of Parliament.[2] John Stuart Mill sat by my side while I was eating, and we had a social conversation together. He was very strong in his expressions of personal esteem for myself, and hoped I should be able to visit him at his residence at Avignon, in France, where he spends his parliamentary vacation. He is as modest as he is gifted in intellect, though not much as a speaker. I am glad to have made his acquaintance.

Of our trip from London to Paris, and the difficulty we found at midnight to procure lodgings, after abortive applications at various hotels, Frank will give you the particulars. We deemed ourselves in luck, after all, and are well satisfied with our quarters, excepting the incessant travelling through our street until one or two o'clock in the morning; for Paris is crowded with strangers, and every day brings a fresh influx, partly no doubt with reference to the splendid celebration of the Emperor's birthday on Thursday next, when there is to be a magnificent illumination, &c., &c. The price of rooms and board, in decent quarters and with tolerable accommodations, is enormous. We hire a bedroom and contiguous parlor— the latter Fanny occupying at night, using a single iron bed stead; Harry being called suddenly to Munich, having received a letter from his aunt, (which ought to have been sent to him in London several days since, but these careless persons here to whom it was sent lost his address,) stating that his father was in a dying condition; and it is probable he is now not living. These two rooms cost us twenty-six[3] dollars a week, American currency, exclusive of board, washing, &c. Here we expect to remain till the 1st of September. My whole trip will be a heavy one, pecuniarily, in spite of great economy.

We were rejoiced to get letters from you, and William, and Oliver Johnson, on Sunday morning. These we devoured with an eager appetite, and were much refreshed by their contents. You seem to have had no lack of company at Rockledge; and this must have helped to relieve the solitude that our absence would otherwise have created. We feel truly grateful to Julia [Randall] for her kind attentions to you; and are much rejoiced to hear that Mary-Ann [Johnson] is able to be with you again, after her severe and protracted illness. Ellie and darling Agnes you must miss exceedingly until their return. As to William and Ellie going to housekeeping, it is quite natural they should desire to do so; but it will be a step requiring serious consideration as to pecuniary disabilities. I would counsel William not to think of buying Mr. Ellis's cottage, or any other even on mortgage, until my return, unless an extraordinary bargain is offered.[4] My dear S. J. May will doubtless have returned home ere this is received; but I will send him a message of love, at a venture. I owe him a long letter, and must write it soon; and also Oliver. As to Fanny and Frank, I see no special change in their looks, and there is no news to communicate. Our love to the households of Rockledge and Llwellyn Park.

Your own W. L. G.

P.S. Fanny was glad to get a letter from May Addie, who assures us that you are looking uncommonly well.[5] Keep on with your electrical treatment.

ALS: Garrison Papers, Boston Public Library; partly printed in *Life*, IV, 228–229.

1. The reform act of 1867 reapportioned representation in Parliament of a number of English boroughs. Both John Bright and William Ewart Gladstone (1809–1898) spoke for the Liberal party in support of the bill. Gladstone, who had first entered Parliament in 1833, became the acknowledged leader of the Liberal party following the resignation of Lord John Russell in December 1867. The following December he became Prime Minister, a position he was to hold during four separate administrations.

2. John Russell, Viscount Amberley (1842–1876), whose name Garrison misspells, had been educated at Harrow, Edinburgh University, and Trinity College, Cambridge. Between 1866 and 1868 he was the Liberal party representative in Parliament from Nottingham. (*Burke's Peerage and Baronetage*, London, 1975.)

John Russell, first Earl Russell (1792–1878), was a distinguished British statesman whose parliamentary career began in 1813. During the Civil War, as foreign secretary, he endeavored to maintain neutrality with the North and the South, though he did in effect recognize Confederate independence by advocating an offer of mediation between the belligerents in September 1862. At Garrison's London breakfast in 1867, he acknowledged his error in a speech. Lord Russell served twice as Prime Minister (1846–1852 and 1865–1866). (Spencer Walpole, *The Life of Lord John Russell*, London, 1889, II, 348–352; *Proceedings at the Public Breakfast Held in Honour of William Lloyd Garrison . . .* , London, 1868, pp. 31–33.)

Charles Thomas Longley (1794–1868), a graduate of Westminster School and Oxford, served as vicar in several parishes before becoming successively headmaster of Harrow, bishop of Ripon, archbishop of York, and, in 1862, archbishop of Canterbury.

3. The number written was originally "thirty-five," which was crossed out and "twenty-six" substituted above the line in another hand.

4. Mr. Ellis is probably Charles Mayo Ellis (1818–1878), a Harvard graduate of the class of 1839 who became an attorney with offices in the Old State House in Boston. He is supposed to have aided in the defense of fugitive slave Anthony Burns. In the directories his address is given as "house, Highland, near Hawthorne," and his mother's as "living at Ellis near Hawthorne." The cottage for sale may have been the mother's. (Roxbury directory, 1866; letter to the editor from Nancy Sahli, researcher, July 22, 1972.)

5. May Addie has not been identified.

213

TO SAMUEL MAY, JR.

Paris, 21 Rue d' Anten, Aug. 20, 1867.

My dear friend May:

Your very delightful and most interesting letter has too long remained unanswered; but it is not too late to thank you for it, although it may be to apologize for the delay. The truth is, that what with home correspondence, and the necessity of answering multi-tudinous notes and letters, and the prolonged fatigue of the journey from London to Scotland, (via Manchester and Newcastle-on-Tyne,) and back again, and attendance upon parties and meetings, and sight-seeing in every direction, and a procrastinating dislike of the use of the pen, and many other hindrances, I have been obliged to abandon almost all hope of writing to any of my friends in the United States during my absence.

I felt much relieved in mind to learn from your letter, that the noble company of friends and co-workers who so kindly came to give George Thompson and myself their fraternal farewell at the time of our embarkation, made so little of the drenching rain they had to encounter during their excursion down the harbor. At least one of their number has since been called from earth, it may be to receive the greetings of loved ones in Spirit-land; I allude to my very early and attached friend Isaac Winslow. It was owing exclu-sively to his liberality that I was enabled to publish my "Thoughts on African Colonization" in 1832. I am shocked to hear that he died in an Insane Asylum at Augusta, Me. He was at the funeral of our lamented friend Thankful Southwick, at Grantville, a few days be-fore I left for Europe, and seemed to be in remarkably good condi-tion at his advanced age. His memory is blessed.

I have endeavored to keep you posted as to my movements and reception meetings, by sending you sundry newspapers along my route. Had I chosen to accept them, I could have had welcome pub-lic greetings in every considerable town in Great Britain; but I came over for no such purpose, and unfeignedly shrink from all such manifestations. I could not, however, without almost seeming affectation, decline the breakfast at St. James's Hall in London,[1] and the similar ovations at Manchester, Newcastle, Edinburgh, and Glasgow; though I felt very foolish and very much out of my ele-ment on each occasion, in consequence of so many compliments having been showered upon me. In no instance did I make the slightest preparation as to what response I should make, except pencilling down impromptu one or two points at St. James's Hall; and, indeed, it would have been useless for me to have done so, for my memory is like a sieve, and cannot retain half a dozen consecu-tive sentences or propositions. It was, therefore, most confounding to me to be forced to speak under such circumstances, especially before such select and intelligent assemblies; and I read with some feelings of chagrin and mortification what I said in so rambling a manner, especially as the reporters for the press made terrible botch-work of my utterances. Some of their blunders were equally comical and atrocious. Unfortunately, I had no opportunity, even in a single instance, to make any revision; and it was useless afterward to attempt to give a correct version. If you had been present, you would have been abundantly satisfied that it was no formal demonstration of personal respect, but a spontaneous outburst of warm appreciation and high enthusiasm, the all-pervading spirit being peace and good will towards the United States. The St. James's affair was indeed very remarkable, on the score of talent, character, and numbers. I regret to hear that Earl Russell's exceedingly creditable speech on the occasion was characterized by Mr. Phillips, in the Anti-Slavery *Standard,* as "maudlin talk—point to no point!"[2] This is his estimate of a manly confession of having been wholly in the wrong, and President Lincoln entirely in the right in his treatment of the great rebellion. Nothing is more rare—not even "the gold of Ophir"[3]—than such a frank confession of error and misapprehension from the lips of a distinguished statesman like Lord John Russell; and it is very painful to me to see Mr. P. so lacking in magnanimity in his reference to this confession. It would very much redound to his credit if he had the grace to imitate so noble an example.

The presentation to me of the "freedom of the city" by the Lord Provost and Magistracy of Edinburgh was a notable mark of respect, taking me utterly by surprise. It has been rarely conferred, and is made a great deal of in the city. It is rather curious that the person who preceded me in receiving it was Prince Alfred, Lord Palmerston preceding him. It was given to the illustrious John Hampden. You see, therefore, that different considerations lead to its bestowment. It was most worthily given to George Thompson several years ago. Of course, it possesses no interest or value to me beyond its being a high official recognition of the rectitude and grandeur of the Anti-Slavery movement in the United States, and through me, a vindication of American abolitionists generally.

Believing it to have been the best judgment that could have been rendered in the case, I was very glad to hear that the Court had decided to give Mr. [Francis] Jackson's bequest entirely to the New England Freedmen's Aid Commission, notwithstanding Mr. Phillips's strenuous efforts to the contrary. It was a curious point that he made, that not a single daily paper in *New York* printed an entire speech of mine delivered in *Brooklyn!* As if it could reasonably have been expected, or furnished any ground for complaint! When he stated that I and my friends had to go to the *Standard* to get it printed in full, he was wholly inaccurate, and did me a positive wrong; for I neither made, nor thought of making, any such request of the *Standard.* You will recollect that Aaron M. Powell presided on the occasion. As we were leaving the platform, he asked leave to print my lecture in the *Standard,* without abridgment. I told him that I had already promised my manuscript to the Editor of the Brooklyn *Eagle*[4] (who was present,)—but gave him permission to get it, if he chose, in case only an abridgment of it appeared in the columns of that paper. As that proved to be the case, he accordingly got the manuscript, and printed it in the *Standard* of his own motion. I am sure Aaron will confirm every word I have said about it. But it was a foreign and most ridiculous issue to have been made on the occasion.

Fanny and Frank have been with me in all my journeyings. We lost our projected tour to the Scottish Highlands, in consequence of bad weather. At Edinburgh, my dear friend Elizabeth Pease Nichol took us readily to her heart and home, and left nothing undone for our comfort and enjoyment. In Glasgow we had "a right good time" with William Smeal, Andrew Paton, and the [William] Andersons, and found them all well except Catharine Paton. On our return to London, Miss [Mary A.] Estlin (fearing she should have no other opportunity of seeing us) kindly came all the way from Bristol, and spent several days with us. She has had some thoughts of making a visit to the United States, but shrinks from going on account of our hot air furnaces, the dry heat of which she thinks would be unendurable, if not perilous in her case, as she is easily affected about the lungs. It is not very improbable, however, that she and Eliza Wigham will be tempted to cross over next May or June. I strongly solicited Mrs. Nichol to the same thing; but there is some trouble with her heart, and she is afraid to make the experiment. I have also urged dear R. D. Webb to make us a visit, and feel quite sure it would give him unspeakable pleasure to do so, were it not for the expense. To all these friends I have given your loving regards, in accordance with your request. Would that you could have been with me!

I am postponing my trip to Switzerland &c, (with the children,) till after the Anti-Slavery Conference, which comes off on Monday and Tuesday next, 26th and 27th inst. Only two sessions will be given to the deliberations of that body. Probably there will be few delegates from organized bodies, but Mr. Chamerovzow now informs me that more than a hundred persons have signified their intention to be present. The part I intend taking in its proceedings will be a very subordinate one, having reference chiefly to the cause of the American freedmen. How we shall get along with different dialects, I do not know; but they will greatly abridge the freedom of intercommunication. Here, for instance, I am in a city with nearly two millions of inhabitants, with not one of whom can I intelligibly carry on any conversation,—an exceptional case, like that of Prof. Laboulaye, being very rare. Even he, though accurate, is a good deal fettered and limited in his English speech.

Mr. Villard is at present in Munich, administering aid and comfort to his father [Gustav L. Hilgard], now beyond hope of recovery, though he may continue awhile longer.

We spent last evening very pleasantly with our old anti-slavery friends, Sarah and Rebecca Bradford, of Roxbury. They have been residing for a year in the south of France and in Switzerland, accompanied by their brother.[5] Sarah will sail to New York in a Havre steamer on the 4th of September, leaving Rebecca behind for another year, with reference to her health.

There have been very many Americans in Paris this summer, and they are still coming. Senator Doolittle is here, and Hon. Moses Kimball and family of Boston.[6] Also, Col. [James] McKay of New York.

You can imagine how chagrined I was at the reception of Andy Johnson in Boston. He is still headstrong and defiant as against Congress, and ought to have been impeached and removed long ago.

I get good news as to the state of my dear wife's health. Trusting that all is going well with you at home and sending our united regards to your wife and children, and to your venerable father and mother, I remain,

Affectionately yours,

Wm. Lloyd Garrison.

Rev. Samuel May, Jr.

☞ My present calculation is to leave Liverpool for Boston on the 26th of October.

☞ When I go to Birmingham in October, I will endeavor without fail to see Mr. Goddard.[7]

Handwritten transcription: Garrison Papers, Boston Public Library; partly printed in *Life*, IV, 221–222.

1. For details of the breakfast see Introduction VII, "Honors and Awards: 1867."

St. James's Hall, designed by Owen Jones in the Moorish Alhambra style, was built in Piccadilly (on the site of the present Piccadilly Hotel) in 1857; it was used for large meetings and especially for concerts. The building was demolished in 1905. (Edward Walford, *Old and New London*, London, n.d., IV, 254.)

2. Wendell Phillips' comment appeared in a column headed "Notes" in the *National Anti-Slavery Standard*, July 27, 1867, as follows: "We copy from the London *Morning Star* a full report of Mr. Garrison's reception in England; an interesting

chapter in the history of the Anti-slavery movement, and a well deserved tribute to his eminent services in the early and darkest days of the cause and through its weary noon. From the picture given of the present state of the question, we, of course, dissent and only wish that melancholy facts did not so sadly and fully contradict it. On Lord Russell's maudlin talk—point no point—it would be waste of time to comment."

3. A phrase to be found in various parts of the Bible, including Chronicles 29:4, Job 22:24, Job 28:16, and Psalms 45:9.

4. Thomas Kinsella (1832–1884), Irish by birth and a printer by trade, worked as a compositor for the Cambridge *Post* in western New York until 1858, when he joined the staff of the Brooklyn *Eagle,* the Democratic evening paper founded in 1841 and once edited by Walt Whitman. Kinsella rose rapidly from typesetter to reporter, and in 1861 he was appointed editor to replace proslavery Henry McCloskey. The paper thrived under his editorship for more than two decades. He supported President Johnson and was repaid by being appointed postmaster of Brooklyn for a brief period. In 1868 he became a member of the city's Board of Education, and in 1870, a member of Congress. (*S. M. Pettengill's Newspaper Directory and Advertiser's Handbook,* New York, 1877; Mott, pp. 354–355.)

5. Extensive search has not revealed the identity of the Bradford brother.

6. Moses Kimball (1809–1895), the son of David and Nancy Stacy Kimball of Newburyport, became in 1833 the publisher of the *New England Galaxy;* subsequently he specialized in publishing engravings of historic paintings. With his brother David, he opened the Boston Museum, a very successful theater, in 1841, and for the next fifty years he sponsored public amusements. Kimball was also a politician who served in both city and state governments; for sixteen years he was a member first of the House and then of the Senate of the Massachusetts legislature. By his wife, Frances L. A. Hathaway, whom he married in 1834, he had seven children. (Justin Winsor, *The Memorial History of Boston,* Boston, 1881, IV, 58, 373.)

7. Samuel Aspinwall Goddard (1797–1886), the brother of Mary Goddard May (Mrs. Samuel May), was a prominent resident of Birmingham, England. He was the author of a series of letters on the Civil War, which were first printed in the Birmingham *Post* and subsequently in London and Boston as a book entitled *The American Rebellion* (1870). (*Life;* obituary, Boston *Transcript,* August 9, 1886; *National Union Catalogue, Pre–1956 Imprints.*)

214

TO HELEN E. GARRISON

Chillon, (Lake of Geneva,) Sept. 4, 1867.

My darling Wife:

This is a memorable day to me, it being the thirty-third anniversary of our marriage. Sitting by the side of this indescribably beautiful lake, and within hailing distance of the famous but hideous old prison (a thousand years old) which Byron has immortalized in verse,[1] I have had my thoughts running back to the hour when our epistolary correspondence first began—to the many happy hours we spent together in loving courtship—to the marriage scene and ceremony at Brooklyn under the roof of your revered parents,[2] and all who were then present, with our beloved friend Samuel J. May to tie a knot legally which we had already in heart and spirit tied indissolubly—to the birth of our first-born, with all its thrilling associations, and that of our other dear children—to the sad removal by death of our darling Charley and Lizzie[3]—to the various scenes and vicissitudes through which we have been called to pass—down to the present hour, with the wide Atlantic between us—I seeking recreation for a brain long severely tasked, and recuperation for my physical system so much injured last year by my unfortunate falls; and you confined at home by paralysis, yet serene and patient in your helplessness, but none the less yearning in spirit to have the hour of reunion arrive, that we may again be by each other's side, and with Fanny and Frank to join us in the gladsome event. I have gratefully remembered what a loving, faithful, helpful wife you have been to me, always doing for me whatever affection could suggest, and contriving to economise in every way in view of my limited means; in the darkest and most perilous days of the Anti-Slavery struggle never once intimating a wish that I would yield somewhat to the pressure of an infuriated public sentiment as a matter of prudence, but always ready to stand by me in accordance with my convictions of duty. With similar feelings of gratitude, I have remembered what a mother you have been to your children—so exemplary, so affectionate, so devoted, so unwearied in efforts to see them supplied with all needful comforts, and to make our home "the dearest spot of all the earth"[4] to them, as it has ever proved to be. You are entitled to be crowned among the best of wives, among the most loving of mothers. With my benediction resting upon you, I pray that you may yet be restored to the use of your limbs, and that your declining years may be full of blessedness and peace.

The last letters received from you and William were dated August 11th. They came just in season to enable me to decide, without any misgiving, to remain on this side of the Atlantic until the 26th of October, seeing Switzerland and the Rhine, &c. The assurances they contained as to the improving state of your paralytic side gave us all fresh hope and joy. Of course, we do not mean to cherish too sanguine expectations for the future in regard to your case, lest disappointment may follow; nevertheless, the signs of change for the better as narrated by yourself and Mary-Ann [Johnson], (whose kind and affectionate letter I will reply to by another mail, and whose regard for you and me has been shown in so many ways,) are of the most encouraging kind. The letters all came at the time of the Paris Conference. As to the Conference, I can only say, now, that it excited no local interest or curiosity, no reporters being present for any of the daily papers, excepting Galignani's, which contained

only a brief report of the proceedings.[5] There were but two sessions, and most of the speaking was in the French dialect, and,
therefore, unintelligible to me. Even Hon. John G. Palfrey made
his remarks in French, to the disappointment of such of the audience (about one third) as understood the English language.[6] The
venerable Duke de Broglie[7] (too old to be present) was made Honorary President, and Prof. Laboulaye Acting President. Both Laboulaye and M. Cochin spoke in an admirable manner, and paid me
and other American Abolitionists handsome tributes for our labors
in the Anti-Slavery cause. Any allusion to me was always responded to in a very flattering manner, but no resolution was proposed in reference to the peculiarity of my case,—probably because the whole affair was managed by the Committee of the British
and Foreign A. S. Society. I spoke once, for about forty minutes,
and what I said was well received by those who understood English. I believe Frank sent William two copies of Galignani doubtless, the London A. S. Reporter[8] for October will contain a pretty
full account of the proceedings. It was a great oversight, on the part
of those having the matter in trust, not to have had a competent reporter present.

We all left Paris a week ago to-night, (Thursday,) taking the night
train for Geneva, where we arrived at 11 o'clock next morning. At
early dawn we entered the defiles of the Jura mountains, and during the remainder of our ride feasted our eyes upon the wildest
most picturesque and sublime scenery we had ever witnessed. Mr.
and Mrs. Blanchard,[9] (the latter a sister of Sarah Pillsbury,[10] and
bearing a very close resemblance, and Richard D. Webb, (who
came to the Conference with Miss Estlin, of Bristol,) accompanying
us, and who are still with us—making our party quite a delightful
one. I have no time or room for particulars of what we have seen. At
Chamounix we were very near Mont Blanc, the Mer de Glace, and
other famous localities. We made two lofty ascensions on the backs
of mules, and rode on the same for twenty-two miles on Tuesday
from Chamounix to Chillon over a mountainous range, surpassing
in wildness and grandeur anything I have ever dreamed of. It is all
witchery and enchantment every step of the way. We are just leaving for Vevey, Lausanne, Berne, and Interlaken. The last named
place we shall probably reach to-morrow, where we shall remain at
least a week, and where we hope to get letters from home. Nothing
further from Harry. He hopes to meet us at Interlaken.

☞ We all continue in excellent health. Harry will probably take
Fanny to Munich from Interlaken. Love to George, William, Ellie,
Wendell, Lucy, Mrs. Johnson, &c.

☞ I trust Fanny's letter will give you other particulars that you may wish to learn.

AL: Garrison Papers, Boston Public Library.

1. Garrison refers to Byron's "The Prisoner of Chillon." He is correct about the age of the castle, part of which was built in the ninth century. (*Dictionnaire historique et bibliographique de la Suisse*, Neuchatel, 1924.)

2. Helen's parents were George Benson (1752–1836) and Sarah Thurber Benson (1770–1844). Benson, a prominent Providence merchant who had retired to Brooklyn, Conn., in 1824, had been an active abolitionist since the late eighteenth century. He served as president of the New England Anti-Slavery Society in 1833–1834. Mrs. Benson, a shy and reserved woman whose personality and character had left their imprint on her daughter Helen, was a devoted wife and mother.

3. Elizabeth Pease Garrison (1846–1848), the second Garrison daughter, had been a sickly child who died of "lung fever" preceded by influenza. (*Life; Letters*, III, 549–550.)

4. James Montgomery, *West Indies*, Part III, line 67, adapted.

5. *Galignani's Messenger*, dedicated to the improvement of relations between France and England, had been founded in Paris in 1814 by Giovanni Antonio Galignani (1752–1821) and was currently being managed by his two sons, Jean-Antoine (1796–1873) and Guillaume (1798–1882).

6. John Gorham Palfrey (1796–1881) had one of the most varied careers of his day. He was an abolitionist, active in the American Anti-Slavery Society; a Unitarian minister; an editor of the *North American Review;* an historian, author of the four-volume *History of New England* (1858–1875); and a politician. He had been secretary of the Commonwealth of Massachusetts (1844–1847) and member of Congress (1847–1849), and was currently postmaster at Boston.

7. Achille Charles Léonce Victor, Duc de Broglie (1785–1870), after a career of public service to the liberal French monarchy in various offices, including that of foreign minister, was spending his last years in retirement, engaging in literary and philosophical pursuits. During the 1840s he had served as the president of France's only antislavery body, the *Société pour l'Abolition de l'Esclavage*. (Howard Temperley, *British Antislavery, 1833–1870*, London, 1972, pp. 186–187.)

8. The *British and Foreign Anti-Slavery Reporter* was published by the British and Foreign Anti-Slavery Society, later called the Anti-Slavery and Aborigines Protection Society, between 1840 and 1909. Although the editorship was officially by committee, much of the content was supervised by a managing editor, at first J. H. Hinton, then John Scoble, and, since 1852, Louis Alexis Chamerovzow. He had attempted to heal the rift between the Garrisonians and the British New Organizationists, but although he received some approval from British Garrisonians, the attempt was unsuccessful. By 1860 the subscription list had dwindled to 700, of whom only eighty actually bought the paper, which had become little more than a digest of information from American sources, British Parliamentary papers, and other publications; in 1868 the *Reporter* became a quarterly. (Temperley, *British Antislavery*, pp. 83, 230, 242.)

9. George Augustus Blanchard (1824–1897) of Concord, N.H., married Frances Ann Brown Sargent (born in 1829 and still living in 1908) in 1849; she was the daughter of Dr. John L. and Sally Wilkins Sargent of Tamworth, N.H. Blanchard held a variety of jobs (woodworker, railroad clerk in Ohio, shipping clerk in Illinois). At the time of Garrison's letter the couple were on a two-year tour of Europe, after which they returned to Concord, where Blanchard managed his father's churn manufacturing firm. In 1893 they moved to Boston, where he became the eastern representative for the Mosely folding bathtub manufacturing company. (Ezra S. Stearns, ed., *Genealogical and Family History of the State of New Hampshire*, New York, 1908, pp. 785–786.)

10. Sarah H. Sargent married Parker Pillsbury on January 1, 1840. They had one

daughter, Helen Buffum (born 1843). Like her husband, Mrs. Pillsbury was an ardent abolitionist. (*Biographical Review . . . Merrimack and Sullivan Counties*, Boston, 1897, pp. 47–48.)

215

TO WILLIAM LLOYD GARRISON, JR.

Interlaken, (Switzerland,) Sept. 11, 1867.

My dear William:

Letters from you, and Ellie, and your mother were received yesterday—the latest date being Aug. 27th. The speed and regularity with which correspondence is carried on at such a great distance—an ocean of three thousand miles intervening, and foreign countries to be traversed—are indeed remarkable.

I have read your statement as to the Testimonial Fund, and the various views of the Trustees as to the bestowal of it. I remember the proverb, "You must not look a gift horse in the mouth," and, therefore, shall be bound thankfully to acknowledge whatever may be done with it. But, I confess, "the bloom of the peach," if not its flavor, will be taken away, if the whole amount contributed, instead of being handed over to me on my return, to be invested as I may deem safest and best, in concurrence with any *private* suggestions the Committee may kindly suggest, and also with our convictions as a family, shall be held in the hands of a Committee, subject to stringent limitations and restrictions in the use of it, putting me in fact under guardianship, and virtually saying to the world that they consider me as either incompetent to manage it, or as liable through a disposition to extravagance to squander it at no distant day.[1] I must earnestly express the hope that I shall not be placed in any such position. I am not sure that I would rather not receive a farthing of the money; and I am not unwilling that the Committee, as a body, should be apprised, with all possible respect, deference and gratitude, of my feelings about it. It is all well meant, I am sure, but I think it is not well considered. I wish you to give my thanks to Mr. [Samuel] May [Jr.] and Mr. [Samuel E.] Sewall for suggesting the only course that seems compatible with the dignity and specialty of the Testimonial. I beg that it may not be reduced to the level of an eeelemosynary charity, in behalf of a worthy but helpless or incompetent individual, which therefore needs to be carefully doled out in a scanty pittance from quarter to quarter, so as to prevent wastefulness. On the whole, I cannot consent to receive any such charity while health, strength and reason are left to me, and while I have any children left to care for me. The Testimonial stands upon its own merits, and I hope it will be allowed so to stand, for the sake of its historical character. If there is anything in my character or habits that renders it inexpedient or unsafe for me to receive it in full, then it ceases to be a Testimonial, and ought not to be so proffered, but only as a charitable contribution to save me from want! It matters not whether I am to receive the benefit of it in the shape of an annuity or of interest money. In either case, it is resolved into guardianship and a charity; and if such be the final arrangement made, then I must respectfully but firmly decline the Testimonial.

I appreciate, to the fullest extent, the desire to have the fund the most judiciously invested for my benefit and that of my family; but that desire we shall all feel in an eminent degree, and, animated by it, as a family, we ought to be presumed capable, with such friendly advice as might be given to us, of assuming its responsibility.

I am particularly sensitive on this point, because whatever failings I may have, the misuse of money has never been one of them. While I despise a parsimonious spirit, I have always endeavored to be as thoughtful and conscientious in the use of the means in my possession as in the discharge of any of the duties of life. No man may do as he pleases with what is his own, except as a steward who is to render an account of his stewardship in the matter of well-doing. Forty years of struggle, and poverty in childhood and youth, have taught me the need and begotten the habit of an economical use of money. Your mother and all of you know my manner of life in that respect. I have given way to no indulgence of any kind, but, having a horror of getting in debt, and a growing family to provide for, with very limited means, and a newspaper on my hands struggling against wind and tide, I have been habituated to economical considerations; and these are not likely to be lost at my time of life —a time which, with decreasing energy and growing infirmities, is rather calculated to deepen circumspection and excite anxiety as to the future. However, this has little or nothing to do with the Testimonial, and its honorable bestowal; except as the proposition to provide out of it a fixed annuity, or the interest money only, may seem to imply a misapprehension as to my habits, or a distrust as to my personal competency.

We are having a charming time in Switzerland. You may look for us at home about the 8th of Nov. Love to all as one.

Your loving father,

Wm. Lloyd Garrison.

P.S. I do not mean to be understood as saying, that it is derogatory to any man to receive an annuity, or interest money on an investment made by his friends in his behalf. No. But I am not willing to have what assumes to be a token of national respect hedged up by any such limitations or conditions. It is, however, for the Committee having the matter in charge to make such conditions as in their judgment they may deem best; and then it will be for me to decide whether I will accept the overture. After what I have said, of course I shall not be willing to accept it, except it be made freely, confidingly, and without restriction as to the use that may be made of it.

☞ Fanny and Frank fully concur in the sentiments I have expressed.

☞ If I were so unfortunate as to be owing creditors who might be disposed to avail themselves of the Testimonial, then it would be a wise precaution to guard it against this liability. But I owe nothing.

P.S. Frank and I have engaged our passages on board of the Java, which sails from Liverpool for Boston on the 26th of October. Anne Warren Weston will accompany us.

ALS: William Lloyd Garrison Papers, Massachusetts Historical Society; a two-page handwritten transcription of extracts from this letter, apparently intended to be read at the testimonial meeting, is preserved in the Merrill Collection of Garrison Papers, Wichita State University Library.

1. Garrison was not embarrassed; the entire fund was placed at his disposal. (*AWT*, pp. 311, 375.)

216

TO ELLEN WRIGHT GARRISON

Interlaken, September 12, 1867.

My dear daughter Ellie:

Among the gratifying letters received from home the day before yesterday was yours, dated Auburn, Aug. 20th. Accept my thanks, and also this hasty reply to it. Every item of intelligence communicated by you was, of course, read with eagerness. The only drawback from the pleasure it gave us all was the statement made in regard to dear Eliza[Wright]'s feeble condition. We can only hope that, by the time this reaches you, she will have fully recovered her health.

The date of my letter, and the place where I am, indicate that I am in glorious, beautiful, sublime, wonderful Switzerland; and, consequently, that, on receiving the family injunctions to be sure to make the present tour, I abandoned my plan to return home in September; fixing Saturday, Oct. 26th, as the day on which to leave Liverpool for Boston with Frank, and, possibly, with Harry and Fanny; for Harry's father died a week ago on Monday, and I know that Harry is anxious to get back to the United States at the earliest practicable period after the settlement of his father's affairs. We expect him here on Friday, to spend a few days with us, and perhaps to take Fanny along with him to Munich, first going with us to Lucerne. But nothing can be definitely settled as to future movements until he comes. Watching so long and so intensely by the bedside of his suffering father, it (with the sad event itself) has greatly prostrated him, and shattered his nervous system.

I am glad to hear that William and you have abandoned the idea of going to housekeeping the present year; for, although it is natural that, however pleasant it may be at Rockledge, you should both desire to be under your own roof, yet the present expenses of independent housekeeping are too great to be assumed on slender means, and [I] strongly admonish against a hasty committal in that direction. I trust you have found it, and will continue to find it as long as you remain with us, as near to being perfectly at home as possible. Only I surmise that you have felt unnecessarily delicate and anxious about the possible return of Harry and Fanny this fall, lest they should need the room you occupy, and so put us and them to some inconvenience. I beg you to give yourself no solicitude whatever on that score. I have not the slightest idea that Harry will settle down with us, at any time, beyond a mere temporary visit; or, if he should conclude to do so, that he will wish to board at Rockledge. Should he return this fall, (and this seems now to be probable,) he will have to hurry to Chicago, and no doubt from thence to Washington, leaving Fanny for some time, perhaps for the winter, at Rockledge; she occupying, of course, the chamber she formerly had. So, give yourself no uneasiness about being in the way; and let us all patiently wait to see what another season will bring forth. It will be very difficult for me to be separated from darling Agnes at any time in the future. I do yearningly hope that she will not wholly forget me before my return home; and if my photograph can help her little memory in that respect, I trust it will be often pointed out to her.

I take it for granted that this letter will find you all at Rockledge, and also our beloved Wendell and Lucy, and baby Lloyd, (whose head is said to so strikingly resemble his grandfather's in shape,) and dear Mrs. McKim. What a grand time you will all have together!

And how happy dear wife will be made by the event! I send love, kisses, benedictions for all, from us all.

You will learn from Frank's long and minute letter how we have been enjoying ourselves for some days past, and I need not repeat particulars. Yesterday we went to Berne, with Mr. [Richard D.] Webb, to see that old and quaint looking city, and had a glorious trip of it. The sail on the lake was indescribably lovely, and the mountain views superbly grand.

Fanny has made what purchases she could for you, in accordance with William's request, and it has given her great pleasure to do so. Of course, I mean to be a partner in that matter.

You will see what I have written to William concerning the disposal of the Testimonial. I trust my views will meet the approbation of all the family. I wish William to hand the letter to Mr. [Samuel] May [Jr.] or Mr. [Samuel E.] Sewall, saying that, having received it from me, he deems it proper that the Committee should be apprised of my feelings before coming to any definite conclusion about the Testimonial.

I may have to draw upon William for some money on getting to England, but I hope for an amount not exceeding $500.

Mr. Phillips has, at last, publicly broken the chain of friendship so long subsisting between us, by his imputations upon me in his comments upon my letter to Mr. May concerning the Jackson Testimonial.[1]

Yours, lovingly;

                                        Wm. Lloyd Garrison.

P.S. Dear wife sustains herself nobly, and seems to be getting along hopefully. Frank has dreamed that he saw her clasp something with her paralyzed hand.

ALS: Garrison Papers, Sophia Smith Collection, Smith College Library.

1. On August 10, 1867, a letter, dated July 24, 1867, from Robert Purvis of Byberry, Pa., was printed in the *National Anti-Slavery Standard*. In it he protested the master in chancery's decision on the Jackson bequest and asked who was responsible for misdirection of the funds. Directly following this letter was a reply by Wendell Phillips, who gave his account of the court proceedings. Referring to the decision as "a robbery of our treasury" and "a gross perversion of the fund," he cited the cause as the unwillingness of a "minority" of the trustees to grant freedom of opinion to the "majority," and the appeal by the minority to the outside authority of a prejudiced court. Phillips noted specifically that the master based his decision in favor of the freedmen upon "the letter Mr. Garrison left on his departure for Europe."

By the request of Garrison's sons, the letter Phillips cites (Garrison to Samuel May, Jr., May 7, 1867) was printed in the *Standard* on August 24, 1867, giving Garrison's opinion that the total bequest should be allotted to the New England Freedman's Union Commission. Directly following Garrison's letter was a comment by Wendell Phillips, which was most probably the statement Garrison refers to as having "publicly broken the chain of friendship." Phillips said that "Mr. Garrison acted as if he were the sole Trustee," and repeated the charge that he appealed to a "prejudiced and pro-slavery Court."

Garrison made no immediate reply in the *Standard,* but after reading a letter to the *Standard* from David Lee and Lydia Maria Child, dated January 1, 1868, and printed February 15, which sympathized with the society as being "unjustly deprived" of the bequest funds, Garrison wrote a defense in the form of a review of his actions. This letter to the *Standard,* dated February 25, 1868, was printed on March 14 without reply.

---

2 1 7

TO HELEN E. GARRISON

Frankfort-on-the-Main, Oct. 3, 1867.

Dear Wife:

On Sunday last, we all bade adieu to Lucerne, with its beautiful lake and sublime mountain scenery—the day previous ascending the Rigi, from the summit of which we had the most stupendous and extended view of the Alps, the chain extending for hundreds of miles, and every summit covered with snow. We passed the night there, witnessing a brilliant sunset, and the next morning a glorious sunrise, baptizing peak after peak with a flood of light. My feet were somewhat crippled by the effort, but I was compensated many times over.

From Lucerne we went to Zurich, where Fanny sojourned so many weeks last year, and spent three or four hours in examining what was noteworthy in the place. It is delightfully situated, and presents many attractions; but it has been scourged by the cholera all summer, so that it is almost wholly avoided by travellers, and all its splendid hotels are empty. We arrived at Shaffhausen that evening, and the next morning spent some time in looking at the falls, the features of which were peculiarly fascinating. Monday evening we arrived at Constance, and saw many things to interest us, as it is a remarkably quaint old town, and noted as the place where John Huss and Jerome of Prague were burnt for their Protestant heresies.[1] The lake is many miles in extent, and surpassed in size and beauty only by lake Leman. Tuesday morning we separated from Harry and Fanny, they going directly to Munich, and we to Stuttgart. As I was only seven or eight hours' ride from Munich, (by railroad,) I was strongly inclined to visit it, but decided not to make the attempt for lack of ample time. Harry and Fanny will probably remain only a few days there, and then will perhaps go to Paris. It is still problematical whether they will return to the United States the coming winter, or remain in Europe. Much will depend upon the answer of Mr. [Horace] White, of the Chicago Tribune, to a letter sent to him by Harry. Perhaps that answer will be received before I leave England, so that I can bring you definite intelligence on the subject. Nothing deters Harry from returning but the high price of genteel living in the United States; and he prudently and properly wishes to see his way clear before taking leave of the continent. We expect to get a letter from him or Fanny to-morrow. They are both in very good health.

Tuesday evening Frank and I reached Stuttgart, and found it to be a large, populous, and in some parts very handsome city, with numerous fine residences, the most admirable railway station we had ever seen, and a royal palace, a large portion of which we interiorly examined the next morning, and were much impressed by its elegance, taste and grandeur.[2] Wednesday we took the cars for Heidelberg, reaching there at 6 P.M. Early this morning, (Thursday,) we visited a famous ruined castle, of immense extent, and walked through the principal street, nearly three miles long, seeing many handsome residences, but not meeting any Americans; and at noon left for this city, arriving at half past 2, P.M. We went immediately to the office of the American Consulate, and found letters from you and Mary-Ann [Johnson], and a note from William, as late as September 17th, as well as several letters from friends in England. All these were eagerly devoured. Frank is now writing to you at the same table with me, as we have barely time to save the mail which leaves for the Liverpool steamer of Saturday to-morrow morning.

I desire you to give Mary-Ann my thanks for her comforting and most encouraging letter in regard to your condition, and the favorable symptoms attending it. I am sure she does not desire or mean to awaken any unwarranted expectations, and I have very great confidence in her judgment and knowledge. I am glad to hear that "Dr. Rush" speaks hopefully as to your restoration, and I trust in order to facilitate it you will not be faithless but believing, thus assisting with your will-power the efforts of Miss [Marcia A.] Houghton, who, it seems, is equally sanguine of final success.[3] Any how, her treatment is undeniably helping your general health, and that is of very great importance. Persevere until I return at least, and resolve to make the most of it. Your hearty co-operation will be of great value.

It is gratifying to know that you have been kindly remembered by Dr. [George] Putnam and Mrs. [George] Simmons in the matter of fruit, and you will give them my thanks from this side of the Atlantic. It is equally pleasant to be informed as to the various friends who have called at Rockledge, as it is next to seeing them. They must have served to make the time go pleasantly with you, and I gratefully appreciate their loving attentions to you.

Your letter is written with Wendell, and Lucy, and noble baby Lloyd, and dear Mrs. McKim, and Ellie, and darling Agnes, and William, and George around you. The circle must be a happy one indeed. I am glad to know that you think Lloyd is a premium babe, (to say nothing about his resemblance to me, which, *of course,* is personally very gratifying!) and equally delighted to learn how charmingly Agnes is developing in mind and person.

We shall leave Frankfort on Sunday for "Bingen on the Rhine," remain there a day or two, then for Coblentz, from thence to Cologne, thence to Brussels, thence to Ostend, and thence across the Channel to London, arriving there next week Friday. On Monday evening, 14th inst., I am to meet a select number of those most interested in the Freedmen's cause, (chiefly Quakers,) at the Friends' Institute;[4] on Tuesday evening 15th inst., I am to have a special reception by prominent friends of the Temperance cause; on Wednesday 16th, I go down to Birmingham, and on Thursday morning, 17th, am to have a public breakfast, and to address a great Freedmen's meeting in the evening, on Friday, 18th, I shall see, with Frank, what is most interesting in the city; on Saturday, 19th, go to Leeds to spend a quiet Sunday with my old anti-slavery friend, Joseph Lupton, Esq.;[5] and on Monday attend a tea party of prominent gentlemen and ladies at the principal hotel, and then go to another large Freedmen's meeting, in Victoria Hall,[6] which I am to address, George Thompson promising to be there also. On Tuesday, 22d, I shall go to Manchester, to speak at an immense gathering in the Free Trade Hall, remain there on the 23d; proceed to Liverpool on the 24th; on the morning of the 25th, a public farewell breakfast will probably be given me in that city, but this is not yet quite certain; and on Saturday, the 26th, embark with Frank for Boston and Rockledge. You see, therefore, what a programme of labor and excitement I have to look in the face during the present month. I hope not to break down in health and am at present feeling and looking very well.

With the most loving regards to you all, and affectionate remembrances to all the friends, I remain,

Your own W. L. G.

☞ Frank regrets that he will not be able to see Charley McKim in Paris before his return home. He has written to him.

☞ It was a very pleasing coincidence, the anniversary of the marriage of Wendell and Lucy while they were with you at Rockledge.

ALS: Garrison Papers, Boston Public Library.

1. John Huss (c. 1373–1415) was the Bohemian leader of the Reformation, a man of peasant background, who had by 1396 received three degrees from the University of Prague. He rose rapidly in the hierarchy of the university and of the Roman Catholic church, until he became so much influenced by the radical theology of John Wycliffe that in 1408 he was forbidden to participate in priestly functions. A series of conflicts followed, culminating in a trial for heresy by the Council of Constance and his execution in 1415.

Jerome of Prague (died 1416) was a slightly younger associate of Huss, supposedly of noble background. Following his studies at Oxford, where he was greatly influenced by Wycliffe, he traveled extensively in Europe, preaching his reformatory doctrines, and in 1415 came to Constance to aid Huss. He was himself imprisoned, but after a recantation was released; he continued, however, to expound his heretical ideas, was soon imprisoned again, condemned, and executed a few months after Huss.

2. Garrison refers to the new palace, finished in 1807.

3. Garrison may refer to a séance at which Benjamin Rush (1745–1813), the famous Philadelphia physician, was believed to have appeared.

4. A reference to the central office and library of the Society of Friends, located in Devonshire House at 12 Bishopgate, London. (FJG, October 14, 1867.)

5. Joseph Lupton, a wholesale cloth merchant, was a Unitarian and a follower of Garrison. He was closely associated with Mary Estlin and Sarah Pugh. In 1853 he was a founder of the Leeds Anti-Slavery Association. (Letter to Richard D. Webb, September 12, 1846, *Letters*, III, 410, n. 2.)

6. A reference to the auditorium in the town hall at Leeds, a building in the Greek style dedicated by Queen Victoria in 1858.

218

TO FANNY GARRISON VILLARD

22 Southampton Street, Bloomsbury, W. C.
London, Oct. 11, 1867.

My dear Fanny—

You will see, by the date, that Frank and I are at our old quarters, where we arrived on Wednesday evening at 6¼ o'clock, making our trip through that day from Brussels to Calais by railroad, and crossing the Channel to Dover, the trip from shore to shore being a little rough but short. I had previously written to Mrs. Levitt of our coming, and happily found the front parlor and back chamber that we had before all in readiness for us, with a comfortable soft-coal fire.[1] She was all pleasantness, and rosy as usual, and inquired particularly after you and Mr. Villard. The servant-girl, Ann, was absent pro tem., to get something for her younger sister, who sails for

America on Monday next, and who unfortunately had her pocket picked of twenty-one shillings and sixpence while doing a little shopping. It seems, now, as if we had not been absent at all; the same street cries saluting our ears, the same smoky state of the atmosphere prevailing, the same nastiness under feet, &c., &c.

We left Frankfort on Sunday morning, and took the steamer on the Rhine at Castel, (opposite Mainz,) intending to stop that night at Coblentz, but went through to Cologne, in consequence of the unpropitious state of the weather. We had a very strong head wind to contend with all the way, and the weather was piercing cold, making it very uncomfortable (as it occasionally rained) to be on deck; nevertheless, we were fortunate in getting very good views all the way, and were much delighted and impressed with what we saw. For some time I was considerably disappointed, as the scenery did not compare with much to be seen on the Hudson river; but as we continued down the river to Bingen, Bonn, &c., we had to acknowledge the superiority of the Rhine in proximate grandeur and picturesque scenery, to say nothing of old towers, castles in ruins, and other feudal monuments. The loveliest and most attractive portion of the river appeared to be Bingen and its vicinity, where one might spend some time very pleasantly, especially if influenced by the romantic.

We stopped at Cologne Sunday night at the hotel Holland,[2] and occupied Monday forenoon in seeing what we could of the place, particularly the principal churches and the great Cathedral, the last being truly wonderful as a structure, and the only object we saw worth looking at. It rained hard all the time, and the streets (rather lanes) were exceedingly nasty, and everything was calculated to stimulate the population to commit suicide *en masse,* and without delay. It is the most detestable place to reside in I ever saw. No doubt the wretched state of the weather had something to do in affecting the judgment. At noon we gladly took the cars for Brussels, where we arrived at tea-time, stopping at the hotel de l'Europe.[3] It rained heavily all the way, and we found the streets in anything but a nice condition. The weather was very cold and forbidding, feeling much more like December than October. We remained in Brussels from Monday night till Wednesday morning, and were more pleased with it, (in spite of the rain,) than any place we had seen, except Paris.

Yesterday we went to the Star office, and got a bundle of letters that had been waiting for us—among them one from your mother, dated 23d ult., and yours to me of the 5th inst. There is nothing new at Rockledge. Your mother expresses a good deal of sympathy for

Harry and Emma [Xylander], in view of the death of their father, and also of pleasure that you are with them—adding, "Fanny will be able to see the dear aunt [Anna-Maria Pfeiffer] and sister, to whom she became so tenderly attached before leaving Munich. Tell her to give my love to them, and my sympathy in view of their great bereavement. I have felt so much for the aunt in her lameness, and hearing from Fanny about her, that she seems as if she was my blood-relative."[4] Mrs. McKim, and Lucy, and Lloyd, had all left that day for Orange, William accompanying them to New York. Your mother extols Lloyd afresh, and says I shall soon be "singing his praises as a noble, beautiful boy, destined to be something grand in the world"! Mrs. [Caroline W. H.] Dall had pronounced Lucy's head "much handsomer than Mrs. Chapman's"! Your mother joins. in Lucy's praise, and says, "She is really lovely now, and I think Lloyd will be splendid *when a year old"!* Good for the first grandson, especially as he is said strongly to resemble his grandfather! Of Agnes your mother writes—"She delights everybody with her prattle. She dances—takes hold of her dress each side, and has no fear of strangers. She smacks when she kisses, and laughs heartily." Among those who had called were Edmund Jackson and his wife, Sarah Grimké, and Mrs. Dall.[5] Also, a nephew of Henry Ware, whom came to see Lucy, as he is a proof-reader of her book of negro melodies she and Wendell are getting out.[6] John Ritchie had passed an evening at Rockledge. He expects Mr. [John A.] and Mrs. Lewis to sail quite soon for home. I will enclose a part of your mother's letter, containing a few additional items of intelligence, if the weight will allow of it.

All day yesterday Frank and I occupied in endeavoring to find our trunks (the one from Paris, and the other from Lucerne) at some one of the various receiving houses connected with the London Bridge Station;[7] but we can get no intelligence of them. Frank has written to Bowles, Drevet & Co., and I have written to the Station Master at Lucerne. Of course, we are taken "all aback." We have also telegraphed to Newhaven, to know (which is not improbable) whether the trunks are detained for examination there; and, if so, to apprise us of the fact, and we will send the keys. It is more than twenty-four hours since we telegraphed, but as yet we get no reply. Moreover, the box (containing the carved boxes I bought) that Harry and Frank sent through the post, at Lucerne, has not been received at the London office, and it seems doubtful whether we shall ever get it.[8] Our trunks are of much more consequence, especially the one sent from Lucerne. Tell Harry I owe Mr. Murphy, at Frankfort, 36 Kreuzers for postage on letters he has sent me since I

left.[9] If H. can pay him, I will make it good. Thanks for your interesting letter. Am glad to hear the dear aunt is better. Frank joins me
in love to one and all.

Your loving Father.

P.S. I am to have a social reception meeting on Monday evening,
and another on Tuesday evening, and shall go on Wednesday to
Birmingham. A letter addressed to the care of Arthur Albright, Esq.
will reach me there.[10]

AL signed "Father": Villard Papers, Harvard College Library.

1. Garrison's landlady, Mrs. Levitt, has not been identified.

2. Not identified.

3. The Hôtel de l'Europe was located in the Place Royale in the upper part of
Brussels. (Karl Baedeker, *Belgium and Holland,* Leipzig, 1901, p. 75.)

4. Helen E. Garrison's letter of September 23, 1867, from which Garrison quotes,
has apparently not been preserved.

5. Edmund Jackson (1795–1875) married Mary H. Hewes (c. 1803–1877) in 1827.
They had eleven children, five of whom died before the age of three. (Letter to the
editor from Ruth E. Cannard, director-curator, Jackson Homestead, Newton, Mass.,
November 17, 1972; FJG, April 6, 1877.)

Sarah Moore Grimké (1792–1873), sister of Angelina E. Grimké, was born to the
slaveholding family of John Faucheraud Grimké in Charleston, S.C. In 1821, with
her sister, she moved to Philadelphia, relinquishing the Episcopal church and becoming a Quaker. Partly through the influence of Garrison, she moved in 1836 to
New York and became a professional abolitionist. In 1838 Angelina married Theodore D. Weld, and Sarah joined the Weld household, occupying herself with anti-
slavery duties and later with the care of the Weld children. In 1848 the Welds and
Sarah Grimké began operating a boarding school in their New York home; later they
moved to Perth Amboy, N.J., and conducted a school there. In the 1860s they moved
to the Boston area, where they taught for several years in Dio Lewis' school for
young ladies. Although of the two sisters Angelina was the more distinguished orator, Sarah's contribution to the antislavery movement was substantial and far-reaching. (*NAW.*)

6. Henry Ware, Jr. (1794–1843), a graduate of Phillips Academy, Andover, and
Harvard, was the well-known minister of the Second Church (Unitarian) in Boston
and professor at the Harvard Divinity School. He was one of the founders and at one
time the president of the Cambridge Anti-Slavery Society. In addition to being a
poet, he was the author of many books on religious subjects, including the popular
On the Formation of the Christian Character (1831). By his second wife, Mary Lovell Pickard, whom he married in 1827, Ware was the father of six children, one of
whom was Charles Pickard Ware (1840–1921), whom Garrison mistakenly calls his
nephew. Charles Ware was head of the record department of the American Bell Telephone Co. in Boston. With William Francis Allen and Lucy McKim Garrison he
edited *Slave Songs of the United States* (1867). (See the introduction to *Slave Songs
of the United States;* Emma Forbes Ware, *Ware Genealogy; Robert Ware, of Ded-
ham, Massachusetts, 1642–1699, and his Lineal Descendants,* Boston, 1901.)

7. Garrison refers to an early station on the London and Greenwich Railway, located on the south bank of the Thames between Tooley and St. Thomas streets. It
was built in 1836 and reconstructed in 1851. (Karl Baedeker, *London and Its Environs; Handbook for Travellers,* London, 1885, p. 32; Nikolaus Pevsner, *The Buildings of England: London,* Harmondsworth, 1952, p.60.)

8. The box and trunks were recovered on October 14. (FJG, October 14, 1867.)

9. William Walton Murphy (1816–1886), born in Canada, was brought to New
York state early in life; as a youth he moved to Michigan, where he entered politics

in 1844 as state representative. For years a strong Democrat, he was led by his abolitionist views to become a Free-Soiler in 1848. In 1854 he threw his support to the
burgeoning Republican party and thereafter was a loyal member of that party. In
1861 President Lincoln named him consul-general for Frankfurt. In that post
Murphy used all his influence to further the Union cause in Europe.

The kreuzer was a unit of money used in southern Germany, three kreuzers being
the equivalent in value of one English penny. (Karl Baedeker, *The Rhine from Rot-
terdam to Constance,* Coblenz and Leipzig, 1873.)

10. Arthur Albright (1811–1900), a Birmingham Quaker, was a successful manufacturer of phosphorus. He was an active philanthropist and reformer, who devoted
much of his energy to abolition and peace. During the Civil War he helped many
slaves escape from the Confederate states, even on occasion traveling to the United
States on their behalf. (Christine Bolt, *The Anti-Slavery Movement and Reconstruction: a Study in Anglo-American Co-operation, 1833–1877,* London, 1969, pp. 63–
64; letter to the editor from W. A. Taylor, city librarian, Birmingham Public Libraries, March 29, 1976.)

219

TO FANNY GARRISON VILLARD

Rockledge, Nov. 12, 1867.

My dear Fanny:

"Home again, home again, from a foreign shore,"[1] to find all the
dear ones in good health, and every thing looking as naturally as if
there had been neither separation nor lapse of time. I found your
mother looking as fair and rosy as could be desired, and waiting impatiently at the window for our arrival, and overjoyed to see Frank
and me returning in such good condition. We got to the house a little after nine o'clock on Wednesday evening last, and found it brilliantly illuminated with all that the gas fixings could do, the parlor
and sitting-room set off with plants and flowers, and splendid bo-
quets contributed by Mrs. [Dora] Brigham, (who was on hand,) and
a handsome entertainment prepared by the family. William and
Ellie came for us in a carriage at the wharf in East Boston, but we
did not get our luggage till the next day. Just before the Java
reached the outer lighthouse in the Bay, a steam-tug came along
side, and several gentlemen connected with the Custom-House got
on board, and immediately inquired for me, bringing me a message
from Collector [Thomas] Russell to the effect that, much to his regret, he could not meet me on my arrival, as he was detained at
Provincetown; but through them saying everything would be done
for my accommodation, to prevent unnecessary delay, &c. He also
had previously given William a note to be presented to the Inspec-
tors, requesting them to allow my luggage to be sent to William's

store for examination, or whatever other place I might designate; being significant of a wish to let them go unexamined. Anne Warren Weston had three large trunks, which she also wished to have included with ours, and succeeded with but a formal examination. It seems that the government regulations are very stringent, and each passenger is expected to certify as to the dutiable articles he has with him. I had to do with Major [Lt. Col. Charles B.] Fox, (who was with the 54th or 55th Colored Regiment,) who, while seeming anxious to give me as little trouble as possible, and undesirous of unpacking my trunks, nevertheless wished me to certify to what I had, which was equivalent to submitting everything to his personal inspection.[2] I told him that I knew not what was dutiable, and what was not; that I had made some few purchases of Swiss boxes, &c., of no great value, for family presents, as well as some other articles; but I preferred his examination of everything, rather than to make any certificate in the dark. He, finally, asked me if I had any silks. I told him I had a silk dress for my wife. "Is it not cut?" he asked. "No," I said, "it is in the piece." Of course, that was dutiable, and so I had to pay eighteen dollars in addition to the first cost—I mean eighteen in American currency. I had entirely forgotten that there was also a silk dress for Ellie, and so no charge was made upon it. No further examination or inquiry was entered into, and I was fortunate in getting off so cheaply. You will wonder why I did not get Mrs. Nosworthy to cut your mother's dress, in accordance with your advice; but there was no time to do so, and the trunk containing it was not accessible.

The various presents I brought have been disposed of as judiciously as possible. They have given great satisfaction. Ellie is highly gratified with the articles you purchased for her, and finds them very nice and very cheap, and is "ever so much obliged" to you. She admires the cloak you purchased for her at Munich. That is my present to her.

Your mother was equally pleased with the shawls and other presents. She prizes the covering for the sofa cushion which you wrought so skilfully and with so much labor, and thinks the pattern "a perfect beauty," as all the rest of the household do. She tells me that, in writing to you, she has inadvertently forgotten to refer to it. Much as she longs to see you, she is satisfied that you have decided wisely in remaining behind until Harry can accompany you home.

On Saturday evening, William and Ellie left us to enter upon housekeeping for themselves, within five minutes' walk from Rockledge. They have a very neat, commodious house, and have taken a lease of it for two years. Fortunately, just at this time, Thomas Mott having broken up at Roadside, and sold his splendid house and domains, in order to reside with his family several years in Paris, (doubtless you will soon find them out, as they are already on the way, and will be glad to have them to call upon occasionally,) he and his wife have sent Ellie all sorts of things for the kitchen and other rooms, so that William has been saved a considerable expense in furnishing his house.[3] William left us with reluctance, but Ellie was glad to go, I think. At least, she expressed nothing to the contrary. How they will get along remains to be seen. They are expecting the arrival, to-day, of Mrs. [David] Wright and Lucretia Mott. Mrs. W. will remain some weeks with them.

I have scarcely made any calls, or seen any of the friends, since my return. As no distinct announcement was made of my arrival in any Boston paper, but only "Mr. L. Garrison and son" appeared in the printed list of passengers, there are very many, doubtless, who are yet ignorant that I have got back. I have seen the [Samuel] Mays in Hollis Street, Daniel Thaxter, Percy [Scarborough] and Theo., (Lucy [Thaxter] being away at Brooklyn, [Conn.]) Mrs. [Wendell] Phillips and Lizzie Simmons, but neither Dr. [George] Putnam, nor the Cobbs, as they were absent when I called.[4] We had at tea, Sunday evening, Mrs. Nowell and Joseph,[5] Mr. [Robert F.] Wallcut, John Ritchie, and Miss Cannan. This morning I have had a pleasant call from Theodore Tilton, who is lecturing in this region. Yesterday I caught a glimpse of Wendell Phillips, but he did not see me. To-day I am to be at a reception party given to Lord and Lady Amberley by Hon. Josiah Quincy, at his residence in Park Street.[6] Perhaps you will recollect that I was introduced to Lord A. (who is Earl Russell's eldest son,) at the House of Commons. He is examining our schools, prisons, and various public institutions with a good deal of pleasure and interest. This evening, Charles Sumner (who has recently had a narrow escape of his life by being thrown from the cars while the train was in motion, and was badly bruised) is to lecture before the Parker Fraternity. Henry Vincent, is to lecture to-morrow evening. I am to lecture before the Fraternity the last of November, in consequence of a serious mishap to our friend Rev. Samuel Johnson, who was recently thrown from a train, and dreadfully battered, his jaws being broken, his shoulder dislocated, &c.[7] Of the sudden death of Gov. [John A.] Andrew you will have been apprised before receiving this. He is universally lamented. Mrs. [Louise] De Mortie is also dead, of yellow fever, in New Orleans.

I have said nothing of our voyage. It was the roughest I have ever made—a succession of gales from Liverpool to Boston—but I never once vomited, nor lost a single meal. Frank stood it bravely. We were eleven days and a half. Thanks, many thanks, darling, for your affectionate and interesting letters received at Liverpool and Queenstown, which it was not possible for me to reply to.

☞ We trust you like your new quarters in Paris, & that all is going well with you & Harry.

☞ Everybody inquires after you and Harry, and are eager for all particulars of our tour.

AL: Villard Papers, Harvard College Library.

1. M. S. Pike, "Home Again," line 1, *Lincoln Literary Collection, Design for School-Room & Family Circle,* ed. J. P. McCaskey (Freeport, N.Y., n.d.).

2. Charles Barnard Fox (1833–1895), born in Newburyport and a resident of Boston, was a civil engineer in Boston and the South before becoming a major and then, by brevet, a lieutenant colonel in the 55th Massachusetts infantry. After the war he, was to have several occupations: cotton planter in the South, inspector of the custom house in Boston, real estate broker, and member of the state legislature. (Obituary, Boston *Evening Transcript,* March 30, 1895.)

3. Thomas Mott (1823–1899) was the second son by that name of James and Lucretia Mott, the first having died in 1817. In 1846 Thomas married Mariana Pelham (c. 1826–1872), his first cousin, the daughter of Martha Coffin Pelham Wright, Lucretia's sister. The Garrisons were therefore related to the Thomas Motts, since Mariana Pelham was Ellen Wright Garrison's half-sister. (Anna Davis Hallowell, *James and Lucretia Mott, Life and Letters,* Boston, 1884.)

4. Theo[dore] has not been identified, although he may have been Percy Scarborough's brother.

Lizzie Simmons (born 1845) was probably the daughter of neighbor George Simmons. (FJG, passim, and especially the entry for November 8, 1877.)

Samuel Crocker Cobb (1826–1891), long a resident of Highland Street, entered politics in 1861, when he was elected to the Roxbury Board of Aldermen. He continued to represent Roxbury when in 1867 that town's board was merged with Boston's. Two years later he became a member of the Boston Board of Directors for Public Institutions, serving in this capacity until he was elected mayor of the city in 1873. (Obituary, Boston *Evening Transcript,* February 19, 1891; James M. Burger, *The Memoir of Samuel Crocker Cobb,* Boston, 1892.)

5. Sarah J. Nowell, who came originally from Portsmouth, N.H., was apparently a widow living with her children in Cambridgeport. Mention is made in FJG, beginning in 1868, of James (the elder son, who died in 1877), Joseph, and Sadie.

6. Lady Amberley was Katharine Louisa Stanley (1842–1874), daughter of Edward John Stanley, second Baron Stanley of Alderby; she had been married to Lord Amberley since 1864. (*Burke's Peerage and Baronetage,* London, 1975.)

Josiah Quincy (1802–1882) was the brother of Edmund and the son of Josiah; he was married to Mary Jane Miller Quincy. A graduate of Harvard in the class of 1821, he had been mayor of Boston (1845–1849) and subsequently president of the Common Council. Although not so active in the cause as his brother, Josiah was also an abolitionist; in fact, it was he who presided at the jubilee meeting at the Boston Music Hall, February 4, 1865. (*Life.*)

7. Samuel Johnson (1822–1882), a graduate of both the college and the divinity school at Harvard, became minister of a free church in Lynn in 1858, a post he held until 1870. He published several volumes on religious topics. (Obituary, New York *Times,* February 21, 1882.)

2 2 0

TO HENRY VILLARD

Rockledge, Nov. 12, 1867.

Dear Harry:

I received at least two letters from you before leaving Liverpool, which I tried very hard to find time to answer; but with the constant and pressing civilities which were shown to me, and the various letters I had to write, I found it to be utterly impracticable to do so. Not even a farewell line to Fanny. But I got Frank to be my substitute; and as he apprised you how I was situated, I am sure you have not been disposed to chide me on that score.

One single reference to your letter, dated Munich, Oct. 13th, in which you express surprise and grief that I should have deemed you lacking in gratitude with reference to my prolonging my visit abroad, so that your wishes might be met in regard to Fanny. Please consider the whole matter dropped and buried when I say, that it was no thought or purpose of mine to bring any such accusation against you, and I am very sorry that you have been pained in this manner.[1]

In regard to your location, whether it be abroad or in the United States, it is for you and Fanny to determine, according as means and circumstances may seem to require. Neither my wife nor I would urge you, for one moment, to come back on our account; but we shall rejoice when you can do so, seeing your way clear pecuniarily, &c. For your frank statement respecting your father's affairs, and the moderate inheritance received from him, accept my thanks. I know your expenses in Paris will be unavoidably considerable, (though not so large as in this country at hotels or boarding-houses,) and therefore you and Fanny will need to be careful in regard to current expenditures, especially as your health is precarious, and you are such a sufferer from your terrible neuralgic attacks. What I want to say is, that William and Ellie having gone to housekeeping, the chamber they occupied is vacant; and if you can so arrange matters as to be with us at Rockledge, provided you should prefer being on this side of the Atlantic, "other things being equal," you can board with us as long as you choose at the rate of one hundred dollars a month in American currency, washing included. I do not name a less sum, because you would not wish it, and more I should not feel willing to take, if proffered. If preferred, you and Fanny might have her former room, and the long one adjoining for your writing-room. This is not to urge you away from Paris, but only to enable you to calculate expenses, in case of returning home. We are hoping you may have received satisfactory intelligence from Mr. [Horace] White. The articles you sent to Mrs. White[2] will be forwarded to her in a few days, in care of Miss [Martha] Rand. No duties were paid on them.

Should you happen to see Mr. and Mrs. [George A.] Blanchard, give my warmest regards to them. They added much to our pleasure in travelling. Frank will write soon. All send loving remembrances to you and Fanny.

AL: Villard Papers, Harvard College Library.

1. For another reference to the friction between Garrison and his son-in-law, see the letter to Fanny Garrison Villard, October 15, 1867 (micro.).

2. Martha Root White (died 1873), the first wife of Horace White, was from New Haven, Conn.

221

TO HENRY C. WRIGHT

Roxbury, Dec. 9, 1867.

My dear H. C. W.:

Your letter from Cleveland is just received. I am glad to hear that you got safely to your place of destination, though it seemed rather hard you should leave us on the morning of Thanksgiving Day. Not because of the turkey, the plum pudding, the pies, &c., &c.; not because we are to be thankful on one day of the year more than another; but because there are pleasant associations connected with the festival, and it is a time for special social enjoyment.

I regret to receive an account of the bitter, malignant colorphobia still holding mastery over the popular mind in Ohio, such as you send in your letter. This vulgar, brutal, unnatural prejudice is the opprobrium of our civilization and Christianity. It is as poison to the blood, as leprosy to the body. It is, moreover, positive and terrible retribution for the enslavement of the colored race; and it will continue to smite us as a people until we learn, accept, and act upon the great fundamental truth of human brotherhood, "God hath made of one blood all nations of men, to dwell on all the face of the earth."[1]

As compared with only thirty years ago, great progress has been made in changing public sentiment on this subject; still, it strongly controls every part of our country. Its main concentration is found in the so-called but utterly spurious Democratic party; and this because that party is very largely made up of the ignorance and depravity abounding in the land. It is deplorable to see how badly the Irish are cursed by it; they themselves the most despised next to the negroes. Of course, they are nearly all Democrats, the victims of Romish priestcraft on the one hand, and of political demagogues on the other.

The recreant occupant of the White House has exceeded himself in his Presidential message, in his usurping assumptions and defiant language.[2] That message Congress should have either sent back to its author, or branded as soon as read in fitting terms officially placed upon their records. Instead of this, they proceed to declare, by a vote of three to one, that Andrew Johnson has done nothing worthy of impeachment![3] And the decision is every where hailed as satisfactory. The primary difficulty, then, is not with Congress, (which is organically not an independent but a representative body,) but with the people. Let the latter be called to account rather than the former. Judgment must begin with them.

If you will address a letter to "Elizabeth Pease Nichols, Huntly Lodge, Edinburgh, Scotland," she will readily get it. I think it would gratify her to receive one from you as a token of your remembrance of her kindness, and good words and works.

It gives me great delight to read what you have communicated respecting my dear and beloved friends, Thomas and Mary Jones, and their children. I believe it is a little over twenty years since I was so dangerously ill under their roof; but a thousand years will not obliterate from my memory the grateful recollection of their tender and watchful care of me during that protracted sickness.[4] It gave me great pleasure to call upon them when I was in Cleveland two years ago, but this was diminished on account of my not being able to commune with them longer. I regard them as among the best people I have ever known; and when you see them again, give them my affectionate salutations and my warmest regards.

Remember your age, and be careful of your health. Accept our household love.

Yours, for light and liberty,

Wm. Lloyd Garrison.

H. C. Wright.

ALS: Garrison Papers, Boston Public Library.

1. Acts 17:26.

2. Garrison refers to the third annual message to Congress, December 3, 1867, in which Johnson expressed his concern that all the states be restored to their proper relationship with each other and to the federal government. The policies proposed by the radicals, he was convinced, would not achieve this result. The radical politi-

cians proposed, in effect, not only to confer on Negroes the right to vote but also to disenfranchise a sufficiently large number of white citizens to give the Negroes a clear majority in the southern states. Johnson also pointed out that if Negro governments were in fact established, it would require a strong standing army to hold the white people of the South in subjection. (New York *Times*, December 3, 1867.)

3. The Senate Judiciary Committee had introduced in November 1867 a resolution for Johnson's impeachment, which had been defeated four days after his message of December 3 by a vote of 108 to 57. (Lloyd Paul Stryker, *Andrew Johnson: A Study in Courage*, New York, 1929, pp. 511–518.)

4. See *Letters*, III, 526–528.

222

TO OLIVER JOHNSON

Roxbury, Dec. 11, 1867.

My dear Johnson:

Thanks for your letter, with its hospitable invitation, which, going or coming, it will give me very great pleasure to accept. I infer that you will be looking for me this week Friday. If so, let me correct the mistake by stating, what I wrote to Wendell, that I shall not be able to go to New York until next week Friday, 20th inst. I shall defer to his wishes about going out to Orange that night. "Other things being equal," I should prefer to remain with you, especially if the weather should prove severely cold or stormy. But it shall be exactly as he wishes. It is not an agreeable time of the year to travel; but I am eager to see the dear ones at the Park, especially that remarkable baby [Lloyd McKim Garrison] who looks so like his grandfather—in baldness, perhaps! I also very much desire to see you and other friends in New York.

For a fortnight past I have been feeling very unwell, and am at present "good for nothing." It would almost seem as if I was going through the process of being acclimated. I want to write an article for the Independent as soon as I can use the pen.[1]

En passant—the Boston *Post*, of this morning, sarcastically says, "Tilton is having as much difficulty with the 'position' of the Independent as a dancing-master with a stupid pupil." Inasmuch as the Independent disclaims being the organ of any religious denomination, I hope neither Tilton nor Bowen will try no more to satisfy certain clerical bigots on the score of "evangelical" soundness.[2] What does confession or protestation amount to with such? Ignore them utterly, and let the paper speak for itself. Nine-tenths of the contributors appear to be orthodox clergymen; but even this disproportionate number seems to produce no satisfaction with the cavillers referred to.

The "impeachment" of the traitor at the White House is, what he called Forney, a "dead duck."[3] All honor to those who gave their votes in the affirmative! It is humiliating to see such a pitiable ending of this matter, but it is clear that there is no public sentiment demanding the impeachment, and Congress cannot be expected, as a representative body, to disregard or run counter to that sentiment in so grave a matter. But, alas! for the nation itself!

I hold that the Presidential bully and usurper deserves to be impeached and removed for his recent mutinous and insulting message to Congress, if for no other reason. But the obvious state of popular feeling, and the timidity of the Republicans, as shown in the vote on impeachment, will only the more embolden that bad man.

Give my kind regards to Mary-Ann, and the household at Mrs. [Augustus] Savin's.

Ever faithfully yours,

W. L. G.

ALS: Garrison Papers, Boston Public Library.

1. The *Independent* did publish on January 30, 1868, an article by Garrison about John Henry Hopkins, entitled "The Late Bishop Hopkins."

2. Henry Chandler Bowen (1813–1896) had been a successful New York silk merchant before founding the *Independent* in 1848, a paper that, along with the Brooklyn *Union,* he owned for many years. As proprietor of the paper Tilton edited, Bowen was destined to become famous for his connection with the Tilton-Beecher scandal.

3. John Wien Forney (1817–1881) was a self-made journalist and frustrated politician. Beginning his career in Lancaster, Pa., as printer and then editor of the Lancaster *Intelligencer,* he had a wide-ranging career as writer and editor for a series of papers: the Philadelphia *Pennsylvanian,* the Washington *Daily Union,* the Philadelphia *Press,* the Washington *Sunday* and *Daily Morning Chronicle,* and the weekly Philadelphia magazine *Progress.* In 1856 he supported James Buchanan for the presidency, but under Buchanan's administration he was not offered the kinds of positions he wanted. He actively supported Lincoln in the columns of both the *Chronicle* and the *Press;* for a time he also defended Andrew Johnson but later urged his impeachment. In addition to magazine and newspaper articles, he also published several books.

2 2 3

TO FANNY GARRISON VILLARD

Roxbury, Dec. 12, 1867.

Dear Fanny:

This day I complete my 63d year, and I cannot employ a portion of it more pleasantly than by writing to you. Mrs. [David] Wright, William & Ellie are coming to take tea, participate in stewed oyesters and ice creams, and spend the evening. Julia Randall and Charlotte Coffin are with us. The ground is covered with snow, the day stormy, and the mercury nearly at zero. For a week past we have had weather, which, for severity, belongs to January and February. Perhaps they will be mild in proportion. Jack Frost is playing his most fantastic tricks with the window panes, and pinching feet, hands, ears, noses in a way to make them tingle. I have not been into Boston for several days, in consequence of such inclemency. In Paris you may have, at this season, a good deal of disagreeable weather, but, of course, nothing approximating to this Siberian spell. Pleasant indeed has it been to us all to hear from you to-day, through letters received by Mrs. Wright from Thomas Mott and his wife. They speak of the visit you and Harry had made to them with much pleasure, and mention that you are both thinking of going to Italy this winter. Doubtless your next letter, which we are now hourly looking for, will give us exact information about what you have in prospect.

Well, darling, I am sixty three years nearer my earthly exit than I was at my advent. That is twenty years more than the average of life, and only seven years short of three score years and ten. Of course, my pilgrimage below cannot be greatly extended. At the longest, the period must be comparatively short. It would be foolish and unreasonable for me to wish it otherwise; but it is for that reason I long to see as much of you as I can. Harry will not chide me when I say, that, ever since your marriage, I have missed you from the household almost like a mortal bereavement. So has your mother. Indeed, in her crippled state, and so much needing to be kept cheered up in her spirits, she necessarily feels your absence even more than I do. But neither of us would hurry you back on our account, or to the inconvenience of Harry. He must consult his means and his possibilities; and your first and paramount duty is to consult his wishes, and do all in your power to make him happy as a loving and faithful wife, and also to make his burdens as light as possible. Both of us feel assured that he and you will come back to us as soon as circumstances are propitious—that is, by next April or May, according to your present intentions. We should shrink from having you cross the Atlantic during the inclemency of winter; and March is as blowy and disagreeable a month as any of the twelve. In the mean time, occupy yourself as assiduously as you can in acquiring a better knowledge of the French language, and still greater proficiency in music. Do not presume on your past exemption from sickness to make you reckless on the score of health. It will be likely to go hard with you when you break down, and your safety will be found in acting upon the maxim, that an ounce of prevention is worth a pound of cure.

We have ceased having any "treatment" for your mother at present, her general health being so good, and a pause being deemed expedient.

I have lectured only once since my return home, (before the Parker Fraternity—subject, "Abroad and at Home,") but am to lecture at Melrose on Monday evening, and at Worcester on Thursday evening, next week. It is difficult for me to decide exactly what to do; and Frank is in the same uncertainty—"only more so." Next Friday I shall make another attempt to visit the McKims, and Wendell and Lucy, and the baby [Lloyd McKim Garrison] that looks so like his grandfather, (it must be in point of baldness, I think, though he may have more hair than I suppose,) and then we will have a sort of family confab. as to the future. The Freedmen's Union wishes me to enter the lecturing field in its behalf, but I do not see my way clear to do so, pressing as is the exigency in regard to the Freedmen's cause; the message of Andrew Johnson to Congress, respecting that cause, being calculated to bring fresh persecution upon the poor unoffending blacks. But I am really not well enough to encounter the rigors of winter in travelling and speaking to any extent. I must seriously try to commence upon my History of the Anti-Slavery Struggle.

The beautiful pattern for a cushion for the sofa that you worked with so much skill and labor for your mother has been made up for that purpose by Julia [Randall], in a manner evincing nice taste. It will attract the notice of all comers. Mine was the first head to lie upon the cushion after it was completed to-day; and then your mother laid her head down with mine, and thus the gift was consecrated.

We shall think of you and Harry on the coming holidays; and though this will arrive too late to enable us seasonably to wish you a merry Christmas, it will be in time for us to wish you a happy New Year. The only way I can send you a trifling gift is to ask Harry to draw upon me, at sight, through Bowles, Drevet & Co., or in any other way he prefers, for one hundred francs in gold. Take it for your own use, with my benediction.

After the 1st of January, Boston is to incorporate Roxbury as its Fifteenth Ward.

The Copperheads carried Boston in the recent election for Mayor;[1] and all over the country that party is now jubilant, and confident of succeeding at the next Presidential election. The Republicans are evidently cowed, and, what is worse, very much divided as to the policy to be pursued, and the candidate to put in nomination. Judge [Salmon P.] Chase has a strong party; but Gen. Grant will in all probability be nominated by the National Republican Convention, to be held at Chicago next Spring.[2] In his case, his partisans are strongly inclined to non-commitalism as to any pledges on his part.

I hope you see Mr. and Mrs. Blanchard occasionally. They added so much to the enjoyment of our trip to Switzerland while they remained with us, that I shall always remember their companionship with unalloyed gratification. I heard from their children, the other day, through Mrs. Dr. Morrill of Concord, N.H.[3] She said they were doing well under the almost motherly watchfulness of Mrs. [Parker] Pillsbury, who omits no exertions in their behalf.

Frank has just received a long and characteristically humorous letter from dear R. D. Webb, in which he says—"I had a pleasant letter from that darling little woman, your sister; but as she took six weeks or more to answer my preceding one, I am standing on my dignity, and am waiting for three before I answer her."[4] It will be hard work for him to hold back so long, he seems to delight so much in letter-writing. He has a great fancy for "the pleasant little body," as he calls you.

I have written to Mr. [George] Thompson but once since my return, but get no answer as yet. He is more dilatory than I am in the matter of epistolary interchange. Mrs. [John A.] Lewis saw him a week later than I did—the day she sailed from Liverpool; and says he was looking quite feeble and dejected. I am pained to think of his situation, and know not how he will be able to get along pecuniarily. When I left, there was some talk in Leeds and Manchester about getting up a subscription for him. I hope it will not end in talk.

I could wish that you might find time occasionally to correspond with Mrs. E. P. Nichols at Edinburgh, and the Mawsons at Newcastle-on-Tyne.[5] How pleased they would be to be thus remembered!

My "Testimonial" will be closed this month, and invested according to the best judgment of the Committee. The whole amount collected is about $31,000. Of this amount, $3000 were paid last year to redeem our house from the mortgage upon it. The expense of collecting will probably be $1000, including Mr. [William] Hooper's services and travelling expenses, though not a cent was realized from his efforts. This leaves $27,000 as capital. I hope to be able, with the interest thereon, to earn enough not to lessen that amount. But I may have to do so, nevertheless. The gift is larger than I expected it would be by at least one half. Mr. [Samuel] May [Jr.] has labored in season and out of season to secure it; and, instrumentally, I owe every thing to his friendship.

William and Ellie like their new quarters. They live on Lambert Street, next below Porter, on the left hand side, by the passage way this side of the stone cottage. Agnes is fast learning to talk.

All our love to dear Harry.

Ever your loving father,

W. L. G.

ALS: Villard Papers, Harvard College Library.

1. Nathaniel Bradstreet Shurtleff (1810–1874) was a graduate of the college and medical school of Harvard. A Democrat, he served three terms as mayor of Boston (1868–1870), the last time without the support of his party. Long a member of the Massachusetts Historical Society, Shurtleff was a distinguished antiquarian who edited the many volumes of records of both the Massachusetts Bay and the Plymouth colonies. He was also the author of *A Topographical and Historical Description of Boston* (1871). (J. M. Bugbee, "Boston Under the Mayors," in Justin Winsor, *The Memorial History of Boston*, Boston, 1881, III, 276–277; Charles C. Smith, "Memoir of the Hon. Nathaniel B. Shurtleff, M.D.," *PMHS*, 1st ser., 13: 389, December 1874.)

2. At the National Republican Convention in Chicago, May 20, 1868, Ulysses S. Grant was nominated unanimously for President and Schuyler Colfax for Vice President. (*American Annual Cyclopaedia and Register of Important Events, 1868*, New York, 1873.)

3. The George A. Blanchards had two daughters: Lucretia Tilden, who was eventually to live in Belmont, Mass., and Grace, who was to become a librarian in Concord. (Ezra S. Stearns, ed., *Genealogical and Family History of New Hampshire*, New York, 1908, I, 785–786.)

Eliza Ann Cate Morrill married homeopathic physician Dr. Alpheus Morrill as his second wife in 1838; they had three children: Shadrach Cate (1839–1904), Annie (already identified), and Mary. (Stearns, *Genealogical and Family History*, p. 717.)

4. The reference is to Richard Davis Webb's letter of November 30, 1867 (Merrill Collection of Garrison Papers, Wichita State University Library), and the quotation is accurate, although Garrison improves the punctuation.

5. John Mawson (died 1867) was a prominent citizen of Newcastle, a druggist and chemist, member of the Town Council, and ultimately sheriff. He was also a member of the Peace Council and an ardent abolitionist. His second wife, whose maiden name was Swan, was the niece of his first wife, Jane Cameron, as well as the sister of Mawson's business partner. As sheriff, Mawson was disposing of some explosives that ignited accidentally, killing him on December 18, 1867. (Obituary, Newcastle *Daily Chronicle*, December 19, 1867.)

224

TO LYMAN ABBOTT

Roxbury, Dec. 14, 1867.

Dear Mr. Abbott:

I am very much obliged to you for your earnest letter, pertaining to the present state of the Freedmen's cause, and the need of renewed efforts for its furtherance. Of course, it will give me great pleasure at all times to do what I can for it; but I cannot at present commit myself to attending any series of public meetings in its behalf. First, because I have been more or less unwell ever since I got back from Europe; and I do not feel that it would be prudent for me, at this inclement season of the year, to be travelling about, running no inconsiderable risk from fatigue and exposure. Secondly, having been so long absent from home, I do not feel justified in leaving it so soon, especially in view of the crippled condition of my wife, arising from paralysis; and, therefore, I have declined many advantageous overtures to lecture at the West this winter. Thirdly, I am now seriously thinking of commencing with the new year my projected History of the Anti-Slavery Struggle; in which case I must bring a special consecration to the work.

I will not, however, go into any further reasons or specifications at this time, as I am expecting to be in New York at the close of next week, when I will call at your office, and confer with you and Mr. [J. Miller] McKim on the subject.

The atrocious sentiments expressed in the recent message of President Johnson to Congress, relative to the freedmen, cannot fail to subject them to fresh persecutions on the part of the Southern whites.[1] Yet, out of this great evil I shall look for the hand of a wonder-working God to bring forth great good to that unoffending and afflicted race. No less guilty will be the evil-doers.

Yours, in the cause of the oppressed,

Wm. Lloyd Garrison.

Rev. Lyman Abbott.

ALS: Abbott Memorial Collection, Bowdoin College Library.

Lyman Abbott (1835–1922) was a New York lawyer turned Congregational clergyman and editor. Ordained in Maine in 1860, he went that same year to Terre Haute, Ind., where he remained during the Civil War. In 1865 he moved to New York to serve as corresponding secretary of the American Union Commission, an organization composed of ministers and laymen dedicated to helping the federal government in the process of Reconstruction, and as pastor of the newly organized New England Congregational Church on Forty-first Street. In 1870 he became editor of the *Illustrated Christian Weekly*, and six years later he joined Henry Ward Beecher in editing the *Christian Union* (subsequently the *Outlook*). Following Beecher's death Abbott became pastor of the Plymouth Congregational Church in Brooklyn.

1. Johnson sent his message to Congress on December 3, 1867. The "atrocious sentiments" to which Garrison refers are probably statements like the following on the subject of Negro suffrage: "The foundations of society have been broken up by civil war. Industry must be reorganized, justice reestablished, public credit maintained, and order brought out of confusion. To accomplish these ends would require all the wisdom and virtue of the great men who formed our institutions originally. I confidently believe that their descendants will be equal to the arduous task before them, but it is worse than madness to expect that negroes will perform it for us. . . . Of all dangers which our nation has yet encountered, none are equal to those which must result from the success of the effort now making to Africanize half of our country." (New York *Times*, December 3, 1867.)

225

TO JACOB HORTON

Roxbury, Dec. 14, 1867.

My dear Friend:

A few days ago, as I was leaving home for New York by the way of Providence, I received a line from Mr. Coffin, in regard to preparing a suitable obituary of your beloved and lamented wife [Harriet Farnham Horton], for insertion in the Newburyport Herald.[1] I regretted that I had not then time to carry out the suggestion, which was so much in accordance with my own feelings; and it is now too late to attempt anything of the kind for the public eye. I was both sorry and disappointed that neither of the ministers, upon whom devolved the funeral services, made any reference to the deceased, either as a mother or wife. I felt there was much due to her memory in both those relations, which she sustained in so excellent a manner; and I would gladly have borne my testimony on the occasion, if any intimation had been made to me that it would be acceptable from my lips.

In the bereavement which you and your children have suffered, I shall always largely participate. Born under the same roof with Harriet, growing up with her from childhood, and for many years an inmate of her parents' family, she was almost like an own sister to me, and always treated me very much like a younger brother. Although later in life we have seen comparatively little of each other, I am sure our early attachment never suffered any abatement. All my recollections of her are of the pleasantest kind. She was a darling child, jubilant as a singing bird; a beautiful girl, with sunshine in her heart and upon her face; a handsomely developed woman, with all wifely qualities and a strong motherly nature. I remember her, in my boyhood days, as a quickening spirit in every circle. She had great magnetic power over those with whom she came in contact; so that, in truth,

> "None knew her but to love her,
> None named her but to praise."[2]

She had a ready wit, without any satirical bitterness; a large fund of mirthfulness, without any tendency to frivolity. Her friendship was marked by unshaken adhesiveness, and by rare generosity. Few have lived on earth more devoid of selfishness, or more ready to do for others, with a noble self abnegation. The buoyancy and goodness of her disposition were alike remarkable; and in her zeal to serve others, she was apt to forget the limitations of physical endurance, to her own injury. Such self-sacrificing natures are too rare in the world. But why should I attempt to portray her character to you, or to your children?[3]

What she was as a wife, you can testify from a full heart. What she was as a mother, they can never forget, and will ever remember with filial love and gratitude. There is a large vacancy in your household; an empty chair at the family table; an absent one from the fireside circle. The silver cord is loosed and the golden bowl broken.[4] The eye that shone with such brightness is dimmed; the voice that had such musical cadences is hushed; the face that was ever so smiling in joy, and so sympathetic in sorrow, has been changed; and the form that enshrined so much intelligence, affection and love laid away forever in the tomb. What then? That which is mortal must return to the dust and the spirit to God who gave it.[5] Beyond a peradventure, Harriet is still living; for, as it respects our spiritual destiny—

> "There is no death; what seems so is transition."[6]

It is only an exchange of spheres, from a lower to a higher plane. In due season we shall follow her, let us hope and believe, to have a blissful reunion, beyond all language to depict.

Be cheered by this conviction, my dear friend; accept this inadequate tribute; give my sympathetic regards to your sorrowing children, and to Mr. French;[7] and believe me

Ever truly yours,

Wm. Lloyd Garrison.

Jacob Horton, Esq.

Handwritten transcription: Garrison Papers, Boston Public Library.

1. The Newburyport *Herald* (founded 1794) was a paper with which Garrison felt a personal identification, since it was the paper in which he was first published and on which he served his apprenticeship beginning in 1818. (*AWT.*)

Efforts to establish the identity of Mr. Coffin have been in vain.

2. Fitz-Greene Halleck, "On the Death of Joseph Rodman Drake."

3. Harriet Farnham and Jacob Horton, who were married August 8, 1824, apparently had only two living children at the time of Garrison's letter: Harriet Elizabeth (born 1825) and Charles French (1834–1892); three other boys by the same name died in infancy. (Letter to the editor from Wilhelmina V. Lunt, curator, Historical Society of Old Newbury, July 6, 1974.)

4. Ecclesiastes 12:6.

5. Ecclesiastes 12:7.

6. Henry Wadsworth Longfellow, "Resignation," stanza 5, line 1.

7. It has not been possible to identify Mr. French with certainty, although he was very likely a relative of the Horton family and may have been Charles French (1798–1884), for whom the Horton boys were presumably named. (Letter to the editor from Wilhelmina V. Lunt, July 6, 1974.)

226

TO WENDELL PHILLIPS GARRISON.

Roxbury, Dec. 18, 1867.

My dear Wendell:

Your letter, enclosing a very pressing one from Mr. [J. Miller] McKim, was received yesterday.

I also received a letter from Oliver [Johnson], saying they would expect me to stay at Mrs. [Augustus] Savin's on Friday night. I have written to him that it will give great pleasure to accept the proffered hospitality, but telling him not to take the trouble to be at the depot on my arrival, as I know my way to his home in East 12th Street perfectly well.

I will be at the office of "The Nation" in good season Saturday forenoon; only do not arrange to have the carriage meet me at Orange at 12.30 that day, as at that very hour I have an appointment with Mrs. Vizcarrondo, at 23 West Tenth Street; and so will go out to Orange with you in the afternoon, at your usual time. Mrs. V. is the wife of one of the Spanish delegates whom I met at the Paris Anti-Slavery Conference.[1] I presume she is on a mission to this country with reference to the abolition of slavery in Cuba.

You must have had a severe time of it, last week, in getting to and from New York. The Park is a beautiful rose indeed, but with a sharp thorn to it.[2]

Kisses for Lucy and Lloyd, and the most affectionate regards to Mr. and Mrs. McKim.

I am at present unable to decide whether to return home on Tuesday night, or to spend Christmas with you. On some accounts I should like to be at home on that festival; but I hardly feel reconciled to making you so hurried a visit.

Last evening I attended a meeting of the Ladies' Freedmen's Society at Cambridge,—taking tea first with Charles Eliot Norton. There was a very respectable audience, but largely composed of ladies. Mr. Norton presided, and made an excellent introductory speech, occupying about forty minutes. He then referred to me in a very complimentary manner, and read Lowell's verses, "In a small chamber," &c.,[3] and invited me to the platform. Strange to say, I had never before addressed an audience in Cambridge. I was very warmly received, and spoke for about three quarters of an hour; my remarks being well received. Richard H. Dana followed me in a handsome reference to my anti-slavery career, and in an able and forcible appeal in behalf of the Freedmen's cause.[4] He was followed by Dr. [John G.] Palfrey in a similar strain. It was a very interesting occasion.

Ellie and her mother [Mrs. David Wright] have gone to West Medford to spend the day. Darling Agnes is with us. Of course, you have been apprised that Mrs. [Richard P.] Hallowell has given birth to a son, whose name is to be James Mott.[5]

William has been doing a very satisfactory business in wool the present month.

Your loving father,

W. L. G.

ALS: Garrison Papers, Boston Public Library.

1. Julio Vizcarrondo y Coronado (1830–1889) was a Puerto Rican who had been educated in the United States and had married Philadelphian Harriet Brewster. In 1863 he and his wife went to Madrid to found the Spanish Abolitionist Society and its journal, *El Abolicionista Español,* Sra. Brewster de Vizcarrondo being instrumental in organizing a female committee. The society called for the immediate abolition of slavery in the Spanish Antilles. (Arthur F. Corwin, *Spain and the Abolition of Slavery in Cuba, 1817–1886,* London, 1967, pp. 154–171.)

2. The sharp thorn in the rose of Llewellyn Park was probably its inaccessibility to New York City in bad weather. The New York *Times* on December 13 reported "the severest snow storm in many years," which disrupted city and suburban travel.

3. See James Russell Lowell's poem "To W. L. Garrison."

4. Richard Henry Dana (1815–1882), best remembered for his firsthand account of a sailor's life, *Two Years Before the Mast* (1840), was also a world traveler and a distinguished lawyer, an expert in admiralty and international law. His most influential works include *The Seaman's Friend* (1841) and an edition of Wheaton's *Elements of International Law* (1866). Dana was active in politics, but his formality and reserve prevented his gaining high public office. Although not an abolitionist, he was sympathetic to the antislavery movement.

5. James Mott Hallowell (1867–1928) became a lawyer and assistant attorney general for Massachusetts. (Massachusetts Division of Vital Statistics.)

Index of Recipients

(References are to letter numbers)

Abbott, Lyman, 224
Andrew, John A., 54, 101

Banks, Nathaniel P., 102
Bowditch, Henry I., 29
Brown, Annie, 24
Butler, Benjamin F., 99

Chace, Elizabeth Buffum, 41
Chapman, Maria W., 130
Cheever, Henry T., 13
Child, Lydia Maria, 117

DeGrasse, John V., et al., 8
Dickinson, Anna E., 30, 31, 32, 33
Downing, George T., et al., 8

Emerson, Ralph Waldo, 51

Forbes, John M., 77, 103
Friend, Julia M., 38

Gardner, Francis, 72
Garrison, Ellen Wright, 170, 216. See also Wright, Ellen
Garrison, Francis J., 19, 184, 186, 194
Garrison, George T., 19, 62, 66
Garrison, Helen E., 2, 16, 19, 36, 45, 46, 47, 48, 60, 83, 84, 85, 86, 87, 88, 97, 109, 110, 111, 112, 118, 128, 131, 132, 133, 134, 135, 136, 137, 138, 139, 141, 142, 144, 146, 147, 165, 180, 181, 191, 198, 199, 200, 201, 202, 203, 212, 214, 217
Garrison, Helen Frances (Fanny), 19, 44. See also Villard, Fanny Garrison
Garrison, Wendell P., 11, 19, 40, 42, 79, 92, 114, 143, 150, 166, 171, 173, 177, 226
Garrison, William Lloyd, Jr., 19, 206, 211, 215
Gibbons, James S., 6
Godkin, Edwin L., 164
Greeley, Horace, 63, 73

Herndon, William H., 145
Horton, Jacob, 108, 225

Jenkins, Howard M., 106
Johnson, Oliver, 1, 5, 7, 10, 14, 17, 21, 22, 39, 43, 49, 52, 58, 65, 74, 82, 89, 90, 98, 113, 116, 152, 160, 188, 210, 222
Julian, George W., 34, 69, 161

Kennedy, John A., 196

Lincoln, Abraham, 104, 105
Lowell, Janes Russell, 185

McKay, James, 27
McKim, James Miller, 15, 71, 120, 122, 124, 129, 140, 172
McKim, Lucy, 93
May, Samuel, Jr., 175, 187, 192, 197, 205, 213
May, Samuel J., 18, 55, 64, 96, 148
Miles, Henry, 126
Morris, Robert, et al., 8
Mott, Lucretia, 193

Nell, William C., 195
Newman, Francis W., 94, 95
Nichol, Elizabeth Pease, 56, 127, 209
Norton, Charles Eliot, 100

Phillips, Wendell, 153
Powell, Aaron M., 9, 37, 67

Rarey, John S., 4
Ricketson, Daniel, 59

Sedgwick, Charles B., 35
Smith, Gerrit, 12, 68, 78
Stanton, Edwin M., 123
Steinthal, S. Alfred, 208
Steward, Ira, 169
Stowe, Harriet Beecher, 158
Studwell, Edwin A., 174
Sumner Charles, 3, 20, 23, 81, 91, 151, 162

Tappan, Arthur, 70
Tappan, Sarah S., 156
Thompson, George, 25, 26, 28

Index of Recipients

Tilton, Theodore, 53, 61, 159, 168
Townsend, Milo A., 57
Trask, George, 115

Villard, Fanny Garrison, 155, 157, 163, 167, 176, 178, 179, 182, 183, 189, 190, 218, 219, 223. *See also* Garrison, Helen Frances
Villard, Henry, 119, 121, 149, 220

Webb, Richard D., 204, 207
Welles, Gideon, 80
Whipple, Charles K., 107
Whittier, John Greenleaf, 50
Wilson, Henry, 76
Wright, Ellen, 75. *See also* Garrison, Ellen Wright
Wright, Henry C., 125, 221

Yerrinton, James Brown, 154

Index of Names

The following symbols and abbreviations are used: *, identified; AASS, American Anti-Slavery Society; MASS, Massachusetts Anti-Slavery Society; HEG, Helen Eliza Garrison; WLG, William Lloyd Garrison; WPG, Wendell Phillips Garrison.

Abbott, John S. C., 6
Abbott, Lyman, *563–564; letter to, 563
Abolicionista Español, El, 567
Abolitionists: and Civil War, 35–36, 39–40, 41, 65–66, 69–70, 79–82, 111–112; and Conway-Mason negotiations, 161–162
Academy of Music, Brooklyn, 187, *188
Adams, Charles Francis, 10, *12; and ironclads, 147
Adams, John, 12, 230
Adams, John Quincy, 12, 77, *79
Addie, May, 529
Adelphic Union Society, Williams College, 102, 109, *111
Adie, Julia Perkins, 285
Adirondack Mountains, N.Y., 126
Adrian, Mich., WLG lectures at, 327
Agassiz, Louis, 470
Akron, Ohio, WLG lectures at, 320
Albright, Arthur, 549, *550
Aldrich, J. M., 89, *90
Alexander II, of Russia, *502; assassination attempt on, 500
Allegheny Literary Society, Meadville, Pa., 307, *309
Allen, William Francis, 41, 549
Amberley, John Russell, Viscount, 527, *529, 552
Amberley, Katharine Louisa Stanley Russell, Lady, 552, *553
American and Foreign Anti-Slavery Society, 174, 175
American Anti-Slavery Society, 6, 45, 106, 124, 164, 169, 174, 249, 273, 281, 322, 323, 326, 341, 440, 449, 497, 537; meetings, anniversaries, celebrations, 16, 18, 144, 149, 150, 152–153, 163, 171, 172–173, 175–176, 178, 181, 200–201, 203, 271–272, 374, 375, 449–450, 451–452, 453, 483, 486; finances, 29, 242; divided on Lincoln, 213; to continue

after Emancipation, 247–248; WLG regards mission of as ended, 265; and Jackson bequest, 453
Executive Committee, 19, 20, 91, 129, 130, 142–143, 165, 171, 274; decision on *Standard*, 21–22; policy during Civil War, 35, 39–40, 41; will send copies of *Standard* to Congress, 46–47; defends *Standard* against Phillips, 214–215; discusses union of *Liberator* and *Standard*, 239–242
American Colonization Society, 24, 26
American Congregational Union, 203, *204
American Contraband Relief Association, 354
American Equal Rights Association, 116, 156
American Freedmen's Aid Commission (Society), 273, 289, *290, 297, 298, 299, 300, 301, 304, 305–306, 308, 309, 322, 324, 325, 328, 337, 339, 347, 348–349, 361, 408, 410, 464
American Freedmen's Union Commission, 408, 440, 441, 560
American House, Burlington, Vt., 125, *128
American Missionary Association, 290, 323
American Peace Society, 105, 164, 177
American Purity Alliance, 28
American Union Commission, 349, 408, 563
American Woman Suffrage Association, 116
Ames, Charles Gordon, 103, *105–106
Anderson, Charles, 266, *268
Anderson, Robert, 246, 266, 267, *268, 296, 409
Anderson, William, 515, *516, 532
Andrew, Miss, 468, 477, 498
Andrew, John Albion, 140, *141, 186, 263; letters to, 141, 251; and Thomp-

Andrew, John Albion (*continued*)
son testimonial, 194; WLG endorses
for Cabinet post, 254, 256–257; and
WLG testimonial, 366–367; death of,
552
Andrews, Charles, 49, *51
Ann (English servant), 546
Anthony, Anne Keene, 9, 31, 276, *277
Anthony, Edward, 113, *114, 154,
203, 346, 462
Anthony, Mrs. Edward (Helen Maria
Hastings Grieve), 114, 460, 462
Anthony, Frederick Eugene, 285, *409
Anthony, George Henry, *285
Anthony, Henry, 30, *31, 114, 277, 283,
285, 370, 390, 395, 404, 410, 459
Anthony, Mrs. Henry (Charlotte Ben-
son), 31, 283, *285, 370, 404, 407,
410, 459, 461
Anthony, John Gould, 31, *277
Anthony, Joseph Bowen, *285
Anthony, Susan B., 114, 153, *156, 179,
201, 202
Anti-Slavery Bugle, 22, *23, 45
Anti-Slavery Conference, Paris. *See*
World's International Anti-Slavery
Conference
Anti-Slavery Festival. *See* National Anti-
Slavery Subscription Anniversary
Festival
Appleton, Mrs., 459
Apthorp, Eliza, 134
Arago (ship), 246, 247, 264, *265, 266
Argyll, George Douglas Campbell, 8th
Duke of, 441
Arkansas, 226
Arlington Heights, Va., 210, *211
Arthur's Seat, Edinburgh, 426, *427
Ash, J. P., 330, *331, *332
Ashby, William, 434, *437
Ashby, Mrs. William (Ann Babcock),
434, *437
Ashley, James M., 439, 448
Atkinson, George, 41
Atkinson, Sarah C., 134
Atkinson, Wilmer, 41
Atlantic Monthly, The, 250
Austria, 420, 422
Avery, Abraham, 485

Bacon, Leonard, 55, *56
Bailey, Edwin C., 123, *124
Bailey, Harriet, 50
Bailey, Isaac, 426, *427–428
Bailey, Jenkins and Garrison, 354
Bailey, Joseph T., *526

Baker, Edward Dickinson, 53, *54
Ball, Cyrus, 346, *348, 349
Ball, Mrs. Cyrus, 346, *348
Ballou, Adin, 347, *349
Baltimore, Md., 11, 113, 207–208, 209;
WLG remembers imprisonment in,
173–174, 205–206, 210, 372, 373
Banks, Nathaniel Prentiss, 143, *144,
375, 388, 389; letter to, 252; policies
in Louisiana, 231–233, 234, 245, 249,
252–253
Barker, Stephen, 455–456
Barker, Mrs. Stephen (Louisa Jane
Whiting), 454, *455–456
Barnard, William, 98
Barnes, George, 237, *238
Barnes, Mrs. George (Rebecca S. Heer-
mans), 237, *238
Barney, Nathaniel, 461, *463
Barnum, Phineas Taylor, 57, *58
Bascom, John, 109, *111
Bassett, William, 311
Bates, Edward, 20
Beattie, William, 479
Beattie, Mrs. William (Jane), 479
Beecher, Edward, 520, *521
Beecher, Henry Ward, 4, 11, *12, 23,
144, 158, 159, 171, 269, 306, 461,
563–564; and Tiltons, 39; and eman-
cipation, 48; to be editor of *Indepen-
dent*, 55; and Thompson testimonial,
140; and George Thompson, 187,
188; at Ft. Sumter ceremonies, 246,
247, 266; supports Negro and woman
suffrage, 349; praises Andrew John-
son, 392, 394; opposes policy of *In-
dependent*, 521
Beecher, Mrs. Henry Ward (Eunice
Bullard), 266, *268
Beecher, Lyman, 12
Belfast Natural History and Philo-
sophical Society, 13, 16
Bellows, ?Charles, 104, 106
Bellows, Henry Whitney, *306–307
Bellows, Josiah Grahme, 375
Bennett, James Gordon, 37, *38
Benny, 110
Benson, George, 9, 535, *537
Benson, Mrs. George (Sarah Thurber),
9, 535, *537
Benson, George William, 31, 96, 157,
*204, 207
Benson, Mrs. George William (Cath-
erine Knapp Stetson), 30, *31, 95, 96,
157
Berne, Switzerland, 542
Bertin, Edouard-François, 500, 503

Bethune, Richard, 338
Bethune, Mrs. Richard (Joanna Graham), 338
Bigelow, Elisabeth T., 126, 127, *128
Bigelow, George H., 127, *128
Bigelow, Henry Jacob, *450; examines WLG, 452–453
Bigelow, Lawrence Goodhue, 125–126, 127, *128
Bigelow, Lawrence L., 127, *128
Bigelow, Lucius L., 127, *128
Bigelow, Susan A., 126, 127, *128
Billings, Edwin T., *470; portrait of WLG by, 469, 484
Birmingham, England, WLG's engagements in, 545
Birney, James G., 23, 144
Bismarck, Otto Edward Leopold von, 496, *497
Black, James Wallace, 469, *470, 484, 501
Blackwell, Alice Stone, 116
Blackwell, Henry Brown, 116
Blair, Mason, 20
Blair, Montgomery, 75, *164, 210
Blanchard, George Augustus, 536, *537, 555, 561
Blanchard, Mrs. George Augustus (Frances Ann Brown Sargent), 536, *537, 561
Blanchard, Grace, 561, 562
Blanchard, Joshua P., 163–*164
Blanchard, Lucretia Tilden, 561, 562
Bliss, Mr. and Mrs. ?Zenos, 340, *341
Bois de Boulogne, Paris, 500, 503
Bolívar, Simón, 92, *93
Bond, Hugh L., 209, *210–211, 272, 294, 324, 353, 437
Booth, John Wilkes, 247
Border Ruffians, 10, 11, *12, 468
Boston, Mass., petition from, 10–11, 12; WLG welcomes Stanton to, 295; Sherman visits, 421; mob, 481
Boston *Commercial Gazette*, 481, *486
Boston *Common*, *98
Boston *Courier*, 11, *12, 37, 47, 76
Boston *Daily Advertiser*, *459
Boston *Evening Traveller*, *63, 101
Boston Female Anti-Slavery Society, 242, 272, 481
Boston *Journal*, *119, 125
Boston Latin School: WPG seeks post at, 30, 49; military drill at, 178, 184
Boston *Morning Post*, 37, *38, 47, 125, 557
Botta, Giuseppe Guglielmo, *251, 258
Boutwell, George S., 448

Bowditch, Henry Ingersoll, *84, 285, 366; letter to, 83
Bowditch, William Ingersoll, 20, 22, *23, 130, 213, 214, 239, 475
Bowen, Henry Chandler, 557, *558
Bowles, Drevet and Company, 524, 483, *486, 491, 510
Bowly, Samuel, 516
Boylston Hall, Boston, *184
Boylston Market, Boston, *31
Bradford family, 343, *344
Bradford, Mr., 533
Bradford, Augustus W., 105
Bradford, John, 344
Bradford, Mrs. John (Sarah Whitwell Tyler), 344
Bradford, Rebecca, 344, 421, 533
Bradford, Sarah, 344, 421, 533
Bradshaw, Mrs. Andrew (Martha), 425, *427
Brady, Mathew B., 461, *463
Bragg, Braxton, 352
Braintree, Mass., WLG speaks at, 124
Bramhall, Cornelius, 115, *116, 154, 203, 461
Bramhall, Mrs. Cornelius (Ann Rebecca Reed), *116, 134, 154, 427, 461
Bramhall, Marcia, 427
Breckinridge, Robert J., 33, *34
Bridget (servant), 436
Brigham, Dora Taylor (Mrs. Levi Brigham), 271, *273, 482, 502; stays with HEG, 419; séance at house of, 446–447; sees WLG off for Europe, 477, 483; welcomes WLG home, 550
Bright, John, 65, *70, 141, 441, 493; contributes to WLG testimonial, 442–443, 444, 458; WLG hears speak, 527; supports Reform Bill, 529
British and Foreign Anti-Slavery Reporter, 536, *537
British and Foreign Anti-Slavery Society, 141, 147, 465, 537
British West Indies, emancipation of: George Thompson and, 23, 505, 506; celebrations of, 32, 101, 102, 103, 165, 166
Broglie, Achille Charles Léonce Victor, Duc de, 536, *537
Brooklyn Committee, 187
Brooklyn (N.Y.) *Eagle*, 532, *534
Brooks, Erastus, 48
Brooks, James, 48
Brown, Annie, *63; letter to, 62
Brown, Charles, 320, *322
Brown, Mrs. Charles (Julia A. King), 320, *322

Brown, Ellen, 63
Brown, George Center, 109, *110–111
Brown, John, 2, *6, 63, 154, 263, 267,
    468, 470; anniversary of execution of,
    5, 6–7; grave of, 125, 126, 128, 204;
    failure of testimonial for family of,
    367, 443, 444
Brown, Mrs. John (Mary Anne Day),
    *63, 128
Brown, Sgt. John, 263
Brown, Oliver, 63
Brown, Salmon, 63
Brown, Sarah, 63
Brown, Watson, 63
Brown, Wells, 105
Brown, William Wells, 103, *105, 135
Browne, Albert G., Jr., 117
Brownlow, William Gannaway, 208,
    *209
Brownson, Orestes A., 92, 101, *102–
    103
Bryant, Mr., 340
Bryant, Arthur, 341
Bryant, Austin, 341
Bryant, John Howard, 339, 340, *341
Bryant, William Cullen, 138, 141, 186,
    *187–188, 339, 441
Brussels, Belgium, 547
Buckingham, Joseph T., 12
Buell, Don Carlos, 126, 128
Buffum, Miss, 328, 329
Buffum, Anne Vernon, 329
Buffum, Arnold, 107, 325, *326
Buffum, Mrs. Arnold (Rebecca Gould),
    107
Buffum, James Needham, 453, *455
Buffum, Mary Lee, 329
Buffum, William, 325, *326, 328
Buffum, Mrs. William (Ann L. Shel-
    don), 325, *326, 328
Bunker Hill, Mass., 98
Bunker Hill, N.Y., 98
Burlington, Vt., 127
Busteed, Richard, 118, *119
Butler, Benjamin Franklin, 143, *145,
    213, 234, 387, 450; letter to, 243
Byron, George Gordon, Lord, 534

Cambridge, Mass., 567
Camel's Rump (Hump), Vt., 119, 121,
    126
Cameron, Simon, 20
Cannan, Anne, 238, 343, 502, 552
Canterbury, Charles Thomas Longley,
    Archbishop of, 527, *529
Carleton, William Tolman, *257
Catlin, Henry, 318, *319–320

Caughey, Andrew Harvey, 312, *313
Chadwick, John White, 460, *462
Chace, Arnold, 107, *108
Chace, Edward, 107, *108
Chace, Elizabeth Buffum (Mrs. Samuel
    Buffington Chace), *107–108, 375;
    letter to, 106
Chace, Harvey, 108
Chace, Samuel Buffington, 107, *108
Chace, Samuel Oliver, 107, *108
Chace, William, 206, *207
Chace, Mrs. William (Harriet Hall),
    206, *207
Chambers, William, 518, *520, 531
Chamerovzow, Louis Alexis, 510, *511,
    532, 537
Chamerovzow, Mrs. Louis Alexis, 510
Chamounix, Switzerland, 536
Channing, William Henry, 522, *526
Chandler, Elizabeth M., 324, *326
Chandler, Thomas, 324, *326, 327
Chapin, Edwin Hubbell, *299
Chapman, Henry Grafton, 309, *311
Chapman, Mrs. Henry Grafton
    (Eleanor Jay), 311
Chapman, John Jay, 311
Chapman, Maria Weston (Mrs. Henry
    G. Chapman), 20, *29, 130, 242, 422;
    letter to, 309; WLG's gratitude to,
    309–310; sees WLG off for Europe,
    477, 483–484, 507
Chapman, Mary Gray, 310, *311, 331,
    422, 484, 507
Charleston, S.C.; WLG hopes for fall
    of, 167; WLG visits, 246–247, 269–
    270, 411; WLG mounts slave steps
    from, 262, 263
Charleston *Mercury,* 76, *78–79
Chase, Salmon P., 20, 75, 205, *207,
    210, 349, 421, 441, 561; and WLG
    testimonial, 367, 413, 443
Chase, Supply, 328, *329
Cheever, George Barrell, 17, *18, 35,
    149
Cheever, Henry Theodore, 3, *36; let-
    ter to, 35
Chesson, Frederick William, *150–151,
    492, 493, 501, 504
Chesson, Mrs. Frederick William
    (Amelia Thompson), *150, 465, 490
Chicago, Ill.: WLG lectures in, 333–
    338; described, 334, 358–359
Chicago *Republican,* 334, *336
Chicago *Times,* 334, *336, 338
Chicago *Tribune,* 267, *268–269, 334,
    335, 336, 358, 544; and Henry Vil-
    lard, 359, 495, 523

Child, David Lee, 18, 282, *283, 543
Child, Lydia Maria (Mrs. David Lee
    Child), 18, 129, *130, 134, 543; letter
    to, 282
Chillon castle, 534, 537
China (ship), 501, *503
Choate, Rufus, 109, *110
Christian Commission. *See* United
    States Christian Commission
Christian Examiner, 235, *236
Church of the Messiah, Syracuse, N.Y.,
    355, 357
Cincinnati, Ohio, 113; Phillips attacked
    at, 91, 92; WLG lectures at, 352, 353
Civil Rights Bill, 409
Civil War: WLG's reaction to, 1–4, 6,
    17, 19–20, 27, 28–29, 127, 170–171;
    and abolitionists, 35–36, 39–40, 41,
    65–66, 69–70, 79–82, 111–112; use
    of balloons in, 53; British attitudes
    toward, 60–61, 64–74, 79–82; nonre-
    sistance and, 106–107, 108; conscrip-
    tion and volunteering in, 107, 108,
    110; policy of *Liberator* and *Stan-
    dard* during, 111–112; and Emanci-
    pation Proclamation, 116
Clay, Henry, 174
Cleveland, Ohio, WLG lectures at, 321
Cleveland *Leader*, 321, *323
Cleveland Library Association, 307,
    309
Cleveland *Plain Dealer*, 321, *323
Clifford, John Henry, *372
Cobb, Samuel Crocker, 552, *553
Cobb, Mrs. Samuel Crocker (Aurelia L.
    Beattie), 478, *479
Cochin, Pierre-Suzanne-Augustin,
    491, *493, 508, 510, 536
Cochin, Mme. Pierre, 510
Cochrane, John, 235, *236
Codman, John, and Jackson bequest,
    449, *450, 474, 483, 542
Coffin, Mr., 564
Coffin, Charlotte, 50, *51, 127, 143–
    144, 163, 237, 238, 263, 264, 312,
    335, 352, 357, 385, 415, 477, 502, 559
Coffin, Levi, 337, *339, 408
Coffin, Peter, 51
Coffin, Thomas, 157
Coffin, Mrs. Thomas (Anna), 157
Coignet, Clarisse-Josephine Gautier,
    500, *503
Coleman, Lucy Newhall, 154, *158
Coles. *See* Cowles
Colfax, Schuyler, 195, *196, 349, 392
Collier, William R., 334, *336
Collins, Mrs. Robert, 283

Collyer, Robert, 334, *336
Cologne, Germany, 547
Colored National Convention (1855),
    26
Commonwealth, 129, *130
Comstock, Addison J., 326
Comstock, Edwin, 324, *326, 327
Confederacy, the: WLG condemns, 75–
    77; and Great Britain, 99, 132–133,
    136, 146, 147; and Conway-Mason
    negotiations, 132–133, 161–162, 165,
    220; Blanchard defends, 163. *See
    also* South
Confederate Constitution, 77, 79
Congregational Union. *See* American
    Congregational Union
Congressional Temperance Society, 470
Conway, Moncure D., *88–89, 102,
    103, 130, 135; and negotiations with
    Mason re Great Britain, 132–133,
    137, 138, 161–162, 220–221; charac-
    terized, 146, 165; *The Rejected
    Stone, The Golden Hour*, 146, 147
Cook, Burton C., 448
Cooper Institute (Union), N.Y., *18
Copperheads, 143, 145, 165, 171, 316,
    391, 392, 397, 451, 561; term de-
    fined, 142
Corinth, Miss., battle at, 118, 119
Corn Laws, 505, 506
Cotting, Benjamin Eddy, 453, *454
Cow Hill, Vt., 118
Cowing, Sarah, 134
Cowles, Edwin, 321, *323
Cox, John, 41, 42, 43, *44
Cox, Mrs. John (Hannah Peirce), 42,
    43, *44, 206
Cox, John William, 43, *45
Craft, Ellen, 282, *283
Craft, William, 282, *283
Craig, James, 331
Crandall, Prudence, 372
Crane, L., 330, 331, *332
Cresswell. *See* Creswell
Creswell, John Angel James, 392, *394,
    399
Crittenden, John J., 12
Crittenden compromise, 12
Crosby, Uranus H., 451
Crystal Palace, London, 516, *517, 525
Cuba (ship), 464, *465, 480, 487;
    WLG's departure on, 476–477, 506–
    507
Currier, Mrs., 333
Curtis, Caleb, 485
Curtis, Mrs. Caleb (Caroline Matilda
    Agry), 485

575

Curtis, George William, 151, 503
Curtis, Mrs. George William (Anna Shaw), 503
Curtis, John, Jr., 331, *332
Curtis, Thomas, 42
Cutting, H. P., 52, *54

Dall, Caroline Wells Healey (Mrs. Charles H. A. Dall), *407, 548
Dana, Richard Henry, 151, *567
Darlington, Chandler, 42, 43, *44
Darlington, Mrs. Chandler (Hannah Monaghan), 42, 43, *44
Dartmouth College, 421
Davies, Charles, 266, *268
Davis, Andrew Jackson, 101, *102
Davis, Mrs. Andrew Jackson (Mary Robinson Love), 102
Davis, Edmund, 326
Davis, Edward M., 43–44, *46, 285, 468
Davis, Mrs. Edward M. (Maria Mott), *46, 285
Davis, Garret, 391, *393
Davis, Henry Winter, *394; WLG attends ceremony honoring, 392, 399
Davis, Jefferson, 37, *38, 77, 79, 120, 137, 247, 508
Davis, Perry, 325, *326
Davis, Thomas, 6, *7, 29
Davis, Mrs. Thomas (Eliza Chace), 7
Davis, Mrs. Thomas (Paulina Kellogg Wright), 6, *7, 29
Davis, William Howard, 200, *202
Davis, William M., 284, *285
Declaration of Independence, 3, 68, 72, 73, 163–164
Declaration of Sentiments, AASS, 175, 176, 320, 335, 424
DeGrasse, John V., *26; letter to, 24
Delaney, Mr., 328
Delavan, Edward C., *313
Delavan House, Albany, N.Y., 311, *313
Democratic party, 91, 123, 124, 125, 555–556
De Mortie, Louise, 451, *452, 552
Denham, Butler, 341
Denham, Elizabeth S., 341
Denham, Lucy Storrs, 341
Denham, Mary B., 341
Denis. *See* Dennis
Denison, Charles Wheeler, 176, *177
Dennis, Fred, 356, *357
Dennis, Mrs. Fred (Anne or Anna McKim), 9, 41, 356, *357, 390
Dennison, William, 349

Denyer, Robert J., 154, *157
Detroit, Mich., WLG lectures at, 324–325, 327–328, 337
Devereaux, Horace ("Homer"), 404, *405
Devil's Mountain (Hill), Vt., 119–120, *121
Dickinson, Anna Elizabeth, 42, 43, *45, 61, 149, 150, 175, 179, 205, 206; letters to, 85, 86, 88, 89
Dickinson, John, 45
Dickinson, William Edmund, 155
Dickinson, Mrs. William Edmund (Elizabeth Stone White Grey Sargent), 155
District of Columbia: abolition of slavery in, 53, 54, 91, 92, 226; suffrage in, 382
Dix, John Adams, 266, *268
Dixon, James, 400
Dodge, James George, 269, *270
Doggett, Kate Newell (Mrs. William E. Doggett), 333, *335
Doggett, William E., 333, *335
Donisthorpe, George Edmund, 519, *521
Doolittle, James R., 400, 495–496, *497, 533
Doubleday, Abner, 266, *268
Douglas, Joshua, Jr., 318, *320
Douglas, Mrs. Joshua, Jr. (Lavantia Densmore), 318, *320
Douglas, Stephen A., 121, 345, *346
Douglass, Frederick, *50–51, 272; speaks at Syracuse, 49; WLG distrusts, 153, 156; quoted, 223–224
Dow, Joseph, *275, 284, 314, 333, 407, 409
Dow, Mrs. Joseph (Eliza F.), 333, *335
Dowling, Miss, 500
Downing, George T., *26; letter to, 24
Draper, Ebenezer (Eben) D., 271, *273
Draper, Mrs. Ebenezer D. (Mary Boynton), 273
Draper, Mrs. Ebenezer D. (Anna Thwing), 271, 273
Drew, Thomas Bradford, 103, 106, 501–502, *503
Drew, Mrs. Thomas Bradford (Mary), 501–502
Drummond, William Hamilton, 13, *16; *The Rights of Animals . . . ,* 13, 16
Duffield, George, 328, *329, 337
Duffield, Mrs. George (Isabella Graham Bethune), 337, *338
Dugdale, Joseph A., 42, *44

Dugdale, Mrs. Joseph A. (Ruth), 44
Dunham, Carroll, 425, *427
Dunlap, Mrs. James (Elizabeth Freeman), 344
Dunlap House, Jacksonville, Ill., 343, 344
Durfee, Mr., 325, 326

East, the, contrasted with West, 325
East India Company, 505, 506
Eddy, Eliza Jackson Merriam (Mrs. James Eddy), 491, 492, *493, 501, 511
Eddy, James, 493
Edinburgh, Prince Alfred Ernest Albert, Duke of, 518, *520, 531
Edinburgh, Scotland, WLG at, 518, 530, 531
Edinburgh Ladies' Emancipation Society, 147, 518, *520
Edmundson, Joshua, 304
Edmundson, Mrs. Joshua (Mary Wigham), 304
Eight-Hour League. *See* Grand Eight-Hour League
Ellenville (N.Y.) Convention, 112, *113–114
Ellis, ?Charles Mayo, 528, *529
Ellis, John Millot, 344
Ellsworth, Elmer, 20
Emancipation League of Boston, 130
Emancipation Proclamation, 59, 60, 114, 116, 131, 134, 143, 162, 170, 222, 226, 230, 245; and McClellan, 123, 124; Massachusetts legislature urged to support, 141–142; English support for, 137, 138; Newman criticizes, 179; WLG disappointed in, 442
Emancipator, 177
Emerson, Ralph Waldo, 20, 83, *84, 88, 92, 469; letter to, 135
Emerson, William, 20
Empire Hotel (House), Akron, Ohio, 320, *322
Empire State (ship), 264, 265
Encore Club, Quincy, Ill., 307, 309
Endicott, William, Jr., 321, *323, 414, 483, 510–511, 524
England. *See* Great Britain
Erie, Pa., WLG lectures at, 318
Essex County Anti-Slavery Society, 497
Estlin, John Bishop, 465, 505, *506
Estlin, Mrs. John Bishop (Margaret Bagehot), 465
Estlin, Mary Anne, 464, *465–466, 536, 546; criticizes George Thompson,

505, 511–513; visits Garrisons in London, 532
Evangelist, 177
Everett, Joshua Titus, 453, *455
Eugène Louis Jean Joseph, Prince, 496,*497
Eugénie, Empress of France, 496, *497
Europe, WLG's trip to, 476–549

Fairfield, Edmund Burke, 330, *332
Farnum, Katherine Earle, 134
Faustin I (Soulouque) of Haiti, 26
Fayerweather, Sarah Harris, 371, *372
Felton, Cornelius Conway, 30, *31
Female Sewing Circle. *See* Philadelphia Female Anti-Slavery Society
Ferris, Peter W., 340, *341
Fessenden, Samuel, 191, *192, 195
Fessenden, William Pitt, 191, *192, 210, 256
Field, Kate, 128
Fields, James Thomas, 404, *405, 406
Fields, Mrs. James Thomas (Annie Adams), 404, *405
5th Rhode Island Regiment of Heavy Artillery, 243, 250
55th Massachusetts Regiment, 160, 276, 277, 292
54th Massachusetts Regiment, 160, 276, 277
Finney, Charles G., 144
First of August celebrations. *See* British West Indies, emancipation of
1st North Carolina Heavy Artillery, 243, *244
Fish, Benjamin, 326
Fish, Mrs. Benjamin (Sarah D.), 326
Fish, William Henry, 115, *116, 264
Fish, Mrs. William Henry (Anne Eliza Wright), 115, *116
Fisk, Photius (Phocious), *198; WLG intercedes for, 197–198, 199, 215–216; assaulted, 361, 362
Fitzhugh, Miss, 235, 236
Fitzhugh, James, 236
Fitzhugh, William, 33
Flint, Isaac, 41
Floyd, John B., 78
Follen, Charles, 501, *503
Follen, Mrs. Charles (Eliza Lee Cabot), 503
Follen, Charles, Jr., 20
Forbes, John Murray, *194; letters to, 193, 253
Forbes, Mrs. John Murray (Sarah Swain Hathaway), 194
Forney, John Wien, *558

Forster, William Edward, 458, *459, 516, 526
Fort Donelson, Tenn., 78
Forten, James, 96
Fort Sumter, S.C., 264, 265, 269; flag-raising at, 246, 296, 409, 410–411
Foss, Andrew T., 123, *124, 298
Foss, Eugene Kincaid, 123, *124
Foster, Abby Kelley (Mrs. Stephen Symonds Foster), 23, 123–124, 129, *130, 134, 175, 326; rejoices for Garrisons, 284; speaks at festival, 374
Foster, Daniel, 103, *105
Foster, Stephen Symonds, 23, 130, 175, *176, 326; critical of Lincoln, 202; at AASS anniversary, 203; speaks at festival, 374; attacks WLG, 453
Fourteenth Amendment. *See* United States Constitution
Fox, Charles Barnard, 551, *553
Fox, Kate, 157
Fox, Margaret, 157
Fowler, Philemon Halstead, 101, *102, 109
France: WLG in, 489–513, 527–533; landscape of, 490; people of, 507
Francis, Abby, 134
Free Christian Church, London, 522, 526
Freedmen's Aid Commission. *See* American Freedmen's Aid Commission
Freedmen's Bureau, 294, 349; bill extending, 364–365, 391–392, 397–399, 400, 422, 423
Freedmen's Inquiry Commission, 149, *150
Freedmen's Record, 300, *301
Freedmen's Union Commission. *See* American Freedmen's Union Commission
Freer, Lemuel Covell Paine, 333, *335
Freer, Mrs. Lemuel Covell Paine (Esther Wickes Marble), 333, 335
Free Trade Hall, Manchester, England, 525, *526, 545
Frémont, John Charles, 4, 33, *34–35, 37, 43, 81, 115, 123, 131, 143, 145, 179, 202, 235, 387; proclaims emancipation, 39, 41; WLG and Phillips disagree over, 185; Phillips supports for President, 213
French, Mrs., 237
French, ?Charles, 565, 566
Friend, Julia M., *100; letter to, 99
Friends' Institute, London, 545, 546
Friends of Freedom, 164

Frost, John, 333, *336
Frothingham, Octavius Brooks, 154, *157, 201
Frothingham, Mrs. Octavius Brooks (Caroline Elizabeth Curtis), 481, *485
Fugitive Slave Law, 27, *28, 74, 114, 139, 152, 283
Furness, Frank, 357
Furness, Horace Howard, 46
Furness, William Henry, 43, *46, 356, 357
Fussell, B., 41

Gage, Frances D., 384
Gage, Matilda Joslyn, 157
Galesburg, Ill., WLG lectures at, 342
Gaglignani, Giovanni Antonio, 537
Gaglignani, Guillaume, 537
Gaglignani, Jean-Antoine, 537
Gaglignani's Messenger, 535, 536, *537
Gardner, Francis, 30, *31; letter to, 184
Garnaut, Eliza Jones, 238
Garnet, Henry Highland, 364, 394, 396, *400
Garrett, Thomas, 41, 97, *98
Garrison, Abijah, 157
Garrison, Mrs. Abijah (Frances Lloyd Garrison), 154, *157
Garrison, Agnes, *418, 423, 425, 427, 433, 436, 461, 467, 477, 492, 498, 501–502, 511, 526, 528, 567; birth, 416; WLG's love for, 435, 541; described, 430, 545, 548; WLG misses, 484; learning to walk, 562
Garrison, Ellen Wright (Mrs. William Lloyd Garrison, Jr.), 9, *190, 272, 276, 284, 352, 359, 385, 407, 425, 427, 501, 511, 526, 528, 545, 559, 567; letters to, 403, 540, *see also* Wright, Ellen; engaged to William, 188–189; and Lucy McKim, 217; has neuralgia, 322, 327, 454; gives birth to Agnes, recovers slowly, 416, 417, 419, 422, 423; is a good mother, 433; is missed, 467; sees WLG off for Europe, 476, 477; WLG wants advice of, 525; postpones moving from Rockledge, 541; meets WLG and Frank, 550; pleased with Fanny's gifts, 551; moves from Rockledge, 551–552, 554; likes new living arrangements, 562
Garrison, Francis Jackson, *9–10, 23, 30, 104, 143, 163, 189, 206, 298, 312–313, 321, 322, 331, 335, 340, 341, 343, 352, 354, 384, 385, 386, 389,

Garrison, Francis Jackson (*continued*)
394, 415, 467, 542, 552, 554, 561; letters to, 51, 433, 444, 468; Francis
Jackson's bequest to, 50; gives WLG
photo album, 52; has diphtheria, 137;
and military drill, 178, 184; studies
for admission to Harvard, 302; visits
Philadelphia, Washington, 390, 392;
in poor health, 417; on walking tour,
419, 420, 421; in Germany, 429, 432–
433; medium reports on, 434–435;
and Hilgard relatives, 444–445, 447;
sends WLG travel directions, 488;
meets WLG in Paris, travels in Europe, 490–549 passim; unchanged by
life in Europe, 495; agrees with
WLG on testimonial, 540; uncertain
as to future, 560

Garrison, George Thompson, *9, 30,
31, 101, 103, 110, 189, 263, 264, 265,
267, 272, 302, 352, 354; letters to, 51,
160, 166; not a nonresistant, 106; en-
lists, 132, 160; WLG's feeling for,
160, 167; leaves with regiment, 167;
with WLG at Charleston, 246, 247,
270; and Anne Anthony, 276, 277;
and his regiment, 292; on furlough,
296; and orphan boy, 298; should
marry, 502; WLG wants advice of,
525

Garrison, Helen Eliza Benson (Mrs.
William Lloyd Garrison), *9, 103,
134, 163, 176, 508; letters to, 8, 42,
51, 94, 117, 119, 122, 125, 152, 202,
204, 207, 209, 211, 212, 236, 263,
269, 271, 283, 304, 311, 314, 316,
317, 320, 324, 327, 330, 333, 339,
341, 346, 350, 353, 389, 423, 425,
460, 476, 479, 487, 489, 494, 497,
527, 534, 543; WLG's concern and
affection for, 8–9, 189, 292, 314, 317,
429, 534–535; and children, 8, 110,
160, 167, 189, 291, 371, 419, 434,
456–457, 535, 551, 559; beloved by
friends, 205, 305; her letter-writing,
327, 341–342; 436, 452; charmed by
grandchildren, 545, 548; sympathizes
with Hilgards, 547–548; welcomes
WLG and Frank from Europe, 550
   health and treatment: 47–48, 49,
      143, 187, 188, 190–191, 195, 218,
      291, 293, 302, 314, 360, 410, 467,
      468, 533, 542, 560; has stroke,
      133; treated by healing medium,
      237–238; treated by Dr. Dow,
      263, 275, 282, 283; confined by
      paralysis, 385; treated by Dr.

Munroe, 414–415, 417; WLG
   cannot leave, 563
Garrison, Helen Frances (Fanny), letters to, 51, 114. *See also* Villard,
   Fanny Garrison
Garrison, James Holley, 157
Garrison, Katherine McKim, 42
Garrison, Lloyd McKim, 42, *486, 492,
   501; birth of, 484; at Rockledge, 541;
   resembles WLG, 545, 557, 560;
   praised, 548
Garrison, Lucy McKim (Mrs. Wendell
   Phillips Garrison), 9, *41–42, 292,
   305, 327, 338, 343, 346, 370, 372,
   385, 390, 419, 427, 454, 460, 484,
   490, 492, 501, 560; letter to, *see*
   McKim, Lucy; engaged to Wendell,
   217, 218–219, 302; WLG sends
   money for, 345; wedding of, 354,
   356, 358; plays piano for WLG, 424;
   at Rockledge, 429, 541, 545, 546;
   edits slave songs, 548, 549
Garrison, Philip McKim, 42
Garrison, Wendell Phillips, *9, 41–42,
   43, 123, 141, 143, 176, 189, 201, 203,
   264, 272, 292, 302, 305, 308, 311,
   327, 338, 343, 357, 380, 385, 389,
   419, 427, 429, 454, 458, 461, 501,
   548, 560; letters to, 30, 51, 103, 108,
   196, 216, 276, 345, 360, 391, 406,
   409, 416, 566; job prospects, 30, 31,
   49, 158–159; on walking tour, 104,
   109; a nonresistant, 106; has diphtheria, 137; described, 158, 169; on lecture tour, 169; writes for *Liberator*,
   197; engaged, 217, 218–219, 302;
   and *Nation*, 278; decides wedding
   day, 335; wedding of, 354, 356, 358;
   WLG on future career of, 360; Phillips paid Harvard education of, 368;
   WLG visits, 423–425, 460; WLG
   wants advice of, 525; at Rockledge,
   541, 545, 546
Garrison, William Lloyd:
   reflects on his own career: 260,
      261, 265, 303–303, 310, 360, 472,
      534–535; on honors and adula-
      tion, 153, 262–263, 514, 517–
      518, 530, 531; contemplates writ-
      ing antislavery history, 291, 292,
      366, 404, 406, 408, 409–410, 560,
      563; resists growing old, 312,
      356–357, 360, 435, 559
   his love and concern for home and
      family: 8, 52, 120–121, 127, 167,
      206, 217, 218–219, 265, 267,
      286–288, 291, 292, 314, 317, 328,

Garrison, William Lloyd (*continued*)
334–335, 340, 360, 405, 430,
559–560
his affection, admiration, and gratitude toward friends: 137, 242,
282, 295–297, 302, 309–310, 363,
369–370, 444, 466–467, 482, 515
health: 5, 47, 49, 90, 190, 241–242,
324, 343, 345, 347, 355–356; defends homeopathy, 62; teeth
pulled, 283–284; injures shoulder seriously, 404, 406, 407, 409,
414, 417, 421, 452–453; improved by trip to Europe, 517;
unwell since return from Europe, 557, 560, 563
money matters: 50, 310, 311, 315,
318, 319, 320, 331, 345, 351, 354,
358, 406, 417, 457, 483, 490,
524–525, 527, 528, 554–555, 560,
562; *see also* National Testimonial
comments on lectures, speeches,
and audiences: 100–101, 314,
316–317, 318, 319, 322, 330, 331,
333, 353, 530; advises Anna
Dickinson, 87; lecture topics:
"The Abolitionists and their Relations to the War," 55, 56; "Our
National Visitation," 101; "The
Past, Present and Future of Our
Country," 308; "Liberty Triumphant (Victorious)," 386, 390,
391, 395–396, 404, 405; "On the
State of our Country . . . ," 405;
"Our National Situation," 461,
462; "Abroad and at Home," 560
pleasures and hazards of travel:
scenery, 109, 118, 119–120, 126–
127, 235, 237, 330–331, 489,
490; encounter with heifer, 118;
mountain climbing, 119–120;
fellow passengers, 120, 266–267,
311–312, 480–481; Lake Champlain, 126–127; on board *Arago*,
266–267; on sleeping car, 304;
lost luggage, 318, 548; pick-
pocket, 351; trip to Nyack and
Tarrytown, 425–427; departure
for Europe, 476–477; seasickness, 476, 478, 487; on board
Cuba, 479–482; no one speaks
English, 490, 533; down Rhine
to Cologne, 547. *See also* Paris
comments on miscellaneous subjects: animals and their treatment, 13–16; capital and labor,

401–402; country life, 117, 118;
death and immortality, 435, 466,
565; Divine Providence, 418;
doing good, 360; letter-writing,
49, 111, 403, 530; love and marriage, 8–9, 286, 371; military
demonstrations, 500; the press,
37, 47, 53, 76, 334, 338, 530–
531; reform, 401; spiritualism
and clairvoyance, 5, 6, 99, 109,
429, 434–435, 446–447; tobacco,
278–279; wine-drinking in
France, 495, 507–508; worldliness,
418–419, 456
writings mentioned: "Sonnets for
the Times," 406, 407; four unti-
tled sonnets, 450, 451; *Thoughts
on African Colonization*, 26, 530
Garrison, William Lloyd, Jr., *9, 110,
163, 176, 177, 276, 284, 302, 313,
317, 331, 335, 351, 352, 354, 359,
407, 415, 432–433, 456, 477, 484,
492, 486, 528, 545, 548, 559; letters
to, 51, 509, 521, 538; a nonresistant,
106; has diphtheria, 137; engaged,
188–189; in charge of *Liberator*, 206;
WLG distributes circular for, 331;
travels in West, 403; and birth of
Agnes, 416; and wool business, 422,
430, 436, 454, 458, 567; sees WLG
off, 476; handles WLG's finances,
483; consulted on Henry Villard's financial problems, 523–525, 526;
postpones moving from Rockledge,
541; to consult testimonial committee, 542; meets WLG and Frank,
550; moves from Rockledge, 551–
552, 554; likes new living arrange-
ments, 562
Gaskins, Mr., 316, 317
Gasparin, Agénor-Etienne, comte de,
491, *493
Gay, Elizabeth N., 134
Gay, Sydney Howard, 6, 18, 20, 130,
136, *138, 140, 158–159, 214
Geffard, Nicholas Fabre, 24, *26
Geist, Christian F., 414, *416, 417
Geneva, Switzerland, WLG visits, 536
Genius of Universal Emancipation, 18,
192, 326
Germany, WLG in, 543–546, 547
Gibbons, James Sloan, *20; letter to, 19
Gibbons, Mrs. James Sloan (Abigail
Hopper), *20, 113
Gibbons, Julia, 20
Gibbons, Lucy, 20
Gibbons, Sarah H., 20

Girard College, Philadelphia, 43, *45
Girard, Stephen, 45
Gladstone, William Ewart, 527, *529
Glasgow, Scotland, WLG at, 514, 515, 517, 518, 530, 532
Glasgow Emancipation Society, 521
Gloucester, James, 103, *105
Gloucester, John, 105
Goddard, Samuel Aspinwall, 533, *534
Godkin, Edwin Lawrence, *389; letter to, 386
Godwin, William, 485
Goodell, William, 156, 200, *202
Goodrich, ?John Z., 271, *273
Goodrich, Mrs. ?John Z., 271
Goodwin, Frederick, 493
Gottheil, Gustav, 513, *514
Grand Eight-Hour League of Massachusetts, 401–402, *403
Grand Hotel, Paris, 491, 493
Grandey, George W., *299
Grant, George Monro, 480–481, *484
Grant, Mrs. George Monro (Jessie Lawson), 480, *484
Grant, Ulysses S., 78, 114, 143, *144, 178, 202, 246, 254, 255; and Freedmen's Bureau, 399, 400; candidate for President, 561, 562
Great Britain: danger of war with, 57, 58; attitudes toward Civil War, 60–61, 64–74, 79–82; and Confederacy, 99, 132–133, 136, 146, 147; effect of Emancipation Proclamation on, 116, 137, 138; Conway-Mason negotiations and, 132–133, 137, 138, 161–162, 220–221; treaty with, 226; WLG in, 487–490, 513–533, 546–548
Great Eastern (ship), 464, *465
Greeley, Horace, 6, 58, 92, *155, 158–159, 474; letters to, 161, 185; speaks at AASS meeting, 153; for Union over abolition, 171; and Jefferson Davis, 508
Green, Beriah, 175, *176, 333, 336
Green, Samuel, 103, *105
Green, William, 423–424, *425, 461
Green Mountains, Vt., 126
Greene, Anna Shaw, 134
Greene, Benjamin, 138
Greenwood Cemetery, Brooklyn, 461, *462
Grew, Henry, 45, *95
Grew, Mrs. Henry (Kate Merrow), 45
Grew, Mrs. Henry (Susannah Pitman), 96
Grew, Mary, 41, 43, *45, 95, 175, 204, 339, 464, 465

Grew, Susan, 95, *96
Griffing, Charles Stockman Spooner, 352
Griffing, Emma, 352
Griffing, Josephine Sophie White (Mrs. Charles Stockman Spooner Griffing), 351, *352
Griffith, Martha (Mrs. Albert G. Browne, Jr.), 115, *117, 134, 154
Grimes, James Wilson, 193
Grimké, Angelina. *See* Weld, Mrs. Theodore D.
Grimké, John Faucheraud, 549
Grimké, Sarah Moore, 96, 156, 548, *549
Grinnell, Moses Hicks, 426, *427
Grinnell, Mrs. Moses Hicks (Julia Irving), 427
Grozelier, Leopold, portrait of WLG by, 351, 352
Gurowski, Adam, *Slavery in History*, 93, *94

Hahn, Michael, 234
Haiti, 24–26, 92, 93–94, 226
Hale, Albert, 347, *349
Hale, John Parker, 210, *211
Hall, Newman, 141
Halleck, Henry, 112, *114, 126, 143, 387
Hallowell, James Mott, *567
Hallowell, Mrs. Richard Price, 417, *418, 567
Hambleton, Alice Eliza, 97, *98
Hamilton, Charles Smith, 387
Hamlin, Hannibal, 194, *195
Hammond, C. G., 441
Hammond, Henry Laurens, 333, *336
Hammond, Mrs. Henry Laurens (Elizabeth Gordon Pattee Lovejoy), 333, 336
Hampden, John, 518, *520, 531
Hampton, Wade, *380
Hansen, Peter Andreas, 45
Harlan, James, 349
Harper, Frances Ellen Watkins (Mrs. Fenton Harper), 271, *273, 454–455
Harper, Ida Husted, 157
Harpers Ferry, 2
Harris, Edward, 276, *277
Harrisburg, Pa., 113
Haskell, Daniel M., 484
Haughton, James, 504, *506
Hayball, Samuel, 327
Hayti. *See* Haiti
Heaton, Jacob, 321, *323
Heidelberg, Germany, WLG visits, 544

Helmer, Mr., 316, 317
Helper, Hinton Rowan, *The Impending Crisis of the South,* *473–474
Helper, Mrs. Hinton Rowan (Marie Louisa Rodriguez), 474
Hepza (servant), 371, 385, 415
Herald of Freedom, 114
Herald of Progress, 101, 102
Herb, 110
Herndon, Annie M., 350
Herndon, Beverly P., 350
Herndon, Elizabeth R., 350
Herndon, Leigh W., 350
Herndon, Mary F., 350
Herndon, Nathaniel J., 350
Herndon, Nina Belle, 350
Herndon, William Henry, 331, *332, 345; letter to, 349; entertains WLG, 341, 347–348
Herndon, Mrs. William Henry (Anna Miles) 347, *350
Herndon, Mrs. William Henry (Mary J. Maxcy), 350
Heywood, Ezra H., 37, *38, 57, 58, 480
Higginson, Thomas W., 145
Hilgard, Ferdinand Heinrich Gustav. *See* Villard, Henry
Hilgard, Gustav Leonhard, *278, 302, 419, 428, 437, 495, 499, 519, 523, 524, 525, 528; welcomes Fanny and Frank, 444–445, 447; illness and death of, 488, 533, 541
Hilgard, Mrs. Gustav Leonhard (Katherine Antonia Elisabeth Pfeiffer), 291, *292
Hill, Samuel L., *31
Hillsdale, Ohio, WLG lectures at, 330
Hillsdale College, Ohio, 330, *332
Hilton, Mrs. Gustavus (Jennie C. Beattie), 479
Hinton, J. H., 537
Hinton, Richard J., 62, *63
Holley, Sallie, 122, *123–124
Holmes, James H., 10, *11
Holmes, Theresa, 10
Hook Mountain, N.Y., 426
Hooper, William R., 347, *348, 359, 562
Hopedale Community, 116
Hopper, Edward, 285
Hopper, Mrs. Edward (Ann Mott), 285
Hopper, Isaac Tatem, 20, 154
Hopper, Mrs. Isaac Tatem (Sarah Tatum), 20
Hopper, John, *20–21, 113, 154, 201, 202, 272

Hopper, Mrs. John (Rosa De Wolf), 20, 115, 272
Hopper, Maria, 284, *285
Hopper, William De Wolf, 154, *157
Horton, Charles French, 565, 566
Horton, Harriet Elizabeth, 565, 566
Horton, Jacob, *263; letters to, 262, 564
Horton, Mrs. Jacob (Harriet Farnham), 564–565
Hotel de l'Europe, Brussels, 547
Hotel du pont de l'Europe, Paris, 491
Houghton, Marcia A., 477, *478, 498, 502, 544
House of Commons, WLG welcomed at, 527
Hovey, Charles Fox, 23
Hovey Committee, 22, 23, 260–261
Howard, Jacob Merritt, 325, *326
Howard, Mrs. Jacob Merritt (Catherine A. Shaw), 325, 326
Howard, Oliver Otis, *294–295, 391
Howard, William A., 12
Howe, James, 349, *350
Howe, Mrs. James (Hannah Wilstach), 350
Howe, Julia Ward (Mrs. Samuel Gridley Howe), 36
Howe, Samuel Gridley, 35, *36, 150, 437
Howland, Joseph A., 112, *113
Hunter, David, 60, 93, *94, 115
Huntington, Frederic Dan, 109, *110
Huntley Lodge, 302, 515–516
Huntsman Hall, La Porte, Ind., 331, *332
Huss, John, 543, *546
Hussey, C. G., 324
Hutchinson, Asa, 116, 206
Hutchinson, James, Jr. 122, *123, 125, 420
Hutchinson, Mrs. James, Jr. (Abby E. Flint), 122, *123, 125, 420
Hutchinson, John Wallace, 116, 205, *206
Hutchinson, Mrs. John Wallace (Fannie B. Patch), 207
Hutchinson, Judson, 116, 206

Illenden, Richard, 329
Illenden, Mrs. Richard (Sarah Grant), 327, *329
Illenden, Richard, II, *329
Illinois College, Jacksonville, 342, *344
Illinois Conference Female Academy, 342, 344

Illinois State Central Hospital for the Insane, 342
Illinois State School for the Blind, 344
Illinois State School for the Deaf, 343, 344
Independent. See New York *Independent*
Interlaken, Switzerland, 536
Ireland, 70, 71, 72
Irish, Elisha H., 353, *354
Irish, William Beckford, 354
Irish, Mrs. William Beckford (Lydia Cadwallader), 354
Irving, Catharine Ann, 426, *427
Irving, Mary Elizabeth, 426, *427
Irving, Sarah, 426, *427
Irving, Washington, 426, *427
Island Grove Park, Abington, Mass., 103, *105

Jackson, Edmund, 130, 453, *455, 475, 548, 549
Jackson, Mrs. Edmund (Mary H. Hewes), 548, *549
Jackson, Francis, 4, 20, 22, *23, 37, 44, 40, 311; bequest of, 6, 440, 449, 453, 474–475, 483, 520, 531, 542–543
Jackson, Josephine A., 285
Jackson, Mary, 134
Jacksonville, Ill., WLG at, 342–343
Jacksonville (Ill.) Female Academy, 342, 344
Jameson, Anne, 104, *106
Jameson, Thorndike Cleaves, 243–*244, 251, 258
Jameson, Mrs. Thorndike Cleaves (Lucinda Lawrence Otis), 104, *106, 251, 258, 335
Jamison. *See* Jameson
Jarvis, Edward, 375
Jarvis, ?Mrs. Edward (Almira), *375
Jay, John, 272, *273–274
Jefferson, Thomas, 79, 230
Jenkins, Charles E., 429, *430–431, 526
Jenkins, Mrs. Charles E. (Nancy W.), 430
Jenkins, Charles E., Jr., 429, *430–431
Jenkins, Howard M., *260; letter to, 259
Jennison, Charles Ransford, 62, *63
Jerome of Prague, 543, *546
John (orphan), 298
Johnson, Andrew, *209, 440, 442; nominated for vice president, 208; policies of, condemned, 299, 382, 395–

396, 409, 422; and Freedmen's Bureau, 364–365, 397–399; Washington's birthday speech, 365, 399–400; Civil Rights Bill veto, 409; and impeachment, 412, 433, 439, 447, 450, 458, 462, 533, 556, 558; messages to Congress (1866), 435, 437–438, (1867), 556–557, 560, 563, 564
Johnson, Eastman, 51
Johnson, Giles B., *148
Johnson, Jonathan Eastman, 313
Johnson, Oliver, *6, 23, 42, 43, 90, 140, 159, 196, 204, 308, 346, 406, 469, 471, 478, 566; letters to, 5, 16, 21, 29, 36, 46, 54, 57, 100, 111, 129, 135, 149, 165, 186, 200, 213, 214, 239, 274, 280, 362, 380, 450, 517, 557; WLG's respect and affection for, 37, 239, 242, 363; to present memorial to Lincoln, 97; trip with WLG to Vt. and N.Y., 117–120, 125–127; wants to merge *Standard* and *Liberator*, 239, 248; resigns as editor of *Standard*, 274, 275; testimonial for, 276, 277; aggrieved at treatment by Phillips, 280–281; and last number of *Liberator*, 362–363; and *Independent*, 521
Johnson, Mrs. Oliver (Mary Anne White), *6, 29, 42, 43, 55, 113, 136–137, 354, 363, 380, 477, 482, 498, 535; has visions, 5, 6; to stay with HEG, 469; illness and recovery, 519, 528; WLG grateful to, 544
Johnson, Mrs. Oliver (Jane Abbott), 6
Johnson, Philip C., 313
Johnson, Mrs. Philip C. (Mary K.), 313
Johnson, Samuel, 552, *553
Johnson, Ziba, 117, *118
Johnson, Mrs. Ziba (Sally Lincoln), 118
Johnson, Ziba Leonard, 118, *119, 120
Jones, Benjamin Smith, 43, *45
Jones, Mrs. Benjamin Smith (Jane Elizabeth), 43, *45
Jones, James F., 232–233, *234
Jones, Mrs. John, 451, *452
Jones, Thomas, 321, *323–324, 556
Jones, Mrs. Thomas (Mary Ann), 321, 323, 556
Journal des Debats, 500, 503
Julian, George Washington, *91–92, 173, 385; letters to, 90, 172, 382
Julian, Louis Henry, 173
Jura Mountains, Switzerland, 536

Katy (servant), 322, 352, 431, 436, 478
Kavasales, Philipangos. *See* Fisk, Photius
Kean, Charles John, 328, *329, 337
Kean, Ellen Tree (Mrs. Charles Kean), 328, 329, 337
Kelley, William Darrah, 266, *268, 270, 385
Kelly. *See* Kelley
Kennedy, John Alexander, 17, *18, 54, 56, 165–166, 473; letter to, 472
Kennedy, Thomas, 408
Kentucky, 226
Keyes, Henry, 120, *121
Kiliani, Otto, 45
Kiliani, Mrs. Otto (Lilian Bayard Taylor), 45
Kimball, David, 534
Kimball, Mrs. David (Nancy Stacy), 534
Kimball, David, Jr., 534
Kimball, Moses, 533, *534
Kimball, Mrs. Moses (Frances L. A. Hathaway), 533, 534
Kimber, Abby, 42, 43, *44
Kimber, Emmor, 44
King, Leicester, 320, *322–323
King, Mrs. Leicester (Julia Ann Huntington), 322
Kinley, Isaac, 350–351, *352
Kinley, Mrs. Isaac (Jeanne Adams), 351, 352
Kinsella, Thomas, 532, *534
Kinsley, Edward W., 263
Knight, Holland Lorenzo, 56
Knight, Mrs. Holland Lorenzo (Jane Charlotte), 56
Knox, Thomas, 453, *454–455

Laboulaye, Edouard-René Lefebvre de, 441, 491, *493, 501, 508, 533, 536
Lackshefka. *See* Zakrzewska
Ladies' City Mission Society. *See* Ladies' Union Aid Society
Ladies' Freedmen's Society, Cambridge, Mass., 567
Ladies' Union Aid Society, St. Louis, 307, 308
Lafayette, Ind., WLG lectures at, 346–347
Lake Champlain, 126, 127
Lake Constance, 543
Lander, William W., 394, *395
Lander, Mrs. William W., 394, 395
Lane, Mr. and Mrs., 461
Lane, James Henry, 421, *422

La Porte, Ind., WLG lectures at, 330–331
Lathrop, James, 137–138
Lavinia, 206
Lawson, William, 484
Lawrence, William, 448
Leavitt, Joshua, 176, *177, 264, 521
Leeds Anti-Slavery Association, 546
Leeds, England, 545
Lee, Robert E., *265–266
Lee, Mrs. Robert E. (Mary Ann Randolph Custis), 265–266
Leggett, Augustus Wright, 337, *338
Leggett, Mrs. Augustus Wright, 337, 338
Levitt, Mrs., 546
Lewis, John Allen, 196, *197, 469, 491, 548
Lewis, Mrs. John Allen, 196, 469, 491, 548, 561
Lewis, Richard A., 461, *462
Liberator, The, 30, 80, 308, 322, 359, 376, 378, 386; superscription changed, 3; policy of, during Civil War, 111–112; has fewer subscribers, 113; and Democratic convention, 123, 124; subscription price raised, 129; and Thompson testimonial, 141; WLG decides to end, 183–184, 248; WLG uneasy about, during absence, 206, 315; merger of *Standard* and, considered, 239–242, 248; financial troubles of, 261, 309, 310, 311, 315; WLG reviews career with, 302–303; WLG prepares last number of, 362–363; J. B. Yerrinton and, 369–370; Purvis rejects, 390
Liberia, 226
Liberty Club, Cleveland, 324
Light, George Washington, 464, *465
Light, John, 465
Light, Mrs. John (Nancy), 465
Lincoln, Abraham, 10, 11, 20, 74, 81, 91, 97, 136, 141, 142, 162, 165, 170, 191, 201, 206, 240, 247, 263, 332, 345, 388, 531; letters to, 255, 257; note to WLG from, 259; WLG criticizes policies of, 3, 4, 19, 37, 47, 53, 57, 59–60, 93, 112–113, 114–115, 143; WLG explains policies of to Thompson, 67–68, 69, 76; Blanchard opposes, 163; WLG supports, 178–180, 181–182, 202, 203, 221–226, 228–233; Phillips opposes, 179, 181, 182, 202, 213, 214–215, 225; WLG received by, 183, 209–210, 211–212;

Lincoln, Abraham (*continued*)
Thompson supports, 186; renominated, 208; AASS divided on, 214; assassination of, 246–247, 270, 409, 411; WLG cannot influence, 254; WLG admires, 256, 257–258; WLG delivers eulogy on, 281, WLG visits tomb of, 348, 349, 350
List, Charles, 272
Llewellyn Park, Orange, N.J., 424, 566
Lockport, Pa., WLG lectures at, 316
London: breakfast for WLG in, 151, 441, 529, 530, 531, 533; WLG stays in, 489–490, 517–526, 546–549
London Anti-Slavery Reporter. See *British and Foreign Anti-Slavery Reporter*
London *Daily News*, 380, *381
London Emancipation Society, 138, 139, *141, 150
London *Morning and Evening Star*, 492, *493, 547
London New Broad Street Committee, 464, *465
London Temperance League, 516
Long, Jessie, 136, 137
Long, James, 333–334
Longfellow, Henry Wadsworth, 470
Longfellow, Samuel, 469, *470
Longshore, Dr., 85
Long Wharf, Boston, 476, *478
Longwood Progressive Friends: meetings, 42–*44, 101, 102, 150, 159, 205, 517; present memorial to Lincoln, 97, 98
Lord Provost of Edinburgh. See Chambers, William
Loring, Louisa, 134
Lothrop, Olivia, 481, *485
Lothrop, Samuel Kirkland, 481, *485
Louis Napoleon. See Napoleon III
Louisiana, 226, 228; Banks's policy in, 231–233, 245, 249
Louisville (Ky.) *Journal*, 174
L'Ouverture, Toussaint, 94
Louvre, the, 492
Love, Alfred Henry, 176, *177, 390, 458
Love, Mrs. Alfred Henry (Susan Henry Brown), *177, 458
Love, William Henry, 177
Love, Mrs. William Henry (Rachel Evans), 177
Lovejoy, Charles Perkins, 341
Lovejoy, Elijah P., 34, 521
Lovejoy, Elijah Parish, 341
Lovejoy, Ida Taylor, 341

Lovejoy, Owen, 33, *34, 195, 333, 339
Lovejoy, Mrs. Owen (Eunice Storrs Denham), 339, *341
Lovejoy, Owen Glendower, 341
Lovejoy, Sarah Moody, 341
Lovejoy, Sophia Mappa, 341
Lowe, Charles, 289, *290, 293
Lowe, Thaddeus S. C., 53, *54
Lowell, Charles Russell, 503
Lowell, Mrs. Charles Russell (Josephine Shaw), 503
Lowell, James Russell, *250, 444, 567; letter to, 442
Lowell, Mass., WLG speaks at, 262, 263
Lowrie, Walter, 319, *320
Lucas, Samuel, 493
Lucerne, Switzerland, 543
Lundy, Benjamin, 191, *192, 326, 474–473
Lupton, Joseph, 545, *546

McCarthy, Justin, 493
McClellan, George B., 53, *54, 118, 123, 124, 126, 235, 236, 240
McClennan, Mrs. John H. (Angeline S. Beattie), 479
McCombe, John, 401, 403
McDowell, Irvin, 126, *128
McGill. See Magill
McIlvaine, Charles Pettit, *306
McKaye, Henry Goodwin, 493
McKay(e), James Morrison, *78, 150, 203–204, 493, 533; letter to, 75
McKay(e), Mrs. James Morrison, 491, *493
McKim, Charles Follen, *42, 284, 424, 430, 545
McKim, James Miller, *41, 43, 196, 217, 219, 302, 322, 353, 356, 410, 419, 423, 437, 441, 454, 460, 461, 464, 560, 563, 566; letters to, 39, 175, 288, 293, 297, 307, 337, 407; WLG visits, 304–306; and *Nation*, 389; corresponds with Mary Estlin about Thompson, 505, 512–513
McKim, Mrs. James Miller (Sarah Allibone Speakman), *41, 43, 208, 217, 219, 305, 356, 390, 454, 560, 541, 545, 548
McKim, Lucy, letter to, 218. See also Garrison, Lucy McKim
McNeally, Mr. and Mrs. Cyrus, 328
Madden, Mrs., 431, *433
Madison House. See Matteson House
Magill, Edward H., 30, *31

Maine, 309

Manchester, England, WLG honored at, 514, 525, 530

Mann, Birney, 115, *116, 285

Mann, Daniel, 116, *285, 298, 417; pulls WLG's teeth, 283–284

Mann, Mrs. Daniel (Maria Dimock), 116, 285

Mansfield, Leroy D., 425, 426, *427

Marin, Matthias C., 361, *362

Marriott, Charles, 169

Marriott, Henry, 169

Marriott, Maria, 168, *169

Marshall family, 104, 106

Martin, J. Sella, 103, *105

Martineau, Harriet, *381, 386

Mary (servant), 115, 267

Maryland, 19, 20, 226; congressional elections in, 430, 431

Mason, James Murray, 137, *138; and *Trent* affair, 58; and controversy with Conway, 88, 132–133, 161–162, 165, 220

Massachusetts, George Putnam on, 431–432

Massachusetts Anti-Slavery Society, 7, 30, 31, 164, 450, 451; arrangements with Anna Dickinson, 85; annual meeting (1864), 185–186; Phillips and WLG clash over continuance of, 364, 374–375, 377; WLG assailed at meeting of, 453, 454

Massachusetts Homœopathic Society, 61

Massachusetts legislature: urged to support Emancipation Proclamation, 141–142; Phillips tries to influence, 451

Master in Chancery. *See* Codman, John

Matteson House, Chicago, 333, *336

Mawson, John, 561, *562

Mawson, Mrs. John (Miss Swan), 561, *562

May, Adeline, *41

May, Edward, *41

May, Mrs. Edward (Mary M. Blodgett), 41

May, Elizabeth Goddard, *41

May, George Emerson, *51, 163

May, Mrs. George Emerson (Alice Haven), 51

May, Mrs. George Emerson (Caroline M. Mathews), 51

May, John Edward, *51

May, Mrs. John Edward (Kate Pomroy Horton), 51

May, Joseph (infant), 51

May, Joseph, 49, *51, 312, 313, 315, 357

May, Mrs. Joseph (Harriet Charles Johnson), *51, 312, 313, 315

May, Joseph Russell, *41

May, Josephine, 315

May, Louisa Forman, 315

May, Samuel, 435, *437, 508, 533, 552

May, Mrs. Samuel (Mary Goddard), 134, 155, *437, 508, 533, 534

May, Samuel, Jr., 20, 37, *38, 39, 88, 89, 130, 142–143, 152, 175, 271, 483, 510, 524; letters to, 412, 448, 463, 474, 506, 529; disagrees with Howland, 112, 113; favors union of *Liberator* and *Standard*, 239, 240; controversial letter of, 274, 275; and National Testimonial, 366, 367, 469, 538, 542, 562; sees WLG off, 477

May, Mrs. Samuel, Jr. (Sarah Russell), *41, 134, 271, 465, 508, 533

May, Samuel J., 38, *50, 116, 175, 264, 307, 316, 357, 359, 528; letters to, 49, 142, 162, 235, 355; Fast Day sermon, 50, 51; controversy with Blanchard, 163–164; WLG visits, 237, 312, 314, 315, 404; is ill, 312, 317; insures WLG, 355, 366; and Testimonial, 366; married WLG and HEG, 534–535

May, Mrs. Samuel J. (Lucretia Flagge Coffin), 50, *51, 237, 238

Meadville, Pa., WLG lectures at, 318–319

Mechanics Hall, Worcester, Mass., 469, *471

Medill, Joseph, 269

Mendenhall, Isaac, 42, 43, *44, 201, 204

Mendenhall, Mrs. Isaac (Dinah Hannum), 42, 43, *44, 98, 201, 204

Mercantile Library Association, Boston, 436, *438

Merriam, Charles D., 493

Metzger, Mr., 448

Miles, Henry, *301; letter to, 300

Mill, John Stuart, 441, 458, *459, 527

Miller, Ann Fitzhugh, 138

Miller, Charles Dudley, 136, *138

Miller, Mrs. Charles Dudley (Elizabeth Smith), 136–137, *138, 195

Miller, Gerrit Smith, 138

Miller, William Fitzhugh, 138

Missouri, 226

Missouri Compromise, 12

Mitchell, Lebbeus Horatio, 83–*84
Monument Square, Baltimore, 208, *209
Moore, John Wilson, 391
Moore, Rachel Wilson (Mrs. John Wilson Moore), 390, *391
Morgan, Edwin Denison, 210, *211, 400
Morrill, Alpheus, 375, 562
Morrill, Mrs. Alpheus (Eliza Ann Cate), 375, 561, *562
Morrill, Anne (Annie), *375
Morrill, Mary, 562
Morrill, Shadrach Cate, 562
Morris, D., 448
Morris, Robert, *26; letter to, 24
Morse, James Herbert, 20
Morse, Joseph B., 63
Mott, Adam, 45
Mott, Mrs. Adam (Anne), 45
Mott, Emma (Emily), 284, *285
Mott, Isabel, 285
Mott, James, 41, 43, *45–46, 306; WLG given photograph of, 95; wedding anniversary of, 467
Mott, Lucretia Coffin (Mrs. James Mott), 41, 43, *45–46, 171, 175, 552; letter to, 466; is an unmatched character, 95; looks saintly, 306; differs from WLG, 390; helps Thompson, 464; WLG's affection and admiration for, 466–467
Mott, Maria, 285
Mott, Thomas, 285, 468, 551–552, *553, 559
Mott, Mrs. Thomas (Mariana Pelham), 190, 285, 552, *553, 559
Mount Auburn Cemetery, 348, *349
Mount Mansfield, Vt., 119, 120, 126
Munich, Germany, 432, 434
Munroe, Dr., 414, 417
Munroe, William F., 416
Munroe, William H., 416
Murdock, John Nelson, 123, *124
Murphy, William Walton, 548, *549–550
Murray, John, 431, *433
Music Hall, Boston, 5, *7, 262, 263
Myers, Mr., 325

Napoleon III, 420, *422, 496, 497, 500, 528
Nation, The, 41, 277, *278, 346, 386, 389, 520
National Anti-Slavery Standard, *18, 362, 453, 461, 462, 520, 531, 532; AASS to continue publishing, 21–22; masthead changed, 22, 23; financial difficulties, 29; copies to be sent to Congress, 46–47; policy during Civil War, 111–112; must raise subscription price, 129; Phillips and, 182–183, 213, 214, 215, 280–281; future of, 183–184; merger of *Liberator* and, considered, 239–242, 248; Johnson resigns as editor of, 274, 275; and Jackson bequest, 440, 449, 474–475, 542–543
National Anti-Slavery Subscription Anniversary Festival, 5, 7, 29, 129, 130, 134, 135
National Convention of Loyal Women, 154, *157
National Freedmen's Aid Commission, 288, 290, 293, 294
National Freedmen's Relief Association, 272, *273, 290, 353
National Loyal Convention. *See* National Union Convention
National Republican Convention, 561, 562
National Temperance League, *516, 525
National Temperance Society, 516
National Testimonial for WLG, 469; is organized, 366–367; WLG's reactions to, 412–414, 415, 436, 443, 458, 472, 476–477, 538–540, 542, 562
National Union Convention, 207–208, 223
Needles, John, 205, *206, 207
Needles, Mrs. John (Mary Bowers), 205, *207
Needles, Mrs. John (Eliza Mathews), *207
Needles, Mrs. John (Lydia Smith), *207
Needles, John A., 205, *207
Nell, William Cooper, *471, 477, 478–479; letter to, 471
Nelson, George S., 421, *423
Newburyport, Mass., 262
Newburyport *Herald*, 564, *566
Newcastle-upon-Tyne, England, 514, 530
New England Anti-Slavery Society, 143, 144, 152, 326, 537
New England Freedmen's Aid Society, 289, *291, 293, 294, 300
New England Freedmen's Commission, 449

New England Freedmen's Union Commission, 440, 453, 455, 474, 475, 531, 542
Newman, Francis W., *227; letters to, 220, 228; WLG's correspondence with, discussed, 179–181; WLG defends Lincoln's policies to, 220–226, 228–233
New Mexico, 10, 12
New Orleans, La., 113
New York City, draft riots in, 165–166, 473
New York *Evening Post*, 140, *141
New York *Express*, 47, *48
New York *Herald*, 37, *38, 47, 54, 55, 56, 76, 191, 193, 461, 462
New York *Independent*, 21, *23, 55, 113, 159, 386; and Thompson testimonial, 140, 141; WLG writes for, 380, 385, 406, 407, 450–451, 453; under attack, 520, 521, 557–558
New York *Journal of Commerce*, 37, *38, 47, 59, 76
New York state: Democratic committee in, 33; election in, 312, 313
New York *Times*, 377
New York *Tribune*, 57, *58, 140, 141, 153, 155, 158–159, 161, 162, 461
Nichol, Elizabeth Pease (Mrs. John Pringle Nichol), *147, 556, 561; letters to, 145, 301, 515; WLG's affection for, 302; gives set of *Liberator* to British Museum, 303, 304; and WLG Testimonial, 367; Garrisons visit, 515–516, 518, 532
Nichol, John, 301, *303–304
Nichol, John Pringle, *147, 303
Norfolk (Va.) *Day-Book*, 76, *79
North, the: attitude toward South, 19–20; pro-slavery feeling in, 37; British attitude toward, 60–61, 67, 79; opposition to emancipation in, 77, 442; election of Lincoln a triumph for, 81; "satanic democracy" of, 113; colorphobia prevalent in, 143; division of sentiment in, 170
North American Review, 249, *250, 252
North Becket, Mass., 30
North Elba, N.Y., 126, 204
North Ferrisburgh, Vt., 299, 300
North Western Freedmen's Aid Commission, 290
Norton, Charles Eliot, *250, 567; letter to, 249
Norton, Daniel, 400
Notre Dame de Paris, 492

Nosworthy, Frederick A., 482, *486, 487, 489
Nosworthy, Mrs. Frederick A. (Louisa Thompson), *465, 482, 486, 487–488, 551
Nowell, James, 553
Nowell, Joseph, 552, 553
Nowell, Sadie, 553
Nowell, Sarah J., 134, 552, *553
Noyes, George C., 330, *332
Nyack, N.Y., 425–426

Oakford, Charles, 462
Oakford, Edward G., 462
Oakford, Helen, 462
Oakford, Mrs. John (Helen M. Anthony), 460–461, *462
Oak Ridge Cemetery, Springfield, Ill., 348, 349, 350
Oglesby, Richard James, 345, *346, 347
Ohio, colorphobia in, 555
Old Colony Railroad, *265
Olmsted, Frederick Law, 294, *295
Oneida, N.Y., WLG speaks at, 404
Oneida Institute, 333, *336
Oneida lake, 235
Opdyke, George, 153, *155, 186
Osborne, David Munson, 190
Osborne, Mrs. David Munson (Eliza Wright), 189, *190
Osborne, Thomas Mott, 190
Osgood, John Felt, 481, *485
Otis, George A., *251, 258, 336
Otis, Mrs. George A. (Lucinda Smith), 127, *128, 325, 336
Otis, James Frederick, 176, *177
Otis, Mary Amy Georgina, 134, 335, *336
Owen, Robert, 484
Owen, Robert Dale, 150, 480, *484–485
Owen, Woodland, 324, *325–326, 327, 330
Owen, Mrs. Woodland (Jane Parton Illenden), 327, *329, 330
Owens. *See* Owen

Palfrey, John Gorham, 536, *537, 567
Palmerston, Henry John Temple, Viscount, 518, *520, 531
Papineau, Mrs. Seth L., 337, 339
Paris, France: described, 491–492, 495, 507; lodgings in, 528
Paris Exposition, 457, 459, 467, 492, 494–495, 496, 508
Parker Fraternity, 57, *58, 552

Parker, Lydia M., 134
Parker, Theodore, 5, *7, 11, 58, 351, 470. *See also* Twenty-eighth Congregational Society of Boston
Parkman, John, 289, *290
Parkman, Mary Jane, 134
Parsons, Theophilus, 469, *470
Paton, Andrew, 518, *521, 532
Paton, Catharine, 532
Patton, Abigail Jemima Hutchinson (Mrs. Ludlow Patton), 115, *116, 461
Pavilion, Boston, 421, *423
Payne, Daniel Alexander, 480, *484
Peabody, Mrs. ("Saunty"), 429, 430, 434; séance, 446–447
Peabody, Andrew Preston, 83, *84
Peacham, Vt., WLG and Johnson visit, 117–120
Pease, Joseph, 147
Peixotto, Benjamin Franklin, 321, *323
Pelham, Mariana. *See* Mott, Mrs. Thomas
Pelham, Peter, 157
Pennypacker, E. F., 41
Pennsylvania, election in, 316, 317
Pennsylvania Anti-Slavery Society, 36, 38, 39, 87, 241, 338, 339
Pennsylvania Society for the Abolition of Slavery, 459
Percy, Charlotte Henry, 115, *117
Percy, Edward R., 95, *96, 113, 115
Percy, Mrs. Edward R. (Anna Elizabeth Benson), *96, 115, 154
Perkins, Benjamin, 415, *416, 477–478
Peterboro', N.Y., 236–237
Pfeiffer, Anna-Maria, 428, *430, 437, 495, 499, 524, 528, 549; kind to Frank and Fanny, 444–445, 447; HEG's sympathy for, 548
Phebe, 115, 116
Phelps, John Wolcott, 131, 143, *145, 387
Phi Beta Kappa, WLG made member of, 284, 285
Philbrick, Edward S., 289, *290–291, 293
Philadelphia, Pa., 113
Philadelphia *Christian Recorder*, 232–233, *234
Philadelphia Female Anti-Slavery Society, 44
Phillips, Henry C., 415, *416
Phillips, Wendell, *6, 7, 11, 17, 20, 23, 40, 41, 49, 88, 103, 130, 135, 149, 150, 152, 159, 165, 175, 186, 187, 201, 204, 208, 260, 325, 374, 386, 453, 470, 552; letter to, 368; in danger of assault, 5; speeches of, 17–18, 54–58, 101, 102, 152–153, 155, 203; on western tour, 91, 92; urged to go to Britain, 132, 136–137, 138, 150; and Thompson testimonial, 140; replies to Blair, 164; opposes Lincoln, 179, 181, 182, 202, 213, 214–215, 225; WLG's relations with, 181, 182, 185, 203, 245, 248, 271–272, 339, 364, 368, 377–379, 381, 385, 462, 531–532, 542, 543; and Photius Fisk, 197, 199, 216; and *Standard*, 182–183, 213, 214, 215, 280–281; denounces Banks's policy, 252–253; and continuation of MASS, 364, 374–375, 377; and *Nation*, 386, 389; and Sumner, 387–388; and Jackson bequest, 440, 449, 475, 542–543; on Fourteenth Amendment, 451, 452; on Lord Russell's apology, 531, 534; on WLG's reception in England, 533–534; *Speeches, Lectures, and Letters*, 388
Phillips, Mrs. Wendell (Ann Terry Greene), 136, *138, 369, 552
Pierce family, 95, *96
Pierce, Charles W., *96
Pierce, Edward Lillie, 284, *285
Pierce, Mrs. Edward Lillie (Elizabeth H. Kingsbury), 284, *285
Pierce, Joseph S., *96
Pierce, Joshua, *96
Pillsbury, Gilbert, 269, *270
Pillsbury, Helen Buffum, 538
Pillsbury, Parker, 23, 112, *114, 154, 175, 203, 339; critical of Lincoln, 202; editor of *Standard*, 274, 275
Pillsbury, Mrs. Parker (Sarah H. Sargent), 536, *537–538, 561
Pitman, Isaac, Sr., 96
Pittsburgh, Pa., WLG and Thompson speak at, 353–354
Pittsfield, Mass, 109
Place, William Henry, 83, *84
Plymouth Church, Brooklyn, 12
Popp, Richard, 428, *429, 444–445, 447
Popp, Mrs. Richard (Anna Dorothea Friedrike Hilgard), 430
Port Henry, N.Y., 126
Portland, Me., 421, 422
Post, Isaac, 154, *157
Post, Mrs. Isaac (Amy), 154, 157
Potter, Ray, 340, *341
Powell, Mr., 327, 330
Powell, Aaron Macy, *28, 112, 113, 114, 127, 176, 271, 275, 460, 462, 532; letters to, 27, 97, 168

Index of Names

Powell, Mrs. Aaron Macy (Anna Rice), 27, *28
Powell, Elizabeth, 27, *28, 169
Powell, George T., 27, *28
Powell, Townsend, 27, *28
Powell, Mrs. Townsend (Catherine Macy), 27, *28
Powell, William Peter, 32, *33–34
Powell, William Peter, Jr., 32, 34
Pratt, Mary, 10
Princeton, Ill., WLG lectures at, 339–340
Progressive Friends of Longwood. *See* Longwood Progressive Friends
Prussia, 420, 422
Pugh, Sarah, 41, 42, 43, *44, 546
Pullman, George M., 306
Purvis, Hattie, 95, *96
Purvis, Robert, 41, 95, *96, 149, 150, 154, 155, 175, 339; estranged from WLG, 390; and Jackson bequest, 542
Purvis, Mrs. Robert (Harriet Forten), 95, *96
Purvis, Robert, Jr., 95, *96
Putnam, Miss, 434
Putnam, Alfred Porter, 460, *462
Putnam, Caroline F., 122, *123–124
Putnam, Caroline R. (Mrs. Joseph Putnam), 374, *375, 496, 497
Putnam, George, 356, *357–358, 359, 431–432, 479, 481, 502, 544, 552
Putnam, Mrs. George (Elizabeth Ware), 358

Quincy, Edmund, 17, *18, 20, 130, 152, 214, 271, 281, 311, 478; supports WLG on *Liberator-Standard* merger, 239, 240; and National Testimonial, 366, 367, 413; retires as president of MASS, 374; sees WLG off to Europe, 441, 477; and Jackson bequest, 475
Quincy, Ill., WLG lectures at, 342
Quincy, Josiah, 18, 552, *553
Quincy, Mrs. Josiah (Mary Jane Miller), 553

Rand, Mrs. 115
Rand, George Curtis, 481, *485, 491
Rand, Mrs. George Curtis, 481, *485, 491
Rand, John, 481, *486
Rand, Mrs. John (Betsy Babcock), 486
Rand, Martha Loring, 481, *485, 491, 555
Randall, Dexter, 405, 469, *470
Randall, Mrs. Dexter (Eliza Thurber), 405, *470

Randall, Julia, 404, *405, 407, 425, 457, 469, 477, 498, 528, 559, 560
Rarey, John Solomon, *16; letter to, 13
Reconstruction, 282, 299, 361–362, 435, 469; Act, 440, 475
Redpath, James, 26
Reed, Maro McLean, 343, *344
Reed, Mrs. Maro McLean (Elizabeth Lathrop), 344
Reform act of 1867, British, 527, 529
Remond, Charles L., 248, 271, *273, 497
Remond, Edmund Quincy, 496, 497
Remond, John, 273
Remond, Mrs. John (Nancy), 273
Remond, Sarah Parker, 134, 496, *497
Remond, Susan, 374
Republican party, 6, 17, 91, 171, 316, 561
Rhine River, 547
Richmond, Ind., WLG's pocket picked at, 350–351, 354, 358
Richmond, Va., 167
Richmond (Va.) *Enquirer*, 76, *79
Ricketson, Daniel, letter to, *151
Rigi, the, Switzerland, 543
Ristori, Adelaide, 429, *430
Ritchie, John, 481, 482, *486, 548, 552
Ritchie, Mrs. John (Caroline Poole), 486
Ritchie, Mrs. John (Rosa Schoepffer), 486
Ritchie, Uriah, 486
Ritchie, Mrs. Uriah (Susan White Rand), 486
Robie, Hannah, 484, *486
Robie, Samuel, 486
Robie, Thomas, 486
Robinson, Marius R., 22, *23
Robinson, Rowland T., 299, *300
Robson, William, 509–510, *511
Robson, Mrs. William (Margaret), 511
Roby. *See* Robie
Rock, John Swett, 103, *105, 435
Rockland Female Institute, 425, 426, *427
Rockledge, 433, 484, 492, 494, 522, 528
Rockville, Conn., WLG lectures at, 404
Rockwood, Mrs., 446
Rogers, Dr. and Mrs., 461
Rogers, Charles O., 119
Rogers, John, "The Wounded Scout," 453, *455
Roman Catholic Church, 164
Roper, John, 485
Roxbury, Mass., 561
Rush, Benjamin, 544, 546

590

Russell, John Russell, 1st Earl, 527, *529, 531, 534
Russell, Nathaniel P., 41
Russell, Mrs. Nathaniel P. (Sarah Tidd), 41
Russell, Thomas, 477, *478, 507, 550–551
Russell, Mrs. Thomas (Mary Ellen Taylor), 271, 273
Russell House, Detroit, 327, *329
Rust, Richard Sutton, *408

St. Eustace (Eustache), Paris, 492
St. James's Hall, London, 441, 530, 531, *533
Sanborn, Franklin Benjamin, 454, *455
Sarah (servant), 238, 394
Sargeant. *See* Sargent
Sargent, Christiana Keadie, 155
Sargent, Epes, 484
Sargent, Henrietta, 134, 421, 484
Sargent, John Turner, 152, 153, 154, *155, 239, 271, 453, 454
Sargent, Mrs. John Turner (Mary Elizabeth Fiske), 134, *155, 271
Sargent, Mrs. John Turner (Charlotte Sophia White), *155
Sattara, Rajah of, 506
"Saunty." *See* Peabody, Mrs.
Savannah, Ga., 269
Savin, Augustus, *48
Savin, Mrs. Augustus (Sarah S.), 47, *48, 113, 389, 426, 519, 566
Savin, Carrie, 48
Savin, Frank W., 48
Savin, Harrison, 48
Sawyer, ?Gamaliel Bradford, 126, *128
Scarborough, Percy E., 429, *430, 552
Scarborough, Theodore, 430
Scarborough, Mrs. Theodore (Caroline Simmons), 430
Schouler, William, 135, *137
Schurz, Carl, 225, *227
Scotia (ship), 487, *488
Scotland, 70, 71
Scott, Thomas, 117, *119
Scovell. *See* Scoville
Scoville, Samuel, 26, *268
Scoville, Mrs. Samuel (Harriet Eliza Beecher), 266, 268
Seaver, Francis, 100, *102, 331, 340
Seaver and Lothrop, 102, 115
Second Baptist Church, Detroit, 328, *329
Sedgwick, Charles Baldwin, *93, 237,

313, 316, 357; letter to, 92
Sedgwick, Mrs. Charles Baldwin (Deborah W. Gannett), *93
Sedgwick, Mrs. Charles Baldwin (Ellen Chase Smith), *93
Sedgwick, Charles Hamilton, *93
Sedgwick, Ellen Amelia, *93
Seven Weeks War, 420, 422
Severance, Theodoric, 269, *270
Severance, Mrs. Theodoric (Caroline M. Seymour), 134, 269, *270, 375
Sewall, Louisa Winslow, 219
Sewall, Lucy Ellen, 219
Sewall, Samuel Edmund, *219, 272, 463, 476, 486, 524, 538; WLG visits, 218; and National Testimonial, 367, 542
Sewall, Mrs. Samuel Edmund (Harriet Winslow List), 218, 219, 271, *272–273
Sewall, Mrs. Samuel Edmund (Louisa M. Winslow), 219, 272
Seward, William Henry, 20, 75, 93, *94, 210, 365, 387, 439–440
Shaffhausen (Schaffhausen), Germany, 543
Shaw, Francis George, 130, 441, 500, *503
Shaw, Mrs. Francis George (Sarah Blake Sturgis), 129, *130, 134, 503
Shaw, George R., 285
Shaw, Robert Gould, 167, *168, 503
Sheridan, Philip Henry, 254, *255
Sherman, William Tecumseh, 254, *255, 421
Shipherd, Jacob Rudd, 288, *290, 293, 353
Shurtleff, Nathaniel Broadstreet, 561, *562
Sigel, Franz, 131, 143, *145, 387
Simmons, George A., 502, *503, 544
Simmons, Mrs. George A. (Belinda P.), 502, 503
Simmons, Lizzie, 552, *553
Simpson, James W., 401, 403
Simpson, Matthew, 294, *295, 297, 298, 305, 306
Sims, Thomas, *151–152
Sixteenth Republican Ward Association (New York City), 153, *155
Slidell, John, 58, 132, 137, *139
Sloane, James Renwick Wilson, 149, *150, 154, 155
Smalley, George Washburn, 136, *138, 140, 158–159, 275, 280
Smalley, Mrs. George Washburn (Phoebe Garnaut), *138

Smeal, William, 518, *521, 532
Smith, Dr., 120
Smith, Mrs., 419
Smith, Caleb B., 20, 75
Smith, Evelina, 134
Smith, Gerrit, *33, 57, 149, 150, 156, 169, 176, 319, 403; letters to, 32, 170, 194; urged to go to Britain, 132, 136–137; values Union above abolition, 170–171; contributes to Thompson testimonial, 193; WLG visits, 235, 236–237
Smith, Mrs. Gerrit (Wealtha Ann Backus), 33
Smith, Mrs. Gerrit (Ann Carroll Fitzhugh), *33, 136–137
Smith, Greene, 235, *236
Smith, Henry Martyn, 267, *268
Smith, Henry Mitchell, 56, 113, *114
Smith, Mrs. Henry Mitchell (Victoria Knight), 55, *56, 113, 114
Smith, James C., 282, 283
Smith, James McCune, 32, *34
Smith, Joshua Bean, 453, *455
Smith House, Hillsdale, Ohio, 330, 332
Snow, Mrs., 498, 502
Snow, Benjamin, 481, *485, 487, 489, 496, 500, 511
Snow, Mrs. Benjamin (Mary Boutelle), *485
Snow, Mrs. Benjamin (Margaret Pollock), 481, *485, 487, 489, 496, 500, 511
Snow, Francis Huntington, 485
Snow, William, 485, 489, *493
Social, Civil, and Statistical Association of Colored People of Pennsylvania, 386
Soule, William L., 204
Soule, Mrs. William L. (Mary Benson), 204
Soules. See Soule
South, the: no compromise possible with, 10–11, 47; North's attitude toward, 19–20; WLG condemns rebellion by, 67–74; has not destroyed nation, 75–76; is not to be trusted, 340, 361–362, 382; is instrument of God, 376; Black Codes in, 442; and Fourteenth amendment, 451; Negro persecution in, 563
South Carolina, 2–3, 263
Southwick, Joseph, 103, *106, 272, 406
Southwick, Mrs. Joseph (Thankful Hussey), 103, *106, 272, 530
Southwick, Sarah Hussey, 134, 271, *272

Spalding, Rufus Paine, 321, *323
Spooner, Bourne, 499, *502
Spooner, Mrs. Bourne (Hannah Bartlett), 499, *502
Spooner, John Adams, 313, *314, 499
Spooner, Mrs. John Adams (Lydia Sylvester), 313, *314, 490, 499
Springfield, Ill., WLG at, 345, 347–348, 350
Springfield (Mass.) *Republican*, 182
Stacy, George Whittemore, 103, *105, 333
Stacy, Theodore, 333, 336
Standard. See *National Anti-Slavery Standard*
Stanley, Edward John Stanley, 2d Baron, 553
Stanton, Daniel, 153, *157
Stanton, Edwin M., 75, 150, 183, 190, 191, *192, 205, 246, 264, 267, 391, 392; letter to, 295; receives WLG, 210; WLG's admiration and appreciation of, 295–297
Stanton, Mrs. Edwin M. (Ellen M. Hutchinson), 391, 394
Stanton, Elizabeth Cady (Mrs. Henry Brewster Stanton), 153, 154, *156, 179, 201, 202, 461
Stanton, Gerrit, 153, *157
Stanton, Harriot, 153, *157
Stanton, Henry, 153, *157
Stanton, Henry Brewster, 153, *156
Stanton, Margaret, 153, *157
Stanton, Robert, 153, *157
Stanton, Theodore, 153, *157
Stearns, George Luther, 468, *469–470
Stearns, Mary E., 134
Stebbins, Giles Badger, 325, *326
Stebbins, Mrs. Giles Badger (Miss Fish), 325, 326, 328, 330
Steinthal, S. Alfred, *514; letter to, 513
Steinthal, Mrs. S. Alfred (Miss Haworth), 514
Stephens, Lemuel, Jr., 43, *45
Stephens, Lemuel, 45
Stephenson, John Hubbard, 104, *106, 193, 194
Stephenson, Mrs. John Hubbard (Abigail Southwick), *106, 134
Stephenson boys, 104, 106, 109
Stetson, James A., 31
Stevens, Thaddeus, 385, *386
Stevenson, Thomas Greely, 153, *155, 387, 388
Steward, Ira, *402–403; letter to, 401
Stewart, William M., 400
Stickney, John Newton, 404, *405

Still, William, 458, *459
Stoddard, Arthur Francis, 515, *516, 518
Stoddard, Mrs. Arthur Francis (Frances E. Noble), *516
Stoddard, Solomon, 516
Stoddard, Mrs. Solomon (Sarah Tappan), 516
Stone, Captain, 480
Stone, Lucy (wife of Henry Brown Blackwell), 115, *116, 154
Storrs, Richard Salter, Jr., 266, *268
Stowe, Calvin E., 376
Stowe, Harriet Beecher, *376, 521; letter to, 376; *Uncle Tom's Cabin*, 103, 105, 376
Strawn, Jacob, 344
Strawn's Opera House, Jacksonville, Ill., 342, *344
Studley. See Studwell
Studwell, Edwin A., 187, *188, 461; letter to, 410
Sturgis, Nathan Russell, 130
Sturtevant, Julian Monson, 342, *344
Stuttgart, Germany, 344
Sumner, Charles, *11, 37, 55, 57, 118, 120, 124–125, 140, 151, 153, 155, 183, 192, 205, 210, 256, 285, 319, 365, 385, 552; letters to, 10, 52, 61, 199, 215, 361, 383; attacked by Boston *Courier*, 11, 12; and Crittenden compromise, 12; urges emancipation, 39, 41; WLG encourages and advises, 53; and *Trent* affair, 58; criticized in *Liberator*, 199, 200; WLG praises, 215, 383–384; and National Testimonial, 367; and Phillips, 387–388
Supreme Judicial Court of Massachusetts, and Jackson bequest, 474, 520
Sutliff, Milton, 320, *322
Swain. See Swayne
Swasey, Isaac Nathaniel, 459, *460
Swasey, Mrs. Isaac Nathaniel (Lucy Richardson), *460
Swayne, Noah Haynes, 266, *267–268
Sweet, Stephen, 458, *460
Switzerland, 526; WLG in, 534–542
Syracuse, N.Y.: Douglass speaks at, 49; landscape around, 237; WLG speaks at, 403–404, 405

Taft, Augustine, 273
Taney, Roger B., 226, *227
Tappan, Colonel, 312
Tappan, Arthur, 144, *174, 176, 372–373, 518; letter to, 173
Tappan, Lewis, *176–177
Tappan, Mason W., 12
Tappan, Sarah Salisbury, *373; letter to, 372
Tarrytown, N.Y., WLG and Tiltons visit, 426
Taylor, Dr., 461
Taylor, Bayard, 43, *45, 291
Taylor, Mrs. Bayard (Marie Hansen), 43, *45
Taylor, Edward G., 462
Taylor, Edward T., 273
Taylor, Mrs. Edward T. (Deborah Davis Millet), 273
Taylor, John T., 462
Taylor, Ira H., 283
Tennessee, 226, 230
Thaxter, Daniel, *238, 335, 343, 352, 552
Thaxter, Mrs. Daniel (Lucy Scarborough), 238, 429, 335, 343, 352, 429, 430, 431, 552
Thayer, Abijah W., 174
Thayer, Caroline C., 134
Thayer, David, 61, *62
Theodore (?Scarborough, Jr.), 552
Thirteenth Amendment. See United States Constitution
Thomas, Francis, 448
Thome, James Armstrong, 321, *323
Thompson, Edith, *465, 490, 512, 522
Thompson, George, 22, *23–24, 133, 201, 207, 209, 247, 269, 270, 271, 272, 281, 303, 322, 324, 338, 352, 441, 452, 457, 467, 469, 471, 479, 481, 483, 487, 501, 506, 507, 509, 530, 531, 545; letters to, 64, 70, 79; WLG's letters to, discussed, 60–61; understands American affairs, 64–65; efforts to raise money for, 137, 139–140, 193–195, 415, 443, 463–464; supports Union cause in Britain, 144; Phillips attacks, 182; supports Lincoln, 183; WLG makes speaking arrangements for, 183, 186–187, 188; visits Washington, addresses Congress, 190, 191–192, 193; speaks at AASS meeting, 203; accompanies WLG to Ft. Sumter ceremonies, 246, 263–265, 266, 267, 296; meets WLG unexpectedly in Cleveland, 321–322; speaks at Pittsburgh, 353–354; has heavy lecturing schedule, 355, 357; and National Testimonial, 366; attends séance, 434–435, 446–447; lec-

Thompson, George (*continued*)
tures at Fitchburg, 437; departs with
WLG for Europe, 476–477; close
friendship between WLG and, 482;
Mary Estlin criticizes, 505, 511–513;
honored at Edinburgh, 518; uncer-
tain of future, 519–520, 522, 561
Thompson, Mrs. George (Anne Erskine
Spry), *465, 490, 496, 512; "broken,"
519; WLG visits, 522
Thompson, Herbert, 463, *465, 496,
519
Thompson, Joseph P., 55, *56
Thompson, William Lloyd Garrison,
*465
Thwing, Ebenezer Withington, 502,
*503
Ticknor, William Davis, 404, *405
Ticknor and Fields, 366, 404, *405,
408, 409
Tillinghast, James, 285, 405
Tillinghast, Mrs. James (Sarah Benson
Anthony), *285, 404, 405, 407
Tilton, Theodore, 12, *38–39, 55, 56,
57, 101, 136, 150, 175, 196, 204–205,
256, 269, 270, 308, 346, 374, 380,
406, 519, 552; letters to, 139, 158,
377, 396; as editor of *Independent*,
23, 557; WLG's affection for, 37–38,
97; and Thompson benefit, 137, 186;
WLG praises speech of, 153, 159;
and WLG call on Lincoln, 183, 209,
211, 212; at Ft. Sumter ceremonies,
264; and Johnson testimonial, 276;
and last number of *Liberator*, 363;
excursion with WLG, 425–427; invites WLG to write for *Independent*,
450; opposes Fourteenth Amendment, 451; lecture tour of west, 451,
458
Tilton, Mrs. Theodore (Elizabeth Rich-
ards), 12, *39, 204–205, 425, 519
Todd, Francis, 192, 209
Todd, John, 109, *110
Toledo, Ohio, WLG stops at, 324
Toledo Library Association. *See* Young
Men's Association (Toledo)
Tourgueneff. *See* Turgenev
Towne, Edward C., 469, *470
Townsend, Edward D., 264, *265
Townsend, Milo A., letter to, *148
Townsend, Mrs. Milo A. (Elizabeth
Updegraph Walker), *148
Townsend, William Comstock, 285,
*459–460
Townsend, Mrs. William Comstock,

(Mary Gould Anthony), *285, 458,
459–460
Train, George Francis, 120, *121
Trask, George, *279; letter to, 278
Travelli, Mr., 347
Tremont Temple, Boston, 5, *7
Trent affair, 58, 70, 132
Trowbridge, R. E., 448
True American, 318, *319
Trumbull, Lyman, 391, *393, 397, 399
Tuileries, Paris, 492
Turgenev, Nikolai Ivanovitch, 491,
*493, 500, 508
Turgenev, Mme, 500–501
Turner, Nat, 2
Twenty-eighth Congregational Society
of Boston, 7, 85, 87, 88

Underground Railroad, 26, 28, 33, 41,
45, 108, 273, 300, 323, 339, 341, 359
Underhill, Ann Leah Fox, 153–154,
*157, 196
Unitarian Church of Philadelphia, 356,
*357
Unitarian Convention, 264, 265
United States, compared to Europe,
495
United States Christian Commission,
288, 290, 337
United States Congress: should propitiate loyal slaveholders, 36; emanci-
pates slaves in D.C., 53, 54, 91, 92;
efforts of, to abolish slavery, 171,
173; and equal pay for Negro soldiers, 192–193; Thompson addresses, 193; WLG attends sessions
of, 210, 387, 391; and Negro suffrage,
382, 385, 449; and Freedmen's Bureau, 398–399, 422, 423; and President Johnson, 409, 435, 447, 556,
557, 558; Johnson's messages to,
(1866), 435, 437–438, (1867), 556–
557, 560, 563, 564
United States Constitution, 131–132,
257; South has no claims on, 67, 68,
74, 76, 77; government fighting to
uphold, 69; Lincoln guided by, 230;
Thirteenth Amendment, 173, 240,
241, 249, 254, 256, 260, 326; Fourteenth Amendment, 383, 384, 385,
440, 449, 451, 452
United States government: and Southern rebellion, 67–74, 162; should
proclaim emancipation, 75–78, 91;
British attitude toward, 79. *See also*
Johnson, Andrew; Lincoln, Abraham

United States Sanitary Commission, 288, 290
United States Supreme Court, 68
Universal Peace Society (Union), 177

Van Doorn, John K., 342, *343
Venice, Italy, 420, 422
Vergennes, Vt., WLG speaks at, 297, 299
Vermont, WLG tours, 117–127
Vermont Anti-Slavery Society, 300
Versailles, 496, 499–500
Vevey, Switzerland, 432, 433, 536
Vickers, Mr., 430, 434
Vickers, Mrs., 430
Victoria Hall, Leeds, 545, *546
Villard, Fanny Garrison, *9, 43, 104, 110, 143, 163, 189, 235, 272, 283, 284, 311, 317, 331, 334–335, 343, 348, 351–352, 354, 356, 358, 369, 392, 407, 410, 437, 441, 465, 467, 488; letters to, 370, 374, 384, 414, 418, 420, 428, 431, 452, 456, 546, 550, 559, *see also* Garrison, Helen Frances; gives WLG photo album, 52; visits New York, 113; has diphtheria, 137; nurses HEG, 206; visits S. J. May, 237; is engaged, 276–277, 286–288, 292, 302; WLG's love for, 277, 287–288, 359, 559; prepares for marriage, 315, 320; wedding, 370–371; in Washington, 375; writes often, 404; en route to Europe, 418–419; and Hilgard family, 428–429, 444–445; studies music, 447; meets and travels with WLG in Europe, 488, 490–543 passim; is unchanged, 495, 499; unable to return home with WLG, 519, 525; WLG pays travel expenses of, 524; agrees with WLG on testimonial, 540; plans uncertain, 541, 543–544; shops for Ellen, 542; works cushion for HEG, 560
Villard, Henry, 9, 42, 141, *277–278, 283, 284, 302, 317, 321, 335, 336, 337, 343, 348, 356, 384, 385, 386, 389, 391, 394, 395, 441, 445, 447, 448, 465, 488, 536, 548, 560–561; letters to, 286, 291, 358, 554; engaged to Fanny, 276–277; WLG welcomes as son-in-law, 286–288; WLG's affection and respect for, 291, 292, 351–352; is able to afford marriage, 315; Fanny should check generosity of, 315, 457; and Chicago *Tribune*, 359, 495, 523; marries Fanny, 371; in

poor health, 392, 410, 456, 511; en route to Europe, 418–419; is good husband, 429; and family name, 436, 438; meets and guides WLG in Paris, 490, 494, 507; calls on Cochin with WLG, 510; is in financial difficulty, 523–524; is recalled to Munich, 528, 533, 543; future plans uncertain, 544; WLG has misunderstanding with, 554; WLG discusses living arrangements with, 554–555; must be Fanny's first consideration, 559–560
Vincent, Henry, 435–436, *438, 552
Virginia, 19, 20
Vizcarrondo y Coronado, Julio, *567
Vizcarrondo, Harriet Brewster de, 566, *567
Von Arnum, Elizabeth, 134

W., Mr. (butcher), 30
Wade, Benjamin Franklin, 210, *211, 385, 391, 393
Walden, John Morgan, 298, 337, *339
Walker, David, *Walker's Appeal*, 2
Walker, J. M., 326
Walker, Thomas, 381
Wallcut, Robert Folger, 44, *46, 151, 335, 502, 552
Walton, Jacob, 327, *328
Ward, Artemus (Charles Farrar Browne), 328, *329, 337
Ware, Charles Pickard, 41, 548, *549
Ware, Henry, 548, *549
Ware, Mrs. Henry (Mary Lovell Pickard), 549
Warner, Ellen Bliss, 285
Warren, Ohio, WLG lectures at, 320
Washington, George, 230
Washington, D.C., 113, 384–385; WLG visits, 209–212, 364–365, 391–392, 396–400. *See also* District of Columbia
Washington House, Washington, 210, *211
Washington Lecture Association, 92
"Watch Meeting, Waiting for the Hour . . ." (painting), 255–256, 257, 259
Waterhouse, S., 298, 299
Waterston, Robert C., 476, *478, 506–507, 508
Waterston, Mrs. Robert C. (Anna Cabot Lowell Quincy), *478
Watts, Isaac, 467
Watts, John S., 12
Webb, Alfred, *513

Webb, Richard Davis, 16, 55, *105, 366, 465–466, 509; letters to, 504, 511; accompanies WLG to Switzerland, 536, 542; is fond of Fanny, 561
Webb, Mrs. Richard Davis (Hannah), *505
Webster, Daniel, 109, *110
Weddell House, Cleveland, 321, *323, 338
Weld, Theodore D., 41, 96, 133, 142–143, *144, 149, 150, 153, 156, 166
Weld, Mrs. Theodore D. (Angelina Grimké), 41, 96, 144, 153, 154, *156, 549
Weld, Theodore Grimké, 143, *144
Welles, Gideon, 20, 75, *198, 199, 255, 349, 362; letter to, 197; and Photius Fisk, 215–216
Wesselhoeft, Robert, 416
West, the: WLG makes lecture tour of, 248–249, 307–308, 316–354, 358; contrasted with East, 325
Western New York Anti-Slavery Society, 105
Western Virginia, 226
Western Freedmen's Aid Commission, 339, 353, 354, 408
West Indies. *See* British West Indies
Weston family, 507
Weston, Anne Warren, 20, 130, 239, *242, 284, 540, 551
Weston, Deborah, 271, *272
Weston, Warren, 272
Whipple, Charles King, 20, 23, 30, *31, 44, 130, 214, 315; letter to, 260; helps with *Liberator*, 206; opposes merger with *Standard*, 239; and Jackson bequest, 449, 475
Whipple, John A., 501, *503
White, Mrs. Broughton, 354
White, Horace, 335, *336–337, 358, 523, 544, 555
White, Mrs. Horace (Martha Root), *555
White, Joseph, 346
Whiting, Anna (Anne) Maria, *212, 454
Whiting, William, 212, 455
Whiting, Mrs. William (Hannah Connant), 212, 455
Whiting, William, Jr., *212
Whitlock, Antoinette, 335
Whitney, James S., 123, *124
Whitson, Thomas, 41
Whittier, John Greenleaf, 23, 116, *134, 174, 334, 336; letter to, 134
Wiggin(s), Mary, 434, *437, 468–469
Wigham, Eliza, *147, 303, 304

Wigham, Henry, 304
Wigham, John, 147, 304
Wigham, Mrs. John (Jane Richardson), 147
Wigham, Mrs. John (Jane Smeal), *304
Wigham, John, Jr., 304
Wigham, John (III), 304
Wightman, Joseph Milner, 5, *7, 47
Wilberforce University, 480, *484
Wilbur, Charlotte, 202
Wild, Edward Augustus, *167
Wild's Brigade, 167–168
Wilkes, Charles, 58
Wilkinson, Alfred, 237, *238, 315
Wilkinson, Mrs. Alfred (Charlotte Coffin May), 50, *51, 238, 312, 315
Wilkinson, Alfred, Jr., 315
Wilkinson, Marion, 315
Wilkinson, Morton Smith, 210, *211
Willey, Ephraim, 478
Willey, Mrs. Ephraim (Mary Noble), 478
Willey, Mary, 134, 477, *478, 483, 502
William I of Prussia, 496, *497, 500
Williams, Thomas, 448
Williams College, WLG and Fowler speak at, 109
Williamstown, Mass., 110
Wilmot, David, 98
Wilson, Billy, 19, 20
Wilson, Henry, 62, 140, *141, 155, 166, 171, 183, 205, 269, 270, 362, 363, 385; letter to, 190; and pay for Negro soldiers, 191, 192–193; welcomes WLG in Washington, 210; receives news of Lincoln's death, 247; WLG defends, 388; and Freedmen's Bureau bill, 392, 394; supports temperance, 469, 470
Wilson, James, 448
Wilson, John, 104, *106
Winni (servant), 238, 322, 352
Winslow, Charles Frederick, 421, *423
Winslow, Isaac, 476, *478, 530
Winter, (?)Julius, 52, *53–54
Wise, Mr., 311
Women's Loyal National League, 156, 201, *202, 204
Woman's Journal, 116
Wood, Charles Greenleaf, 481, *485
Wood, Fernando, 47, *48
Wood, John, 342, *343–344
Woonsocket, R.I., WLG lectures at, 453, 454
World's Anti-Slavery Convention, London (1840), 464, 504

World's International Anti-Slavery
Conference, Paris (1867), 441–442,
457, 459, 463, 467, 483, 508, 532,
566; described, 535–536
Wright, Charles, 190
Wright, David, *158, 189, 190, 272
Wright, Mrs. David (Martha Coffin),
154, *157–158, 189, 190, 272, 276,
417, 425, 427, 467, 552, 553, 559
Wright, Eliza, *190, 540
Wright, Elizur, 144
Wright, Ellen, letter to, 188; *see also*
Garrison, Ellen Wright
Wright, Frances, 485
Wright, Francis, 7
Wright, Frank, 189, *190, 284
Wright, Henry Clarke, 20, 122, 130,
154, 326, 335; letters to, 298, 555;
clairvoyant warns against trip to En-
gland, 99–*100; speaks at Abington,
103; supports WLG in AASS contro-
versy, 248
Wright, Matthew Tallman, 189, *190
Wright, William Pelham, 189, *190
Wyman, Mrs., 429

Xylander, Robert V., *430, 444–445,
447
Xylander, Mrs. Robert V. (Emma Ottilie Friedrike Hilgard), *430, 437,
444–447, 499, 548

Yates, Richard, 391, *393
Yerrinton, James B., 31, *242, 313, 315;
letter to, 369; WLG's gratitude and
admiration for, 369–370
Yerrinton, James Manning Winchell,
30, *31–32, 57, 149, 150, 200, 242,
315
Young Men's Association (Chicago),
307, *309
Young Men's Association (Toledo),
307, *309
Young Men's Christian Association,
Lockport, Pa., 316

Zack, Dr. *See* Zakrzewska
Zakrzewska, Marie, 416, *418, 432, 434
Zurich, Switzerland, 432, 433, 543